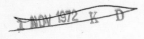

THE DYNAMICS OF INTERNATIONAL POLITICS

THE DYNAMICS OF
INTERNATIONAL POLITICS

SECOND EDITION

NORMAN J. PADELFORD
Massachusetts Institute of Technology

GEORGE A. LINCOLN
United States Military Academy

THE MACMILLAN COMPANY,
COLLIER-MACMILLAN LIMITED, *London*

Fourth Printing, 1969

Earlier edition © 1962 by The Macmillan Company.
Based on *International Politics*, copyright 1954 by The Macmillan Company.

Library of Congress catalog card number: 67–13592

The Macmillan Company
Collier-Macmillan Canada, Ltd., Toronto, Ontario

Printed in the United States of America

Preface

This book is a revision of the previous edition published in 1962 which, in turn, grew out of an earlier volume that first appeared in 1954. This revision is generated by the changing times and the availability of many suggestions from teachers who have found the previous edition useful.

Our purpose in writing this volume is essentially twofold: first, to show the dynamic characteristics of the present international scene; second, to provide some assistance for those who may be called upon, whether as citizens or as officials of government, to deal with a world in which they will have harsher realities and more difficult choices to make than at any time in history. We believe that our country is improving in its comprehension of world affairs, and we hope that this book will contribute to that comprehension.

Our approach is essentially a pragmatic one within a broadly defined framework of political analysis. In this edition we have expanded our treatment to take account of such changes as shifts in power relationships, the multiplication of states, the increasing dominance of events occurring since World War II, and the rising importance of development and nation building. The book has been largely rewritten to update the content, and to underline those aspects of international politics that now seem most important to us in the ongoing conflict between the powers, the rapid shift in the equation of power in the world, the racing pace of technological change, the population explosion, the search for ways of controlling conflict, and the slow progression of mankind toward larger community.

Part I provides a framework for analysis by demarcating the field of study. It also provides a newly constructed conceptual basis for ordering the data and suggests in broad outline some of the principal items of revolutionary change conditioning international politics. Part II examines the major factors and forces operating within and cutting across the field of international politics, shaping the values and purposes of states and affecting their responses to events. Attention is given to the impact of technology and to implications of the rapidly expanding world population. Part III discusses the decision-making process by which foreign policy is determined and action programs are formulated in the principal political systems. Part IV discusses the instruments used to translate national foreign policies into action programs. In this part we have included a new chapter on power politics and the balance of power, recognizing that these are still important dynamic elements in world politics. Part V considers the efforts of states to organize the international community in order to achieve the objectives of security, welfare, and peace. Here we have also added a new chapter on the search for peace, a central concern of states, including a discussion of the problem of arms control.

In writing this book we continue to be impressed by the hope expressed by Sir Winston Churchill in his introduction to *The Gathering Storm* that the new generation will "repair some of the errors of former years and thus govern, in accordance with the needs and glory of man, the awful unfolding scene of the future." Knowledge is essential to the task set for this generation by Churchill, a point made by one of America's most eminent statesmen nearly two generations ago. Elihu Root said that there is one "inevitable condition" for an effective diplomacy by a popular democracy—the people "must acquire a knowledge of the fundamentals and essential facts and principles upon which the relations of nations depend. Without such knowledge there can be no intelligent discussion and consideration of foreign policy and diplomatic conduct. Misrepresentation will have a clear field and ignorance and error will make wild work with foreign relations."

The views which are set forth in the succeeding pages do not purport to present the policy view of the United States Government or of any branch or agency thereof, although the focus of our attention is at all times on the dynamics of international politics as they affect the interests and goals of the United States. The authors are writing as private citizens.

We have incorporated the suggestions of numerous teachers who have used the previous books, as well as those of our publisher and of our colleagues who have generously read portions of the drafts for this edition. We are indebted to these friends for counsel, criticism, and assistance as this volume has progressed, as well as to our students for their suggestions.

We make no attempt to list the names of all who have helped us. Our indebtedness to some has been expressed in the previous books. At the Massachusetts Institute of Technology we have received assistance in particular from Ithiel De Sola Pool, Desmond P. Wilson, Eric Hansen, and Thomas P. Carroll. Sarah Holyoke typed much of the final manuscript and Rosamond Smith helped with the task of proofreading. At the United States Military Academy colleagues to whom we owe particular gratitude include William M. Wix, Frederic J. Brown, James Buck, William L. Hauser, Amos A. Jordan, Verda Lare for her patient secretarial support, James W. Mann, Allen D. Raymond, Sam C. Sarkesian, Donald R. Sherk, John R. Sisson, K. Wayne Smith, William P. Snyder, William J. Taylor.

We are especially indebted to Zeb B. Bradford for details of arrangements for illustrations and other assistance. We thank the *Christian Science Monitor*, *The New York Times*, and other sources indicated with the illustrations for permission to utilize them. We also express our warm appreciation to Dorothy M. Clegg for editing the manuscript, to Mrs. Edward Colt for preparation of the index, and to William Layman at The Macmillan Company for assistance on many details when the book was in production. The efforts of these friends and associates have saved us from many pitfalls and contributed materially to the volume.

We, of course, take responsibility for the opinions and judgments expressed and for any errors of fact.

This book has been written on a line-by-line collaborative basis. The give and take of this exchange has been a rewarding learning process to the authors. We believe it has provided a presentation of increased precision and usefulness. Finally, we recognize the encouragement our wives have given us and the sacrifices they have accepted while we have pursued the lonely tasks of authorship.

N. J. P.
G. A. L.

Contents

Part I
THE SETTING OF INTERNATIONAL POLITICS TODAY   1

PREAMBLE   *1*

1. The International Political System   5

Introduction   *5*
The International Political System   *6*
The Problems of Order and Change   *17*
Adjusting the International System   *19*
Dynamic Elements in Contemporary World Politics   *23*
Conclusion   *27*

2. Toward a Theory of International Politics: A Framework of Analysis   29

Introduction   *29*
The Historical Approach   *30*

Three Systemic Approaches   *31*
Normative Approaches   *37*
Policy Science Approaches   *43*
An Eclectic Approach to International Politics   *47*

Part II

BASIC FACTORS AFFECTING THE POSITIONS AND POLICIES OF STATES   **51**

PREAMBLE   *51*

3.   **Attitudes, Beliefs, and International Politics**   **53**

Introduction   *53*
The Role of Values, Attitudes, and Perception   *54*
Ideas and Ideology in World Politics   *59*
Social Structure, Politics, and Change   *64*
Conclusion   *69*

4.   **Nationalism as a Force in International Politics**   **70**
Introduction   *70*
What Is Nationalism?   *70*
Roots of Nationalism   *72*
The Evolution of Political Nationalism   *76*
Nationalism, Internationalism, and Supranationalism   *86*

5.   **Imperialism, Colonialism, and Anticolonialism**   **88**
Introduction   *88*
The Problem of Definition   *89*
Western Imperialism and Colonialism   *92*
Communist Imperialism   *98*
The Ambivalence of Anticolonialism   *102*
Conclusion   *103*

6.   **The Role of Geography and Physical Environment**   **105**
Introduction   *105*
Geography as an Approach to International Affairs   *106*
Geographic Elements and World Affairs   *112*
Other Elements Affecting Power and Security   *116*
Natural Resources   *118*
Conclusion   *122*

7. Population and World Politics   **123**
Introduction   *123*
Distribution, Size, and Growth of Population   *124*
Ways of Dealing with Population Increase   *130*
A Caution on Statistical Forecasts   *134*

8. The Economic Base of Power and Foreign Policy   **136**
Introduction   *136*
The More-Industrialized World   *137*
The Less-Developed World   *142*
Importance in World Affairs of Investment   *147*
Some Patterns and Problems of Trade   *150*
A Changing World Economic Order   *157*

9. The Technological Factor   **160**
Introduction   *160*
A Major Factor in World Affairs   *160*
Communications   *168*
Spread of Industrial Technology   *169*
Military Technology   *170*
Conclusion   *176*

10. The Search for Security   **177**
Introduction   *177*
The Meaning of National Security   *178*
Military Power and Security   *182*
Some Nonmilitary Aspects of Security   *187*
Security Produces Insecurity   *191*
The Changing Nature of National Security   *192*

Part III
DECISION MAKING FOR FOREIGN POLICY   **195**

PREAMBLE   *195*

11. The Nature and Role of Foreign Policy   **197**
Introduction   *197*
Aspects of Policy   *197*
Relation of Domestic and Foreign Policy   *203*

Sources of Policy   204
Yardstick of Choice—The National Interest   208
Guidelines to Choice   212
The Process of Formulating Foreign Policy   214
Limitations and Requirements of Foreign Policy   217

12. The United States Foreign Policy Process   219
Background of United States Policy Formulation   219
The Chief Executive and the Policy Process   223
The Responsibilities and Functions of the Executive Branch
    in the Policy Process   229
The Congress and Policy Making   238
The Public   242
Categories of Foreign Policy Decisions   244
Conclusion   246

**13. The Formulation of Foreign Policy in the Parliamentary
      Democracy   249**
Introduction   249
Key Feature of Policy Making in the Parliamentary or Cabinet
    System   249
Policy Making in the Two-Party System: Great Britain   250
The Prime Minister and the Cabinet   251
The Foreign Secretary and the Foreign Office   255
Parliamentary Control over Policy and Policy Makers   257
Parties and Policy: Conservative and Labor   258
Public Opinion and Foreign Policy   260
Variants in Policy Process in Other Parliamentary Systems   261
Conclusion   266

14. The Foreign Policy Process of the Great Communist Powers 268
Introduction   268
The Soviet Union: Politics and Policy   269
Government and Policy Making   273
Basic Factors in Soviet Foreign Policy   276
Communist China: Introduction   280
Basic Factors   280
Decision Making in Communist China   281
Flow of Decision Making in Communist States   286
Future of Sino-Soviet Relations   287

Part IV
INSTRUMENTS AND PATTERNS OF FOREIGN POLICY   291

PREAMBLE   *291*

15. Power Politics and Patterns of Policy   293
Introduction *293*
The Meaning and Use of Power *294*
The Balance of Power *296*
Evaluation of the Balance Concept *303*
Limiting Forces in Power Politics *307*
Patterns of Policy *309*
Conclusion *311*

16. Diplomacy and the Conduct of Foreign Affairs   313
Diplomacy and Foreign Policy *313*
The Evolution and Transformation of Diplomacy *314*
The Actors in Twentieth-Century Diplomacy *318*
The Basic Functions of Diplomacy *321*
Negotiations—The Art of Diplomacy *324*
The Level and Setting of Negotiations—New Styles in
  Diplomacy *332*
Successful Diplomacy Stems from Sound Policy and Effective
  Programs *338*

17. International Communication as an Instrument of Policy   340
Introduction *340*
Attitudes and Ideas in World Politics *340*
Propaganda as an Instrument of Policy *342*
Propaganda and Policy *348*
The Operation of Information and Propaganda Systems *352*
Cultural Relations as an Instrument of Policy *353*
Conclusion *357*

18. The Economic Instruments of Foreign Policy   359
Introduction *359*
Policies and Instruments Affecting International Trade *361*
International Agreements *368*
Foreign Economic Assistance *372*
Case Study—The United States Balance of Payments *380*
Conclusion *382*

19. The Military Instrument and Its Management in Foreign Affairs   384

The Military Instrument Described   384
The Nuclear Dilemmas   390
The Management of the Military Instrument   391
Military Strategy   398

Part V
ORGANIZING THE INTERNATIONAL COMMUNITY   407

PREAMBLE   407

20. The Search for International Peace   409

Introduction   409
Some Aspects of Conflict Control   412
Peacekeeping   414
Peaceful Settlement of Disputes   416
Arms Control   417
Conclusion   423

21. The International Rule of Law   425

Introduction   425
The Nature of Contemporary International Law   426
The Observance and Enforcement of International Law   433
Role of Law in International Politics   434
Some Contemporary Problems of International Law   436
The International Court and International Law   444
Toward World Law   445

22. Limited-Purpose International Organizations   447

Complex Pattern of Organization   447
Wellsprings of Organized Cooperation   450
The Mechanism of Cooperation   453
Western European Cooperation   454
Nonlocalized Political Association   458
The United States as a Focus of Organized Cooperation   462
International Communist Organization   473
Conclusion   474

23. Organizing the World Community: The United Nations   **476**

The Rationale of International Collaboration   *476*
The Nature and Politics of the United Nations   *478*
The United Nations and the Maintenance of International
Peace and Security   *488*
Promotion and Development   *495*
Change in the United Nations   *498*
Conclusion   *502*

24. Change and Challenge   **504**

The Rapidity of Historic Change   *504*
The United States in the Changing World   *507*
—Conclusion   *513*

Appendix A   The Flow of Policy Making in the Department
of State   **516**

Appendix B   North Atlantic Treaty   **525**

Appendix C   Nuclear Test Ban Treaty   **529**

Appendix D   Inter-American Treaty of Reciprocal Assistance
(Rio Pact)   **532**

Appendix E   United Nations Charter   **537**

Appendix F   Protocol of Amendments to Charter   **566**

Appendix G   References   **569**

Index   **591**

Illustrations and Tables

FIGURE

1–1 Gross National Product 1964   12

1–2 Population 1964   13

3–1 "All These Foreigners Look Alike . . ."   56

4–1 How Nationalism Has Remade Maps   82

5–1 Africa—Sequence of Sovereignty   97

5–2 Possible Chinese Territorial Interests   100

6–1 Mackinder's Heartland   108

6–2 The Disputed Areas on India's Northern Border   114

6–3 Strategic Materials from Other Free Nations Are Essential to United States Industry   121

7–1 World Population: The Past 35 Years . . . The Next 35 Years   126

7–2 Population by Age Groups   129

7–3 Food and Population Growth in the Less-Developed Countries   132

8–1   Latin America—Personal Income and U.S. Economic Assistance   143

8–2   India's Food and Population Problem   146

8–3   Trade Within and Between Industrial and Nonindustrial Areas   153

11–1   The Strategists   200

12–1   National Security Organization Within the Executive Branch   228

12–2   The Department of State   232

12–3   The Department of Defense   235

13–1   The Government of Great Britain   252

13–2   Structure of the French Fifth Republic   265

14–1   Government and Party in the Union of Soviet Socialist Republics   270

14–2   Government and Party in Communist China   283

14–3   Factors in the Dispute Between Peking and Moscow   288

15–1   Population and Power Centers   306

18–1   Foreign Assistance Act Expenditures as Percent of U.S. Gross National Product   375

18–2   Assistance Received by the Developing Countries   376

18–3   Trends by Area of U.S. Assistance   378

18–4   United States Balance of Payments   381

20–1   The Spreading Threat of Nuclear Bombs   420

22–1   The Two European Trade Areas   457

22–2   Organization of American States   463

22–3   The North Atlantic Treaty Organization   467

22–4   Western Alliances—The Major Mutual Defense Treaties   471

23–1   The United Nations and Related Agencies   481

24–1   Ten Major U.S. Foreign Policy Commitments Around the World   508

TABLE

1–1   The Community of States   9

5–1   Newly Independent Countries   95

7–1 Estimated Population of World's Four Largest Countries (in Millions) at Continued Present Trends 127

8–1 Estimates of Gross National Product: Summary for Non-Communist Countries 138

8–2 Distribution of U.S. Exports in First Half of 1964 152

8–3 Some "One-Commodity" Export Countries at the Beginning of the 1960's 154

10–1 "40 Wars Since '45" 183

11–1 The Foreign Policy Process 202

19–1 How Vulnerability Affects Deterrence 392

22–1 Sample Contemporary Regional and Other Limited-Membership Organizations 449

23–1 UN Organization Voting Blocs 485

PART I

The Setting
of International Politics
Today

Preamble

A REVOLUTION OF *momentous proportions is taking place in world politics. The policies of states now flow in numerous strong currents. Nationalism continues to divide the globe politically, making international cooperation difficult and raising the possibility of further conflicts among states. This force is heightened by a militant Communism which holds to a doctrine of protracted world conflict, but is now polarized within its own domain. At the same time, traditional conceptions of the state system are changing as new states become independent, many without the traditions of the older states, many lacking conditions of stability, and all driven by an urge for rapid development. The inrush of more than two score new states has changed the complexion of the United Nations and shifted the balance of numbers from the older powers of Europe and America to newer states of Asia and Africa. The end of the line of new states is not yet in sight. An additional score or more may yet make their way into the community of states. Meanwhile, differences among the Great Powers go on largely unabated, while many of the newer states adhere to policies of neutralism and nonalignment, and the influence of the politically mature middle powers is diminished within the world*

1

organization. What the future of international relations will be as a result of the confluence of these various forces is difficult to foretell.

A revolution of equal magnitude is occurring in the realms of natural science and engineering. The recent developments in nuclear science and in military, space, and communications technology have injected a new dimension into the politics of nations, as has the expanding world population to which the new technology has contributed. The ability of man to project scientific devices beyond the earth's atmosphere, and even beyond the solar system, is symbolic of the change that is occurring in the equations of those factors which comprise the study of world affairs.

Among these changes, forces are at work tending to focus upon new forms of international cooperation centered on regional groupings of states. The concept of community, moreover, is being given new meaning in Europe and the Atlantic area, and counterforces born of national pride and prestige continue to undercut international collaboration.

The comprehension of these changes is both challenging and sobering to serious-minded citizens, who see them as having created two problems: first, how to preserve the institutions which embody established national values, and second, how to shape the world environment toward a more stable and secure international order. Other nations are confronted with these same questions, posed, however, in the context of their own objectives and perspectives.

In approaching the problems of international politics, there are at least four fundamentals we believe necessary to understanding. (1) An awareness of history. Regardless of the argument over the relevance of the past to the present and the future, the leadership of the present does have a sense of history and is influenced by it. (2) A knowledge of the structure of the world society of states and of the processes of political interaction within it. (3) An awareness of the effects of certain basic factors, such as geography, economics, demography, attitudes and ideology, power politics, and technology, which cut across and shape the environment of world politics. (4) A grasp of the motivations, sometimes termed national goals, born of internal forces and institutions, which shape the foreign policies and actions of individual states.

No single book can treat adequately all these matters, but it can strive to bring the various dynamic elements into proper perspective. This we shall try to do in the pages that follow. Difficult though it may be to comprehend all of these matters, their existence is a reality, and they form an integral part of any analysis of current situations.

Though the old international political system is in a process of accel-

erating change, traditional factors and forces still need to be considered. But we need more than traditional wisdom to comprehend the new dynamics of racing technological change, the growing political awareness of once dormant peoples, the rapidly expanding state system in which each state seeks prestige, the driving urge for betterment in the minds of millions of people, and the totality of the global thermonuclear threat. These and other forces are producing new trends in state actions, new goals of international action, and new methods of cooperation.

There have been, and are, a considerable number of theories claiming to explain relations among states. Recent advances in the social sciences have contributed to understanding these relations, and it appears that a disciplined approach to the theory and practice of international politics may be feasible. But thus far none of the formulated approaches seems to present a sufficiently adequate image of world affairs of today and tomorrow.

We believe that for the rapidly changing world of this generation the soundest method of approach to international affairs is essentially pragmatic. This is no revolutionary idea. It is an accepted approach in examining internal political systems. This approach can proceed by asking the questions: How can one usefully describe the international system? What are the forces and factors moving and changing it? What is the process by which decisions are reached on matters of foreign relations; how does this compare between countries operating under different political systems? What are the instruments and other ways by which states operate in, and attempt to influence, that system? What can be discerned as to the emerging patterns of national and international behavior? What are the institutional means available to states for advancing their interests, facilitating cooperation, and settling international disputes? Are these institutionalized procedures adequate for the tasks being thrust upon them and for modern conflict control?

This method of approach may be termed a theory *dealing with a method of approach. It is not a theory of causality and prediction. We believe, however, that it offers the surest technique for analyzing the complex data of contemporary international political affairs. Our approach derives in part from a close observation of decision making and of management of international affairs at national policy levels over a considerable period. It also derives from the teaching of international relations to large, selected bodies of students, many of whom will have to live and work in the milieu of international affairs.*

The authors have by deliberate design provided only a skeleton of analysis. Many articles and books have been written on the topics of each chapter. In a very active and changing world, current events can often give more pointed illustrations than classical historical allusions. Hence the reader is invited to fill out the picture that is sketched in the succeeding pages by reference to the suggested readings appearing at the end of the book and by continual attention to the developments in the contemporary world scene reported in the press.

CHAPTER 1

The International Political System

INTRODUCTION

International politics as a field of study has few fixed bounds with respect to time, space, or the relevance of data. It can be viewed as stretching from the past, through the present, to a future whose long-term course is difficult to predict because of the powerful forces of change that are at work in human affairs.

At any one time relations among states extend along a front ranging from limited contacts because of lack of related interests or physical separation, through varying degrees of persuasion and accommodation, either to cooperation and alliance or to friction, conflict, and sometimes open violence. The texture of these relationships often changes over time, as has that of Germany and the United States, formerly wartime enemies and now closely cooperating allies.

The purposeful use of means (strength) ranging from persuasion to instruments of violence along the front of international contact is an exercise of power. Power is, in large part, possessed and exercised by states, although it can be argued that some international agencies, such as those

5

of the European community, may acquire an independent measure of power.

Strength exercised without purpose is senseless. Strength exercised with purpose through foreign policy and foreign relations is the primary substance of international politics. Other elements in the picture are personalities and chance. This book is about the totality of international politics.

THE INTERNATIONAL POLITICAL SYSTEM

Nature of the System.   States and the interaction of their policies and relationships form the international political system. These relationships differ from those within national and subnational systems in several respects. In the first place, the central fact about international politics is that it is politics among independent national states, of which there are today more than 120. Each of these states, being sovereign and independent (at least in principle), has a leadership pursuing its own national interests as it sees them. The actions of states are the result of many factors—the judgment of the state authorities, the power available to the state, the limitations which the state has accepted and is willing to abide by in the form of treaties and agreements, the influence of world opinion and morality, and the constraining counteractions of other states or groups of states acting singly or in concert. Differing historical experiences, political ideologies, economic systems, and stages of economic growth interact with other factors—such as religion, race, culture, and territorial position—to affect the decision making and action of states.

In the second place, interstate relations differ from those within a state, where hierarchical and obligational political arrangements backed by the power of government prevail. International politics form largely a horizontal system of relationships involving coordination rather than subordination. Power is not operatively concentrated at any central point. There is no supranational authority governing states.

In the third place, because the interests and goals of states differ, there is continual competition and conflict among them. This sometimes leads to violence. Although the system has arrangements for facilitating interstate communication, adjustment depends upon the goodwill and cooperation of states. International agencies lack the power to enforce settlement of disputes, to impose solutions, and to prevent the use of force and war. Professor Quincy Wright of the University of Chicago estimated that more than 278 wars (involving 50,000 troops or more) occurred between 1500 and 1940.[1] Chapter 10 contains a list of forty wars or near wars occurring in the twenty years after 1945. It must be acknowledged that the international political system functions with more organized violence and coercion among its parts than do well-ordered domestic political systems. The international order is now complicated by wars of proxy and of "liberation" being waged within states by militant subversive groups in league with external powers, such as the Vietcong operations in South Vietnam.

Rivalries between states with substantially the same objectives are often controlled, eroded, and ultimately resolved. Peaceful procedures are routine in the absence of the high tensions that exist when states fear the possibility of the outbreak of violence. For instance, the conflict between the United States, on the one hand, and the French and British governments, on the other, over the attack of the latter on Suez did not include the possibility of war between the parties. An understanding and accommodation among these powers was eventually worked out. This has not always been true among others, as the long succession of conflicts and wars of the past three centuries shows.

States—The Actors. The actors in the international political system are the independent nation-states. Normally these states recognize one another and carry on relationships through diplomatic channels. Even without recognition and during war relationships exist.

It has been customary to define the state as a sovereign political entity. That is to say, the state must have supreme political power within its own boundaries, be independent of others, and be capable of marshaling some resources for public purposes. It normally must have a measure of unity with a government controlling its territory and people. Sovereignty, however, has shades of meaning. Political realities often produce superior-inferior relationships between one power and another—as between India and Nepal.

The preceding definition arose in the classical, restricted European context. Today there are broad variations in the degrees of political cohesion, sovereignty, and independence that states enjoy. What is essential is that the state, whatever its size, possess sufficient independent means of decision making to qualify as a sovereignty. It must have enough people, territory, and resources to sustain statehood. It must be prepared to accept commitments and obligations. And it must be recognized by others. In addition to these qualities a state should have a symbol of separate

[1] Quincy Wright, *A Study of War* (Chicago: University of Chicago Press, 1942), Vol. I, Appendix XX.

statehood in the form of a flag; a seal with which to impress legality upon documents and agreements; and a press to print money and public information. From the list of states given in Table 1–1 it is apparent that the definition needs qualification. There is greater political unity in the United States or the Netherlands, for instance, than there is in the Congo or the Sudan. There is greater freedom from external influence in the Soviet Union or France than there is in Mongolia or Cuba. There is little comparison between the magnitude of strength possessed by Britain or China on the one hand and of Upper Volta or Malé (the Maldive Islands) on the other.

There is an old saying in the state system that "Geneva is the equal of Russia." This is technically true. In other words, the smallest independent entity is regarded as being the political and legal equal of the largest. In the United Nations Assembly the vote of Togo counts the same as that of the United States or the Soviet Union, irrespective of differences in national income, development, power, population, and other factors. The Great Powers can be, and sometimes are, overwhelmingly outvoted at the United Nations.

States vary in all attributes, including the numbers of people, size of territory, character of the political system, resources, ideology, and judgment. On the one hand, we can identify them within certain broad categories. There are the *Great Powers*, which can also be called superpowers, having large nuclear arsenals and delivery systems and vast strength, and the lesser Great Powers, lacking overwhelming strength. In the first category one would put the United States and the Soviet Union today. In the second would come China, Britain, France, Germany, and Japan.

Then there are the *middle powers*, which trail the Great Powers in some important characteristic, such as population, national income, or the size of their armed establishments. In this category belong Argentina, Australia, Brazil, Canada, India, Italy, Pakistan, Poland, Sweden, and others. Most of the states of Europe fall in this middle grouping.

There are the so-called *small powers*, some of which—such as, Ethiopia, Peru, and the Sudan—are not small physically. In industrialization, national income, modern armaments, and other qualities, they rank below the middle powers. Most of the countries of Asia, Africa, and Latin America fall into this classification, although with enormous differences among them. The total of small powers far exceeds that of the Great Powers and middle powers combined. At times the small and middle powers may have considerable influence, particularly when acting together or when the Great Powers are divided.

Among the small powers there are some countries so small in physical

TABLE 1-1

The Community of States

AFRICAN		ASIAN	
Algeria	Malawi	Afghanistan	Laos
Botswana (Bechnld.)	Mali	Burma	Malaysia
Burundi	Mauretania	Cambodia	Malé (Maldive Is.)
Cameroun	Morocco	Ceylon	Mongolia
Cent. Afr. Rep.	Niger	China	Nepal
Chad	Nigeria	Ntl. Rep. (Twn.)	Pakistan
Congo (Bzvl.)	Rwanda	Peoples Rep.	Philippines
Congo (Lpldv.)	Senegal	India	Singapore
Dahomey	Sierra Leone	Indonesia	Thailand
Ethiopia	Somalia	Japan	Vietnam
Gabon	So. Africa	Korea	Rep. of:
Gambia	Sudan	Rep. of:	Peoples Rep.
Ghana	Tanzania	Dem. Peoples Rep.	
Guinea	Togo		
Ivory Coast	Tunisia		

		MIDDLE EASTERN	
Kenya	Uganda	Cyprus	Kuwait
Lesotho (Basutld.)	Untd. Arab Rep.	Iran	Lebanon
Liberia	Upper Volta	Iraq	Saudi Arabia
Libya	Zambia	Israel	Syria
Madagascar		Jordan	Turkey
			Yemen

NORTH AMERICAN	OCEANIAN
Canada	Australia
United States	New Zealand
	Samoa

WESTERN EUROPEAN	
Austria	Ireland
Belgium	Malta

CARIBBEAN	
Cuba	Denmark	Netherlands

Dominican Rep.	France	Norway
	SOUTH AMERICAN	Germany, Fed. Rep.	Portugal
Haiti		Greece	Spain
Jamaica	Argentina	Iceland	Sweden
Trinidad & Tobago	Bolivia	Italy	Switzerland
	Brazil	Luxembourg	United Kingdom
	Chile		Vatican State

CENTRAL AMERICAN	
	Colombia
Costa Rica	Ecuador

EASTERN EUROPEAN	
El Salvador	Guyana
Guatemala	Paraguay	Albania	Hungary
Honduras	Peru	Bulgaria	Poland
Mexico	Uruguay	Byelorussia	Rumania
Nicaragua	Venezuela	Czechoslovakia	Soviet Union
Panama		Finland	Ukraine
		Germany, Dem. Rep.	Yugoslavia

POLITICAL ENTITIES WITH QUALIFIED STATUS			
Aden (Fed. of S. Arabia)	Bhutan	Bahrein	British
Liechtenstein	Muscat	Monaco	Honduras (Beliz)
Rhodesia	Mauritius	Swaziland	Qatar
Andorra	San Marino		Trucial Oman

size, population, and resources they may be aptly termed *mini-states*. These miniature states, of which Malé (the Maldive Islands), Guyana, Togo, Kuwait, Samoa, and Trinidad and Tobago are examples, have attributes of statehood. They are independent, recognized by others, and enjoy diplomatic relations. Many are members of the United Nations, each with a vote equal to that of the United States and the Soviet Union. Their ability to contribute substantially to security, the support of international bodies, and to the economic growth of others is, however, limited.

Over and beyond these categories of states are a number of *political entities with qualified status*. These include protectorates like Monaco, Liechtenstein, and San Marino, principalities left over from former days that are enclosed within larger states and usually have their foreign affairs conducted for them by the protector. The Vatican State may be placed in this category, although its spiritual and temporal power is in a different category from others. Its integrity and neutrality are protected by Italy.

Finally, though not to be classed as states, there are the *international bodies* set up by states that have acquired distinct political personalities and often have their own representation. Examples are the United Nations Organization, NATO, and the European Economic Community, the Organization of American States, and the World Bank. A few, notably the EEC, have some supranational qualities. Others are instrumentalities of states for the performance of designated functions. But their executives are sometimes accorded a standing of their own and perform missions that involve more than national representation.

The international political system, then, comprises the states, and political entities just described, and the interrelationships and interactions among them.

Figures 1–1 and 1–2 show the Powers by gross national product and by population (cf. pp. 12–13). The correlation between power status and gross national product is readily apparent from Figure 1–1. This status is, however, also derived from rate of expansion of gross national product. For example, United States GNP currently expands in approximately two years as much as total Chinese Communist GNP.[2] By and large, GNP is about as near to the political-economic and military realities of states as one can get. Power status is also related to population growth, as will be pointed out in succeeding chapters.

The Guiding Role of the National Interest.   The most immediate guiding element behind the policies and actions of states is the furthering of what their leaders in decision-making positions believe to be the *national*

[2] See *The Economist*, June 4, 1966.

interest of the state. There may be differing views on what the national interest is and requires in a particular situation. Concepts of the national interest are centered on core values of the society, which include the welfare of the nation, the security of its political beliefs, national way of life, territorial integrity, and its self-preservation. These goals must be implemented by specific policies and programs which seek to create and preserve a favorable international environment. Past experiences and attitudes also condition the judgment of the circumstances on which leaders base their policy decisions.

Some states attempt to protect what they conceive to be their national interests by defending a given status quo, some by enlarging their territory or sphere of influence, some by attempting to reduce a foreign threat or danger, others by striving to dominate weaker states. These policies sometimes involve making alliances. Still other states seek to reconcile their interests with the international environment by adopting policies of isolation, nonalignment, or neutralism. The fact that states have similar objectives tells us little about the methods they may follow to achieve them.

The Nature of Power.   Power is a means and not an end in itself but has meaning only in terms of its purpose. The *power* of a state is, first, relative to the power of other states. Second, it is conditional, depending on a variety of factors, such as nationalism, which may operate where power is to be applied. Third, it is situational, depending on the specific international case where, regardless of the strength commanded by a state, the power available may be appropriate or inappropriate to the circumstances. Power in the international political sense has to be defined in terms of the *relationships* of particular states in particular circumstances. Strength composed of economic, psychological, moral, military, and political elements, successfully directed to the furtherance of national interests, constitutes national power. An appraisal of a state's actual power in a given situation requires a much more complex analysis and judgment than can be derived from a simple listing and measurement of these elements.

Broadly speaking, the factors of national power can be grouped in two categories: (1) those concerned with physical elements, such as location, natural resources, productive capacity, the military establishment, and population; and (2) those concerned with intangible elements, such as national character, morale, leadership, prestige, and the international appeal of a state's policies. These two categories correspond respectively to (a) elements that are concrete enough to be quantified to some extent, and (b) elements that are primarily qualitative of which the statecraft of leadership is the most important single element.

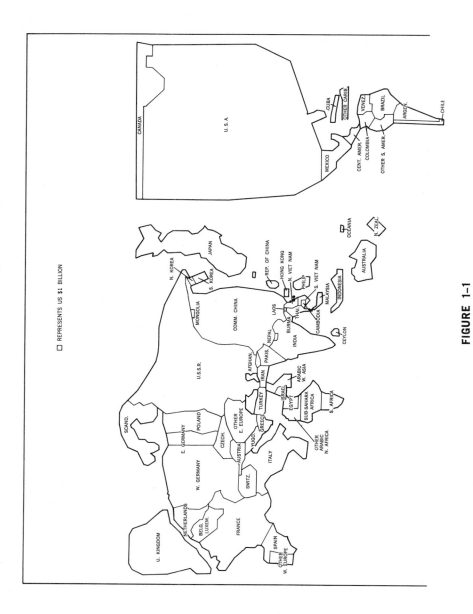

FIGURE 1-1

Gross National Product 1964 (*Designed by Edwin O. Reischauer. Reprinted by permission*)

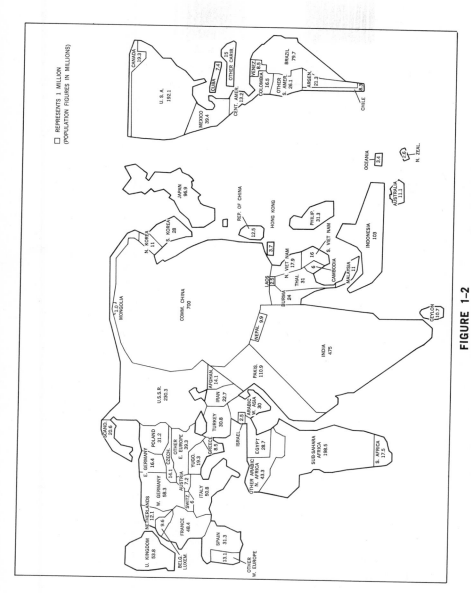

FIGURE 1-2

Population 1964 *(Designed by Edwin O. Reischauer. Reprinted by permission)*

In thinking about power relationships it is helpful to make two distinctions. First, power in the sense to which the press and public usually refer, is the total visible capacity to achieve a purpose in the interstate political process, regardless of consensus. Essentially this is power to influence or to coerce, that is, the capability to resist and to impose one's will upon others who may be weaker or who do not agree with the values or objectives of the state possessing the power. Second, there is a type of power that is often overlooked, based upon consensus in shared values. This power takes the form of voluntary agreement among states to follow a given course of action desired by one or more of them. Consent is given because the parties share certain values or interests in a particular situation. For instance the power of the North Atlantic states depends largely on a consensus of values and ends which complements their strength in weapons and economic resources. Also the African states, despite other divisions, are a significant element in international politics because of the sheer numbers they comprise and their general agreement on the issues of anticolonialism and nonalignment. In terms of effective military strength there is no comparison between the coercive tone available to the NATO countries and the African states. But in terms of political lobbying and voting strength at the United Nations or other international gatherings, the African states have an influence that is out of proportion to their military manpower, industrial capacity, and technical skills. The combined voting strength of the thirty-seven African states and other nonaligned countries is greater than that of the NATO members and other economically advanced states. This was demonstrated in the resolutions on development assistance at the Geneva Conference on Trade and Development in 1964. The practitioner of *Realpolitik* may wryly comment that majority control in international gatherings has drifted toward groupings with only a small proportion of world productive capacity, sometimes only a small proportion of the population, and often with unstable governments.

Power in international politics is above all the ability to influence international actions. And like those who seek high office in domestic politics in order to influence the choice of policies and action, states employ their available elements of strength in order to gain their ends, advance their interests, and shape international decisions and actions to their values, goals, and desires.

National and international politics share many concepts. But national politics, as practiced in the North Atlantic area, are more likely to be moderate and orderly, being carried on within a constitutional framework of government and law enforcement. They are rarely characterized by organized rebellion and violence, as they may be in some of the newer states and in countries lacking a strong consensus or sense of political unity. International politics, being politics among sovereign states, are less restrained by established institutions and shared values. Having few agreed rules by which the widely differing interests and objectives of states are regulated, and few governing mechanisms, international politics have long been characterized by differences, disputes, and conflicts.

The question as to whose values or whose ends will prevail in international politics is determined finally by the relative power positions of the parties. For as values help set men's purposes, so the use of power in its various forms—political, moral, economic, and military—is a means of achieving a state's ends. In the broad sense, power is used by states to act upon their environment, to bring about situations or patterns of relationships which best satisfy their value objectives. This is why power is necessary to freedom—which means, of course, freedom to act in accordance with one's values.

Because national power is continually being brought to bear in international relations to achieve or advance national interests and values, international politics are inherently power politics.

Prestige.   An important element associated with power is the *prestige* which accompanies its possession and use. The essence of prestige is the respect in which a state is held by others. This may include affection or close friendship. United States prestige has been high although specific United States attitudes and actions have not always been popular. Prestige is usually derived from successful use of power to achieve desired results—that is, a reputation for success. At the same time, great power tends to generate jealousy, criticism, misunderstanding, and sensitivities among lesser states. But a Great Power can be respected and have a dependable reputation.

Prestige, unlike the relatively stable nature of the national interest, is a volatile phenomenon. It is psychological and considered in relation to specific political situations and actions. Prestige can decrease rapidly with loss of territory or failure to keep commitments or match the scientific achievements of others. Not all states hold another in the same esteem. With over 120 states in the world, the United States or any other country cannot expect its prestige at any one time to be high with them all.

The power in a state's prestige comes partly from respect for the strength of a state and partly from the desire of other states to be identified with the purposes, or to emulate the accomplishments, of a successful and powerful state. Because prestige augments power, it is sought and defended by statesmen as an important adjunct of policy.

The Idea of Community.   The international political world is sometimes spoken of as the "society of states." Parts of it are called the European community, the North Atlantic community, the American states, and the Soviet bloc. These terms imply that there are common interests and objectives among specific groups of states and among all. What is community—a familiar idea among individuals—and how much community exists in interstate relations?

A *community* can be defined by its ends—that is, its common values or purposes. Values embody what men esteem. When men agree on values, ideals, or purposes, they form a community and usually cooperate to win these common ends. Differences are adjusted by peaceful procedures. A political community is committed to this core value: a political order with procedures for resolving disputes and effecting changes. When there is no agreement on these fundamentals there is unlikely to be a stable situation.

The present society of states has four features. First, the community is loosely structured. It has few common values. Most states do respect the principles of international law most of the time in accordance with their respective interpretations. Second, the community does not assure continued existence of political entities as independent states or that they will be free from internal subversion or violent change. Many entities in the past have failed to survive, the Austro-Hungarian Empire being an example. Third, the society of states has few central political organs, and these have generally been weak. In the nineteenth century there was the Concert System of the European Great Powers; in this century, the League of Nations and the United Nations. All three institutions have depended on their member states for the implementation of the resolutions and agreements reached diplomatically in their meetings. Within the international community there is an increasing trend toward the use of institutional arrangements for facilitating relationships. But the ultimate power in international relations resides with the states. Fourth, the society is sharply divided within itself. The Communist powers are not only ranged together against the West, but also have their own dissensions. The nonaligned nations combine sometimes with the West, sometimes with the East, and sometimes with neither. And the Western camp is not united.

Smaller groupings of states within international society, like the European Economic Community, share a considerable body of values and purposes. Canada and the United States form a sort of community in the

American hemisphere having common interests in preserving the integrity of the North American continent, their democratic institutions, and high standards of living. Similarly, the members of the Organization of American States and the North Atlantic states form nascent communities, though with somewhat fewer shared values than those of Canada and the United States. The *free world* is a vague term denoting little formal community but some mutual interests among its states. The world community, however, incorporates no shared values other than avoidance of nuclear war and the aspiration for economic and social advancement, even though the United Nations Organization is a universal political instrument.

THE PROBLEMS OF ORDER AND CHANGE

One of the principal problems in world politics is to adjust between the views of states that favor the existing international order and those proposing change. This is crucial when some powers are determined to maintain the status quo (which is to their advantage), whereas others are no less determined to change the existing order, by use of force and violence, if necessary, to improve their political position. In such cases, for example in the 1930's and 1940's, power politics may reach its most dangerous and violent phases with the outbreak of total war.

The Concept of the International Order. The arrangement of relations among states at a particular time is often spoken of as the *international order* at that time. Any order tends to reflect the values and interests of the stronger and more influential states, for it is shaped by their relative power. If the existing order is to continue, it must be upheld by that power, that is, the power of those states whose interests and purposes it serves. The United States ignored this principle when it withdrew its support from the international order established at Versailles in 1919. This was an order to be based on collective security rather than on balance-of-power politics agreed to by the Allies because it had been proposed by the United States.

A universal order was established under the Roman Empire that extended Roman citizenship and law to others. This order was supported by the military power of Rome and by some agreement on values. When Roman power proved insufficient, the system collapsed. Similarly, in the nineteenth century a world order based on European values was maintained by European power. After 1945 the power of the metropolitan states in Europe declined and the old order crumbled as nationalism spread to Asia and Africa. In place of the old order a new one developed to accommodate fifty new sovereign, independent African and Asian states, and a greatly changed pattern of power positions among states.

Peaceful versus Violent Change.   When a state finds its values reasonably satisfied by the international order, it will ordinarily help to uphold that order and will work for the adjustment of relations as power positions change. When a state does not accept as right or just the principles on which the order is based—as Adolf Hitler did not accept the Versailles Treaty terms—it will use whatever means, strategies, and power lie within its command to attempt an overthrow of the order.

States which are satisfied with a stabilized order and wish to preserve it become status quo powers, often appealing to law, order, and peace to justify their stand. Those seeking a radical change are viewed as revisionist or revolutionary powers. Both sides may insist that their object is the preservation or attainment of a legitimate international order. Revolutionary powers may claim that their values or purposes are more important than the existing order and justify resort to violence.

Today Communist China poses the principal challenge to the existing order. Its leaders state they seek not merely an adjustment, but a complete transformation of world order—if necessary, by violence.

The conflict between order and justice as interpreted by revisionist states contributes to the dynamism of world politics and demands that states consider seriously the problem of peaceful political change. Failure of the Versailles order to effect an adequate adjustment by peaceful means was a major reason for World War II.

In stable domestic societies orderly procedures for change are usually institutionalized through a constitutional system. Laws and order emerge as the political process transforms the situation. In international politics the procedures for change are far less formalized. More depends upon the power states can throw into the situation. When pressure for change becomes serious enough to threaten peace and security, someone is likely to appeal to the United Nations for emergency measures to prevent or to control hostilities. These steps have become particularly significant in a world sensitive to the contagious effect of hostilities and the existence of destructive weapons capable of rapid deployment anywhere. It is the function of diplomacy and of international organization to encourage states to seek change through peaceful procedures and to deal with violence when it occurs. This problem of adapting the existent order to legitimate demands for change is one of the major tasks of statecraft.

Peace, Security, and World Order.   Peace is not necessarily synonymous with national security. Security exists when a state neither fears attack nor anticipates other states overturning the basic framework of relations between states to its disadvantage. For any one state security is the concomitant of an international order in which all other states with important relationships affecting that state, and with the power to change these relationships, are reasonably satisfied with the existent order—that is, they find the order consonant with their own basic interests. Where this consensus is lacking or where some powerful state or group of states is deliberately seeking to overthrow or subvert the order or is aiming to attack another state, there obviously cannot be a full sense of security. Because security arises from a state's perception of its relations to others, it is a psychological phenomenon.

There is general agreement that peace and security are the primary purposes of a world order, but there is not agreement on the nature of the present world order. And the type of future world order is a controversial issue. There are two generally opposed viewpoints—those of the Western states on the one hand, and of the Communist states on the other. There is a third viewpoint held by the loose grouping of states that tend toward neutralism and nonalignment. Communist doctrine teaches that non-Communist states are not to be tolerated, but "liberated" and added to the Communist group. The Western states, if they had their way, would probably stabilize an order based on the national independence and equality of states. The "middle third," which includes more than a third of the world's population, seeks independence, self-expression, and development.

Peace may be the "most important assignment of the century," as President Johnson has said, but it cannot be attained merely by saying, "Let there be peace." For states seek other ends which may be valued even more than peace. So in the study of international politics we must give considerable attention to the policies states pursue in their effort to achieve national security.

ADJUSTING THE INTERNATIONAL SYSTEM

The same states that sometimes cooperate and sometimes conflict in exercising their power form the system for maintaining order and accomplishing change in international affairs. This system is not sharply defined and scholars do not agree about its nature and theory of operation.

Traditional Diplomacy and the Balance of Power.   Traditionally the international political system has functioned through the medium of diplomacy and by the exercise of power politics. This is understandable because the purpose of gaining and exercising political power is to influence the behavior and actions of other states.[3] In this system each state seeks to advance its own interests and pursue its own goals as it sees fit, utilizing the procedures of diplomacy supported by whatever power it is able to bring to bear. This has customarily meant dealing with other states through negotiations and the operation of agreements. Diplomacy also involves concerted actions when the interests of several states converge.

A society of sovereign states, each practicing power politics in pursuit of its national interest, suggests anarchy and conflict. However, states are interdependent and their interests often coincide. One of the recognized characteristics of the international system is a tendency toward a *balance-of-power* situation by which state relationships move in dynamic equilibrium. Such a balance is rarely static. The balance-of-power concept as a principle of international politics will be discussed in Chapter 15. Here we shall briefly outline its history.

The European states have been the main practitioners of the balance of power, whether seeking equilibrium or overthrow of the balance. Napoleon strove to dominate Europe through his Grand Army campaigns from Spain to the gates of Moscow. Other states formed the Quadruple Alliance in an effort to preserve their freedom and finally re-established the equilibrium of the European Concert by breaking Napoleon's power.

During the nineteenth century British governments believed it to be in the national interest for Britain to function as a "balancer" between any group of powers on the Continent. Britain joined in opposition to Napoleon, realigned with the French and Sardinians against Russia in the Crimean War, and later formed the Triple Entente, with France and Russia counterbalancing the Triple Alliance of Germany, Austria-Hungary, and Italy.

World War I and then Hitler's drive for European hegemony destroyed the balancing system in the twentieth century. Attempts were made in the nineteenth century to extend the operation of the balance of power beyond Europe to the competition among European powers for colonial possessions and to British maneuvers against the expansion of Czarist Russia around the rim of Asia from the Black Sea to the Sea of

[3] See Franz Neumann, "Approaches to the Study of Political Power," *Political Science Quarterly*, June 1950. See also Martin Wight, *Power Politics* (London: Royal Institute of International Affairs, 1949); and Robert Dahl, *Modern Political Analysis* (Englewood Cliffs, N.J.: Prentice-Hall, 1963).

Japan. After World War II international politics ceased to be primarily European. One of the principal questions in this new context was whether some equilibrium would be reached between the Communist powers and others.

The power of the United States is now central to the successful functioning of most regional balances and any global balance. The Greek-Turkish Aid Program, the Berlin crisis in 1948–1949, NATO, the Korean War, the Cuban missile crisis in 1962, Vietnam, the division of Germany, bipolarization in the Communist camp, and the independent line taken by General de Gaulle can be related to the tendency of state leaderships to seek a favorable balance of power. The equation of world relations is further complicated by the large number of new nonaligned nations and the growth of international organizations. Power politics and balance-of-power maneuvers have not been superseded by the United Nations, which has both helped and hindered power struggles.

Collective Security and a New Universal Approach. At the close of World War I, under the leadership of Woodrow Wilson, the League of Nations was created to be a universal instrument to effect order and change with peace and justice. The League was an attempt to establish a concert-of-power system, operating by agreed principles, to replace the old order dominated by balance-of-power considerations. Wilson insisted on formalizing in the League the concept of *collective security*. The new system was based on the participation of all the principal states, establishment of machinery for peaceful change, and willingness to employ sanctions and collective force against threats to peace and security and acts of war.

The League's usefulness was limited. It eventually broke down for a variety of reasons, including the refusal of the United States to participate, British and French differences, Hitler's rearming of Germany, and Japanese and Italian aggression in Manchuria and Ethiopia. Efforts to re-establish balance replaced the Wilson formula for a new order, eventuating in World War II.

At the close of World War II, again under the combined leadership of the United States and Britain, but with the support of Russia, China, and France, the victorious powers agreed to set up an improved system of collective security to be called the United Nations Organization. The U.N. Charter was based on the expressed intent of the Allied powers to stand together and to use and support the United Nations in the maintenance of international peace and security. The U.N. design is studied more closely in Chapter 23.

The United Nations has had some success in dealing with threats to international peace and security. The organization has helped bring about a number of cease-fires, notably in Palestine and Suez. Peacekeeping forces have been recruited under U.N. auspices for use when international peace has been threatened, although disputes and serious financial difficulties have arisen for the organization in some instances. A United Nations command was created for forces called to defend the Republic of Korea. Although violations of international agreements have been exposed in the forum of the U.N. there has been no certain decrease in tension or even an assured reduction in conflicts between smaller powers because of such exposures. In fact these are continued in corridor diplomacy and open debate of the U.N. The arms race has not abated despite efforts to maintain peace and security and to resolve conflicts.

Meanwhile, the powerful coalition that defeated the Axis powers has partly disintegrated. The former enemy states have been welcomed as allies of the West. And the Soviet Union, with its own alignments in some disarray, has turned first toward, and then away from, Communist China. Collective security has been weakened by mutual suspicions, the Communist desire for world leadership, Western fears, and lack of common values and bonds.

Rules of the Game. The rules and principles of the international political system are not codified, and not all of them are clearly defined or universally accepted. Even the generally accepted rules are subordinate to the paramount consideration of national interest in a crisis.

There are at least four generally recognized sources of the rules of the game: diplomatic practices, international law, morality, and world public opinion. Diplomacy and international law are discussed in Chapters 16 and 21. The significance of morality and world opinion is difficult to determine. The behavior of states and agreements among them sometimes reflect a moral consciousness and respect for world opinion. No nation likes to stand condemned before the bar of world opinion, and so states will go to great lengths to refute charges of amoral or immoral conduct. Morality is a component underlying the goodwill and confidence which affects the image and prestige of a state.

However, moral considerations have only a limited effect in world politics when each state is the ultimate guarantor of its own existence and holds that defense of its own national interest is its highest moral duty. The cumulative influence of religion, law, humanitarianism, enlightened self-interest, and a disposition to define some aspects of international relations in terms of broad principles of universal applicability have brought some conceptions of moral "oughtness" into the realm of international politics. To say that the field of international politics is served only by selfishness, brutality, self-righteousness, and unrestrained appetite for power is not only overly cynical, but unrealistic. Man's moral nature and his aspirations for a better world do exert an influence upon the course of international relations.

Morality implies the acceptance of certain standards of behavior. These vary among cultures, ideologies, and states, and even within states. One of the most difficult questions in international relations is to what extent states recognize moral obligations toward each other.

In sum, the rules of diplomatic practice, international law, morality, and world opinion are interpreted and enforced by the states themselves and may often be ignored with impunity. They are least likely to be dominant in the vital issues of security, peace or war, but do provide guidelines for the routine conduct of interstate affairs.

DYNAMIC ELEMENTS IN CONTEMPORARY WORLD POLITICS

Since World War II, new forces or elements have developed in the international political system affecting its operation and the nature of the world order. Some of them, briefly mentioned, follow.

Rapid Nation Building and Development. History may designate the last half of this century as the "Era of Nation Building." Never in a comparable period have so many new states entered international society as in the period since 1950. More than fifty new political entities have been created out of the old colonial empires of Europe. In Africa alone there are over thirty-five states, compared with less than half a dozen in 1948. At the time of the Congress of Vienna in 1815 there were less than twenty modern states in the entire world.

Most of these new states, which are a result of the spread of nationalism and the decline of former colonial empires, define their primary interests as full independence, faster progress toward modern industrialization and a rapid increase in standards of living. Most of these states are underdeveloped in comparison with Western standards. Yet the "revolution of rising expectations" exists everywhere. Development may in fact be slow and difficult, for it usually involves major social, political, and economic changes.

The relationships between the economically advanced and the

developing states, the rich and the poor, the haves and have-nots have become one of the main problems of contemporary politics. Much of the capital and technology necessary for development must come from the advanced states. International relations are complicated by this increase in interdependence and the clash between Communism and democratic forces in the development field. There may be marked differences in the national interests of developed and developing countries. Many states consider the interstate aspects of development more important than alignment in any struggle against Communism. The developing countries tend to favor socialist ideas and practices in government and neutralist foreign policies. Rapid development and stable democratic government are difficult to achieve simultaneously. Social and economic revolution often spells political instability and consequent uncertainty in international affairs. A substantial number of the newer states have been beset with coups, revolutionary shifts, temporary dictatorships, and other forms of instability since becoming independent. These tendencies may continue for years. The development of new institutions, a foreign policy, and experienced leadership is a slow process.

The increase in population and availability of politics to largely illiterate masses through modern communication techniques has added to the political unpredictability of some of the new countries. In Algeria, 61 per cent of the population is under twenty-five, compared with 43 per cent in the United States. When the pool of potential leadership in a country includes only a few college graduates and experienced administrators—as in Libya, the Congo, and several other states when they became independent—and when foreign policy can come under the direct pressure of the mass of politically inexperienced citizens, the hazards to world politics are certain to be increased. With the increase in population, modern technology has also enabled political leaders and aspirants to reach the masses and work upon their emotions where before only a few could be reached. Democratic institutions also permit masses of semiliterate persons to vote and thus determine the policies and destinies of their countries.

The nature of the newly emergent nationalism of Asia and Africa is still somewhat obscure and shows significant differences of emphasis from country to country. There is considerable point, however, to the statement of the late Prime Minister Nehru of India that this new nationalism is essentially an "antifeeling," turned primarily against the West and suspected manifestations of neocolonialism. If one of the dynamic elements of world affairs were not a Communism committed to world conquest in its doctrines and in the self-professed goals of its leaders, the new nationalism could be viewed with equanimity. But some of the states are vulnerable and hence a cause of concern.

Political Instability. In a nation state system as interdependent for security and welfare as ours has become, and with its global and regional power realities, any suggestion that governments are not interested in the internal affairs of other states is a myth. The stability of individual governments and the processes by which power is passed internally are of concern to others and important internationally.

Over half of the political entities now present in the world have experienced rapid change since 1955. Many of these are without lengthy experience in self-government. It seems likely that a significant portion of these states may be characterized by unstable governments and turbulence incident to struggles for internal power between the in's and out's during the near future.

Since the wave of independence swept over the former colonial empires there have been well over one hundred revolts, coups, uprisings, and insurgencies within states in addition to armed clashes between states. Coups overthrew established governments in nine African countries in 1965 alone. Most of this unrest has occurred south of a line drawn through the Mediterranean and the 35th parallel, in lands where per capita income is less than $250 U.S. a year.

The recurrent nature of forceful and irregular change suggests that political instability is a condition statesmen must reckon with for some time. Economic growth, social advancement and transformation of traditional conditions may come more slowly than the new ruling elites have prepared their peoples to expect. Unrest and tendencies to seek quick answers by violent means may be widespread. The danger is that alien elements may attempt to fish in these waters, as they sought to do in the Congo, or that local politicians will stir up troubles with other states in order to distract attention from intractable conditions at home which they cannot change, with resultant threats to peace and security. Some degree of crisis decision relative to new regimes, or some other aspect of U.S. relations with the country concerned, may therefore confront the Secretary of State several times a year.

The Conflict of Ideologies. The beliefs which men hold form a powerful incentive behind their actions. Specifically structured and doctrinaire beliefs are called ideologies. Today the global struggle between the forces of Communism, on the one hand, and of democracy and practically all other political systems, on the other, is a central feature of world politics. Many see this struggle as determining the scope and nature of contemporary world politics. "Peaceful coexistence" does not imply absence of conflict, but is a slogan for nonviolent conflict, implying Communist confidence that the non-Communist world can be taken over peacefully. It is a face-saving position on which Soviet Communism can fall back should the non-Communist world prove too tenacious, or Chinese Communism become more of a threat than the continued existence of a free world. Chairman Mao Tse-tung's government in China has declared that "war of annihilation is the fundamental guiding principle" of Communist strategy and includes the waging of "people's wars" in Asia, Africa, and Latin America. For the present generation the conflict between the non-Communist states and Communism is likely to remain a feature of international politics.

Within the sphere of Communist influence a new dynamic has arisen in the polycentrism, i.e., the lessening of Soviet control over the national Communist movements in Eastern Europe, and in the conflict between the two Communist giants—China and the Soviet Union. The outcome of the Sino-Soviet struggle is by no means clear, but it has a profound effect upon international politics and the international political system.

Technology. A third dynamic element in contemporary international politics is burgeoning technology, especially in the West and the U.S.S.R. It is usual nowadays to stress the exponential increase in technological knowledge. Its application in ways directly and indirectly affecting international relations is on such a massive scale as to constitute a unique phenomenon of our time. Although most people think initially of the effect on military power, the first impact to be considered should be on the arts of communication. The revolution in the methods and the extent of mass communication affects both domestic and international politics. These effects sometimes include passing over leadership in direct appeals to peoples. Technology has made propaganda and "public information," the influencing of mass opinion at home and abroad, a major instrument of policy. The mass media have made foreign affairs both a big business and a business present in the lives of peoples everywhere. Through the radio and television there are now few audiences that cannot be reached almost instantaneously by one or another of the modern media.

Advanced technology, once the private preserve of the states of the West, can now be used effectively by all peoples with a reasonable modicum of skills. Knowledge of a written language is not necessary to listen to oral appeals or to learn how to employ machines. Industrialization is no longer a monopoly of a few states. Nor is the operation of modern military weapons any longer a Western monopoly.

At the same time as industrialization has been spreading geographically, technology has facilitated the "population explosion" which is occurring in many of the underdeveloped countries where population growth rates are close to or exceeding economic growth rates. The world's population has doubled within the past sixty-five years. It is estimated that by the year 2000, the world population may be over 6 billion. More than 1 billion of these people are expected to live in mainland China before then. The most serious aspect of the "population explosion" is that many of the highest growth rates are in countries least able to support the new "unbidden guests at the table of life," as Pope Paul VI phrased it in his address to the United Nations General Assembly. In these countries there will be dangerous pressure on existing food supplies, creating critical problems of public health, political stability, international cooperation, foreign aid, and the maintenance of international peace and security.

International Institutions and the Political Process.　One of the notable features of the present-day system is the increase in the number and use of international institutions. The United Nations Organization and its multitude of specialized agencies, conferences, and related bodies is the prime example. With a membership of approximately 120 states, the U.N. has become a forum where the world's statesmen gather to exchange views, to debate controversial issues, and to seek solutions of differences through a multiplicity of efforts and methods. In addition to the United Nations there is an ever-increasing number of functional bodies, regional organizations, and other multilateral institutions whose business ranges from the exchange of information, to the regulation of coal and steel production, adjustment of tariffs, establishment of international air traffic schedules, and collaboration on mutual defense arrangements. The huge web of international organization, and its activities, is one of the newer dimensions of world politics. It has no parallel in previous history.

CONCLUSION

The nineteenth-century system of world politics has disintegrated. The world is still evolving to a new system and the characteristics of the transition are not clear. They include an increasing dependence of peoples on an effective system of world politics and a greatly increased mass sensitivity to world affairs. There is a new pattern of sovereign states. There is an acceptance of drastic change whose trends can be guided and assisted, but not checked. Tension and often conflict are inherent in this fluid situation. The outcome of these tensions and conflicts will determine whether the next reasonably definable system of international relations will be shaped by the forces believing in the values of free institutions and peaceful cooperation in accordance with the principles of the United Nations Charter, or alternatively, whether the system will succumb to the forces that seek to destroy the independence of states. Or will the system be one of compromise and temporary accommodation among power groupings operating like the classical balance of power? These are among the possibilities facing mankind in the last third of this century.

CHAPTER 2

Toward a Theory of International Politics: A Framework of Analysis

INTRODUCTION

Historians and political thinkers have long sought to order the chaotic data of international politics. Early theories of a political order were contributed by Plato, Confucius, and the Indian scholar Kautilya. Thucydides describes in his *History of the Peloponnesian War* the politics and diplomacy of the ancient Greek city-states.

Today there are a number of approaches and theories for studying international politics. The older approaches emphasize the traditional methods of political science, economics, and law. But as scholars and observers have sought to shed new light on the forces underlying the practices of states, they have begun to consider behavioral factors, systems analysis, and to strive for a comprehensive theory of international relationships. More knowledge of the cross-disciplinary areas of the social sciences such as political psychopathology, and the use of mathematical models, have suggested new methods for handling data and new techniques for appraising political and social forces. The study of international relations is currently in a state of ferment. Theorizing has become the order of the day. Serious efforts are being made to utilize social science techniques in order to establish verifiable propositions.

This book is not designed to be primarily a study of theories or systems of analysis to explain future patterns of development. It is instead focused on central concepts, relationships, and facts operative in international affairs today. Regardless of differing viewpoints on the way to approach the study of international politics, there is no question of the existence and importance of international politics.

In the following pages we will describe five ways of organizing the data of international affairs: (1) the historical approach; (2) a systemic approach; (3) the normative or philosophical approach; (4) the policy science approach; and (5) an eclectic approach.

THE HISTORICAL APPROACH

The historical approach, which places major emphasis on diplomatic history, has been the principal traditional approach to international politics. Contemporary foreign affairs are heavily conditioned by views and precedents inherited from the past and projected through the present into the future. They are influenced by ties and conflicts of former years as well as by principles of interstate relationships that have grown up through long use. Diplomatic history is particularly rewarding in revealing how statesmen have succeeded and failed in the past, what they have found safe and useful, and what they have found dangerous and illusory.

One of the principal values of the historical approach lies in its exposition of the changes which have taken place since the last half of the nineteenth century. As international affairs moved through the previous century, the practice of diplomacy, formerly restricted to a limited circle of political relationships, was carried on by a small corps of professional diplomats in a slow-moving international framework dominated by a few great powers. This traditional system of European politics has within a few decades become a global system. There has been a geometric progression in the pace of history and the pace of relations among states. Relationships have been multiplied by the increase in participating states, by the advent of international agencies, and by the growing concern on the international level with the expansion of foreign affairs in the economic, military, ideological, and cultural fields. Action programs now extend far beyond the traditional purview of foreign offices and professional diplomats alone.

Diplomatic history can still serve as a useful vehicle for studying the evolution of international relations. It is a helpful means of tracing the courses of different policies, programs, and responses in their historical context. The historical approach can also afford an effective matrix for examining the extent to which the practice of nations has conformed to the norms and goals proclaimed as the bases of policies. History is also helpful in discovering how decisions were reached, in following public opinion and group interests, and in observing what has happened to the various inputs and outputs in the decision-making process.

History is a laboratory for examining the relationships between cause and effect in world politics. The consequences of given policies and actions can be seen if it is remembered that each situation is unique and that history never exactly repeats itself. But history, or any other single academic discipline, cannot tell statesmen precisely how men will act or react under new circumstances and with different actors at the helm. History cannot teach decision makers what they ought to decide in any given situation. It can suggest possible courses by giving focus to past events, trends, and demonstrated interests. Decision making is a political process that must be carried out in the context of the times—a context that always has some new elements in it.

History emphasizes two important aspects of international relations: that there is always change and that there are no permanently fixed directions in which politics operate. In the modern scene the study of diplomatic and other history, although still useful, is an inadequate approach taken alone. The student of politics needs to know more about the art of decision making and bargaining in the context of present forces than historical writing about the past can tell us.

THREE SYSTEMIC APPROACHES

Few will deny that there is some coherence, regularity, and order in international affairs. The controversies are primarily about the generalizations which describe the real world of international politics, and on the direction of movement of that world. The following sections describe three views or models of how the state system should be organized and operated. No one of them is wholly adequate for portraying the present international order exactly. The reader will recognize that the present system includes characteristics of each of the systems described. International affairs seem generally to emphasize a pattern which includes one or the other of these variants.

The Balance of Power. The most durable concept of a system ordering international politics in the era of the modern state has been that of the balance of power. This arrangement, described in more detail in Chapter 15, has evolved out of the concurrent existence of a group of sovereign states, each pursuing its own interests through whatever means and with whatever power it can summon.

Some see in contemporary international politics a continuation of the balance-of-power system which largely governed the relations of European states in the eighteenth and nineteenth centuries. This observation stems from the fact that the primary actors in world politics are states. Because relationships between states are often competitive in character, it is assumed that they are conducted in terms of power—that is, of strengths purposefully applied to practical relationships. Power struggles are typical of human relationships and form the only possible basis for the continued independence of national sovereign states. The continued existence of small states and the absence of major wars are the alleged benefits of the system, provided statesmen conform to its special rules of procedure. The rationality and skill of statesmen and diplomats are vital components of the order, for it is they who perform the delicate art of "balancing" power in changing world circumstances.

Nationality made balance-of-power politics legitimate by setting limits upon the aspirations of statesmen to extend their domains. In the age of monarchy the doctrine of the "divine right of kings" provided an ideological base for the perpetuation of the system, for if foreign armies could topple one, domestic mobs could topple others. Wars rarely were aimed at the extinction of an opponent, lest his strength be needed on a later occasion to help meet a threat of aggression from some other quarter.

In the golden age of the balance of power, world politics centered in Europe. Dynasties and diplomats intermarried with little regard to nationality. French was the common language spoken by most leaders, who were often more closely tied to one another across state boundaries than to the humble masses who spoke the tongues of particular countries. Only Christian states were involved until the inclusion of Turkey, China, and Japan in the system in the nineteenth century. Furthermore, European society generally accepted certain common values, such as the right to live and let live, private enterprise, and the profit motive. When the crusading zeal and mass armies of the French Revolution challenged the social structure of Europe few restraints were placed upon the processes of politics. But then European affairs reverted again to a comparatively orderly system for another century after the brief interlude of Napoleon.

In the classical model of the balance-of-power system, Great Britain frequently played the role of "balancer." Her island position, her mobile armed forces, principally dominant sea power, and her extensive interests abroad fitted her for the role.

The diplomacy of the balancing system was sometimes rough and treacherous. The effects, nevertheless, were more preservative than disintegrative. None dared go too far in provoking wars when uncertain about the good faith of others. With the exception of the Napoleonic Wars, most of the fighting from the Peace of Westphalia in 1648 to the outbreak of World War I occurred outside Europe or was quite limited in character. Those who argue that this model still describes world politics take care to point out that Napoleon and even Hitler were resisted and eventually stopped when other states combined to oppose the destabilizing force.

The balance-of-power system is an empirically derived theory. The concept was most valid when applied to the comparatively small and homogeneous European region in the eighteenth and nineteenth centuries. Then small elite leaderships dominated the foreign policies of their respective states, shared approximately consistent concepts and objectives, and understood the rules of the game. Now international politics are worldwide. Application of the theory by regions as well as globally is very difficult. The forces cutting across the equations of state power and international politics, such as the new nationalism, Communism, modern mass communications, international collaboration, and others, involve factors that change the picture considerably from the simplistic model of the balance of power as known in the past. The influence and interaction of these forces are such that the older conception of the balance of power taken by itself no longer affords an adequate explanation of or approach to the study of international politics today.

Bipolarity. A second type of system which at times has prevailed in international politics can be described as bipolarity, where potentially decisive power is lodged in two controlling power centers. A bipolar conception of international politics in the middle of the twentieth century begins with the cold war conflict between Communist states and the anti-Communist states. Another example is the opposition of the Allied states to the Axis powers from 1942–1945.

Bipolarity is in one sense a particular kind of balance-of-power system. Although several powers or power centers are desirable in the traditional balance pattern, often with a "balancer" and with emphasis upon flexibility in their relationships, the bipolar model tends to group as many states as possible around one or the other of the Great Power centers or configurations. The United States is allied with some forty states, the Soviet Union with twelve. The "balance" which this represents has been a confrontation of two organized systems, one dominant in industrial power but comparatively loose in organization, the other smaller in terms of industrial output but initially more tightly organized. Despite the disparity in total available resources, military technology has ensured a rough approximation to military stalemate, or balance.

In a "tight" bipolar situation, the states at the periphery are viewed as components of one or the other side. Until after the Korean War, Communists termed countries not members of their bloc as "lackeys of the imperialists," no matter how independent their policies. As for the viewpoint of the United States, Secretary of State John Foster Dulles expressed the view that neutrality "between good and evil" was "immoral." Since the mid-1950's the power blocs have become more tolerant of the positions of the nonaligned states. Ties have loosened within the blocs—even to the extent of a new bipolarity between Moscow and Peking. Should an acute crisis occur, however, the bipolar theory assumes that those states which value their autonomy would be forced to take sides with that power or group of powers which least threatens their vital national interests.

Among many of the states which compose each of the two-power systems, there are bases of community and cooperation. In both the Atlantic complex and the Communist camp there has been political, economic, and military coordination. With varying degrees of intensity, efforts have also been made to extend links outside these limits to other regions. The United States supplements the NATO relationship with the Rio Pact, and with ANZUS, SEATO, and CENTO. Moscow and Peking have each sought through local Communist Party ties to extend their influence and controls abroad.

Bipolarity has not been free from problems and has undergone erosion on both sides in recent years. In the West, President de Gaulle has progressively withdrawn French forces and cooperation from NATO in opposition to integration under U.S. leadership. In the Communist orbit Sino-Soviet differences, along with nationalism, have severely strained the ties between the two principal powers and helped to further the polycentric movement in Eastern Europe.

Bipolarity does not explain the totality of international relations. There is too much communication, and even significant cooperation at times, between the various parts of the world. The bitter accusations by Peking against Moscow's "collaboration with the United States imperialists" show that some cooperation between Moscow and the West might sometimes be as meaningful as the relationships between the two great Communist powers.

A more accurate description of the world is a "loose" bipolarity which allows for rivalries between the Soviet Union and China, differences within NATO, and nonalignment among the African and Asian states. States do in fact cooperate and conflict, and revolutionary changes continue to occur, as in Africa and Asia, for reasons that have little to do with the conflict between the two Great Power blocs. The conflict between the superpowers, with their opposing ideologies, does, nevertheless, overhang international politics. As President John F. Kennedy said in November 1963, however, not all international relations can be encompassed or described by it. In his words,

Yet lasting peace between East and West would not bring peace to the family of man. Within the last month, the last four weeks, the world has witnessed active or threatened hostilities in a dozen or more disputes, independent of the struggle between Communism and free choice—disputes between Africans and Europeans in Angola, between North African neighbors in the Maghreb, between two Arab states over Yemen, between India and Pakistan, between Indonesia and Malaysia, Cambodia and Vietnam, Ethiopia and Somaliland, and a long list of others.[1]

Universalism.   A third system of world politics can be described as universalism or international community. Rome at the height of its power endeavored to bring the greater part of the then known world within its system of law and order. Territories stretching from the Near East to England were incorporated in the Empire and peoples of many diverse backgrounds were made Roman citizens or given common rights under Roman rule and law. In the medieval period following the downfall of Rome, the Holy Roman Empire sought to perpetuate the concept of a universal system linking church and state. Its domain was never as all-encompassing as that of Rome because of the schism between the Roman and Orthodox churches and the Turkish invasion of Europe. This empire system was both a universal and an absolutist one that in theory left little room for either freedom of conscience or of civil rule. There was never sufficient centralized power in the Middle Ages to enforce the system, however. The principalities and petty kingdoms waged the Hundred Years War partly against this universalism. The war ended in the Peace

---

[1] *Public Papers of the Presidents*, John F. Kennedy (Washington: Government Printing Office, 1963), p. 839.

of Westphalia, led to the founding of the present sovereign-state system, and was followed by the birth of nationalism.

In the twentieth century many thinkers and statesmen have been moving toward the idea that an unorganized state system is incapable of operating by cooperation alone and therefore cannot satisfy all the needs of man. Taking their germinal ideas from Madison, Monroe, Jefferson, and other founders of the American constitutional system, advocates of the universal ideal have argued that just as governments are needed within societies to direct political activities, to provide orderly means of adjusting disputes, and to regulate actions in the common interest, so in the international sphere parliamentary-type conferences and councils, arbitral and judicial tribunals, and administrative agencies are needed to promote attainment of mutual goals. Some argue that the logical extension of this increasing community in the distant future is an eventual world government.

Helped by the impact of these ideas, a series of formalized international bodies has been progressively founded for a variety of administrative, economic, political, and social purposes. These have included the Universal Postal Union, the Permanent Court of Arbitration at The Hague, the League of Nations, the International Labor Organization, the World Court, and the United Nations and its family of affiliated specialized agencies.

The United Nations has contributed to diffusing and blurring bipolarity and to enabling additional points of view to bear upon world problems. A greater consensus has been generated on such matters as racial equality, national independence, economic development, and anticolonialism. By hastening the demise of colonialism, this consensus has helped to fragment the world into a much more complicated system of states. Only time can determine whether the resulting international arrangement will move to some universal system which is an orderly replacement for the balance-of-power system or whether some other system or, combination of systems, will evolve.

Limitations of the Systemic Approaches. The preceding three systems provide frames of reference that are useful in the study of international politics. But they provide at best only a beginning to understanding. "There are more things in heaven and earth, Horatio, than are dreamt of in your philosophy," said Hamlet. The systemic approaches are severely limited in their ability to take account of all the forces moving in the world. They do not, for example, afford adequate explanations of the underlying reasons for, or the impact of, the psychological and sociological forces that move societies or affect the operations of political systems. They do not give the necessary insight into the operations of the decision-making process in various states or the motives that guide statesmen in their choices among alternatives. Furthermore, the systemic approaches do not provide sufficient answers to the problems being raised by the changes taking place in technology or economic progress. This is where other disciplines and methods of analysis are needed to fill out the picture.

NORMATIVE APPROACHES

Under the heading of *Rules of the Game* in Chapter 1, it was stated that the disposition to define some aspects of international relations in terms of universally applicable principles has brought some conceptions of moral "oughtness" into the realm of international relations. The standards and rules, the norms, for conduct of international relations have been the subject of scholarly discussion for centuries. The resulting enunciation of norms, has not by any means always been based on moral "oughtness." Generalizations have, for instance, been based on the theses of historical determinism, the dominance of an inevitable struggle for power among states, and on other interpretations of the state system in operation. There have, however, been significant components of idealism among the flow of scholarly contributions.

The following pages mention some of the philosophical thought concerning interstate affairs and describe two approaches—power politics and international law and organization—which depend significantly on the premise that interstate affairs should conform to certain definable guidelines.

Some Philosophers and Their Ideas. Niccolò Machiavelli (1469–1527) in *The Prince* gave counsel on how rulers should deal with others if they were to advance the interests of the state. Rejecting the norms of ethics and religion as being appropriate to the affairs of states, Machiavelli urged sovereigns to be prepared to employ whatever means necessary to obtain the interests of the state. To succeed, the prince must not hesitate to use deceit. "If they lie to you, lie more to them," was his counsel drawn from diplomatic experience among the Italian Renaissance city-states. If conditions change, the prince would be justified in breaking a promise made to others. Let the prince keep in mind the preservation of his own life and that of the state, and all the means he found necessary to do this would be judged honorable by the world. It is natural, Machiavelli added, for the state to desire, and hence to be prepared to take, territory. Only by facing "stern realities" in a realistic fashion could the prince advance the interests of his state. His book was soon translated into many languages and read by rulers and diplomats. Machiavelli should not, however, be judged too harshly. He was setting forth the details of following enlightened self-interest in the harsh and deceitful atmosphere of Italian city-state relations.

Francis Bacon of England (1561–1625) urged strength, expansion, and practice of the warlike arts among sovereigns. "No body can be healthful without exercise," he wrote. "Neither natural body nor politic, and certainly, to a kingdom or estate, a just and honorable war is the true exercise." A foreign war, Bacon wrote, "is like the heat of exercise and serveth to keep the body in health; for in a slothful peace, both courage will effeminate and manners corrupt." Such counsels of robust exercise may have been reasonable in the days of the pike and crossbow. They are hardly so in the nuclear age.

In the age of enlightenment, David Hume (1711–1776) exhorted states to end trade protectionism, arguing that a free trade policy that results in the increase of riches and commerce in any one nation "instead of hurting, commonly promotes the riches and commerce of all its neighbors." His arguments initiated the free-trade–protectionism debate carried forward by such succeeding British scholars as Adam Smith and continuing to the present time.

The problems of peace and war have been of particular concern to many philosophers. Rousseau (1712–1778) regarded tyranny and war as the "greatest plagues of humanity." To him liberty was the most precious of all political ends and he believed war for its defense was not only just but a sacred obligation. Immanuel Kant (1724–1804) in *Perpetual Peace* proposed an organized international society in order to get out of the state of nature which breeds conditions of war. He also counseled states to institute universally valid laws. For states having relations with one another, he said, "there can reasonably be no other method of escaping from the lawless condition which connotes only wars than by renouncing their uncivilized lawless freedom, like private individuals, and subjecting themselves to compulsory public laws, thus forming an international state which would gradually extend and finally include all the peoples of the world." Supporters of world government and world peace through world law have advanced little since the days of Kant in their intellectual arguments for this course of international politics. Kant reversed the teaching of Machiavelli and believed that good faith is essential in all public dealings and that morals can never be discarded. "Right must be held sacred by man," he said, "however great the cost and sacrifice to the ruling power. Here is no half-and-half course. We cannot devise a happy medium between right and expediency, a right pragmatically conditioned." [2] Reinhold Niebuhr in our day, in his *Moral Man and Immoral Society*, has essentially focused on the same problem as Kant.

Hegel, although considered an idealist by some, provided for Marx the concepts which the latter warped to the "universal idea" expounded in the Communist doctrine that the class struggle will eventually lead to a dictatorship of the proletariat and then to the withering away of the state. After fifty years of practice in Russia this condition does not seem nearer attainment than when Lenin first seized power.

Idealism. United States thinking concerning international politics has been much more conditioned by political heritage than by any specific philosophic thought. That thinking has been significantly influenced by a "liberal idealism" for which Woodrow Wilson was the principal leader in thought and action. Idealism particularly conditioned American thinking about international politics between World Wars I and II. Idealism has significantly underlain the approaches of an international system based on law and effective international organization. The flavor of this idealism pervades the Preamble to the Charter of the United Nations. Idealism is not a structural system or theory and tends to stress judging of states and state actions by the same standards that are applied to individuals in our society. Things are "good" and "bad,'" or "right" and "wrong," in contrast to the seeming impersonality and amorality of power politics. Communist theoreticians speak in terms of "correct" or "incorrect," a reflection of their deterministic ideology and belief in their monopoly of truth. The philosophy of idealism is more an approach to international politics as they ought to be rather than as they are.

Philosophers and idealists have enriched the thought of man, but they have not brought him much closer to a universally acceptable theory of international relations than existed at the beginning of the state system. The statesman still has to struggle with those difficult and never-ending questions of what his national interests and goals require under a continually changing environment. Justice Holmes' statement that "general propositions do not decide concrete cases" seems increasingly applicable in the world of international affairs today.

[2] Immanuel Kant, *Perpetual Peace*, translated by M. Campbell Smith and edited by A. Robert Caponigri (New York: Liberal Arts Press, 1948), Part II.

Power Politics. Accepting the premise that power is the primary factor underlying international politics and that each state employs it wherever needed to achieve its goals and satisfy its interests, international politics can be seen as a struggle for power.

The late Nicholas J. Spykman, professor at Yale University prior to 1942, insisted upon realism in thinking about international relations. The "preservation and improvement of its power position in relation to other states," wrote Spykman, must be a state's "primary objective." In his *America's Strategy in World Politics*, Spykman declared that whatever might be the order resulting from World War II "international society will continue to operate with the same fundamental power patterns. It will be a world of power politics. And, however unstable and always changing the equilibrium of forces may be, it is an indispensable element for an international order based on independent states."

Professor Hans Morgenthau argues systematically in his *Politics Among Nations* and other studies that interest and power are the basic ordering concepts and norms of international politics. Accordingly, those who engage in politics inevitably come into conflict with others similarly engaged in seeking to further their values or goals through power. There being no external authority to restrain the powerful from aggrandizing at the expense of others, a policy looking to the development of counter-vailing power offers the greatest probability of maintaining peace. At the same time, Professor Morgenthau accepts that moral restraints and law do operate upon the use of national power.

The logical extension of the struggle-for-power thesis is that force is a major, even dominating, factor in state relations. Clausewitz's statement that "war is a continuation of politics by other means" is a truism. So, perhaps, is a statement by the late Soviet Marshal Shaposhnikov that "if war is a continuation of politics only by other means, so also peace is a continuation of conflicts only by other means." [3]

But the spectrum of force has now become very broad and complex, extending from the nuclear threat of vast destructive power through the ambiguities of so-called wars of liberation and clandestine activities. The line between force and persuasion and accommodation has been blurred. The accession of many new countries to the society of states has brought with it further emphasis on the norms of peace and development, together with criticism of the older norms of unrestricted power politics.

The rise of shared values among groups of states forming limited

[3] Raymond L. Garthoff, *Soviet Strategy in the Nuclear Age* (New York: Praeger, 1958), p. 6.

purpose international communities is related to these norms receiving increased emphasis. The European Coal and Steel Community, the European Economic Community, and Euratom are examples of increasing cooperation and even integration among nations which formerly were involved in long drawn-out struggles for power. Other groupings are similarly developing in the Americas such as the OAS, in Africa in the OAU, and in the Atlantic area. As these groupings mature, they may evolve concepts of relationships and norms of conduct that are different from the traditional norms of power politics.

Accordingly, it seems that a view of world politics based exclusively on a struggle for power in the older sense affords too narrow a perspective for explaining the sweep of forces now shaping international relations. As we have stated earlier, where goals and values are not broadly shared, power of one type or the other will be the final arbiter. But the consideration of international politics is more meaningful if attention is not altogether restricted to the power relationship. It should look at the values and goals which unite nations as well as at the differences that divide them and lead to conflict, important as these differences are.

International Law and Organization. International law has attempted to codify norms of international conduct. For those whose purpose is an understanding of the "whys" of international politics today and the probable course in the future, it is fair to say that most states do conform to what they regard as international law. Hugo Grotius' treatise on *The Law of War and Peace*, published two decades before the Peace of Westphalia, laid a basis for systematic inquiry into the relations between states, with a view to discerning principles and practices having the force of law. In deducing a law of nations from the practices of states, Grotius, like the Church fathers before him, sought to impose a set of norms or code of behavior upon princes and states. From his assemblage of customs, practices, and precepts, supplemented by the works of others that followed, there grew a new body of jurisprudence known as the law of nations. This in turn gave rise to the view that the study of international law affords a fruitful approach to international relations.

A long line of jurists have argued that law is the key to order and should be observed by nations in their interest. Authorities like Hans Kelsen, and Judge Philip C. Jessup of the International Court of Justice, have reasoned that the "rule of law" is the essential ingredient to international order and that there is an obligation upon states to abide by it and advance it. The advocates of a stronger law have tended to stress the doctrine of *ubi societas, ibi jus* ("wherever there is society, there is law").

Starting from the thesis that law is universal, learned men have argued that abiding peace can be attained only through strengthening world law. They, therefore, emphasize that moves to enlarge the rule of law should be taken wherever possible. Those taking a more restricted view of the law argue that the law of nations is but one of the limiters upon power, not the key to international politics as a whole.

The development of international institutions, both regional and universal, has been one of the principal constructive steps toward building a more orderly world during the twentieth century. Among these institutions the United Nations, the World Health Organization, the World Bank, the International Development Association, the Organization for Economic Cooperation and Development, and such regional systems as the Organization of American States stand out. It may be argued that these institutions are essentially instrumentalities for coordination of relations among nations. But some of them have acquired separate international personalities and are able to exert considerable influence on the course of international relations.

The organizations have been slow in acquiring a capacity for decisive action against aggression and war, especially when the Great Powers are involved. But they do provide a common meeting ground where good offices and collective diplomacy can be exerted. And they do exercise some implicit restraints on actions when members are called upon to conform to the norms agreed upon in their charters.

The role of international organizations in legitimizing actions, in concerting collective measures, and in promoting agreement upon standards of behavior, should not be overlooked. The U.N. resolutions outlawing nuclear weapons in space, its repeated calling for disarmament talks and for cessation of nuclear testing, its condemnation of Soviet intervention in Hungary in 1956, its calls for cease-fire and withdrawal of troops on a number of occasions, and its appeals for international cooperation in assisting economic development have exercised significant influences upon national policies and international conduct. From such steps fresh norms may be evolving. To these should be added the efforts of the specialized and functional agencies, and of regional bodies.

As in other cases, a study of international organization alone does not provide a formula for understanding all the factors and forces which generate and condition interstate relations today. Stanley Hoffmann has cited two major limitations which make the international organization approach inadequate. "There is no sudden mutation in world politics, and the forces that may someday break the crust of the nation-state can only be helped, not created, by international organization." And, he adds, "the mushrooming of international institutions will not solve the fundamental issue of security." [4] We will discuss the usefulness of some of the international organizations at greater length in Part V.

Most international politics originate outside international institutions, but these do provide a forum and an arena. International institutions remain a creation of their members, and their business and effectiveness is determined by their members. Quite apart from the question of the relative effectiveness of the present organizations, the international organization approach provides only a partial explanation of world politics taken as a whole.

POLICY-SCIENCE APPROACHES

With the increasing recognition that no one academic discipline provides a sufficiently comprehensive approach to international relations, the search for a body of theory has turned to the combined use of several academic disciplines and techniques in what is termed the policy-science approach. This approach increases the systemization of knowledge concerning the environment, particularly governmental, the motivations of peoples and their leaderships, as well as the bases of interaction. It is not yet clear whether the policy-science approach adds anything to theory other than identification of some new factors and more precise definition of known ones. New developments in the behavioral sciences and techniques of analysis, such as gaming, are incorporated in this approach.

Behavioral Analysis. The disciplines of sociology, anthropology, and psychology provide analytical tools for examining changing social structures and distributions of political power. These analyses deal with the underlying cultural, emotional, and other environmental pressures which motivate individual and group behavior under varying circumstances. Significant variables in any given situation can be identified by research based on the social sciences. This approach contributes to the construction of theoretical models for the study of international politics, although resulting interactions cannot be altogether accurately predicted.

Beginnings have been made in studying concepts of national character and national style, although care is needed lest these produce merely additional stereotypes of dubious value. Opinion surveys are able to

[4] Stanley Hoffmann, "The Role of International Organization: Limits and Possibilities," *International Organization*, Vol. X, No. 3, August 1956, pp. 357–372.

develop interesting information about popular images that condition attitudes and responses toward leaders and toward foreign countries. Investigations made before and after crises have shown that the images of the national characters of opposing states undergo marked alteration in the minds of even sophisticated elements of the public. Examination of foreign observations about Americans and public-opinion samples here and abroad has led Professor Gabriel Almond to conclude that volatility of public mood is a particularly distinctive trait of Americans. This conclusion raises intriguing questions about when public opinion is a useful, and when a dangerous, guide to the conduct of foreign policy. The late Professor Sigmund Neumann pointed out that those who are emotionally disengaged in society, the crisis strata, are the potential supporters of the revolutionary upheavals that exacerbate world affairs. Hitler's mobilization of the disaffected elements in prewar German society and their subsequent violent actions against the Jews and others may be recalled. This fragment of analysis suggests that domestic social measures could play a part in the stability of international politics.

Communications studies measuring the flows of information and comprehension suggest perceptions of factors and trends relating to community building and disintegration. These measurements and the construction of "cohesion" and "influence" matrices help identify the cohering groups and the sources of influence. These may help determine the kinds of bonds between states that are durable and those that are not.

Examination of data concerning elites can provide clues to leadership qualities in various countries and may illuminate the kinds of stresses and actions of these groups in varying circumstances. Nathan Leites has deduced, for example, that there is an "operational code" of behavior among Soviet leaders which combines traditional elements of Russian character with the dialectical-materialist philosophy of Marx. The analysis of elites may similarly enable one to posit a number of possible roads which a given country might follow in the future, somewhat as a road map enables one to see several possible routes for a journey.

If sociology and psychology could inform us with assurance who was gaining power and how power would be used, political scientists could perhaps calmly plot the future. These studies are not yet sufficiently developed to satisfy all needs. Individual personalities continue to baffle trained psychologists. There is much more complexity in the interactions among the leaderships of 120 states than there is between five or twenty, for there are the domestic interactions between the leaders and their own people in addition to the interactions at the interstate level. When all of these elements are added together the parameters in the total situation stretch toward infinity. Nevertheless the behavioral science studies can be useful in studying international politics by throwing light on certain factors not susceptible to analysis by other modes of investigation.

Scholars able to combine the more orthodox methods of economics, political science, and historical and legal research with the disciplines of sociology and psychology can do a good deal to clarify the decision-making process and to tap the behavioral patterns and motivations that underlie state actions.

Game Theory. Game theory is one of the more recently developed techniques in the study of international politics. This technique originated in the war games developed for training military staffs and their commanders. By assigning individual participants roles to play in real or imagined international crises, decision making can be simulated in such a way as to take account of a wide range of variables in the international process in the search for solutions. This technique has some, though limited, usefulness in predicting policy measures. Games usually bring out the hard problems rather than provide clear policy guidance.

Analysis of Systems and Subsystems. Balance of power, bipolarity, and universal systems of international politics have been empirically described. Policy scientists have utilized the concept of a system, or a subsystem, consisting of given actors or entities, known sets of variables (political machinery, attitudes and interests, and policies), and values which set parameters. With these, empirical data can be examined for systematic regularities. A system exists when describable regularities characterize the relationships of the variables to each other. Having identified a system (the Inter-American System, NATO, the international "system"), the analyst can alter the variables (facts, attitudes, decisions, etc.) and study the resulting changes that occur in the behavior of the system as a whole with a view to estimating its equilibrium. The system will continue as long as there is some sort of dynamic equilibrium.

A system or subsystem can be strictly defined as a theoretical model with nonessential aspects of the real world eliminated for purposes of simplicity. One might take, for example, a model of the present world containing an organized third force, such as the nonaligned powers united between Communism and the West. Again, one might take the analogy of a bridge designer describing the effects of putting in or taking out a limited number of struts in a bridge design. If pressed too far the analogy is misleading, for we are not certain of the load or stress factors that would be put into the system. The international system is continually changing and has innumerable variables rather than constants. Projection of the effect is complicated. The complexities and the risks of a change in a few variables departing too far from reality are emphasized by the considerable investment of talent and effort that the United States government puts into any simulation of the system in operation. The United States executive branch does use what amounts to some forms of political gaming to aid the policy-planning process. To simulate the operation of a subsystem over a relatively short period of time, dozens of experts in many fields contribute a great deal of time. In the end, however, in real-life situations the President and his aides must take the lonely road of reaching policy decisions on their own, with the benefit of the best information and counsel they can assemble for the occasion. There is then little time for simulation exercises amid the pressures of high public office.

Decision Making and Policy Planning. One of the more useful contributions of the policy sciences has been the stress they have laid upon close examination of the foreign-policy decision-making process and of the forces influencing the decision makers. Emphasis is placed upon the interaction of organization, procedures, and personalities involved in decision making. Organized study of these factors is difficult because they are frequently changing for reasons external to foreign affairs. Long, and often fruitless, controversy may develop out of the question of how a decision is made and who caused it to be made.

Where leaders are pressed to make decisions there may often be incomplete or obscure information about some of the factors involved. There can even be obscurity about the actual working of the decision-making process. Even if all factors and forces are reasonably defined, there is no assurance that the decision makers in another country are operating on a given theory or assumption about international politics shared by the other side. Arthur Schlesinger, Jr., who was in daily touch with President John F. Kennedy during his short administration, has said, "nothing in my experience of working for Kennedy was more chastening than my attempt to penetrate into the process of decision." In retrospect, he adds, "I shudder a little when I think how confidently I have analyzed decisions in the ages of Jackson and Roosevelt, traced influences, assigned motives, evaluated roles, allocated responsibilities and, in short, transformed a dishevelled and murky evolution into a tidy and ordered transaction." The "sad fact is," he concludes, "that in many cases the basic evidence for the historian's reconstruction of the really hard cases does not exist—and the evidence that does exist is often incomplete, misleading or erroneous." [5]

The practitioners of long-range foreign policy planning and steering strategic plans through the decision-making process have been responsible for the development of an analysis of world politics sometimes called the "policy-planning" approach. This is primarily a way of approaching the formulation of foreign policy and is action-oriented in the framework of a particular country's interests and objectives. Although this is not an approach to the study of international politics generally, the policy-making approach has contributed usefully to education through the writings of professional policy planners in the United States. We know considerably less about policy planning in other states and societies. This eclectic and nondoctrinaire approach, taking the world as the practitioners see it, is discussed more fully in Chapter 11 and in Part III. The policy planners of the Kremlin would almost certainly employ a quite different theory of international politics if they were to write for publication. Policy planning has little effect on the real world unless the plans are coupled with decisions for their execution and with programs to carry these out.

Both decision making and policy planning focus on the operation of international affairs rather than on an analysis and explanation of the system as such. A knowledge of how decision makers and policy planners think aids the understanding of international relations but excludes the forces and factors beyond the cognizance or control of decision makers and policy planners. The "policy sciences" examine in detail parts of the continually changing flow of domestic and foreign politics to provide a picture of the total flow. But they do not yet afford a theory encompassing all of the phenomena of international affairs. With them must be coupled the methods of data handling known to the older disciplines as well.

AN ECLECTIC APPROACH TO INTERNATIONAL POLITICS

As indicated in the preceding pages, the authors do not believe that any monistic theory can provide an adequate rationale of the full flow of international politics. In their view, attempts to make all important components of that flow consistent with any one body of theory merely result in misleading distortion. On the other hand, each of the various approaches

---

[5] Quoted by William V. Shannon in "Controversial Historian of the Age of Kennedy," *The New York Times Magazine*, November 21, 1965, p. 135.

discussed contributes something to understanding. No scholar has yet made a synthesis encompassing all the essential components of the various approaches into a satisfactory general theory of international politics. To be pertinent, such an analysis would have to vary with time and circumstances—presenting a multidimensional, dynamic problem. Various of the theoretical approaches provide useful tools of analysis, but neither singly nor together do they form a complete "tool kit" for the complexities of today's world.

We agree with the suggestion of Stanley Hoffmann, made in his article entitled "International Relations, The Long Road to Theory," that there are four significant components to the focus or field of world politics: (1) the political structure of the world at any given moment; (2) the forces that are cutting across the units of this structure and may be reinforcing or changing it; (3) the relationship between domestic and foreign policies of the respective units; and (4) the resultant patterns of relationships among the first three components, which are properly called international relations.[6]

These four categories do not comprise a theory. They list the components of the field of international relations which need to be examined at any given point. The categorization is therefore a method of developing an adequate framework and perspective for the study of international politics, not a method of direct analysis. What we have to say about the four components of Hoffmann's succinct summary is woven into the pattern of the following chapters.

States are the principal actors in international politics. International politics are principally among states, even when carried on through international organizations. We believe the best way to begin the study of international politics is with analysis of the factors and forces which impinge on those states. We then proceed to discuss how individual states, pressed by both domestic and external environments, determine how to act or react in world affairs. The book then moves on to examine the way states use various instruments for attaining their goals in international affairs and the interplay of state interests and instruments. Our study concludes with a discussion of the formal organization of the contemporary world community.

This approach places initial emphasis on understanding the environment, the real world, which shapes national policies and international politics. In order to think usefully about international politics the student

[6] Stanley Hoffmann, "International Relations, The Long Road to Theory," *World Politics*, Vol. XI, No. 3, April 1959, pp. 346–377.

must have a mental inventory of facts and ideas and some system for ordering them. This book attempts to show the kinds of facts that are needed with examples supporting the generalized analysis. The discussion of some central concepts like national interest and power is integrated into the discussion of the topics indicated by the chapter headings. Such is the way that these concepts are applied in reality.

The approach is both pragmatic and analytical. It attempts to provide a method of approach to clearer understanding of international relations in an area where both great complexity and dynamic change are among the chief characteristics of those relations. This method of approach does not reject theory. On the contrary, it invites the use of theory when appropriate to analysis. The approach is therefore eclectic.

The continuing search for power and influence to support the national purposes of states and the pre-eminence of national interest are central concepts. These do not require further demonstration—even though the search for power does not explain all aspects of international relations. The importance of the decision-making process, and of the decision makers and the factors that sway them, is apparent. Yet one must guard against looking upon these processes as static or autonomous. No model of decision making can adequately account for the impact of a powerful individual personality upon policy. Economic considerations are likewise significant, but they do not support a thesis of economic determinism in international affairs. Idealism is the expression of the ultimate values of freedom, peace, welfare, justice, and security, although these goals are not accepted in the same manner and with the same meanings by all states.

The approach to world politics through pragmatism and analysis of the underlying forces and interests is the approach attempted by the United States policy planner. It is a nondoctrinaire method starting from observation and analysis of basic factors in the world. This approach implicitly accepts certain values and objectives. At the same time it recognizes that the values and objectives of other entities in the international scene may be different and may conflict. The chapters that follow are directed primarily to facts and analysis concerning matters of particular interest to the United States. Furthermore, because the principal power struggle in the world is between the United States, on the one hand and Moscow and Peking, on the other, the chapters give special emphasis to this problem and the dynamic forces contributing to it. They also attempt to give a comparable, objective view of the forces influencing the developing countries in their struggle to make the great transition from stagnation and dependence to modern independent societies able to speak with authority on the international stage. In studying the interaction of the many factors and forces operating in world politics through this pragmatic and eclectic approach, we hope to assist the reader in gaining realistic insights into the dynamics of international politics.

PART II

Basic Factors Affecting the Positions and Policies of States

Preamble

A PRACTICAL APPROACH to international poli-
tics begins with the identification and study of the principal factors which
combine to make up the internal and external environments of states and
affect international politics.

Factors which affect international affairs, such as those of geography,
population, social characteristics, economics, and the like, may operate
primarily upon the characteristics and capabilities of states. A factor may,
on the other hand, be a "force" which, guided by policy, can be a dynamic
element influencing interstate relations. Again, a factor like economics
may both affect capabilities, be an active force, and at the same time serve
as an instrument of foreign policy.

In Part II two types of factors are discussed. First there are the more
"subjective" factors, such as social elements, nationalism, imperialism and
anticolonialism, and the search for security. Then there are the more
"objective" factors, such as technology, physical environment, population
and economics. These factors vary in their dynamism, geography being
comparatively static, nationalism and technology being highly dynamic.
These factors both shape and cut across the patterns of international relations.

51

The relations of states are partly the interaction of the way the people and leaders of one state view the world situation and respond to it, as contrasted with the ways other peoples and leaders view the same situation and factors. Viewpoints differ and are "riddled with ambiguity," in the words of Dr. Charles Malik of Lebanon, as are such terms as free elections, human rights, arbitrary, democracy, nation, government, war-mongering, progress, peace-loving, peaceful coexistence, peace, justice, freedom, and truth. Out of a long experience as a scholar, foreign minister, and ambassador, Dr. Malik concludes that "there is no meeting of minds on fundamental issues today" and "the world actually displays conflicting interpretations which often mean radically different things by the same term." [1] *The key to the similarity or difference of attitudes among states often lies in their appraisals of the basic factors discussed in the following chapters of Part II.*

Leaders and peoples strive to appraise the basic factors of their external environment in order to influence that environment in a manner they consider to be to their national interest. This interest is not an objective fact, but a situational judgment which depends on the appraisal of the forces operating in the external environment, some of which we will discuss in the next eight chapters. For any state, the body of conclusions about the national interest is really a consensus of the judgments of the leaders and other influential people, made in the perspective of their national values and goals, which were discussed in Chapter 1. For specific policy issues the judgment that counts internationally is generally that made by a few leaders, such as the President of the United States and his immediate advisers. But we shall discuss the decision-making process in Part III. Here in Part II our primary concern will be with those factors and forces which influence the environment and shape the alternatives with which the statesman must deal in his search for courses of action that are in the national interest.

[1] Charles Malik, *Independence: Reality and Myth, The Legacy of Imperialism* (Pittsburgh: Chatham College Press, 1960), pp. 88–89.

CHAPTER 3

Attitudes, Beliefs, and International Politics

INTRODUCTION

The interaction of attitudes, beliefs, and social environment is a basic influence on the behavior of states. These elements determine men's perception of and response to physical and political environments. The customs and traditions of the social environment give rise to attitudes, which lead to beliefs. Attitudes and beliefs together define the values men hold and the ends they seek. Common experiences and shared beliefs and values also condition the ideas men have about their institutions, loyalties, and interests; and these affect men's observation of the behavioral characteristics of others.

Values are the standards men consider right and desirable, so political action is driven both by and toward them. The human impulse causes men to act upon their external environment, generating international political action through the interaction of subjective and objective elements, that is, of values in the context of particular environmental situations.

The focus in this chapter is upon the role of attitudes, traditions, ideas, and beliefs as well as social environment in conditioning the behavior of states.

53

THE ROLE OF VALUES, ATTITUDES, AND PERCEPTION

Anyone interested in understanding international political behavior must start from the premise that there are different attitudes, beliefs, and values among human groups. Men live in different social, political, economic, and physical environments. These surroundings suggest who are one's associates and one's opponents, and indicate in the limited resources available to each group how man should adapt himself to survive. Traditions of cooperation and political and social values and institutions are formed against this background.

It is important to consider why men hold certain values and how, under the impact of another culture or of other forces, values may change. The degree to which clusters of attitudes, values, and purposes are shared within a nation determines the measure of consensus that prevails among the various social groups. This in turn affects the stability of political institutions. The degree of accord that exists on these attitudes, values, and purposes among two or more states determines the degree of community that prevails among them. Relationships among states are likely to be conciliatory, cooperative, and peaceful where attitudes and values are shared. A condition of potential instability and conflict exists when there is little or no sharing of attitudes and values.

Basic Orientation of Man Toward His Environment.   Peoples and leaders hold opinions on a wide variety of matters affecting their external affairs, such as peace, war, imperialism, race, capitalism, nuclear weapons, and foreign aid. These attitudes are based on values held, and they determine what means are used to gain ends consistent with those values. Past experiences have much to do with shaping these perceptions, attitudes, and the responses that are made to them, as do communications within the group and the interplay of group relationships.

Stereotyped Images—"Pictures in Our Minds."   Attitudes may clarify or distort reality. Men respond to what Walter Lippmann has called their "pseudo-environment," the world that is "politically out of reach, out of sight, out of mind," that has to be "explored, reported, and imagined."

What each man does is based not on direct and certain knowledge but on pictures made by himself or given to him. If his atlas tells him that the world is flat he will not sail near what he believes to be the edge for fear of falling off.[1]

[1] Walter Lippmann, *Public Opinion* (New York: Macmillan, 1921), p. 17.

Two things limit our ability to view the world with objectivity. The first is man's limited access to facts. His knowledge is imperfect and his ability to perceive and understand and to act more soundly is limited by lack of time, experience, contacts, and skill in language to communicate the complex reality of events. Lippmann observes, "Inevitably our opinions cover a bigger space, a longer reach of time, a greater number of things, than we can directly observe." We therefore have to depend upon what "others have reported and what we can imagine." [2] The problem is made more difficult when two individuals with the same facts reach opposite conclusions about the action indicated.

The second limiting element is more subtle and ambiguous, being in effect a complex of psychological factors. Our ability to perceive reality is limited by our preconceptions and prejudices, our stored-up images, the stereotyped patterns into which we generalize and fit the realities of the world. Men tend to fit their limited understanding into their preconceptions of their own world. These preconceptions serve as a defensive mechanism enabling people to preserve the image of the world to which they have become adjusted. "A world which turns out to be one in which those we honor are unworthy, and those we despise are noble, is nerve-wracking," Lippmann observes. Therefore, the human mind possesses a power to disguise the purposes of its own thoughts and actions. It is here that the fields of psychiatry and psychoanalysis become relevant to the student of international politics.

Perhaps the most significant attitudes which affect political actions are those which can be categorized as the stereotyped images. These are judgments accepted from others before one has sufficient personal experience to judge for himself. People think in stereotypes like "the French," "the Soviets," "the military mind," "foreigners," "bolsheviks," "warmongers." These evoke distinct characteristics. Word stereotypes of this nature are frequently employed in group relationships in times of tension or crisis. Stereotypes are often substituted for reasoned opinions, for men tend to "pick out what our culture has already defined for us and we tend to perceive that which we have picked out in the form sterotyped for us by our culture." Such images are as common concerning nations as they are concerning individuals.

Distrust of foreigners and their aims is a traditional characteristic of peoples and is especially marked among those who have been, or have believed themselves to be, victims of foreign rule or exploitation. Neutralism in Asia and Africa today is a more complex phenomenon than merely a

[2] *Ibid.*, p. 59.

FIGURE 3-1

"All these foreigners always look alike. . . ." (*Reprinted from the
New Statesman & Nation of 31 March 1956 by permission
of the* New Statesman, London)

desire to avoid war or be neutral in the event of a Great Power war. There
is a deep-seated urge to assert independence of the Western powers which
have ruled and exploited Asians and Africans in the past and to establish a
political force to counter Western influence. Latin American distrust of
the United States is a subjective attitude that combines fear and envy of
the "Colossus of the North" and resentment of past United States interventions and of some American business practices. It grows out of not only
historical experience, but also different sets of values based on different
cultural and social patterns.

Prejudices and Preferences.   Western states have developed close
political associations among themselves, having common cultural and historical ties and some consensus on values and political systems. Communist
powers subscribing to Marxist-Leninist ideas have opposite preconceptions
of the nature of society, and may even disagree among themselves, as have
China and the Soviet Union. Between states having basic differences on
such matters it is difficult to obtain lasting understanding and agreement,
though the countries may maintain correct and formally "friendly" relations.

Basic to corporate attitudes is a feeling of "we" versus "they," which
is reinforced through group living, the idea of nationalism, modern communications, history, symbolic ties, tradition, and other psychological

elements. In democratic societies these may substantially influence the government and limit its freedom of foreign policy choices, especially in times of crisis or tension or when there is internal dissension.

States that feel secure toward their neighbors can usually adjust differences that arise between them by peaceful means. When a state's interests are believed to be threatened it is more difficult to reconcile differences, particularly if there is no history or tradition of cooperation with the state threatening it. Canada and the United States have a long tradition of friendly relations that has facilitated extensive mutual arrangements. Formal diplomatic relations exist between Russia and Turkey. But a history of competition for control of the Turkish Straits has led Turkey to be suspicious of Russian intentions and to maintain a vigilant defense and membership in NATO. Collaboration between Pakistan and India has been made more difficult by the bitterness engendered in the long dispute over Kashmir.

Morality and International Affairs. Morality has neither universal definition nor universal application. Ethical and moral standards of behavior are unique to particular cultures and civilizations. Not all the same standards and values are found among the Anglo-American communities as in the Soviet bloc countries or among the Afro-Asian countries. In each society men apply different standards of conduct to interstate affairs and to their relationships with family, religious, and business groups.

Morality in interstate relations is not equivalent to individual morality, yet it is a real element in such relations. Leaders sometimes consider international morality in their formulation and conduct of foreign policies. They generally attempt to present their conduct as moral and humanitarian.

Persistence and Change in Attitudes Toward Foreign Affairs. The individual may approach external affairs dogmatically, using his beliefs or ideas learned from school, church, political party or other group. He may be unwilling or psychologically unable to accept a reality which does not conform to what he has long held to be "true."

Alternatively, the individual may be willing to examine each case on its merits and adjust his perceptions accordingly. He may be ready to shed a "beautiful theory" when it has been accosted by what Herbert Spencer called a "gang of brutal facts." This is a pragmatic and more flexible approach, not a rigid adherence to stereotyped images.

Differences in attitudes toward the external environment create a major problem in international affairs, where flexibility in tactics is a criterion of success. After the Bolshevik Revolution the Soviet Union was as rigid and doctrinaire in its approach to the outside world as Communist China is today. Despite their arbitrary and doctrinaire beliefs, Soviet leaders have been willing to adopt a more pragmatic position since the death of Stalin. The need to adapt to world realities has become more apparent with the development of nuclear power, the destructiveness of modern war, and the rise of Communist China.

British policies have often been noted for being pragmatic and flexible. In 1848 Lord Palmerston said,

> . . . it is a narrow policy to suppose that this country or that is to be marked out as the eternal ally or the perpetual enemy of England. We have no eternal allies and we have no perpetual enemies. Our interests are eternal, and those interests it is our duty to follow.

In stable and mature societies fundamental attitudes on foreign relations change slowly, for aspirations and impressions from the past influence decision making. For more than a century the United States pursued a policy of neutrality and isolation toward Europe, but since World War II it has participated in the Marshall Plan, the United Nations, and NATO. French attitudes, long bitter toward Germany, have changed considerably since both countries joined NATO and the European Economic Community.

Gauging Attitudes, Objectives, and Responses.   In order to pursue national objectives and determine policy actions in foreign affairs, statesmen must gauge the attitudes, objectives, and likely responses of others as best they can.

Much is known about the Communist theory of international relations and something about the general attitudes of the Soviet and Chinese leaderships toward the Western powers and the underdeveloped countries. There is no comparable knowledge about the precise intentions of these leaders in their choice of actions in specific circumstances, nor certainly is there knowledge that would enable us to predict their tactics. The two major Communist powers have behaved differently toward India and the development of Southeast Asia. The Soviet Union supported India with arms when it was invaded by China. It mediated between India and Pakistan at Tashkent at a time when Communist China was encouraging Pakistan to continue the war upon India. And the Soviet Union has joined with the United States in establishing the Asian Development Bank. If there is orchestration of Communist tactics, it is not apparent. Differences in attitudes predominate, stemming no doubt from the different backgrounds and outlooks of their leaderships.

The mature democracies may not always act as one would predict, as for example the abortive French and British attack on Suez in 1956 in the face of American, Canadian, Indian, and Soviet opposition. In many of the new countries and in some of the countries of Latin America the beliefs of the elites in power have not crystallized. In others rapid changes in leaderships, military coups, administrative incompetence, and disputes among politicians contribute to political instability—making prediction of their courses of action hazardous.

There is a complex interaction between the attitudes of peoples and their leaders toward external affairs. Leaders are to some extent captive to the attitudes of their peoples. This is important to remember in assessing what countries do in particular situations. Strong leaders are usually able to shape the attitudes of their people to support their direction of foreign policy, as the American Presidents have persuaded Congress to support most of their foreign policies. It is much harder to predict the direction of policy in countries like Nigeria or Indonesia, where there are conflicting internal forces and where much depends upon those who may be in power at a given time. Yet actions are based on predictions and these initiate chain reactions of moves and countermoves affecting the entire sphere of international relationships. It is for this reason important to form appraisals that are as accurate as possible of the attitudes of people and their leaders, for these are significant inputs in the decision-making process.

IDEAS AND IDEOLOGY IN WORLD POLITICS

We turn now to one of the most basic means of articulating values and attitudes in their societal context, namely, ideology. We define *ideology* as a body of ideas concerning economic, social, and political values and goals, which posit action programs for attaining those goals. Contemporary international politics are distinguished by the ready availability to mass opinion of systems of ideas about responses toward foreign affairs. They thus are one of the principal dynamics of world politics.

The Power of Ideology. Ideology is based on certain assumptions about the nature of man and society from which concepts of order and mission are evolved. Ideology also offers preferred solutions for difficult economic, social, and political problems of society. Ideology binds individuals and groups in a society to common purposes and ways of action by gathering together widely shared beliefs and inculcating new ones.

In most Western democracies there are widely shared beliefs and objectives concerning political affairs. It is generally possible to compromise differences in order to achieve unity of purpose in the face of a foreign threat and enable society to make ordered progress. A consensus enables a country to amass and exercise maximum power in international affairs through harnessing and directing the energies of its people, as after the attack upon Pearl Harbor in 1941. Great power emerges when ideas and goals are shared among groups of nations, as in the North Atlantic alliance at the peak of its unity.

The belief systems prescribed by doctrinaire theorists of party or government in authoritarian societies usually lack the resiliency and strength of a popularly based consensus.[3] Strong leadership at the center combined with massive propaganda, a tight political machine, and a hard core of dedicated followers can fashion power behind central rule, as has been done in Russia, China, and in prewar Fascist Italy and Nazi Germany. Dogmatic ideologies often rest upon assertions or visions of reality which their followers are trying to make come true. These visions are more effective if the assertions have firm and widespread support.

The ideological strength of Communism is its apocalyptic vision and "scientific" explanation of history. The ideology promises victory to the "working classes" over a vaguely defined capitalism and "imperialism." This is the appeal of Communism in immature societies, where there are ill-informed masses preoccupied with trying to improve their conditions. The true Communist state is unlikely to be achieved within the lifetimes of the present Soviet and Chinese leaders, but the vision nevertheless reinforces the preconceptions and images their people hold of their environment. The appeal of the ideology is multiplied by mass communications made possible by modern technology.

Conditions are fertile in many of the developing countries for new ideas and popular movements which promise rapid change and improvement. To mobilize large-scale popular support for radical change, such as a national uprising against colonial rule, the establishment of a new form of government, or the accomplishment of an economic leap forward, the Communist ideology offers a convenient, appealing tool for translating vague aspirations into rapid results and a rallying point to justify demanding obedience and discipline.

Constitutional Democracy.   The conflict between the ideas of constitutional democracy and of Communism is one of the chief realities of contemporary world politics. Understanding the essence of the beliefs in-

[3] See Z. Brzezinski and S. P. Huntington, *Political Power: U.S.A./U.S.S.R.* (New York: Viking, 1965).

herent in these systems is indispensable to a comprehension of what the conflict is about and the stake the free world has in its outcome.

The present theory of liberal constitutional democracy has its origins in the common Western tradition of classical humanism and Judeo-Christian heritage. Its evolution has been influenced particularly by the development of British, French, and American thought since the latter part of the eighteenth century. Democracy is not a precise creed with precise content, but the liberal democratic tradition contains a common body of premises and principles based on historical experience and the writings of great political thinkers and leaders like Washington, Jefferson, Lincoln, and Roosevelt. These principles are found in documents such as the Magna Carta, the American Declaration of Independence, the Federal Constitution and Bill of Rights, the Federalist papers, the Emancipation Proclamation, and legislation like the Civil Rights Act.

There are several central beliefs included in the basic framework of democracy. These include the following. (1) The individual human being is of unique worth, and protection and promotion of his liberty, dignity, and welfare is the obligation of the state. (2) Government derives its just powers from the consent of the governed. Therefore, a people is entitled to govern itself through elected representatives and to have free choice in its form of government. (3) It is the responsibility of the constitutional order to promote justice, to assure the rule of law, and to safeguard the "inalienable" rights of the individual against arbitrary action. (4) The individual is entitled to the opportunity for a decent social and economic life, which it is the duty of the state to promote. (5) Differing views and attitudes of individuals and groups may be freely expressed—and this freedom should be guaranteed by the state. (6) The system is evolving and will adapt ways of maintaining its values to new circumstances. (7) Democratic values embrace rights considered universal.

These beliefs form a basis for political discourse and common acceptance of certain fundamental values, goals, and means of adjusting rights and duties. Change is facilitated by the nature of the beliefs themselves and by a pragmatic approach to the political process. The adjustment of conflicts is institutionalized by peaceful means through compromise and consensus.

Communist Ideology.[4]   The principles of Communism as revealed through the writings and statements of Marx, Lenin, Stalin, Khrushchev,

[4] We are indebted to Study No. 10, "Ideology and Foreign Affairs," prepared for the Senate Committee on Foreign Relations series on *United States Foreign Policy* (86th Congress, 2nd Session, Washington: Government Printing Office, 1960), by the Center for International Affairs at Harvard University, for the enumeration of principles.

and his successors, and by Mao Tse-tung and other Chinese ideologues, embody the following key concepts. (1) History is a continuous conflict in which the "progressive" forces of Communism oppose the "reactionary" forces of capitalism, whose overthrow will be assured in the "class struggle." (2) There is a basic conflict between Communism and liberal constitutional democracy that can be resolved only by the ultimate triumph of Communism. Party and state must use the means at their disposal to assist the struggle, with Lenin's proviso that "decisive engagement" is to be avoided when "victory is uncertain," and there is to be no "absolutely" decisive engagement which risks the "destiny" of the Soviet nation. (3) Communist ideology proposes the creation of a "classless" society and the ultimate withering away of the state, for through Communism capital wealth will be redistributed to the poorest working classes, economic growth achieved, and "exploitation of the masses" ended. (4) The Communist Party, representing the "dictatorship of the proletariat," is the chosen instrument for the achievement of Communism in all countries and is an absolute good, justifying absolute obedience. (5) Power and the struggle for power are key concepts both in the methods and goals of Communism. Lenin, Stalin, and Mao Tse-tung wrote primarily about the strategy and tactics of gaining and consolidating power. (6) Tactical flexibility is permissible for the achievement of ideological and party goals. Adherents may use whatever means are needed to achieve the goals of Communism, to overthrow non-Communist systems, to exploit the differences between antagonists, and to encourage the creation of "revolutionary conditions" in developing as well as advanced societies. Communist tactics have been set forth by an official Chinese publication in the following way.

In order to lead the proletariat and working people in revolution, Marxist-Leninist Parties must master all forms of struggle and be able to substitute one form for another quickly as the conditions of struggle change. The vanguard of the proletariat will remain unconquerable in all circumstances only if it masters all forms of struggle—peaceful and armed, open and secret, legal and illegal, parliamentary struggle and mass struggle, etc. It is wrong to refuse to use parliamentary and other legal forms of struggle when they can and should be used. However, if a Marxist-Leninist Party falls into legalism or parliamentary cretinism, confining the struggle within the limits permitted by the bourgeoisie, this will inevitably lead to renouncing the proletarian revolution and the dictatorship of the proletariat.[5]

Within the Soviet Union and other Communist-ruled states, ideology

[5] *A Proposal Concerning the General Line of the International Communist Movement,* June 14, 1963 (Peking: Foreign Languages Press, 1963), published in John Wilson Lewis, *Major Doctrines of Communist China* (New York: Norton, 1964), p. 251.

is used as a justification of the party's continued monopoly of power and to identify the historical validity and wisdom of its politics and actions. In Communist satellite states ideology serves as an instrument of Soviet influence and direction. In non-Communist countries it is an instrument for controlling the hard core of party members, swaying mass opinion and catering to local discontents. Social and economic progress in Russia and the European satellite countries may have contributed to increased flexibility in interpreting Communist doctrine in these countries. But the Communist Chinese leaders are unsympathetic to deviations from orthodox statements of Marxist-Leninist principles. They consider liberalized interpretations by Soviet spokesmen "revisionism," betraying the Communist cause. There are limits to how far a Soviet delegation, even the highest ranking, can or will go in dealing with the Western powers. But these limits give considerably more flexibility today than formerly. They are more than the Communist Chinese are willing to tolerate.

The interplay of conflicting ideologies is relatively open and institutionalized in the West. In France, Italy, and other countries, Communist parties are legal and attract popular support. By manipulating popular discontent and with the help of propaganda these parties frequently pull large blocks of votes. But nowhere has Communism been freely voted into power, nor is it likely to be in any Western democracy in normal circumstances.

On the larger scene of world politics, Soviet advocacy of "peaceful coexistence" with non-Communists is partly a maneuver to persuade the West to relax its vigilance, and partly to convince the newly independent countries that the Soviet Union has abandoned the Stalinist aggressive policies in order to stabilize the status quo. Meanwhile, Communism continues the struggle with the West directly by means of economic, political, and propaganda weapons, and indirectly through rivalry in the developing countries. The outcome of the struggle may be determined in large measure by what happens in the developing countries. Aid programs, cultural relations efforts, and political support all play a part in seeking the friendship of these countries and attempting to guide their steps to the future.

A factor unforeseen in the world ideological struggle before 1959 was the widening conflict between the leaderships of Peking and Moscow. Refusal on the part of Peking to accept the Soviet leadership as the "vanguard" of world Communism and as the principal exponent of Communist ideology runs counter to the lexicon of Marxism-Leninism, on which Russian Communists have been brought up. The schism between the two great Communist powers has thus shattered the ideal on which the "fraternal" partnership between the U.S.S.R. and Communist China was first erected. Its effects have been more far-reaching, however, than the two powers alone. For it has set up stresses within the world Communist movement, forced the Party leaderships of the smaller states into difficult positions, and paved the way for Sino-Soviet rivalries and conflicts in Asia and Africa, of which the differences over the war in Vietnam and between India and Pakistan have been prominent examples. The hope of an ever-growing world Communist movement marching down the road arm in arm against the West appears to have given way before the deeper-set differences springing from past history, national attitudes and traditions, and deeply engraved suspicions and misunderstandings which political pride refuses to give up. Secretary-General U Thant of the United Nations in speaking of China recently commented that, "In such a delicate stage, countries will sometimes show certain emotions, certain strong reactions, certain rigidities, and even a certain arrogance." [6]

Amid the changing world scene of the mid-1960's an experienced American scholar, Dr. Marshall D. Shulman of the Harvard Russian Research Center, was led to write in his book *Beyond the Cold War,*

The frenetic and simplistic preoccupation with the Cold War . . . has long since shown how gravely it defeats the true American interests. The Cold War has changed its character not only because Soviet policy has been evolving in response to changes in the world environment, but because the . . . Western allies are becoming aware that anti-Communism is not an adequate response to the total situation in which we live . . . the lesson of past experience with the Soviet Union would be lost if we did not understand and respond to the sources of conflict that go far beyond Communism.[7]

The emphasis upon ideology which events reveal suggests that these idea systems are influenced by the operation of other factors and forces in the total environment. Nuances in their application can occur, and these changes may be very important.

SOCIAL STRUCTURE, POLITICS, AND CHANGE

Relationships between social groups within a national society are structured upon religion, social traditions, the economic system, and other bases. The

[6] U Thant, quoted by James Reston, "Washington: The Mind of Asia," *The New York Times,* January 23, 1966.
[7] Marshall D. Shulman, *Beyond the Cold War* (New Haven: Yale University Press, 1966), excerpts quoted from review article in *The Saturday Review,* January 22, 1966.

relative power of the various groups will largely determine the dominant values of the society. In most states there is a spectrum of social and political structures along which societies may be delineated in terms of their flexibility and value systems.

Three Stages of Social Organization: [1] The Traditional Society. Social structure in traditional societies, such as those of Yemen, Saudi Arabia, or Somalia, is based upon personal connections and honored customs rather than upon contractual relationships or the objectives of political party platforms. Tradition influences behavior and binds the largely immobile society, which is ruled by a small elite. Reinhold Niebuhr has said, "Traditional cultures moderate the demands which men make upon life by custom and habit." [8] Those who depart from the customary way of doing things may face sanctions, as in Islamic law, being invoked in the name of the supernatural. Literacy and rational ideas of causation threaten structures that have built-in impediments to change. Niebuhr further observes,

No situation . . . represents a perfectly just solution to the claims and counter claims of men in a community. Men do not usually challenge the solution either because they do not realize the depths of the injustice or because they are hopeless about the possibility of altering the social situation.

Once groups begin to think that their position in society is unjust, or no longer resign themselves to their lot, they are likely to challenge the traditional order. The paradox of traditional societies is that they are both the most politically stable and the most vulnerable to instability once a change has been initiated. In these societies there are few institutional arrangements to limit conflict, only the application of time-honored custom in face-to-face relationships. When these cease to restrain conflict the basis of stability is broken. Most traditional societies today are being penetrated by forces making for change. A few, such as those of Somalia and Afghanistan, remain dominated by traditional characteristics.

[2] Transitional Societies. The majority of the world's population is in the developing states, which can be said to be in a transitional condition. They include countries such as Turkey, Egypt, Ethiopia, India, and China, which have had some contact with the values and methods of Western civilization, whose societies are fluid, and whose leaders have seen the need for popular education, industrialization, mass communication, and modernization of government. Old values are being questioned, attitudes

[8] Reinhold Niebuhr, *The Structure of Nations and Empires* (New York: Scribners, 1959), p. 220.

of fatalism and resignation are being rejected, and the "revolution of rising expectations" is forcing leaders in these countries more toward economic and social advancement. The entry of militant religious organizations into politics is evidence of the struggle in transitional societies, where there is a search for values and institutions to cope with change. There is a very long inventory of value conflicts between old and new in many transitional societies. In India the struggle over the caste system and the traditional prohibition against slaughtering cows are examples.[9] Language and regional differences disrupt efforts to centralize government and promote education and threaten national unity in countries like India, Nigeria, Sudan, and the Congo. Agrarian unrest is created by large absentee landholdings, heavy indebtedness, and usury.

Large landowners resist pleas for land reform and educational systems, and the economies are not yet sufficiently developed to provide adequate professional training and employment, so instability is increased. The Shah of Iran has enforced land redistribution, but this has not satisfied all demands. Additional difficulties arise if the peasants are too poor to maintain food production with the implements at their disposal. An initial commitment to "agrarian reform" like that in Castro's Cuba may stimulate moves for expropriation, confiscation, and nationalization of both indigenous and foreign-held properties and assets, dislocating the domestic economy and giving rise to disputes with other countries. The training and education of young men in the modern armies of Turkey, Iran, and Pakistan, together with the impact of foreign experts and indigenous university graduates, further accelerate the loosening of old ties and create ferments of change that press upon domestic and foreign policy.

A transitional society is often controlled by a revolutionary leader who wants to hasten the transitional process by reshaping national values. As Turkey had its Atatürk, so Egypt has had its Nasser, Kenya its Kenyatta, and Indonesia its Sukarno. Political unrest is likely if progress is slow and frustration spreads to disaffected and restive student and military groups opposing the government in power. Transitional societies in the process of reshaping and restructuring values may have long periods of instability that offer attractive ground for alien exploitation.

[3] Modern Societies. States that have progressed to the stage of modern democratic societies are generally industrialized, have mass participation in their social and economic processes, and institutional means of change and adjusting conflicts.

---

[9] See Harold Isaacs, *India's Ex-Untouchables* (New York: John Day, 1965).

[a] DEMOCRATIC SOCIETIES. In contrast to the transitional societies, the Western democracies have considerable political stability that reflects a broadly shared consensus of values among social groups. Political party systems have a consensus with respect to the means by which political change is to be accomplished. It is generally agreed that the government has responsibility for the welfare of its citizens, although opinions may differ about the proper extent of that responsibility. Social-security legislation, fair-trade practices, and civil rights enactments are examples of United States commitment to the idea of a welfare state. This commitment tends to level social strata and enhance political stability, enabling pressures for change to be accommodated within the political order.

[b] AUTHORITARIAN SOCIETIES. Left-wing or conservative, authoritarian societies usually centralize political power in a single party. The social hierarchy reflects the ranks of party and government bureaucracy. Ideology or party decree provides the cohesive values among social groups. Revolt against the system is unlikely to succeed unless the ruling elite fails to agree or to maintain its disciplinary apparatus. To contain domestic unrest or bolster support, the leadership may sound alarms of foreign threats or plots or may turn to foreign ventures like Indonesia's confrontation policy against Malaysia. In the Soviet bloc pressures for change may come from intellectuals, workers, and religious leaders, and gradual change may ameliorate the rule. Nationalism has focused the many centers of power that might replace monolithic rule. Social structure, belief systems and ideologies, and the political organs which express these are all powerful elements both of change and of stability in authoritarian societies. Considerable fluidity may develop in modern authoritarian societies. However, accord and adjustment of conflicts between Communist and democratic states are now very difficult because of the structural rigidity of authoritarian regimes and their surrounding ideologies. Still with time some accommodation of international differences between these societies may occur.

Crisis and Stability. A crisis or a period of rapid change often serves as a catalyst and energizer for extremist elements because it leads to fragmentation of the community and the existing order. New leaderships, unsupported by immediate political or dynastic traditions, are generally able to impose their ideas and control upon states in periods of political, social, or economic crises. The identity of revolutionary groups differs in every situation. At the center is a militant elite that believes a radical solution is necessary to change government policies and leadership. Surrounding this core are idealists, including the frustrated, the emotionally disengaged, and the unemployed. Professor Sigmund Neumann has called these elements the "crisis strata" in society. The revolutionary elite forms them into a militant action group to heighten crises or to overthrow the existing leadership. This is how Lenin steered the Russian revolution and how Mao and his followers overthrew the Kuomintang in China. Essentially the same characteristics mark the Vietcong efforts in South Vietnam and the Communist thrusts for power in Indonesia, Venezuela, the Sudan, the Congo, and elsewhere. Extremist elements may attempt to rise at almost any point during a dictatorship to overthrow it in favor of another dictator or of a different form of government.

Throughout both the germinal and activist phases of rapid change there may be incidents involving foreign countries or their nationals or property. Foreign policy may be forced to move in a new direction, from a pro-Western to neutralist or even to a Communist orientation. Political struggles have resulted in such changes in some of the Asian countries. In September of 1965, Indonesian military leaders resisted Communist efforts to seize power, and President Sukarno was eventually compelled to acquiesce in removal of Communists from influential positions and to permit the country's foreign policy to be oriented away from Peking. Similarly, after the Cuban revolution Premier Castro turned Cuban policy away from the United States.

We conclude that radical change in political leadership that is likely to produce sharp transformations in foreign and domestic policy creates tensions and a new body of ideas. Arbitrary prejudices and alignments may replace reason and the real interests of the states. These ideas may moderate with time or be reinforced by events or the acceptance of a totalitarian ideology.

Our analysis of the degrees of consensus on values in various social structures suggests some underlying social and economic conditions that influence the probabilities of particular groups of people retaining extended control over the policies of states. In democratic countries with a high per capita income and in the Communist world, opposition to the established order is discouraged from prompting change through revolution. In developing societies where lack of general agreement produces instabilities, and incompatibilities between goals and the resources needed to attain them exist, conflict and crisis are likely to be fairly frequent. Periodic upheaval may become endemic where there is habitual dictatorship, no demonstrable progress toward better economic and social conditions, and no political tradition. This has been the story in large parts of Latin America, the Middle East, China, and Africa. Transitional societies exist in a situation of potential crisis, with little continuity in leadership, outlook, or foreign policy.

Many of the traditional and transitional societies are in slow evolution that can be ordered through widening perception, mature leadership, the development of skills and stable employment, expanding production, and direct assistance from the more advanced states or aid through international institutions. An American presence, multilateral technical assistance, and the fortunate discovery of petroleum helped Libya survive after independence. Turkey and Iran have been able to preserve their integrity while effecting the transition from traditional to more modern forms of social organization, and have associated with the Western powers and received large amounts of foreign assistance.

CONCLUSION

We have defined international politics as the interaction of the policies of states. Relationships between states are determined by their objectives, the policies adopted in pursuit of them, and the bearing these have upon the interests and actions of other states. Although the actual conduct of international politics is by a relatively small number of individuals in each state, it involves relationships between entire societies, for mass communications have stimulated national consciousness and made ideologies, emotions, and symbols relevant to international politics. Interstate relationships are basically affected by the beliefs, the attitudes, and the feelings of peoples and leaders; by the dynamics of group behavior; and by the interaction of emotions, predispositions, and outlooks in response to the stimuli of particular circumstances.

It is important to understand the various dynamic forces operating within societies and their interaction with external forces penetrating national boundaries. In world politics continual change is the predominant note. Relatively stable societies can accommodate themselves to new circumstances. Communist ideology claims to have discovered objective "laws of history" that explain the correlation between forces and define the concepts of order and justice.

The democratic ideal contains no apocalyptic vision. It is founded on basic values of liberal rule and respect for human rights. Concepts of law and justice are drawn from the political and social environment. Democracy believes that the future remains to be discovered and can be shaped through peaceful change and orderly progress.

CHAPTER 4

Nationalism as a Force in International Politics

INTRODUCTION

Nationalism is one of the principal dynamic forces of political change and action in world affairs. It was a dominant factor in shaping the nations of Europe and America and has been at the root of many wars. Modern nationalism has brought the empires of nineteenth-century Europe to an end, and in their place the peoples of Asia, Africa, and the Middle East have claimed the right to sovereign independence. The world has now entered an era of "pan nationalism." Through nationalism disunited and subject peoples seek unity and independence. At the same time the force of nationalism also encourages the maintenance of parochial attitudes as well as barriers to trade, communication, and collaboration. The enlightened humanism characteristic of nationalism in the Age of Reason is absent from much of the modern nationalism.

WHAT IS NATIONALISM?

Nationalism as a political force is an amalgam of an ideology about the idea of nationality and the political institutionalization of that ideology in

70

the national state. The strength of nationalism depends on a feeling of national unity that may stem from race, language, common history and experiences, or religion. The national state reflects the political and social organization of its members, has coercive power over them and claims in their name sovereignty over the territory in which they live.

Although the idea of nationality is rooted in history, the concepts of modern nationalism and nationality originated in the Western world in the seventeenth and eighteenth centuries. Events in the twentieth century have shown the mobility of these concepts that can be adopted by peoples everywhere, in any stage of cultural, social, and political development. The force of nationalism has appeared in different forms. The totalitarian nationalism of Nazism and Fascism is distinct from the nineteenth-century liberal nationalism of the Italian *risorgimento* and the American struggle for constitutional rights. Nationalism in Asia and Africa today has characteristics that are found neither in totalitarian nationalism nor in the Western European movement toward integration into larger communities. In Communist-influenced areas nationalism has some aspects that differ from the nationalism of free societies.

Nationalism is hard to define because of its varied forms. Hans Kohn has termed it a "state of mind" in which the individual feels he owes his supreme loyalty to the nation-state. Nationalism is a "feeling" which reflects a national consciousness and inspires loyalty to one's nation. The individual feels loyalty because he identifies his well-being with that of his nation and his life is given greater meaning and direction through participation in the purposes, successes, and even failures of his nation. Nationalism is the consciousness which groups of people have of belonging together.

Boyd Shafer, in *Nationalism: Myth and Reality*, sums up the spirit of nationalism in these words—a nation includes a "certain defined (often vaguely) unit of territory (whether possessed or coveted) . . . and a belief in a common history (it can be invented) and in a common origin (often mistakenly conceived to be racial in nature) . . . [and] a hope that the nation will have a great and glorious future (usually in territorial expansion). . . ."

Nationalism makes the political and cultural values of the nation supreme. Loyalty is measured by patriotism. Independent statehood is the key objective of nationalism among subjugated peoples. As a political movement nationalism asserts a people's "claim to a distinctive national identity, entitling it to live its own life in its own fashion."

ROOTS OF NATIONALISM

Before discussing the historical development of nationalism as a political force, we should note some of the factors underlying nationality.

Language, Literature, and Nationalism.   Language and literature are important stimulants to nationalism, although nations do develop without having a common language. Switzerland has four languages and the Soviet Union over 150, although Russian has been made the official language. Many African countries have several dialects and no common written language. The development and use of a national language is generally stressed when a nationalistic feeling is aroused. The revival of Irish nationalism has been accompanied by a demand to use Gaelic rather than English. In Israel, Hebrew is emphasized as the official language. When colonies break away from alien rule, nationalistic sentiment may lead to abandonment of the language of the former rulers in favor of a native tongue. English and French have been retained as the principal languages in countries that were formerly parts of the British and French empires. However, in the more advanced of these countries there are pressures to make a local language the official one, for example, Hindi in India. This creates serious problems where the language is not understood by masses of the people. In India riots followed the proclamation of Hindi as the official language, leading the government to reverse the decision.

Through language people communicate with one another, and pass ideas, values, objectives, memories, and traditions from one generation to the next. The syntax, word sound, and rhythm of the language express the temperament, moods, and general emotional life of the group and intensify the group's uniqueness.

Since the time of the ancient Greeks, scholars, historians, poets, and philosophers have played important roles in building national sentiment and fostering the spirit of nationalism. Plato, Aristotle, the Greek tragedies, and the Homeric poems helped create the "soul" of Greece, and the Norse sagas, with their embodiment of the traditions and memories of a great past, inspire national pride and fervor in Norway.

William Shakespeare is not always thought of as an ardent exponent of nationalism, but these lines of Shakespeare's can be considered as an expression of national sentiment:

> This happy breed of men, this little world,
> This precious stone set in the silver sea,
> Which serves it in the office of a wall,

> Or as a moat defensive to a house,
> Against the envy of less happier lands,
> This blessed plot, this earth, this realm, this England.
> (*King Richard II*)

Shakespeare's verse and drama reinforce the English people's love of their nation in much the same way as do the classical literature, folk music and folk lore of other nations.

Men have long smiled at Gilbert and Sullivan's refulgent additives to English pride and prejudice in their tuneful operettas. But they did have a nationalistic tongue in cheek when they wrote:

> He is an Englishman!
>
> For he himself has said it,
> And it's greatly to his credit,
> That he is an Englishman!
>
> For he might have been a Rooshian
> A French or Turk or Proosian,
> Or perhaps Ital-ian.
> But in spite of all temptations
> To belong to other nations,
> He remains an Englishman.
> (*H.M.S. Pinafore*)

In the United States the writings of Francis Parkman, James Fenimore Cooper, Henry Wadsworth Longfellow, Benjamin Franklin, Mark Twain, Harriet Beecher Stowe, and Robert Frost have helped impart a love of country to generations of Americans.

Religion and Nationality. In some places there is a close connection between religion and nationality. Most Pakistanis are Moslems, and most Indians are Hindus. Indeed, the division of the subcontinent into Indian and Pakistani states was largely drawn along religious communal lines. Before 1945 Shinto was closely identified with Japanese nationalism. Common religious ties have also helped nations unite. Western European collaboration was encouraged by the strong support of predominantly Roman Catholic Christian Democratic Parties in France, Belgium, Italy, Germany, the Netherlands, and Luxembourg.

Organized religion usually supports national policy when emergencies confront the state. The Church may preserve and foster national sentiment against another nation or ideology. Throughout the history of Poland, the

Roman Catholic Church strongly opposed Czarist and Communist attempts to dominate national life. Archbishop Makarios fired Greek national feeling in his leadership of the Greek Cypriots in their struggle with the Turkish minority in Cyprus.

Nationalism may develop irrespective of religion, for in many countries nationality and religion are not closely identified. It can also develop into a chauvinistic force despite formal religious opposition, as happened in Germany under the Nazi regime.

National Unity Through Conflict.   Feudal and dynastic wars played a considerable part in shaping nationalism in Europe, by strengthening loyalties, developing leadership, and accentuating group feelings. Wars force people to work together to preserve their national existence and hence create a sense of unity through shared insecurities and privations. Many nation-states in Europe were formed after the Thirty Years' War and conditions developed that favored the growth of nationalism in the eighteenth and nineteenth centuries. American nationalism grew out of the Revolutionary War, the War of 1812, the Mexican War, and the struggles on the Western frontier. The Mexican War also stimulated the development of nationalism in Mexico. War and the threat of invasion have nearly everywhere been factors in fashioning national sentiment and in forging new nations.

The communal rioting which accompanied the transition from British rule to Indian and Pakistani independence quickly led to mutual fears, reinforcement of group differences, and growth of strong national sentiments. The Indian-Pakistani fighting in 1965 caused Hindus and Moslems in India to come together in the interests of the nation. When Palestine was partitioned and the state of Israel created, war soon developed out of the fears, suspicions, and animosities between Jews and Arabs. Both Arab and Jewish nationalism has increased as a consequence of the tensions that have arisen on both sides of the border.

Race.   The idea of race is sometimes associated with nationalism. The Nazis propagated the theory that true German nationality rested on the Aryan race. Believing in the myth of a "superior" race, they claimed the right to rule "inferior" races and nations, notably the Jews, Poles, and Russians. Racist theories are rejected by reputable authorities, although the concept of race is difficult to define. It is generally held that there is no empirical basis for equating nation and race. But as Reinhold Niebuhr points out, ethnic kinship is one of the most important and least controllable elements in determining the organic basis for the existence of a community. When race becomes equated with color, as in much of the new African nationalism, feelings of kinship and antagonism are quickly aroused and reinforced. Some mixed populations are hampered in their progression to statehood by racial problems.

The Mystique of the Nation. Scholars have contributed to the growth of nationalism by creating an imagery of mystical qualities about the nation. Philosophers like Fichte in Germany and Mazzini in Italy contended that the nation was created by God as part of a divine scheme for a world of harmony and peace. Hegel argued that the nation was a "spiritual organism," and Rénan called it a "soul, a spiritual principle." These were among the *avant-garde* of their time, and their writings helped to awaken a sense of national consciousness and to inspire political leadership to action. These men had humanitarian ideals and would probably have rejected the militarist spirit that grew out of the nationalism inspired by their writings.

Symbols of Nationalism. Identification of the individual with a given nationality takes place through group communication and assimilation, fostered by the manipulation of symbols and the arts of communication. Art, literature, folklore, and music help to cultivate and perpetuate "historical memories," giving them a particular national meaning and scope. Heroes add to the growth of national sentiment and the communication of a sense of nationality among individuals. This national spirit is transmitted from one generation to another through commemoration of heroes like Washington, Jefferson, and Lincoln in America; Kosciusko in Poland; Mazzini and Garibaldi in Italy; Napoleon in France; and Nelson in England. National shrines like Mount Vernon, the *Arc de Triomphe*, Westminster Abbey, and Lenin's tomb, along with such slogans as *liberté, égalité, fraternité*, national flags, anthems, and military uniforms also communicate feelings of attachment and loyalty to a national group.

National Character and National Style. There is some validity in the idea that nations have a certain national character and style. A given environment, certain historical experiences, and a definite pattern of social and legal institutions tend to produce a degree of group uniformity. If a group exists long enough within common political frontiers, unique traits of national character will develop, although nations may share similar values and objectives. England and the United States, Canada and Australia, Norway and Sweden have different national personalities. National style describes how a nation typically attempts to solve its problems through recurrent behavior patterns.

Nationalism Defined by Ability to Communicate. Professor Karl Deutsch has argued that the customary empirical descriptions of nationalism reveal neither its real sources nor objective information on which to base predictions. Deutsch considers the essential aspect of national unity to be "complementarity," or relative efficiency, of communication among people. This is a functional view that measures cohesion of a community by the ability of its members to communicate more effectively and widely with each other than with outsiders. Nationality is defined by performance rather than its components.

Critics of this approach contend that nationalism is an historical process and a sense of nationality is formed by subjective factors that defy measurement. Yet wherever the sense of nationality has become a potent political force, it has included a particular set of ideas, attitudes, and outlooks that are communicated first by individuals and then by interest groups. The Sons of Liberty and the Committees of Correspondence played a key role in the development of an American national consciousness when the colonists were trying to achieve American independence. Gandhi and his followers differentiated themselves by wearing homespun cloth and promoting nonviolent resistance, and used their Congress Party as a means to communicate a sense of national uniqueness to the Indian people. Martyrdom may occur in the process of crystallizing and spreading national sentiment. Many nationalist leaders have been imprisoned or exiled, including Gandhi and Jomo Kenyatta.

Effective social communication, by whatever means, does enhance a nation's political power and unity.

THE EVOLUTION OF POLITICAL NATIONALISM

The identity of individuals and groups with political societies precedes the national state. In ancient history, the Medes, Persians, Greeks, and Romans formed political associations. The national state is the successor of the tribe, city-state, feudal lord, monarch, emperor, and church, which have previously claimed supreme loyalty. It has acquired political and legal aspects which include territoriality, sovereignty, and the right of self-determination.

Liberal Nationalism and National Self-Determination. The intellectual roots of modern Western nationalism lie in the seventeenth- and eighteenth-century Age of Enlightenment and the Age of Reason. Such philosophers as Montesquieu, Voltaire, Locke, Rousseau, and Jefferson protested against the feudal idea of a divine right of kings and held that men should be governed by natural law, from which rights and social and political responsibilities are derived. Their writings were the source of Western liberal or humanitarian nationalism that contained the seeds of the democratic idea.

The political expression of these concepts was set forth in Thomas Jefferson's wording of the American Declaration of Independence.

When in the Course of human events, it becomes necessary for one people to dissolve the political bonds which have connected them with another, and to assume among the powers of the earth, the separate and equal station to which the Laws of Nature and of Nature's God entitle them, a decent respect to the opinions of mankind require that they should declare the causes which impel them to the separation.—We hold these truths to be self-evident, that all men are created equal, that they are endowed by their Creator with certain unalienable Rights, that among these are Life, Liberty and the pursuit of Happiness. That to secure these rights, Governments are instituted among Men, deriving their just powers from the consent of the governed. That whenever any Form of Government becomes destructive of these ends, it is the Right of the People to alter or abolish it, and to institute new Government, laying its foundations on such principles and organizing its powers in such forms, as to them shall seem most likely to effect their Safety and Happiness.

The idea of national self-determination developed out of liberal nationalism and of democracy. If a body of people did not wish to be a part of the state that exercised political power over them, they had a "right" to choose which state should govern them. The ideals of liberal nationalism were later articulated by the rising middle classes in Europe who united to acquire the political and economic power of the landed aristocracy and clergy.

In England the transition to a liberal representative government occurred without violent revolution, except for the Cromwellian period. The French *ancien régime* was deposed by the Revolution which brought a temporary vacuum of political and economic power. The ousted nobility, supported by the armies of foreign nobles, opposed the Revolution and nationalism for the first time engulfed the masses and shaped a national unity. The force of French nationalism stimulated efforts to spread the ideals of the Revolution throughout Europe.

Stirred by the principles and the spirit of the French and American Revolutions, other peoples began to generate political pressures against the "old order." The Latin American peoples broke away from Spain and Portugal in the early nineteenth century, and there were revolts in Belgium,

Italy, and Germany in 1830. Revolution again reverberated in France, Germany, Italy, and the Austrian Empire in 1848. Italy and Germany finally found unity through nationalism.

Liberal nationalism influenced internal political and social change. In Western Europe it sought to limit the power of government and to secure civil and property rights for the rising middle class. In Middle and Eastern Europe, there was only a weak middle class between the feudal aristocracy and rural peasantry, and nationalism remained a mystique. Greeks, Serbs, Poles, Czechs, and Hungarians fought for national freedom against the Ottoman, Hapsburg, and Romanov empires, but these were not completely destroyed until 1919. Then many new states were established in Central and Eastern Europe on the basis of peoples' demands for self-determination.

From Liberal to Totalitarian Nationalism. As strong national governments emerged at the end of the nineteenth century and as nationalism permeated the social fabric to gain mass support, many nations became less liberal and more highly nationalistic.

Liberal nationalists had envisioned a world order of independent constitutional governments giving legal protection to private property and free enterprise and permitting free trade. However, international trade became increasingly subject to protectionism and economic nationalism in the period between the two world wars.

Following World War I the appearance of Communism in the Soviet Union, Fascism in Italy, and National Socialism in Germany led to totalitarian systems of nationalism. All regarded the state as the supreme instrument of power to which the rights of the individual were subordinated. The humanitarianism of the liberal nationalists was replaced by *étatisme* and dictatorial rule.

In Germany this totalitarianism paved the way for the brutality of the Nazi (National Socialist) regime. In Italy it enabled Benito Mussolini and his Fascist "Black Shirts" to erect an authoritarian order. In Germany the worst aspects of this nationalism were carried to extremes as the whole people were indoctrinated to accept concepts of bloodlust and aggressive war as desirable ends of life. These fateful aberrations were brought to an end only after nearly the entire world had been plunged into total war resulting in an enormous loss of life and some of the most heinous crimes against mankind. The cost of this experiment in totalitarian nationalism is without equal.

Nationalism and Communism. Shortly after the Bolshevik seizure of power, Lenin issued a declaration of self-determination for the various nationalities within the U.S.S.R. Czarist policies of Russification were temporarily abandoned. Although national expression was formally permitted for some of Russia's 150 nationalities, they were politically subject to the dictates of the government and the Communist Party. Stalin progressively curtailed the autonomy of the republics and liquidated his opponents. At the onset of the German invasion in World War II, Stalin appealed to nationalism to arouse the Russian people. "Let the courageous image of our great ancestors inspire you in this war" was an order of the day to the Red armies. When the defense of Communism proved insufficient to encourage resistance, Stalin called for unlimited faithfulness to the "mother country." Forgotten heroes of Russian history were revived, including the authoritarian czars, and every device of propaganda was used to stir national emotions.

Soviet patriotism is a messianic combination of Marxist-Leninist ideology and historical Great Russian chauvinism, fostered through press, radio, literature, symbols, and all the apparatus state and party have been able to mobilize. Russia claims the role of the chosen nation, destined to liberate and lead the proletariat throughout the world. The thrust of Soviet nationalism is felt in imperialism in Eastern Europe, the Middle East, and Asia, and in the machinations of Communist intrigue designed to establish worldwide Communism.

National Communism. National forms of Communism have developed in Eastern Europe, following Stalin's death in 1953 and the rise of the Sino-Soviet conflict. Yugoslavia first resisted Soviet interference and Marshal Tito severed relations with Moscow in 1948. Encouraged by this example, others later pressed for a larger measure of freedom than Stalin had been willing to concede. Titoism, combined with rugged Yugoslav nationalism, first showed the possibility of national influences weakening the monolithic orthodoxy of Soviet Communist rule. National uprisings in Poland and Hungary followed Premier Khrushchev's exposure of Stalin's "crimes" at the Twentieth Party Congress in 1956. Popular demonstrations for Gomulka and preparations to resist Soviet military intervention compelled a reluctant Khrushchev to accept more autonomy for the Polish regime. The Hungarian patriots, under the leadership of Imre Nagy, were not so fortunate. When Nagy admitted non-Communists to his government and asked for Hungary's release from the Warsaw Pact, Soviet tanks and artillery rolled into Hungary and put down the nationalists. But the world did not soon forget the patriotism of the freedom fighters of Hungary. By the mid-1960's, some of the restraints which were placed on the Hungarian people after the uprising were eased.

The Polish uprising illustrates the compatibility of proletarian internationalism, or Communism, with Polish nationalism. Hungarian bourgeois nationalism, on the other hand, was seen to be incompatible with the Communist system.

In Rumania the spirit of nationalism caused considerable relaxation of bureaucratic controls and encouragement of international trade and communism. The national Communists pursued this policy cautiously, aware of the threat and protection of Soviet armed forces near its borders. Eastern European Communists recognize their dependence on Soviet protection and the uncertain course of world politics. They, accordingly, are aware that there are limits beyond which it is not wise to press for the time being. Hence, they have had to reconcile the urgings of nationalism with the realities of power politics. But out of these stirrings has come a measure of acceptance of polycentrism by the leadership in the Kremlin.

The Chinese have evolved a nationalism based on ethnic factors rather than political ideas of a nation-state. They have a traditional attitude of superiority that assumes ultimate Chinese expansion from their ancient Middle Kingdom. Specific claims include extensive territories outside present Chinese borders in South Asia, parts of Soviet Central Asia, the Soviet Maritime Provinces, and Taiwan. Traditional Chinese chauvinism is now reinforced by the strong central government and Chinese belief that one or more Great Powers are antagonistic toward them. Maoism has replaced Confucianism as the principal Chinese doctrine.

Sharp differences have arisen between Peking and Moscow over Marxist dialectics, programs for economic advance, and policies with respect to the Western powers. Differences in economic growth and industrialization and maturity of their revolutions have contributed to the Sino-Soviet disagreements. These are also nationalistic and ideological. The current Moscow-Peking dialogue appears to focus on conflicting claims to supremacy. We shall consider these differences at some length in Chapter 14. Suffice it here to say that national ambition, pride, and historic enmities lie behind the Sino-Soviet conflict.

Communist relations with non-Communist states continue to exhibit national characteristics and concern for prestige, power, and influence. Strains among the Communist states and the open conflict between Peking and Moscow have brought into question the validity of the assumption that national Communist policies are pursued in the interests of international Communism rather than of national objectives much of the time.

The New Nationalism of the Non-Western World.   Ironically the force of nationalism which drove European colonialism into Asia and Africa has been turned against the colonial powers.

The nationalist revolution which has spread to Asia, Africa, and Latin America since 1945 has certain unique characteristics that differentiate it from both liberal and totalitarian nationalism. The principal ones are a sense of independent worth and self-respect, an insistence that political equality be recognized, and local leaders be free to determine domestic policy. Anticolonialism remains a feature of the new nationalism to prevent re-establishment of colonial rule. Suspicions extend to the polices of governments and the policies of investors and large corporations seeking markets, raw materials, and new facilities.

The success of the anticolonial movement does not assure that stability and full independence can be maintained. Countries like the Congo and Sudan have experienced subversion, exploitation, internal dissension, and political weakness. Agents of Communist China have been trying to drive a wedge into Africa to take advantage of "situations ripe for revolution," in the words of Chou En-lai. Communist Chinese agents quickly entered tiny, strategically-located Burundi after independence and used it to infiltrate arms and propaganda into neighboring lands until they were expelled. Some African leaders are aware of the dangers. Jomo Kenyatta, for example, replied to Chou En-lai, "Kenya intends to avert all revolutions irrespective of their origins."

Features of the New Nationalism.   As a mass political movement, the nationalism of the newly independent nations is weak, even though leaders and groups may be very assertive. It is difficult to create a "national consciousness" where men's lives have traditionally been bounded by family, tribe, caste, village, or petty principality. There are few broadly-shared values apart from anticolonialism and the desire for political integrity and equality.

In the Western European and North Atlantic areas, nationalism was nurtured in a culture already being transformed by the industrial revolution. It embodied values shared by all social classes. In most of Africa there are no bases for appeal to freedom and individual liberties and few past glories that can be recalled to kindle a militant national spirit. In parts of the Middle East and Asia, nationalism does find support from an embryonic middle class and from intellectuals, professionals, and politicians. The masses of the uneducated peasantry remain politically inarticulate. Most of the political and economic institutions of the new countries are not indigenous, but have been adopted from former rulers.

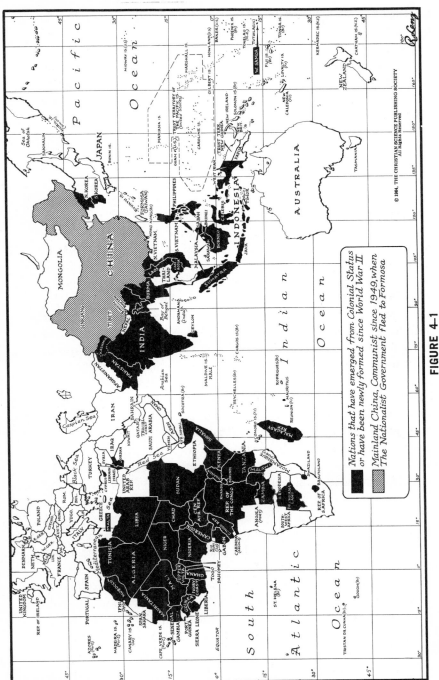

FIGURE 4–1

How Nationalism Has Remade Maps *(Reprinted by permission from The Christian Science Monitor © 1964, The Christian Science Publishing Society. All rights reserved)*

In most of the newly independent countries the colonial powers did not plan political development and often discouraged or forbade political activity and imprisoned native leaders. Democratic institutions may not be suitable to local circumstances nor be able to function successfully. The political and economic institutions through which a democratic and pluralistic society functions are the products of long social evolution. The United Arab Republic, Ghana, and Guinea have turned, at least temporarily, to authoritarian rule. Few have traditions of democratic participation in national government or guarantees of individual liberty and personal rights. Deeply rooted tribal loyalties and differences compounded by suspicions of foreigners and of central control inhibit the growth of democratic political institutions.

The new nationalism does not determine in what form economic development should be pursued. It often impedes economic growth by curtailing access to foreign goods, skills, and capital through fear of alien intrusion and neocolonialism. The rising middle classes in some areas of Asia, Africa, and the Middle East are superimposed on a large, poor, and uneducated peasantry prone to resist changes in traditional relationships.

Charismatic Leadership in the New Nationalism. Some of the leaders associated with the new nationalism have fashioned an almost mystical quality about their personalities and actions. Gamal Abdel Nasser of Egypt, Sukarno of Indonesia, Jomo Kenyatta of Kenya, and Emperor Haile Selassie of Ethiopia are but a few examples of such leaders.

This type of leadership can become a benevolent or authoritarian dictatorship unless opposition and a broadly based democracy develop as a result of popular education. Illiteracy, poverty, and lack of experience in responsible government attract revolutions and coups that attempt to depose dictators. Such leadership, accompanied by strong one-party rule, can thus be a benefit or a liability to a new country. The temptations before leaders of this type are either to rule with an iron hand imprisoning or outlawing political opposition, as in Nkrumah's Ghana, or to flirt with unworkable socialist or more extreme schemes and drive the country into virtual bankruptcy, as Sukarno did in Indonesia. The leader can imagine himself to be indispensable and think that he always knows what is best for the country, which may be chiefly for his own pocketbook or political fortunes. Although charismatic leadership may be a rather natural thing in a country undergoing transition and having a large uneducated populace, it can also lead to political and economic difficulties for the future.

The New Nationalism and Ideology. Many Asian and African leaders educated in the traditions of Western liberalism question its appropriateness and that of the free-enterprise system for their countries. These leaders stress the preoccupation of their people with rudimentary social and economic problems that make economic development at the earliest possible time their prime objective. Under these circumstances variations of socialism involving government planning and controls appeal to these leaders as more suitable for meeting their needs.

In recent years the Soviet Union has expressed its support of the new nationalist movements. Communist China has also tried to align itself with them and particularly with their sentiments of anticolonialism. Leaders of both Communist powers have vied in wooing the new states and in seeking footholds there. Each has invited students and young people to come to their land with all expenses paid. The personal histories of such figures as Mao Tse-tung, Tito, Rakosi, Kadar, and other Communist leaders who have spent part of their youth in Moscow stand as a warning of what may be expected in the future from some of those who pursue "studies" in the Communist countries. Lumumba, Ben Bella, and Odinga may be but the beginning of a new political sequence in Africa. A few countries, including India, Guinea, Egypt, Morocco, and Kenya, have tried to keep Communist activities under strict control. Some leaders, such as Tshombe in the Congo, Kenyatta in Kenya, and Boumadienne in Algeria, have openly rejected Communism, as have most of the military figures brought to power by coups in various parts of Africa. Whether others who are trying to play the East off against the West will be able to preserve their freedom of action at crucial moments only the future can determine. The hope of many is pinned on a vigorous nationalism asserting independence when it is threatened, as it has in not a few instances.

The New Nationalism and Neutralism.   Two other characteristics of the new nationalism deserve note. One is the desire to become members of the United Nations. Membership in the world organization is often second only to the objective of national independence. This has been responsible for no less than thirty-four African countries being admitted to the United Nations. Membership in the U.N. is a symbol of prestige. It gives the newly independent nations a status of equality with their former masters; the right to cast a vote that is the equivalent of that of Britain or France. Membership also provides the opportunity to use their collective power to press for greater economic and technical assistance, for actions against remaining colonial powers like Portugal, and against the hated racialist practices of South Africa.

The second characteristic is the trend toward neutralism and nonalignment. This concept is not well defined and is often thought to include pro-Soviet or pro-Peking bias. The policies of neutralism and nonalignment incline the countries to refuse participation in formal military alignments with the West, although some have sought aid from both the West and the East when their security has been threatened, as India sought arms from London, Washington, Moscow, and anywhere else when it was attacked by China and threatened with renewed fighting. In the cold war many of the new countries have attempted to steer clear of involvement, although some of them have considered it their right to mediate when they can. Bias against the West is rooted in suspicion of the former colonial powers and lack of real experience with Soviet and Chinese imperialism. The limitations of a neutralist policy are recognized by some. Jomo Kenyatta is quoted as saying,

It is natural that we should detest Western colonialism, and associate the word "imperialism" with the West. But if we are truly nonaligned we must not avoid making friends with those Western countries which extend an honest field of cooperation and trade. To do this is just to prove that we are not free and cannot separate good from bad. It proves that we still suffer from a colonial mentality.[1]

Although new states are eager to exclude the Great Powers from their affairs, they have tried to impress their views and policies on the Great Powers. In 1961 the new states succeeded, for example, in passing a resolution at the General Assembly calling on the Powers to reconvene the disarmament negotiations at Geneva. In 1964 a bloc of seventy-six developing countries at the Geneva Conference on Trade and Development caused the Great Powers to establish a continuing machinery for discussion and action on these matters. At the time of the Rhodesian crisis in 1965 most of these same countries rejected British opposition to a draft resolution of the United Nations calling for a boycott of Rhodesia and demanding the use of force against the white minority government and passed it by a large majority.

Another area in which the new nations become involved in the power struggle is that of economic and technical assistance. Their aspirations confront them with hard choices. Assistance from international agencies like the World Bank may not be adequate or on terms which suit their needs or capabilities, nor is it sufficient to meet their desires. They can turn to the Communist bloc, as Nasser did after being rebuffed by Secretary Dulles. Or they can look to the North Atlantic countries. Or, again, they can attempt to "play the field," generating competition

---

[1] See Lawrence Fellows, " 'Harambee,' Says Kenyatta—'Let's All Pull Together'," *The New York Times Magazine*, November 7, 1965.

between East and West. The developing countries have tried hard to increase the assistance available through multilateral U.N. channels where their influence is substantial, rather than taking aid through bilateral pacts where weak countries are often at a bargaining disadvantage. Thus far in the so-called Development Decade the Great Powers have been unwilling to step up their contributions to the U.N. funds by very much, fearing that the funds will not be as efficiently expended or controlled. As a consequence, the new countries must continue to look to the principal sources of assistance and make the best they can of whatever arrangements the granting countries stipulate. This is a large area of incessant political bargaining.

Xenophobia and Racialism. The new nationalism is explosive when the emotions of the public are exploited by demagogic leaders seeking to advance their own interests or to divert attention from pressing economic and social needs. During the early stages of independence, nationalism has sometimes exhibited xenophobic tendencies directed against Western "exploiters."

Such xenophobic emotionalism is compounded of numerous psychological strains, including resentment based on feelings of inferiority vis-à-vis the West. With responsibility for coping with the staggering problems of poverty, health, illiteracy, population pressures, economic development, and effective political organization being suddenly thrust upon governments where there is no political system rooted in tradition, it is occasionally tempting to try to shift the blame for present ills to outside powers. This may bring the solution of these problems no nearer, but it can give momentary alleviation by conjuring up scapegoats. Racialism intensifies these attitudes. Anti-white feelings engendered during the colonial era have been heightened in Africa by the apartheid policies in South Africa, the domineering behavior of the white minority in Rhodesia, and even the problems of the Negro in the United States.

Despite the xenophobia exhibited now and then, the Western countries on the whole enjoy the friendship and respect of the new countries of Asia and Africa. However, the unstable elements associated with some of the new nationalisms make relations between the governments delicate.

NATIONALISM, INTERNATIONALISM, AND SUPRANATIONALISM

Nationalism is a dominant force that is unlikely to decline and may always create problems of change and conflict.

Liberal nationalism can be a constructive force, bringing groups of states together into larger political communities to promote law and order, economic development, and social welfare. Totalitarian and xenophobic nationalism, on the other hand, can narrow outlooks and generate fears, hatreds, and suspicions that can lead to war.

International organization cannot solve the problems of narrow nationalism, although it may assist states to reach accommodations of their differences. Neither security nor welfare is compatible with complete self-determination. A selective approach to a transnational functional internationalism must first grow out of the development of meaningful communities of values, objectives, and actions. The nations of Western Europe and the Atlantic area have been moving hesitantly in the direction of a larger community in organizations and movements like the European Coal and Steel Community, the European Atomic Community, and the North Atlantic Treaty Organization. The African states have formed the Organization for African Unity. Five of the Central American states are developing cooperative economic and political arrangements. The British Commonwealth of Nations and the French Community are each seeking to preserve and cultivate mutual interests across national boundaries. But the resurgence of a parochial French nationalism and search for "grandeur" under President de Gaulle in relation to the European Economic Community and NATO warns that supranationalism is a very fragile thing among even the most advanced and sophisticated and that the appeals and passions of nationalism remain a fundamental and dynamic force in world politics.

Unbridled nationalism can easily become a handicap to the advancement of the underdeveloped states without domestic means of growth. Political conflicts generated by nationalism can lead to tensions and conflicts that divert urgently needed resources to armaments, as in the Indian-Pakistani conflict over Kashmir. The ultimate problem of twentieth-century nationalism is whether war between the superpowers, whether occasioned by direct controversies between them or as a by-product of conflicts involving the new nations, can be avoided. Political realism suggests that conflict cannot be averted, but only channeled and directed. Humanism suggests that man is the master of his fate and can avert or prevent war if he will do so. Nationalism is a far greater force than internationalism at the present time. The increase in number of states in the world, the sensitivity of the new states, and the expansion of communications contribute to the growth of nationalism as a political force. It is likely to remain the most important single force in world affairs for the foreseeable future.

CHAPTER 5

Imperialism, Colonialism, and Anticolonialism

INTRODUCTION

Like the force of nationalism, colonialism and imperialism spring from the self-consciousness of nation-states and their inclination to seek additional power and influence abroad. Most prominent states have at some time sought territories or possessions outside their own borders.

The spread of nationalism has resulted in the development of forces opposing colonialism and imperialism expressed in the movement for independence from colonial rule. Since World War II nationalism has disintegrated the empires of Britain, France, Belgium, and the Netherlands and has led to the large congregation of new states that have been formed in Asia, the Middle East, and Africa. Appealing to the philosophy of anticolonialism is a convenient way of organizing opposition to remaining colonial powers and to real or suspected policies of neocolonialism. Recently independent peoples are sensitive to foreign influence, fearing renewed domination through their dependence upon foreign economic and administrative assistance.

Imperialism and colonialism have left a legacy of emotional forces that are easily exploited through anti-imperialist propaganda. The Soviet

Union and China incite these forces in an effort to align the new states with Communist policy. The memories of imperialism and colonialism, real and imagined, constitute a dynamic element in international politics today.

THE PROBLEM OF DEFINITION

Imperialism and colonialism are difficult to define because they are emotive terms that convey certain images to different areas and peoples. Imperialism is used by Communists to describe and condemn Western policies or programs generally, regardless of their objectives. Charges of colonialism are often made when a Great Power is thought to be seeking special privileges or concessions in former colonial areas. "Economic imperialism" and "cultural imperialism" are slogans used by Communists and some newly independent elements against the Western powers. They are derived from socialist theory that attributes the cause of imperialism to capitalist economics.

Historically, imperialism was the creation of an empire in which one country extended its rule over peoples of differing nationality outside its own borders. Colonialism has traditionally implied a movement of nationals from a metropolitan or home country to a territory abroad, as in the colonizing of North America by England and France. These terms are now used loosely and often interchangeably. They have been applied to situations where a foreign power does not legally rule but exerts considerable influence. Colonialism describes the rule of a minority of colonists over the local people, as in Rhodesia under British rule, where white settlers were outnumbered thirty to one.

Imperialism. We define a policy of imperialism as one in which a nation imposes its rule or its views upon others regardless of their will. Once such a rule is established and coercive power is employed to retain that rule contrary to the will of the inhabitants, an imperial-colonial relationship results. It is imperial for the ruler and colonial for the ruled, as in the Italian conquest of Ethiopia in 1935.

This rule can be extended in a variety of ways, including indirect political control such as the Soviet Union exercises over the Eastern European states through the Communist Party apparatus. The term *rule* must be clarified in order to make the definition of imperialism useful.

Professor Carl Friedrich of Harvard University has defined rule as "institutionalized political power," which "consists of . . . coercive power." [1] In Chapter 1 we identified coercive power as "the capability to (1) resist and (2) impose one's will upon others who may be weaker or who do not agree with the values or objectives of the state possessing the power." And we contrasted this with power which is based upon a "consensus in shared values."

There are two general types of institutionalized power relationships between states. Some interstate relationships have regularized the conformities of conduct through the application or the threat of coercive power by the stronger state. In this situation the stronger state is exercising rule over the weaker states in an imperial-colonial relationship. Hitler's domination of Europe from 1939 to 1945 was an instance of imperialism by this definition. Other interstate relationships regularize conformities of conduct through a consensus in shared values. NATO, the European Economic Community, and the Alliance for Progress are examples. Neither imperialism nor colonialism is present.

Many interstate relationships involve elements of both coercive and consensual power, and each relationship must be examined in its own context to determine which is the predominant form of power. Relationships often change with time and with alterations in the objectives and practices of the states, for example, the evolution from the British Empire to the Commonwealth of Nations. In this case imperialism and colonialism gave way to a measure of consensus in shared values among political and legal equals terminating the old relationship and institutionalizing a new one.

Colonialism.   There can be subtle differences between a policy of colonialism and a policy of imperialism. Imperialism is present where coercive force is necessary to overcome local opposition, retain a colony, or exert influence. Where this power is not employed, when claiming and settling largely uninhabited territories and finding no resistance to foreign rule, the action is one of colonialism. The United States exercised colonial rule over Puerto Rico and the Philippines after their acquisition from Spain. The distinction between colonialism and imperialism is subjective and depends partly on the reactions of those concerned.

The following kinds of rule are not generally considered as imperial or colonial.

1. The administration of Trust Territories under agreement with the

---

[1] Carl J. Friedrich, "Political Leadership and the Problem of the Charismatic Power," *The Journal of Politics,* Vol. 23, No. 1, February 1961, pp. 9, 10. In this article Friedrich is concerned with the internal politics of a state. However, we believe his treatment of rule and power is useful in analyzing international politics as well.

United Nations. The United States administration of the Pacific Trust Territories taken over from Japan is a case in point.

2. Temporary intervention in the territory of another, without intent to impose rule, for a short-term objective of securing the life and property of nationals located there or for peace-keeping or peace-enforcing. The United States intervened in the Congo in 1964 to help rescue missionaries held as hostages by rebel forces, and with the cooperation of the Organization of American States sent forces to the Dominican Republic in 1965 to calm a civil war situation. Unilateral intervention is vulnerable to the charge of imperialism even if the external power is invited in by an independent government, as when British forces were invited into Zambia in 1965 to protect that country from possible troubles with the rebel Rhodesian government. To allay these charges states now tend to seek international approval for their action. Temporary United Nations peace-keeping forces in the Congo, Cyprus, and the Near East have not been so vulnerable to charges of imperialism because of their broadly based international character and the explicit approval of the local government for their presence. Moreover, it is recognized that their mission is to help restore or keep peace on behalf of the international community. This can hardly be called imperialism in the sense in which the term has historically been understood.

Economic Imperialism. Barbara Ward has suggested that economic imperialism be defined as an outside power taking over local resources and using them "mainly or exclusively for its own benefit." It is recognized that such a definition is very broad and that today's economic interdependence of nations gives rise to new political and moral dilemmas.

Foreign economic influence can take place through private capital investment and through governmental economic operations. The degree and the methods of control are important considerations. A few great industrialized powers control the capital, markets, and distribution systems of the international economy largely through private enterprises. Oil has been extracted from the Middle East by the operations of foreign private corporations, although local political units have gained from these activities. The way economic effort is carried out determines whether it can properly be classified as cooperative development or "imperialistic exploitation."

The rapid growth of government foreign assistance programs has led to charges of aid with strings. These charges often come from reluctance to undertake needed economic and social reforms. Increasing standardization of requirements for receiving aid has been blunting such cries. The United States has promoted this standardization, and international lending agencies like the World Bank make equivalent or more rigid stipulations. There is undoubtedly an element of influence connected with modern aid giving. But this does not include an intent to exercise political rule over the recipient, at least in the case of Western assistance.

Charges of economic imperialism are sometimes made against private investment and excessive dependency on one country's purchases of a principal export. Foreign private investors in weak countries now often seek guarantees from their own state against expropriation and establish joint companies with local nationals to protect themselves against nationalization. Notwithstanding such precautionary measures, countries are still sometimes suspicious of what they call "economic imperialism" and are at times vulnerable to the demagogic use of this issue in their internal politics.

WESTERN COLONIALISM AND IMPERIALISM

Motives of Western Colonialism and Imperialism.   No single political or economic motive provides sufficient explanation of Western imperialism. The idea of a Christian missionary goal, and assumption of the "white man's burden" to improve the lot of subject peoples have sometimes been used to rationalize imperialistic actions, for trade and political control usually have followed missionary endeavors. Altruistic motives have combined with power and economic objectives. Some overseas ventures have offered outlets for sheer "adventurous, bored, often lazy, often maladjusted people." [2]

Colonies and spheres of influence spelled increased power and prestige for many states in the nineteenth century, although not every dependency was an asset. France acquired strength and tangible resources from North Africa, and Japan material resources from Manchuria. But some dependencies paid off only in terms of the intangibles of position and prestige, as for example in Libya, Somaliland, Bechuanaland, and the like.

Defense of vital interests has also impelled searches for territories abroad. United States concern for the safety of the Panama Canal led to acquisition of bases in the Caribbean, such as Guantanamo and the Virgin Islands. Britain acquired possessions in the Mediterranean and the Indian

[2] D. W. Brogan, *The Price of Revolution* (London: H. Hamilton, 1951), p. 271.

Ocean in order to protect her lines to India, Singapore, Hong Kong, and Australia.

Exponents of colonialism argue that colonies afford an outlet for surplus population. The argument is invalidated by statistics in many instances. Germany in 1914 had 931,000 square miles of colonial holdings in Africa, yet only some 20,000 Germans lived there amid a native population of 12 million. There were in fact more Germans resident in Paris. Similarly, by 1931 there were more Italians living in Manhattan than in all of Italy's colonies (Libya, Eritrea, and Somaliland). The argument is often more a rationalization than it is a statement of fact.

Imperialism sometimes leads to additional imperialism. It is said that Bismarck encouraged France to seek compensation in Africa for the loss of Alsace-Lorraine to Germany after 1871. The partition of Africa that soon followed resulted from a race among the Great Powers to fill the power vacuum in Africa, on the assumption that if one did not take a given piece of territory, others would do so and thereby upset the balance of power. Hitler, Mussolini, and Tojo later claimed that as "have-not" powers they were entitled to overseas possessions too.

Thus a variety of political and strategic justifications were given for the colonialism and imperialism of the pre-1939 era. No one formula was everywhere employed. Each had a seeming measure of justice at the moment, although in many instances arguments were not lacking for rejecting the claims.

Economic Theories of Imperialism. It has been argued, especially by Communists, that economic motives have been the cause of much Western imperialism. There may be some element of truth in this in some instances, although it is easy to overstress the reasoning. English economist John A. Hobson laid the foundation of the economic theory of imperialism in his book *Imperialism, A Study* (1908). He attributed imperialism to the propensity of the capitalist system to oversave. Private enterprise, he argued, seeks to "utilize political power for outlets in external markets, and as foreign independent markets are closed or restricted, the drive to the acquisition of colonies, protectorates and other areas of imperial development becomes a more urgent and conscious national policy." [3] Today Hobson's thesis is reversed as old colonial areas demand capital which is difficult to divert from profitable employment in the industrialized countries.

Lenin later adapted Hobson's thesis in the Communist doctrine that

[3] J. A. Hobson, *Imperialism, A Study,* 3rd ed. (London: Allen and Unwin, 1938), pp. xxii–xxiii.

imperialism is the product of the "monopoly state of capitalism" and reflects the crisis of "overproduction or underconsumption."

Cases can be found of territorial annexations primarily for economic motives, such as the Japanese seizure of Manchuria, with its rich coal and iron resources. But the history of imperialism seems more usually patterned on other motives. Early colonialism was certainly not a result of overproduction of goods and a search for markets for them. It occurred before the birth of modern capitalism. Imperialist adventures did not invariably coincide with the export of private capital from Europe. Governments have employed capital to further their foreign policy objectives more often than private capitalists have been able to obtain government support for their objectives. From an economic point of view it is not necessary for capitalist states to own their foreign markets. W. W. Rostow observes that "it is perfectly evident that, whatever the economic troubles of the capitalist societies, they do not stem primarily from a dependence on imperialism." [4]

The Dissolution of the Western Colonial Empires. Britain has carried out the most effective decolonization policy, granting independence to over 530 million people. By 1966 the British Empire possessions were some 30 miniscule dependencies with less than six million inhabitants and a chance that some of these might move to mini-statehood. Through carefully phased withdrawal, it was hoped that newly independent states would emerge with stable governments, effective administrative systems, an educated elite, and associations with the Commonwealth that would permit continuity of shared interests and actions. The transitions have generally taken place without open conflict, although the native leaders were sometimes imprisoned and harassed for periods of time before independence, as were Gandhi and Nehru in India, and Kenyatta in Kenya. Only Rhodesia has made a unilateral declaration of independence without British support. The Commonwealth relationships have been strained as the membership has expanded and South African racist policies have exacerbated relationships with the Asian and African countries. Withdrawal of South Africa from the Commonwealth took place in 1964 under pressure from the black African States. The Rhodesia issue succeeded South Africa as the most controversial problem confronting the Commonwealth.

The dissolution of the French Empire took place somewhat less smoothly. In Indochina, where Japanese occupation during World War II

[4] W. W. Rostow, *The Stages of Economic Growth* (New York: Cambridge University Press, 1960), p. 156.

TABLE 5–1

Newly Independent Countries

If you were born in 1945, you are older than these countries:

Jordan	1946	Central African Republic	1960
Philippines	1946	Congo (Brazzaville)	1960
Pakistan	1947	Cyprus	1960
India	1947	Gabon Republic	1960
Burma	1948	Senegal	1960
Ceylon	1948	Mali	1960
Israel	1948	Nigeria	1960
Korea ‡	1948	Mauritania	1960
Vietnam ‡	1949	Sierra Leone	1961
Laos	1949	Tanganyika †	1961
Cambodia	1949	Western Samoa	1962
Indonesia	1949	Algeria	1962
Libya	1951	Burundi	1962
Sudan	1956	Rwanda	1962
Morocco	1956	Jamaica	1962
Tunisia	1956	Trinidad-Tobago	1962
Ghana	1957	Uganda	1962
Malaya *	1957	Zanzibar †	1963
Guinea	1958	Kenya	1963
Cameroon	1960	Malawi	1964
Togo	1960	Malta	1964
Malagasy Republic	1960	Zambia	1964
Congo (Leopoldville)	1960	Gambia	1965
Somali Republic	1960	Singapore *	1965
Dahomey	1960	Malé (Maldive Islands)	1965
Niger	1960	Guyana	1966
Upper Volta	1960	Botswana	1966
Ivory Coast	1960	Lesotho	1966
Chad	1960		

Dates show year nation achieved independence.

* Malaysia was formed in 1963 by the union of Malaya, Singapore, Sarawak, and North Borneo (Sabah). Singapore withdrew from Malaysia in 1965.

† Tanzania was formed in 1964 by the union of Tanganyika and Zanzibar.

‡ The Geneva cease-fire accord of July 21, 1954 divided Vietnam into the Republic of Vietnam (South) and Democratic Republic of Vietnam (North).

The Republic of Korea (South) was formally proclaimed on August 15, 1948. The People's Democratic Republic of Korea (North) was formed on May 1, 1948.

had weakened the French hold, the military gains of the Communist Vietnamese resulted in the division of the area into four states in 1954, North and South Vietnam, Laos, and Cambodia. War developed over French efforts to hold Algeria, before General de Gaulle reversed French colonial policy in 1958 and gave it independence. Under his leadership a French

Community was created, similar to the British Commonwealth idea. All French African territories were granted independent statehood, and with the exception of Guinea, voted initially to remain in the Community. But influenced by their African nationalism, they soon loosened or severed their political ties.

Indonesian independence of the Netherlands was granted in 1949, and in 1962 a U.N. Temporary Administrator aided the handing over of West New Guinea to Indonesia.

The United States granted independence to its principal colonial possession, the Philippines, soon after World War II. Puerto Rico was given commonwealth status, and Alaska and Hawaii were admitted as states of the Union. The United States retains overseas only the Virgin Islands, American Samoa, Guam, the Pacific Trust Territory, and a few small islands in the Pacific.

Yielding to the pressure of African nationalism, Belgium gave independence to the Congo in 1960, despite lack of Congolese preparation for self-government. Political chaos ensued and the presence of a United Nations Force was used to allow time for the government to become stabilized. The alertness of Western diplomacy and the swiftness of the United Nations response saved the political independence of the Congo from a Communist take-over.

The Spanish and Portuguese colonial empires remain. Portugal has proclaimed Angola and Mozambique to be provinces of the home country, though this has not satisfied African critics of colonialism. Little is being done as yet to prepare the people in these possessions for independence. Spain has been moving cautiously in its possessions. For the time being she is not being placed under the same pressures as Portugal and South Africa, however.

Probably the most serious confrontation between African nationalism and neocolonialism lies along a line drawn from the Angola-Congo border in the West along the Zambezi River to the Mozambique-Malawi and Tanzania boundaries in the East. Here, as Waldemar Nielsen has said, a symbolic battleline has been traced out between the forces of Black Africa and white rule.[5] There are responsible, widely experienced diplomats, like Lord Caradon of Britain, who see not only potential African war, but world conflict as well in the offing if one side or the other does not moderate its stand on the issues that come to a head along this line.

The outcome of the era since 1955 has been an explosion of new

[5] Waldemar A. Nielsen, *African Battleline: American Policy Choices in Southern Africa* (New York: Harper & Row, 1965), for the Council on Foreign Relations.

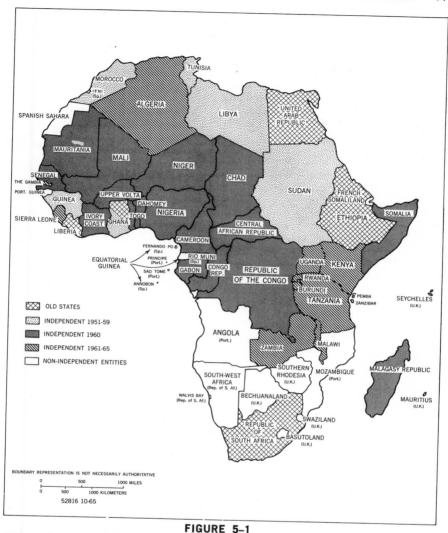

FIGURE 5–1
Africa—Sequence of Sovereignty (Adapted from a map in *Geographic Bulletin No. 6* of The Geographer, Office of Research in Economics and Science, Bureau of Intelligence and Research, U.S. Department of State)

states out of the old empires. The end has not yet been reached, although most of the larger, more populous lands have now won their independence. Though many of the new entities are lacking in the essentials of stable independent existence, the pressures for freedom, equality, and position have been too great to resist. These are facts of international life.

COMMUNIST IMPERIALISM

Ironically, a new force of imperialism has arisen while the old has been disappearing, namely Soviet and Chinese Communism. Approximately 800 million people have gained independence from the Western powers since 1945, and about the same number have come under Communist domination. Communist theory is imperialistic in that it proclaims that force and revolution should be used to establish a worldwide dictatorship of the proletariat. According to Marxist-Leninist doctrine, a single Communist "state union" will be formed after inevitable collisions between the Communist and bourgeois states.

To attain their goal, Communists use a wide variety of policies based on a conviction that eventually all states will become first socialist and then Communist. Communist leaders consider the status quo to be a fluid situation. Walter Lippmann wrote after an interview with Nikita Khrushchev in 1958,

> Whereas we think of the status quo as the situation as it exists at the moment, he thinks of it as the process of revolutionary change which is in progress. He wants us to recognize the revolution not only as it is but as it is going to be.

In 1965 James Reston observed that Premier Kosygin branded all Western actions as "wrong" and Soviet policies or programs as "correct" and reasonable.

Communist imperialism occurs in the imposition of political, military, and economic controls over the nominally independent states of Eastern Europe, North Korea, Outer Mongolia, and North Vietnam, and in the exploitation of Asian, African, and Latin American nationalist revolutions in an effort to bend these toward the ultimate establishment of Communist regimes.

Soviet Imperialism in Eastern Europe. Soviet imperialism in Eastern Europe has followed a general pattern. From 1945–1947, when the Communists were establishing and consolidating their power, there was relative ideological permissiveness. The "people's democracies" were allowed to follow "different roads to socialism" under the watchful protection of the occupying Red Army. A drastic tightening of controls took place during the last years of Stalin's rule. Following the dictator's death a brief respite occurred, culminating in the quasi-rebellion in Poland and the revolt in Hungary. Subsequent preoccupation of the Soviet Union with the Sino-Soviet conflict and concern over China's growing nuclear power have provided opportunities for national Communist leaders to experiment with freer ways of handling their economies and opening their frontiers to trade and foreign visitors. A hard-core Communist elite has retained firm central control, however, in each state. Although the scope for public discussion has increased, these countries are still within the Soviet preserve. Institutionalized economic ties with the Soviet Union are as significant as the political and military ones in perpetuating the satellite relationship.

Soviet Strategy Toward the Underdeveloped Areas. Communist strategy outside the Soviet bloc has sought temporary alliance with nationalism as a means to Communist penetration. Communist leaders hope then to take over from the bourgeois national liberation movements.

In the first stage Communists try to expand influence through trade, economic assistance, the example of Soviet economic growth, and through infiltration of government and influential groups. Trade with the underdeveloped countries is increasing. Soviet assistance is usually in a tangible form that maximizes the political impact and prestige, like the building of the Aswan Dam in Egypt and a modern steel mill in India. Propaganda emphasizes the Soviet Union as a model of rapid industrialization in the twentieth century.

Soviet policy anticipates that in the second stage the underdeveloped countries will make the transition to Communism. With rapid change and mounting internal tensions, it is hoped that conditions will ripen for the Communists to seize power. As "liberation" proceeds it is anticipated that the world balance of power will be altered, with the West becoming unable to stop Communism's bid for dominion. Soviet policy seems to accept Lenin's prophecy that the outcome of the struggle will be determined by control of the majority of the world's population, which lives in Russia, India, and China.

Chinese Communist Imperialism. Empirical evidence indicates that Communist China is likewise striving to expand its influence and rule abroad. Three methods are being employed to accomplish this. These are (1) military pressure outward from the traditional borders; (2) attempts to lead the newly independent nations; and (3) seeking leadership of the world Communist movement and control of its apparatus. China is in conflict with the Soviet Union in varying degrees in each of these methods.

[1] Territorial Expansion. Traditionally, China is expansionist, regarding its territory as the "Middle Kingdom," the center of the world. With the decline of the Manchu dynasty, Chinese power was forced back

FIGURE 5–2
Possible Chinese Territorial Interests (From The New York Times,
September 6, 1964. Reprinted by permission)

from Central Asia, Siberia, and Southeast Asia. Since Communism was
established, however, China has extended its rule to Tibet. Its influence has
been established in North Korea; its military forces have thrust across the
borders of India, claiming territory long occupied by the latter. The Na-
tionalist-held islands of Quemoy and Matsu have been placed under

imminent attack, and Formosa has been claimed to be a Communist Chinese possession. Peking's influence has pressed upon North Vietnam, Cambodia, and Laos. Declarations affirm that parts of the Soviet domain in Central Asia once were Chinese and must ultimately be returned. Peking has urged Ho Chih-Minh to use every effort to force American withdrawal from Vietnam. Published reports indicate that Peking was implicated in the abortive attempt of the Indonesian Communists to assassinate the top army leaders of that country with a view to seizing power there in September 1965, a move that was nipped at the last moment by strong army action against the local party leadership. Along the borders of Burma and Thailand pressures have been mounted that can be increased at almost any time through encouraging guerrilla activities or military invasion. A basis has been laid by which pressure can thus be exerted at many points on the periphery of China in South and Southeast Asia. This can be orchestrated with political action to promote the goals selected at a given moment by the Politburo in Peking.

[2] Chinese Attempts to Lead Developing Countries. In the political field Chinese leaders have sought to enlist the newly independent countries in setting up a "zone of peace." At the Bandung Conference of Asian and African nations in 1955, Peking tried to seize the leadership of this movement and China had clearly hoped to secure closer relations through a second Afro-Asian Conference scheduled to be held in Algiers in 1965. This conference was cancelled, however, as a result of the Algerian coup which unseated Ahmed Ben Bella, and Moscow's assertion of a right to be present as an Asian power. The cancellation was a blow to Chinese hopes.

In 1965 Premier Chou En-lai toured several African countries telling their leaders that Africa was "ripe for revolution." This did not appeal to local leaders who had just achieved their positions by various forms of revolution. They did not welcome the prospect of change implied in the statements and so informed the Chinese visitor. The succession of rebuffs subsequently suffered by the Communist Chinese in several African countries as one after another closed their doors to Chinese missions was a serious setback to Communist ambitions. This was nowhere more evident than in Ghana, where on the overthrow of Kwame Nkrumah, the large Chinese mission was expelled while the Soviets were invited to remain. But it would be premature to expect Peking to give up its goals. Rather, it may bide its time to try again, and elsewhere, wherever targets of opportunity present themselves. The Chinese philosophy is that their revolution provides a "successful lesson" for making a national democratic revolution followed by transition to a socialist revolution under the leadership of the proletariat.[6]

[3] Chinese Drive for World Communist Leadership. Chinese Communism has a long-term goal, namely world Communist leadership. The doctrinal competition between Peking and Moscow is one element of a power struggle between the Communist titans. China, looking forward to possession of nuclear delivery power that Russia had denied her, and modern industrialization, has little to lose and much to win in attempting to gain leadership of the world Communist movement at Russia's expense, by posing as the true exponent of Marxism-Leninism and as an aggressive force, in contrast to a more restrained Soviet leadership.

The militancy of Chinese propaganda and subversive activity in the underdeveloped countries has placed the Soviet Union on the defensive. Chinese tactics are based on Mao's thesis that in pressing "peoples' wars" and "national liberation movements" aggressively the day of Communist victory can be hastened.

The Chinese Communists are principally opposed to the United States as the main obstacle to their bid for supremacy in Asia and Africa. The containment of Communist Chinese imperialism is likely to be a more difficult problem than was the stopping of Soviet expansion in Europe, however. For it must occur in areas whose people have other values than those of the West and who may be as reluctant to have the Western powers come into their countries to save them from a Chinese threat as they are to have the latter take them over. Containment of Communist Chinese imperialism in Asia and Africa must contend with the widespread policies of neutralism and nonalignment, which were not seriously present in Europe. The clashes incident to effecting this containment and the events that may occur if containment is not successful are likely to shape the course of international affairs for most of the lifetime of those now living.

THE AMBIVALENCE OF ANTICOLONIALISM

The attitudes of many new states are ambivalent. They admire and wish to attain the development and standards of the West. On the other hand, there is a large legacy left by the superior-inferior relationship of colonial rule. The result is exhibited in anti-Western attitudes and in lingering

[6] See speech of Deputy Premier Lin Piao, September 3, 1965. *Peking Review*, September 3, 1965.

suspicions and hesitation to engage in political collaboration with the West.

The burden of anticolonialist sentiment presently borne by the Western powers is advantageous for Communist relations with the new states. Communism lacks the appeal of the ideal values of Western civilization that emphasize peaceful adjustment of differences, tolerance of pluralism and diversity, and respect for individual dignity and aspiration. "Ultimately, the question is whether the ideal values of Western civilization . . . [will become] more vital than they have appeared in this century." [7] The generation of such vitality is essential to offsetting the stigma of colonialism.

Anticolonialism is not a new phenomenon invented by Africans. "Big Bill" Thompson campaigned for the mayoralty of Chicago in the 1920's on the theme that if elected he would "punch King George on the nose." This was a considerable time after the thirteen North American colonies successfully fought their Revolutionary War with England. "Big Bill's" constituents so loved the imagery of his campaign that they elected him mayor. The stereotyped memories of colonial suffering are likely to last a long time and be used in local politics of new countries.

CONCLUSION

The Continuing Dilemma—Interdependence and the Responsibilities of Power. There are responsibilities in world affairs which can be discharged only by the more powerful states. Reinhold Niebuhr has observed that no international constitution can "prevent the gradations of power among the nations from creating some kind of hierarchy of authority, more inexact than, but nevertheless analogous to, the hierarchy of authority in any national community." [8]

Lesser powers can voice considerable criticism of world affairs. They form a majority in the United Nations and in any large international gathering. If the international community is to function on an effective cooperative basis, a significant proportion of new states must act with a modicum of restraint and statesmanship, for responsibility goes with power. In failing to uphold the Charter at the time of the crisis over Article 19,

---

[7] Herbert J. Muller, *The Uses of the Past* (New York: Oxford University Press, 1957), p. 346.

[8] Reinhold Niebuhr, *The Structure of Nations and Empires* (New York: Scribners, 1959), p. 13.

the nonaligned states contributed to a weakening of the United Nations, their best assurance of security and a voice in international affairs.

The United States and the Colonial Revolution. The United States has been placed at times in the difficult position of having to choose between its European allies and the new countries. The American people have been conditioned by their historical experience and political values to sympathize with the aspirations of colonial peoples for independence. They may not always appreciate the magnitude of the difficulties the new states face. But certainly no country has poured out more economic and technical assistance for the new states than has the United States. The United States, Britain, and France have a tangible interest in the success of the developing countries in solving the economic, social, administrative, and political problems with which they are confronted. For on their ability to solve these problems hinges the question of whether they will survive as viable, democratic states.

The awakening of the long-dormant lands and the desire of their people to express themselves as political equals in world affairs are realities of the second half of the twentieth century. To help them attain their goal of development is in the interests of the United States and the Western powers. The contemporary struggle between the West and Communism over the former colonial world is for political influence in shaping the values of the new states and helping them decide in which direction they will go in the years to come.

CHAPTER 6

The Role of Geography
and Physical Environment

INTRODUCTION

Since the time of the Greeks man has speculated on the nature and effects of his relationship and that of human institutions to the surrounding physical world and universe. Aristotle urged men to consider the relation of environment to human character and to the necessities of states.

For an understanding of international relations one must have a geographic point of view as well as an historical perspective. Practitioners and observers of international relations need an atlas showing population, raw materials, communication routes, and other data, and an ability to interpret maps.

A national consciousness of geography is usually derived from historical perspective, relations with neighbors, and economic activities. This can, however, lead to misleading and outmoded concepts of the world as a whole. For generations the United States felt geographically detached from Europe and conducted its foreign affairs on a principle of isolationism similar to the neutralism of some of the new countries today. After isolationism had become an inappropriate policy, United States adherence to this principle contributed to the disastrous course of events from 1939 to 1945.

Physical geography is one of the more constant conditioning factors in world politics and affects the power, the needs, goals, and policies that states follow in pursuing their respective interests. The political map of the world has undergone many changes, and man is now learning how to master exploration in outer space. Meanwhile, topography, climate, and other physical characteristics themselves change little. The significance of these "unchanging" facts can vary, however, with new political, economic, and technological developments.

We do not intend to discuss geography itself. It is essential, nevertheless, to be able to identify and apply certain concepts and facts of geography to the problems of international relations. The meaning and influence of geography must be interpreted in the perspective of other factors like attitudes, social and political institutions, economic factors, as well as technology and population. Because all these factors are continually changing, geography is a dynamic influence.

GEOGRAPHY AS AN APPROACH TO INTERNATIONAL AFFAIRS

At the beginning of the twentieth century, scholars began to evolve systematic concepts of relationships between geography and state actions. These came to be known as geopolitics. The study of geopolitics had a considerable appeal before 1945 but has fallen into disfavor recently. The decline in interest is probably due to the increased emphasis on nongeographic factors such as ideology, technology, nationalism, and leadership, and recognition that no single factor dominates international relations. There are differences in the philosophy of security and other aspects of foreign policy that are based on the relationship of geography to power and policy. Geographers no longer accept the notion that nature determines human action, but they do consider that there is an interrelationship between environment and politics and that this influences individual and state actions, values, and preferences.

Rudolf Kjellén of Sweden first coined the term *geopolitik* in his 1916 study entitled *The State as a Form of Life.* He defined geopolitics as "the theory of the state as a geographic organism in space."

Some geopolitical writers have proposed that international relations are inherently linked to the principal reference points of geography. Professor Nicholas J. Spykman of Yale commented more realistically before World War II that the "geographical determinism which seeks to explain by geography all things from the fourth symphony to the fourth dimension paints as distorted a picture as does an explanation of policy with no reference to geography."

Geopolitics is an attempt to bridge the area between earth science and political science. It endeavors to appraise geographic relationships in terms of international politics, national interests, and strategy. After much effort Professor Stephen B. Jones of Yale admits that he is "unable to split the hair that separates political geography from what might be called geographical politics." He considers that there must be a continuum between geography and politics.[1]

We shall use the term *geopolitics* to indicate an approach to the study and analysis of the power and policies of states. This is one of several coordinated approaches sometimes used in strategic analysis, although the term is probably not in the operative lexicon of most foreign offices today.

Mackinder's Ideas. Sir Halford Mackinder, the English geographer and politician (1861–1947), was largely responsible for the development of modern geopolitical thought. He made a scholarly analysis of certain geographic characteristics of the world's land masses and their relationships to the seas, suggesting that certain geographic realities would tend to mold the development of future world affairs. His views were first presented in 1904, modified and published in the book *Democratic Ideals and Realities* in 1919, and adjusted to later developments in 1943.

Mackinder classified Europe, Asia, and Africa as the World Island (see map). He defined the Heartland of this land mass as the interior area of Eurasia, extending from Western Germany through Soviet Europe to Central Siberia. He classified the fringe of Eurasia, from Eastern Siberia through Southeast Asia, India, the Middle East and Western Europe including Norway, as the Inner Crescent or Rimlands. To this he added Africa, to form what he called the World Island. The areas beyond this, including the Americas, he designated as the Outer Crescent. He later named another region the Fulcrum of World Power, covering the north temperate region extending in a westerly direction from the Yenisei River in Siberia to the Missouri River. Mackinder also conceived of the sparsely settled areas of deserts, mountains, and the subarctic as a Mantle of Wilderness. He hoped that some day this area might come to support part of the world's expanding population. He might have emphasized this even more had he read present estimates of world population now made for the year 2000.

[1] Stephen B. Jones, "A Unified Field Theory of Political Geography," *Annals of the Association of American Geographers*, Vol. XLIV (1954), pp. 112 ff.

Mackinder believed that the era of dominant sea power was about to end. In the premissile age he noted that the Eurasian Heartland would be comparatively free from attack, and with its vast resources and manpower, would be able to generate great power. He argued that, other things being equal, the Heartland was the key area of the world.

> Who rules East Europe commands the Heartland;
> Who rules the Heartland commands the World Island;
> Who rules the World Island commands the World.

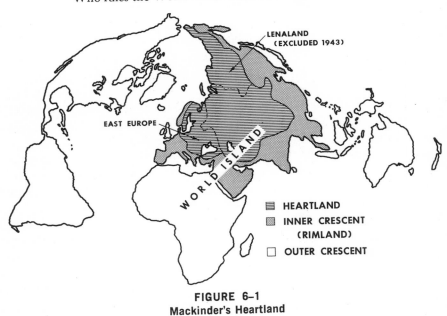

FIGURE 6–1
Mackinder's Heartland

During the Versailles Peace Conference, Mackinder warned that Germany might rise again to encompass European Russia, and control the Heartland. In 1943 he warned that if Russia acquired dominance of Germany, she could conquer the Inner Crescent, and then move toward world empire. These fears were aroused when the Red Army occupied Central Europe and Eastern Germany after World War II. As a consequence of the Communist coup in Czechoslovakia in February 1948, the Western European countries, Canada, and the United States formed the NATO alliance. The containment policy of the Truman Administration, the Truman Doctrine, the NATO, SEATO, and CENTO alliances were, viewed in the framework of Mackinder's analysis, measures to hold the Rimlands from being overrun by power from the Heartland.

Mackinder's ideas are useful as a model for visualizing the power potential of the Communist world were it to extend its way from Europe throughout Asia. If the Soviet Union and China were able to act in close union, Mackinder might be judged prophetic. His thinking was essentially Europe-oriented, for he disregarded America as a great power center. Later he did recognize the development of a North Atlantic Heartland. Mackinder placed a simplistic emphasis on military power, but history has not yet altogether consigned his analysis to the files.

Mahan and Seapower. U.S. Admiral Alfred Thayer Mahan (1840–1914), drawing on precedents from the history of British sea power, made a scholarly geopolitical analysis that stressed the importance of sea power. This approach was in marked contrast to Mackinder's premise about the decline of sea power. Neither predicted, however, land, sea, air, and missile power being integrated into one military power instrument, as has occurred in recent times.

Mahan's ideas were based on the proposition that no continental power of Europe or Asia could successfully challenge the maritime leadership of Britain or America. He believed that no nation with strong neighbors across its land frontiers, such as France, Germany, and Russia, could control the seas. The cost of maintaining sufficient land armaments to protect an exposed frontier virtually eliminated the possibility of competing with a nation with no land frontier to defend, such as Britain and the United States, which could concentrate defense activities on establishing a large navy. Great Power wars, Mahan believed, were decided at sea. He believed Britain could not permanently retain her naval predominance and urged the United States to build a large navy, capable of fighting any war away from home. President Theodore Roosevelt was interested in Mahan's ideas, but United States policy was not based on them. Kaiser Wilhelm of Germany was also interested in Mahan's ideas and with his combined land and naval power managed to devastate Allied shipping during World War I.

The victories of World Wars I and II were significantly dependent on the efficient United States and British navies, which were able to fight at a great distance from home, thereby vindicating Mahan.

Airplanes, intercontinental ballistic missiles, atomic weapons, modern industrialization, the strategic importance of the Arctic area where air power dominates human movement, globe-circling satellites, and the expansion of power struggles to include major economic and ideological components, now qualify some of Mahan's premises and propositions. United States strategy, nevertheless, continues to be premised on the need for capability to project economic, psychological, and military power far from home. This involves global commitments, responsibilities, and actions to preserve the integrity of threatened states and territories.

Mahan's principle of building military power capable of flexible operation at a distance from home would have much to commend it were it adapted to include air power and other mobile forces. The applicability of his thinking to today's world is attested not only by United States and British policies, but also by the buildup of powerful naval and air forces by Germany and Japan in World War II, and by Soviet construction of a large navy, merchant marine, submarine fleet, and strategic air and missile power since 1947.

If Mahan were writing today he would probably argue that the capability of rapid deployment of military and other power overseas is a primary strategic requirement for a country that holds or seeks global power.

Spykman and America's Position.   Professor Nicholas J. Spykman (1893–1943) was particularly concerned with the relationship of world geographic and political factors to the United States' strategic position and to its foreign policy. His opinions preceded the development of strategic air and missile power, awareness of the strategic position of the Arctic, and the potentialities of nuclear science.

Spykman stressed geography as the "most fundamentally conditioning factor" in the formulation of foreign policy. In his principal work he emphasized what is now more generally understood, that the relative power of states depends not only on military forces but on many other factors —size of territory, nature of frontiers, population, raw materials, economic and technical development, financial strength, ethnic homogeneity, effective social integration, political stability, and national spirit.

When many Americans still favored a policy of isolation, Spykman was pointing out that unless the United States employed its capability in cooperation with Britain to create a world balance of power, Old World forces might be sufficiently organized to encircle the New World. Spykman considered that America's policy should be to prevent dominant power from being established in the continental Rimlands of Europe, the Middle East, Africa, South Asia, and the Far East. He thought that if a hostile Great Power developed in any of these areas, it would constitute a threat to United States interests. If the United States and Britain allied, each possessing considerable sea power, they might establish control over Mackinder's old Inner Crescent, termed by Spykman the Rimland. Then, said Spykman, "Who controls the Rimland rules Eurasia; Who rules

Eurasia controls the destinies of the world." Spykman was not pleading for American domination of the world. He wanted a world at peace with a balance of power within Eurasia itself. Since Spykman's time it has become clear that any local power balance is subordinate to a world power balance, and that United States power is essential to that balance.

The Haushofer Geopolitik. The German geographer Karl Haushofer (1869–1946) was an outspoken writer on geopolitics and is presumed to have had a considerable influence on Nazi thought. For Haushofer and his associates, *Geopolitik* was a mystique centered on Kjellén's theses that the state is important in itself and that power is the most important attribute of the state. To these ends Haushofer rationalized a case for *Lebensraum* (space for living) for the "superior" German race, self-sufficiency in material resources, and control of the European Heartland. Because British and Allied sea power and Russian land power stood in the path of these German objectives, war was considered a justifiable means for the German state to take. Haushofer's influence came to an end with the Nazi defeat. In summary, he supported the land mass theory and distorted geopolitical analysis to provide a rationale for Nazi aggression. There is little in his reasoning that can be applied to present conditions.

Communism and Geopolitics. Communist methods seek absolute power, but Communist writers have not adopted the doctrine of geopolitics. Rather, their faith is pinned to the dialectical process of history and the ability of the proletariat to win the class struggle. Communist leadership obviously understands geography from the pragmatic standpoint of power politics, however. The Soviet Union used the opportunity given by the outcome of World War II to create a zone of subordinate buffer states in Middle Europe and to gain possession of the Kurile Islands and Southern Sakhalin. It also tried, but without success, to establish a foothold at the Turkish Straits, in northern Iran, and on Bornholm Island in the Baltic. Communist China, for its part, has been pressing into South and Southeast Asia, demanding withdrawal of all "imperialist" powers from the area and claiming territories in inner Asia from the Soviet Union.

The logical route for Communism to Paris may lie from Peking through penetration of the Eurasian Rimland. If at the same time Communist bridgeheads can be developed in Africa and the Americas, the "inevitable triumph" of Communism might be hastened. This was undoubtedly in the background analysis of the Kennedy Administration when it risked nuclear war to forestall Soviet basing of long-range missiles in Cuba, and of the Johnson Administration when it decided to send American troops to South Vietnam and to intervene in the Dominican Republic.

Speaking on the anniversary of the Japanese surrender in 1945, Lin Piao, Vice Premier of Communist China, outlined a strategy for Communist world conquest that had certain geopolitical concepts built into it. Noting that Mao Tse-tung's strategy for the Communist victory in China had involved establishing rural revolutionary base areas from which the cities were later encircled and then overpowered, the Vice Chairman declared,

> Taking the entire globe, if North America and Western Europe can be called "the cities of the world," then Asia, Africa, and Latin America constitute "the rural areas of the world." Since World War II, the proletarian revolutionary movement has for various reasons been temporarily held back in the North American and West European capitalist countries, while the people's revolutionary movement in Asia, Africa, and Latin America has been growing vigorously. In a sense, the contemporary world revolution also presents a picture of the encirclement of cities by the rural areas. In the final analysis, the whole cause of world revolution hinges on the revolutionary struggles of the Asian, African, and Latin American peoples who make up the overwhelming majority of the world's population. . . .[2]

Taking the Chinese scene as atypical, and ignoring the factors in the larger world picture that make this quite different from the situation prevailing in China from 1937 to 1949, the Chinese Communists imagine that their now-idealized experience with Japan and the Kuomintang provides an appropriate blueprint for advancing their interests on the world scene. This illustrates how geopolitical thinking can be overlaid with stereotypes and images based on a past that has little similarity to problems of the present. But it is with such "pictures in the mind" that others must contend in world politics.

GEOGRAPHIC ELEMENTS AND WORLD AFFAIRS

Topography and the State System. Topography has had a significant influence in the definition of the modern state system. Islands and physical barriers on the continents have defined natural areas for the evolution of some sovereign states such as Japan and Spain. Topography may

---

[2] Speech entitled "Long Live the Victory of People's War." Text in the *Peking Review*, September 3, 1965. Abbreviated version in *The New York Times*, September 4, 1965.

form a unique local consciousness; examples of this are provided by the attitudes of the Andorrans in the Pyrenees and the Montagnards in the highlands of Vietnam. Modern means of communication have decreased the significance of topographical divisions but have led to few larger political unities. In both Africa and the Middle East the dividing lines inherited from the colonial period have largely become the boundaries of present-day states. There has been little political combination save in a few areas. Many new political boundaries seem less logical than partitions based on topography.

Barriers and surface communication routes are important in the affairs of states, although rivers, mountains, jungles, and deserts are less significant obstacles today than in the past. Still they do influence international affairs by the fact of their traditional importance.

Topographic boundaries are associated with the search for security. Missiles with atomic warheads can make all topographical barriers meaningless. Yet many countries act as if this were not true and concern themselves with the possible consequences of a non-nuclear attack. The Hindu Kush Mountains and the Alps, together with the Khyber and Brenner passes, are likely to remain important for security reasons for some time to come. Interstate rivers, the seas, and the narrow connecting waters of straits and canals are essential highways of an economically interdependent world. Control of, or threat of interference with, navigation through the Danube, the Baltic, the Turkish Straits, and the Suez Canal remain critical issues in world politics.

The Importance of Boundaries. Basic to international affairs is each state's possession of a specific area of the earth's surface. Each state has boundaries common to areas under the political control of other sovereign states or which extend along international waters, and each state asserts control over the air space above its territory.

These boundaries are symbols of national power, independence, and the ability of the state to maintain security. Crossing a border always has a critical symbolism in international affairs. Borders have been traditional sources of friction, for they represent the finite territorial limits of national sovereignty. Guards are usually posted along these boundaries to prevent unauthorized crossing, to require the presentation of passports and customs documents, and to require the fulfillment of such formalities as the state deems desirable. Boundaries are sometimes heavily fortified, or are even sealed off with walls, barbed wire, and mines to prevent unauthorized crossings, as in Berlin and along other portions of the Iron Curtain.

Movements toward regional integration, particularly in Europe, have been reducing the importance of some barriers to the flow of commerce and of people. Radio communication transcends boundaries; and the automobile, combined with improved roads, and the airplane have expanded international tourism enormously.

There remain difficult and dangerous boundary problems in international politics. Only in the Antarctic have the nations succeeded in subordinating national claims to the interests of scientific exploration and international collaboration. Such boundaries as those between China and Russia, China and India, Egypt and Israel, India and Pakistan, to mention only a few, are critical friction zones.

Thousands of miles of international boundaries, some of them not agreed on, have been added with the creation of the new states in Asia and Africa. The Kashmir problem, the Arab-Israeli conflict, the Somali-Ethiopian-Kenyan dispute, and the restrictions on movement introduced by the new nationalism in Africa, are examples of the frictions and disputes that are caused by new or undefined boundaries.

Boundaries have sometimes been drawn to take advantage of natural features, such as those of the Czechoslovakian-German and Congolese-Tan-

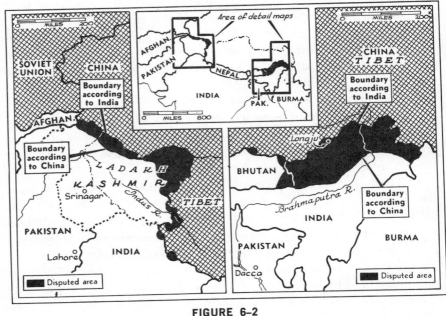

FIGURE 6–2
The Disputed Areas on India's Northern Border (From The New York Times, October 31, 1959. Reprinted by permission)

zanian borders. Political and historic considerations are often the only explanation for boundaries, such as those on the North European plain or those resulting from the partition of Africa in the period of European imperialism.

Some boundaries are drawn where opposing military power has reached approximate equilibrium or has been stopped by political action. Consequences of this type of situation are the Italo-Yugoslav border, the division of Germany, and the line between North and South Korea.

Ethnic considerations sometimes govern the choice of boundaries. The Pakistani-Indian boundaries were determined primarily by religious and communal considerations. The concept of self-determination of peoples was influential in deciding national limits after World War I. An exclusively ethnic division is usually difficult because peoples are often intermingled without respect to geographical lines. In the Trieste area, the city and villages were primarily Italian, whereas the countryside population was predominantly Yugoslav. Czechoslovakia and Poland chose to solve the problems along their boundaries with Germany after World War II by expelling 8 million Germans from the Sudetenland and the Polish administered land east of the Oder River.

In Chapter 21 some of the problems concerning the maritime boundaries of states and their jurisdiction over air space will be discussed.

Stability of Boundaries and Problems of Change. Economic and security considerations have now made original reasons for many boundaries obsolete. Yet there are few boundaries drawn primarily for economic reasons. And material shifts in boundaries do not occur readily, except by force. To relinquish even a minute area appears a national loss and raises an emotional political issue. Some cases have been successfully decided by arbitration or plebiscite. The latter was used in the Saar in 1955 and has been recommended for the Kashmir dispute. The primary means of radical change is through delineation in treaties of peace following war.

Some states have entered into conventions defining methods for dealing with boundary disputes. These conventions usually apply to minor matters like changes caused by a shift in a river channel. Boundary disputes can be referred to the United Nations organization through provisions in the Charter and in the Statute of the International Court of Justice. There is no formula for dealing with major readjustment of boundaries desired by one state and opposed by another, as the Polish-German boundary has repeatedly shown. Boundary disputes are still a threat to world peace and afford some of the most complex issues for world politics.

OTHER ELEMENTS AFFECTING POWER
AND SECURITY

Climate and Human Effectiveness.   It has long been argued that the climate of the temperate zone is conducive to energetic and industrious activity, whereas in the polar climates more effort must go into sustaining life. Extensive research in the far North and in the Antarctic shows that with modern technology the effects of low temperature climates can be overcome, although the costs of production of other than indigenous raw materials are comparatively high.

Similarly, it has been argued that the enervating effects of tropical climates inhibit development of powerful states. Yet India, Morocco, Egypt, and Nigeria are tropical states and have considerable influence in world affairs. With disease control, capital development, and improved diet, literacy and technical skills, states in the tropics should be able to match the productivity of temperate zone countries.

Size and Location of States.   A state's power and prosperity do not depend on its size alone, although having an area capable of supporting the potential increase in population is an important consideration. Population, raw materials, development, and quality of leadership are other essential factors to take into account. There is a greater possibility of natural resources being discovered within a state's territory if it is reasonably large. The discovery of oil in barren and seemingly useless parts of Libya, Saudi Arabia, Canada, Algeria, and Australia is an illustration. Where internal power and communications cannot effectively control total area, size can be a liability.

With capable leadership and ingenuity in foreign relations even a small sized state like Switzerland, Britain, or Japan can gain prosperity and influence and even large power.

Size is relevant in considering defense against modern weapons. Some states are so small that modern military aircraft can hardly operate within national boundaries. A small state is highly vulnerable to attack and can be overrun by a hostile neighbor in a few days or even hours, as was the Netherlands in 1940.

Security against aggression is important along the borders of adjacent states in a condition of existing or potential conflict. The cold war has focused world attention on the historic friction zone between East and West Europe.

The trend toward social, economic, and even ideological interaction among neighboring states may lead to additional problems. States like Finland and Iran, close to the U.S.S.R., are continually under pressure to shape their policies to suit their large neighbor. Propinquity to a state with an expansionist policy creates psychological difficulties for a government, for it has to deal with subversion and unrest and the tacit threat of force. Some of the smaller states of Southeast Asia exist in this relationship to China. Combined with nationalism, racial or cultural differences may generate rivalry, animosity, or repulsion. On the other hand, propinquity may encourage close social, economic, and political associations, as in the case of Canada and the United States.

Location and Security. Spykman's judgment that "power is local" is no longer true where strategic air power, nuclear weapons, and long-range missiles are used. Power is effective only if it is present in the right place at the critical time.

In world affairs today the most effective instruments of policy and of power are those that can be shifted quickly and used at a distance. Great Powers, or an international agency supported by Great Powers, are generally the only possessors of these military, monetary, or other instruments. Even in limited war, where great states voluntarily restrict the military power they will employ, military power can be quickly projected to distant places through the use of air and sea power as demonstrated in Vietnam.

Until power is put into action, its force is subjective, and the presence of a Great Power in an area can constitute such a force. The United States' system of alliances and bases provides this kind of power presence. The Soviet Union has found effective methods to project its power without acquiring direct access to open seas, but if it were to gain control of the Turkish Straits, that would have a considerable impact on world affairs.

Collective security arrangements compensate some states for disadvantages in location and defenses, as for example Belgium and the Netherlands wedged in between France and Germany, and Denmark and Norway caught in between the Soviet Union and the Western powers. It is now recognized that a Communist advance, even though it is minor, is part of a larger, long-range program of world conquest and must therefore be contained, lest this lead to a more ambitious aggrandizement. Hence the defense concept of most Western countries now extends to more than their own territory.

Outer Space and International Politics. The affairs of this earth are so disordered that there is strong argument for concentrating on them, rather than providing resources and attention for outer space. Yet the

United States and the Soviet Union are in a space race with uncertain implications. Vast expenditures of human and economic resources are being devoted to advancing a technology which decreases national privacy and increases vulnerability to attack. Orbiting vehicles can already observe considerable detail on the earth below, and can carry weapons that can be readily and secretly dispatched. Such vehicles could become a serious instrument of intimidation. The problem of nuclear weapons in space is perplexing, for their presence cannot be easily checked. To the extent that such implements exist, or may exist, in space, they constitute the equivalent of missiles already launched, like ready bombers in the air, but criss-crossing a country every few hours as a sort of doomsday patrol. Space technology is the same whether for military or peaceful purposes.

Expenditures on a space program indicate availability of enormous resources. Through space technology, meteorological observation and forecasting are being conducted. Furthermore, communications techniques have advanced to the point that messages can be received from vehicles 50 million and more miles away, as well as television programs relayed from Europe and Asia to the United States and vice versa. Space technology has greatly increased the worldwide togetherness of mankind.

NATURAL RESOURCES

The economic pattern and international policies of states are conditioned by their natural resources—soil and water and their products, together with minerals. Without an adequate supply of natural resources, a state must resort to extensive foreign trade in order to achieve a high standard of living for its people and military strength for its defense. National strength can be attained only by industrialization, which in turn is dependent upon availability of an adequate supply of raw materials.

Distribution of Industrial Raw Materials.   The states of the world are not equally endowed with raw materials and no country has a sufficiency of all essential raw materials. The three principal industrial minerals —coal, iron, and petroleum—are quite unequally distributed. A state without adequate supplies of these must acquire them through international arrangements or develop substitutes. This is not always possible without large means or ample credit. Furthermore, a great diversity of raw materials, particularly minerals, is required to support a modern industrialized economy. Many of these minerals have come to the fore only during recent times. The industrial and military use of titanium (jet engines), germanium (transistors), and uranium (nuclear weapons and power) are examples of fairly recent developments.

How does the variation in supplies of raw materials affect international relations? Does it indicate rivalry among states for what they regard as sufficient quantities of those materials in which they are lacking? Or does this variation point toward the development of freer trade policies and regional trade agreements? Can states enter into mutually acceptable relationships which will assure sources and markets for their materials? Or are imperial powers likely to use these arrangements as a means for gaining political influence? Some answers may be found in an examination of fundamental trends in the supply, use, and trading of raw materials.

Depletion and Expansion of Supplies. The quantity of minerals, fertile soil, and fresh water in the world is being rapidly depleted. Concurrently, the demand for these resources is expanding in two ways—the population explosion and the pressures for increased industrialization. Until recently, North America and Western Europe were the only appreciable consumers of minerals. In the future these essential materials will be a primary target of interstate relations as they become increasingly short in supply. Before adopting a thesis of "raw-materials determinism," however, one should consider other pertinent trends.

The overall total reserves of raw materials are still far from exhausted and new supplies are continually being discovered and exploited. Probably more emphasis will be placed upon increasing the known reserves of usable raw materials through new methods of exploration, exploitation, and more efficient utilization. The newly discovered reserves of oil in Libya, Australia, and Algeria are vast, and many think there are rich deposits in Canada and under the North Sea. These discoveries can have a considerable effect on world affairs. Western Europe may be largely supplied with oil from quite different sources in the next few years than in the past. A decrease in demand from the Middle Eastern fields could change the strategic importance of Middle East stores and of the Suez Canal. An entirely new situation may result for the Middle Eastern states which have depended for most of their foreign exchange on sales of oil to Europe. The depletion of the high-grade iron ore in the Mesabi range near Lake Superior has been paced by development of very large new ore discoveries in Quebec, Labrador, Venezuela, Brazil, and in West Africa. At the same time, the development of benefaction methods is permitting practical use of the vast reserves of lower-grade taconite iron in the Mesabi area. Likewise, the opening up of alternative reserves of manganese has relieved the United States, Britain, and Germany of dependence on Soviet supplies. New reserves of nearly every mineral are still being discovered faster than existent supplies are being exhausted, and in some cases, such as the oil reserves of the United States, the known amounts of the existent reserves are considerably greater today than they were twenty-five years ago. The development of engineering techniques for cheap extraction of oil from shale, and for large-scale conversion of saline water to fresh water, may shortly revolutionize the supply picture of these essential resources.

Another trend is the development of new uses and substitutes for raw materials. Uranium has only recently become useful and valuable and is only on the threshold of enabling nuclear engineers to utilize atomic energy for commercial power use. The atomic industry may also soon revolutionize the means of propulsion of vehicles bound for far reaches of outer space, even as it has already been applied to submarines enabling them to traverse under the polar seas and around the world submerged. As the carbon fuels are now being supplemented by atomic power, so in the future solar and tidal power may be harnessed by man. Substitution continually affects demands. Consider the effect of synthetics on the Japanese silk industry and of glass and plastics on tin production. Substitution of aluminum and plastics for steel in construction and in the automobile industry has altered the pattern of demand for bauxite (aluminum ore), iron ore, and manganese.

Raw Materials and National Policies.   The problem of balancing imports with internal production of raw materials is an example of the interaction of domestic policies with world politics. The United States is a major importer of petroleum, iron ore, sugar, manganese, copper, chrome, and bauxite, although these commodities are also produced in the United States. A slight change in pricing or purchasing policies can be very serious to the supplying countries. Internal raw-materials policies of heavily industrialized countries are also foreign policies.

Availability and costs of materials from abroad depend on time, distance, and bulk. Equally important are the dangers of interruption of supply caused by economic or political forces, hostilities, or other forms of pressure; Egypt's refusal to allow passage through the Suez Canal to ships bound to or from Israel is an example. Water transportation is necessary to cover long distances with many essential raw materials like petroleum, iron ore, and bauxite, whose mass presents a tonnage problem. Some states may encourage and subsidize their merchant marine fleets in order to have adequate bottoms available for carriage of necessary commodities in peace and war.

One way of insuring against interruption in supply is through a stockpiling program. The United States' stockpile is valued at approximately $8 billion and includes over seventy raw materials, ranging from aluminum and zinc to selenium and tantalum. Several underdeveloped countries have benefitted economically from United States' purchases for this stockpile. Domestic politics also requires that a considerable quantity of the materials be procured from domestic sources. In 1965 estimates of military and industrial requirements in time of national emergency were half the value of the stockpile. This gives the United States some control of the world materials markets on which many states depend. The United States can use the inventories, as it did with Bolivian tin and U.S. aluminum, to check what is considered an unwarranted rise in prices.

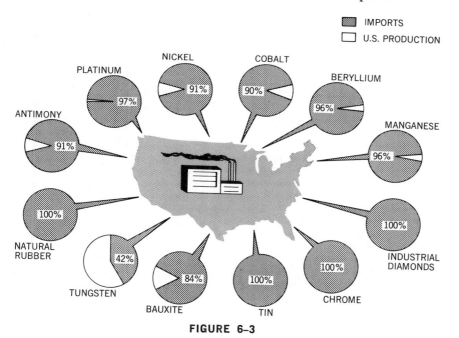

FIGURE 6–3

Strategic Materials from Other Free Nations Are Essential to United States Industry
(*From Public Services Division, United States Department of State, Washington, D.C.*)

Raw materials are the main export of many countries and their policies are conditioned accordingly. Some countries earn most of their foreign exchange—their ability to pay for imports—from the export of a single commodity, such as Chilean copper, Brazilian coffee, Bolivian tin, Malaysian rubber, Iranian oil, and Egyptian cotton. Any increase in U.S. production of these commodities, or of development of substitutes for them, is bound to affect conditions in these countries. Because economic depressions and political upheaval can result, there are increasing attempts to devise long-term bilateral and multilateral commodity arrangements that will dampen price fluctuations.

The importance of raw materials in national and world affairs is indicated in the 1952 report of the President's Material Policy Commission, "There is no such thing as a purely domestic policy toward materials that all the world must have; there are only world policies that have domestic aspects."

CONCLUSION

Specific geographic factors do exert an influence upon the policies and behavior of states and on the equation of power among states. But there has not yet been a geopolitical theory that satisfactorily explains all international relationships.

The forces of nationalism, group dynamics, propaganda, economics, and technological innovations are new considerations that have contributed to the industrial growth of the United States and the Soviet Union and the political explosion that has given rise to many new states in Asia and Africa. These have been largely overlooked by geopolitical theory. The geopolitical writers also give no adequate explanation for the growth of regional and international cooperation and the movement toward international community. However, the Communist Chinese concept of encirclement of the Great Power areas from the rural regions is a geopolitical idea worth consideration.

Although geography affects a nation's power and military planning, and its ability to capitalize on its assets, its influence is modified with every development in the exploitation of air and space. These applications of science and engineering need, therefore, close attention by political scientists to read and interpret the pertinent lessons that should be drawn from them for decision making on foreign affairs.

Supplementary to the facts of geography are political skill and the ability to exploit or obtain resources, and to develop cooperation among states. Geographical factors may be valuable assets or they may limit a state's opportunities, restrain its freedom of action in a given situation, and condition the responses of decision makers in times of crises. But one must be careful not to claim too much for these geographic factors alone. They are but one component of a very complex equation. Other elements must be considered as well. To these we turn in other chapters.

CHAPTER 7

Population and World Politics

INTRODUCTION

Population characteristics affect the politics of states and are included in the calculus of national power. Not all the characteristics can be quantified. Although a large population does not guarantee influence in international affairs, small states are usually at a disadvantage compared to the larger and more populous ones. If the less developed states attain their economic and social objectives, state power might become more commensurate with population. Pakistan, Indonesia, Brazil, and perhaps even Nigeria could eventually acquire Great Power status.

Race, Religion, Literacy, Health, and Other Characteristics. Some personal characteristics contribute to international cooperation or conflict. Race and religion can be as significant as nationalism and other ideologies. Racialism, when associated with anti-white or anti-Western feeling, is a disturbing element in world affairs, and religion has exacerbated Middle Eastern and Indian-Pakistani differences.

Such acquired characteristics as literacy and health are vital to progress in the less-developed countries. Statistics about literacy rates are often inaccurate and not very meaningful, because literacy may be defined as minimal education. In 1960 Afghanistan was reported to have only 4 per cent of the five- to nineteen-year-old age group enrolled in school, whereas India was said to have 29 per cent of this age group in school, and the United States had 81 per cent. These figures, however, do not tell whether the lower percentage groups were in school on a full-time basis, or how many of them passed beyond the lowest grades.

Health, measured in part by statistics on infant mortality and longevity, is relevant to economic productivity, as well as to population changes. In his 1966 State of the Union address President Johnson emphasized that programs of assistance to the developing countries should focus on education, health, advice on population control, and development of modern agricultural methods and food production. Again statistics fail to tell much about malnutrition and the percentage of a population that is physically incapacitated or unable to work because of insufficient food or diseases not reported to public health authorities. In short, the yardsticks for measuring capacity to produce are on the whole poor and more in the nature of generalizations than of specific labor power or arms-bearing capability.

DISTRIBUTION, SIZE, AND GROWTH OF POPULATION

Trends in population, especially growth rates and age distribution, have a vital bearing on prospects for economic development, industrialization, and higher standards of living.

Distribution. A population map of the world shows a very uneven distribution over the principal land areas, as shown in Figure 1–1. About half the world's population lives in the southeast corner of Asia, on about one tenth of the world's land, and about one fifth lives in Europe. Approximately 6 per cent are in Canada and the United States.

Intense concentrations of population live in such restricted areas as the Nile Valley, Japan, the north China plain, Java, Haiti, Puerto Rico, London, and New York City. Some places like Greenland, Northern Canada, the extremities of South America, the Sahara, and most of the interior of Latin America, have very low density rates.

Explanations of these differences are not hard to find. There is a general coincidence between concentrations of people and areas of high agricultural productivity that are themselves traceable to fertile soils, suitable climate, and adequate water. People have not settled in large numbers where it is difficult or impossible to make a living through agriculture or industry, as in the Sahara or Afghanistan or the upper Amazon River valley. There is a high poulation density where means of transport are good or where there have been no serious domestic disturbances or disastrous wars. Areas rich in raw materials or favorable for manufacturing, such as the Ruhr, the Don basin in Russia, and the Pittsburgh-eastern Ohio complex, attract large numbers of people to work in the industries developed there. Large numbers of Chinese have been moved by the Communist regime to sparsely settled Sinkiang to develop newly discovered mineral resources there, but this has hardly been a popular policy.

The settling of people in particular environments is partly determined by their attitudes, objectives, and technical abilities. The pattern of world population distribution is affected by numerous economic, social, cultural, and political factors, none of which is a sufficient explanation of all settlement and migration patterns.

Size and Growth of World Population by Regions. It is estimated that the world's population in 1750 was approximately 700 million; 150 years passed before this number doubled. Sixty-five years later the population had doubled again. On the basis of United Nations demographic studies it is now estimated that at existing rates of growth the present 3.3 billion population may double within the next thirty-five years. If present trends continue, by 1980 the world population will be increasing by more than 100 million a year, and by 2000 will be increasing by over 200 million a year.

Experts are alarmed at the decreasing interval in which the world's population is doubling and the enormous increases needed in food, housing, education, and other facilities to sustain future populations. For the computations estimate that if present trends continue, the world population may reach as much as 7 billion by the year 2000.[1]

Over 85 per cent of the increase is attributed to the low-income countries of Latin America, Africa, and Asia that have a high birth rate. By the year 2000 four fifths of the world population will live in these areas. Then the gap will be accentuated between the high-income, industrialized nations of North America, Europe, and the Soviet Union, and Japan and the poorer, developing countries of the southern half of the globe. In the first group there is an approximate balance between controlled birth rates and

---

[1] Much of the information for this chapter is based upon the *Provisional Report on World Population Prospects as Assessed in 1963*. The United Nations Demographic Service, New York, 1964. See also periodic analyses in the *Population Bulletin*, Washington, D.C.

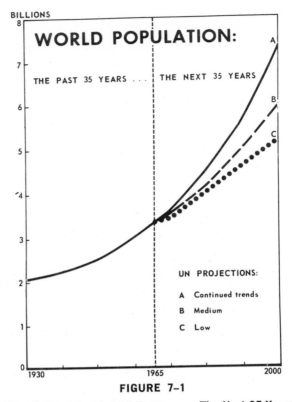

FIGURE 7-1

World Population: The Past 35 Years . . . The Next 35 Years (*From Population Bulletin, Vol. XXI, No. 4, published by Population Reference Bureau, Inc., Washington, D.C. Used by permission*)

low mortality rates. In the underdeveloped countries the adult mortality rate has been lowered through improved medical facilities and public health efforts, while birth rates continue high, from 39 to 50 per thousand population a year. In the economically more advanced countries birth rates are from 17 to 35 per thousand a year. Death rates are relatively high in the lower-income countries, at 10 to 30 per thousand population a year, but are in some cases moving toward the lower rates of 8 to 12 per thousand a year found in the more advanced states. In the developing countries projections of future population could be exceeded if the birth rates remain high and death rates progressively decrease and if there is no great disaster to curtail population growth. The "low" projection "C" shown in Figure 7-1 is based on an assumption that in many of the developing countries both fertility and mortality will decline between now and the year 2000. Should this happen, the population will be two thirds greater than the 1963 world population. By contrast, if fertility rates remain at their present high levels, the totals could amount to twice the numbers projected for the year 2000, barring the intervention of any extraneous forces or pandemic disease cycles. This rate of growth would sorely test the world's ability to feed, clothe, and house its burgeoning populace.

TABLE 7–1

Estimated Population of World's Four Largest Countries (In Millions) At Continued Present Trends

	U.S.	U.S.S.R.	India	China
1965	194	234	484	710
1980	252	295	694	935
2000	362	402	1,234	1,408

Source: *U.N. Provisional Report on World Population Prospects, cit. supra.*

The Population Explosion. Although population is increasing throughout the world, the phenomenon that demographic experts call the "population explosion" is occurring chiefly in the underdeveloped countries. The population of Costa Rica, for instance, is currently expanding at the rate of 4.3 per cent per year and that of Latin America as a whole at a rate of over 3 per cent, doubling population in twenty-five years or less. China and India are increasing at a rate of approximately 2 per cent or more. By contrast, the United States, the Soviet Union, Europe, Australia, New Zealand, and Japan are growing at less than 2 per cent. There are wide variations in Africa, but population is moving at a rate by which it will double in the next thirty to thirty-five years.

The decrease in death rates, which we have noted, is a result of modern public health technology, through mass treatment of many of the diseases which have traditionally contributed to the high death rates, and through use of DDT, antibiotics, and vaccines. Improvement in nutrition decreases infant mortality. In over half the world, life expectancies that used to be less than thirty-five years are approaching those of the Atlantic world, at sixty-five years or more.

Expansion of population must be controlled if countries hope to provide a broadly based public education, savings for capital investment, and the other elements which lead to higher standards of living and a modernized society and economy. At the present time population growth still closely resembles Newton's principle of uniform motion in a straight line little relieved, as yet at least, by birth-control measures.

Age Groupings. Sex and age are significant in population growth. In monogamous societies the balance between males and females of child-bearing age determines the population in the next generation. Wars, because of casualties and the decrease in births, alter population trends. The population pyramid of the U.S.S.R., as seen in Figure 7–2, shows a marked drop in the ten- to nineteen- and thirty-five- to forty-four-year-old age groups, which suffered the most severe losses during World War II, as a consequence of the fighting. In the lower age group the reduced numbers represent the children not born because husbands were not available for women of childbearing age.

Relative age distributions within countries are also important factors in population growth. Where there are comparatively high percentages of childbearing ages and a large number in the lowest age groups, populations are likely to increase considerably in the next three decades. Figure 7–2 indicates that this is true for the underdeveloped areas. In these countries high fertility coupled with declining mortality rates is producing a high proportion of children. This will create increasingly serious educational, food, employment, and social problems.

Unprecedented numbers in the developing lands are reaching the age level of military service, childbearing, voting, and industrial labor. This is particularly noticeable in China, Southeast Asia, certain countries in Latin America, and parts of Africa. These population groups pose special problems for schooling and profitable employment. The large numbers could lead to politically unstable and highly nationalistic conditions. The West and the U.S.S.R., in contrast, have higher percentages of their people over forty-nine. Those over sixty-five are generally not part of the labor force, but are provided for through costly social security programs.

Conjunction of Population Explosion and Other Revolutionary Trends. A strong nationalism is accompanying the population explosion in some areas of Asia, Africa, and Latin America. People have been led to expect that independence will lead to rising standards of living. However, if the population is increasing by 3 per cent per year, an equivalent rise in national production merely maintains present low living standards. To achieve real progress, production increase must almost double the proportion of population increase.

The population surge coincides with a major social change. The industrialization that accompanies economic advance requires a shift of people to urban centers. These requirements strain traditional ties and enhance potential instability among the younger groups that are uprooted.

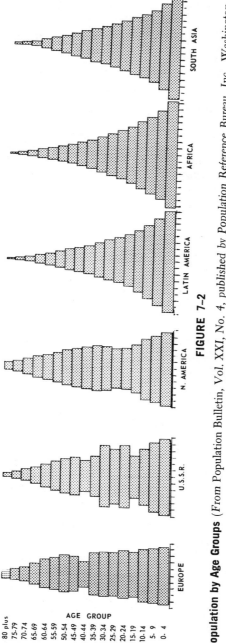

FIGURE 7-2

Population by Age Groups (*From Population Bulletin, Vol. XXI, No. 4, published by Population Reference Bureau, Inc., Washington, D.C. Used by permission*)

Turkey, India, and China each exhibit some of the difficulties that accompany such transitions.

The irony of the situation is that despite economic and technical assistance, and laboriously constructed national plans, population growth threatens economic and other social development before results can be achieved. Prime Minister Nehru declared not long before his death, "Our five-year plans have no meaning if population grows at a rate no one can ever catch up with."

There are salient points in an economic analysis of the problem. A high birth rate means a high proportion of the population is under fifteen and are consumers and economically dependent on the rest of the population. More than 40 per cent of the population of most free-world Asian and Far Eastern countries are under fifteen. In Australia, New Zealand, and Japan about 30 per cent are in this group. To maintain a steady per capita output, investment, which comes from internal saving and import capital, has to double as population doubles. Poor countries, kept poorer by rapid population increase, find it difficult to achieve such savings, beginning from their impoverished conditions, while population is rising rapidly. They have even greater difficulty in providing the additional capital needed to increase per capita incomes. Development therefore is likely to lag in a population-explosion state, unless the country is able to enjoy large and continuing assistance. Foreign aid could contribute more to development if at least a portion of the aid were used for population control.

WAYS OF DEALING WITH POPULATION INCREASE

Three broad courses of action for dealing with rising population pressures are migration, an increase in production (particularly agricultural production), and population control.

Migration.   Some theories affirm that population pressures encourage expansionist policies, which are aimed at acquiring sufficient land and resources. Nineteenth-century policies of colonialism and imperialism may have included these ideas to some extent, although relatively few people emigrated at that time to most overseas possessions. The Soviet Union and China are filling vacant lands within their own borders with their own peoples. Population pressure in Puerto Rico is being alleviated somewhat by migration to the continental United States. Australia and Canada are still encouraging the migration of skilled workers from Europe. But most countries are now unwilling to accept appreciable numbers of immigrants, either because of employment or internal political factors. Migration does not appear to hold out much prospect for large alleviation except possibly within individual countries.

Increased Production of Food. Increased production of food is essential if the population explosion is to be accommodated. About two thirds of the world's population is undernourished. One estimate is that a world food production increase of at least 2.25 per cent per year is required. In the late 1950's an estimate placed the rate of world increase at 0.9 per cent. A rate of increased agricultural production of 2.25 was only achieved in the United States during two short periods of this century—not that the United States with its agricultural surpluses has thus far needed such a rate of increase. The United States agricultural industry is characterized by farm mechanization, labor-saving techniques, heavy investments of capital, use of fertilizers and pesticides, coupled with large operating farm units. Applied to the underdeveloped areas, the United States approach would require social and economic changes that may be beyond the means of many countries for decades to come, even with foreign economic assistance. Reports concerning China indicate that massive redirections of national manpower have thus far failed to satisfy the nation's food needs. Large imports of wheat have had to be purchased from Australia and Canada to make up the deficit. Increased outputs often have to be achieved from increased production per acre, because all arable land is already under cultivation. Current food production per capita in the Far East is less than in 1939.[3]

The supply of food is an increasingly important instrument of policy in world politics. The United States, Canada, Australia, and a few other countries have the capacity for producing export surpluses of general-purpose foods. The United States has made available large quantities of government-owned surpluses through its Food for Freedom legislation (Public Law 480). In the ten years after 1955, for example, the United States made $3 billion worth of food available to India alone.[4] In a single program President Johnson promised Prime Minister Indira Gandhi an extra allotment of 3 million tons of grain to alleviate starvation. It is said that unless an average of one 25,000-ton shipment of grain is received in Indian ports every day of the year, starvation will occur. Australia and Canada, in

[3] Address by B. R. Sen, Director-General of the U.N. Food and Agriculture Organization, entitled, "Food, Population and Human Rights," World Population Conference, Belgrade, August 30, 1965.

[4] United States Information Service, "Fact Sheet on U.S. Economic Assistance to India," New Delhi, June 25, 1965.

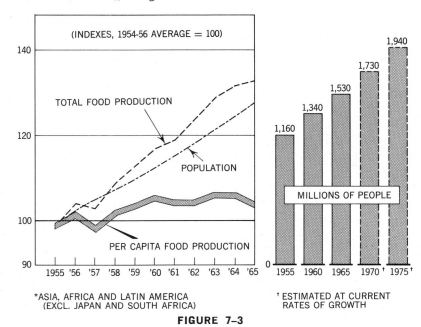

FIGURE 7–3

Food and Population Growth in the Less-Developed Countries (*From Agency for International Development, Summary Presentation to the Congress, March, 1966*)

contrast, have disposed of most of their large crops of wheat through sales and credit arrangements on the world market, with large sales going to Russia and Communist China. Foreign assistance programs are giving more emphasis to agricultural production as the serious food problem is recognized. The Director-General of the U.N.'s Food and Agriculture Organization, Dr. B. R. Sen has pointed out the danger:

> In some of the most heavily populated areas the outbreak of serious famines cannot be excluded. And it is a simple arithmetical conclusion that if food output everywhere just kept pace with population growth at the present level of consumption, by the end of this century the number of people who would be subject to hunger and malnutrition would be double what it is today.

One of the many obstacles in the way to a secure and stable world order is the dependence of many underdeveloped peoples on food shipments from developed countries.

For all of their separate and collective efforts the food-surplus nations are only partly filling the needs of the food-deficient and famine-prone countries. To alleviate the need, the problem must be tackled on several fronts simultaneously. Production must be stepped up in the needy countries. More supplies must be gotten into the picture. Greater efforts need to be put into the conversion of sea water for irrigation and human use. New drought-resistant strains of crops need to be developed. And withal, education must be stepped up to improve land use, to reduce the numbers employed in subsistence farming, and to develop more economical use of resources. Clearly there are large roles to be filled by national effort, bilateral foreign assistance, and multilateral agencies of the United Nations and the specialized regional bodies.

Among the principal obstacles to increasing food production in low-income countries are the social and educational barriers that exist to detraditionalizing agriculture. The problem is not lack of technology, but inadequate ability to apply existent technology. The poor and uneducated are slow to cast off inefficient, time-sanctified methods of production learned from their forebears. The lack of savings, coupled with the burden of accumulated indebtedness under which most peasants must operate, discourages experimentation and the outlays of capital needed to purchase new equipment, fertilizer, and better seed. Thus, all too often a "vicious circle" sets in to oppose extensive change. Breakthroughs can be accomplished only with inputs of foreign aid, technical assistance, and enlightened leadership.

Population Control. Population control is a third method of dealing with the problem and, in the underdeveloped countries, requires government support in order to be feasible in the short run. Eugene R. Black, former President of the World Bank, said before the Economic and Social Council of the United Nations,

Population growth threatens to nullify all our efforts to raise living standards in many of the poorer countries. . . . Unless population growth can be restrained, we may have to abandon for this generation our hopes of economic progress in the crowded lands of Asia and the Middle East. This is not a field in which international agencies can do much.

Attitudes toward population control are becoming less sensitive, and many consider this the only means to keep the rise in world population commensurate with the increase in food and development. Governments in more than a dozen countries, including Latin American countries, like Honduras and Chile, have adopted policies and programs designed to decrease birth rates. The effect of an efficient national program is seen in Japan, where the birth rate per thousand fell from 33.7 in 1948 to 18.5 in 1956. The governments of India and the Soviet Union are supporting population control measures, but the program in India has moved slowly, for such reasons as shortage of doctors and illiteracy. Illiteracy hinders population-control policy, for traditional values and customs encourage a maximum birth rate. The population explosion is coextensive with areas with low literacy, which complicates the task of communication and promotion of new ideas such as population limitation. A *New York Times* report states that Communist China has switched to a policy of population control which discourages families of more than three children. It may be that an authoritarian government can impose an effective population-control program despite illiteracy. If China is successful, the resulting increase in her power is an even more sobering consideration.

The United States government and private agencies have been assisting foreign governments that have requested aid in population-control programs; India and Turkey are examples. External assistance can hardly do enough under present designs, however, to insure a large early decline in the world birth rate where it is most needed. Warning both the advanced and the developing nations, the former President of the World Bank declared, "There is scope for governments to act. It is time that they gave earnest attention to this threat to their aspirations." [5] The double problem of economic development and population control demands planning and vision on a scale as large as the atom bomb development project known as the Manhattan Project of World War II.[6]

A CAUTION ON STATISTICAL FORECASTS

There are enormous risks in making predictions about the variable factors in world population affairs. A few decades ago it was estimated that the world population in the year 2000 would be about 3 billion. Today it is predicted that it will be more nearly 6 to 7 billion. An eminent economist has estimated that if world population growth should slacken off to no more than 1.5 per cent a year, there could still be 25 to 30 billion people competing for the world's food, water, space, and finite goods by the year 2100.[7] This seems unlikely, but is statistically and humanly possible. One of

[5] Quoted in *U.S. News and World Report*, May 8, 1961, p. 83.
[6] See Robert C. Cook, "World Population Projections, 1965–2000," *Population Bulletin*, Vol. XXI, No. 4, October 1965, p. 93.
[7] J. J. Spengler, "The Economist and the World Population Question," Presidential Address, *American Economic Review*, Vol. LVI, No. 1, March 1966, pp. 1–24, esp. 18.

the reasons for the changed estimates is the acquisition of more and better data on population. It has now become evident that the populations of most of the less-developed countries are expanding at an unprecedented rate, which is likely to continue. Should endemic famine or pandemic disease strike these crowded areas, predictions could be thrown awry. An all-out nuclear war among the Great Powers could radically change the world population situation, but this would most probably affect chiefly the areas where population is controlled.

Statesmen have formerly underestimated the magnitude of the population problem and may not yet be looking at it with proper perspective and sufficient concern, particularly in relation to the development objectives of the less-developed countries. President J. J. Spengler, of the American Economic Association, has observed that,

Technology, prudence, and reason could generate a bright future. That it will be bright, however, is questionable, given the unfettered stork, together with continuing escalation of submarginal man in a world of Freudian irresponsibility and distribution according to alleged need rather than demonstrated performance.[8]

With available cultivatable land space, potable water supplies, and stores of irreplaceable minerals shrinking, the outlook for the long run may be only conditionally optimistic. If man is to continue multiplying as he is, if he is to go on using up the rich storehouse provided by nature, and to crowd himself into vast concrete megalopolises, a point may come where the dismal prophecies of Malthus may loom on the horizon. Moreover, out of the frustrations born of such living could spring new conflicts among the nations. It would, indeed, be the epitome of fate if in the age of man's venture into outer space he were to become essentially spaceless, that is, without sufficient living space, on earth. We conclude, therefore, that mankind and its population trends remain not only a very proper study of the student and practitioner of international politics, but one of increasing urgency.

[8] *Ibid.*, pp. 16–17.

CHAPTER 8

The Economic Base
of Power and
Foreign Policy

INTRODUCTION

The economic factor is the most pervasive and continuously operative factor in international affairs. International economic dealings now vitally affect the internal welfare of peoples as well as the security of states. Hence states are deeply concerned with such economic matters, making them necessarily a primary subject of international politics. In addition states with private-enterprise economies are pressed by their citizens, actuated by the profit motive, to intervene in international economic matters. Boundaries no longer conform to requirements for self-sufficiency as states become more economically interdependent. But states seek to avoid becoming subordinate to other states economically, striving to limit the influence of others over their internal economic situation. In the process they generally seek to attain some sort of balance of income and outgo.

Although practically every state is significantly penetrated by economic effects from other states, its own situation depends largely on its degree of industrialization, its measure of primary resources, and its fertile agricultural land. Other pertinent factors are the capital available or procurable for development, and the often complicated interaction between internal and external affairs.

136

During the two decades after World War II, the world tended to be divided into thirds politically: the Communist, the North Atlantic and Japan, and the so-called middle third or underdeveloped world. This division is loosening with the bipolarization of the Communist portion and other polycentric trends. The economic world, once as divided as the political, trends toward a division into a northern portion which is industrialized, in need of primary commodities excepting a few food imports, and is an exporter of capital. The southern and eastern portion depends heavily upon primary products for export, is nonindustrialized but seeks industrialization, and is generally deficient in both capital and food production for its growing populations. The Communist states cut across the economic division of the world. Such a division is oversimplified, however. Some states of the southern half, such as Brazil, India, and South Africa, are underway on industrialization. Figure 1–1 (page 12) gives a schematic picture of the relative economic size and strength of states. It is suggested that the reader refer to this.

This chapter is not a substitute for a text in international economics, which is recommended for supporting reading. But because a summary discussion will provide a useful sensing of the economic factor, we shall describe briefly first the industrialized portion of the world; second, the underdeveloped portion; third, the importance of investment in world affairs; fourth, international trade; and finally some conclusions concerning the emerging economic order.

THE MORE INDUSTRIALIZED WORLD

The Atlantic States. More than 60 per cent of the total world production occurs in the United States and Western Europe, together with Japan. These countries are likely to maintain this relative position notwithstanding the growth rates of the U.S.S.R., China, and the Central European countries. The West and Japan are experiencing the greatest growth in production. They are the greatest trading areas and have large capital resources for investment, along with experience in the management of international finance.

Since 1949 Western Europe has become an economic center comparable to the United States, with greater production than the Communist countries. Western Europe has regained a strong competitive position in world markets and achieved an annual growth rate of over 5 per cent. The revival of the competitive industrial technology of West Germany has been particularly phenomenal. Europe has moved with the help of the Marshall

TABLE 8–1

Estimates of Gross National Product Calendar Year 1964 in Current Market Prices (Dollar Equivalents)

SUMMARY FOR NON-COMMUNIST COUNTRIES

	GNP Total ($ Millions)	GNP Per Capita (Dollars)	Population Mid-1964 (Millions)
Western Europe	$ 462,694	$1,320	350.6
Africa	37,369	145	257.4
Near East	20,271	239	84.7
South Asia	53,408	87	611.4
Far East	100,238	273	366.6
Oceania	26,756	1,556	17.2
Latin America	73,759	327	225.8
United States			
50 States	628,700	3,272	192.1
Other (incl. Puerto Rico)	2,878	1,086	2.6
Canada	43,440	2,258	19.2
Other North America	186	1,005	0.2
TOTAL	1,449,699	681	2,127.8
Memo:			
25 Developed Countries	1,210,004	1,947	621.5
Less Developed Countries	239,695	159	1,506.3

General Notes:
1. National currencies have been converted into U.S. dollar equivalents by use of official exchange rates in most instances; where official rates were not applicable, effective rates were used.
2. GNP per capita is an indicator of the per capita production of goods and services of the countries shown; it is not a measure of the standard of living of their inhabitants.

Source: Agency for International Development, February 18, 1966.

Plan from economic prostration following the war to the acquisition by 1960 of adequate gold and dollar balances, except for the chronic foreign-exchange difficulties of Britain. Coincident with the improvement in the European position, the United States began in the late 1950's to experience increasing problems with its balance of payments.

Along with strong recovery and growth, Western Europe has made significant progress in forming an economic association transcending political boundaries. The six countries (Belgium, France, West Germany, Italy, Luxembourg, and the Netherlands) joined in the European Economic Community, or Common Market, have been seeking to facilitate regional trade and economic integration, whereas the so-called Outer Seven, or European Free Trade Association countries (Britain, Norway, Sweden,

Denmark, Portugal, Switzerland, and Austria) have been striving for a looser trade arrangement. Accommodation between the "sixes and sevens" has moved hardly at all since the accession of President de Gaulle to power in France. He opposed the inclusion of Britain and others in a continental arrangement and has asserted the continued supremacy of national sovereignty over supranational integration within the Community.

The Organization for Economic Cooperation and Development now linking Western Europe, Japan, the United States, and Canada provides a means for coordinating provision of investment capital for developing countries. But the tendency has been for North Atlantic private international investments to move largely within its own area with its lower hazards and high returns. Part of the impetus for United States investments has undoubtedly been not only the high returns available in Europe, but a desire as well to establish a competitive position inside the Common Market.

The United States. United States foreign investments in 1964 were about $75 billion, of which over one half was in Western Europe and Canada.[1] About one third was in the Middle East and Latin America, principally in oil and other extractive industries. The total was made up of direct investments by United States companies, long-term and short-term bank loans, and net purchases of foreign securities. In the mid-1960's the United States government tried to brake the flow of capital to Europe, and its consequent adverse impact on the balance of payments, and to encourage investment in the less-developed countries in support of the political objective of nation-building.

The United States is more self-sufficient than Western Europe, although it also requires large export markets to absorb its mass production and to provide payments for imports. The greater part of the trade is with Western Europe and Japan. Imports from the underdeveloped areas are mainly raw materials which are not produced in sufficient quantity, or at all, in the United States. The United States now imports about one third of its iron ore, all its tin, and all but a small proportion of its chrome, bauxite, and manganese ore. The same trend prevails in one measure or another in most West European countries and Japan.

The United States economy grew from 1953 through 1961 at an average rate of about 2.5 per cent. During the four years after 1961 the growth

[1] *Survey of Current Business*, September 1965, pp. 22–28. Data included in this chapter have been obtained from recent issues of the following sources: IMF, *International Financial Statistics*; IMF, *Directions of World Trade*; U.N. *World Economic Survey*; GATT, *International Trade*; *Federal Reserve Bulletin* and the *Survey of Current Business*.

rate increased to an average of about 5 per cent (5.5 per cent in 1965). The Soviet economy, on the other hand, grew at nearly twice the United States rate from 1945 to 1960, but dropped back to less than the United States rate after that time—with consequent muting, for the time being at least, of Soviet boasts about surpassing the United States.

But statistics alone can be misleading. During the 1950's 75 per cent of U.S. production went into consumers goods, as compared to 55 per cent of Soviet production. A larger fraction of Soviet production and investment went to the military establishment and to heavy industry expansion. Whereas only 17 per cent of United States production went to investment, the Soviets committed 27 per cent of their production to an investment area which emphasized the production of capital goods. From a small industrial base and under a policy which permitted only a slow increase in output of goods for consumption, the Soviet Union achieved a rapid increase in industrial output. This pattern of growth is widely known to the underdeveloped world and is continually being evaluated by its leaders. The Soviet rate of growth decreased significantly, however, in the first part of the 1960's without significant increase in the proportion of production going to consumption. According to some experts this was due to poor investment planning. There are some indications that a larger percentage of Soviet productive capacity is being used for consumers goods lately in an overdue response to the demand of the Russian people.

The American dollar has dominated international exchange since World War II with the British pound sterling moving to a secondary position. Many foreigners and governments hold their liquid reserve assets in dollars, although the booming Western European economies have drained gold and dollars from the United States. In 1965, for example, United States short-term liabilities to foreigners were in excess of $27 billion, over half of which were owned by foreign central banks or other official institutions. The stability of the American dollar, a matter closely tied to the national economy and internal governmental policy, is an important aspect of United States foreign policy, as well as a matter of vital concern to the rest of the world. With world trade and investment flow increasing at a rate even higher than the rate of production increase there is a need for consequent increases in money and credit to carry on business. The United States position as the world's banker does have the hazards of a run on the bank and in the long run of being inadequate for the needs. There has been increasing study and discussion of the establishment of some sort of international credit system which would provide increased liquidity in support of world trade.

Japan.   As the leading industrialized power in Asia, Japan has drawn heavily upon Western industrial technology while capitalizing on its own native genius. Like the United Kingdom it is heavily dependent upon continued expansion of its export trade in order to acquire the raw materials and food which it must import to keep its industries running at high capacity and to feed its people.

Japanese economic policy includes a highly sophisticated industrialization, aggressive competition for foreign markets, and a successful population-control program—the first successful program in a large country. Japan's economic growth rate is the highest of any industrialized country—sometimes running as high as 9 to 12 per cent a year. It is the largest producer of ocean shipping, a large exporter of a wide variety of manufactured goods including textiles, electronics, small cars, motorcycles, and machinery, as well as frozen and canned fish. Japan is competitive with any other country in a wide variety of items and has investment capital to export and is contributing to Asian development. Since World War II, Japan's trade system has not significantly included China, although the latter is a tempting potential market, as it was before the war. Trade is predominantly with other Asian countries and with the United States, from whom she buys more than she sells. An economic rapport between Japan, the factory of Asia, and Communist China may be a fantastic thought, but it is one disturbing enough to warrant continued interest in Japan's economic success in other parts of the world.

The European Communist Bloc.   Overall productive efficiency in Soviet industries and agriculture is low by Western standards, as is the quality of some of its products. But the Soviet Union does have an output of some 12 to 14 per cent of the world's production. This is less than half that of the United States. The European satellite states have a combined production of approximately half that of the Soviet Union; about the same as that of India and China taken together.

The Soviet Union under Khrushchev proclaimed itself confident of surpassing the United States. A resolution of the Twenty-First Congress of the Communist Party cited the next seven years as being the "decisive stage in the peaceful competition with capitalism" and expressed confidence that the competition would be won. Then, when the Soviets had "cleared the way forward it will be easier to advance." But the United States growth rate has since gone up; at the same time the Soviet growth rate has fallen so that its stated goal has not been achieved. Although there has been massive use of a total internal economic policy to further external aims and programs, the Soviet Union has not solved its food production problem. Despite quite adequate soil and cultivable areas, agriculture has been the U.S.S.R.'s greatest failure.

Trade between the Soviet bloc countries and the Free World has been expanding as controls in the Eastern European countries have been lessening. But all of these countries have closely managed economies and are state traders. The Communist system of a rigidly managed economy enables the leadership to avoid any participation in external trade which might permit external economic matters to interfere with internal management. The European Communist bloc has been handicapped when it attempts to compete in a relatively free trading system, partly because the ruble and other Communist currencies are usually inconvertible. Furthermore, the Soviet Union does not have extensive trade connections with the free world, although some of its European satellites, notably Czechoslovakia and East Germany, have had some facility in these matters.

The trend of trade is along the line of increasing penetration of the Iron Curtain, making it increasingly porous. Western European countries have been dissatisfied with United States pressure to restrict trade with Eastern Europe and have sought to revive the pre-World War II pattern of Middle European trade directed to the West and not to the U.S.S.R. President Johnson stated in his 1966 State of the Union address that in "building bridges to Eastern Europe," he would ask Congress for authority to remove special United States tariff restrictions on trade with that area.

THE LESS-DEVELOPED WORLD

Depending on the yardsticks used for *development* there are seventy to one hundred states and, with the underdeveloped Communist states such as China, on the order of two thirds of the world's people in the less-developed area. This group of people is experiencing the main impact of the population explosion and is expanding, both relatively and absolutely.

Many of these countries are generally unindustrialized, as are those of Africa, or only partially industrialized, as in the cases of Brazil and India. Great difficulty in increasing their low agricultural productivity characterizes many of them. One study shows, for instance, that only four Latin American states raise enough food for their people. Societies in the underdeveloped countries range from tribal to fairly modern, and their political systems vary from the new to the older constitutional systems like those of Latin American countries and to authoritarian monarchies like Ethiopia and Saudi Arabia. There is a wide variation in development within many countries by geographic areas and strata of society. For example, the Brazilian state of Sao Paulo is a modern industrial center, whereas Brazil's northeast has 30 million people with an average annual per capita income of less than $200.

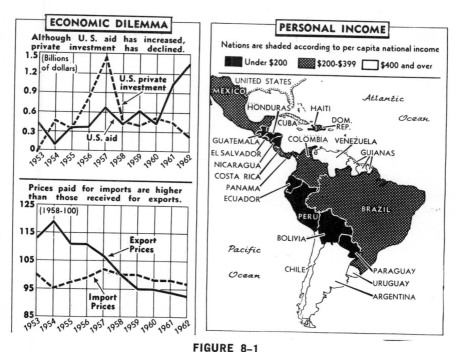

FIGURE 8–1

Latin America—Personal Income and U.S. Economic Assistance
(*From* The New York Times, *November 17, 1963. Reprinted by permission*)

Development, simply stated, is the progress of traditional societies through the modernization barrier. But, as the preceding discussion indicates, generalizations about these societies and, even more, about their progression, are difficult and subject to questioning and many exceptions. As an example, the criterion of an annual per capita product of less than $200, which is sometimes used for differentiating between the underdeveloped and more developed, is an unreliable yardstick, and the criterion of per capita product is a misleading item of single factor analysis. The rate of change, rather than the absolute amount, is often more pertinent. For instance, the Chinese Nationalist Republic (Taiwan), with an annual per capita product of less than $200, is judged to be taking off on a stabilized growth no longer requiring United States economic assistance inputs. Yet there are literally dozens of other countries with approximately the same, or higher, annual per capita product which are not in a situation of assured stable economic growth—and are often even less stable in the areas of political and social development.

Dynamic Impact of Economics of Developing Countries.   The developing countries driving for higher standards of living and modernization have less than one quarter of the world's production but two thirds of its population. Their numbers count in the equations of world politics, where they comprise more than a majority of the international community. Their concerns for security overlap those of the industrialized powers, but their primary interests are far from congruent. Development is their primary goal. Because they cannot themselves provide the capital or the know-how for their rapid expansion, they have had to look to the "have" powers for loans, advice, and many other forms of assistance.

The development drive is an international force cutting across more than economic lines. Social, political, and economic development are all interrelated. Furthermore, there is the added question of whether these countries will shift toward the Communist way, the Western way, or a way developed by themselves. This question is a backdrop of the entire development situation. There is a consensus that there should be some sort of order in international efforts to promote development, but far from a consensus on what the order should be. For example, should political and social change have precedence over economic growth, can all three proceed together, or is some political stability essential to economic growth?

The dynamics of the development problem include the burst of nationalism which conditions choices of ways to progress; governments that have difficulty in administering the functions of government; and the lack of adequately planned development programs. In places, socialist and sometimes Communist doctrinaires are in leadership positions. In others residual anticolonialist thinking inhibits acceptance of Western assistance or collaboration.

In 1965 the annual per capita production of the United States was about $3,000, that of the developed free world about $2,000, and that of the underdeveloped free world about $150. Poor states press the rich ones for assistance, yet it seems certain that the absolute economic gap between them will widen. The ambitions of leaderships frequently outstrip possible timetables of economic advance, making disappointments probable and rash policies more likely. In the milieu just described, scholars search for a theory of economic growth to guide the pertinent components of international relations.

Requirement for Economic Growth. Development economics has become an increasingly favorite area of study. What is a viable theory of development? W. W. Rostow in his book *Stages of Economic Growth* argues that a common pattern can be traced among societies as they emerge from a primitive agricultural economy or traditional society through the stages of transition, to take off into self-sustaining growth and a mass consumption economy. But Dr. Rostow would not argue that industrialization is the only requirement. The transition from subsistence to market agricultural economics has thus far proved more difficult to achieve than advance on industrialization.

Very few countries have achieved self-sustaining growth since World War II, hence case studies are scarce. Professor Neil Jacoby concluded that Nationalist China (Taiwan) reached the takeoff stage because of the native talents and industry of the Taiwanese people, the infrastructure and human resources (such as education) provided by Japan, the professional administrative abilities and ambitions of the mainland Chinese immigrants, stable government, economic policies favorable to private enterprise, and United States assistance.

Growth must proceed from a very small economic base in most of the underdeveloped countries. The goal of growth is quantitative in terms of total production, and qualitative in terms of diversification of production, particularly in the direction of industrialization. Economic growth is not automatic. Growth in the underdeveloped world stems in significant part from (1) the acquisition of skills and organizational ability, (2) imported commodities and services which are, in turn, a product of exports and foreign loans and grants, and (3) investable resources which can be generated by internal savings or foreign investment.

Development Problems Vary by Geographic Region—China and India. The less-developed world can be considered by regions: partially developed Latin America, underdeveloped Africa, the partially developed Middle East, developing and strife-torn Southeast Asia with old societies, and the more special cases of India, Pakistan, and Communist China.

The comparative records of India, with about a fifth of the free-world population, and mainland China, with nearly a quarter of total world population, have been suggested as a test race between the Western and Communist economic systems. Both have about the same low per capita income. Both, but perhaps more particularly China, could become large industrial powers without achieving broadly expanded development for the masses of their people. In following the path of Stalinist regimentation, China has been seeking industrial growth with little increase in private consumption and with almost no outside aid, because Soviet assistance was terminated some years ago.

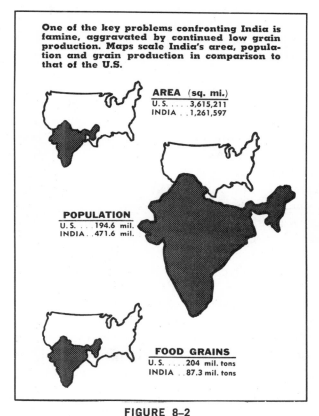

One of the key problems confronting India is famine, aggravated by continued low grain production. Maps scale India's area, population and grain production in comparison to that of the U.S.

AREA (sq. mi.)
U.S. 3,615,211
INDIA . .1,261,597

POPULATION
U.S. . . .194.6 mil.
INDIA . .471.6 mil.

FOOD GRAINS
U.S. ....204 mil. tons
INDIA . 87.3 mil. tons

FIGURE 8–2

India's Food and Population Problem (From The New York Times, *April 3, 1966. Reprinted by permission*)

India, by contrast, has followed a mixed system of free enterprise and British socialistic theory, with large inputs of capital from the West and some assistance from the U.S.S.R. India's agricultural program has not yet succeeded in producing enough food to feed her booming population. The same has been true of Communist China. Both countries have been compelled to seek food in large quantities from the Western world. There has been a slow and steady industrial growth rate in India and a more rapid one in China until 1959 with no significant increase during the first half of the 1960's. Neither country has established a significant margin of achievement over the other.

IMPORTANCE OF INVESTMENT

Many economic problems recur in each area of the world, although with different impacts. These problems include the decreasing availability of raw materials discussed in the previous chapter and the extent and quality of technological advance discussed in Chapter 9. International investment and international trade are two other great problem categories.

Growth Related to Investment. Capital combined with raw materials, requisite technical skills, and managerial arrangements provides additional increments in production and economic growth results. The increment of capital goods added to or subtracted from a state's total capital stock is determined by the amount of net capital investment, taking into account any depreciation. The supply of capital goods can only be increased if a continuing supply of investment funds is made available in the economy. These funds are provided by savings from internal production or by imports in the form of goods and services paid for by loans or grants. The growth of the United States economy and that of the U.S.S.R. stems from a high rate of saving. Growth in Western Europe stems from both internal saving and heavy United States investment. Along with capital the less-developed countries also need skills and institutions necessary to get things like power plants and modern credit systems under way. National market economies suitable for application of mass production methods are also needed as industrialization proceeds.

Economic growth must be sustained if standards of living are to be maintained and raised. We have already spoken about the bearing of the population situation on this in the preceding chapter. If, as has been estimated by several scholars, an investment of 3 to 4 per cent of national product is required to maintain the per capita output [2] where population is increasing at 1 per cent a year, it is clear that countries with population expanding at rates of 2 to 3 per cent, or even more, per year with annual per capita incomes of the order of $200 are going to find it extremely difficult to save the needed funds except with stringent controls, if then. Not

[2] See W. Brand, *The Struggle for a Higher Standard of Living* (New York: Free Press), cited in Senate Foreign Relations Committee, Study No. 1, *op. cit.*, p. 57. See also Charles P. Kindleberger, *Economic Development* (New York: McGraw-Hill, 1958), p. 34.

much can be saved out of per capita incomes of less than $80 (India) or even $200 a year unless such methods are used. The needed rate of saving must be even higher than that achieved in the United States with its per capita product of over $3,000 but its lower population increase. The higher the population growth rate, the higher the needed rate of investment to achieve a gain in per capita product. Hence, the issue of population control is close to the heart of the problem of economic development.

Problems of water, irrigation, better and more fertilizers, better seed, improved machinery, better roads and transportation facilities, and wider networks of inexpensive public utilities are needed in virtually all of the developing countries in order to register solid advances in agricultural production. These all require investments of capital where short-term profit gains are doubtful. Hence they are not likely to be areas for quick, major private investment. Public finance can be the only solution in the low-income countries.

In most of the underdeveloped world significant increase in per capita income depends upon large inputs of external resources. A crude measure of this dependence is the net flow of $9 billion per year from advanced to less-developed countries. This is equal to a quarter of their gross investment and nearly a third of their imports. Over two thirds of this total has been in public loans and grants, the remainder in private investment.

An increased flow of capital is thus needed if development is to be achieved. The flow from Europe and Japan has not increased appreciably in the 1960's. The United States for its part has been feeling the impact on its balance of payments of the large proportion of the flow which it has already provided. In the short term, external capital is a matter of provision through (1) private foreign investment when there are competing demands for that capital in developed countries, where profits are high and risks low, (2) international lending agencies principally financed by the developed countries, (3) bilateral grants and loans which have come in greater part from the United States, and (4) export surpluses. The problem, in the longer term, will be compounded by rising interest and repayment requirements.

Sources and Methods of Transfer of Investment Capital. The United States, Western Europe, Japan, and the Soviet Union are the prospective sources for foreign investment both in the form of capital goods and fund transfers. Roughly 1 per cent of the production of the industrialized countries seems likely to be adequate to support the capital development needs of the free emerging states. This does not seem much in light of the needs and the political and security hazards involved. But the problems of means of transfer, of efficient use, and other difficulties such as the effect on the balances of payments are severe. The distinction between the two related types of investment transfer, capital goods and funds, is made to underline the point that states are often concerned over how their export capital will be used. If transferred in the form of goods home industries are helped and the balance of payments is affected not at all or, at least, less unfavorably. A transfer of funds, unless tied to expenditure in the transferring country, may be spent in a third country, with consequent impact on the balance-of-payments situation.

By the early 1960's private capital was moving readily among the already industrialized states. Development capital was provided for the less-developed areas from government assistance programs—principally those of the United States—and from international lending agencies, financed primarily by the industrialized states with the United States usually the principal subscriber. The World Bank is the senior, and the largest, international lending agency. The Western European capital flow has tended to go to areas having political connections with the source of supply. Thus British capital has gone largely to Commonwealth countries, and French capital has largely gone to the former French colonies. The few loans and grants the Soviet Union made in the first twenty years after World War II were almost all for political objectives. In 1966 the Soviet Union did subscribe to the Asian Development Bank. The expanding Soviet capability is considerable in the light of the modest requirements in the sensitive underdeveloped areas.

Broadly speaking, resources can move internationally in the form of goods, loans by a state or an international agency, private investment in the creation of factories and other production capital, purchase of stocks and bonds, and by transfer of cash balances among banks. These overlap. The last way mentioned is particularly quick and fluid, permitting funds to move overnight under the impetus of a shift in interest rates unless the exporting country exercises controls. Some underdeveloped countries have a major problem in that their nationals tend to transfer their capital abroad, where investments are less hazardous and sometimes more lucrative. Every state is concerned about its balance of international payments and hence about the outflow of funds.

Transfers of capital and funds by states and international agencies to developing countries now usually involve some "strings." The World Bank and other international lending agencies are preferred to bilateral lending by countries sensitive to what they feel may be economic imperialism or to what they consider may be too open association with one of the contenders in the cold war. But the international agencies require assurance of sensible expenditures and sometimes of reforms in economic practices, for example, checks on an internal inflation. The terms of transfer are an important item. The World Bank has generally made hard loans with interest and repayment terms somewhat comparable to private investment. The loans made by the development banks—for example, the Latin American Development Bank and International Development Association, a subsidiary of the World Bank—and by the United States have been deliberately softer, with lower interest and a longer time to pay.

Private investment has encountered serious difficulties in some developing countries. Because of sensitive nationalism and resentment of absentee ownership, foreign capital sometimes feels it necessary to act jointly with indigenous partners in certain lands. This often requires additional time and effort to arrange. In some places expropriation of foreign investments has occurred. The United States recognizes the right of a government to nationalize foreign-owned property, but insists on a correlative right to adequate repayment. Because of the hazards of loss the United States has undertaken to guarantee selected investments against expropriation. Again, some states close off large sections of their economy to private investment, preferring state ownership instead. India is an example. Local bureaucratic practices and threat of inflation also hamper private investment.

Mention should be made of the United States surplus agricultural commodity program—Food for Freedom. With few exceptions, sales are made for local currency, most of which is then loaned within the country, usually for development purposes, thereby contributing to internal capital stock without requiring any dollar transfers. A day may come when some of these loans may have to be forgiven or repaid.

SOME PATTERNS AND PROBLEMS
OF TRADE

We turn next to some patterns and problems of international trade. Trade is vital to the economic prosperity and international security of most states, and is therefore a part of international politics.

The Rationale of International Trade.   In oversimplified terms, a state strengthens itself by international trade through concentrating its resources and efforts upon producing the goods it is most efficient at producing, and trading its surplus of these goods to other states for items it either cannot produce at all or is comparatively inefficient at producing. Trade is also essential, of course, for procuring vital raw materials or manufactured items which cannot be gotten at home. Even the United States, long regarded as self-sufficient, is obliged to import large quantities of certain key materials. Foreign trade represents a much smaller share of the United States gross national product, with imports averaging less than 4.5 per cent of gross national product, than in the case of most countries. For example, the trade of the Netherlands and the United Kingdom equals 50 per cent and 20 per cent of the respective national products. By using substitutes and submarginal supplies, the United States could get by without foreign trade by somewhat lowering and changing its standard of living. A nation as physically crowded and dependent on trade as the United Kingdom could exist without a significant part of its trade. But its standards would be drastically lowered and changed.

If a nation had all the raw materials it needed within its borders, there would still be a powerful case for international trade, for if each nation concentrates on producing the items in which it has a comparative advantage and trades its surpluses, the resulting international division of labor would be to the economic benefit of each country. Considerations of national defense and of undesirable interdependence aside, to gain economically each state should, therefore, seek to maximize its international trade, for thereby it can enlarge the total supply of resources available to it for production, consumption, and defense purposes.

Theoretically, free trade creates the most advantageous situation, in that it maximizes world production. But despite its attractiveness as an economic ideal, free trade has never gained universal acceptance. The United Kingdom, which adopted it in the mid-nineteenth century, has retreated progressively from this policy since the depression of the 1930's. The pressures against free trade are both political and economic. Some producers are always hurt by foreign competition and seek relief. If some states do not choose to play the game, they can turn the willingness of other participants to follow free-trade policies to their advantage by keeping their own barriers high while selling in countries with lower barriers. Hence, the realistic political approach to freer trade necessitates negotiation of simultaneous reduction in barriers. In the so-called Kennedy Round of trade negotiations, the trading nations have been seeking to maximize the area of free-trading practices. Moreover, economic objectives such as maximizing real personal income or gross national product, may be placed second to other noneconomic objectives. Former Premier Khrushchev, for instance, declared that the Soviet Union valued trade not for its economic advantages but because of its political utility.

General Trade Pattern and Trends. As might be expected given the size and diversity of American industry, the United States is the greatest exporter of manufactured goods.

TABLE 8–2

Distribution of U.S. Exports in First Half of 1964

Canada	18.4%
Latin America	13.6
Western Europe	29.5
Asia	17.1
Middle East and Africa	5.3
Sino-Soviet	1.9
Other	14.2

Source: International Monetary Fund, *Direction of Trade*, Nov. 1965, p. 90.

Western Europe has been the world's largest trader as a region. In 1964 its exports amounted to $53.7 billion; its imports to $58.8 billion. Not surprisingly, Western Europe sends a majority of its exports to other Western European countries. The underdeveloped areas sell a large part of their products, chiefly raw materials, to Western Europe and most of the remainder to the United States, which is the largest single purchaser of primary commodities. These underdeveloped areas are not yet heavy importers of primary products, although they must become so as they achieve their objective of increased industrialization.

It can be argued that traditional patterns of trade are not significant. Trade flows where the resources are, where the markets are, and where the best profits can be made. But historically patterns have been slow to change except under the impact of a shock like the world depression or world warfare. Once private enterprise connections are established, they tend to continue. Any competitor trying to establish himself in the pattern must expend considerable time, money, and ingenuity to be successful. Industrial goods paved the way for replacement parts and additional goods of the same models or manufacture. Some foreign investment has had the purpose of providing products for export to the home country of the investor. The development of foreign bauxite, iron ore, and Latin American oil supplies by United States investors are examples.

Trade is, of course, affected by various kinds of government controls, subsidies, and direction whether chosen for political or economic reasons.

Even Adam Smith made an exception of measures for defense in his support of laissez-faire free trade as a principle. For security reasons the United States for two decades after World War II pursued a fairly complete boycott of trade with the Communist bloc. The doctrinal reluctance of the Soviet Union to trade without close Soviet control has already been mentioned.

State trading is almost certain to involve some noneconomic considerations. The United States government built its large stockpile of raw materials in the 1950's for security reasons. This stockpiling proved to be to

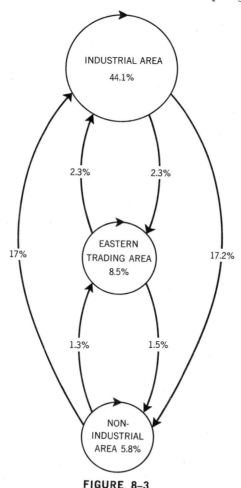

FIGURE 8–3

Trade Within and Between Industrial and Nonindustrial Areas
(*From* International Trade 1962, GATT, 1963, p. 7)

the economic advantage of the underdeveloped countries to which the business was directed. In a similar fashion the United States gives, sells, or lends abroad, on a selective basis, portions of its surpluses of agricultural commodities.

The methods of influencing the direction of trade are complicated and numerous. It is conceivable that state trading capabilities can cause a sudden drastic shift of a trade pattern. A state as powerful as the Soviet Union has the capability to make long-term contracts to absorb large quantities of a product, specifying deliveries of goods in return. If this type of operation becomes more prevalent, economists may take back seats to the political analysts.

The Trade Predicament of the Underdeveloped Countries.   Most underdeveloped countries need diversified imports and are dependent on the exports of a few, sometimes only one, commodity. These commodities often go to only one or a few countries. Coffee provides an example. It is the principal export of Brazil, of five other Latin American countries, and of

TABLE 8–3

Some "One-Commodity" Export Countries at the Beginning of the 1960's

Country	Commodity	% of Total Exports
Bolivia	Tin	65
Brazil	Coffee	56
Chile	Copper	69
Cuba	Sugar	79
UAR	Cotton	70
Ethiopia	Coffee	64
Ghana	Cacao	63
Indonesia	Rubber and Petroleum	71
Pakistan	Jute	49
Burma	Rice	68
Colombia	Coffee	72

Source: International Monetary Fund, *International Financial Statistics, Supple-*ment, 1962/63, Washington, 1963, pp. 255–259.

several African and Middle Eastern countries, with the United States as the principal customer for most of these countries. World overproduction, a sudden decline in real demand for any reason, or an interruption in trade can mean depression and internal political difficulties. In the late 1950's there were at least twenty-five countries each with over 50 per cent of their exports in not more than two primary commodities.

An unfavorable aspect of dependence on export of primary commodities for the underdeveloped countries is that the price fluctuations in their commodities tend to be severe. For example, coffee fell from over $0.70 a pound in 1956 to $0.45 in 1959. Wool fell from $0.55 a pound in 1957 to $0.35 in 1959 and rose again to $0.45 in 1960. Copper fell from $0.44 a pound in 1955 to $0.25 in 1958, rising to above $0.30 by 1960. Low prices of primary commodities over a prolonged period can cause major economic and social crises; hence political crises. Because of the severe price fluctuations outlined here many countries are interested in worldwide commodity agreements that include agreements on prices and export and import quotas, preferably long-term, between countries that are suppliers and their principal customers. The risk of price fluctuation highlights the essential role of the International Monetary Fund (IMF) in providing short-term credits to meet temporary balance-of-payments crises in foreign exchange experienced by these countries. Most countries dependent on export of raw materials are vulnerable to fluctuations in the economy of the United States, which is often their principal customer. Thus, the health and growth of the United States economy is an economic factor of primary importance to many countries, a point underlined by the reported comment of a Latin American diplomat, "When the U.S. economy catches cold, Latin America has pneumonia."

Gains and Hazards of Interdependence. Growing interdependence in international economic affairs, although stimulating to growth and development in many areas, is not without its economic hazards. The economic welfare of the individual and the growth of the economy have become the accepted goals and responsibilities of an increasing number of governments. States seek policies and programs to further these objectives. If these goals and responsibilities are to be realized, there must be increased utilization of international economic measures to reduce the hazards resulting from interdependence. A state may choose the policy of autarky, or relative self-sufficiency through conquest, a policy seemingly discredited by the fall of the Nazi empire. The Soviet trade bloc has tended to be autarkic, but increasing industrialization could lessen concern over dependency and bring Eastern Europe progressively back into the world trading community. A second course of action centers around attempts at global management and arrangements open to practically all nations, illustrated by the General Agreement on Tariffs and Trade (GATT) and the International Monetary Fund (IMF). A third line of action falls under the general heading of economic regional arrangements, of which the

European Economic Community (EEC) is the most effective. These three general categories of courses of action tend to lessen the hazards, while improving the management, of economic interdependence. Policies for dealing with economic interdependence are not mutually exclusive and can be pursued simultaneously. They are applicable not only to trade but also to capital investment and economic development. The Inter-American Alliance for Progress is a case in point of regional cooperation for development.

The Balance of Payments.   Four points are to be noticed with respect to the balance of payments, which, of course, is closely tied to the flow of world trade.

Every state is concerned about the inflow and outflow of resources and the relationship between the two. There is always a balance, in that any seeming imbalance is filled by debt transactions or transfers of gold and foreign exchange.

If these transactions and transfers continue to be adverse over a considerable period, the credit situation of the country may deteriorate and it may lack funds with which to conduct its international trade. International lenders are less likely to provide needed capital, and foreign policy and operations may be inhibited. For example, one of the reasons for tying United States capital-assistance loans to expenditure in the United States has been the need to minimize the impact of United States overseas operations on the balance of payments. One of the major reasons for governmental action in many countries to check inflation is the need to keep price levels low enough to be competitive in foreign markets, thereby avoiding an adverse effect on the balance of payments.

Many less-developed countries have chronic balance-of-trade problems. The wants of their citizens have shifted toward import consumption goods (e.g., automobiles) which, unless some controls are exercised, may use up the foreign exchange needed for import of production goods. The problems of these countries are compounded by the repayment obligations they incur for development and other purposes. These in turn affect their balance of payments, particularly if the payments must be in the hard currencies.

Governments have now assumed, or had pressed upon them, a responsibility for welfare of their peoples and consequently for economic stability—a term which includes an assumption of economic growth. The outcome is a much-increased interest in managing international economic affairs. The balance of payments is the principal yardstick for gauging the course of this management.

A CHANGING WORLD ECONOMIC ORDER

The pre-World War II economic world, dominated chiefly by the colonial powers and the United States, was characterized by an emphasis on private enterprise supported occasionally by individual state policies. There was little positive attempt by governments to manage either their external or internal economies and even less attempt to coordinate these two facets of a state's total economy.

Much of the world had little or no political bargaining position in international economic affairs. Very few states, or their dependencies, were critically dependent, particularly in the short run, on world trade. There was a rapid change in this situation in the first two decades after World War II, during which the United States temporarily dominated the international economic scene and provided resources for rehabilitating the war-torn world. By mid-1965 a new economic era seemed to be appearing with characteristics materially different from the pre-World War II situation.

Some Dynamics of Economic Change. Some trends can be distinguished in the world economic system.

First, international trade, investment, and other interstate economic activity have expanded much faster than population and production, increasing interdependence and vulnerability. This encourages states to attempt to manage international economic affairs and insure against disturbing fluctuations.

Second, there has been a political fragmentation of the economic world. Old dependency relationships have been swept away by the demise of colonialism and the rise of sovereign states, some of them highly nationalistic. This change has taken place at a time marked by requirements for increasing economic interdependence because of expanding populations and increasing desires for industrialization. There is pressure in the less-developed states to meet the "revolution of rising expectations." These expectations involve both a demand for increasing standards of living and for higher levels of industrialization. In the 1930's the clash between the "have" and "have-not" states was a great power clash. In the 1960's the "haves" are the industrialized powers; the "have-nots" are the remainder who look to the "haves" for assistance that will one day make them industrialized competitors. At the Geneva Conference on Trade and Development in 1964, for example, seventy-six "have-nots" lined up against the twenty-six economically more advanced states to demand more assistance and a larger voice in world economic affairs.

Third, states are no longer willing to rely on the old self-regulating mechanisms in internal and external economic matters. In the external field, new international economic organizations and arrangements have partially supplanted the reliance on the gold standard and on trade solely for profit and other economic considerations in regulating the flow of both goods and international exchange between states. Internally, governments have taken a new interest in and an increased responsibility for economic matters. Levels of unemployment, standards of living, economic growth, the economic problems of depressed areas, availability of resources, and the welfare of the citizenry are now all matters of national concern. Although all states have accepted the legitimacy of some governmental control in these areas, one of the basic differences between states today is the degree to which the government takes direct responsibility for these problems and objectives. This degree varies, of course, from the limited free-enterprise system of the United States to the state-dominated economies of the Communist countries. Not all of these objectives, internal and external, are compatible at all times. It is this incompatibility which gives rise to significant problems of public policy.

Fourth, there is a rising economic power in Eastern Europe which if permitted, without political restraint, to develop in interstate trading will increasingly erode channels through the Iron Curtain, as has already happened in Rumania's economic relations with Britain and France. Alternatively, this power may be used in state trading practices toward both short- and long-range political goals, as seen in Soviet economic and technical assistance to Egypt for construction of the Aswan Dam. The political and ideological realities of this Communist economic potential add to the bargaining position of the nonaligned countries.

Finally, within the world community there are now three great forces which did not concern the classical international economist of yesterday. These are (1) the population explosion, which makes the pressure of the underdeveloped areas for growth a double problem; (2) the psychological and political elements involved in international economic affairs through the Communist drive, and the characteristics of the new nationalism; and (3) technology, which has increased interdependence for capital, raw materials, markets, and technology itself.

The United States and the Changing Economic Order.   Defined geographically, the major changes of the international economic environment with regard to the United States are (1) the return of Western Europe to a strong trading position with capacity to export capital; (2) the powerful forces—economic, demographic, social, and political—in the underdeveloped areas that press for growth; and (3) the expanding Soviet-bloc economic capability in international affairs.

Although it no longer dominates world economic affairs, United States action, or inaction, is the keystone of the free world economic system. United States economic policy a generation ago was considered useful for increasing our standard of living, and, in times of crisis, for fighting wars. A growing economy is now essential for maintaining the international political position of the United States, as well as its security. Foreign economic policies need to be shaped and administered to accomplish two sets of objectives: the furtherance of American internal growth and prosperity, and the promotion of the economic health and political stability of the free world. These two sets of objectives pose a challenge, taxing both the technical competence of our economists and the wisdom of our political leadership.

CHAPTER 9

The Technological Factor

INTRODUCTION

This is a technological world and international affairs are affected by applied science. Technology generates change in population, security, and in economic affairs. Formerly, the "time span of important change was considerably longer than that of a single human life. Thus mankind was trained to adapt itself to fixed conditions. But today this time span is considerably shorter than that of a human life and accordingly our training must prepare individuals to face a novelty of conditions." [1] The rapidity of change is even greater today and it has been estimated that scientific knowledge doubles every ten or fifteen years. The effect of this technological advance is felt in world affairs as most of the world now attempts to use modern technology.

A MAJOR FACTOR IN WORLD AFFAIRS

Definition. Technology, sometimes defined as applied science, covers applications of the physical and biological sciences to engineering, in-

[1] Alfred N. Whitehead, "On Foresight," quoted in Wallace B. Donham, *Business Adrift* (New York: Whittlesey House, 1931), Introduction.

dustry, and other human activities, and can also be applied to the uses of the other sciences. The applications of the social sciences in international relations are discussed in other parts of our analysis.

Why not stress pure science rather than technology? Societies and international relations receive the impact of science only through technology. It is the engineer, and other technical practitioners, rather than the professor or the pure research expert, who turns knowledge into a form which enables it to be used as power. There is at least one caveat to these statements, phrased by Professor Warner Schilling.

Just as a reputation for military power yields political results above and beyond the forces on hand, so too may the Soviet Union be expected to reap political benefit from its "scientific prestige," especially among the underdeveloped states where scientific and technological achievements stand as symbols of the good life they hope to achieve.[2]

Technology—Generator of Change. Professor Raymond Sontag, distinguished historian, suggests that world events between World Wars I and II were dominated by three great themes: nationalism; the drastic changes stemming from the events of 1914–1919, causing a discontinuity in the flow of history; and technological change. Those themes have continued since World War II and others have been added, including the rise of Communism and the development of international organization. We are concerned here with technological change but must remember that this change has been paced by a surge of nationalism. Technology, nationalism, Communism, and other forces can be seen as the instigators of change that has broken the apparent continuity of history.

Technology has pervaded all aspects of life, so that some values that once influenced international politics no longer have the same impact. The increasing desire for satisfaction of material wants often supersedes religious and even perhaps ideological objectives as a guiding force in politics. The demise of absolute military security is a product of the technology that has also produced the advances in communications and industry contributing to social unrest. Europe and America became dominant in world affairs as their technology advanced. Now the technological advance is being adopted by the non-Western World and is being combined with its nationalism, creating a force of uncertain power in world affairs.

---

[2] Warner R. Schilling, "Science, Technology and Foreign Policy," *Journal of International Affairs*, Vol. XIII, No. 1, 1959, p. 16.

The quantitative measure of the revolutionary drive in the area of technology is indicated in a study of the Organization for Economic Development estimating that in 1962 both Russia and the United States were employing more than a million people on research and development, and Western Europe about one half million. An annual increase of at least 5 per cent in both manpower and expenditure is probable. Over 60 per cent of the United States effort is in the military and space fields, but other areas have received some "spin off" benefits from progress in these fields. The United States government pays for over 65 per cent of all research and development, but private industry does over 70 per cent of the total work; universities do another 13 per cent; and government institutions provide the remainder. It should be noted, however, that although United States educational institutions conduct a minor share of total research and development, their efforts are guided by federal expenditure. In 1963, federal funds sponsored nearly 75 per cent of the total research and development effort in colleges and universities, including federal contract research centers.[3] The technological revolution has made university research, by its own choice, significantly dependent on support of government funds.

Harold and Margaret Sprout in *Foundations of International Politics* cite that, unlike the applications of the social sciences and humanities, technology tends to be cumulative, accelerative, irreversible, and to diffuse widely and quite rapidly from the country of origin. There is a likely chance that Western military and industrial technology will be widely engraved on underdeveloped societies in a generation, but not so high a probability that there will be a similar adoption of its political principles. Nor will technology be likely to be forgotten; even the devastation of World War II did not set back Europe and Japan for long. Matters pertaining to technology can usually be proven by demonstration. Matters political, social, and even economic cannot be proven so easily, if at all. Technological matters are often little affected by cultural and linguistic barriers. Hence, technology can and does readily flow internationally providing the needed accompanying resources such as literacy and capital are available.

Not long ago there was a fairly prevalent myth that other than Western peoples could not apply modern technology. For instance, in the years between World Wars I and II there was some belief that the Japanese could not manufacture and operate modern warships and planes. Today,

[3] National Science Foundation. *Federal Funds for Research Development and Other Scientific Activities. Fiscal Years 1964, 1965, 1966.* Vol. XIV, 1965. NSF 65-19, pp. vii, 148, 149.

Japan leads the world in shipbuilding and there is no doubt of the Japanese ability to utilize the most modern technology. Provided literacy, organization, and capital are available, the states which are late-comers to the use of modern technology can rapidly lessen the technological gaps between .hem and the advanced Western states. The precise effects of such a progression are certainly speculative. But some of the likely effects can be identified. States become more interdependent; for example, advancing industrial technology creates demands for both foreign markets and foreign raw materials (see Figure 6–3). There is a turn-around in implicit assumptions concerning the world division of economic activities. Once it was assumed that backward states supplied raw materials if anything, while the industrialized West provided the manufactured goods. Now there is a race among both industrialized states and also among private corporations to provide technology to backward states, both because of the long-run political implications and long-run profit opportunities. Technological cooperation among individuals and corporations can go forward despite political coolness or differences among their respective states. There is an increasing web of technological and economic relationships, in addition to political ones, not easily defined or appraised but having some characteristics comparable to the effect of intermarriages on international politics in earlier centuries.

There have been deliberate efforts by states to restrict the interstate flow of technology, particularly military technology. The most recent major example undoubtedly concerns the technology of nuclear weapons. The United States, for instance, has sought to persuade allies to refrain from exporting "strategic" items to Communist countries. Some two centuries ago Britain forbade the export of machinery and techniques for making woolen cloth. Such policies can be effective in the short run. But over the longer run technology flows across national boundaries. Some of that flow is derived from espionage. But once scientists and engineers know of an accomplishment, their efforts are often redoubled to emulate it. Technology flows with export capital. And, while a state may not have the inventors, it may have the competence to reproduce similar and equally good items as seen in the success of the Japanese in electronic products. The lower labor costs in most late-starting countries increase the likelihood that they will be competitive in the international economy.

The "revolution of rising expectations" includes an expectation on che part of governments that their states will possess and be able to manage modern technology. This expectation extends far beyond the realm of military weapons to industrial and communications technology. The impetus is more than a desire to reduce interdependence, it is also a desire for the prestige status believed to exist in possessing technology. Thus, India presses the development of a steel industry. Indonesia and Brazil may soon do likewise—Brazil, with her large proven ore reserves, being more likely to succeed.

Population characteristics, some elements of geography, and many economic facts, can be presented by maps, charts, and tables. Technological position cannot be so presented but must be, in part, inferred from pertinent indicators. One of these indicators is the proportion of a state's population engaged in agriculture. If this is high, it can normally be assumed that agricultural technology is backward or that industrial technology, being backward, has not created a competing demand for increased labor, or both. Another indicator is the per capita gross national product varying from over $3000 for the United States to less than $100 for some countries in the southern part of the world. Still another indicator is the per capita consumption of energy (coal, oil, hydroelectric, and other forms of power). The United States per capita consumption of energy is on the order of three times that of Western Europe and of the U.S.S.R., fifty times that of India, and six times that of Japan. Such overall indicators should not be cited, however, without the comment that by concentrating available technological resources on one or a few priority objectives a state may be able to attain a status, for these few objectives, with the more technologically advanced states. Thus, Communist China has achieved atomic explosions.

Technology and World Affairs.   What are the likely principal effects of technology on a nation's relations with the surrounding world? We suggest five categories of such effects which will continue into the future.

First, technology tends to change assumptions and goals, with the significance of the technological advance not always understood at the time. The United States abandoned its isolationist policy at the same time the country's vulnerability was increased by new technology. Prevention of war has become a more significant objective as technology has made total war more disastrous. The recognition of the existence and availability of technology is one of the main wellsprings of the revolution of rising expectations in the southern part of the world. Technology has made "one world" a disturbing reality of quite a different nature from the concepts of those who suggest that we should institute a world government insuring peace under law. Our current "one world", generated by almost instant communication and great interdependence, makes every friction and conflict a concern to almost everybody else. This situation expands the interests, sometimes the "vital" interests, of states from their immediate geographic vicinity to a much wider, even global, arena. Figure 11–1 gives a cartoonist's cryptic summary of one aspect of this reality. We can neither work our will by force alone nor can we pretend that the issues in once distant lands are not now our interests.

Second, technology influences other objective factors, such as the economic factor, and the relative importance of geographical locations, and of population. For example, oil-producing areas have traditionally been considered as strategically important; their strategic priority may change with the advancement of atomic power. Longer ranges of vessels and missiles, and the techniques of supply from floating bases, and air refuelling, have decreased the significance of naval and air bases. Iceland and the Azores, for example, were once vitally important to United States air power, but now have become relatively unimportant as air bases.

The geographic factor of distance has lost a considerable part of its traditional meaning. There is practically instantaneous transmission of messages, news, and pictures. Individuals can move halfway around the world in a matter of hours. Two generations ago, for example, there was a common practice of sending warships on friendly visits to show the flag, as President Theodore Roosevelt did. Now it is easier and cheaper to send a Secretary of State or a Prime Minister for talks with others for the few days he can afford to be away from his capital. The seas were not long ago a significant barrier to both communication and aggression. They no longer separate countries but rather tie them together; Tokyo, for instance, is closer to Washington than to Peking. Now the seas are no barrier to radio and television and much less a barrier to people and goods than land areas since their surface and the airspace over them is international. The difficulties, for instance, to Britain's communications with her remaining interests around the Indian Ocean are not the seas but the need for rights to overfly relatively short land distances.

Turning to the relationship of technology and population, the meaning of the latter turns in great part on the command of technology. This command, as mentioned above, can be broadly measured by per capita gross national product (see Figures 1–1 and 1–2). Population alone casts a short shadow beyond a country's borders except in unusual cases when the state leads a revolutionary movement, as for example, the U.S.S.R. and perhaps Nasser's U.A.R. But population coupled with technology gives a strength which can cast a long shadow of power across the world. Those states which would be great powers must keep up in the technological race. This is one of the many post-World War II problems of Britain.

Third, technology has affected the subject matter of foreign policy and its supporting programs; for example, through international coordination of technological matters, technical-assistance programs, increased emphasis on arms control, technological intelligence, development of international law to cover the use of outer space and communication satellites, and export earnings attained through technical exchanges. The United States, for instance, has an export balance in fees for technology of over half a billion dollars.

Fourth, technology is a primary instrument in nation-building. It gives the industrialized countries the capacity to create and export capital and is a major determinant of the capability of less developed countries to absorb capital. There is considerable movement of publicly financed national and international technicians between countries and a steady increase in private and public international technological activity for both humanitarian purposes and profit. Development, a primary goal of over 70 states, is really a striving for technological, as well as political and social, advance.

Fifth, technology has had an almost revolutionary effect on the methods of conducting foreign policy. Radio and television propaganda, technical assistance and scientific exchange, space and other projects for prestige, contrast with earlier diplomatic methods. Speed in communications is the most dramatic change. For example, Thomas Jefferson, while Secretary of State, had occasion to comment that nothing had been heard from our ambassador to Madrid for over two years. If another year went by without any word, Jefferson proposed to write to him.

Technology—Both Factor and Instrument of Policy. Although the material effects of technology are apparent, there is no universally accepted rationale relating technology to the evolution of world political events. This rationale is unlikely, for technology is a means and not an end. It has little international meaning itself but has to be assessed in relation to economics, security, and other factors. This assessment is ultimately a political judgment. Statesmen may understand sufficient technology to weigh the factors in making judgments, but good technologists are not, *ipso facto*, good statesmen.

Applied scientific knowledge has become a desirable instrument for states. The export and import of technological methods under the Marshall Plan, later United States assistance programs, United Nations technical advisory programs, Soviet technicians abroad, and education for students from underdeveloped countries all combine with policy to advance national interests. Some technology is comparatively simple and inexpensive to transmit to other nations. More complicated technology, such as the utilization of oil shale and the desalinization of sea water, requires a large and sustained effort that only large industrialized power can provide. Although long-term programs for sharing technology and providing capital investment are necessary, domestic politics may require the government to apply a short-term approach.

The development of advances in modern technology is complex and expensive in terms of manpower and resources. Advances in pure science and engineering require more than a large reserve of potential competence in individuals. Ability must be recognized, developed, and utilized, usually with large inputs of capital. It appears that only economically advanced societies have the capacity to stimulate and support continued technological development. American spending for research and development was about $20 billion in 1965, more than the gross national product of any single Latin American country. Only the United States and the Soviet Union have had the human and material resources to press large-scale rapid advance in certain technological areas such as nucleonics and exploration of space.

It is not without reason that the most complex and prolific chemical and plastics industries exist in the United States, Britain, and West Germany. These have required enormous investments in money, manpower, and resources. Their development requires a close coupling of the most advanced scientific knowledge, technological skills, extensive research, and tremendous reserves of capital funds which, in free world countries, have been commanded only by great corporations existent in larger and more developed states.

The Impact of Technology on World Affairs. No effort will be made in this chapter to discuss all the types of technology now influencing international politics. Our primary purpose is to engrave the thought that technology is an important factor and likely to be increasingly so. To emphasize this point the succeeding sections do discuss three important and interrelated types of technology: communications, industrial technology, and military technology. First, however, we mention other types of the same order of importance.

The effect of the health sciences is largely responsible for the population explosion, making population control and food two of the critical long-run aspects of international affairs. The two types of technology which may prove most important to world affairs of the future are those pertaining to agriculture and population control. If the social and behavioral sciences achieve more precision and facility in supporting development of modern institutions, they could greatly assist the transition of the developing states through the modernization barrier. At present, however, there seem to be no certainly effective formulas and it is even for discussion whether Western political and social patterns are closely applicable to many of the modernizing countries.

COMMUNICATIONS

There has been a tremendous expansion in air transportation, and in the transmission of information and ideas by electrical and electronic communications. Communications are making a particular impact in the timely application of power, diplomacy, and propaganda.

The more tangible instruments of power include technological resources as well as economic and military strength. New developments in transportation have led to some surprises for policy makers. Interventions may now sometimes be less popular politically but have been made operationally easier by modern technology. The speedy United States military intervention in Korea was an unexpected technical and political shock to the Communists. When Salvador was damaged by an earthquake in 1965, United States air-transported assistance arrived within a few hours. Communications made possible a faster United States build-up in Vietnam in 1965 than was accomplished in North Africa in the same period in World War II. The rapid movement of United Nations forces into the Congo in 1960, and the sending of Soviet arms to Guinea, oil to Cuba, and technical missions to African countries show that the technology of transportation combined with modern communications have made defeat in a local crisis possible within a few days. Air transport also makes possible an extraordinary interchange of goods and devices throughout the world.

Both the diplomatic freedom of action of the ambassador and some of his responsibilities have decreased as a result of developments in electronic communications and air transport. In addition, the press interview and other statements over radio and television now receive as much public attention as the traditional diplomatic methods of notes and private conversations. An efficient diplomat today must have some technological knowledge, and many diplomatic missions include technical experts, for modern diplomacy is concerned with technological matters like arms control and economic development.

It is now routine for leaders of one state to appeal directly to peoples of another state, with or without the permission of the other state, through the medium of the radio and television. The United States Secretary of State could be seen on television by anyone in the North Atlantic area answering questions about Vietnam from reporters sitting in London, Paris, Rome, Bonn, and Washington. Although many people are illiterate in some parts of the world, news is accessible through the transistor radio. Through Telstar, intercontinental television now can bring the President of the United States and other international leaders face to face with everyone having access to a television receiver. The communications, weather, and other satellites will soon enable everyone to talk to, listen to, and see everybody and everything that the satellite operators choose to project. The privacy of states has been irretrievably shredded by technology. High-speed printing technology has made possible the distribution of a massive quantity of books, pamphlets, and news releases, for propaganda and cultural relations.

SPREAD OF INDUSTRIAL TECHNOLOGY

The march of technology has globalized the industrial revolution. Two of the major questions concerning the future development of industrial technology are (1) how this technology will be transmitted to the underdeveloped countries, and (2) what its impact will be on international relations.

In the past, technology has filtered to the underdeveloped parts of the world through private enterprise and initiative. The industrial revolution spread slowly but was accompanied by accelerating production and rising living standards. It can be argued that the less-developed areas, many of which have passed recently from colonialism to independence, ought to be able to develop by self-help as Japan did prior to World War II. However, technology is now more complicated, and the social and political pressures for advance are much more urgent than previously.

Industrialization is a product of the complementary resources of technology and capital input. Transfer of modern technology usually needs an input of capital. The United States, for example, failed to realize in 1949 that technological success through the Point Four program depended on the provision of at least a modicum of capital goods. Technological knowledge accompanies capital for foreign investment and is shared with recipient countries by the growing number of private business enterprises with international activities, one of the most dramatic recent examples being the agreement of Italy's Fiat company to provide production in the U.S.S.R. for several hundred thousand cars a year. Capital input and technology are potent instruments of policy whose combined effects on future international relations are still uncertain.

Energy has been the single most important element in economic and social advance. It provides the power for production, for turning on the lights, and for driving the family car to school, the country club, and the hot dog stand. This power is derived from coal, natural gas, water, and increasingly from oil. Someday atomic power may rank with the other sources. Until that time petroleum and the areas where it is produced will continue to be important in international politics.

Technology is a primary factor in generating energy; available energy creates a demand for technology to utilize that energy for productive purposes. Economic modernization is, in considerable part, a problem of the generation and use of energy. State power is, in considerable part, the acquisition and use of energy. Britain's power decline might be checked by the development of North Sea natural gas supplies replacing the production of her high-cost coal industry.

Expanding industrial technology expands the number of states needing to import raw materials and increases the total requirement. At the same time, science and technology are striving to develop substitutes, such as synthetics, for primary raw materials such as minerals. Success can, in the shorter run, cause the gravest difficulty to states with significant reliance on the affected materials for markets and sources of foreign exchange.

Another aspect of the diffusion of technology is its ready adoption in lower wage areas. The resulting flow of lower cost export goods may compete strongly with the older industrialized countries. For example, United States technology, along with capital, exported to Europe in the years after World War II under the European Recovery Program have helped the competitive position of Europe in world markets as well as augmented its industrial and military power. The same is true for Japan. In sum, industrial technology is a significant dynamic in international affairs even as it is for internal affairs.

MILITARY TECHNOLOGY

A crucial aspect of modern technology is the effect that it has had upon military power. Until the twentieth century, military technology changed slowly. The principal method of transportation, the horse, remained constant for over 3,000 years. Weapons and ways of attack and defense remained roughly in balance. Military power was generally both limited and local, its effectiveness decreasing geometrically in relation to the distance from a home base. The coming of the industrial revolution fostered greater reliance on technology as a source of military power. European military technology provided a military advantage facilitating the establishment of the great colonial empires of the nineteenth century. But technological and military change were evolutionary during those years; it was not until this century that accelerating technology resulted in a surge of change in the nature and meaning of military power in interstate relations. The characteristics of this change can be listed under four headings—the discontinuity in weapons capabilities, new dimensions in limited war and in rate of change, increased interdependence, and as an element of the arms control problem.

The Discontinuity in Weapons' Capabilities. First, there is a revolutionary change in the immediacy and scope of the threat of military destruction that forms the strategic background to any conflict. The components of this change include the sudden increase in weapon power and the ability to deliver weapons quickly over great distances. The impact area of these new weapons extends to the economy and civilian populace. Even if these weapons are not employed, the social and economic measures which accompany any attempt to create an effective defense may destroy important values.

In a decade, weapons development moved from explosives with a maximum power of a few tons of TNT to warheads with the power of a million or more tons. Geography has become much less important in estimating the significance of total military power. In World War II a 300-mile per hour plane with a 2,000-mile operational radius was considered advanced; today, enormously destructive power can be delivered thousands of miles in a few minutes. A megaton warhead can devastate over 100 square miles and contaminate a larger area with radioactive fall-out. In testimony to the House Armed Services Committee in 1965, Defense Secretary McNamara estimated that a nuclear attack on the United States in 1970 could kill from 20 to 70 per cent of the population. One of the salient facts of international life is that, although states have moved to attain offensive nuclear power, they have not thus far taken comparable defensive measures. This suggests that faith in political action preventing a nuclear holocaust is superior to the threat born of technology.

Military force in action has often been a blunt instrument. Now that military technology has given military force the power to effect enormous destruction in a short time, there is even more point to the late Dr. James Shotwell's suggestion that the changing nature of society has made war an anachronistic instrument of policy. "Now war is as uncertain in its direction as in its intensity, or its spread. It is no longer a safe instrument for statesmanship." Dr. Shotwell continued, "In short, war which was once a directable instrument of policy has now changed its nature with the nature of modern society and ceases to be controllable and directable—it becomes a contagion among the nations; and one cannot safely use a contagion as an instrument."

New Dimensions of Limited War. A second less dramatic but significant area of change is in the military power that is less than totally destructive. This is sometimes called "limited-war force." There is a great increase in conventional firepower and in ability of armed force to move and act quickly. Although technology has provided the massively destructive weapons, it has also contributed to the increasing emphasis on speed, flexibility, firepower, and professionalism of both individuals and conventional military units.

Military power is, because of military and communications technology, no longer local. The *Economist*, noting the new United States C5A military air transport, commented that ten of these planes could have handled the entire Berlin airlift in 1949 and that forty-two could lift a division to Europe in half a day, a task that required 234 aircraft and took two and a half days in the early 1960's. "For the first time, an army and everything it could conceivably use, including its vehicles, its helicopters, and the rest, can be flown rapidly across the world." The fast deployment logistics ships being built by the United States increase capability to "Git Thar Fustest With the Mostest". Although they cannot provide depot support for sustained fighting, they reduce cost and frictions over foreign bases. The double turbine helicopter, able to lift large loads including artillery into and from small clearings, and onto mountain tops, may change the face of military power as much as supersonic jet planes. Current history demonstrates that limited use of force for limited objectives is practicable, and, as most nations do not possess the means for nuclear war, their resort to force does not risk escalation to nuclear war unless nuclear powers enter the controversy. Lesser states may now invoke military force more readily than the Great Powers.

The Pace of Military Technology. The uncertainties contributed by the scientific revolution are compounded by the exceedingly rapid pace of that revolution. Roger Hilsman comments that in the field of military policy, since World War II half a dozen military innovations "have followed each other so rapidly that efforts at adaptation are hardly begun before they must be scrapped." Thus a succession of generations of fast-winged planes were followed by generations of air-breathing missiles, few of which became operational before the proving of ballistic missiles, which in turn had a rapid rate of obsolescence as solid-fuel rockets were developed to make the dynasty of liquid-fuel missiles comparatively short. Herman Kahn in his book *On Thermonuclear War* has suggested that as far as weapons are concerned, World Wars III through VIII have already been fought. Two main effects of rapid obsolescence are the high cost of armaments and the conventional weapons that are out of date, by the yardstick of racing technology, but have high prestige and military effectiveness in some localities. These weapons are available for the Great Powers to distribute to states lacking the industrial capacity to produce their own. Thomas Finletter comments in the same vein, noting that military technology has been "so fast-moving as to make almost impossible the task of military men whose responsibility it is to anticipate the future. Military planning cannot make the facts of this future stay long enough to analyze them." Nor does the rapidity of change permit the military establishment to assimilate fully the characteristics and effects of a particular weapon before a new innovation becomes operational. Usage in World War II was required to cause full acceptance of the tank and airplane first employed in World War I. There may be a serious and widening discontinuity within modern armed forces that possess sophisticated post-World War VIII weapons but remain at the World War II level of assimilation.

After World War II the United States had to adjust its security thinking drastically, abandoning its primary dependence on its great, but slow-moving, civilian industrial power and on distance, which no longer gave safety from direct attack. Part of the adjustment was dictated by worldwide shifts in power, but a great part of the adjustment derived directly from military technology.

If the security situation of a state depends on the modernity of a weapons system, military security can be compromised by the potential opponent getting a technological advantage that provides a better class of weapons. The opponent may develop muzzle loaders rather than bows and arrows, jets rather than piston planes, nuclear explosives rather than conventional explosives, and antimissile defense rather than a defense against winged carriers. The state then has two alternatives—buy the more modern weapons system from a third party or look ahead in research, development, and production to match the opponent. Long-range foresight is required, for years now elapse between the research stage of new weapons and their operating installation. Lead time in weapons development and production is one of the imponderables in the problem of proliferation of nuclear weapons and a major aspect underlying arms control and related inspection systems.

Increased Interdependence. A third area of change is the increased interdependence of states for security. Both the scientific and industrial technology involved and the costs of production make modern weapons the monopoly of a few powers. Given these weapons, most states can operate them. There is, therefore, an increasing emphasis on (1) collective security and other interdependent arrangements and (2) use of military power through the strengthening of third parties. Because of the dangers of direct conflict among the Great Powers, and the importance of time, military collaboration with friends becomes a continuing necessity rather than a crisis phenomenon.

Small countries cannot compete either in the research and development or in the industrial aspect of military programs. Even the industrialized NATO powers have found a considerable pooling of efforts in military technology essential. The realities of science, geography, industry, supply, training and operations encourage interdependence and cooperation. States will take political and economic risks to satisfy the dominant urge to possess arms. Thus Egypt's Nasser acquired arms from the Soviet Union, and India has bought weapons from both the Soviet Union and the West.

When a great state such as the United States has the same security objectives as small states, and technology now enables military power to be moved and applied rapidly, it can be asked to what extent the lesser states need be allied. Might they not safely, from their standpoint, continue a political attitude of neutrality? India, certainly not a small state, followed this policy and yet was quickly supported by the U.S. when Communist China pressed against India's northern border. If a state sees only a limited amount of difference in being an ally and being a neutral, it may find the gains of political independence balance the equation on the side of neutrality.

Small states which formally link their security with great states are open to pressures and threats and the greater risk of a thermonuclear exchange between the large states. Technology has generated a *de facto* military confrontation between the Great Powers, and because of the totality of thermonuclear war smaller states can reasonably question how much a great ally will risk to support a smaller state when attacked. This question has been part of the problems of NATO. A French strategist, Pierre Gallois, has argued, for instance, that nuclear weapons have made alliances obsolete, because no state will jeopardize its survival for another.

Interdependence brings more dilemmas to the Great Powers than it does to the small ones. They become third parties to conflicts among allies, as was the case during the Greek-Turkish conflict over Cyprus, and they can conceivably be embroiled with another Great Power through the unilateral actions of a small ally. Rapid technological changes have contributed to the weakening, as well as to the strengthening, of some premises underlying collective security arrangements. Advanced technology has made some of the NATO bases, perhaps some of the allies, militarily less essential. Among the dynamics of international politics in the future are the real, yet unclear, cross-currents generated by technology in connection with interdependence.[4]

Technical personnel and training arrangements have generally accompanied transfer of weapons to all the nonindustrialized countries. This places the transferring country in a favorable position to influence the armed forces, often one of the most administratively competent and most organized groups in an underdeveloped country, and even to influence the recipient's social and political fabric.

Technology and Arms Control. One of the political effects of the swift advance in technology has been the greatly increased international pressure for arms control, to which technology can also provide an approach. It is not unreasonable to turn to the cause in search for a cure. The Geneva convention on poison gas was based on a technological definition, and the naval disarmament agreements of the early 1920's were founded on such technological characteristics of warships as tonnage and size of guns. The early post-World War II plan for keeping Germany and Japan disarmed was to control or prohibit industry for producing modern weapons.

The rate of change of military technology is gravely reducing the usefulness of technological criteria as arms-control measures. By the time that a policy position based on technological assumptions has been evolved, cleared with allies, and negotiated, new technology can render the original assumptions invalid. This factor has been particularly potent in arms-control discussions.

Technology may in itself provide a *de facto* arms control through the mutual restraint imposed upon nuclear powers by the weapons of mass destruction. On the other hand, the lack of technology constitutes an indirect restraint on use of the more modern arms by the nonindustrialized powers. This restraint depends on the willingness of the few highly industrialized powers to prohibit or limit the provision of such weapons

[4] See Henry A. Kissinger, *The Troubled Partnership* (New York: McGraw-Hill, 1965).

to countries that cannot produce their own arms. This requires an operating unanimity among the producing powers and raises difficult questions about the right of each state to use force in its own defense and have the arms to exercise that right.

We have mentioned the problems of arms control, which will be discussed further in Chapter 20, because military technology has underlined its importance. Applied science must contribute to any progress on arms control, but the key requirements for progress are in the psychological and political fields.

CONCLUSION

Technology, as much as any factor, has provided the current dynamics to international politics. It is one of the most international of human activities with limited regard for boundaries and sovereignty. Technology provides hope for advancement to the developing nations. It has made the world interdependent for markets and raw materials. Technology has made possible the military confrontation of states geographically widely separated and has made every state more penetrable than in the past. Boundaries have been made more anachronistic. Electronic communications now enable everybody to talk directly to everybody else. Technology has caused a rapidly shrinking world in which the affairs of each state are interlaced with, and penetrated by, the affairs of many other states.

CHAPTER 10

The Search for Security

INTRODUCTION

National security is the fundamental concern of every state and is a principal focus of the interaction among the basic factors in world politics. This is evidenced by the facts that most states maintain defense establishments; that many seek alliances and coalitions in order to attain a favorable distribution of power; and that they place emphasis upon collective security, regulation of armaments, and establishment of a stable international order. Security was a primary object in founding the American constitutional system. One of the seven purposes set forth in the Preamble of the Constitution is "to provide for the common defense." Some degree of security is essential to welfare and the other purposes of government.

Each state is responsible to its citizens for their collective, as well as their individual, security. Security for one state is a matter existing in the external environment of other states and may involve countering some states and cooperating with others. Hence the problem of security cuts across interstate relationships.

The confluence of the forces we have been discussing in previous chapters has produced the present era of frictions, conflicts, and interdependence. The paradox is that in the process insecurity may have increased.

The meaning of security has undergone change in an era President Eisenhower described as one of "perpetual crisis." As Professor J. H. Herz has put it, "The decisive change is from 'distinctiveness' and 'separateness' to 'pervasion,' to the absolute permeability of each unit by each of the others, so that the power of everyone is present everywhere simultaneously."

The search for security involves diplomatic, psychological, economic, and military means. The policies and programs adapted to this end will be discussed in Part IV of the book. In this chapter will be discussed the sources of increased insecurity today and their consequences and implications.

THE MEANING OF NATIONAL SECURITY

The meaning of security is suggested by the fact that concern for it occupies a major portion of United States foreign policy operations and by the fact that a major portion of the federal budget is allocated for its preservation. This does not disclose, however, what is being "secured."

Arnold Wolfers has suggested that security "points to some degree of protection of values previously acquired." Quoting Walter Lippmann, Wolfers says, "A nation is secure to the extent to which it is not in danger of having to sacrifice core values, if it wishes to avoid war, and is able, if challenged, to maintain them by victory in such a war."

This description helps but is incomplete in an era in which there may be no victory if there is atomic war. Security embodies other elements in addition to attack and defense, and peace is more than ever a "core value" to most peoples. Maintenance of international peace is the stated objective of the United Nations. "Peace" is also an emotional symbol which each of the contestants in the world power struggle tries to capture.

Security for the individual and the state embodies both "freedom from fear," in the words of the Atlantic Charter, and the freedom of a state to pursue its own interests by its own methods. To nations bent upon increasing their power and position, security implies being able to compel others to act in accordance with their demands. This may mean the incorporation of other states in a *de facto* empire, as the Eastern European states were compelled to acquiesce to Soviet domination after 1945. Or it may mean enforced political alignment, cession of territory, or the granting of special concessions.

When we turn to the range of values that a state may strive to make secure, the calculus becomes complicated and contradictory. Most Americans prefer a policy which provides both the value of security and the value of some disentanglement from the costs and complications of worldwide involvements. A state may accept some limitations on its freedom of action in order to further certain social and economic values. Yet states have generally been concerned with avoiding dependency upon others wherever possible, lest today's friend become tomorrow's ruler. Many of the outwardly puzzling shifts of the European balance of power have come out of this paradox.

The governments and peoples of not a few small states may indeed feel as did the mythical ruler in "The King and I" by Rodgers and Hammerstein that it is a "puzzlement" whether to permit their nation to be secured, lest they wake up some day to discover they had been protected out of what they had owned. Absolute security is a goal unlikely to be achieved.

Professor Wolfers has observed that security is a value "of which a nation can have more or less and which it can aspire to have in greater or lesser measure." This judgment has validity for security from military attack, providing one bears in mind that the realities of modern military power make absolute military security no longer practicable for any state. The costs of armed forces, the complications of alliances, and the likely reactions of potentially hostile powers cause every state to be continually making decisions as to how to pursue its own military security. These decisions are rarely explicit. They are instead implicit in budgetary actions, in alliance policies, and in other actions in foreign affairs. The measures to further the security of one set of values almost inevitably infringe on another set. Thus there was a controversy in the United States in the late 1950's over whether or not it would be best to spend more money for military forces, despite the chance that so doing could give rise to economic troubles which would weaken the overall power position of the nation. There was similar concern in 1966 over the impact of the cost of the war in Vietnam on the administration's program for the elimination of poverty.

Internal Security. If a nation's leadership or people believe that other states are unfriendly to their system of internal order, a feeling of insecurity is likely to result. This feeling can be aroused within a country by skillful leadership. Such was the situation in Communist China, where the leadership quickly turned attitudes against the United States, which had long been friendly to the Chinese people. Similarly, the Cuban viewpoint concerning the external environment was changed almost overnight by the Castro regime, so that the traditional Cuban feeling of security shifted to one of insecurity and accompanying hostility toward the United States.

The concept of internal security traditionally includes concern over insurgency, subversion, espionage, and sabotage. Internal security includes the aspect of stability and continuity of the regime. In the present day, security includes a concern over nonmilitary threats to social, economic, and cultural systems, with a consequent distrust and even hostility toward states which are the source of the threat. Because few common values are shared and national purposes are often opposed, distrust frequently prevails between Communist and non-Communist states. This is not always so with some of the newer states which have had little experience with subversion or other pressures on cherished institutions. They are sometimes skeptical of warnings of dangers to their security from this source until subversive elements threaten to overthrow their governments or saboteurs begin to undermine them.

Where there is distrust of professional military elements as a potential threat to the values of a free society, people have to become persuaded that in order to preserve their security and freedom it may be necessary to accept endangering some values in order to attain others. The important role of the armed forces in many of the emerging countries lacking strong institutions illustrates this dilemma. At the same time it is fair to observe that the military has in some countries of Latin America, Asia, and Africa been a guardian of internal stability and constitutional government.

Domestic political factors, traditions, ideologies, and the extent of shared consensus on national goals within a society all help determine the range and priority of the values that include security.

Feelings and Attitudes.   One of the basic facts about security is that it is essentially subjective. Military security undeniably is closely tied to the strength a nation can assemble to deter an attack or to defend itself in combination with the strength of allies and sometimes of the United Nations. The sense of security or insecurity fluctuates with the concern a people and its government have about the strength of other potentially threatening nations.

Any state may develop a feeling of insecurity if it feels that a foreign power has embarked upon a program which may lead to aggressive designs upon it or states friendly to it. We pointed out in Chapter 3 how stereotyped attitudes may tend to narrow perception and objective evaluation. Tension tends to exacerbate feelings of insecurity and evoke latently hostile attitudes. Security is partly a state of mind of a people and of its leaders and may not be the same for the two groups. In the late 1950's, for example, one wing of the British Labor Party expressed much more concern over the resurgence of German armaments than did the official leadership.

There are three related components in the concept of security as a state of mind or attitude, all having to do with confidence—confidence in the nation's strength, confidence in the relative strengths and intentions of friends and opponents, and confidence in being able to maintain a secure situation in the face of future trends. Attitudes concerning security can be derived from knowledge, from an ignorance of the external environment that leads to unwarranted complacency, and from individual and national conditioning. These attitudes are a product of far more than the quantitative equations of strengths involved. They are the product of effective power and an appraisal of intent. Professor Frank Tannenbaum says, "The United States is very much stronger than Canada, but American power to control Canadian policy is limited by public opinion at home and abroad, by the non-imperialistic sentiments of the American people, by the existence of the Commonwealth, the United Nations, and so on."

The subjective nature of insecurity permits the use of fear as an instrument of both internal and external policy. Militant leaderships use alleged threats to the security of their nation to distract people's attention from troublesome internal affairs. Pre-World War II France used the fear of Germany and its military preparations to direct attention away from its own political bickerings and weakness. Almost all states are sympathetic to the expressed fears of another state. A state may allege coercion or fear of aggression as a reason for acting, or not acting, in its external affairs, seeking to rally other states to its support. The allegation sometimes expresses a real, although not always warranted, concern, and at other times it is a deliberate move in international politics. An interesting corollary to such tactics is the effort of aggressive Great Powers to appear as the peacemaker. "A conqueror," said Clausewitz, "is always a lover of peace; he would like to make his entry into our state unopposed."

Because of worldwide desire for security, a state loses prestige and influence if it is known as a "warmonger." It gains in prestige and security if it is a strong supporter of peaceful methods. This attitude inhibits the use of armed force to swing the balance in local power conflicts. Proclaiming "peace" and "peaceful coexistence" as a policy has probably contributed to political successes of some states with the uncommitted nations.

Fundamental Security Objectives. National survival is the predominant duty of a state and the first security objective. Security is a negative concept in that it protects, and positive in that it provides confidence and contributes to a sense of freedom. In Chapter 1 security was defined within the context of the international order or external environment of a state. In searching for security, a nation endeavors to establish or align itself with that external environment in a way conducive to the pursuit of its national goals or purposes, and internally, to preserve the continuity of the regime in power and those social, economic, and other institutions it values. The idea of national security implies preserving the national life, independence, and territorial integrity of the state free from outside interference, including freedom from subversion, so that the nation can enjoy certain moral, cultural, and material standards of its own choice and maintain its national position in world affairs. Security is both a means to the satisfaction of the other ends and an end in itself.

Traditionally, national security has been closely equated with military security, and military power has been the principal arbiter. In recent times, however, the concept of national security has become broadened and security has been complicated by the interaction of new forces. As one consequence the meaning of military power has become somewhat more ambiguous.

MILITARY POWER AND SECURITY

The recurrent use of armed force for the solution of conflicts and the advancement of national interests, usually in the name of national security, has been a central feature of international politics since the beginning of the state system. Military force has been the ultimate sanction in world politics, and it is an underlying factor in an appraisal of nonmilitary forces.

By its very existence military power is both protective and coercive, reassuring and disturbing, a measurable reality and a major psychological element in international affairs. Military power can vary from passive existence, to some means of creating an awareness of its presence, to threatening actions and active employment of force. Modern political methods often combine nonmilitary techniques with the sobering shadow of military power.

Violence in International Affairs.   Voltaire once complained that history is written primarily as the record of violence, destruction, human suffering, and death. Whether or not one accepts this philosophy, the fact remains that mankind lives in an international society charged with disputes and conflict. In relations among sovereign states, there has been frequent overt use of armed force. From 1820 to 1929, eighty-two wars or "deadly quarrels" have been counted, in each of which more than 10,000 people were killed. The United States has been engaged in at least seven international wars since 1775, in addition to its Civil War.

TABLE 10–1
Forty Wars Since 1945

Place & Date	Opponents (Winner in Italics)
Indonesia 1945–47	Netherlands v. *rebels*
China 1945–49	Nationalists v. *Reds*
Kashmir 1947–49	India v. Pakistan
Greece 1946–49	*Govt.* v. ELAS rebels
Israel 1948–49	*Israel* v. Arabs
Philippines 1948–52	*Government* v. Huks
Indo-China 1945–54	France v. *Viet Minh*
Malaya 1945–54	*Britain* v. Red rebels
Korea 1950–53	*U.N. & South Korea* v. Red China & N. Korea
Formosa 1950–current	U.S. v. Red China
Kenya 1952–53	*Britain* v. Mau Mau
Sinai 1956	*Israel* v. Egypt
Suez 1956	G.B. & France v. *Egypt*
Hungary 1956	*Russia* v. rebels
Quemoy-Matsu 1954–58	Chinese Nationalists v. Chinese Communists
Lebanon 1958	*U.S. & Lebanese* v. rebels
Tibet 1950–1959	*Chinese Communists* v. Tibetans
Cyprus 1955–59	Britain v. *EOKA rebels*
Algeria 1956–62	France v. *rebels*
Cuba 1958–59	Govt. v. *Castro rebels*
Laos 1959–current	Government v. Pathet Lao
Kuwait 1961	*Britain* v. Iraq
Goa 1961	*India* v. Portugal
Yemen 1962–current	Royalists v. government & Egypt
Congo 1960–62	*Govt. & U.N.* v. mutineers & secessionists
Cuba 1961 (Bay of Pigs)	Cuban refugees & U.S. v. *government*
South Vietnam 1959–current	U.S. & S. Vietnam v. Viet Cong & N. Vietnam
Himalayas 1959–62	India v. *Red China*
Angola 1960–current	Portugal v. rebels
West New Guinea 1962	Netherlands v. *Indonesia*
Colombia 1960–current	Government v. rebels
Cuba 1962	Russia & Cuba v. *U.S.*
Algeria-Morocco 1963	Algeria v. Morocco
Venezuela 1963	*Government* v. rebels
Malaysia 1963–current	Britain & Malaysia v. Indonesia
Congo 1964–current	Govt. v. Simba rebels
Thailand 1964–current	Govt. v. Red terrorists
Dominican Rep. 1965	Govt. & U.S. v. rebels
Peru 1965	Government v. rebels
Pakistan-India 1965	Pakistan v. India

Courtesy TIME; © Time Inc. 1965.

During the first twenty years after World War II there were at least forty armed conflicts, including the United Nations action in Korea, in which the United States experienced the fourth highest number of casualties of any war in its history. One characteristic of international violence since the surprise attack on Pearl Harbor in 1941 has been the initiation of hostilities without formal declaration, increasing the ambiguity of the situation as well as gaining a military advantage. There was no formal declaration of war between states in the first twenty years after World War II. An example of the ambiguous use of armed force is the progressive development of hostilities in Vietnam, from low-level guerrilla activity in 1960 to the 1965 regimental-size Vietcong operations backed by North Vietnam before it was generally accepted that there was a war situation.

States are powerfully motivated to satisfy their needs and interests. When peaceful means fail to bring satisfaction, the availability of weapons and their effectiveness provides an alternative that is at times attractive to those in charge of the affairs of state and to political groups striving for power and recognition. The use of armed force can appear to be the only way to defend the body politic and its interests or to achieve seemingly legitimate ends. The weak organization and political instability of the community of states where international law recognizes the right of self-defense and self-help is another aspect causing states to maintain instruments of force for use in international affairs.

Limited War of the Past.   In the past the average citizen was often relatively little concerned with warfare, except when his local community was involved. The Prussian peasant cared little about the success or failure of Frederick the Great in subordinating other German principalities or in adding to his prestige through foreign ventures. Wars were the preoccupation of kings and rulers and often the result of dynastic quarrels or disputes over royal domain.

Between the fifteenth century and the French Revolution, European armies were small professional bodies, sometimes bands of mercenary adventurers hired out to the highest bidder. Neither deep hatreds nor dedication to differing principles were usually involved in pitting soldier against soldier. War and the profession of arms were managed as arts in the seventeenth and eighteenth centuries. Adept maneuvering and expert disposal of forces were the determining factors, not heavy expenditures of resources or the ability to sustain many casualties.

The French Revolution brought about, and later Napoleon developed, techniques for raising and supporting mass armies. The rise of nationalism motivated these mass armies, which were made possible by the increased population growth and the industrial revolution, with the result that the conduct and scale of war were fundamentally changed.

Influence of Nationalism. Some of the effects of Western nationalism have already been noted in Chapter 4. The growth of nationalism out of the turmoil of the French and the American revolutions was largely responsible for the identification of personal with national interest. It justified the development of popular armies and was one cause of the mass character of modern war. Edward H. Carr said of the late nineteenth century that, "The socialization of the nation, the nationalization of economic policy, and the geographical extension of nationalism" combined to produce the totalitarianism of our times. One manifestation of this is total war.

Twentieth-Century War. War in the first half of the twentieth century involved entire societies and became predominantly total war in which mass armies were conscripted, equipped, and thrown into battle. In World War II Germany, the Soviet Union, Japan, the United States, and probably China, each put more than 8 million men into uniform. Women participated in the armed forces of several nations, and Soviet women even bore arms at the fighting front.

The modern "nation in arms" blurred the traditional distinction between soldier and civilian, ending the immunity civilians in the West enjoyed in the nineteenth century as long as they avoided being caught in the crossfire of battle. The staggering demands of mass, mechanized warfare required involvement of every able person in the total national effort that supplied the armed forces of the Great Powers in World Wars I and II. Only by mobilizing all sectors of the economy could the demands of modern warfare be met. Both hostilities and psychological warfare were increasingly carried to the home front of the enemy to bring about defeat and demoralization. By arousing popular zeal the necessary sacrifices were achieved and the enormous destruction and losses sustained.

The precedents from World Wars I and II color our conceptions of the future, perhaps misleadingly. World War III is likely to be seen in terms of a World War II pattern of international hostilities with the addition of nuclear weapons. Under such circumstances the home front might suffer while military forces remained comparatively unharmed. Popular attitudes have changed with time, except for a few special cases such as China, to a realization of the grim meaning of war. World War I was the last time in the Western world when nations went to war with bands playing and civilians cheering.

There is a type of warfare that has received increasing emphasis since 1945—insurgencies and "wars of liberation." Communism has often supported these wars through internal subversive and insurgent efforts. This form of conflict has generated a counter-use of armed forces in combined political, economic, and military roles, teamed with political and other nonmilitary instruments of policy, because insurgency and guerrilla warfare are not conducted by force alone. There is a trend to limited use of highly professional forces with some of the most modern military technology other than nuclear weapons. This is more like warfare in the nineteenth century than the massive conflicts of World Wars I and II. Nuclear power is a deterrent against a third world war but provides little security for small states unless a Great Power possessing nuclear weapons considers its security to be involved.

Objectives of War—Unlimited and Limited.   Warfare, when total in terms of the involvement of all national resources, can be total in its objectives. The goals of Great Power war today can include more than defeat of armies in the field, exaction of reparations, and the shifting of boundaries. They can now incorporate the complete subjugation of the enemy's people, the destruction and dismantling of his heavy industries and war potential, the reorganization of his government, and the changing of his ideological concepts. The outstanding characteristic of defeat in World War II was the extent of political, economic, and even social and cultural changes ensuing for the defeated peoples. The most pronounced of these changes were imposed on Japan by the Allied powers and on the Central European states by the Soviet Union. The terms and measures taken warn that in the future the total national way of life of states may be radically changed by war, even though these states are not always voluntarily participants.

Societal changes as an objective of modern war, including "wars of liberation," are one of the major modern developments in the nature of war. They increase insecurity and apply not only to the defeated but to the neutral and victorious states. For the social and economic disruption occasioned by war may bring revolutionary change, even without military defeat. Modern total war risks total defeat, which may be in the form of obliteration. The main energizing characteristic of World Wars I and II was that of comparatively unlimited political objectives resulting in unlimited use of military means. If there is to be any check on use of means, objectives must also be limited. Following the timeless truth that he who presses an enemy against a closed door must be prepared for a death struggle, future hostilities are likely to be paced by strong political efforts to stop the fighting before the antagonists become totally committed. If the United Nations had not been born in 1945, we would be creating one now as a message center and dampening device for international crises.

Limitation by Rules of Warfare. Between the seventeenth and twentieth centuries, elaborate rules for the conduct of wars were worked out by international lawyers in order to minimize the hazards of combat. Learned treatises, such as Grotius' epochal work *The Law of War and Peace* (1625), elaborated rules and regulations for the governance of armies and hostilities. Limitations were imposed on the use of certain weapons and procedures by international conventions at The Hague in 1899 and 1907, and at Washington in 1922.

In the twentieth century many of these limitations broke down in the national and racial hatreds generated by both mass hostilities and new technologies. The rules are less easy to apply and enforce in ambiguous wars carried on by proxy or subversion or when violent conflict occurs without formal declaration of war by any party.

Each state is the ultimate judge of its own actions and can be expected to adhere to treaties and agreements on rules of warfare only as long as it believes the gain is greater than that which would be obtained from nonadherence. In the struggle for existence a state may be under great pressure to forego adherence to agreements made in happier times. Military necessity is the prime consideration when defeat or disaster threatens. It must be recognized that there are some sanctions supporting agreements on rules of war. No state, even a victorious one, cares to have a reputation for breaking agreements. States are sometimes interested in reciprocity, and there is often a danger of reprisals. The Germans in World War II hoped their prisoners would be treated well by the Americans, and this may have affected their treatment of American prisoners. A professional military leadership will tend to follow its peacetime indoctrination. If that indoctrination has followed certain rules, the leadership will follow them until state policy changes them.

The obstacles to making any effective legal approach to war less dangerous to civilian security include the advance of military technology and the tactics of insurgent war which often do not distinguish between military and civilian.

SOME NONMILITARY ASPECTS OF SECURITY

Concern over security is usually expressed in military terms. But other forces can penetrate the security of a state and create the same policy dilemmas.

Negative Power Influence. There is a positive aspect of power that can extend to the use of violence. There is also a negative aspect insofar as one state can withhold its support or power from another state that is dependent on it. Today all states have some dependency on others for markets, raw materials, and such subsidies as foreign-assistance programs. A substantial share of the national income of some states, as in Latin America, comes from single commodity exports. Suppose other countries take action to decrease or terminate the essential relationship. If, for example, the United States suddenly stopped the export of dollars to Israel or the import of coffee from Brazil, or if it stopped its arms-assistance program to a country which fears local attack and which has no arms industry or hard currency to buy arms in the world market, what would happen? There are alternatives. An affected country can make internal adjustments or ally with a third country. When Premier Castro decided to sever traditional Cuban ties with the United States, he found alternative sugar markets and sources of arms in China and Russia. This made his country economically dependent on these powers to at least the same extent it had been on the United States. The changes do not necessarily alter the inherent posture of insecurity.

Population and Production. A neighbor's increase in relative strength is likely to arouse feelings of insecurity even though relationships continue to be outwardly friendly. For large powers, such as the United States, the Soviet Union, and China, the "neighborhood" is the world. Traditional relationships have not always been friendly. Population and production strengths can conceivably be quickly used to exert pressures destabilizing any existent balance of power, and their growth in one country is of concern to others, particularly when there are no historic ties of friendship and common purpose. Even a high rate of economic growth in a neighboring state may be a disturbing internal influence. An example of this is provided by the contrasts between Israel and the Arab states; China and the free countries in Asia; and perhaps the effect of the Cuban experiment, should it succeed economically, on other Latin American countries.

Feelings concerning security were often conditioned materially by the size and rate of growth of the military manpower pool—the eighteen to thirty-four age group—of a neighboring or potentially hostile state. Military strength is no longer so closely geared to the ability to raise mass armies, so this element no longer has the same significance for the Great Powers, although it may continue to be vital for some lesser state relationships, such as in the Israeli-Arab relationship. For the Great Powers this concern for manpower has been replaced to some extent by a concern for scientific and technical progress, which in the long run may affect the relative power status of competing states even more.

Ideology and Subversion. A powerful and hostile ideology is a traditional source of insecurity for communities. This was true in the religious wars in Europe, the Roman suppression of Christianity, and the antipathy between Athens and Sparta. More recently, the idea of liberal nationalism was considered a threat by the autocratic governments of the Holy Alliance in the early nineteenth century, and the aggressive drives of the Axis powers threatened the democratic countries in Europe, Asia, and America after the mid-1930's.

Although aggressive nationalism continues to be a source of tension, Communism has replaced it as the ideology creating the most widespread sense of insecurity in contemporary history. We have discussed its tenets and purposes in Chapter 3 and its tactics in the new nations in Chapter 5. It would be misleading to suggest that all peoples, or all leadership groups, understand these tactics, or the capabilities and ultimate objectives of Communism. Optimistic opinions about the extent of insecurity deriving from this source do exist in some parts of the world.

Social Uncertainties. The impact of the industrial and social revolutions upon economically underdeveloped or colonial lands creates additional insecurity. Individual feelings of insecurity are aroused as ancient cultural and social patterns are disrupted and masses of people move into crowded cities, factories, and mining centers and their livelihood comes to depend on a monetary economy subject to commercial and political fluctuations. These feelings of insecurity and uncertainty, when combined with rising and even extreme nationalism, can easily be exploited by leaders who seek to play on the individual's sense of insecurity by blaming domestic maladjustments on foreign powers, particularly former colonial rulers.

The Insecurity of Smallness in a Great-Power World. There are many countries whose peoples and leaders feel that they can sometimes do little directly about their own security, especially if it involves the Great Power blocs. The outwardly detached attitude of the nonaligned states may sometimes have substance and sometimes be only a convenient fiction. Few would accept that Ireland is not an opponent of Communism. Recognition by small states of their insecurity in a Great Power conflict has been reflected in policies of nonalignment, alliance patterns, strong support of arms control and the United Nations, and in an adverse reaction to threats of armed action by states anywhere.

The ultimate security of most nonaligned states depends materially on the power of the United States and a few other states. President Eisenhower, in his telecast of October 10, 1960, quoted these appropriate words of a neutralist head of state, "when we really get into a jam all the neutral peoples of the world really look to the United States to see that her strength is used for maintaining the peace and establishing and maintaining order and some respect for law and for the United Nations in this world." One of the most important sources of insecurity is the possibility of a major United States depression which would decrease the power of the country, divert the attention of its leaders inward from external affairs, and depress the economies of many countries dependent on exports to, or assistance from, the United States.

Vulnerable Geographic Position.   The significance of geographic factors to national security is continually changing. Vital lines of communication become insignificant, or shift, as overseas sources of supply and allies change and subject territories become independent. Deserted areas are no longer a protection, for they can become feasible avenues of attack. The margin of security that the surrounding ocean gave to nations like Britain, Japan, and the United States has rapidly decreased. The North Polar region can be called the Arctic Mediterranean and seen as a "pivot area" of world strategy.

Modern military technology has enabled destructive weapons to cross geographic barriers and even buffer states in minutes, making security much more penetrable. However, security is still a concept held by people and their leaders, and they may continue to have a traditional geographical approach to security until put to some test which defines the realities. Americans were much more concerned over Soviet missiles in Cuba than in Russia, even though the military threat may not have been drastically increased. The political and psychological effect of such proximity of Soviet power would have been considerable.

The United States, in striving to contain Communist imperialism, feels its security affected by two opposing blocs with large and tightly disciplined populations, and advantageous geopolitical positions facilitating thrusts over contiguous land areas into Europe and the Asian Rimland. Another principal concern for security is against nonmilitary threats, such as aggression through insurgency, infiltration, and progressive detachment of free areas. Drastic alteration in the world balance of power might result, with the United States ultimately becoming an isolated island lacking sufficient resources and power to maintain its values. For the United States and other parts of the free world, the boundaries of the concept of national security have expanded.

SECURITY PRODUCES INSECURITY

Both Strength and Incompatibility of Purpose Create Insecurity.
The traditional means to security has been the building and maintaining
of national armed forces. When a state has values or objectives which conflict with those of another state, and one or both might be willing to use
force, there is mutual insecurity. Armed forces and a sense of insecurity
generate counter armed forces, resulting in an arms race and a search for
allies.

Without force in being, there is no security in a world containing
one state willing to use force to effect the changes that are basic to its purposes. Force is of no value unless accompanied by an apparent willingness
to use it. Power, appropriate strength plus the intent to use that strength, is
essential to security, although it will also generate insecurity if the purpose
seems aggressive to another state.

Intent Is a Critical Element. Appraisal of the element of intent is
important in determining whether increased security for one state affects
favorably, adversely, or not at all the feeling of security of other states.
The strengths and weaknesses of the United States since World War II
have generally been strengths and weaknesses to Canada, the Western
European states, and other free world states. A paradox of this condition
has been the reluctance of some of the benefiting countries to expend resources on their own security. In the 1950's the umbrella of United States
strength made possible the policy of neutralism that India and some other
states followed. The strengths and weaknesses of Egypt have been respectively the weaknesses and strengths of Israel, and prior to World War II
the same was true of France and Germany, and of Poland and Germany.

Intent is related to trust and shared values, of which there are only
limited quantities even among states. There seems to be an almost natural
desire among states for a power-balancing arrangement which keeps one
state from becoming too dominant. The very powerful states generate a
natural jealousy and distrust by their power alone, as seen perhaps in General de Gaulle's mistrust of American power and leadership and his determination to have an independent striking force in Europe.

Search for a Security for All. What can be done to increase the
security of states as a group, and for individual states to increase their security, without increasing the insecurity of other states? This is one of the
vital questions of world affairs today. The search for this security must find
a general solution that is not a formula that bases the security of one state

on the insecurity of another. Some argue that technology has now made security depend primarily on measures to control force, rather than the pursuit of force. Each state is responsible for its own security and no state has yet found an adequate control of the force which might be used against it.

Some of the African and Asian states have chosen policies of neutralism and nonalignment. This always retains the option of entering an appropriate alliance. Neutralists can be useful third parties in dampening those conflicts which might erupt into war. Collective security agreements, political arrangements for moderating and settling disputes, and arms control are methods that states will emphasize, because unilateral security is no longer practicable. The basic purpose of the existing groups of great states conflict, leaving no short-term alternative but to maintain a dynamic equilibrium of military power while continuing efforts to strengthen instrumentalities such as the United Nations and regional collaboration, which will be discussed in Part V.

THE CHANGING NATURE OF NATIONAL SECURITY

Not by Arms Alone.   The military aspects of security are the most dramatic, overshadowing all others. They have been drastically changed in recent decades, principally by the thrust of modern technology. But these military aspects have been penetrated by and intertwined with political, psychological, and economic considerations. The management of military power has become an interdisciplinary profession of great complexity. Also, security threats and counters thereto may have little connection with overt armed force. The political and economic aspirations of many states are, in varying degrees, subject to dependence on policies and actions of other states. The cultural and information program can be a weapon. Policies pertaining to such matters are sometimes security policies, illustrated by the title during the 1950's of the United States program for economic and technical, as well as military, assistance—the Mutual Security Program.

Efficacy of the State as a Security Instrument.   The late George C. Marshall, when Secretary of State, stated the foreign policy of the United States "in its simplest form is concerned with those conditions abroad which affect or could affect the future security and well-being of our nation. . . ." His successor, Dean Acheson, defined the fundamental objective of United States foreign policy as the "improvement of the security of the American people by assisting and bringing about conditions which will make for peace."

One of the principal classical reasons for the existence of the state is the provision of physical security for its citizens and protection of their institutions and values. Some states such as the United States and the Soviet Union can still guarantee a high probability of security in the short term. The long-term prospects are less certain. Most states are dependent for their security on alliances, international organizations, or circumstances that leave them, like Switzerland, temporarily in a bayou off the mainstream of struggle. The individual national state can no longer provide the physical means to carry out its responsibility for the security of its people.

This suggests that a consciousness of shared insecurity on the part of nations and individuals may result in the decline of the modern state system and an evolution toward some type of world order more appropriate to meeting the threats to human survival and values. If this were so, our definition of international politics as being primarily concerned with relations among states would then become obsolete.

Decision Making for Foreign Policy

Preamble

WE HAVE BEEN *considering ways in which certain basic factors affect the positions and attitudes of states. These factors make up the environment in which governments formulate and pursue their foreign policies using their own political systems and processes.*

Part III deals with the nature of foreign policy and the political processes through which national decisions are reached on matters relating to foreign affairs. We shall attempt here to provide a basis for understanding the interaction between internal affairs and the foreign policies of states.

A state's foreign policy is the totality of its dealings with the external environment. Foreign policy is more than a collection of official documents, formal records of actions, and public statements. A foreign policy statement can be simple and succinct, such as "54–40 or fight," or it may be complicated and imprecise, as is the case with policy on regulation of armaments. Policy is the overall result of the process by which a state translates its broadly conceived goals and interests into specific courses of action in order to achieve its objectives and preserve its interests.

The decision-making processes of many states do not readily lend themselves to systematic analysis. In some dictatorships policy is primarily the product of one man's judgment rather than that of a consensus developed through a discernible political process. In other states the political structure and foreign policy processes are not yet formed or are subject to recurrent coups d'état. It is possible, however, to examine some features common to most systems.

The governmental systems of the principal states are of three main types—the presidential system functioning under a constitutional-separation-of-powers doctrine; the cabinet system of government with a ministry responsible to a popularly elected parliament; and authoritarian rule. This section begins with a consideration of the nature of foreign policy and of decision making as such. It then proceeds to a comparative study of decision making in sample representatives of the three political systems, examining in the process some of the principal variables affecting the choices open to policy makers in the West and East.

CHAPTER 11

The Nature and Role of Foreign Policy

INTRODUCTION

The foreign policy of a state is the part of its national policy that relates to other countries and is based upon *a priori* conceptions of national interest. Each state must decide what course it will pursue in world affairs within the limits of its strength and the realities of the external environment. Failure to make this decision leaves the initiative with others and may endanger vital interests.

Foreign policy is the key element in the process by which a state translates its broadly conceived goals and interests into concrete courses of action to attain these objectives and preserve its interests.

ASPECTS OF POLICY

Goals and Objectives. States function in a world system with given characteristics that even the most powerful state cannot wholly change. The basic goals of many states are similar. However, there are differences in the meaning attached to certain stated objectives and in the means to attain them.

197

Broad declarations of policy, such as the Monroe and Truman Doctrines, are used to outline objectives that a state will seek in its foreign policy. Under the Monroe Doctrine and its corollaries the United States declared that the Americas were to be no longer subject to colonization or the extension of the European political system. This statement implies that firm action will be taken to meet any challenge. Its effectiveness depends upon this action. Military aid to Greece was given by the United States under the Truman Doctrine when Greece was being attacked by externally supported Communist guerrilla forces.

National Interests.   The basis of all foreign policy is concern for the protection and advancement of what are believed to be the national interests of the state. Secretary of State Charles Evans Hughes said in 1922, "Foreign policies are not built upon abstractions. They are the result of practical conceptions of national interest arising from some exigency or standing out vividly in historical perspective."

The concept of the national interest is complex and capable of different definitions. The national interest can be considered as the general long-term and continuing purpose of a state, although its precise nature and how to further it are political decisions made by those in power.

Four common denominators can be identified among the wide range of perceived interest—national security, economic welfare and advancement, the safeguarding or augmenting of national power in relation to other states, and national prestige. The traditional characteristic of conflict in international politics is the product of different interests, conflicting objectives, and the policies and programs states adopt in pursuit of them.

The differences in policies and programs that lead states into conflicts include such matters as trade, rivalry over markets and sources of raw materials, competition for influence and power, conflicting territorial objectives, and opposing ideologies. These and other differences spring from basic concerns for the safety, strengthening, and advancement of their own societies. But lest the existence of conflict be overstressed, it should be added that states have increasingly found ways to cooperate on policies and programs which further their common interests. The great expansion of international organization and of peaceful interstate relations attests to this. There is more cooperation than conflict in the world today.

Conflicts within a country over the choice of foreign policies and programs to further its interests often pose difficult choices for the policy maker. This was illustrated in the Vietnam War in at least four crucial decisions which had to be made—(1) whether to go into the country with ground forces to engage in overt hostilities with the Vietcong or to restrict

U.S. support to military advisers to South Vietnamese troops, whose will to resist further was deteriorating; (2) whether to authorize the aerial bombing of North Vietnam or to restrict actions to South Vietnam; (3) how far to escalate hostilities in an effort to cause Hanoi to negotiate a peace settlement that would accept the territorial and political integrity of South Vietnam; and (4) to what extent to try to continue the Great Society program of internal United States development while engaging in war in Vietnam.

Each of these decisions found domestic political concerns in some conflict with external political and security concerns. There was criticism on and off college campuses opposing use of U.S. forces in Vietnam and demanding the negotiation of a peace—without giving any formula for accomplishing this. At the other extreme there was criticism for not deciding on greater escalation. Meanwhile, the President and his advisers were also faced with the difficult task of appraising United States interests in Vietnam in the context of interest in the larger conflict going on within Asia and the world, of which Vietnam was not the cause but simply one of the effects, and of developing a suitable long-range policy. For the struggle in Asia may go on for a generation. James Reston summarized the problem in these words, "The need now is for a redefinition of purpose, to see Vietnam in the perspective of Asia, to see what we are doing in relation to what we are willing to keep on doing and where we want to be at the end of 1975, to differentiate between cause and effect." [1]

Some fear that failure to commit resources to Southeast Asia, including Vietnam, would result in a collapse of all free nations there, with a consequent shift in the balance of power, and serious effects on U.S. security. Determination of the national interest in the context of making such choices is one of the most trying, as well as one of the most challenging aspects of the conduct of foreign affairs. But decisions must sometimes be made in such a context.

Policies. Foreign policy is more than a bundle of official papers or a series of pronouncements by high officials. Foreign policy is a country's way of dealing with its external environment. C. B. Marshall, in his book *The Limits of Foreign Policy,* has described the responsible formulation of foreign policy as the "forming of our intentions—as distinguished from our ends—regarding the world external to our national jurisdiction."

Intentions include actions as well as statements of principles and aspirations, and actions depend upon capabilities and commitments. The

[1] James Reston, "Long-Range Asia Policy Sought," *The New York Times,* December 29, 1965.

THE STRATEGISTS

FIGURE 11–1

(© 1966 Mauldin—Courtesy of the Chicago Sun-Times.)

focal point is the relationship of intentions and capabilities to the fact that a state must deal with circumstances and forces beyond its own national jurisdiction.

Policy is formulated by choosing, deliberately or by default, between alternative courses of action. Refusal to make a conscious choice among alternatives is in itself a choice. Selection among available programs and techniques, and their management, is limited by what is considered necessary and possible. The resources and the strength available to the state, as well as the internal governmental processes, the character of national leadership, and other factors discussed in Part II, condition this selection.

Walter Lippmann once wrote, "A policy has been formed only when commitments and power have been brought into balance. . . . Without the controlling principle that the nation must maintain its objectives and its power in equilibrium, its purposes within its means, and its means equal to its purposes, its commitments related to its resources and its resources adequate to its commitments, it is impossible to think at all about foreign affairs." [2]

The process of choice for many states may sometimes result in what is only the "least undesirable alternative." Only rarely does a feasible alternative fail to conflict with some value objective, because most courses of action involve the expenditure of resources. The United States, although supporting the principles of democracy, has at times found it necessary in its national interest to give assistance to friendly dictators.

States strive to anticipate and prepare long-run policy with sufficient astuteness to enable them to realize their basic purposes and objectives. Success depends upon accurate estimation of the effect of the forces shaping the external and the internal environments.

Policies and actions may be in response to present circumstances, or they may be anticipatory. Any action, whether taken because of immediate or because of long-term goals, significantly affects subsequent action. Present alternatives may not be feasible in the future because of the effect of short-term measures. Long-run consequences of present actions must always be considered; no present opportunity is likely to be duplicated.

If a state adheres to a theory which predicates the direction of forces at work in the international scene, as the Communist states do, it will strive to match its actions with what its leaders consider to be the "force of history."

[2] Walter Lippmann, *U.S. Foreign Policy: Shield of the Republic* (Boston: Little, Brown, 1943), p. 7.

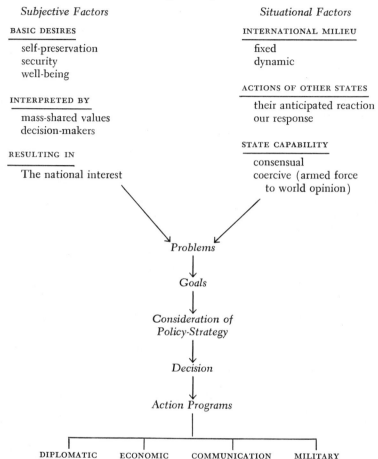

TABLE 11–1

The Foreign Policy Process *

Subjective Factors	*Situational Factors*
BASIC DESIRES	INTERNATIONAL MILIEU
self-preservation security well-being	fixed dynamic
	ACTIONS OF OTHER STATES
INTERPRETED BY	their anticipated reaction our response
mass-shared values decision-makers	
	STATE CAPABILITY
RESULTING IN	consensual coercive (armed force to world opinion)
The national interest	

Problems

↓

Goals

↓

*Consideration of
Policy-Strategy*

↓

Decision

↓

Action Programs

DIPLOMATIC   ECONOMIC   COMMUNICATION   MILITARY

* This diagram is schematic and oversimplified. But it has been found useful as a basis for discussion.

Programs and Commitments.   A successful policy must be appropriate to the desired objectives of the state in the perspective of its own strength and the realities of the world environment. The means applied must be adequate and appropriate to the end in order to bring the power of the state into effective focus. To do this, power must be made explicit through the construction and implementation of concrete programs.

Andrew Goodpaster, for six years Staff Secretary to President Eisenhower, once summarized the essential relationship between policy and program in this comment, "Show me your programs and I will tell you what your policies are." He might have said, "Show me your programs and I will tell you whether you have a viable policy."

A foreign policy program can be defined as a pattern of administrative and operational actions to achieve a defined objective that promotes specific national interests. The Marshall Plan of aid for the postwar economic reconstruction of Europe fits this definition. The characteristics of a program include timing of the tasks to be performed and specific indication of the means to be employed—in terms of men, money, or other resources—for these tasks. Programs may vary from the routine protection and administration of the interests of citizens abroad to the large economic, military, and space programs of the Great Powers.

The United States pursued an "Open Door" policy of commercial opportunity and territorial integrity toward China from 1898 to 1948, but it had few action programs apart from general statements made by Presidents and successive Secretaries of State. In 1931, when the Japanese Army invaded Manchuria and subsequently established a puppet regime in violation of Chinese sovereignty, Secretary of State Stimson announced that American policy would be one of "nonrecognition" of Japanese aggression. When the Japanese invaded China in 1937, the Secretary of State stated that the United States would not assist the Japanese to enjoy the fruits of their aggression, but nothing was done to help the Chinese preserve their territorial integrity. An announced policy not supported by an action program may be regarded lightly by others. Strong action behind U.S. policy in Vietnam made that policy more credible.

RELATION OF DOMESTIC AND FOREIGN POLICY

Foreign policy and domestic policy do not exist in separate compartments. Both are related products of the same leadership and have their origin in the same basic national purposes. Foreign and domestic policy must be mutually supporting to be successful. Economic development of the new countries depends upon foreign investment and machinery. Ability to exert military strength actively over any considerable time depends upon a diversified domestic industrial structure and a sound economy—or help from allies with such resources. Both sets of policies, foreign and domestic, are conditioned by the same ideologies and popular attitudes. Domestic affairs may enhance or damage a country's foreign policy. Hanoi and

Peking can be misled about U.S. resolve by a few American protests against the government's Vietnam policy or by the burning of a few draft cards. Denial of voting rights to Negroes in the Southern states and racial violence have hurt America's image abroad. When the United States redeemed its promise of independence to the Philippines, domestic sugar growers demanded a high protective tariff on Philippine sugar. This illustrates the complications that can arise in the policy process because of the inseparability of domestic and foreign interests. Policy produces inconsistencies also. India and Egypt have jailed Communist leaders while seeking and accepting aid from the Soviet Union for domestic economic development.

External policies do have certain distinguishing characteristics. They are concerned with relationships with other states. Domestic policies are directed toward individuals and groups under the control of the state concerned. Such policies are often embodied in legislation and administrative regulations having the force of law which citizens are obliged to obey. Foreign policies, on the other hand, are executed through negotiation, persuasion, compromise, or coercion; and foreign states have no obligation to collaborate except as their own interests dictate. There is considerable difference between these two situations. There is no certainty that foreign policy objectives can be attained or conflict avoided.

Because it is the chief function of foreign policy to preserve the supreme value of national existence, foreign policy and security policy need always to be considered together.

SOURCES OF POLICY

Tradition, Precedents, National Style, and History. Traditions and precedents are powerful elements in molding people and their leaders. United States traditional suspicion of power politics conditioned its relationships with Europe for over 100 years. Britain's historical role as the "balancer" in European politics has made it difficult for her to adjust to a weakened power position. Many European conflicts in the last 300 years have originated in suspicions and antipathies born of past conflicts, for example, those between the French and Germans, Slavs and Germans. These traditions and precedents make present-day cooperation difficult and underlie foreign policy thinking.

Most foreign policies have an element of inertia ingrained through tradition. Countries that have been allied tend to remain allied or to return to an alliance after periods of interruption. Good-neighbor policies tend to continue. Given a certain orientation, a state tends to maintain its course. Traditionally, friendly relations exist between England and Norway, the United States and Canada, Brazil and Chile. One could speculate that a traditional attitude of hatred for the United States might grow out of Communist China's political campaigns, undertaken since 1949, to inculcate systematically such attitudes among her people.

W. W. Rostow has supported the thesis that nations have a "national style" in their manner of formulating and conducting foreign policy. Americans tend, for example, to think that foreign problems can be solved if American ways are adopted to deal with them. "National style" seems to be a product of tradition, precedent, sense of history, and ideology. Several countries have been changing their national style. For instance, France under President de Gaulle has been exhibiting a highly centralized and personalized policy process in place of the more institutionalized style followed in the Third and Fourth Republics. It is not clear what styles will develop in the new states of Asia and Africa; whether these will be institutionalized, bureaucratic, or highly personalized and hence dependent on those who may obtain power.

Attitudes are formed from interpretations of history as each individual searches for precedents and "truth." The record of the past is not always applicable to present events. Yet interpretations of history are used in reaching judgments on foreign policy. Hence in formative societies historians can influence attitudes and policy formation. Whoever provides the history books and instruction in the new countries may thereby advance across another ridgeline in the struggle for men's minds.

Image of the External Environment.   A state must always adjust its images to the environment of the real world. The government agencies in Washington, although agreed on the overall purposes of national policy, can differ substantively in their estimates of world trends. Allies like Britain and Canada can disagree even further because their backgrounds and perspectives are different. The question for policy is often not, "What is reality?" but rather, "Whose image of reality is the correct one and which one will prevail?"

George Kennan in *The Realities of American Foreign Policy* notes the American tendency to be pragmatic about internal affairs and utopian about external affairs. He suggests that in internal affairs we have recognized that the best we can do will be far from meeting abstract principles. In external affairs it has often been assumed that high principles should prevail. Mr. Kennan thinks this is a dangerously unreal doctrine to apply today. For the world environment is at the same time sane and rational and one where traditional principles are violated in the interests of survival. Mr. Kennan suggests that this situation has given the United States a sort of schizophrenia. Some of the new countries exhibit the same kind of alternation between their desires to live in a world at peace and advance economically, and their wish to eradicate the remnants of white influence and to extend their power.

Looking at the external environment in another way, if the Soviet Union and Communist China are seen as "peace-loving democracies," policies toward them are generally adjusted accordingly. On the other hand, as Mr. Kennan has cautioned, if one views the leaders of these or any other countries as being "aggressors," they are likely to be treated as such and may be left with little choice but to follow such a course. The images acquired become reality to the possessor thereof. Because these images and stereotypes color interpretations of news and condition responses to actions, states invest considerable resources in public information and cultural relations programs, diplomacy, and propaganda in order to create a good image abroad.

Intelligence.   The necessity for understanding the nature of the environment and for having accurate appraisals of the capabilities and intentions of others has long been recognized as essential to the formulation and conduct of foreign policy. Intelligence gathering and interpretation is a proper activity of states. It can be said with considerable truth that most officials, and also many citizens, are to a considerable extent their own intelligence experts. For the individual tends to put faith in his own judgments based on his own knowledge and experience. When knowledge and experience are extensive, there may be a basis for faith in this attitude. Winston Churchill had an extraordinary ability to make almost intuitive appreciations of situations. However, governments cannot trust intuition alone. Judgment needs to be braced with a flow of information and systematic analysis derived from it. For this reason states set up intelligence operations. These operations usually extend to the collection of large amounts of data, systematic analysis of available information in terms of the positions and operations of other states in world affairs, and provision of day-to-day and even hour-to-hour information and estimates to responsible officials.

Although significant espionage certainly goes on, the larger proportion of foreign intelligence work is probably overt, consisting of observation, reporting, and analysis of occurrences in other countries.

Operational military intelligence has generally been guided by a doctrine which includes seeking to determine an enemy's capabilities while passing to some other staff department, or to a field commander, the responsibility for appraising intentions. In the foreign policy field neither capabilities nor intentions are likely to lend themselves to the tidy analysis pattern of operational military intelligence. Intentions sometimes need to be foreseen before the leaderships of other countries have become committed to them or have even formally adopted them. The task of political intelligence and its analysis requires highly talented effort. In the governments of the United States and Britain intelligence studies and reports often have a quality equal to the best articles on international affairs in scholarly journals, even though they may be embodied in secret documents.

Intelligence estimates can influence policy. A misleading intelligence estimate or a failure to flag a developing situation may have a material effect upon a state's position in world affairs; an example of such a situation was provided by Pearl Harbor in December 1941. The Communist attack upon the Republic of Korea may have been partly caused by an erroneous interpretation of United States willingness to defend Korea. The Bay of Pigs episode of 1961 may have been partly caused by faulty intelligence estimates of the strength of forces available to Castro and the weakness of the anti-Castro elements in Cuba.

Correct intelligence estimates do not assure that the choice of policy will be a wise one, or that a selected course will be carried out with maximum effectiveness. But a failure or lack of intelligence greatly increases the hazards of foreign policy.

Leadership. Foreign policy is a material product of leadership. Its formulation and direction lies ultimately with the head of the government or the ruling party of each state. Leadership is supplemented by public opinion and organized interest groups, which may restrain as well as support the policies and freedom of action of leaders. Thus, Arab opposition to the existence of Israel limits President Nasser's policy. In considering the role of leaders, attention should also be given to their schooling, previous experiences, associations, and personal ties, for these also influence their attitudes and their actions and reactions. If a leader has not been outside of his country and has associated with a limited circle of acquaintances, his views are likely to be parochial. The experiences encountered in his rise to power are likely to color his interpretations of foreign affairs, particularly if they have involved clandestine and revolutionary struggle. Thus one must take into account a good many features of background in considering why certain leaders behave as they do and in appraising the policies of their governments.

Political heads of state and their foreign secretaries often travel abroad to meet and to try to influence other leaders. Some states are devoting considerable attention to providing education for talented students from developing countries, some of whom will undoubtedly become leaders. These efforts recognize the important role leadership plays in the formulation of foreign policy.

YARDSTICK OF CHOICE—THE NATIONAL INTEREST

There is no more fundamental element in the decision-making process than identification of the national interest in specific circumstances. Yet the number of available definitions of the national interest indicates that scholars are far from agreed on its precise nature.

Robert Osgood defines national interest as a "state of affairs valued solely for its benefit to the nation." He lists some of these as the preservation of territory, independence, and fundamental institutions; self-sufficiency in the conduct of foreign relations; national prestige; and national aggrandizement. W. W. Rostow says that the "national interest is the conception which nations apply in trying to influence the world environment to their advantage." Hans Morgenthau, one of the principal exponents of the analysis of foreign policy through national interest and considerations of power, declares that the idea of national interest can embrace a whole gamut of meanings determined by the "political traditions and the total culture context within which a nation formulates its foreign policy." Some scholars believe that the national interest coincides substantially with moral principles. Alexander Hamilton had no doubt about the importance of interest to a nation's policy. He said that government is an agent and cannot give away the nation's interests.

It may be affirmed as a general principle that the predominant motive of good offices from one nation to another is the interest or advantage of the nation which performs them. . . . An individual may, on numerous occasions, meritoriously indulge the emotions of generosity and benevolence, not only without an eye to, but even at the expense of, his own interest. But a government can rarely, if at all, be justifiable in pursuing a similar course. . . .[3]

During one of their wartime meetings President Roosevelt is said to have urged Prime Minister Churchill to give Hong Kong back to China.

[3] Alexander Hamilton, *The Federalist Papers*, No. 26.

To Churchill's reply that he could not give away His Majesty's possession, Roosevelt countered that he would see the King about it. Churchill closed the matter, however, by commenting that His Majesty was not permitted to give away His Majesty's possessions. This would compromise the national interest.

The national interest can be described as the total values and purposes of a state applied to a particular set of circumstances, and seen in relation to the means available for their realization.

Problems in Identifying the National Interest. Dealing with the national interest is particularly hard for a democratic government. Popular support must be won for the chosen course of action, and opinions may be sharply divergent. Consensus on the national interest is necessary in fundamental matters relating to independence and security, and on any policy requiring significant resources for its execution. Unless a nation knows its interests and prepares to safeguard them through policy and action, its direction in foreign affairs may be determined more by accident and the actions of other states than by its own choice.

In foreign economic relations, the idea of the national interest is conceived differently by advocates of free trade and of protectionism. In the United States there has been general agreement on the necessity to liberalize trade and extend economic assistance to other countries.

Different conceptions of the national interest have been most conspicuous in the discussions over American policy with regard to Vietnam. Some argued that interests could be secured only if the United States were to engage in an all-out war with the Communists, regardless of world reactions or the possible involvement of China. Others opposed the expenditure of human and material resources and the war itself. The Johnson Administration sought to build a consensus for the idea that limited military action was required by the United States to uphold the independence of South Vietnam and to maintain that country's right to be free from interference from North Vietnam—"neither withdrawal nor massive escalation," as summarized by Vice President Humphrey in March 1966.

Crystallizing National Interests and Objectives. In a democracy conceptions of national interests and objectives become articulated through many channels. The press, members of the legislative body, political parties, patriotic societies, veterans' organizations, business and professional groups, labor unions, and even religious bodies voice opinions and help to crystallize the national interest. In authoritarian societies national interests are determined by the elite in power.

It is not always easy where many groups are free to voice their views and their special interests to identify with certainty what the public regards as the national interest. Attitudes and perceptions are not constant and sometimes change rapidly. Similarly, where the political system provides a structure of checks and balances or a division of powers, as in the United States, opinions within the government may diverge to the point that national action can become stalled until the political process works out a sufficient consensus. The conflicting views of Woodrow Wilson and the Republican majority of the Senate produced a long stalemate on American acceptance of the Paris peace settlement of 1920. In the end, the country refused to follow the President's policy and withdrew from the order which its arms had helped to fashion. In a cabinet and a two-party system of government like Britain's, where the government is made up of the party having a majority in Parliament, there is less likelihood of a deadlock because of disagreements upon the national interest. If government and opposition have nearly equal representation, a cabinet may be compelled to compromise more than usual.

In countries where governments comprise coalitions of several parties, with no party having a clear majority and with fundamental divisions, national policy and action can be rendered unstable or forced into weak or compromising positions. This happened in France under both the Third and Fourth Republics.

Importance of Gauging Interests and Objectives of Others.   One of the most important tasks before policy makers is to gauge accurately the national interests of other states. Allied states must make this assessment in order to work together.

Western statesmen have often been criticized for not perceiving the objectives and strategies of the Communist powers. Major efforts have been made recently to study Communist behavior. Fundamentally, Communist and Western interests are based on differing perceptions of world realities. The long-run objectives of the Communist states are clear in Communist doctrine. They are to overthrow non-Communist governments and establish a Communist world. Short-term intentions are less obvious. These states have employed devious tactics to mask their true intentions and their diplomacy has often been suspect. As a consequence, after deceptions and broken agreements, other states have become increasingly cautious in their relations with the Communist powers.

Permanence and Change in Interests.   The fundamental interests of states tend to persist, but the means by which they are expressed and the methods used to promote them are adapted to circumstances.

Until 1945 there was little doubt in England that British interests lay in control of the seas, possession of bases, and on maintaining a balance of power in Europe sufficient to prevent any single power from dominating the continent. From the seventeenth to the twentieth centuries, Britain maintained the most powerful navy in the Atlantic and allied or associated herself with various European states, including Russia at times, to control the European balance of power. The changing economic, military, and political circumstances since World War II have turned British interests to close military and political ties with the United States, participation in NATO, and dissolution of the empire while emphasizing the Commonwealth association.

United States long-term interests in the integrity of the American continents have persisted. The principles of the Monroe Doctrine have been reasserted by American Presidents and Secretaries of State in the face of a foreign threat. The most striking example occurred in 1962, when President John F. Kennedy found it necessary to face an atomic showdown with Russia over her emplacement of long-range ballistic missiles in Cuba. Unlike the United States situation in the 1930's, when Japan effectively nullified the "Open Door" policy for China, President Kennedy, backed by the people, had both the resolution and the means—an effective program—to support the principle that the Americas are not open to foreign intervention or colonization.

Conceptions of what the national interest requires can change radically. In 1917 and again in 1941 the United States reversed its policy of isolation to participate in World Wars I and II. After World War II the United States continued the association with its allies and made new coalitions—NATO, ANZUS, Rio Pact, etc.—to oppose aggression. Environmental changes obviously affect conceptions of national interest. Development of modern air transport, reducing the significance of time and distance, has increased the scope of states' security interests. Foreign policy thus carries with it the implied proviso of "until further notice" and the implication that it will be reviewed as conditions change.

Sacrificing National Interests. Alexander Hamilton argued that no government will intentionally sacrifice the national interest of its country, although it may misjudge the implications of its own policies or those of others. The exigencies of war may cause a government to end hostilities in a manner that will leave no practical choice but to surrender portions of the national domain to another. A state may find itself with no alternative to war but to make a concession counter to its interests. Czechoslovakia, for example, bowed before Hitler's demands for partition in 1938 and 1939 after it was made apparent at the Munich Conference that neither Britain nor France would support armed resistance to the Nazis. The Finns, on the other hand, determined on war with Russia in the winter of 1939, when Moscow presented them with territorial and political demands they deemed irreconcilable with the preservation of national independence. Poland and other Eastern European states, such as Czechoslovakia in 1938, had little room for maneuver at the end of World War II, when under the Red Army occupation they were compelled to accept Soviet protection and satellite status. No independent state will voluntarily choose such a subservient position, but occasions do arise when there is little opportunity for any other course but to bow to the will of a superior power and hope for a day when the national interests can be served more in accord with the wishes of the people and the traditions of the country.

GUIDELINES TO CHOICE

Political Realism. Are there any general guidelines for charting the relation between national purpose and specific courses of action, other than judging national interest according to the situation? Legalists who favor establishment of world order through law have argued that national policy should be guided by the norms of a world code of law. Others contend that politics must be dealt with pragmatically, using legal means when available and applicable.

Kenneth Thompson, in *Political Realism and the Crisis in World Politics*, writes that the political realist must accept the necessity for facing problems on their merits and in the context of the ways that other actors on the world scene are dealing with them—one of these ways being through choices based on national interest, not some ideal blueprint. It is our belief that political realism offers the most practical approach to the handling of foreign policy questions. Although idealism and morality affect policy through conditioning the attitudes of peoples and their leaders, they are not alone an adequate basis for choice in policy making.

Idealism and Morality. Idealistic formulas have generally been associated with the search for peace, a goal which has become more pressing as the potentials of thermonuclear war have become better known. In the twentieth century, pacifists of the Quaker faith, world federalists, neutralists, and some nuclear scientists have been disturbed by the present nature of international relations. Discussions of disarmament often bring together idealists and realists who argue about peace as the central issue. Woodrow Wilson's approach was idealistic when he declared that, "It is a very perilous thing to determine the foreign policy of a nation in the terms of material interest." And again he said, "We dare not turn from the principle that morality and not expediency is the thing that must guide us." Views such as these rest upon a series of untried assumptions about the rational nature of man and the moral nature of international politics. The Marxist-Leninist doctrine, promising universal peace in a Communist world, is another "idealist" approach to international politics.

George F. Kennan, in *American Diplomacy 1900–1950*, takes issue with Wilson's analysis of international politics. Kennan affirms that one of the causes for the failure of past United States foreign policies was their great emphasis on "moralism." Successful policy depends on considerations of material interests and power, otherwise the nation will be led into foreign crusades, endless commitments, and wars with unlimited objectives.

States do subscribe to some broad declarations of principles, as in the United Nations Charter, and do aspire to a reputation for a morally upright foreign policy. North Korea and China both used progapanda campaigns to try to establish that they were not the aggressors in Korea. The United States has prestige and influence deriving from a reputation for acting on principle. President Harry S. Truman summarized this when he said that the "foreign policy of the United States is firmly based on fundamental principles of righteousness and justice." George Washington's counsel that "honesty is the best policy" remains a practical, as well as a moral, enjoinder. The exercise of moral judgment in making choices in affairs of state is complex, for values of the state must be balanced with those of individuals and the universal objectives of peace and security.

We are inclined to agree with Arnold Wolfers that although personal morality has a relationship to foreign affairs, the ethics of individuals are not always appropriate to problems of state, and relations between states should not be judged on the same basis as those among individuals. Dr. Wolfers comments, "Much of what strikes people as immoral practices of governments may prove to be morally justified by the peculiar and unhappy circumstances which the statesman has to face and which, moreover, he may be unable to change." [4] This is moral realism. It may be shocking to those who hold to an absolute ethic. But the conduct of foreign policy continually involves making choices which, because of circumstances, cannot always be the "best," but must be the "least worst" among the limited choices available. The soundest yardstick for judgment in such situations is generally thought to be the enlightened self-interest of the nation.

[4] Arnold Wolfers, "Statesmanship and the Moral Choice," *World Politics*, Vol. I, No. 2, January 1949, pp. 175–195.

THE PROCESS OF FORMULATING FOREIGN POLICY

The Apparatus of Choice.   Each state has a process for formulating and conducting foreign policy. In some instances this process is highly institutionalized and predictable; in others it is largely personalized and no more predictable than the whim of a leader or dictator.

Policy is generally decided upon and guided by the head of government, whether president, prime minister, or dictator. A government department headed by a major official—called a secretary of state, secretary for external affairs, or secretary of foreign affairs—manages the routine conduct of foreign policy and is usually the primary source of advice on policy matters. Many states have an intelligence organization, sometimes partly concealed in other government agencies, whose function it is to acquire and sift the raw data of information on other countries needed to assist the head of government in making policy decisions.

Other government departments enter into the process of choice in varying degrees. They may be very important at times, as the Department of Defense has been under Presidents Eisenhower, John F. Kennedy, and Lyndon B. Johnson, especially when charged with conduct of programs in support of foreign policy or when charged with executing internal policies affecting external affairs. The Treasury Department of the United States and the Exchequer in Britain have likewise occupied important roles in foreign policy making through their ability to influence monetary policy and foreign economic transactions.

The legislatures of many states have an influence upon policy making through their control of the purse and the power to authorize essential action programs. They also often exercise a negative kind of check through provision of a public forum for questions and criticism, and the authority to approve nominations and treaties. Furthermore, individual members of the legislature often have the ear of the head of government and are able to exercise a personal influence upon policy choices. Such is frequently the case in the United States with such senior members of the Senate as the Majority Leader, the chairmen of the Armed Services and Foreign Relations Committees, and other trusted members of the Congress.

A General Approach to Policy Formulation.   In a well-institutionalized political system the policy process customarily includes the following: (1) A general assessment of the state's international position in relation to other states, neighbors, rivals, and allies. (2) The broad principles of conduct which the state upholds and which it advocates with respect to international affairs. (3) Specific objectives and national interests which the state seeks for itself in foreign relations and for the course of world affairs generally. (4) An appraisal of the state's capabilities and whether they indicate bold action or caution, self-reliance, or political, economic, or military ties with others. (5) The strategies, commitments, and tactics that are undertaken for the realization of the state's objectives and interests.

When the policy process embraces a systematic approach, it tends to provide predictable and reasonably consistent patterns of decision making. When policy depends on the reactions or whims of a single person, such as was the case with President Sukarno of Indonesia, there can be little assurance of a steady pattern of policy apart from certain broad trends like a pro- or anti-Western policy, or neutralism and nonalignment.

Kenneth Thompson sees five common elements or unifying threads in the policy planning approach. The first is that there are few absolutes in international politics. Lord Acton once counseled that an "absolute principle is as absurd as absolute power." The second feature is a respect for the lessons that can be learned from history. A third essential is for the policy maker to understand himself, his nation, and the outside world. A fourth unifying thread, specifically applicable to the United States, is a dissatisfaction with the ideas about foreign affairs which were widely held in the 1920's and 1930's, that power politics and the balance of power are unmitigated "evils" and that the use of force should be abandoned. The fifth unifying thread of the policy-planning procedure is a skepticism about the practical usefulness today of the so-called idealistic approaches to foreign affairs. The troubles of the world are not to be explained by single actions or even single errors in foreign policy. Former Ambassador Kennan supplements this with a warning against looking to the diplomat or the policy planner "for any belief in human perfectibility, for any optimistic philosophy of public affairs."

Policy planning seeks to avoid the restriction of rigid norms of "good and bad." In Ambassador Kennan's words, the sources of conflict and tension are always "specific, never general." They are "devoid of exact precedents or exact parallels." There is the related recognition of the limits to which available policies can affect the international environment and that the flow of policy is really a flow of choices among limited alternatives, none of which are likely to seem wholly satisfactory.

Uncertainty and Risk as Elements of Choice. The formulation and conduct of foreign policy involves some elements of risk. Altogether, the conduct of international politics is an art rather than an exact science.

One of the fundamental principles of policy making is that of the "calcu-lated risk." But the risks are matters of political judgment, and they are seldom worked out in mathematical terms.

The corollary to the principle of risk is the need to maintain some margin for maneuver, that is, to "keep the future open," to be able to adopt an alternative policy or adjust a selected course of action to de-veloping events. This may involve a conflict between the maker and the executor of policy. The former wishes to remain flexible as long as possible because of the imponderables, and the latter needs specific guidance for the provision of resources that involve legislation, appropriations, produc-tion, and the creation of an operating organization.

Seven elements of uncertainty and risk can be identified in connec-tion with foreign policy. First, there is the element of chance, the acci-dental occurrence of some event not foreseen when a policy is being evolved. The occurrence of the Hungarian revolt in 1956 at the time of the British-French attack upon Suez is an example. Policy makers did not see this coming in advance. Second, there is miscalculation. This may be based on wrong information or on faulty judgment of the external situation. The Communist assault on South Korea was a miscalculation of United States willingness to defend the Republic of Korea and of the length of time it would take to bring effective forces to bear on the situation. Third, irra-tional action may cause a state to embark on a course that considerations of reason, rather than emotion, would counsel against. The establishment of East Pakistan, separated from West Pakistan by the land mass of India, is a case in point. This was determined upon emotional and religious grounds. The territories cannot hope to be united and ad-ministration of two such widely separated areas places a heavy drain on Pakistan's resources. Fourth, states may behave in a manner inconsistent with their past practices and commitments. President de Gaulle's request that allied forces and NATO headquarters leave France or submit to her control, although in keeping with de Gaulle's own conceptions of grandeur and independence, was hardly consistent with France's role as a NATO ally and with her policy from 1948 to 1965. Popular agitation and mass demonstrations in foreign countries pose a fifth element of uncertainty and risk in connection with foreign policy. This is illustrated by the forced cancellation of President Eisenhower's visit to Japan in 1960 because of student demonstrations in Tokyo. Foreign policy being a flow through time of relationships and actions, a sixth element of uncertainty is pro-vided by the intangible factors of friendship and suspicion, goodwill and misunderstanding that can arise between leaders and countries, and the sheer uncertainties that must accompany relationships with many countries whose governments are not stable but are subject to coups and frequent change. Finally, a seventh element of risk and uncertainty arises from the operation of foreign policy itself. The decision maker can never be wholly certain what the outcome of his policies and the programs taken to implement them will be. Neither timing nor level of achievement follow a direct cause-and-effect relationship. Racing technological change, with its infinite nuances, compounds other elements of uncertainty in making the outcome of policies and actions unpredictable, for with it come changing perceptions and values, and shifting reactions and judgments.

LIMITATIONS AND REQUIREMENTS OF FOREIGN POLICY

Expanding Requirements for Policy. Only a few countries—and these generally the Great Powers—required an extensive body of foreign policy until recently. Small countries often confined their relationships to a few neighbors and it was possible for some to adopt courses which eliminated the need of many policies. Japan's isolation until the arrival of Commodore Perry in 1854 successfully avoided all foreign policy. The United States isolationist policy provided a simplified course for policy makers. The coincidences of geographic isolation and the checking of power by power within Europe gave the United States a margin of safety in foreign affairs. Bismarck is reported to have once commented that "God takes care of fools, drunkards and the foreign policy of the United States."

Foreign policies have expanded in number and content for several reasons. The demise of colonialism has increased the number of sovereign states. Over fifty independent states are now responsible for foreign policies that used to be made in London, Paris, Washington, The Hague, Brussels, and Rome. The growing interdependence of states leads to an increasing need for external policies. And to these other causes are added the multiplication of international conferences and of international organizations which call upon states to develop policies on an ever enlarging circle of issues. The large agendas and voting procedures of the United Nations involve each state in determining policies on matters they might not otherwise consider.

These circumstances pose difficulties for many of the developing countries. For whereas countries like the United States, Britain, and France can place professionally staffed embassies in many countries at the same time, supplemented by special missions to international conferences, many of the newer states, with their limited means and few trained personnel, have all they can do to staff their Foreign Office, a few embassies abroad, and a United Nations mission. This is one reason why the United Nations forum has become an important clearing house for many of the newer states.

Limitations of Policy.   Referring back to the definition of foreign policy given at the beginning of this chapter, it may be that the best a state can do in affecting its external environment may still fall short of its value objectives. That best may be no better than a recognition of the trends taking place in the environment and the least dangerous adjustment to them.

The choices and effects of policy are limited by the necessity for cooperating with other states having similar objectives, and by the limits which politics and competence place upon decision makers. This is true both for security and also for trade and political matters, as the world becomes increasingly interdependent.

Secretary of State Dean Rusk, in writing about the tasks of the American President shortly before taking office, said,

> If realism requires us to avoid illusions of omnipotence, it is just as important that we not underestimate the opportunity and the responsibility which flow from our capacity to act and to influence and shape the course of events. Involved is not merely a benign concern for the well-being of others but the shape of the world in which we ourselves must live.[5]

It is the function of foreign policy to shape the nature of this world environment as best it can with the means available to it and within the limitations that surround its decision makers and executors.

[5] Dean Rusk, "The President," *Foreign Affairs*, Vol. 38, No. 3, April 1960.

CHAPTER 12

The United States Foreign-Policy Process

BACKGROUND OF UNITED STATES POLICY FORMULATION

The United States approach to world affairs is heavily conditioned by the past. Sources of policy are to be found in the statements of Presidents and Secretaries of State, past diplomatic actions, treaties, executive agreements, laws, operating programs, and domestic and overseas public opinion.

Mass of Foreign Relations. No state has ever dealt with such a quantity of foreign relations as does the United States today. The State Department cable and radio traffic exceeds the combined output of the Washington bureaus of the United Press and Associated Press news services. The United States is associated with approximately 400 international organizations and is represented at an average of fifteen international meetings every day. The foreign policies of other countries are materially affected by United States foreign policy and action, by estimates of United States capability, and by what the country does or does not do.

Both the content and process of policy are complicated by the breadth of modern policy, the necessity that actions prove and support policies, and the institutional arrangements in which decisions are made and implemented.

The span of United States policy has been greatly extended in the second half of the twentieth century by the economic and political interdependence of nations, the ideological struggle, and the requirements of national and joint security with other countries. Dean Don K. Price of the Littauer School of Public Administration at Harvard, speaking of the change that has occurred in foreign affairs, sees the need for a new realism in the American outlook that will acknowledge the limitations on our ability to reform the world environment, although we have reversed our traditional policy of aloofness and accepted the need for alliances and long-term commitments. Still the American people may be only beginning to realize the extent to which they are committed, budgetarily and otherwise, to actions by the implications of accepted policies.

Men and Policy Making.   It is understandable that concern should arise over the effectiveness of our policy-making process. Roger Hilsman, before he became Assistant Secretary of State, observed that, "It is almost traditional in America to view affairs as a problem in public administration," a comment similar to one by the late Whitney Griswold, former President of Yale University, who speculated that this country might be missing some of the important substance of policy in the "organizational redundancy" of the "administrative ant hills in which our foreign policy is defined and the intricate filtration system through which it must pass before it can be executed."

Strong policies are made by individuals who may require the assistance of committees and other staff machinery. Since 1960 somewhat less emphasis has been placed on formal procedures and organized bureaucracy and more on the personal judgments and actions of the President and the Secretaries of State and Defense. The complexity of policy and of its execution demands experienced men able to keep abreast of the rapidly changing world.

Policies and programs depend basically on individuals. At the upper levels of a political system, organization charts are not very significant. Changes in organization may lead to improvements in the quality of staff. They may speed up the process of decision making or insure that programs are more closely integrated with policy. But as former Under Secretary of State Robert Lovett once noted, "No organization chart is a substitute for a sense of common goals."

Most Americans visualize policy making in terms of the structure and procedures of government. Policy making does flow within the institutional framework of the executive and legislative branches and institutional machinery does provide a useful analytical tool for studying the policy process. But policy making stems from the thinking of and relations between individuals working within the machinery, rather than from inanimate institutions as such.

Policy a Product of Overlapping Directorates and Shared Powers.

Professor Richard Neustadt of Harvard's Kennedy Institute of Politics has pointed out in his study *Presidential Power* that our institutional arrangements for foreign affairs were fashioned on a model of power sharing on the assumption that these affairs would be minimal and best subject to a system of "checks and balances." So power in foreign affairs is exercised under the President's authority to initiate and direct foreign policy, the House of Representatives' authority to appropriate funds, and the Senate's right to consent to treaties and to confirm appointments.

Power and responsibility for foreign policy are "shared and overlapping," but the substance of policies and programs ultimately reflect the views of those who are able to wield the principal power, normally the President and the executive branch. Congressional and public support are needed to give any policy an assured stability and continuity. Although there is a high degree of consensus among the American people on the basic purposes and goals of policy, differences do arise over specific ways to achieve these purposes. The American tradition of vigorous public debate can influence external affairs. National security is, according to an old rule, something statesmen should say the least and do the most about. When policy making is conducted openly, with the press and radio not always accurately reporting statements or facts, the effectiveness of decisions and actions can be negated. Yet within this milieu the President and his assistants must achieve a flow of decisions on situations demanding their attention.

The Policy Process Viewed in Operating Perspective.

The process through which foreign policy grows and evolves can be divided roughly into three overlapping parts: (1) "policy formulation," which is the President's special prerogative; (2) "policy direction," by which is meant detailed guidance of the conduct of foreign affairs in ways consistent with overall policies, which is the task of the Secretary of State and the State Department; and (3) "programs of implementation," which are the tasks of many agencies but principally of the Department of State, the Department of Defense, and the foreign assistance administration.

No clean-cut boundary exists between the terms *policy* and *program*. Policy is meaningless without programs to execute it and give it substance. Programs in turn shape the future content and flow of policy. Former Secretary of State Dean Acheson spoke of foreign policy as a "method and a direction," which implies responsibility for the officer routinely applying broad policy concepts to concrete day-to-day problems and to the formulation of programs. In the Department of Defense a "program" is understood to be a combination of activities directed to the objective of executing policy with specifics "as to time phasing of what is to be done and the means proposed for its accomplishment," including budgetary support.

Professor Robert R. Bowie of Harvard University, formerly Director of the State Department Policy Planning Council, has given a schematic model of the thought process by which foreign-policy decisions are reached. This process entails (1) a continuing appraisal of external conditions and how they are likely to develop in ways affecting a nation's interests; (2) the selection of concrete practical objectives related to the political, security, economic, and other goals of the country; and (3) the marshalling of available means for influencing the environment in the direction of the national objectives, when specific situations arise calling for action by the country.[1] These means may extend from the writing of persuasive diplomatic notes and the sending of instructions to officers in the field to the offering of material inducements and, if need be, the deployment and utilization of instruments of force.

In addition to these three interacting variables, the President must also integrate the relevant internal factors into his appraisal. He cannot get too far ahead of the public, nor can he afford to overlook the fact that the continuance of his party in office depends upon the support he can win for his policies and leadership.

The process mentioned by Professor Bowie also involves defining the problem that has to be met and the objectives to be achieved, assembling necessary information relating to these and analyzing ways of dealing with the problem, including developing alternative courses of action and weighing their respective merits and disadvantages, their costs, potential advantages, and risks. A decision requiring financial or other support is not finally made until the resources needed to back it up are assured. And almost any important decision requires that the public be informed in order to obtain backing from this quarter.

Policy making requires more than decisions on general lines. Such decisions may in fact be made implicitly as operations proceed. Policy making occurs within the parameters of what is considered possible. This accordingly involves a careful appraisal of the actions and the means

---

[1] Robert R. Bowie, "The Secretary and the Development and Coordination of Policy", in Don K. Price, *The Secretary of State* (Englewood Cliffs, N.J.: Prentice-Hall, 1960), pp. 51–75, esp. 55–57.

needed to attain desired ends. The officials who have responsibility for carrying out action programs and providing the necessary means need also to be consulted and informed, for as we have said, policy grows as execution proceeds. Such consultation and coordination is not always easy in the large bureaucracy now concerned with foreign affairs in the U.S. political system. The National Security Council, in principle, provides an institutionalized process for facilitating consultation and coordination. But the Council has been ponderous in operation and has been resisted by some elements in Washington. Presidents since Dwight Eisenhower have relied upon other ways of consulting and disseminating information on important policy questions. Some of these other ways of coordinating action will be discussed after describing the operation of the policy-making process.

THE CHIEF EXECUTIVE AND THE POLICY PROCESS

The President—Center of the Policy Process. Within the executive branch of the government the President's leadership and responsibility are clear. Under the Constitution he is responsible for formulating foreign policy, for initiating programs to carry out policy, and within the bounds of law and of resources provided by Congress, for executing policy. Alexander Hamilton claimed that the President has all powers in international affairs "which the Constitution does not vest elsewhere in clear terms." He has a monopoly on the right to communicate with foreign governments, to recognize and break relations with other governments, to negotiate and conclude treaties with foreign governments, although two thirds of the Senate must give consent to make them binding. He also has the authority to make executive agreements, which are less formal than treaties, providing these are within the framework of existing law and do not have to be approved by the Senate. The scope of this latter function is indicated by Secretary of State John Foster Dulles' comment in 1953 that 10,000 executive agreements had been entered into as a consequence of the NATO Treaty.

Only the President can mobilize the raw power of the nation, including the Armed Services; the Foreign Service, with its more than 100 missions overseas; the numerous assistance missions; the Central Intelligence Agency; and the Federal Bureau of Investigation. As Commander-in-Chief of the Armed Forces, the President has the responsibility for military command and action, which can bring the military might of the nation behind his policies. In his person and office the President symbolizes the nation to the external world. He also leads the formulation of public opinion and the shaping of a national consensus on foreign policy. Furthermore, he is responsible for presenting legislative and financial proposals to the Congress to implement his policies.

Each new President on taking office inherits a foreign policy in being from his predecessor and programs for its execution. This body of policy includes elements that go as far back into history as Washington's Farewell Address and the Monroe Doctrine. It includes a national style reflected from past leadership and public opinion as well as extensive operating programs which are bound to become inputs for any new policy. Each President must continue, check, or alter and supplement this policy as he thinks best. Presidents add a personal touch that becomes identified with their administration, as Truman's policies toward Greece and Turkey, Eisenhower's policies toward the Near East, President Kennedy's Alliance for Progress program for Latin America, and President Johnson's "peace offensive" to end the war in Vietnam.

The President is assisted, and sometimes inhibited, in his policy task by the attitudes and actions of the other two main components in the policy process, the Congress and the public. Executive-legislative relations have ranged from President Wilson's stormy battle with Congress over the Paris peace settlement at the end of World War I, to the extraordinarily cooperative Congress which President Johnson had in his first year in office. The American public similarly fluctuates in its support of Presidential policies. There has been a measure of backing for maintaining United States strength in Europe through the NATO alliance, but much less so for implementing the SEATO commitment in Southeast Asia. Foreign assistance has not been a popular foreign policy program, despite the fact that every president has considered it essential to the attainment of America's goals. This lack of public support has no doubt lain behind the grudging acquiescence accorded to foreign aid bills by Congress.

Role of the President's Advisers. The President has at least four groups of advisers available to him on foreign policy matters. These four are (1) the Secretary of State and his immediate senior assistants; (2) the White House staff and certain agency heads in the Executive Office of the President, such as the Directors of the Atomic Energy Commission, the Space Agency, the President's Science Adviser, and the Director of the Bureau of the Budget; (3) the Secretary of Defense and his senior assistants, together with the Joint Chiefs of Staff; and (4) trusted individuals outside of public office, to whom the President may turn for counsel or assistance. Because national security and the availability of military power for supporting foreign policy objectives are a large concern to any president, the advice of the Secretary of Defense and the Chiefs of Staff is pertinent to a significant number of foreign policy problems.

The President can take advice on foreign policy from any source. There have been instances when the President has paid only limited attention to the Secretary of State. A White House adviser, Colonel Edward House, was President Wilson's chief foreign policy adviser during World War I. Franklin D. Roosevelt rarely consulted Secretary Hull and earned the reputation for being his own Secretary of State. He did, however, turn for advice to several personal aides, including Harry Hopkins and Ben Cohen, and to his Secretary of the Treasury, Henry Morgenthau, who was particularly influential on matters pertaining to the treatment of Germany. President Eisenhower at times appeared to be influenced by his Secretary of the Treasury and Director of the Budget, as well as by his Secretary of State, when financial commitments were involved. President John F. Kennedy frequently consulted his brother Robert and other members of his family. President Johnson leaned heavily upon Special Assistant McGeorge Bundy until his departure from government, and sometimes preferred to handle issues himself rather than looking to the Secretary of State. President Johnson also turned to his Secretaries of Agriculture and of Health, Education, and Welfare, as well as to Vice President Humphrey, in building programs for Vietnam and developing support behind them.

These personal advisory relationships emphasize two basic aspects of the policy process: the link between internal and external policy and the President's lonely position of ultimate responsibility for decisions. As President Kennedy once remarked,

> There is such a difference between those who advise or legislate and . . . the man who must . . . finally make the judgment. . . . Advisers are frequently divided. If you take the wrong course, and on occasion I have, the President bears the burden of the responsibility quite rightly. The advisers may move on—to new advice.[2]

When a President fails to press the decision process, whether from weakness on his part or lack of interest, foreign policy is bound to mark time or suffer unless he is aided by a strong Secretary of State who is able and willing to take initiative into his own hands. Such fortunately was true when Warren G. Harding had as his Secretary of State Charles Evans

---

[2] Quoted by Theodore C. Sorensen, *Kennedy* (New York: Harper, 1965), p. 391.

Hughes, runner-up for the presidency against Woodrow Wilson in 1916, and Chief Justice of the Supreme Court after 1923. Nowadays the President is usually surrounded with an able corps of special assistants in the White House staff, appointed by himself, who keep him advised on decisions needing to be made and who assist in alerting and convening his principal policy advisers.

The White House Staff. The President's White House staff includes a group of personal assistants who devote much of their time to matters connected with foreign affairs. Each President determines the size and use of this staff. Relationships with Congress demand politically adept individuals with a broad knowledge of the problems and issues of government.

Most recent Presidents have employed variants of a staff system originated by Franklin D. Roosevelt, in which one or more personal assistants covers each major area of interest and responsibility. President Eisenhower also utilized a White House Secretariat to keep a record of decisions, actions, and opinions and to check on problems and issues on which the President should be informed and advised. President Eisenhower's system was characterized by an absence of foreign policy advisers who might compete with responsible Cabinet officers, such as the Secretary of State. His system emphasized decision making through deliberation strongly oriented toward security considerations. Other Presidents—such as Roosevelt, Kennedy, and Johnson—have included on their staffs experts on foreign affairs and defense and retained for themselves the decision-making function on a wide range of questions. The system of personal assistants has been designed to insure that essential information is brought to the President's attention when it is needed and that the President's views, when formulated, are made known to and understood by executive officials.

It is essential that the President personally devise and maintain a strong leadership in foreign affairs and assure that the machinery of the government carries out policies effectively. Formal and informal meetings of the government officers principally concerned with problems under consideration are held under White House aegis to elucidate for the President major aspects of foreign policy problems and to assist him in reaching decisions.

The National Security Council (NSC). The National Security Council was made the principal Presidential advisory body on national security matters by the National Security Act of 1947. The Council is composed of the President (chairman), the Vice President, the Secretaries of State and Defense, and the Director of the Office of Emergency Planning. The

Chairman of the Joint Chiefs of Staff and the Director of the Central Intelligence Agency are statutory advisers. The President may ask anyone else to attend and use of the Council depends entirely on each President. President Eisenhower made extensive use of the Council, and a subordinate planning system that was created to service it. Presidents John F. Kennedy and Lyndon B. Johnson made little formal use of the NSC, each preferring to operate less formally and more personally, still using the knowledge and counsel of responsible officials and trusted advisers. The NSC is the only statutory advisory body on foreign policy. Too frequent use of the Council invites the contention that the national security aspect is overemphasized.

The NSC is a personal instrument of the President and can be used to whatever extent he desires as a staff and advisory agency to formalize policy decisions. Or it can be largely ignored if the President prefers to function primarily by telephone and other less formal consultation and meetings. The process of policy making at the top level must go on more or less the same, whatever the format chosen by the momentary occupant of the White House. Such organizational arrangements as the Senior Interdepartmental Group designated by President Johnson provide a way for deliberation and coordination. The important thing is that the President have before him all the relevant facts and issues when they are needed and that the consequences of alternative courses be thoroughly explored before important decisions are made.

Importance of the Budget. Preparation of the annual budget is a key aspect of policy formulation. Policies require supporting programs and the budgetary process supplies the required financing. The Bureau of the Budget is the staff arm of the President, preparing the budget and supervising the expenditures of the operating departments. Theoretically, the Bureau has no power in itself. In practice it has very great power, because the President cannot make all the detailed assessments of government programs. In addition, the Bureau usually has an objective for total annual expenditures in keeping with Presidential guidelines, within which all government programs must be fitted. The Bureau not only appraises the more than $50 billion of the defense budget, but also advises on such matters as State Department requests for money for an enlarged Foreign Service, for higher pay, and for so-called representation allowances (called "whiskey money" by some skeptical legislators), which permit American representatives to compete with other countries in their lavish hospitality. Presidential decisions on the allocation of dollars are an important part of the policy process.

The Bureau of the Budget also processes all legislation which the

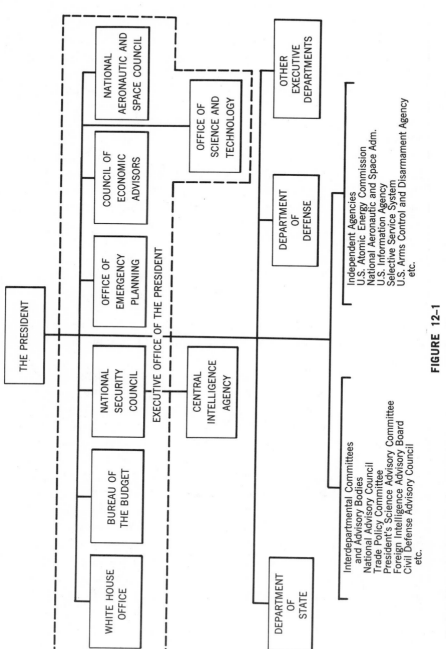

FIGURE 12-1

National Security Organization Within the Executive Branch *(From United States Government Organization Manual, 1966)*

President recommends to Congress, whether originating in the White House or in a department, whether for defense, for the Great Society, or for foreign aid. In this capacity it is impossible at times for the Bureau to avoid giving advice which influences policy. Arthur Smithies of the Department of Economics at Harvard stresses, "Until a country has made its budgetary decisions, it may have objectives, strategies, hopes and fears; but it has not got a policy until it has committed resources to the obtainment of its objectives." [3]

THE RESPONSIBILITIES AND FUNCTIONS OF THE EXECUTIVE BRANCH IN THE POLICY PROCESS

The key foreign policy aide to the President is the Secretary of State. It is his responsibility to serve as adviser on policy and as manager of foreign affairs. The power of the Secretary of State rests primarily upon his role as assistant to the President. Early in his administration, President Eisenhower made this role quite explicit when he said, "I personally wish to emphasize that I shall regard the Secretary of State as the Cabinet officer responsible for advising and assisting me in the formulation and control of foreign policy. It will be my practice to employ the Secretary of State as my channel of authority within the Executive Branch on foreign policy." President Eisenhower stressed more than is usual the "channel" of authority and chose a very strong personality in John Foster Dulles for his first Secretary of State.

The Responsibilities of the Secretary of State. The Secretary of State not only advises the President on policy formulation, but also is a public leader and diplomat. The Secretary must represent the executive branch before Congress on matters relating to foreign affairs. In addition, he is responsible for administering one of the most complicated departments of the government. The Secretary has an extensive corps of senior advisers including two Under Secretaries, several Assistant and Deputy Assistant Secretaries of State, the Policy Planning Council, and many experts. These attempt to maintain and administer national policy and to chart long-run interest and trends for United States policy.

The Secretary of State needs to be compatible with the President and to share a mutual respect. He usually sees the President several times a

[3] Arthur Smithies, "Defense Budgets and the Federal Budgetary Process," unpublished paper delivered at the University of California, May 5, 1960.

week, and when on diplomatic missions sends him regular reports. The Secretary will rarely bring the President good news or an easy problem. Dean Acheson and President Truman; John Foster Dulles, Christian Herter, and President Eisenhower; and Dean Rusk and President Johnson have been highly compatible and have shared a mutual respect. James Byrnes and President Truman were not so compatible, and the relative infrequency of Byrnes' reports from abroad may have contributed to his early replacement by General George C. Marshall.

The Secretary supplements the President's role of making complete and continuous expositions of foreign policy essential in a democracy. Generally, the Secretary is an effective and desired witness before Congressional committees relating to foreign affairs. In democracies with a free press, statements made for domestic information are quickly made available throughout the world. Consequently, the President, the Secretary of State, and the Secretary of Defense must be careful with their use of words in public statements.

The Secretary of State is a diplomat and negotiator as well as a policy adviser. Some argue that the Secretary should concentrate on his other responsibilities and leave diplomacy to the career diplomats. Others consider that high-level negotiation and representation should be principally the task of politically appointed personages who represent the President personally, such as Ambassadors Stevenson and Goldberg at the United Nations. But the Secretary of State cannot avoid engaging in two major areas of diplomacy. First, he is the individual whom chiefs of foreign missions in Washington strive to see on matters of concern to their governments. Second, we live in an era of personal diplomacy, in which foreign ministers meet and confer frequently. The Secretary of State may limit his negotiating activity to a minimum, as Secretary Herter did. Or, depending on the President's wishes, his own confidence in the men on the spot, and his personal involvement in policy efforts under way at the time, he may travel extensively, as did Dulles, and negotiate personally. Policy is certainly shaped and developed by negotiation, and no Secretary is likely to overlook this. His negotiating experience is an important aspect of the foreign policy task. Compared to John Foster Dulles, Secretary of State Dean Rusk did less traveling, preferring to have others come to him in Washington. Under Secretary George Ball and Ambassador-at-Large Averell Harriman compensated for this, however, by carrying on missions abroad at the President's and Secretary's request.

Function of the Department of State. One of the main functions of the Secretary of State is the direction of the Department of State, which is the center of attention of the foreign embassies in Washington. The Department assists the Secretary in his own actions and helps to formulate his views for the President. Its main task, however, is to execute policy through instructions to some 300 offices abroad, including over 100 embassies, and several hundred annual delegations to international conferences and organization meetings. The Department's task also includes providing policy guidance to other departments operating abroad. Because of the increasing mixture of foreign affairs with the responsibilities of the Defense and other departments, both the Secretary and his subordinates are in continual communication with their opposite numbers in other agencies.

In the daily flow of the policy process much of the detailed work must be done without direct reference to the Secretary. Messages always carry his signature but only the most important are seen by him, and relatively junior desk officers now despatch messages which before World War II would have had to be cleared by the Secretary. The mass of business leaves no other recourse. The foreign ambassador resident in Washington and his country's routine relations with the United States are handled by a regional office in the State Department under an Assistant Secretary.

Precedents, treaties, Presidential, National Security Council, and other policy decisions, public statements by the President and the Secretary, all guide the administration of policy. Where there are no precedents, new policy lines must be sought. These may be based on advice from the Secretary of State and his senior aides, including the Policy Planning Council, or from the President or White House staff.

The policy process begins with the Department's appraisal of a situation. This involves consideration of the existing world environment, the domestic situation, and the availability of resources. Even the President must follow essentially the same analytical process. President Truman's rapid decision in 1950, made within a matter of hours, to use United States armed forces in Korea contained all these elements in an incisive appraisal. The difficult decision reached by President John F. Kennedy and his advisers to meet the Soviet missile armament of Cuba with a demand for supervised withdrawal and his order for a naval quarantine of Cuba, with their implicit possibility of the use of armed force, was another decisive appraisal at the highest level. Long-range planning of policies suitable for a rapidly changing world depend on the Secretary of State and the members of the State Department Policy Planning Council. The genesis of the Marshall Plan and the building of the NATO alliance were results of farsighted policy planning. Although much effort goes into systematic long-range planning, adverse shifts in the external environment cannot be

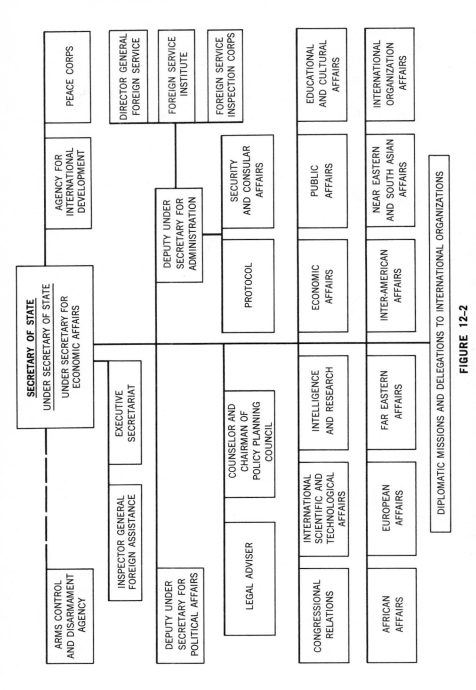

FIGURE 12-2

The Department of State (*From United States Government Organization Manual, 1966*)

attributed to inadequate long-range planning and inflexibility, although the probabilities of such changes should be foreseen.[4]

For a detailed description of the flow of policy-making procedure in the Department of State, it is suggested that the reader turn at this point to Appendix A at the back of the book. There will be found a résumé reproduced from a study prepared by the Brookings Institution for the Senate Foreign Relations Committee describing how the officers of the Department and of other related agencies customarily deal with foreign policy issues. This description is a hypothetical case study of the application of policy in an operational context and is generally valid over time. Another title of the Appendix might have been "Policy in Operation."

Participation of Outside Agencies.   Interest in policy formulation and execution extends beyond the President's office and the Department of State. There is an increased connection between internal and external policies. Tariff and monetary policies are no longer internal affairs, but world affairs. Such internal elements as stability, inflation, economic growth, segregation, and public information are related to foreign affairs and can have a serious impact upon them.

National security considerations are often dominant concerns in foreign affairs, demanding an intricate meshing of political, economic, and military elements of policy. The two decades after World War II have shown that there are no longer any purely military problems.

Execution of foreign policy comprises many different types of operations, from diplomatic representation to foreign assistance programs. Many agencies of the government are now actively involved under the policy direction of the White House and advised by the State Department.

There are as many as fifty agencies, commissions, or departments with an interest in foreign affairs. These range from the Treasury Department, with its responsibilities for customs and monetary policies; to the Department of Commerce interest in tariffs; and to the National Aeronautics and Space Agency, with its tracking stations scattered about the globe.

The complex functioning of the government is bound to produce problems in the flow of policy and the guidance of operations. Inevitably, the continuous policy direction of the State Department and the functions of execution overlap. Herein lies the principal area of friction between policy and execution, to which management experts, Congressional committees, and committees of distinguished citizens have directed a great deal

[4] The genesis of the Marshall Plan is recounted by Joseph M. Jones in *The Fifteen Weeks* (New York: Viking, 1955).

of study. Different administrations have handled these problems in different ways and probably always will. President Johnson initially sought to cope with the situation through his own efforts and an expanded role of his Presidential assistants, particularly Special Assistant for National Security Affairs McGeorge Bundy. But he later shifted to give greater emphasis to the role of the Department of State. The methods change, but the problems persist.

The Role of the Department of Defense.   The influence of security matters, and hence of the Department of Defense, on foreign policy formulation has been one of the major developments of the two decades since World War II. The following observations were made by the Brookings Institution in a study prepared for the Senate Foreign Relations Committee:

No development affecting the contemporary organization of foreign policy-making is more significant than the impact of military affairs on the daily relations between the United States and other governments. This is unprecedented in times of relative peace, and the trend is likely to continue in future years.

In an era when the position of the United States in world affairs rests so substantially on the nature and strength of its military posture and when the pace of weapons development is so swift, it is foolhardy for major military decisions to be made without the most searching considerations of their political and economic implications.[5]

One might add that in a time when national security is overshadowed, as it is now, every hour of every day, by foreign nuclear weapons capable of devastating large sections of our society, and when relations with other countries are important to the preservation of national security interests, foreign policy must be closely linked with security needs and carefully analyzed by those competent to weigh them.

The Brookings report accepts the integrated responsibility of military and State Department policy makers, concluding that

Regular procedures should be established whereby the senior officials of the State Department can, as a matter of course, bring their views to bear on major defense decisions, including choices regarding weapons systems, force levels, and planning for military contingencies that may confront the United

---

[5] *The Formulation and Administration of United States Foreign Policy*, prepared by The Brookings Institution for the Senate Committee on Foreign Relations, Study No. 9. 86th Congress, 2d Session, Washington, 1960.

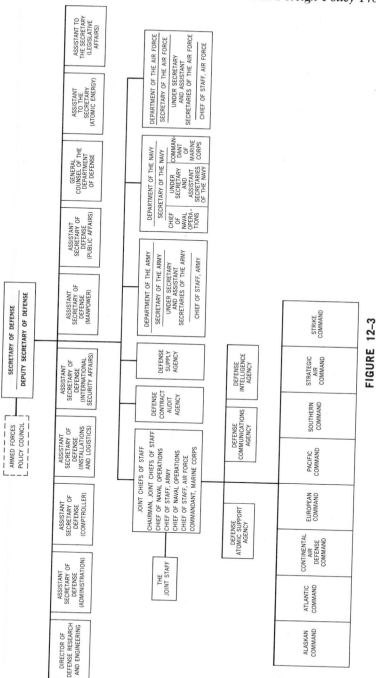

FIGURE 12-3

The Department of Defense (*From United States Government Organization Manual, 1966*)

States. Under modern conditions, these are as much the concern of officials responsible for the nation's foreign policy as political decisions are rightfully the concern of military policy makers.

The result is a need for interaction between departments immediately below the President. This raises a question with respect to the role of the Secretary of Defense. Should he be thought of primarily as a business manager of a more than $50 billion operation? Or should he be considered as a statesman primarily concerned with military affairs, directing enormous resources, and acting as a deputy to the Commander-in-Chief? Secretary Robert McNamara strove to fulfill both roles. He exercised a vigorous managerial direction of the huge operation at the Pentagon and simultaneously served as a principal advisor to the President on foreign policy matters having security implications and involving the use of military resources.

Cooperation is vital between the Secretaries of Defense and State, and at all levels of the two Departments. This is furthered by having an Assistant Secretary of Defense for International Security Affairs and sections corresponding to State Department divisions. There are also staff divisions in the Joint Chiefs of Staff and in the three military service departments to integrate foreign policy into military plans and operations. Several Foreign Service officers fill positions in the Pentagon, one in the Joint Staff, and several military officers hold positions in the State Department, one on the Policy Planning Council. The interlocking of interests is also indicated by the careers of several individuals who have held high positions in both departments, such as General Marshall, Robert Lovett, and Paul Nitze. The military assistance program is operated as a separate "service," subject to State Department guidance and ambassadorial supervision. Military strategy, now heavily conditioned by alliances and political-psychological aspects, is intimately linked to foreign policy. Foreign policy in turn rests heavily on the capabilities of forces in being and on the military budget. The flow of policy must be a two-way proposition between the two departments, and fortunately, this is the case most of the time.

Science and the Policy Process.   As parts of the executive branch, the President's Science Advisory Office, the Atomic Energy Commission, and NASA also participate in the policy process.

Science and applied technology are an inescapable element in policy considerations, as we have noted in Chapter 9, and their influence cuts across the traditional organizational lines of government. Dr. James R. Killian, of the Massachusetts Institute of Technology, formerly President Eisenhower's Assistant for Science and Technology, has pointed out that more Foreign Service officers need to have education in science and engineering and that universities need to make more adequate provision for preparing scientists to occupy policy roles in foreign affairs. Science and engineering have important contributions to make to foreign policy in security, technical assistance programs, the exploration of outer space, and arms control. The race to put a man on the moon, to orbit scientific laboratories, to photograph remote celestial objects significantly affects the prestige and image of the nation as well as having communications and defense values. Exchanges of data and scientific information promote better relations and further the development of space communications, meteorological satellites, and other activities transcending boundaries. The international rapport among scientists is a definite element in foreign relations and plays a substantial part in some types of negotiations, of which arms control is an important example.

There are organizational problems in integrating consideration of science and technology into the policy process, although some progress has been made on these. The Department of Defense now includes many officers having graduate degrees in science, including the social sciences. Over 35 per cent of West Point graduates now achieve advanced degrees in science, for example. The Secretary of State has a Science Adviser, and there are now science attachés at some embassies.

The extent to which scientific experts are consulted in the policy process depends upon the subject under consideration and the personalities concerned. Pressures of time and realities of administration make it easier to consider an element like science through competent individuals in the normal channels of the policy process rather than by depending on special advisers and committees. Science and technology are not ignored in the decision-making process once it is apparent they are relevant and have something to contribute.

Correlation and Coordination of Policy Operations. Efficient administration is a difficult but essential part of the policy process. We do not propose to go into the details of public administration here. But three examples will illustrate the problem and the trend of United States administration of foreign operations. All U.S. government agencies operating in any one country, of which there are fourteen in Brazil, for instance, are now placed under the direction of the ambassador to insure a measure of coordination among operating agencies. Most ambassadors concert policy and coordinate operations by a "country team" organization of the heads of the principal agency missions in their country. As another example, the Bureau of the Budget now requires preparation of foreign programs on the basis of their objectives rather than on the basis of the initiating agency, to permit comparison and integration among all agencies.

As a third example of ways of getting policy both formulated and carried out, President Johnson in 1966 extended to the Washington level the application of the concept of the "country team." A Senior Interdepartmental Group was set up under the chairmanship of the Under Secretary of State, with separate regional groups chaired by the respective Assistant Secretaries of State. The permanent memberships of the groups concerned (State, Defense, Foreign Assistance, Information, Intelligence, plus White House representation) represented agencies carrying on the bulk of operations in foreign affairs. In some ways the design of the arrangement closely resembled the National Security Council operation of President Eisenhower, expanded in responsibility to broader areas of foreign affairs, and adjusted organizationally from the statutory membership and other requirements of the National Security Act to the changes wrought by the passage of two decades. Newspaper reports described the new arrangement as making the Secretary of State the "director" of overseas operations, other than military, affecting two or more departments. The arrangement underlined a point made by former Assistant Secretary of State Harlan Cleveland several years earlier. "We have passed (hardly realizing it) from the era of *foreign relations* to the era of *foreign operations*." [6]

THE CONGRESS AND POLICY MAKING

President Truman once declared to a group of visitors, "I make American foreign policy." What a President can do in law, however, he may be unable to do in politics. The President, as Commander-in-Chief and head of the executive branch, has impressive power to make policy. But if his policy requires legislation, as much policy does, then he must look to the Congress. Even President Johnson, whose relations with Congress set a modern standard for harmony, found himself in some difficulty securing "consent" for his Vietnam policies.

Congressional leverage in the field of foreign affairs is exercised primarily through the advice and consent function of the Senate with regard to treaties and appointments, the appropriations authority of the House of Representatives extending from normal running costs of the State Department to military and economic aid programs, and through resolutions,

[6] Harlan Cleveland, *The Promise of World Tensions* (New York: Macmillan, 1961), p. 155.

hearings, and investigations that can originate in either body. Examples abound of Congressional ability to utilize these powers to help shape important policy measures. Senators Tom Connally of Texas and Arthur Vandenberg of Michigan were members of the United States delegation which drafted the United Nations Charter. Negotiations of the 1963 nuclear test ban treaty were conducted before a panel including several Senators. Within two weeks in 1962, Congress adopted resolutions expressing determination to use all means to defend U.S. rights in Berlin and Cuba. A similar resolution was adopted after the Tonkin Gulf encounter between U.S. naval ships and North Vietnamese torpedo boats. The hearings conducted by the Senate Committee on Foreign Relations under Senator Fulbright's chairmanship on Vietnam and on U.S. policy toward China provide an example of Congressional determination to examine and to influence the President's foreign policy decisions, for Congress, like the British monarch, has "the right to be consulted, the right to encourage, the right to warn."

The development of a consensus on foreign policy involves elaborate processes of bargaining. These are, because of the dispersion of power in American society, as complex and subtle as those required for domestic policy. As Professor Clinton Rossiter has stated, "Ours is just about the only legislature in the world over whose decisions the executive has no final power of persuasion, either in political fact or constitutional theory." [7]

The Overall Role of the Congress. Congress legislates, appropriates, and sometimes helps in the leadership of public opinion. It has the right to formulate general goals in legislation and it can identify major problems and suggest alternative courses of action. It also evaluates past policies and programs through hearings, and it maintains a large flow of informal political contacts with the executive branch and the public.

The great increase in foreign affairs has changed executive-legislative relationships from those envisaged when the Constitution was drafted. It is now impracticable to submit great detail to Congress, and most agreements with foreign governments now take the form of executive agreements, rather than treaties, and do not require the consent of the Senate to become effective. On the other hand, individual members of Congress, such as Senator Mansfield, the majority leader in the Senate, may participate closely in the President's planning and assist in decision making and in conveying personal messages from the Chief Executive to foreign leaders. Such a procedure gives the President an additional channel of contact with

[7] Clinton Rossiter, *The American Presidency* (New York: Harcourt, 1960), p. 54.

foreign leaders when he sees fit to utilize it, as well as giving Congress a feeling of increased participation in foreign affairs.

The Participation of the Congress in the Policy Process. Congressional committees are a primary instrument of legislative participation in policy making. Among the twenty standing committees that deal with international matters, the House and Senate Foreign Relations Committees (called Foreign Affairs in the House), the Armed Services, and the Appropriations Committees are the most central in securing legislation and appropriations, and in advising the President. The legislative process for effective support of foreign policy measures requires an authorizing law, handled by the authorizing committees, for example, Foreign Affairs in each house, and appropriations to support it, handled by different committees (Appropriations). The uncertainty of continuity in policy is frequently increased by Congressional provision of only temporary authorization of a program. Foreign assistance was "temporary" from the Marshall Plan through the mid-1960's. There are a few instances of new policy being initiated by Congressional legislation, but almost all important legislation is recommended by the executive branch. The President's veto is available to block legislation he does not like, although Congress can override this veto. Congress can also exercise a negative influence by refusing to consent to treaties or appointments or by tacking riders onto bills the President cannot veto without great inconvenience.

The advisory and checking functions of Congress, and Congressional leadership of public opinion, do contribute to policy formulation. At the same time, neither Congress nor its committees are organized to operate quickly, and time often counts heavily in dealing with foreign affairs. Neither the parliamentary nor the authoritarian systems have the cumbersome machinery imposed by our system of checks and balances.

In fairness to the Congress, it deserves to be said that some Congressmen working on foreign affairs and related matters often have more experience than executive-branch officials who testify before them, and are often widely traveled in foreign areas of their interest. Leaders such as Senators Vandenberg, Connally, George, Mansfield, Russell, and Jackson have been influential in policy making, in counseling with the President and the Secretaries of State and of Defense, and in molding public opinion. The principal contribution of most Senators and Congressmen is, however, support for executive policies and programs within the Congress.

Foreign policy is not usually a crucial issue in the election of Representatives and Senators, except in time of war. Most Congressmen are therefore reasonably free to vote as they think best on foreign policy matters. The dangers of Congressional attention to foreign affairs include too much consideration, delay, and restraint, particularly on operational details in a rapidly moving and unpredictable world, and in the development of a schism between Congress and the White House, which can hamper executive-legislative cooperation.

Presidential Leadership and Congressional Bipartisanship. The President, the Secretaries of State and Defense, and their assistants are careful to keep key members of Congress advised on foreign policy and national defense. It has been estimated that Cabinet members often spend as much as one sixth of their time consulting with Congress and appearing before its committees. There is no known record of the number of "foreign affairs breakfasts" Presidents have had with Congressional leaders.

Party discipline is often loose on foreign policy matters, even though the leadership of one party rests with the President. For this reason and because foreign policies and their supporting programs are often long-range, extending beyond a given administration, bipartisanship does develop. Republican Senators Dirksen and Leverett Saltonstall repeatedly supported the foreign policy positions of Democratic Presidents Kennedy and Johnson, in the interest of national unity. Such support is particularly helpful in giving maximum credibility abroad. Support of the United Nations, NATO, inter-American policies, and the foreign-assistance programs has extended over three or more administrations, with strong bipartisan support. Bipartisanship becomes particularly important when the Presidency is held by one political party and the Congress by the other, as was the case when the Marshall Plan and NATO were brought forward under President Truman, and during six years of the Eisenhower administration.

The Congressional opposition has the prerogative of withholding support and of criticizing executive policy. This is an opposition's chief stock in trade. Hence it can be argued that bipartisanship works best when reserved for the most important and long-range matters vital to the national interest. Opposition can hinder the smooth flow of the policy process if it comes from within the President's own party, as when Senator Fulbright of Arkansas, Chairman of the Senate Foreign Relations Committee, attacked President Johnson's policies in Vietnam and the Dominican Republic. A President can counter by withholding information, which of course can still be sought through hearings, and by entrusting activities often performed by such senior Senators or Representatives to others. But a schism between the President and senior Senators of his own party on a foreign policy issue is bound to give hope and comfort to foreign opponents and is avoided whenever possible.

Presidents have deliberately cultivated bipartisanship by appointing distinguished members of the opposition party to defense and foreign policy posts. President Franklin D. Roosevelt began this practice by inviting Republicans Frank Knox and Henry L. Stimson to be Secretaries of the Navy and of War in 1941. President Truman made Senator Vandenburg and Governor Stassen delegates to the San Francisco United Nations Conference. Since then it has been customary to have bipartisan representation at the annual meetings of the United Nations General Assembly. This policy has the dual advantage of presenting a united front to foreign countries and of orienting opposition leaders in the hope they will later support the pertinent administration policies. President Truman made John Foster Dulles, later Secretary of State for President Eisenhower, head of the American delegation to negotiate and sign a peace treaty with Japan. President Eisenhower made few appointments from the other party, but Presidents Kennedy and Johnson returned to the practice in some of their appointments.

These are some of the ways in which attempts are made to overcome the divisiveness of partisan politics and to prevent it interrupting the foreign policy process. There is nothing that encourages bipartisan support in the Congress quite so much as the knowledge that the people are strongly behind their President and will resent any Congressional attacks on his efforts.

THE PUBLIC

Public Interest in Foreign Affairs.   Professor Gabriel Almond, in his book *The American People and Foreign Policy*, says that "the function of the public in a democratic policy-making process is to set certain policy criteria in the form of widely held values and expectations," leaving the actual formulation of policy to those who have a positive and informed interest. These values and expectations are defined in the Constitution; in our attitudes toward foreign affairs; and in our ideals, such as peace, democracy, and an orderly free world. It is doubtful that people are willing to leave policy to the government policy makers or that the policy makers should ignore the competence of those outside of government. Personal interest and experience in foreign affairs has expanded greatly. Perhaps 15 million Americans have served overseas in the armed forces, and a million travel to Europe each year.

The private sector's interest in foreign policy is a two-way street. The

State Department and other agencies seek the advice and assistance of private individuals and institutions, and the public, particularly the press media, seek policy expositions from the government. The methods used extend from White House study committees through a wide variety of consultant and contractual arrangements. Such associations draw more completely on the reservoir of wisdom of the country and sometimes help to increase public understanding through the contacts of consultants with the people.

Foreign Affairs and the Public. The public is continually faced with a massive stream of information and interpretation concerning foreign affairs. Newspapers, magazines, radio, television, syndicated columnists, and many speeches of national leaders deal with aspects of foreign affairs. Organizations such as the Foreign Policy Association, World Affairs Councils, the American Assembly, and others help disseminate information and promote public discussion on major issues. Formal college education hardly dealt with international affairs prior to World War II. Indicating the change, the Ford Foundation commented in a 1966 report entitled *Context the World* that college programs dealing only with non-Western regions had doubled in ten years.

One can ask whether the trend of increasing information, education, and public interest enables the American public to make better judgments on specific issues. There is a danger that public comprehension may not keep up with all of the information being poured upon it. Uncritical acceptance can lead to confusion and belief in easy solutions. On the other hand, a well-informed public is the beginning point of support for sound national policies in a democracy such as this.

The public can act as a brake on policy if the President believes that public support is inadequate. It can be an impetus to policy through indications of dissatisfaction with the trend of events, and it can influence specific aspects of policy through the pressures of vocal segments of the public, including pressure groups and the press.

The public-interest groups include columnists, editorial writers, general-interest organizations, and assemblies of prominent citizens. Special-interest groups continually spring up to influence particular policies, like the Zionists and U.S. policy toward the Near East, and the Committee of One Million on China to oppose recognition of Communist China. Some Congressmen have scored the "locust horde" of lobbyists that descend upon them every year to exert pressure for passage of special interest legislation or opposition to governmental policies. The cynic might quote Yeats, "The best lack all conviction, while the worst are full of passionate intensity."

The press is in a unique position to influence the public by what it does and does not publish and broadcast and by forming public attitudes. President John F. Kennedy is quoted as having said of the press,

. . . there is a terrific disadvantage in not having the abrasive quality of the press applied to you daily . . . even though we never like, and even though we wish they didn't write it, and even though we disapprove, there isn't any doubt that we could not do the job at all in a free society without a very, very active press.[8]

Policy makers in Washington take public opinion into account and try to judge the significance of shifts in this opinion. The views and sentiments of organized interest groups are available, as are newspaper editorials, books and articles, and public-opinion polls. These are, of course, only fragments and are at times difficult to interpret as a whole. Probably the views of the public that are communicated to the decision makers through well-informed individuals and the mass of correspondence that pours daily into Washington have as much to do with forming a sense of national consensus as anything.

In the final analysis, continuing support of costly programs can only be maintained as long as there is an informed and enlightened public opinion. Strengthening and preserving this is an indispensable part of the overall policy-making task. This in turn needs to be reinforced with awareness that goals cannot always be attained at once and may require sustained effort. There is relevance to the adage, "Foreign policy problems are not solved; they just wear out as they are replaced by other and more difficult ones."

CATEGORIES OF FOREIGN POLICY DECISIONS

Viewing the decision-making process in the context of the history of United States foreign relations it is possible to distinguish three types of decisions that have confronted those charged with responsibility for conducting the nation's foreign affairs. These three categories of decisions are (1) changes in, or development of, a major basic policy; (2) crisis decisions requiring some massive effort; and (3) routine decisions on day-to-day issues. It may be argued that the last category is not truly decision making but rather the

[8] Quoted by Theodore C. Sorensen, *Kennedy* (New York: Harper, 1965), pp. 313–314.

conduct of foreign affairs. But in a rapidly moving world situation large ends can flow from seemingly small decisions.

The shift of United States policy away from isolation and toward a commitment of great resources to world cooperation and containing Communism was a major policy change. As Joseph M. Jones points out in his book *The Fifteen Weeks*, analysis of the problem, strong executive leadership by President Truman and Secretary Acheson at a time when the Congress was of the opposite party, and a well-prepared information campaign to mobilize public support for the Marshall Plan were inherent in the success of this policy change.

Not all major decisions of this nature are compressed within equally short periods of time. Some, such as the decisions to intervene in World Wars I and II, are the result of a gradual build-up, one crisis after another compelling the country to recognize that a shift away from a previous position is inescapable.

Crisis decision making is illustrated in the decision of the government to break the Soviet blockade of Berlin in 1948 by means of the airlift, a course that could have led to war; the decision to intervene in Korea with armed force when the Republic was invaded by the North Koreans; the decision to extend the American military effort in Vietnam to bombing North Vietnam; and the decision to intervene with force in the Dominican Republic in order to safeguard American lives and forestall a possible Communist takeover following the outbreak of civil warfare in 1965. In this last instance it was appreciated that unilateral United States action would lead to a large outcry in Latin America. But it was felt the stakes were so high that no chance could be taken of having another Castro-type revolution on the American doorstep, and Washington moved immediately to convert the peace-enforcing force to an Organization of American States effort with officers and troops from other republics. In crisis situations there may be little time in which to prepare public opinion in advance. The public may have to be informed simultaneously with other governments, as President John F. Kennedy did in the Cuban missile crisis.

The great mass of decisions in foreign policy are the steady flow of day-to-day actions. This type of decision making is illustrated by the history of the foreign-assistance policy starting with the Greek-Turkish Aid Program and the Truman Doctrine in 1947 and continuing through the years since then by a host of legislative hearings, investigations, and perhaps thousands of detailed decisions on economic and technical aid to other countries. The bulk of the foreign policy decision process comes within this category, whether it pertains to allied, neutral, or other countries.

CONCLUSION

Alexis de Tocqueville, writing in *Democracy in America* over a century and a quarter ago, summed up the difficulties which the policy process faces in this democracy in these words:

> Foreign politics demand scarcely any of those qualities which a democracy possesses; and they require, on the contrary, the perfect use of almost all those faculties in which it is deficient. Democracy is favorable to the increase of the internal resources of the state; it tends to diffuse a moderate independence; it promotes the growth of public spirit, and fortifies the respect which is entertained for law.

Against these advantages de Tocqueville added the following cautionary note.

> But a democracy is unable to regulate the details of an important undertaking, to persevere in a design, and to work out its execution in the presence of serious obstacles. It cannot combine its measures with secrecy, and it will not await their consequences with patience.[9]

There is much in United States history to vindicate de Tocqueville's judgments. United States policies, programs, and policy processes have been criticized for apparent inability to anticipate and plan for future needs in the shifting patterns of international politics.

Some argue that our institutional procedures for dealing with foreign affairs are inadequate. Among the weak links are the hiatus in top-level leadership which occurs every four years, when attention turns to electing a new President; the appropriations process, which is separated from legislative authorizing actions by the Congressional committee system; and the principle that no Congress can bind its successor, thereby limiting assurance of appropriations for defense and foreign affairs to two years. The involved systems of allocating, expending, and checking on funds assure good financial management, but at a pace so slow that it can hamper competition with opposing forces in world affairs. Former Assistant Secretary of State for International Organization Affairs, Harlan Cleveland, has commented,

___

[9] Alexis de Tocqueville, *Democracy in America*, trans. by Henry Reeve (London: Longmans, 1875), Vol. 1, pp. 237–238.

"We know in our hearts that we are in the world for keeps, yet we are still tackling twenty-year problems with five-year plans staffed with two-year personnel with one-year appropriations." There is a need for long-range planning separate from the harried individuals and agencies engaged in "doing." Yet the planning needs to be so integrated with the "doers" as to assure realistic programs.

Some institutional changes might facilitate the conduct of United States foreign affairs by cutting through the red tape that surrounds action at the lower levels. We would suggest, however, that many changes in bureaucracy merely leave things more or less as they have always been. The American Presidents from Truman to Johnson have done a good deal to speed up the process of decision making. They have brought it more directly into the hands of the occupant of the White House. And they have devised procedures for assuring that adequate information is at the disposal of the President when the decisions have to be made and that those are present who should be to give their counsel. The Presidents have also worked at the problem of correlating actions in Washington and in the field among those who are involved in implementing the policy decisions. Advances in the technology of the media of mass communication now enable the President, the Secretaries of State and of Defense, and any others whom they may designate, to reach directly into the homes and offices of the nation via television, the radio, and the press. Simple formulas for resolving the difficult problems of government operations seldom produce lasting results.

Elihu Root remarked after World War I that the United States had been irrevocably thrust into international affairs, and "should learn the business." Another twenty years were needed for the United States really to begin to learn the business of foreign affairs. The learning process which has continued since World War II has included devising ways to use our traditional governmental institutions more effectively. One facet of this has been the increasing responsibility accepted by successive Presidents for taking decisive leadership in this area. The process has also included a great increase in expertise and professional experience among government officers in many agencies, and among Congressmen and their staffs. It has also included a growing realization of the responsibility and the price of being a superpower. In the quarter century following 1940, the United States has provided over \$100 billion in assistance to foreign peoples and sent over 10 million citizens to serve in uniform in foreign lands. With the world and their government brought to their homes, cars, and wherever a pocket radio is carried, the American people have been made aware that foreign affairs are their business. History will judge whether the lessons have been learned in time. A firmer basis exists for an informed consensus to evolve in the United States as the people have increased their understanding. This is the strongest political power that can exist in a democracy.

CHAPTER 13

The Formulation of Foreign Policy in the Parliamentary Democracy

INTRODUCTION

In most democratic political systems, including those of England, Canada, the free nations of Western Europe and the Commonwealth, and many of the new states of Asia and Africa, foreign policy is made and conducted under a Parliamentary, or Cabinet, form of government. In this chapter we shall consider how Cabinet governments formulate and execute foreign policy. We will analyze first the procedures employed in Britain, the "mother of Parliamentary democracies," and then discuss Canadian and French practices briefly to illustrate variations found in other Parliamentary systems.

KEY FEATURE OF POLICY MAKING IN THE PARLIAMENTARY, OR CABINET, SYSTEM

The cardinal feature of decision making in the Parliamentary, or Cabinet, system of government is the responsibility of the Prime Minister and of the Cabinet. These officials are chosen from among the political leaders of the majority party or coalition in the Parliament, thereby permitting a single line of power and responsibility for initiation, execution, and control of national policy. This line runs from the party leadership, through the legislature to the Cabinet, and back to the legislature. The Cabinet includes the Prime Minister, who is the leader of the government, and the heads of the executive departments. Through their membership in Parliament these ministers link together the executive and legislative branches of government. And by being the head of the majority party in Parliament, the Prime Minister, with the assistance of his Cabinet associates, exercises control over the majority of the legislature. In contrast to the American Presidential system, an adverse vote in the legislature on a major policy issue normally will lead a Prime Minister and his Cabinet either to resign and seek a national election or to change their policy. With this unity between the executive and legislative branches, deadlocks are not usually lengthy, in contrast to the situation in the United States, where power is shared by Congress and the President, who may represent different political parties and therefore hold differing views on what is desirable.

When the Parliamentary system operates smoothly and responsibly, it has a good chance of avoiding one of the difficulties which encumbers policy making where division of responsibility and sharing of powers are constitutionally mandatory. The success enjoyed by Parliamentary systems is closely related to the number of political parties. Countries with two political parties normally enjoy a high degree of political stability, as well as the capacity for effective and timely decision making. Countries with multiparty systems are not usually so fortunate. Where Cabinets represent coalitions of several parties, as was usually the case in the Fourth Republic of France, individual members may act with less responsibility, because they do not feel the same loyalty to the Prime Minister as would the members of single-party Cabinets. Recurrent political crises are a frequent accompaniment of multiparty rule due to differences over policy and actions. These can interrupt policy and even lead to complete paralysis.

POLICY MAKING IN THE TWO-PARTY SYSTEM: GREAT BRITAIN

Policy making in Britain has gradually shifted from the monarch, and later the monarch and a group of councillors, to the leaders of the majority party in the House of Commons, who comprise the Cabinet, which is collectively responsible to the House of Commons. The prerogatives of the Crown have diminished from absolute control to "the right to be consulted, the right to encourage, the right to warn." By custom the Prime Minister and Cabinet do not have to accept the views of the reigning monarch—King or Queen as the case may be—but the monarch's views are given respectful attention. There is no longer any question that the initiative and control of policy reside in the Prime Minister and Cabinet.

The monarch, in whom the unwritten constitution rests supreme legal authority, is not, in the actual operation of the government, a person, but an institution known as "the Crown." Foreign affairs, like domestic business, are conducted in the name of the King or Queen. All key decisions are made by the ministers in the Cabinet and the monarch is the titular and ceremonial head of state.

THE PRIME MINISTER AND THE CABINET

The British Prime Minister and his Cabinet are responsible for formulating policy, for reporting it to Parliament and the nation, for introducing and guiding through Parliament legislation in the national interest, for executing the laws, and for directing the administrative departments of government. Detailed decisions on foreign and domestic policy are made in the departments of government.

It is customary for members of the Cabinet to resign as a body if they lose support for their policies in Parliament. This arrangement forces Cabinet members to seek unity and enables Parliament, through the mechanism of a disciplined two-party system, to exercise constant surveillance and constructive criticism of national policy.

Cabinet Composition. Members of the Cabinet are selected by the Prime Minister, normally from among the leaders of his own party in the House of Commons. Members of the House of Lords may be included in the Cabinet, although the most important offices are normally reserved for political leaders from the Commons. In time of war, or when no party has a clear majority, the Prime Minister may invite leaders of the other political party to become members of a national government, as Winston Churchill did during World War II, when the Cabinet contained several members of the Labor Party, including the Deputy Prime Minister, Clement Attlee.

The Cabinet normally contains about twenty members, including the Foreign Secretary, the Minister of Defense, the Chancellor of the

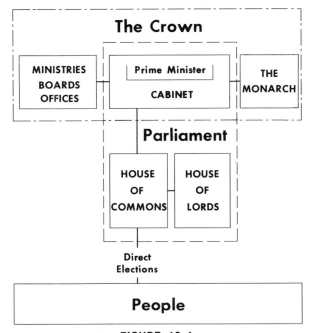

FIGURE 13-1

The Government of Great Britain

Exchequer, the President of the Board of Trade, and other departmental leaders desired by the Prime Minister.

Coordination of Policy. In addition to its primary task of formulating national policies, the Cabinet coordinates the policies and actions of the several ministries to insure attainment of the overall objectives of the government and the nation. Within the Cabinet itself, increasing use is made of standing committees to settle policy differences and coordinate the activities of related ministries without occupying the time of the entire Cabinet. The three most important are the Defense, Legislation, and Policy Committees. The Defense Committee, under the chairmanship of the Prime Minister and normally attended by the Chiefs of Staff in advisory capacity, is a committee on national security, fulfilling within the British Cabinet the functions the National Security Council was designed to serve in the United States. There is no separate committee on foreign affairs, which are the concern of the entire Cabinet.

Foreign affairs normally constitute the first item on the agenda of the weekly Cabinet meetings. The discussion is sometimes limited to a report on the progress of negotiations or on the general international situation. On other occasions the Foreign Secretary may ask for opinions in order to confirm his judgment or to strengthen his hand. Or there may be some development calling for a major political decision, as when a critical stand must be taken at an international conference, when an agreement with serious implications must be negotiated with another country, or when some delicate international issue is due to come up in Parliament.

Contrary to the usual practice in American government, diplomatic papers are normally circulated to the full membership of the Cabinet. This is important in a system where the ministers are collectively responsible to Parliament, and to one another, for all aspects of national policy and administration. It has the added merit of avoiding a situation in which Cabinet members may first learn through the newspapers of important policy positions taken by the head of the government or the Foreign Secretary, as sometimes happens in the United States and France. The possession of adequate information is essential where a Cabinet is intended to be a decision-making body and not merely a gathering of advisers.

Direction by the Prime Minister.   As the leader of the government and the Cabinet, the Prime Minister has final responsibility for the formulation and conduct of foreign policy. Some Prime Ministers have played a dominant role in foreign affairs—Viscount Palmerston in the mid-Victorian era, David Lloyd George in World War I, and Winston Churchill in World War II. Sir Harold Macmillan will probably be remembered as an active participant in personal diplomacy, dealing directly with Eisenhower, Khrushchev, de Gaulle, Kennedy, and other world leaders, and as an advocate of approaches to world peace through summitry.

The ultimate responsibility of the Prime Minister is so fundamental that serious criticism of his foreign policies can destroy his prestige and effectiveness as a leader, even though his policy is supported by the Cabinet and his party. Sir Anthony Eden as Prime Minister in 1956 ordered the abortive invasion of Suez. This was condemned by the Labor opposition, the United States, the Soviet Union, and many members of the Commonwealth, as well as by the United Nations. Although the Cabinet and House of Commons majority stood behind the invasion policy, the Prime Minister suffered such a humiliating loss of prestige that he resigned shortly afterward.

The Prime Minister and the American President.   A comparison of the policy roles of the Prime Minister with those of the President of the United States gives the President two apparent advantages. First, the President has a fixed term of four years, and although he may become unpopular with Congress or with the voters, he has the constitutional right to retain his office and exercise its powers during that time. The Prime Minister has no certain tenure. In theory, Parliament may force him to resign or to hold a new election at any time. Second, the President is supreme within his Cabinet, which may be composed of administrators, and has no constitutional status and need not be consulted. The British Prime Minister must carry with him a Cabinet consisting of political leaders, but once he has its support he can usually hold Parliament in line if his party has a margin of votes and is politically adept.

The advantages held by the United States President are less significant in practice. A Prime Minister who enters office with a safe party majority is, to all intents and purposes, as sure of a sustained period in the job as the President is of his four years. And if the Prime Minister is more restricted by the views of his Cabinet colleagues, he is usually in a position to exercise a preponderant influence in Cabinet deliberations. The Prime Minister's most significant advantage lies in the extent of his control of the legislature. The tightness of party discipline and the power of the Prime Minister to dissolve Parliament are weapons which the President does not possess. Congress is constitutionally an equal partner, jealous of its prerogatives and bound neither in theory nor in practice to support with legislation and appropriations the President's recommendations. Assuming Cabinet support and a legislative majority, the Prime Minister can count on Parliament to carry out his program, not as an equal partner, but as an assembly under his control. Prime Minister Harold Wilson demonstrated this graphically with his Labor Government, which ruled for seventeen months on a majority of only three seats in the House of Commons.

The Prime Minister holds office for a period of up to five years, and he may be elected to an unlimited number of terms. The Prime Minister may call an election short of five years, as Mr. Wilson did in 1966, if he thinks his Party's chances of improving its position in Commons will be advanced by such a maneuver. During his period in office a Prime Minister is subject to constant vigorous criticism both by his opponents in Parliament and by the public media. Above all, the spirit of the unwritten constitution insures that the Prime Minister exercises his powers only so long as he does so with restraint and responsibility. The most important restraint on the powers of the Prime Minister is exercised by the incumbents themselves: the men who reach the top in British politics are deeply committed to the limited powers of constitutional democracy that have evolved over nearly a thousand years.

THE FOREIGN SECRETARY AND THE FOREIGN OFFICE

In the decision-making process under the Parliamentary system, the Foreign Secretary holds a pre-eminent position in foreign affairs. This is due not only to the importance of foreign affairs, but also to the efforts of a distinguished line of Foreign Secretaries, such as Palmerston, Salisbury, and Sir Edward Grey in the nineteenth and early twentieth centuries. These men established a doctrine of continuity in the conduct of foreign affairs which remains a vital factor in British policy.

The Work of the Foreign Secretary.   Sir Winston Churchill once described the Foreign Secretary, who ranks among the top two or three Cabinet members in political prestige, as responsible for the conduct of affairs "under the constant scrutiny if not of the whole Cabinet, at least of its principal members." The degree of freedom any particular Foreign Secretary enjoys in conducting foreign relations depends on his personal relationship to the Prime Minister, his standing with the public, and his position within the majority party. Because it is the Prime Minister who represents the authority and responsibility of the Government before Parliament and the country, the Foreign Secretary must retain the Prime Minister's confidence and be prepared to admit that the Prime Minister may at any time take the initiative in decision making or conduct affairs himself. Within important limits, the Foreign Secretary has general responsibility for the formulation and execution of foreign policy. It is his duty to explain and to defend the Government's policy in Parliament. If the Foreign Secretary is a peer, as was Lord Home in the Macmillan government, he performs this duty in the House of Lords, while the Prime Minister and the Ministers of State for Foreign Affairs perform it in the Commons. Like his counterpart in the United States, the Foreign Secretary is responsible for administering the Foreign Office and for the conduct of affairs abroad. And he must, of course, deal with foreign diplomats. When talks are conducted at the heads-of-government level, he assists the Prime Minister.

The British Foreign Secretary and the American Secretary of State.   The fundamental difference between the Secretary of State in the United States and the Foreign Secretary in Great Britain is that the latter occupies a more institutionally defined office. Whereas the American Secretary of State is directly responsible to the President, serves at his pleasure, and may be overriden by the President at any time, the Foreign Secretary is usually a political figure in his own right. Under both systems there have been those who have been prominent and those who have been overshadowed by their heads of government. It is possible that no British secretary has been or could be relegated to quite the minor role that Robert Lansing occupied in the United States under Woodrow Wilson, or that Edward Stettinius occupied under the second Roosevelt. It is also possible that no present-day occupant of the secretaryship in London could exercise such great and unilateral authority as did Secretary of State John Foster Dulles in the first six years of the Eisenhower presidency.

Aides to Foreign Secretary. In directing foreign affairs, the British Foreign Secretary is assisted by several Ministers of State and Parliamentary Under-Secretaries of State, each a Member of Parliament and therefore changing with each government. The Ministers of State, who do not have Cabinet rank, devote much of their attention to British participation in the United Nations and other organizations and to conferences demanding high-level political representation. The Parliamentary Under-Secretaries assist the Foreign Secretary and the Prime Minister in handling matters on the floor of Parliament and help in maintaining liaison between Parliament and the Foreign Office.

The Foreign Secretary also has the assistance of a large staff of civil servants in the Foreign Office. The senior civil servant, the Permanent Under-Secretary, is a career official who holds office regardless of changes in government, thereby giving continuity to the administration of foreign affairs. The Permanent Under-Secretary is the Foreign Secretary's principal policy adviser, bringing to this task detailed knowledge of the country's policy and foreign relations, current issues, and the intricacies of diplomatic practice. It is the Permanent Under-Secretary's duty to caution the Foreign Secretary on courses of action which might depart from historic policies or on which experts in the Foreign Office believe the nation might be led into difficulties. Under the administrative control of the Permanent Under-Secretary are deputies, assistant secretaries, division heads, and ultimately the whole of the Foreign Service. The office of Permanent Under-Secretary is the ambition of career members of the Foreign Service.

Divisions of the Foreign Office. The British Foreign Office is organized and staffed in much the same way as the Department of State and performs essentially the same functions—analysis of reports from the field, preparation of memoranda for the chief policy officers, and drafting of outgoing cables and instructions. In addition, the permanent staff plays a role in formulating policy, although the responsibility and initiative for policy clearly rests with appointed political leaders.

Other ministries involved in foreign affairs include the Ministry of Defense, the Treasury, the Board of Trade, and the Commonwealth Relations Office. Conflicting interests and differing views are resolved ultimately at the Cabinet level, where all positions are consolidated into a single national policy.

PARLIAMENTARY CONTROL OVER POLICY AND POLICY MAKERS

Parliament and Congress. In Britain, Parliament plays a role in foreign policy formulation quite unlike that of the Congress of the United States. Like Congress, Parliament must pass all necessary laws and enabling acts and appropriate funds for governmental operations. Unlike Congress, it has no special constitutional powers to regulate foreign commerce and consent to treaties. The Cabinet, not Parliament, declares war, although acts of Parliament are needed to enact war legislation. Express consent of Parliament is not necessary for the ratification of treaties, except those involving cessions of territory or expenditures of funds. The chief role of Parliament is to serve as the source from which the leaders of the government are chosen and to be the forum within which the government's policies and actions are scrutinized, attacked, defended, and made known to the public, and the government itself supported or overthrown.

Government versus Opposition. A Government with a clear majority and a well-disciplined party in Parliament knows that it has freedom to pursue its policies as long as it retains the confidence of its party. Well-organized criticism of the Government's policies and administration by the leaders of the Opposition, who have an unofficial "Shadow Cabinet" ready to take over the Government on short notice, is bound to keep a Government attentive to the task of advancing the national interests and in tune with public opinion.

Where the Government has a slim majority in the House of Commons, as Harold Wilson's Labor Government did in 1964–1966, it is inclined to be cautious in controversial policy and programs. Mr. Wilson refused to press one of Labor's traditional domestic policies, nationalization of steel during that period, and moved cautiously in the Rhodesian crisis.

A Government supported by a clear majority cannot ordinarily be defeated by the Opposition on record votes. But persistent challenge by Opposition spokesmen can reveal weaknesses in policy, blunders in administration, and lack of adequate attention to vital issues. The Opposition can also arouse the country to dangers in policy. It is in this area that Parliamentary governments, whether in Britain, Canada, or elsewhere, make their main contribution to foreign policies.

There are seldom prolonged "great debates" on foreign policy issues in Parliament, such as those that took place in the United States Congress on sending troops to Europe in support of NATO in 1950 or on Far Eastern policy after President Truman's dismissal of General MacArthur in 1951. On many occasions opposition parties will support the Government's foreign policy, believing that politics "stops at the water's edge." But the Opposition may at any time bring a question of policy to debate and make the vote on the matter a vote of "confidence" on which the Government must resign or change its policy if it lacks a majority. Conversely, the Government can make any vote one of "confidence" in its policies or administration, and by winning the vote enhance the enthusiasm, morale, and political prestige of the Government.

The power of the Opposition in the House of Lords is slight, for in England it cannot overthrow a Government or hold up legislation indefinitely. Debates in the House of Lords, which operates at a more leisurely pace than the Commons, can be significant in bringing out important points relating to policy or national position.

PARTIES AND POLICY: CONSERVATIVE AND LABOR

Basic Consensus of Parties.   On the fundamental issue of the Soviet threat to the Western democracies there has been little difference between the Conservative and Labor parties. Although vigorous resistance to Communist aggression is usually associated with the Conservatives rather than with Labor, it was under the Labor Government of Clement Attlee that Britain joined NATO and embarked on an expensive rearmament program. On the whole, and particularly when out of office, the Labor Party, whose left-wing members retain strong pacifist commitments, has shown deep concern about the rearmament of Germany and the implications for humanity of nuclear weapons.

A second area of general agreement concerns Britain's participation in NATO and her special relationship with the United States. The Conservatives are staunch supporters of NATO, and although relations were badly strained by U.S. opposition to the Suez intervention, the party has generally supported American policies. Responsible Labor leaders, including

Harold Wilson, Denis Healey, and Michael Stewart, have decried talk of abandoning NATO as "myopic and positively dangerous." To the dismay of some Labor Party members, Prime Minister Wilson supported the United States in Vietnam.

Both parties are concerned with improving prospects for a *modus vivendi* with the Communist bloc and they have vied in attempting to persuade the people of their desire to negotiate a relaxation of East-West tensions. Both parties have been concerned with stopping the spread of nuclear weapons and the Labor Party has shown considerable interest in regional disarmament schemes, including "nuclear free zones" and "disengagement." On the question of Germany, both Conservative and Labor leaders have rejected capitulation over Berlin. The Conservatives have insisted that a reunited Germany must be free to ally itself with the West in NATO, whereas Labor has been receptive to proposals linking German reunification with neutralization.

British foreign policies have been conditioned by the limited resources available since the end of World War II. Both the Conservative and Labor parties are profoundly motivated by a desire to maintain British influence and independence of action in a world in which Britain has lost its primacy as a Great Power and in which overseas commitments have been drastically reduced.

Areas of Dispute.   Despite these areas of agreement, there are some significant differences between the parties. There is a fundamental divergence on the causes of international conflict. Labor foreign policy tends to orient to the Fabian Socialist theory that international tensions can be resolved through the advancement of universal welfare and social equality. It places heavier emphasis on foreign aid and raising the economic levels of the underdeveloped countries. Conservatives tend to reject the premise that social and economic inequities are the underlying cause of conflict, laying heavier stress on the struggle for power. Although the Conservatives are more concerned with defense and diplomacy, their party has nevertheless accepted economic aid as a necessary and useful policy technique.

A second area of difference is revealed in attitudes toward the United Nations. The Labor Party tends to view the world organization as an institution which can temper national policies. The Conservatives have less faith in the efficacy of the United Nations, regarding it as only one of many instruments and adhering more to the traditional techniques of diplomacy and concepts of the national interest.

There are also disagreements about policy toward the developing nations. Labor has contended that the Conservatives still harbor vestiges of old colonialist attitudes, although the Conservatives have greatly assisted independence movements in Africa. Conservatives have shown more concern over the threat of Communism incident to independence in some of the weaker nations than have certain segments of Labor, but this is partly the result of their having been in office when most of these countries gained independence. The difference between the parties is clearly not over freedom versus imperialism, but in estimating the potential development of the world balance of power.

On the matter of Commonwealth ties, neither party has been doctrinaire; both have been eager to maintain them.

Taken on the whole the area of agreement on fundamentals of foreign policy is broad. The differences are chiefly on matters of tactics, timing, choice of procedures, and on degrees of cooperation or opposition.

PUBLIC OPINION AND FOREIGN POLICY

Like all genuinely democratic governments, British governments are responsive to public opinion. The repeated efforts in recent years to arrange summit negotiations, and the reluctance to plunge unreservedly into European integration, reflect widely held hopes and fears. The Government must conduct foreign policy within the tolerable limits of what the public will accept. It may give a lead where public opinion is hesitant, as on the admission of Germany to NATO and its treatment as a full partner in the Western alliance, or the Government may persist in an announced policy in the face of public remonstrance, as when Chamberlain pursued his policy of appeasement of Hitler. In the long run a Government must, however, have public support or face the danger of losing power at the next national election.

Public sentiment is generally conscious of such constants as the need to keep the sea lanes open for the importation of food and raw materials and the need to secure world markets for British manufacturers. It is also united on the strategic necessity of maintaining a balance of power on the Eurasian land mass, the consequent need to contain Soviet expansion through NATO, the desirability of the special partnership with the United States, and more recently it has recognized the vulnerability of the British Isles to nuclear attack and the consequent need to promote negotiations for securing world peace and the relaxation of international tensions. Beyond this, there is the belief that British power and influence should be used affirmatively to insure the maintenance of a world situation in which there will be security for free nations and acceptance of the rule of law.

These values are solidly rooted in the concept of the national interest, and the resulting consensus tends to stabilize and guide British policy irrespective of shifts in government.

VARIANTS IN POLICY PROCESS IN OTHER PARLIAMENTARY SYSTEMS

The Policy Process in Canada. British Parliamentary democracy, particularly its major political institutions, has been widely copied. A general similarity in political institutions does not insure a similarity in process. Natonal circumstances—geography, cultural heritage, religion, and economic processes—tend to transform the operations of basic political institutions. This is illustrated by the policy process in Canada.

Decision making in Canada is modeled after the British Cabinet system, but with significant differences that originated in the unique political history of Canada. In drawing up the British North America Act of 1867, the constitution of Canada, the law makers rejected the idea of a unitary state and left more extensive residual powers with the provinces than the framers of the American Constitution provided for the states. Extensive powers, including defense, transportation, development, and treaty making, were given to the central government, but the Act carefully preserved the integrity of the provinces, so that Quebec today has been able to negotiate a separate cultural agreement with France.

For many years Canada had no occasion to engage in foreign relations, because its representation abroad was handled by Britain. It was not until the 1923 Imperial Conference in London that Canada, with Australia, New Zealand, India, and South Africa, was acknowledged to be coequal with Britain and given the right to separate membership in the League of Nations. Since 1938 Canada has had its own foreign service and embassies established in several capitals, including Washington. Canada's foreign policy independence was firmly asserted in 1939, when the Government delayed in making its own decision to join the war against Germany. In 1942 Prime Minister Mackenzie King and President Roosevelt concluded the historic Kingston Agreement that established the basis for joint defense of the North American continent and sealed the relationship with the United States in a long-term partnership.

Decision making in Ottawa is similar to the British process. Ultimate power over foreign affairs is in the hands of the Prime Minister and Cabinet, who are corporately responsible to the popularly elected House of Commons. The upper house, or Senate, is composed of distinguished citizens and may debate questions relating to foreign policy, but it has no power to force the Government to comply with its wishes. And like the House of Lords in England, it may not delay money bills for more than one session.

Until 1949 the Prime Minister normally held the Ministry of External Affairs in his own hands. Since then, men like Lester Pearson and later Paul Martin have held the foreign portfolio separately. As senior members of the Cabinet, Secretaries for External Affairs have generally conducted their policy independently and earned public respect for their leadership in foreign affairs. Major policy decisions are taken in the Cabinet and reports are made periodically to the Commons, with both the Prime Minister and his Minister of External Affairs needing the support of the House for their policies and actions. There is a Standing Committee on External Affairs in the House of Commons, and since 1963 a Special Committee of Defense has been appointed. These are purely advisory and do not compare with the powerful House and Senate Committees in the United States, although they have produced valuable studies and recommendations. There is also a Cabinet Committee which groups together ministers with responsibilities in foreign affairs and defense.

The pattern of Canadian politics is no longer clearly a two-party, working-majority system, as in England. Of the last five general elections, only one (1958) resulted in an absolute majority for one party. It is difficult to determine if this is an abnormal and temporary situation, or whether it is the beginning of an era in which the party forming the Government will not have an absolute majority. There are some who think Canada may be heading toward multiparty or coalition government.

On the basic issues of Canadian foreign policy there is a good deal of consensus. Both the Liberals and Progressive Conservatives agree on support of NATO and the U.N. The New Democratic Party, the third largest party in the present House of Commons, has been more hesitant in its support of NATO and NORAD (North American Air Defense), and its leader has been critical of United States policy in Vietnam and the Dominican Republic. The Social Credit Party, which has its principal strength in the prairie provinces, would go further than the others in experimenting with socialist policies and turn attention more toward domestic development. Although closely linked to its neighbor, the United States, and to Great Britain, Canada has followed a staunchly independent foreign policy. In spite of American opposition it has sold large amounts of wheat to Communist China. It did not support Britain during the Suez invasion and has been unwilling to break contact with Castro's Cuba. At the Commonwealth Prime Minister's Conference in 1961, Conservative leader John Diefenbaker insisted, against all precedent, upon discussing and condemning South Africa's racial policy.

Among the factors currently affecting Canadian policy are the multiplicity of political parties and increasing regionalization. The latter is emphasized by British Columbia's recent insistence on concluding a separate agreement with the United States for the Columbia-Frazier River power development and the demand of Quebec's Premier Lesage for a Quebec House in Paris to implement that province's cultural affairs. This regionalization may have profound effects in the future.

Multiparty Situations. Parliamentary government is not invariably democratic, or even stable, nor is policy making in most countries whose formal institutions ostensibly conform to a Parliamentary system always conducted in the same way as in Britain. Sometimes these differences stem from variations in formal, constitutional relations among organs of political power and decision; sometimes they arise from local political circumstances of the time. Some political analysts attribute Hitler's rise to provisions in the Weimar Constitution which permitted "constitutional dictatorship." Others lay the rise of the Nazis more to the facts of the political sociology of Germany in the 1930's and the weaknesses in the multiparty system that functioned under the Weimar Constitution. The instability of the French Fourth Republic is sometimes attributed to the unwieldiness of the executive's power of dissolution of the legislature. Although such defects in constitutional engineering may become important during major political crises, such crises usually have roots much deeper in the political community. Significant variations in the operation and success of similar sets of formal institutions can be traced to differences in the nature and degree of the value consensus achieved by the communities under discussion.

A few states with multiparty systems have achieved a substantial measure of stability as a result of one party's maintaining sufficient representation to hold power for a considerable period of time, alone or in coalition, as in the Netherlands and Israel. In the Scandinavian countries, coalition governments somewhat left of center have prevailed much of the time. These governments have been able to function effectively on the whole in foreign affairs because of public agreement on the main outlines of external policy. Finland's political situation is unique because of its delicate position with respect to the Soviet Union, and the fact the Communist Party has been the second largest group in its Parliament. Governments in Finland have frequently rested on coalitions of Social Democrats, Agrarians, Centrists, and representatives of the Swedish People's Party, because no one party has had a sufficient majority alone to outmaneuver the Communists.

In many Asian and African countries policy rests on what might be termed one or one-and-a-half party systems. In India the Congress Party has enjoyed predominant political power, partly because it has been the party of Gandhi and Nehru and was the force that obtained independence for India, and also because the opposition has been too fragmented to offer an effective alternative. The charismatic leadership of the late Jawaharlal Nehru, personifying India's struggle for nationhood and self-development, was vital to the shaping of the Indian political system and its foreign policy.

Traditional French Politics. France has been the outstanding example of a political system laboring under the effects of diverse and irresponsible multiparty maneuvering. Deep divisions on economic and religious policies, and extremist challenges from both right and left, presented the Third and Fourth Republics with the perpetual problem of forming complex coalitions in order to obtain a working majority in the popularly elected Assembly. The virulence of dissension is illustrated by the formation of twenty-two governments, out of nearly a dozen parties, between November 1945 and April 1958. Britain had four Governments during the same period and only one shift of party control in Parliament. During the mid-1950's, instability and party strife were the major features of the French system, with *immobilisme* the natural result. In view of the divergent and competing interests of the democratic parties, there was agreement on little more than resistance to the pressures from the large Communist bloc on the left and the antidemocratic groups on the right.

The sequence of political crisis in France might have been disastrous to French foreign policy but for the very considerable measure of continuity maintained in the Foreign Ministry. Between 1944 and 1954 George Bidault, Léon Blum and Robert Schuman held the office of Foreign Minister. From 1954 until 1958 it was held by four others, and when General Charles de Gaulle came to power he elevated to Foreign Secretary a man who had been the top-ranking career officer of the Quai d'Orsay, Maurice Couve de Murville. In the midst of highly turbulent domestic political maneuvering, France was able to maintain a relatively stable course in foreign affairs. It was able to participate in the European unity movement, to join NATO, to initiate the Coal and Steel Community and later the

European Economic Community, to be a major factor in the European coordinating agency of the Marshall Plan (the Organization for European Economic Cooperation), and to develop a new climate of relations with the German Federal Republic. M. de Murville held office longer than any Foreign Minister under either the Third or Fourth Republics.

Policy Making in the Fifth French Republic.   In the 1958 Constitution of the Fifth French Republic, General de Gaulle attempted to cure the ills of the former system by curbing the powers of the National Assembly and increasing those of the President, enabling him to function as the chief architect of the nation's policies and as its master strategist. The President was given authority to choose whom he would as Premier and Cabinet ministers and was not required to have them invested through Parliamentary approval. These officers became in effect advisers to the President and executors of *his* policy rather than the fountainhead of policy themselves.

Where formerly the policy process stemmed from the Premier and a Cabinet that did not have to remain united but were responsible to the Assembly, the President was an honorific figurehead. Under the Fifth

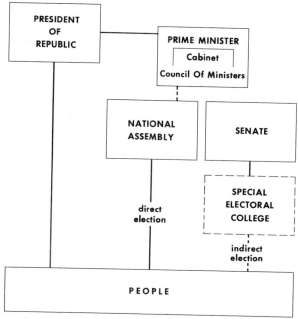

FIGURE 13–2

Structure of the French Fifth Republic

Republic policy flows directly from the President. The Premier, Foreign Minister, and others are his aides.

The 1958 Constitution provides that motions of censure of the Government's policies in the National Assembly must obtain an absolute majority of the total membership. There can be no abstentions and all votes are recorded. The Constitution empowers the President to submit a policy to the electorate in a referendum and to dissolve the Assembly and call a national election if the Assembly refuses to follow the policies proposed by the executive, a sobering threat to any deputy. The National Assembly has thus been placed in a situation where it either must follow the President's lead or risk the prospect of a national election or referendum. The Constitution furthermore vests the President with power to take whatever measures he may deem necessary in the event of national crisis, which he may himself proclaim.

The policy process in France today thus rests in the hands of the President. The foreign policies pursued by the Government with respect to NATO, the European Economic Community, Great Power or other relations are the President's policies. Opponents have been compelled to support those policies, or to resort to sniping operations from the sidelines. General de Gaulle's unique style and role, his personal conception of the dignity of the Presidential office, and his interpretation of his function as savior of the glory of France have been vital to this scheme of government. Former Premier Pierre Mendès France was quite correct in remarking that "the destiny of the nation is in the hands of one man." De Gaulle's election to a second term in 1965, although by a narrow margin, indicated that the French public preferred to entrust its fate to the aging general rather than to an uncertain future and a return to traditional political bickering.

CONCLUSION

In examining some of the variants found in the Parliamentary or Cabinet forms of government, we have by no means exhausted the range of possibilities. Each country has a political system different in some respects from all others. This means that to understand the decision-making process in these nations, one must probe beneath the surface of formal institutions and appearances to the realities of politics. The Prime Ministers and Foreign Secretaries of Britain, France, India, and Japan speak not only from differing national backgrounds and interests, but also from quite different traditions and systems of policy making. Although there are certain deeply ingrained traditions and attitudes in many countries with respect to international affairs, these are affected by the functioning of the political process and the unique characteristics of the party situations prevailing in each country.

CHAPTER 14

The Foreign Policy Process of the Great Communist Powers

INTRODUCTION

The prominence of the Soviet Union and Communist China in world politics makes it important for students of international affairs to examine their decision-making processes. An understanding of Soviet and Chinese foreign policy must be partly derived from an understanding of the nature of Communist society and the values that each ruling Party tries to impress upon its peoples. Both Russia and China underwent social upheaval by means of violent revolutions in which power was seized by a single political group dedicated to the Communist ideology. The revolutions, in 1917 and 1949 respectively, took place in conditions of political instability, where there was comparatively little industrialization and no significant middle class having broadly shared values to give stability and cohesion to the societies. In each case the Communist Party eliminated individual and organized opposition and set about remaking society in the Marxist-Leninist image.

In each of the power centers of the Communist world the decision-making process takes place in a totalitarian setting based on a new "state religion." Added to this common denominator are the unique cultural heritages of Russia and China. It is now fifty years since the Russian revolution, whereas the Communist Chinese regime is only in its second decade. Traditionally, both the Russians and Chinese are expansionist and, because of their geographical propinquity, competitive. A professed common ideology does not exclude divergent interpretations or conflicting policies.

Our primary purpose in this chapter is to examine the policy-making process in each of these powers against this background and in the light of the discussion of ideology and social dynamics in Chapter 3.

Deliberations of the foreign policy makers in the two principal Communist powers are concealed behind a façade. There are few public discussions, little press criticism, and no serious legislative debates. Despite liberalization in the Soviet Union since the death of Stalin, Sir Winston Churchill's characterization of Russia as a "riddle wrapped in mystery and enclosed with an enigma" is still valid in relation to the policy processes of both the Soviet Union and Communist China.

Constitutional arrangements and the formal institutions of government play a lesser role than in the Western democracies. The source of high policy in both countries and the power to carry it into effect comes from the dictatorship of the closely knit elite of the Communist Party.

In attempting an analysis of policy making in the Communist world, one must remember the lack of information about the way the Party elite operates. Our knowledge is based on fragments of evidence and is more an hypothesis than it is a solid body of knowledge. It is important to distinguish between appearances and reality in the operations of the system.

THE SOVIET UNION: POLITICS AND POLICY

It is not our object here to go into details concerning the structure and operation of the Communist Party and of the Soviet government. There is a wealth of literature on both subjects. We shall note only a few of the aspects that are more relevant to the process of decision making on foreign affairs.

The Constitution of the Soviet Union gives to the central government in Moscow authority to determine "the general procedure" governing relations with foreign states. The fifteen Union Republics have a theoretical right "freely to secede" and to enter into direct relations with foreign states. In fact, however, the government in' Moscow controls all aspects of Soviet foreign policy.

Central Source of Power and Policy—The Party. The predominant characteristic of the Soviet system is centralization of power in the Politburo of the Communist Party. It is here that the key decisions are made from which come directives to all echelons of the Party and the Government. Policy decisions considered appropriate are reported to the representative organs of Party and state, either for information or for formal approval, which is normally given without dissent.

In foreign relations the leaders in the Politburo, formerly called the

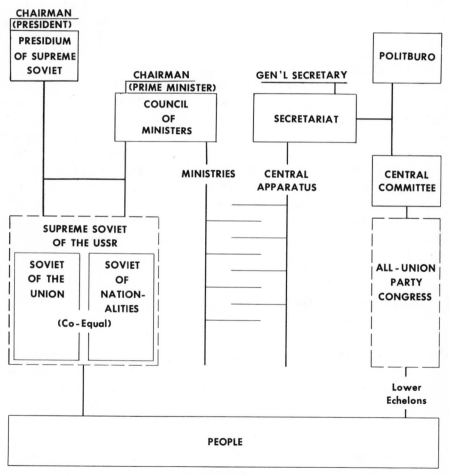

FIGURE 14–1

Government and Party in the Union of Soviet Socialist Republics

Presidium, once they have reached agreement, can bring the full weight of Soviet power to bear. The elite representation in the Politburo roughly reflects Soviet society, supplementing the strength ideology gives to the control by the Party.[1] Although decision making is not conditioned by constitutional restraints, public criticisms, or future elections, as it is in free societies, the decision-making process is not isolated from the interest groups in Soviet society. The monopolistic position of the Party, including government control of all information media, assures that there will be no strong opposition to a decision. The political mechanism of interlocking directorates by which members of the Politburo and other top Party members are also members of the Council of Ministers and are leaders in the Supreme Soviet insures the Party's control and dissemination of doctrine.

In the first forty-five years of the U.S.S.R. three men were ultimately responsible for Soviet policy—Vladimir Ilyich Lenin, Joseph Stalin, and Nikita Khrushchev. Each succeeded in controlling the reins of political power in the Party hierarchy. Stalin ruled in a highly absolutist manner, Khrushchev in a more personal manner, without recourse to Stalin's terrorist methods. After Khrushchev's downfall at the hands of his colleagues in the Politburo, who had become alarmed at his unpredictable ways and the risks he was prepared to take with the United States and Communist China, affairs of state came under the direction of Party leader Leonid Brezhnev and Premier Alexei Kosygin, perhaps indicating more collegial and cautious decision making. The peculiar position of Soviet negotiators is indicated by Secretary of State Herter's comment after meeting with Soviet leaders during the Eisenhower Administration.

. . . the Soviet representative, no matter how highly placed he might be, was bound by the collective decisions on basic policy matters made prior to his departure from Moscow. Any substantive changes in these positions apparently required reference back to Moscow before they could be undertaken.

The Communist Party Politburo. The supreme policy and decision-making body in the Soviet is the Politburo of the Communist Party. This collective directorate has been variously termed the *Politburo* and the *Presidium* throughout its history, but was officially redesignated the Politburo by Party leader Brezhnev at the Twenty-third Party Congress. It is a self-perpetuating body of eleven members who are "elected" by the Central Committee, which in turn is elected by the Party Congress. These

---

[1] Merle M. Fainsod, *How Russia is Ruled* (Cambridge, Harvard University Press, 1961) pp. 334–342.

leaders hold their positions partly because of their prowess in the internal political struggles and intrigues of the Kremlin and partly because of their loyalty to the current leaders. The chairman of the Politburo is the General Secretary of the Party—in the mid-1960's, Leonid Brezhnev. As well as with the attitudes and beliefs engendered by the Communist revolutionary ideology, the Politburo membership has to deal with the aspirations and the problems of an industrializing society.

The members of the Politburo formulate policy on matters ranging from the most crucial issues of state to relatively trivial ones. Available information suggests that policy questions are often routinely considered, that the Ministry of Foreign Affairs reports directly and regularly to the Politburo, and that the General Secretary and the Politburo membership as a whole comprise, in effect, a policy-planning board on major international issues. The Foreign Minister is not always a member, but may be asked to attend to give suggestions or technical advice.

The role of the Politburo is somewhat similar to that of the Cabinet in Britain. However, the Politburo is not responsible to the legislative body, but uses it as a sounding board. And the General Secretary exercises a unique role through his position at the head of the Party's control mechanism. Stalin used this position as a major instrument for exerting dictatorial power over his Politburo colleagues.

The Secretariat.   The Secretariat of the Communist Party ranks second to the Politburo in terms of the active role played in policy decisions. The function of the Secretariat, led by the General Secretary, is to direct and support the professional Party machine. Although its precise operations are not known, the shaping and implementing of plans and proposals, and the special influence of the secretaries as members of the Politburo, seem to be the chief contribution of the Secretariat to the policy-making process.

The Secretariat is also the most important means of communication with Communist Party leaderships in other countries and links Moscow with Communist agents throughout the world to advance Soviet ambitions.

The Central Committee and All-Union Congress.   The Communist Party Congress, composed of over a thousand delegates, is theoretically the supreme authority of the Party. It is empowered to approve and amend the Party policy proposed by the higher executive organs. The Congress is in no sense a policy-making body. It is used chiefly to propagate the broad lines of policy decided upon by the Party leadership.

The Central Committee, comprising 175 full members and 113 candidate members elected by the Congress, includes Party leaders from the various Soviet republics and regions. The Committee's main function is to appoint the Politburo and Secretariat and to serve as another forum for hearing and approving policies decided upon by the members of the Politburo. It does on occasion exercise a real voice in Party matters, as when it voted Mr. Khrushchev out of office and chose Mr. Brezhnev. Shifts in the mode of Soviet external behavior to a more cautious and correct diplomacy followed on the choice of the latter.

GOVERNMENT AND POLICY MAKING

Within the Soviet system, the institutions of government are secondary to the Party leadership in the formulation of high policy.

The Council of Ministers. The Council of Ministers is the chief executive organ. This is composed of a chairman, who is the Premier of the Soviet Union; several deputy chairmen; heads of various ministries, including the Defense and Foreign Ministries; and certain others. The Council directs the work of the ministries and other government agencies, supervises the armed forces, and gives general guidance to foreign affairs within the scope of Party directives. Its significance in the policy process derives from the close relationship of the principal figures at the apexes of the Party and governmental pyramids, insuring that the same policy prevails in Government and Party.

The Supreme Soviet. Technically, the Council of Ministers is constitutionally subordinate to the Supreme Soviet, but in reality this two-chamber legislative body, elected by universal suffrage, exercises little power in policy making. The Supreme Soviet usually meets twice a year for sessions of one to three weeks to hear and endorse ministers' reports, to serve as a forum in which policy statements are made by the leading figures of the U.S.S.R., to vote the annual budget, to name the members of the Council of Ministers, and to elect a Presidium of its own. The First Chairman of this Presidium is constitutionally the titular head of the Soviet state. The Presidium exercises some powers formally vested in the Supreme Soviet, including the declaration of war, the ratification of treaties, the appointment of ambassadors, and the reception of foreign diplomatic representatives. Members of the Politburo and of the Council of Ministers are usually members of the Supreme Soviet.

The Foreign Ministry. Foreign policy decisions are executed by the Ministry of Foreign Affairs, assisted at the highest level by leading Party officials and career diplomats. The position of the Soviet Foreign Minister can hardly be likened exactly to that of either the American Secretary of State or the British Foreign Secretary. He need not be a member of the Politburo, whereas the Secretary of State in Washington is always a member of the President's Cabinet and of the National Security Council. The prestige and the position of the Foreign Minister in Moscow depends on the Party leadership. For many years Marshal Stalin appointed a personal confidant, Vyachyslav Molotov, as Foreign Minister. He was a member of Stalin's Politburo and on some occasions also First Chairman of the Council of Ministers. When Andrei Vishinsky succeeded Mr. Molotov, he was not admitted to membership in the Politburo. The same was true of Andrei Gromyko.

The operating divisions of the Foreign Ministry are similar to those of the United States Department of State and the British Foreign Office. There is a "collegium," or planning and directing staff at the top, that includes the Foreign Minister and Deputy Ministers.

The personnel of the Foreign Ministry and foreign service are generally kept more or less apart from factional Party pressures. Few of the personnel have become embroiled in the political intrigues of the nation's leadership. This is not to say that the Party does not maintain a close supervision of Soviet diplomacy. Every mission apparently has its Party functionaries looking over the shoulder of the professional staff and reporting back through Party channels on their loyalties, efficiency, and reliability. Assignments are checked by the Party Secretariat.

C. L. Sulzberger, writing in *The New York Times*, states that 60 per cent of Soviet officials stationed abroad are career officers of the secret police which also has a Moscow staff of approximately 6,000 persons, and of the military intelligence service. He also states that almost one half of the Soviet envoys to non-Communist governments are affiliated with these agencies. The two agencies are closely supervised by the Communist Party. The secret police have a special directorate of "Disinformation" devoted to the isolation of the United States and generation of discord among Western nations.[2]

Since the death of Marshal Stalin, the Foreign Ministry has acquired a higher position and its service has received added prestige. Important Party officials have been assigned to some top diplomatic posts. As Mr. Gromyko and others have demonstrated, it is possible, however, for a capable but lower-ranking Party member to rise to influential policy-making positions.

[2] *The New York Times*, June 19, 1966.

The Ministry of Defense. The military establishment is a vital instrument of Soviet foreign policy. The separate services are laced together under the central control of the Ministry of Defense, which contains a General Staff and, at the same level, a chief political directorate, which is the principal instrument for Party control of the armed forces. Party influence is assured through attaching political officers to all levels of the services. Whether or not high-ranking officers of the armed services are included in the Politburo, it appears to be national policy to maintain a military establishment capable of posing a constant threat to the free world and to China and a deterrent to attack on the U.S.S.R.

The principal policy decisions on national defense are taken by the Party leaders in the Politburo, with the technical advice and counsel of the military experts. All policy is correlated into a single national plan, and the military is subject to the overall plans adopted by the Party leadership. The dominance of the political element was never more graphically revealed than in the great purge of 1937–1938, when Stalin suspected the loyalty of most of his important military leaders and liquidated them. Since his death there seems to have been a rapprochement between the military and the political leaders. There is occasionally news of military dissatisfaction with the Politburo's policy decisions, such as the one in 1959 to demobilize one and a half million men in order to make more manpower available for the civilian economy and adjust to Soviet weapons progress. On the other hand, the military has great prestige and is unlikely to pursue policies contrary to national interests.

Military power, foreign policy, economic growth, and the advance of Soviet Communism are programs integrated by the Politburo into a single grand strategy to gain greater power for the Soviet Union, to destroy or weaken opponents, and to establish Soviet Communism securely in new areas of the underdeveloped world.

Foreign Economic Affairs. Soviet policy is emphasizing programs of economic and military assistance to meet the challenge of the colonial revolution and the emergence of the underdeveloped nations. A State Committee for Foreign Economic Relations is responsible for the administration of these programs, including development of economic and trade relations, supervision of technical and economic assistance, scientific collaboration, aid in the construction of enterprises abroad, training and provision of specialists, and credit grants. The overall strategic planning of the Politburo extends to these and other aspects of national policy.

The Ministry of Foreign Trade supervises foreign trade, which is frequently used to advance political objectives. The objectives are determined by national economic plans rather than by market conditions, for Soviet trade is conducted almost exclusively by state organs, making it possible to change markets and sources of raw materials quickly for economic or political reasons. When the United States decided to end sugar purchases from Cuba in 1960, Moscow announced within forty-eight hours that it would buy Cuba's sugar.

Economic and scientific progress in the Soviet Union since World War II has significantly advanced the internal strength and military power of the U.S.S.R. This has important foreign political implications, enabling the Soviet Union to cite its rapid development and economic growth as an achievement of the political system and an example for underdeveloped countries. Soviet advances in science and technology, especially the rapid acquisition of nuclear power, the early launching of large satellites, the soft landing on the moon, and the hitting of Venus, demonstrate enormous expenditures of effort and resources and high competence in scientific activity. These impress Asian and African leaders considerably and increase Soviet prestige and power in world politics. The relationship of achievement to prestige seems to be a carefully calculated objective.

The Flow of the Policy Process.   From what is known about the Soviet system, the policy process seems to operate in the following manner. Proposals for policy decision are developed in the ministries concerned and/or in the Party Secretariat, and are approved by the Council of Ministers. The issues and policies are then presented to the Politburo, where they are discussed by representatives of the agencies involved and the members of the Politburo, and decisions are taken there. These then flow back to the Council of Ministers and the ministries involved and to the Party Secretariat for implementation. Reports on policies being pursued and actions taken are made to the Supreme Soviet and, where appropriate, to the Central Committee and All-Union Congress of the Communist Party for information and approval. Uniformity of policy is obtained at all levels, and the various bodies involved are held in line, reinforcing one another.

BASIC FACTORS IN SOVIET FOREIGN POLICY

Soviet foreign policy, like that of other nations, is rooted in a complex of underlying forces, including the environment, political traditions, historical experiences, the personalities and relationships of the Soviet leaders, and the ideological dogma of Marxism and Leninism.

The Heartland Base. The vast area, resources, manpower, and industrialization of the Soviet Union enable the Communist leaders to pursue vigorous foreign policies. The essential effect of Russia's geographical position, combined with her other capabilities, is to make her a superpower in what Mackinder called the Heartland of the Eurasian world island.

Attitudes and Traditions. Soviet foreign policy is conditioned by certain persistent national attitudes. Russian leaders have always been ambivalent toward the Western world. Russia's relative isolation from Europe has fostered deep suspicions and antipathies toward the West. Yet Western ideas and technology have powerfully attracted some Russian leaders and intellectuals. The combination of the Russian tradition of absolutism, which the Soviets have adapted to their own ends, and the messianism of their Marxist-Leninist doctrines also influences foreign policy.

Concern for National Security. The strategic exposure of Russia to attack by Great Powers across its western frontiers and the Arctic and its vulnerability in the Far East and the Black Sea have made Russian leaders sensitive to the problems of defense and security. Their deep preoccupation with the problems of national security has been enhanced by the succession of invasions suffered at the hands of Napoleon, the British and French in the Crimean War, the Polish invasion of 1920, and the two German invasions during the World Wars of the twentieth century. Soviet expansion into the peripheral lands has been partly to create a buffer zone and to achieve an historic Russian goal of drawing Eastern Europe into its empire. The expansion of Soviet domination into the power vacuum left by the defeat of Germany and Japan in 1945 continued the tsarist tradition of five centuries of expansion into areas of weakness. Russion expansion may be contained only when it encounters equal or greater force.

Commitment to Scientific and Industrial Advancement. Since the 1920's the Soviet Union has been committed to a systematic exploitation of its natural, human, physical, and educational resources, to achieve its goals of leading the world in industrial and scientific power. A critical policy decision was made to draw up five-year plans to achieve a major increase in the supply of engineers and scientists as a step toward the transformation of the Russian economy and society. This involved the laborious task of enlarging or building new universities and scientific institutes, of directing student enrollment into scientific studies, and of developing adequate science faculties, research laboratories, and other projects. Concurrently enormous capital resources and much government planning were involved in the construction of new industries to employ the flow of skilled graduates in positions useful to the nation's overall plan.

The first reward of this long-range commitment was seen in the Soviet Union's ability to move entire industries from the Ukraine and Western Russia to the Urals and Central Asia during the desperate days of World War II and to produce large quantities of quality war materials despite restricted productive capacity and the high losses suffered in manpower. It enabled the nation to survive with the assistance of American Lend-Lease. Other early results were the acquisition of atomic and thermonuclear bombs, the development of jet planes, rockets, long-range missiles, and atomic-powered submarines by the mid or late 1950's, and the launching of the first man into space in April 1961. By the late 1950's there were sufficient skilled technicians and industrial equipment to enter the field of economic and technical assistance to underdeveloped countries.

In the Soviet Union high priority is given to the Academy of Science, which is directly responsible to the Council of Ministers. There is some evidence that members of the Academy have the ear of the highest policy-making men of the country on foreign as well as domestic affairs.

Availability of International Communist Apparatus to Support Soviet Aims. The Communists differ with the Western world about international relations, because part of the ideology of Communism is that the traditional state system will crumble and that diplomacy will disappear. Pending the withering of the state system, the Soviets have accepted the need to use diplomacy in dealing with the external environment. Their diplomacy has generally been suspicious and militant, although they did provide good offices for the India-Pakistan hostilities in 1965–1966. *Isvestia* commented, "In all the history of Soviet diplomacy, such activities as took place at Tashkent have been hitherto unknown." The Soviets complement diplomacy by the apparatus of international Communism, appealing directly to the people and institutions of other states. Western democracies have no equivalent to this extradiplomatic instrument for advancing foreign policy. Local Communist parties all over the world, many guided from Moscow, have supplemented the activities of official Soviet missions. In 1960 representatives from eighty-one countries assembled in Moscow, supporting the statement of aims initiated by the Soviet leadership. Coordination and direction are achieved through formal and informal mechanisms that range from institutional Party channels to personal contacts among Communist leaders, and are strengthened by the intangible bonds of Marxist-Leninist ideology. Direction and control of these parties is a major element of the bitter dispute between Peking and Moscow, for a significant element of power is involved, and in some countries Communist parties have split into Moscow- or Peking-oriented factions.

Influence of Communist Dogma. The Marxist-Leninist doctrines of "inevitable conflict" between the Communist and capitalist worlds and of dialectical materialism are continuing bases of Soviet foreign policy, though now complicated by the Sino-Soviet struggle for Communist leadership. The instruments of policy are flexible and pragmatically selected.

Much has been said by Soviet leaders about "peaceful coexistence." Careful examination of statements made to Soviet and Communist audiences reveals that this means coexistence only until Communist forces are able to overthrow regimes now outside their control and to isolate and undermine the West. No cessation of the struggle against the West and no moratorium on efforts to subvert the developing lands is implied in the concept. Soviet doctrine supports "wars of liberation," that is, insurgency against non-Communist governments.

Soviet foreign policy has always been carefully controlled by long-range plans. These establish goals and outline general methodological schemes through which the goals are to be attained. Regardless of apparent flexibility, little deviation is permitted, except tactical digressions. The Nazi-Soviet Non-Aggression Pact of 1939 is an example of a sudden reversal of policy.

A striking feature of the program adopted by the Communist Party of the Soviet Union in 1961 was its revelation of a number of modifications of traditional Marxist-Leninist principles in both the foreign and domestic fields. The doctrine of peaceful coexistence was elevated to the status of Party dogma, challenging the Communist Chinese, who have never accepted peaceful coexistence even as a temporary expedient for dealing with the West. Communist China was not regarded as an equal, but was relegated to a subordinate position in the bloc.

The program also claimed the right to decide when wars should be regarded as "just" and as "imperialist wars of aggression," and to determine when nationalism should be treated as a "political and ideological weapon used by international reaction" and when it should be accepted as a "democratic element directed against oppression."

Peking did not accept the Soviet leadership, despite the efforts of the latter to reach a détente after the departure of Khrushchev. Differences include interpretations of ideology, importance of the nuclear threat, methods of economic and political development, tactics in furthering the

Communist movement, and attitudes and beliefs concerning the world. Although the Sino-Soviet Treaty of Alliance of 1950 has not been abrogated, it is doubtful that all provisions, such as the agreement to consult on all important matters of common concern in international affairs, are being executed. The Soviet leadership, failing in the détente effort, turned to active competition with the Chinese, particularly in the underdeveloped areas. This is a competition for position that can escalate conflicts with the non-Communist world. Two opposing Communisms are not necessarily less dangerous than one. Their doctrinal objectives are still the same.

COMMUNIST CHINA—INTRODUCTION

Communist China's emergence as a dynamic and revolutionary Great Power, with the world's largest population and a large armed force, is an inescapable fact of international politics. Its place in Asia cannot be minimized. In the long run it seems likely to exert an increasingly serious challenge to the nations of the free world. The dynamics of its foreign policy process should therefore be studied.

BASIC FACTORS

Communist Chinese policy is a synthesis of aggressive nationalism and of Communist ideology as interpreted by Chinese leaders. It combines elements of doctrinal Marxism, Leninism, and Stalinism, with an added ingredient of indigenous Maoism—the writings and philosophy of Mao Tse-tung. These are combined with fundamental concepts of Chinese national interests that are derived from the facts of China's location, the size and prospects of its enormous and rapidly expanding population, its history and culture, the political and strategic implications of China's history and position, the status of the nation's resources and of its efforts to progress economically, its suspicions, fears, and ambitions.

The transformation of China from a fragmented nation into a modernizing industrial power mobilized on a continental scale has been, in the words of an authority on China, "one of the most tremendous and startling revolutions in history," one that may have profound effects upon underdeveloped lands far from its borders.[3] History, Marxist dogma, and

---

[3] A. Doak Barnett, *Communist China and Asia* (New York: Harper, for the Council on Foreign Relations, 1960), p. 4.

the lessons of Soviet experience have been galvanized under Mao's guidance to regiment and mobilize the mass of the people to serve the leadership's goals. Through their efforts the leaders are seeking to make the "leap" within one generation from a basically preindustrial and agricultural society to the take-off stage of mass production.

China's leaders have not hesitated to challenge Soviet interpretations of doctrine, and they have not followed Soviet counsel. They have followed their own judgments in their policies toward Taiwan, India, Indonesia, Vietnam, the United States, and Africa. Inner Asia has always been a zone of competition between China and Russia. Rivalries exist over Mongolia, Manchuria, outer Sinkiang, and the Indian borderlands. Tests of Communist solidarity may occur over conflicts of interest in some of these territories, and competition exists in attempts to expand Communist control in Africa, Latin America, and other less-developed areas.

China has at least three times the Soviet population, large conventional armed forces, and the future possibility of nuclear forces. It is driven by a fanatical nationalism. Grounds of rapprochement and consensus between the two powers are no longer clear. It is unlikely, however, that the U.S.S.R. would refuse to participate in a Chinese war that threatened the existence of its Communist regime.

DECISION MAKING IN COMMUNIST CHINA

Decision making in Communist China is more tightly concealed from the West than in the Soviet Union and only the most tentative hypotheses can be advanced.

Commitment to Aggressive Policy. Although China is largely an agrarian and peasant country its regime has utilized radical means to transform it from an agricultural nation to an industrial and military power, and to increase production in both spheres. Communist Chinese aggressive policies have included massive intervention in the Korean War, participation in the overthrow of French power in Indochina, the subjugation of Tibet, military incursions along the border of India and the small states to the south, hostility to the Western powers, active support of the Communist Party in Indonesia, and bold adventures in Africa. As stated by its Minister of Defense on September 3, 1965,

As for revolutionary wars waged by the oppressed nations and peoples, so far from opposing them we invariably give them firm support and active aid. It has been so in the past, it remains so in the present and, when we grow in strength as time goes on, we will give them still more support and aid in the future.

In searching for the genesis of Chinese Communist attitudes, one must take into account China's historical antagonism toward the outside world and its cultural tradition of superiority over alien civilizations. The leadership has been driven by a need to maintain an atmosphere of struggle in order to inspire the masses to the sacrifice required for achievement of national goals. This situation places a premium on programs that present continually fresh challenges to the people, that picture foreign "enemies" pressing upon them, and that offer outlets for venting pent-up frustrations, fears, and animus bred by the shortages of food and material goods, and the recurrent exactions of forced labor.

Pursuit of an aggressive foreign policy is not surprising at this stage of the revolution. Communist China is driven by an urge to establish a position of equality with the Soviet Union, together with an ancient propensity for making China the greatest power in Asia. Being motivated by a revolutionary zeal, China is led to adopt aggressive policies toward others, feeling that it has little to lose by such efforts.

Central Role of the Party.   Like its Soviet counterpart, the Chinese Communist Party is the all-powerful instrument of policy making in China. The highly disciplined elite composing the Party Politburo holds the key power of decision making on both domestic and foreign policy. The government is the instrument for executing the Party will. The Party operates on the principle of exacting complete obedience to the dictates of the top-level hierarchy. As in the Soviet Union, the Party membership comprises a small proportion of the populace—less than 20 million out of approximately 700 million.

The Hierarchy of Power.   The hierarchy of power in China is not unlike that of the Soviet Union.

The Party Constitution declares that the National Party Congress is the "highest leading body of the Party." But the Congress was not convened from 1945 to 1956 and the succeeding Congress met once in the decade after 1956, despite the Constitution's requirement for annual meetings. When the Congress has met, it has done little more than hear speeches, elect a Central Committee, and rubber-stamp resolutions presented to it.

The Central Committee is in theory responsible for directing the work of the Party, but, as in the case of its counterpart in Russia, it normally passes its mandate on to the Politburo and the Secretariat, which it elects. These comprise the core of the policy-making and policy-implementing machinery.

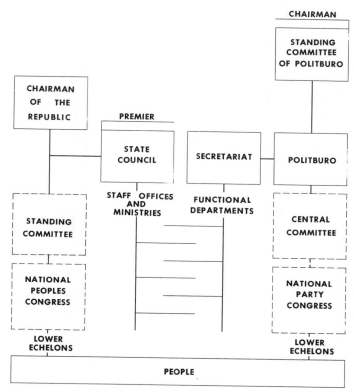

FIGURE 14–2

Government and Party in Communist China

The Politburo is customarily composed of twenty-six members. Here policy issues are thrashed out and become orders and directives transmitted through the Party and government networks. Within the Politburo there is a Standing Committee composed of the highest-ranking members of the larger body. The leadership of this inner core consisted during the early 1960's of Mao Tse-tung, Chairman of the Party; Liu Shao-chi, Chairman of the Republic since 1959; Chou En-lai, Premier of the Government; Teng Hsiao-p'ing, Secretary General of the Party; Lin Piao, Minister of Defense; Ch'en Yun, a leader in economic planning; and Chu Teh, an aging but influential military hero. These men have held the real nucleus of power in Communist China. Decisions within the Standing Committee are probably reached in a highly personal fashion, without recourse to intricate machinery. Major policy decisions on matters of doctrine or foreign relations are apparently taken only with the approval of the Politburo.

The Party Secretariat, under the direction of the Party Chairman, fulfills approximately the same role in policy matters as the corresponding body in Moscow. Through its Propaganda Department there is an extensive program to indoctrinate the masses. Contact is maintained with overseas Chinese in order to advance Peking's objectives. Through the manipulation of Party-controlled mass social and economic organizations, public opinion is mobilized in active and vocal support of the regime and its policies.

The Formal Institutions of Government.　The principal institutions of government involved in the policy process are the National People's Congress, a Standing Committee of the Congress comparable to the Presidium of the Supreme Soviet, and a State Council resembling the Soviet Council of Ministers. "In all departments of state, all decisions on important questions are made on the proposal and according to the directives of the Party." It is the function of the Government to carry out the policy decisions of the Party leadership through uses of the power of the state and the instruments of bureaucracy.

The Chairman of the Republic presides over the National Defense Council and a Supreme State Conference made up of high-ranking government leaders. The Chairman and the Conference comprise a "joint leadership" of the Government. The Supreme State Conference fulfills somewhat the same purpose on the Chinese scene as the Cabinet and the National Security Council do in Washington. The head of the State Council of Ministers is the Premier, who is named by the Chairman of the Republic.

A system of interlocking directorates assures unity of Party and Government. This system obscures the more theoretical distinctions of formal machinery and puts the control of policy in the hands of a few key men rather than in institutional structure.

Ministry of Foreign Affairs.　The Foreign Ministry appears to be more the executor than the formulator of major policies, although it is probably true that as its members gain experience its recommendations carry considerable weight with the Politburo. The temporary recall of diplomats before important Party conferences suggests that professional opinions are solicited by the Party.

In 1958 a Staff Office for Foreign Affairs was established directly under the State Council, composed of the Minister of Foreign Affairs and high-ranking Party men, with the apparent function of coordinating international activities among the various ministries. It may be guessed that one of the purposes of this was to tighten Party control over the conduct of foreign affairs.

National Defense. Although Communist doctrine stresses the supremacy of the Party over the army, the military viewpoint is obviously significant in Chinese decision making. The Politburo and its Standing Committee are the ultimate source of authority in combining questions of defense and armaments into national policy. On the more technical aspects of defense and strategy, the National Defense Council appears to be the determining instrument, aided by the Ministry of Defense, which supervises the operation of the military establishment. The influence the Defense Ministry exercises in policy formation derives from the Party rank of its top officials. A Party Military Committee maintains liaison with the services and articulates policy lines on military matters.

Economic Development. The growing power of Communist China is mainly due to the efforts of the Party to develop Chinese industry and science. Economic policy is formulated by the top Party leadership on the hypotheses of rapid expansion of heavy industry, restrictions on consumption, maximization of investment, and maintenance of large armed forces. To promote the greatest possible increases in output, national planning on a large scale has been adopted, followed by mobilization of the populace to achieve "struggle targets," and "great leaps forward." With these policies and methods, Communist China made rapid economic progress during the 1950's. Poor harvests and planning contributed to the deceleration of progress during the first half of the 1960's.

Scientific and technological advance is stressed and carried out under the direction of a Scientific and Technological Commission. Research and development work are aimed both at catching up and at carrying on fundamental research. Foreign scientists who have been permitted to travel in China have reported on both the apparent influential role of the Academy of Sciences in the shaping of national policy and the massive attempts to build and develop research institutes and laboratories and to train young scientists.[4] China's explosion of a nuclear device in 1964 shows the quick return on investment, although one should bear in mind that Soviet assistance until 1959 was undoubtedly responsible for part of this success.

Solution of the food problem is the most critical of China's needs.

[4] See, for example, J. Tuzo Wilson, *One Chinese Moon* (New York: Hill and Wang, 1959).

But just as the Soviet Union put off for decades satisfying the desires of its people, so the Communist leadership in China may choose to concentrate the greater part of the nation's capital on research and development, heavy industry, armaments, and prestige items in an effort to boost its power and position internationally, while establishing a strong base for future advance in consumption. Unlike the Soviet Union, however, China has a critical population problem, which may divert a much higher proportion of resources to food production.

FLOW OF DECISION MAKING IN COMMUNIST STATES

The nature, the substance, and the procedures of Soviet and Communist Chinese decision making are quite different from those of the Western democracies. The differences stem from the essentially peaceful, defensive, and preservatory objectives of the democracies, as contrasted with the doctrinaire and aggressive objectives of the chief Communist states. The differences in procedures are a function of the constitutional and institutional emphasis found in the liberal constitutional democracies as compared with the personal and totalitarian nature of the Communist regimes.

Policy preparation may begin either in the ministries or in the Party Secretariat. If it begins in the former, it then passes through the Council of Ministers (or State Council in China) to the Politburo. If it begins with the Party Secretariat, policy making may move directly to the Politburo, which may invite or direct the Ministry or Ministries involved to study the matter and submit their views. Once the policy question is decided by the Politburo and the Premier, directives flow back down the line to the Council of Ministers and the Ministries involved and to the Secretariat. If the top leadership considers an official opinion necessary, a meeting of the Party Central Committee or of the Supreme State Conference may be convened. In extraordinary circumstances, the Party Congress may be convened to listen to the leaders and vote approval. For execution the matter then proceeds through the formal channels of Party and Government.

Throughout the process men and not institutions shape the decision, largely free from the pressures of competing groups. The monolithic power of the Party leadership does leave some room for the interplay of differing interests, as between the experts in the state bureaucracy and the political elements in the Party structure, or between the various ministries, or between the Party members on one side and the professional military officers, as well as professional officials, on the other. But all these differences can be controlled by the Party because of the carefully fashioned interlocking directorates and the continual barrage of propaganda poured upon all elements of society.[5]

One feature of decision making in the two principal Communist powers is the ability of their leaderships to effect rapid and decisive shifts in tactics and in policy when these suit their purposes. Negotiating positions can be quickly changed and requests for economic or military assistance by underdeveloped countries have sometimes been acted upon with extraordinary speed. These tactics increase the difficulties for Western policy and programs.

FUTURE OF SINO-SOVIET RELATIONS

The impelling question concerning the foreign policies of the Soviet Union and Communist China is what is going to happen to the relationship between them. We do not presume to have the answer to this question. We only know that the question needs to be put and the most attentive consideration be given to these relations. The consequences of either cooperation or conflict between the Soviet Union and China are bound to affect the interests of the United States, the Western powers, and the nonaligned nations of Asia and Africa.

Classical Marxism-Leninism did not explicitly foresee a situation in which two great Communist-ruled powers would rival one another for world leadership. Lenin and Stalin contemplated only a situation in which the Soviet Union would always be the vanguard, the model, and the Great Power of Communism, with whom all other Communist states would be leagued and to whom all would look for leadership. The validity of this concept for the Soviet elite is still claimed in their statements and actions during the long and bitter exchanges between the Chinese leadership and themselves over policies concerning war and peaceful coexistence.

The schism between the two giants of the Communist world is becoming acute. Rankling under the subordinate rule accorded to their regime by the Soviet Union, the Chinese leaders have asserted themselves as the faithful expounders of Marxist-Leninist doctrine while accusing Moscow's leaders of "revisionism," "Splitism," and "Great Power chauvinism." They

[5] See Philip E. Mosely, "Soviet Myths and Realities," *Foreign Affairs*, Vol. 39, No. 3, April 1961, pp. 341–354.

have charged Moscow with pursuing "a whole series of dirty deals" with the United States, of ardently working for United States-Soviet "collaboration for the domination of the world," and only "mouthing a few words" against imperialism. Most seriously among the attacks on Moscow, the Peking leaders have formally accused the Soviet Union of "aligning" with the United States to "establish a holy alliance against China" and against the Marxist-Leninists and of "disregarding the opposition of many fraternal parties."

The Central Committee of the Soviet Communist Party has published a long list of charges against the Chinese Communist Party. These

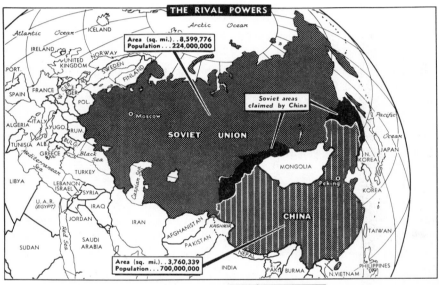

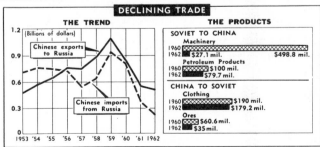

FIGURE 14–3

Factors in the Dispute Between Peking and Moscow (From The New York Times, *February 9, 1964. Reprinted by permission*)

have included Chinese "obstinate resistance" to Soviet overtures for understanding, rejection of programs for normalizing relations, "waging a political struggle" against the U.S.S.R., inducing the Chinese people to believe the Soviet Union is one of their "chief enemies," organizing "subversive activities against the Soviet state and social order," provoking border clashes to "prepare for a military conflict with the U.S.S.R.," blocking the passage of war materials to North Vietnam. Even more than this horrendous catalogue of Marxist sins, the Soviet leadership has alleged that the Chinese leaders want a long war in Southeast Asia to maintain international tensions in order to represent China as a "besieged fortress," and to embroil the U.S.S.R. and the U.S.A., so that the Chinese may, as they say, "sit on the mountain and watch the fight of the tigers." Such policies, according to Moscow, are to serve Chinese "militant Great Power chauvinism and hegemony." [6]

On the question of war the Soviet leaders have sharply contradicted Chinese doctrine by holding that thermonuclear war is avoidable and that the great strength and influence of the "peace loving" Socialist camp has rendered it possible to secure the abolition of war as an instrument of political policy. Soviet statements have criticized Peking's bellicose policies in Southeast Asia as "leftist adventurist actions" retarding progress of the Communist cause.

How far Communist China and the Soviet Union can go on with abusive charges and ripostes of the nature mentioned and still retain friendly relations is an open question. Relations between many countries would totter on the brink of rupture and hostility in the face of such exchanges. This may not necessarily follow in the lexicon of Communist colloquy. The spirit of their politics may be summed up in the Chinese quip, "Our diplomacy simple. We hold door open while slamming it in face of opponent."

China is the only important country added to the Communist bloc without the use or presence of Soviet troops. The communization of China as a result of the military actions of wholly Chinese forces gives China a distinctive place within the camp. By virtue of its size and population, China is the only Communist country that is potentially more powerful than the Soviet Union, and that has experimented widely with communal forms of social living and action. This, plus the fact that its forces have engaged in war with the United States in Korea, has given the Communist Chinese leadership a confidence that it is entitled to share with Moscow the

[6] See *The New York Times*, March 24, 1966, for texts of Chinese and Soviet letters preceding Soviet Twenty-third Party Congress.

leadership of the world Communist movement. Such a position the leaders in the Kremlin have been unwilling to concede.

We have already suggested that the differences in national interests may go deeper than mere doctrinal disputes. That both China and the Soviet Union are Communist ruled does not mean that they will have identical views or follow identical policies. Both are national states, with very different cultural, economic, and ethnic backgrounds. They are also at very different stages of economic development. We have already mentioned possible territorial areas of conflict as well as rival spheres of influence.

A further consideration to be kept in mind as Soviet-Chinese relations unfold is that hard bargaining is a normal characteristic of the negotiations of both powers. They set high demands, use tricks and devices, name-calling and rudeness toward opponents, and appear absolutely uncompromising before the final bargaining. The traditional Chinese feeling of superiority over foreigners extends equally to the Russians, whose historic role in Asia they regard as imperialist and directed against their national interests and aspirations. The higher the stakes and the more important the differences that separate the two powers, the more extreme the tactics of each may become.

If the projections of economic growth and the predictions of the demographic experts match present estimates, from 1975–2000 there could be such an increase in productivity and population in China and the Soviet Union that a revolutionary swing in the balance of world power could occur if these powers were able to heal their split and if the Western nations were no more united than they are now. Even if the two great Communist powers are not able to heal what seems to be a fundamental division, the increasing shadow over Asia of an expansionist China will heavily condition the balance of power in Asia and the course of future interstate affairs. The future relations between the Communist giants are fraught with grave danger to others.

PART IV

Instruments and Patterns of Policy

Preamble

INSTRUMENTS OF POLICY

A POLICY IS MADE *effective by the steps that are taken to make it meaningful. Policies are not self-effecting. They must be supported by action programs which generally operate in the external environment of a state, but domestic programs also support foreign policy. Immigration, tariff, and agricultural-surplus programs are domestic policies with external relevance.*

The programs and actions taken to carry out a foreign policy are the instruments of policy. These instruments, which are discussed in the next five chapters, comprise principally (1) power politics; (2) diplomacy; (3) international communications, including public information and the use of ideology, propaganda, and manipulation of opinion; (4) economic actions; and (5) use of military resources. Harold Lasswell of Yale University once described action programs as covering "force, deals, goods, and ideals."

The instruments of policy are as hard to classify as most social phenomena. A simplistic mechanical analogy would consider communications as the components, and economic and military actions as the fuel. Diplomacy could be likened to a motor driving foreign policy, and power politics to a composite of instruments, selected according to the situation. The definition of interests and goals and the decision-making process would form the control mechanism. International politics, however, is a sui generis *aspect of human affairs which no mechanical analogy can adequately describe.*

Some may wish to give primacy to power politics and diplomacy. We accept that all things are in the end political, but concur with Don K. Price, Dean of the Harvard School of Public Administration that, "Diplomacy is nothing without the military force, the economic support, and the propaganda to back it up—and if the Secretary of State cannot mobilize the help of his colleagues from Defense and Agriculture and Commerce and the rest, he is powerless." The instruments of policy are the principal components of national strength and constitute national power when given purpose and direction. This power determines the degree of success or failure of national policy.

Rarely is any instrument used alone. Diplomacy is often directly supported by economic and military means. A state's diplomacy may be strengthened also by prestige gained from its economic, scientific, and military programs. Inept diplomacy can weaken a state's policies. There are patterns of foreign policies, integrating a variety of individual policies and employing a variety of instruments to further a particular goal or set of related goals. The composite flow of actions and interactions constitutes power politics. This forms the heart of international politics.

CHAPTER 15

Power Politics and Patterns of Policy

INTRODUCTION

In Chapter I it was suggested that international politics are inherently power politics and that the operation of the international political system is significantly conditioned by what may be called balance-of-power considerations. It was said that power is a means, not an end: that it is relative to the power of other states, to a specific situation, and to a variety of other factors, such as national resolve, nationalism, leadership, and availability of resources. Power was defined as strength appropriate to a purpose. Strength can be economic, political, psychological, or military and includes more subtle, nonphysical elements, such as national character and unity, morale, leadership, and statecraft. Prestige—the respect a state enjoys abroad, and the appeal of its policies—is likewise an element of strength. Quantifying and evaluating the different elements is often difficult.

This chapter focuses on the use of power in world politics. A central feature of world politics is the power struggle, the conflicts in which elements of power are used for resolution, among the Great Powers. This struggle can be seen in the present-day conflict between the Western powers and the Soviet Union, between Communist China and the Soviet Union, between Communist China and the United States, and among some of the Western states, including France, Britain, and the United States. There are power struggles between other countries, such as Israel and the Arab states, Pakistan and India, East and West Germany. This struggle pervades many aspects of international affairs. It can be seen in direct intergovernmental contacts and in meetings of the United Nations. Power politics among the Great Powers may seem to be more dangerous to world peace. However, World War I was sparked by the assassination of an Austrian Archduke in a Serbian mountain village. And World War II started with the German attack upon Poland. Small power conflicts can have worldwide repercussions. Not all power politics are necessarily a struggle for power, for there is a type of power, based on consensus in shared values, that can contribute toward greater community.

THE MEANING AND USE OF POWER

An Operational Concept of Power.   Power is an elusive concept. It is an ability to pursue and achieve goals effectively, and to persuade or coerce others to accede to given actions and objectives. This operational aspect of power is a cardinal element in relations among independent states. Decisive elements are the offering of a variety of inducements and the use or threat of coercive power.

In international politics, power involves the application of the state's strength and capacity to the advancement of national interests and the attainment of goals.

In foreign policy calculations, the concept of power is employed in both a relational and operational context; relational in terms of how the initiator evaluates his comparative power and how certain other states estimate it; operational in the sense of how much and what kinds of strength, and what means of employment are necessary to achieve national objectives.

The type of situation must be considered in any appraisal of the specific elements of power. The actor, that is the state leadership, must consider the amount of inducement, or the sanctions required to attain his objectives in particular circumstances. The policy maker must also consider what countries and circumstances would be vulnerable to certain appeals or immune to certain kinds of pressure or persuasion.

Several considerations should be included in an appraisal: (1) each actor's perception and evaluation of the situation; (2) how each actor sees this situation in relation to other situations that are important to him; (3) each actor's perception of his value objectives with respect to the given situation; (4) each actor's evaluation of other actors in the situation—their motives and objectives, and their inducements and coercive power; and (5) an evaluation by actor A of actor B's evaluation of A's perception and evaluation and B's evaluation of his own position.

Problems with the Use of the Concept of Power. Power is not a constant when measured (1) in economic, political, and military terms; (2) in the relative strengths of others; and (3) from the point of view of a given country. In each instance the power factors pertaining to any state have a particular meaning relative to the positions and policies of other states, their interests, attitudes, and goals. It is equally difficult to assign priorities to the various elements.

Geographic position may have more significance for some countries than others. Population size may be less important than national morale or efficiency in managing the internal affairs of one state than it is in managing those of another state. If the power struggle is essentially military, the predominant factors may be relative population, industry, and the strength of forces that are in being. In many situations the military element may have little applicability, as in the conflicts between General de Gaulle's policies and the European Common Market partners. One can also ask whether there is a limit to increments of power that add significantly to the strength of a country? Some consider it unnecessary to extend nuclear stockpiles above the level sufficient to destroy any conceivable enemy.

Intangible elements are also hard to measure and evaluate. In the spring of 1940 England appeared to be a relatively ineffectual land and air power compared with Nazi Germany. But under the leadership of Winston Churchill during the crucial Battle of Britain, British skills, tenacity, and will power were demonstrated to the point that the German air attack was contained and a considerable war effort was mounted. The components of the transformation of French strength after General de Gaulle became President are impossible to assess quantitatively. Confidence, strength, revived morale, and a firmer diplomacy replaced uncertainty and irresolution. Could this all be attributed to one man? And what will happen to French power after de Gaulle? There are few, if any, reliable answers to the calculus involved in computing the weight of these intangibles.

Simulation and game theory are used in an attempt to reduce some of the uncertainties. Interesting suggestions result as to how certain parties may behave under specific circumstances and given assumptions, but there have not been any assured conclusions about many of the vital aspects of the power equation. Conclusions can only be tentative, as they are based on different judgments.

In international politics, as in national systems, reasoning, persuasion, material inducements, bluffing, and bargaining against a background of threatening force are the principal means by which one state seeks to influence the conduct of others for its own advantage. Power politics under these circumstances are essentially psychological relationships in which one party manipulates the symbols of strength in order to convince another to comply with the requests or policies of the first, or to compromise, rather than to oppose them. When persuasion is of no avail, the statesman must decide whether to adjust his own policy to this fact or to attempt coercion that could lead to war. There are attempts to fit the concept of power into quantitative or mathematical frames of reference. Former President Eisenhower commented once that power is a product rather than a sum of elements. If any component applicable to the specific circumstances approaches zero, then the product of the whole combination approaches zero. Vast economic strength without adequate military strength or adequate resolution may be rendered ineffectual.

THE BALANCE OF POWER

Relations between states are often fraught with rivalry, tension, and conflict. One or more states are usually seeking to dominate or to upset the existing order in favor of some arrangement consonant with their concepts of the world. Other states wish to preserve the present order. Alignments based on power develop as states with common interests cooperate to counter those threatening their interests. Balance-of-power politics are in reality efforts to limit other states' use of power.

The Concept of Equilibrium or Balance.   The concept of an equilibrium or balance of power was probably originally suggested by the natural equilibrium between opposite forces in nature. In the solar system man has long observed that a kind of balance of forces holds the stars and planets on their courses in dynamic equilibrium.

In the realm of politics, Aristotle thought that societies were held in equilibrium by the interaction between the rich, the poor, and those with "middle means." A much more recent political thinker, James Madison, believed it desirable for government to seek an equilibrium between elements desirous of change and those wishing to maintain the status quo. Political thinkers have long reflected on the balance of power. Some of their reflections will be noted. It is important to know that such reflection has occurred; whether the reflection has been correct is another matter.

In international politics the balance of power has been seen as a means of curbing absolute power and tyranny. David Hume, in his essay "On the Balance of Power," quotes Polybius as saying a state or ruler should "never be allowed to become so great as to incapacitate the neighboring states from defending their rights against it." Machiavelli counseled in *The Prince*, that whoever "contributes toward the advancement of another power, ruins his own."

Richard Cobden characterized the balance of power as "a chimera," "an incomprehensible nothing; mere words, conveying to the mind not ideas, but sounds like those equally barren syllables which our ancestors put together for the purpose of puzzling themselves about words." The French philosopher Fénelon, on the other hand, said, "To hinder one's neighbor from becoming too strong is . . . to guarantee one's self and one's neighbors from subjugation; in a word, it is to work for liberty, tranquility, and public safety; because the aggrandizement of one nation beyond a certain limit changes the general system to all nations connected with it." Leopold Von Ranke saw the genius of European politics as its ability to meet "pressure on the one side with resistance on the other," through which Europe has "preserved the freedom and separate existence of each state." In a similar vein, in the *History of the Decline and Fall of the Roman Empire*, Edward Gibbon wrote,

The division of Europe into a number of independent states . . . is productive of the most beneficial consequences to the liberty of mankind. A modern tyrant who should find no resistance either in his own breast, or in his people, would soon experience a gentle restraint from the example of his equals, the dread of present censure, the advice of his allies, and the apprehension of his enemies.

Jefferson wrote to a friend in 1815 that "It cannot be to our interest that all Europe be reduced to a single monarchy." So he hoped that "a salutary balance of power may be maintained among nations." The United States held itself aloof from the European system until called on to restore the balance in 1917 and again in 1941. For as Forrest Davis wrote in the *Saturday Evening Post* in 1944 after talking with President Franklin D. Roosevelt,

Our historic interest, like England's, has demanded a European balance of power wherein no single nation commands all the Continent's resources and manpower to our potential disadvantage. Stripped to the bare essentials, we fought in 1917 and are fighting now to prevent the mastery of Europe by one aggressive power.[1]

And that is essentially the way the United States has appeared to view the European and the world scene since Pearl Harbor.

The concept of a balance or equilibrium of power lay behind the Treaty of Westphalia in 1648, the Vienna settlement of 1815, the Versailles Treaty of 1919, and the establishment of the United Nations in 1945. Napoleon, Kaiser Wilhelm, Hitler, and the Communist leaders have striven to substitute mastery for balance.

The leaders of states are often reluctant to claim balance of power as a policy. Statesmen have disavowed their intention of establishing or participating in such a system, even when their policies have in fact been directed toward restraining, offsetting, or surpassing the strength of others. Proclamation of a favorable balance of power as a national objective may encourage others to develop a counter-policy.

Varying Conceptions of Balance and Equilibrium. Professor Ernst Haas of the University of California finds that the concept has been used with eight different meanings: a distribution of power, a balance or equilibrium of forces, hegemony or imbalance, stability and peace, instability and war, power politics generally, a universal law of history, and a guide to policy making.

The following discussion focuses upon the equation of power and on the balance of power as a guide to policy.[2]

The Balance as Equation of Power. In the equation of power there may be either an approximate equilibrium of power between two states or groups of states, or a preponderance of power on one side.

An approximate equilibrium of power existed in Europe in the first decade of the twentieth century, when England, France, and Russia formed the Triple Entente and Germany, Italy, and Austria-Hungary formed the Triple Alliance. This equilibrium was not completely restored after World War I, partly because of the refusal of the United States to associate itself with the European power equation.

---

[1] Quoted by DeWitt C. Poole, "Balance of Power," *Life* Magazine, Vol. 23, No. 12, September 22, 1947.

[2] For an expanded discussion, see Ernst Haas, "The Balance of Power: Prescription, Concept, or Propaganda?" *World Politics*, Vol. V, No. 4, July, 1953. See also G. Liska, *International Equilibrium* (Cambridge: Harvard University Press, 1957); I. L. Claude, *Power and International Relations* (New York: Random House, 1962).

Scholars have debated whether such an equilibrium is conducive to peace or tends to tempt aggressors to upset the equilibrium. The weight of evidence suggests that such an equation of power may keep the peace for a time, but will not in the long run deter a country from a policy of force when it is determined to change the situation and sees a momentary advantage. A balance of power stabilizes a peaceful situation only when peaceful, nonexpansionist states hold a preponderance, that is, a "favorable balance."

The Allied victory in World War II caused the distribution of power among states to change from the prewar equation. The United States and the Soviet Union survived with greatly augmented power relative to other states. Germany, Japan, and Italy had greatly diminished power, and virtually none in the first years following the ending of hostilities; and Britain, France, and other allies also emerged with relatively reduced power. Interstate relations were determined in large part by the difficult evolution of a new balance.

The policy of containment of Soviet Communism undertaken by the United States in 1947 was designed to stop the Soviet drive for European hegemony by erecting a counterpoise of strength through aid to Greece and Turkey, economic reconstruction of Europe under the Marshall Plan, NATO, and U.S. and European rearmament. The containment policy succeeded in Europe but the power struggle extended along the entire periphery of Communism in Eurasia to Korea and Vietnam.

Obtaining a preponderance of power is usually thought to be synonymous with obtaining a "favorable balance of power." Any balance is a relative, fluid, and temporary expedient, not a permanent achievement. A situation deemed favorable by one state may appear as a threat to another state. And any situation is dynamic because each state is continually acting either to maintain or to change the status quo.

Balance of Power as a Guide to Policy. A second meaning associated with balance of power is that a state should endeavor to hold in its hands the balance of power as a goal of policy. This is the sense in which Cardinal Wolsey spoke of that "grand rule, whereby the counsels of England should always be guided, of preserving the balance of power in her hands."

A Memorandum of British Policy, written by Sir Eyre Crowe for the British Foreign Office in 1907, illustrates the principle. After noting the dangers that can arise from a neighboring state's having a predominance of power and an aggressive policy, Sir Eyre observed,

The only check on the abuse of political predominance derived from such a position has always consisted in the opposition of an equally formidable rival, or a combination of several countries forming leagues in defense. The equilibrium established by such a grouping of forces is technically known as the balance of power, and it has become almost an historical truism to identify England's secular power with the maintenance of this balance by throwing her weight now in this scale and now in that, but ever on the side opposed to the political dictatorship of the strongest single State or group at a given time.[3]

Britain has generally followed this policy since 1907, aligning against Imperial Germany before and during World War I, then supporting the recovery of Germany after 1923 while countering French policies in the Near East. Again Britain opposed Germany when Hitler tore up the Versailles Treaty and embarked on his aggressive policies. After 1950 Britain once more aligned with the United States and France to revive an impotent Germany to counter the menace of Stalinist aggression in Europe.

Throughout the nineteenth century Britons saw their safety in holding aloof from lasting alliances on the Continent and in occupying instead the role of "balancer." Since 1945 it has been neither possible nor desirable to pursue this policy. A clear and present danger has threatened from the East, and Britain has been one of the staunchest of the NATO allies, although individuals still favor a balancing role between the U.S. and the U.S.S.R. There have been suggestions that General de Gaulle has also wanted to act as a broker between East and West. But France has lacked sufficient power to tilt the scales decisively. Some of the nonaligned states of Asia and Africa have thought of themselves as balancers between the Great Powers, but except for voting numbers in international gatherings, the combined power of these states is indecisive in differences among the Great Powers.

In theory and practice, any balance-of-power system, whether limited or global, requires "balancers." Most states are committed to one side or the other and the price of asserting the necessary freedom of choice for being a balancer may prove high in the long run. England held aloof too long from the European continent prior to World War I, and India from the East-West confrontation after World War II. India probably did not suffer from her policy because both the United States and the Soviet

---

[3] Memorandum quoted in G. P. Gooch and H. Temperley (ed.), *British Documents on the Origins of the War*, 1898–1914 (London: H.M. Stationery Office, 1928) Vol. III, pp. 397 ff.

Union came to her support when she was threatened by China. Some states do have freedom to move from one side to a balancing position and then back again, but they are rarely free to move back to their original side.

The identity of the balancers is not clear in situations like the Arab-Israeli, Greek-Turkish, Pakistan-Indian, and Latin American tensions. Power external to the geographical area and the relationships, sometimes of the United Nations or other international organizations, may be able to function as the balancing component. The United Nations, as originally conceived, might have provided the balancing element in tensions among lesser powers, through the unanimity of the Great Powers acting in the Security Council.

A "balancer" may have prestige and influence disproportionate to its strength, but that strength must be adequate and accompanied by wisdom to discern when and how to employ the strength, and resolution to commit it. In asserting a position as balancer a state assumes a responsibility that may make it no more of a free agent than if it joined one side to create a preponderant power situation.

Some Postulates of Balance-of-Power Policy. Operations, by any state, in a balance-of-power context rests implicitly on three postulates. A state must be prepared to shift alignments as circumstances change and as new threats appear. Balance-of-power politics rejects ideological prejudices and commitments because they introduce rigidities and distracting elements into the balancing of power. But, again, Communists have imposed their ideology upon nations, so that ideological struggle has become a prominent reality of contemporary world politics. International organizations have also been minimized by proponents of the balance-of-power system lest they deter statesmen from responding to crises on any other basis than calculation of power in the service of national interests. A country may be committed to alliances as Britain was with Japan after World War I, but by accepting an increased association with the United States it became necessary to terminate the alliance. States must be ready to re-examine their own interests and commitments, as General de Gaulle has done vis-à-vis NATO. It even is conceivable that under some circumstances the United States and the Soviet Union might find it essential to their respective interests to join in opposing Communist China, as they did Nazi Germany. Stranger shifts have occurred in history—one being perhaps the alliances of the United States with Germany and Japan.

In the second place, states must be willing to accept conflict and even war, if necessary, to prevent others from so changing the balance as to seriously impair their vital interests. This is the sense in which President John F. Kennedy met the Soviet move to install long-range missiles in Cuba when he said to the American public and to Chairman Khrushchev on October 22, 1962,

> This sudden, clandestine decision to station strategic weapons for the first time outside of Soviet soil is a deliberately provocative and unjustified change in the status quo which cannot be accepted by this country if our courage and our commitments are ever to be trusted again by either friend or foe . . .

Then dealing directly with the threat, the President added,

> We will not prematurely or unnecessarily risk the costs of a worldwide nuclear war in which even the fruits of victory should be ashes in our mouth—but neither will we shrink from that risk at any time it must be faced.[4]

A third postulate springs from the other two and is a corollary of them. If war and other crisis occurs, no state should be so completely destroyed that alien power will be tempted to move into the vacuum and thereby create an unfavorable balance-of-power situation for the victor. That is what happened in 1945 when Germany, Italy, and Japan were laid prostrate. Within five years the Western powers found it necessary to assist the three former enemy powers in order to help redress the balance of power against the Communist threat in Europe and Asia.

Lord Palmerston expressed the essence of balance-of-power policy when he declared that England had no eternal allies and no perpetual enemies, only eternal interests. Professor Nicholas Spykman emphasized the same concept. "He who plays the balance of power can have no permanent friends. His devotion can be to no specific state but only to balanced power. The ally of today is the enemy of tomorrow." He added that one of the charms of power politics is that it offers no opportunity to "grow weary of one's friends." In light of the shifts in associations during and since the 1930's he also might have commented that the system gives some assurance against being estranged forever from present opponents.

Balance-of-power policy, whether equilibrium, equivalence of strength, monopoly of power, or a favorable margin of power, is an exacting exercise in decision making and implementation.

[4] Television address, October 22, 1962. Text in *Department of State Bulletin*, Vol. XLVII, No. 1219, November 12, 1962, pp. 715–720.

EVALUATION OF THE BALANCE CONCEPT

Claims on Behalf of the Balance of Power. Claims have been made that the balance of power has (1) prevented and discouraged wars; (2) preserved the independence of states; and (3) prevented undue domination by one state or group of states and thereby assisted in maintaining the multistate system.

History tends to support the thesis that balance-of-power politics has prevented, delayed, or discouraged some wars. The system has also failed to prevent many wars in the past and is not an assured preventative for the future. The pursuit of such a policy is most defensible on the pragmatic basis that it is the best practical policy alternative to contain an aggressive power or safeguard national security.

Balance-of-power politics has helped preserve the independence of most European states. In this century the system did not prevent Italy from conquering Ethiopia, or Japan from taking over large portions of China. In Europe, the arrangements for accommodation among the Great Powers included agreements at the expense of small states during the 1930's. Czechoslovakia was destroyed at Hitler's demand and Poland partitioned by Germany and the Soviet Union in 1939. Chamberlain and Daladier thought that by "appeasement" war with Hitler could be avoided, but the record of history shows that a state bent on upsetting the existing balance is unlikely to be bought off by accession to its demands.[5]

Criticisms of the System. It has sometimes been alleged that instead of being an effective formula for maintaining peace and security, balance-of-power politics encourages war by making all insecure.

Woodrow Wilson was an outspoken critic of the balance of power. He declared in a speech in January 1917, "Mankind is now looking for freedom of life, not for equipoises of power." There must be, he asserted, "not a balance of power, but a community of power; not organized rivalries, but an organized common peace." In London on December 28, 1918, Wilson declared in a Guildhall address that the men who had fought the war did so to,

---

[5] The reader will find it interesting to read in this connection the Hossbach Memorandum from the captured German Foreign Office Archives and read into the record of the War Crimes Trial on November 26, 1945, recording a 1937 secret conference of Hitler and his top staff on plans for Germany's attack of Europe. See International Military Tribunal, *Trial of Major War Criminals*, Vol. 2, pp. 262–273; reproduced in Seabury, *op. cit.*, pp. 75–87.

. . . do away with an old order and to establish a new one, and the center and characteristic of the old order was that unstable thing we used to call the "balance of power.". . . The men who have fought in this war . . . were determined that that sort of thing should end now and forever.

There must be, he went on,

. . . not one powerful group of nations set off against another, but a single overwhelming, powerful group of nations who shall be the trustee of the peace of the world.

On the other hand, the late Professor DeWitt C. Poole of Princeton University, an experienced career diplomat, wrote that freedom can be had only "in a world in which power is widely distributed and balanced; a world of a complex balance of power."

Some skeptics have debated whether the balance-of-power concept has ever described accurately an existing situation. They question the acceptability of equivalence of power for a particular state, and the practicability of stable, continuing equilibrium when population increase and economic and technological change continually alter the power equation. States exhibit by their policies and actions a desire to achieve an ever-increasing margin of power on their side. They certainly will not adopt programs checking their natural increase in power merely to support an alleged balance situation.

The balance should not be analyzed in moral terms. Woodrow Wilson and others have implied that the balance of power is an immoral concept. National power exists in fact, however, and will continue to do so. Regardless of moral or ethical considerations, a distribution of power prevails at all times among states. Figures 1–1 and 1–2 in Chapter 1 graphically represent some of the bases of the present distribution of power. A moral judgment can only be pertinent to the decisions on use of power rather than the actual strengths. Determination of what will happen in a given situation lies not so much in the balance *per se* as in the interests and resolves that generate action or inaction.

The decisions of sovereign states involved in a balance-of-power system cannot be controlled altogether by their associates. Political leaders may be hesitant or constrained in particular circumstances by domestic political differences or pressure groups. More than one crisis may compete for the attention of a state or states like the simultaneous occurrence of the British-French attack on Suez in 1956 and the Hungarian revolt against Soviet control. Individual states, while cooperating in a balance-of-power situation, may interpret involvement differently, depending on the particular issue, as United States' allies did not agree over the Vietnam situation. The operation of the balance is further complicated by the spectrum of types of power used—political, economic, and psychological as well as military. The reaction needed may be collaboration in support of an ally's foreign exchange situation rather than military support. There are many "qualifiers" that may enter into the decisions of governments on whether to act in support of an associated state. These cannot all be foreseen in advance.

Changing Circumstances. The revolutionary changes occurring in world affairs affect the balance system.

Although Western Europe is still a center of great power, the individual states no longer possess the greatest power. The United States and the Soviet Union possess the most decisive power. Additional centers of power are rising in China, Japan, and India. Other significant power may appear in Brazil, in one or more states in Africa, and in other states having an adequate population base to support appreciable power, as in Pakistan and Indonesia. Groups of individually weak states, like the African states, may exercise significant power in international organizations. The locale of power politics has been globalized. The proliferation of power centers make the establishment and operation of a balance-of-power system, or systems, extremely complex. Balance, if it is to exist at all, depends increasingly on the intervention of a balancer or controller external to some of the geographical areas involved.

The spread of industrialization, the urge for development, and consequent economic interdependence have made the power equation more sensitive to economic factors. Again, the reader is encouraged to ponder the distribution of economic strength as depicted in Ambassador Reischauer's map given in Chapter 1.

The expansion of nationalism and of the susceptibility of peoples to ideological appeals through the medium of mass communications is similarly bound to affect the operation of any balancing system. Modern communications and propaganda techniques, viewed alone, may make shifts from one side to another easier than before. Cuba, for example, moved quickly to opposition to the United States. Russia and the Western powers became allied in World War II, but the absence of common values and objectives made the association a short-lived expedient. Japan and the United States have been allied since 1950, though enemies in World War II. Any balance system needs an element of self-adjustment and that is now much more complex and unpredictable than formerly. There is a conflict between Peking and Moscow and a rise of polycentrism in the Communist world counterbalancing in a sense the disarray that has appeared in the Western alliance because of de Gaulle's policies. The nonaligned states have increased greatly in number. These alterations have introduced an added dimension of uncertainty into the balancing system that was not present in the classical European balance of the nineteenth century.

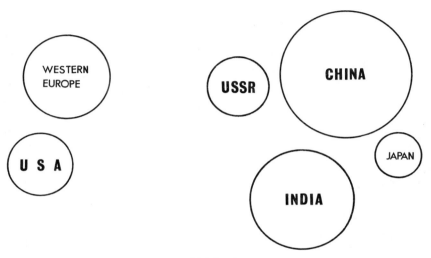

FIGURE 15–1
Population and Power Centers

The vast increase in number of sovereign states, the present-day ideological differences inhibiting the flexibility which was existent in the power politics of Europe in the nineteenth century, some movements toward regional integration regardless of balancing considerations, the cleavages among some states which might reasonably associate in a search for equilibrium, and other complexities combine to provide solid material for debates on the nature and extent of existence of balance of power.

Great Power wars, openly declared, have not been manageable in the twentieth century according to the postulates of the balance of power. They seem even less likely to be manageable between nuclear powers. The management and use of military force in the balance-of-power equation has additional technological as well as political components, as discussed in Chapters 9 and 19. These include more detailed prior consultation and arrangements among allies, as there may be no time for decision making in time of crisis, high military readiness, and a great increase in ambiguity in connection with the use of armed force.

LIMITING FORCES IN POWER POLITICS

Rapidly changing conditions in the latter part of the twentieth century raise questions about the viability of the balance of power as an instrument to maintain peace. Are there other limitations upon power politics?

Morality and World Opinion. As we suggested in Chapter 1, morality and world opinion limit power politics, but it is hard to assess to what extent. International agreements and the desire of most states to win respect, create some international moral consciousness that decision makers take into account. Theologian Reinhold Niebuhr writes in his *Moral Man and Immoral Society* that it is hard to find agreed principles of morality accepted as binding by states. The Genocide Convention proscribes racial extermination, but racial conflicts exist in the Near East, Africa, and elsewhere that might provoke disregard of these humane principles.

Conceptions of self-interest in given circumstances provide the momentum for state conduct. If self-preservation appears to necessitate a course of action contrary to what some regard as standards of morality, states and their agents are likely to follow this action regardless of world opinion. Most international affairs do not, however, raise crucial issues closely related to self-preservation.

Morality and world opinion in themselves lack sufficiently compelling sanctions to deter decision makers from taking those feasible measures which best serve their country's interests as they see it. Morality and world opinion are, nevertheless, valuable complements to other limits on the use of power. The problem confronting the statesman was summarized by Demosthenes in his oration to the Athenians on the formation of Megalopolis in 371 B.C. "Our purposes and our actions," he declared, "should always be just; but we must also be careful, that they are attended with advantage."

International Law. The customs, principles, and agreements comprising the law of nations establish certain rules of conduct and principles of responsibility which states have generally been willing to accept. States acknowledge that actions under these principles are proper for adjudication before courts of law and that the rules are enforceable through measures of self-help and by the collective action of international bodies. States are sensitive to charges of violating international law and will go to considerable lengths to defend the legality of their procedures. Where found wrong, they will often make reparation and conform, even though no power exists to enforce such conduct. In these respects international law limits power politics chiefly through its influence on world opinion.

Tradition and Internal Opinion. Each state tends to follow its own traditional patterns in interstate affairs and is influenced by the environment of its internal opinion and political philosophy concerning the use of power in interstate relations. There is sometimes a tendency to apply internal political philosophy to those relations. After World War I, the United States did not choose to use its maximum available strength in international affairs until Pearl Harbor. In effect, United States power was limited by United States policy. Stanley Hoffmann comments, "The depreciation of the hidden role of force in a liberal community entails a depreciation of other more subtle forms of coercion as well, and a tendency to underrate the element of struggle that persists in any political system." Referring to the United States, Professor Hoffmann writes, "A liberal vision of international affairs suffers from a complete misunderstanding of the role of force in world history." [6] The limiting factors of tradition, internal opinion, and political philosophy are not immutable, witness the major changes in United States policy and ways of employment of power in the last generation.

Collective Measures. A third limiting factor that has come to receive increasing attention is collective action under multilateral international treaties. During the nineteenth century the Great Powers of Europe acting through the Concert of Europe and the Congress system sought to restrict the free use of power. Through these instrumentalities the so-called Eastern Question (Turkey and the Balkans) was handled, and collective measures were mounted to halt Russian and Turkish expansionist activities in southeastern Europe.

The League of Nations represented another collective approach, with its procedures for pacific settlement of international disputes and its principles of collective security.

In the United Nations an attempt has been made to remedy two of the fundamental weaknesses of the League of Nations. All of the principal powers became original members of the U.N., insuring a preponderance of power whenever the Great Powers could agree among themselves. Provision was also made for the assembling of collective international forces to maintain and enforce international peace. But the latter provision has never

[6] L. Stanley Hoffmann, "Restraints and Choices," *Daedalus*, Fall, 1962, pp. 668–704.

been implemented, and as we shall note in Chapter 23, the Great Powers have been divided on most crucial issues.

The United Nations has served useful purposes on many occasions in bringing nations together for discussion of issues. But a universal association of states with widely divergent aims and attitudes tends to emasculate action at crucial points. The balance-of-power equation in the world is more often reflected in the politics within the United Nations than moderated by those politics.

The principle of collective action, as Professor Inis L. Claude of the University of Michigan has pointed out in *Power and International Relations*, is to substitute a universal concert of power for the more biased and less reliable balance of power. The results have not yet established universal collective security as a reliable guarantor of peace, security, and the interests of individual states.

The joining of the nations of Western Europe and North America in the North Atlantic Alliance, together with the ANZUS Pact, the U.S.-Japanese mutual-security agreement, the SEATO alliance, and the Rio Pact, are to some extent arrangements by which the groups may collectively exercise restraints on the use of power by one or more of their members. But their primary purpose is to manage the cooperating power more effectively in the regional and global balance situations. The large and increasing amount of international economic organization in the world seems likely to have a more limiting effect on the ruthless use of economic power than the effect of the United Nations and other agencies on the use of military power.

The balance-of-power policy and the other limiting factors on power politics are useful and necessary in contemporary international politics. They in turn increase the complexity of the changing interstate scene.

PATTERNS OF POLICY

Practically all states adhere to certain techniques and common practices in order to facilitate the conduct of their external affairs. These include (1) the recognition of other states and the exchange of diplomatic and consular officers; (2) the conclusion of treaties and agreements to facilitate intercourse with others; (3) adherence to certain international conventions and protocols and participation in certain international agencies, such as the United Nations; and (4) support of international law. The general adherence to these categories of policy helps to make the actions of states more predictable. Certain broad patterns of policy are distinguishable and can be classified under four headings.

[1] Patterns Concerned with Methods of Conducting International Relations. Some states prefer to conduct the greater part of their relationships with others on a bilateral basis because their bargaining or negotiating position is stronger or more expedient in such a situation. Others prefer to operate extensively on a multilateral basis within international organizations of various kinds. Others dislike multilateral approaches to problems because such action may force them to take a position on a matter on which they might otherwise have remained neutral or which they would prefer not to have raised and perhaps taken out of their hands. Some states decline to join some international organizations or arrangements; others join but attempt to make careful distinctions concerning matters which they prefer to see handled by other means.

[2] Patterns Concerned with Welfare. Economic affairs form a large part of the policy patterns of most states and include concern for trade, discrimination, access to markets, raw materials, and extension and receipt of foreign aid. These patterns of policy extend also to social welfare, such as the promotion of educational, scientific, and cultural cooperation, and opposition to trade that is socially harmful, such as the narcotics traffic.

[3] Patterns Concerned Primarily with Security. Because aggression has become total in the variety of the instruments used, the policies employed to cope with it have become equally diverse, extending from information programs to active use of military force. Policy patterns here include the maintenance of a strong military posture, forming or adhering to alliances and coalitions, or practicing isolation and neutrality. Some states are following policies of nonalignment while retaining freedom to interpose in international conflicts through criticism, recommendations, and various forms of diplomatic action. Again, some states do not hesitate to engage in intervention in the internal affairs of others when they feel this necessary in order to advance or protect their own interests. The patterns of policy include the promotion of peaceful settlement of international disputes, although some states find it necessary or desirable at times to resort to the use of military power.

[4] Patterns of Policy Having Expansionist or Revolutionary Objectives. Some states pursue expansionist and revolutionary objectives in their foreign relations. The design of Nazi policy was one of eventual world domination. Communist policy has a similar doctrinaire objective, which is being pursued by a new imperialism with an ideological drive and use of subversion and a stated policy of undeclared war. Economic and cultural penetration may be a preliminary step to later efforts to obtain political control of other states.

The Interrelation of Policy Patterns. None of these patterns of policy are mutually exclusive; some are complementary; others conflict. That two or more patterns seem to be inconsistent or conflict does not necessarily mean that a nation will not use both of them as its national interests and objectives dictate. For instance, the U.S.S.R. has generally promoted conflict among non-Communist states yet provided good offices for the India-Pakistan conflict of 1965.

Execution of policies inevitably requires adjustment to realities, for "diplomacy is an art of the possible." A policy pattern tends to be a preference in ways to conduct affairs from which a state sometimes diverges in deference to the realities of the situation.

Policies and programs are embedded in traditions, precedents, and a multitude of diplomatic and administrative arrangements, and patterns tend to repeat themselves. States are cautious about change until assured of greater effectiveness. In the current world community of many new states without traditional patterns of policy these elements of tradition and consistency do not always exist. For the older states the fluid world situation requires a continuing reassessment of established patterns in order to adapt these to emergent forces. Shifts in the policy of one state tend to generate shifts in the policies of others. The present revolutionary era is a period of greatly increased dynamism in policy patterns in international affairs. This dynamism derives from the interests of states as defined by their leaderships, which are striving for a balance of power, in their interstate relations.

CONCLUSION

Woodrow Wilson was a leading idealist who thought that power politics could be abolished by the institution of a system based on reason in foreign affairs. But all politics are power politics, and the search for power is deeply implanted within the hearts and minds of political leaders. Nations hold differing, and inevitably somewhat conflicting, aims and values. Rivalry, conflict, and struggle for power are bound to ensue.

The reality was expressed by Ambassador George F. Kennan,

. . . the sovereign national state, this child of the modern age, notwithstanding the mantle of nebulous moral obligation in which it likes to wrap itself, still recognizes in the crucial moments of its own destiny no law but that of its own egoism—no higher focus of obligation, no overriding ethical code.

Mr. Kennan added that the diplomat discovers,

it is not only his own government and not only governments in his own age that are this way; but that governments have been this way for a long time in the past, throughout, in fact, the entire range of history of the national state.[7]

The task in international affairs includes reaching accommodation by channeling these cross-purposes and self-serving actions into orderly discussion and adjustment through the council chamber, the forum of the mediator, and the courtroom where accommodations can be reached.

So long as threats to peace and security and other vital interests remain, the national decision maker must concern himself with safeguarding the welfare and integrity of his own state. For as Alexander Hamilton underlined when the American Constitution was being considered, governments are agents and not principals. In protecting and advancing the interests of the state, power politics remains an indispensable instrument.

[7] George F. Kennan, "Diplomacy and History," *The Review of Politics*, Vol. XVIII, No. 2, April 1956, pp. 170–177.

CHAPTER 16

Diplomacy and the Conduct of Foreign Affairs

DIPLOMACY AND FOREIGN POLICY

Policy, as was indicated in Chapter 11, is the overall course of action a country proposes to follow in its foreign affairs backed by supporting programs. Diplomacy is the primary instrument for carrying out a state's foreign policy with other states with which it is at peace.

Policy and diplomacy are distinct yet interdependent. Many policy makers are involved in the actual conduct of diplomacy, as in meetings of heads of state and of Foreign Ministers. Professional diplomats, on the other hand, sometimes contribute to foreign policy determination, and they affect the policy's success by their skill or lack of skill in carrying it out.

Lester Pearson, Prime Minister of Canada, has stated the relationship in this way. Diplomacy, he says, "does not make policy, it transmits and explains it and tries to negotiate arrangements which embody and secure it." [1] A neat distinction can no longer be drawn, however, between foreign policy and diplomacy, any more than it can between policy and

[1] Lester B. Pearson, *Diplomacy in the Nuclear Age* (Cambridge: Harvard University Press, 1958), p. 2.

313

programs. The art of diplomacy is generally no more than the principal means of accomplishing, in Sir Harold Nicolson's terms, the "executive" rather than the "legislative" part of foreign policy.

Definition. Diplomacy can be defined as the process of representation and negotiation by which states customarily deal with one another in time of peace. Effective diplomacy is supported by, and guides, the total inventory of policy instruments—political, psychological, economic, and military—which a state possessses. It is the focal process of international politics. It is the "accessory" before and after the fact of policy.

In a technical sense, diplomacy can be described as "the business of communicating between governments," to use the words of Ambassador George Kennan. But it serves in a broader sense as the principal organ for adjusting and reconciling differences between states as well as providing the medium of communication.

We shall be concerned in the discussion that follows with the changes that have occurred in the style of diplomacy from ancient times to the present. With the world in transition, different styles have come to prevail. There are today many non-European states participating in diplomatic affairs bringing new traditions and values to the arena of diplomacy. Diplomacy is no longer the exclusive province of the professional diplomat. Some of those engaged in contemporary diplomacy not only play the game differently than it used to be played, but occasionally try to change the rules as well.

THE EVOLUTION AND TRANSFORMATION OF DIPLOMACY

Diplomacy has been popularly associated with intrigue and romance. These elements are included in modern diplomacy, although it mainly follows an unromantic, hard-working, institutionalized pattern that is far removed from the fictionalized image of courtiers soliciting favors from monarchs.

The Formal Institutions of Diplomacy. The establishment of missions, consulates, and other agencies abroad is governed by custom, tradition, and specific agreements between states. Customarily a state has an embassy or legation, usually called a mission, in the capital of each other state it recognizes and with which it agrees to have diplomatic relations. A mission's rank is determined by the importance each country attaches to the interchange, and by reciprocity. Most diplomatic missions are embassies, headed by an ambassador. Legations, which are of a lower rank, are headed by ministers. Consulates, military, and economic assistance missions are provided for by special agreements between the sending and receiving states. In the more important capitals, such as London and Paris, there may be more than one ambassador or both an ambassador and a minister, with the latter tending especially to economic or alliance affairs. Some deputy chiefs of United States missions and also chiefs of economic missions hold ministerial rank. The permanent missions to the United Nations are headed by a representative with the personal rank of ambassador.

Consulates, which essentially handle trading and visa matters, are linked with the embassy in the country in which they are situated and are generally located in port cities. The consular staff is responsible to the ambassador or minister in charge of their country's mission.

The Historical Evolution of Diplomacy. Diplomacy is an old institution, originating in relations between separate political entities. The Greeks and Romans used it extensively. Roman diplomacy was conducted with considerable formality. The most ardent practitioners of diplomacy in the era before national states were the Papacy and the princely Italian city-states of the Renaissance. Through their dealings were fashioned many of the customs and usages associated with diplomatic techniques. Machiavelli's *The Prince* portrays the nature of international relations in that day. Deceit, duplicity, and cunning did characterize some of the diplomacy of that period, and reputation for such procedures continued to haunt the diplomatic profession long after such practices had been replaced by more honest and straightforward dealings between states. The principle of diplomatic immunity began in Greece. Today an accredited representative of a foreign country is accorded immunities from the enforcement of local law.

The Rise of Permanent Diplomatic Missions. Before there were nation-states, diplomacy was conducted by ambassadors appointed on an *ad hoc* basis for particular negotiations. The first resident embassy was established in 1450 between two Italian princely states, but establishment of permanent missions did not become a customary practice until the late seventeenth century. French procedures then became the model of the diplomatic method. Cardinal Richelieu's rules for the diplomatic game were expressed by François de Callières in a manual published in 1716 entitled *De la manière de négocier avec les souverains.*[2] Sir Harold Nicolson

[2] François de Callières, *De la manière de négocier avec les souverains,* etc. (Paris: 1716). English translation published by University of Notre Dame Press, 1963.

has described this as "the best manual for diplomatic method ever written."

De Callières stressed integrity, continuity, good faith, and confidential but honest negotiation by professional diplomats. His description of the tasks of the diplomat has contemporary relevance.

. . . the principal function of the negotiator is to bring about a harmonized union between his master and the sovereign to whom he is sent, or else to maintain and increase existing alliances by every means in his power. He must labor to remove misunderstandings, to prevent subjects of dispute from arising, and generally to maintain in that foreign country the honor and interests of his Prince. This includes the promotion and patronage of his subjects, assistance to their business enterprises, and the promotion of good relations between them and the subjects of the foreign Prince to whose court he is accredited.

De Callières' principles reflected the type of diplomatic practice which lasted until World War I. It was the diplomatic method of equal powers sharing a common civilization, whose leaders and diplomats partook of similar social values. And it was the diplomat's role as an essentially peaceful bargainer that guaranteed his immunities, privileges, and personal security in even a relatively hostile country.

The Transformation of the Diplomatic Method. Methods of the old diplomacy have been transformed by the forces of political and social change since 1919. These forces also include the revolution in technology and communications, the political transformation of societies, and the comparative decline of Europe in international politics.

Developments in communications have decreased the ambassador's role in implementing policy, for reports can be relayed quickly and instructions cabled or telephoned. As liberal democracy developed, the aristocratic traditions of the old diplomacy yielded to more businesslike methods. The practice of diplomacy was placed in the hands of professionally trained career civil servants. The present foreign-service system in the United States was established by the Rogers Act of 1924. Previously, diplomatic appointments were subject to the political spoils system. Today the greater percentage of diplomatic positions of the United States, Britain, France Canada, Japan, and other constitutional powers are entrusted to career foreign-service officers who are recruited in the first instance by competitive examinations following a university education.

Woodrow Wilson condemned secret diplomacy and called for "open covenants, openly arrived at." In so doing he was applying liberal democratic values to the conduct of foreign affairs. He was not pressing for open negotiations on delicate matters, but rather for complete information to the public on the agreements reached. Wilson was not, of course, the first to conceive of open diplomacy. In the time of the Greek city-states, ambassadors negotiated treaties and agreements before sessions of the duly chosen assembly and the terms were publicly discussed. One might speculate on a diplomacy which put foreign ambassadors to a similar test before the United States Congress!

Dimensions of the New Diplomacy. Present-day diplomacy includes what Canadian Prime Minister Lester Pearson has termed "political diplomacy"—that is, diplomacy carried on personally by foreign ministers and heads of state, or by their personal representatives. Negotiations are often covered by elaborate press, radio, and television reporting.

The emergence of Communist power and the new states in Asia and Africa has changed the functions and purposes of diplomacy as well as the "style" of negotiations. Whereas diplomacy used to be a political art practiced primarily by states with a Western tradition, many states today are neither Western nor bound by older traditions. They therefore do not always follow the traditional ways. As former United States Foreign Service Officer Charles W. Thayer comments in his book *Diplomat*, diplomacy has not yet altogether "emerged from its Stone Age, as is occasionally demonstrated by the rocks hurled by mobs of one government through embassy windows of another." [3] Or again, when the delegates of twenty-four African states walk out of the U.N. General Assembly when Britain's Prime Minister speaks, they may be exhibiting more of their own immaturity and lack of responsibility than anything else.

In a world totally involved in international politics, where foreign affairs are subject to public scrutiny and sanction, thanks to the media of mass communications, negotiations and communications may be used for propaganda purposes. This seems often to be the case with international conferences.

Diplomats must be able to deal with the representatives of the press and make information about negotiations available to the public. This sometimes results in two series of meetings taking place simultaneously, one publicly and another privately. The real negotiations take place in the private session. A diplomat's freedom to maneuver can be restricted by public curiosity. The diplomat's lot, never an easy one, has become less so under the glare of publicity.

[3] Charles W. Thayer, *Diplomat* (New York: Harper, 1959).

THE ACTORS IN TWENTIETH-CENTURY DIPLOMACY

The actors in today's diplomacy include heads of governments, Foreign Secretaries and their Foreign Offices, staffs, the diplomatic corps abroad, and military and other expert personnel drawn into international operations. There are other envoys too, such as roving ambassadors, personal representatives, and even tourists. Senate Majority Leader Mike Mansfield gathered information from abroad for President Johnson and presented official views of the President in Paris, Moscow, and Saigon.

Heads of State and of Governments. Heads of state who hold primarily titular positions, such as the British King or Queen, or the President of the Federal Republic of Germany, have essentially ceremonial roles in foreign affairs. Their visits to foreign lands are chiefly to promote goodwill. Heads of governments, on the other hand, often take a personal hand in the diplomacy of their country. Woodrow Wilson, the two Roosevelts, Harry Truman, Dwight Eisenhower, and John F. Kennedy extensively engaged in substantive negotiations at home and abroad when serving as President of the United States. The same can be said for President de Gaulle of France. Prime Minister Winston Churchill was noted for his negotiations with President Roosevelt, Premier Stalin, and other heads of governments. His Foreign Secretary, Anthony Eden, was relegated to a subordinate role in many of Churchill's wartime parleys.

Dictators have been somewhat variable in the roles they have tried to play in diplomacy. Although Stalin had a key role in the summit conferences with Allied leaders at Teheran, Yalta, and Potsdam during World War II, he normally remained in the background and controlled foreign affairs through Foreign Minister Molotov. Premier Khrushchev, on the other hand, sought the center of the stage of world politics by repeated attempts to organize summit conferences with Western statesmen and led his country's delegation to the 1960 United Nations General Assembly. President Nasser of the United Arab Republic assumed responsibility for Egyptian diplomacy, trying to gain recognition as an Arab leader and to organize a neutral bloc able to bargain with the Great Powers.

Reciprocity is an important diplomatic principle that has increasingly drawn heads of government into diplomacy as one responds to the initiative of another. So long as this principle applies, it is likely that those charged with the chief responsibilities for government will remain active in diplomacy much as they are at present. Thus, when Soviet Premier Kosygin invited the late Indian Prime Minister Shastri and Pakistani President Ayub Khan to meet at Tashkent to resolve differences between their countries, there was little choice but for them to meet personally with the Soviet Premier.

Foreign Secretaries. The most preoccupied actors on the stage of diplomacy are the Secretaries of State for Foreign Affairs. Foreign affairs is their business. Their official lives are filled with a continuous round of diplomatic conversations, visits to other countries, attendance at conferences, and preparation for and follow-up of important negotiations. They are responsible for advising their heads of government and keeping them informed on external matters, while conducting their government's policy in accord with the wishes of the heads of government. They also have to administer the large bureaucracies in their Foreign Offices and foreign services, and attend cabinet and other high-level policy meetings.

Since 1945 the Foreign Secretaries of some of the principal powers have spent large amounts of time away from their desks attending international conferences. Secretary of State James F. Byrnes spent approximately as much time away from Washington attending Foreign Ministers' meetings to negotiate the peace treaties for the Axis satellite states between 1945 and 1947 as he did in his office. During his five years in office John Foster Dulles traveled more than 100,000 air miles annually—which would have taken him to the moon and back—while engaging in a continuous round of parleys with other world leaders. Secretary Rusk preferred to minimize his own traveling, causing others to come to Washington.

Professional Diplomats. The professional experts form the largest group of those engaged in diplomacy today. These include the civil servants and specialists who staff the Foreign Offices, and embassies, legations, and consulates abroad. They handle the routine aspects of foreign relations, preparing studies, reports, and instructions; drafting cables; backstopping top-level negotiations; engaging in exchanges with subordinate officials of foreign governments; and staffing delegations to international conferences. In the words of de Callières, their job is twofold, "the first to conduct the business of the master; the second to discover the business of others." Such a corps of professionals is not formed in a day. Time and experience are required to develop a sophisticated and mature foreign service under the pressures of the modern age.

Special Emissaries. Governments occasionally appoint special emissaries to represent them at important ceremonial events or to conduct special negotiations. President Franklin D. Roosevelt dispatched his confidant, Harry Hopkins, on several secret missions to Churchill and Stalin, bypassing both the Secretary of State and the ambassadors in the capitals concerned. President Eisenhower used his brother Milton Eisenhower on a number of special occasions. Similarly, Presidents Truman, Kennedy, and Johnson used Ambassador Averell Harriman, a highly professional diplomat, as a personal envoy on a considerable number of special missions. Three years before he became Secretary of State, John Foster Dulles was given the task of negotiating the Japanese Peace Treaty. These appointments are a prerogative of the head of state and enable him to obtain a direct personal contact with other heads of governments on specific items of business. The special emissary may be more highly skilled than the accredited ambassador in a particular problem area affecting several countries. But he may also diminish the prestige and subsequent effectiveness of the ambassador on the spot; hence, the technique is best used sparingly.

Military and Other Expert Personnel.   With the interrelationships of political, economic, security, and scientific matters that exist in today's complex environment, it is natural that personnel from numerous departments of government should be drawn into diplomatic intercourse as well as policy formulation.

Among the most active supplementary participants in international affairs are members of the armed services and the defense establishments. The Supreme Allied Commander for NATO has a political as well as military role. The Secretaries of Defense of the NATO countries, and their deputies, are engaging in diplomacy when they discuss new defense arrangements at NATO meetings. In a similar fashion, public-health officials meeting at the World Health Organization or Treasury representatives attending meetings of the World Bank are also involved in diplomacy.

Many others engaged in mutual security, cultural relations, and economic and technical assistance operations are similarly involved in diplomatic activities of one kind or another. "A soil scientist from the United States in Afghanistan may, while he is there, do more to influence Afghan opinion on United States policy, for better or for worse, than the United States or even the Soviet Ambassador." [4] Representatives of various government departments are designated as attachés in diplomatic missions and may be part of delegations to international conferences.

The university educated and professionally trained diplomat is more necessary than ever in the greatly enlarged scope and rapidity of contemporary international relations. In technical matters that concern states, additional help is required from scientists, military men, writers, doctors,

[4] Pearson, *op. cit.*, p. 19.

fiscal experts, and agronomists. The problem confronting many governments is how to organize these various elements into an effective team. This is a problem for public administration experts as well as for those charged with the leadership of nations.

THE BASIC FUNCTIONS OF DIPLOMACY

The basic functions of diplomacy comprise (1) protection; (2) representation; (3) observation and reporting; and (4) negotiation. In addition, individuals in diplomatic positions now have many quasi-diplomatic functions as a result of their nation's participation in regional or mutual security arrangements, foreign-assistance programs, or international organizations. For instance, the United States Head of Mission in a country receiving foreign assistance has policy and operational responsibilities in economic and military matters.

[1] Protection. The primary function of the diplomat is to protect and advance the rights and interests of his country and its nationals abroad. He must always be alert to threats or discrimination and see that the reputation of his country is not compromised. This responsibility is carried out through representation, negotiation, treaties, and executive agreements. The officers of diplomatic missions are continually called upon to counsel their own citizens who ask for help and to seek redress where rights have been infringed, wrongs suffered, property seized, or persons injured or not given full protection of the law. Under disturbed political conditions, the protective function may become a heavy responsibility. This may bring into question the use of the embassy or legation as a place of refuge or asylum, as in Hungary, where Cardinal Mindszenty was given asylum in the United States Embassy. When civil or international war is imminent or taking place, missions are expected to do everything in their power to help their nationals reach places of safety or to return home.

When diplomatic relations are broken off between belligerents, neutral states are customarily asked to care for the interests of the contesting parties in one another's territory. During World Wars I and II, Switzerland and Sweden exercised this protective and mediatory function.

[2] Representation. It is the responsibility of an envoy, whether sent to another state or to an international gathering, to represent his country and the interests of its government and people. Representation implies being a symbol and exemplification of his state and government. It is to him that foreign officials as well as private individuals and groups must look as the official source of information and interpretation of his country's attitudes and intentions. He must be able to explain these views with tact, clarity, and precision—even if he himself has a different personal opinion. In playing this role as both symbol and spokesman of his government, the envoy seeks to cultivate friendship and widespread understanding for his state by developing personal associations with the leaders of government, business, society, education, and political life.

Former Ambassador Joseph C. Grew described the diplomat's responsibility in the following words:

> He must be, first and foremost, an interpreter and this function of interpreting acts both ways. First of all he tries to understand the country which he serves—its conditions, its mentality, its actions, and its underlying motives, and to explain these things clearly to his own government. And then, contrariwise, he seeks a means of making known to the Government and the people of the country to which he is accredited the purposes and hopes and desires of his native land. He is an agent of mutual adjustment between the ideas and forces upon which nations act.[5]

Representation implies that the members of a diplomatic mission must be well-informed about their own country and continually providing information where needed. They must be able to expound at social gatherings or in public speeches on such varied subjects as their country's policies on trade and housing, progress in public and private medicine, and the unique qualities of their country's art.

Senior diplomats and heads of mission represent their countries on numerous ceremonial occasions ranging from the opening of the local parliament to university celebrations. They must become acquainted with the host country through travel, and they must entertain widely and attend receptions and dinners in honor of other ambassadors. Care must be taken that invitations are reciprocated and that important members of the government and of commerce are included. Sir Harold Seymour said, "A good dinner goes a great way in diplomacy."

Most countries supply their diplomats with ample funds to spend on cultivating good relations. This has been notably true of the Communist countries. The United States was for many years so niggardly in this respect that only wealthy persons could afford to take the principal ambassadorial posts. Recent adjustments have now made it financially possible for career officers to serve as ambassadors and ministers in the larger capitals.

---

[5] Joseph C. Grew, *Ten Years in Japan* (New York: Simon and Schuster, 1944), p. 262.

Although much business can be accomplished at informal dinners, the social aspect can be overemphasized.

Nowadays in assuming the traditional position as his country's highest official representative, the modern ambassador often has a major administrative and managerial responsibility to perform. A United States ambassador must supervise the activities of several U.S. agencies, for example, as many as fourteen in Brazil, and assume administrative charge of perhaps several hundred officials (even more than that if there is a Peace Corps operation in his country) and their dependents. These tasks can place a heavy drain upon his time.

[3] Observation and Reporting. Diplomats are the eyes and ears of their governments abroad. To enable their governments to proceed intelligently in foreign affairs, and to know in the midst of fluid events where their friends stand and where trouble is to be apprehended, it is one of the principal assignments of every mission abroad to maintain a continual stream of reports to the home office. These cover a wide range of subjects on current economic, political, social, and military conditions; pending legislation; new products and industries; technological achievements; and even trends in education. Governments also require accurate information on developing issues, trends in negotiations, and the significance of political attitudes held by important leaders, responsible officials, and influential segments of public opinion. They need all the light they can obtain on the relationships between the foreign country and other states. Gathering this information requires continual study of all channels of information and statistical data. Its evaluation involves the cultivation of an intimate knowledge of national and local conditions and of key personalities. The combined task of gathering and weighing this information calls for the joint efforts of experts in numerous fields.

A glance at communications coming into the Foreign Office of a major power almost any day would leave one with the impression that the government is receiving a mass of bits and pieces, fragments of knowledge. Considering what arrives on one day from a given country, this is to a certain extent true. However, along with the coded cables, there come longer mailed reports containing reflective interpretations and evaluations. It is the job of the Foreign Office staff, with the aid of intelligence analysts, to piece the parts together and to sift and evaluate the implications of what is taking place abroad. A conversation reported from one capital may appear to have little significance in itself, but when put together with views reported from other quarters, or with some obscure action in another part of the world, it may take on larger significance.

Although their countries may be conducting intelligence activities, secret spying is not usually practiced by the formal diplomatic and consular representatives of most countries. Secret spying is not necessary, because a great amount of information is available from legitimate official, private, and public sources, although subtlety may have to be practiced to obtain it where governments deliberately seek to hide or foreclose customary sources of information, as happens in authoritarian-ruled societies. Communist regimes, however, have shown that they are not averse to using their diplomatic personnel for espionage and subversion, as evidenced by recurrent instances of Communist diplomats being expelled from host countries as *persona non grata*. Furthermore, foreign diplomats operating in Communist countries have often had to contend with wiretapping and the placement of concealed microphones, even within their embassies. United States Ambassador Henry Cabot Lodge illustrated this before the United Nations Security Council when he displayed a United States coat of arms that had been presented to the United States Embassy in Moscow in which the Russians had concealed a tiny microphone.

[4] Negotiation.   Lastly, there is what Ambassador George Kennan has termed "the classic and central diplomatic function, which is the wearisome duty of negotiating between governments." Whether negotiating singly with his counterparts of one government, or simultaneously with several at an international conference, it is the diplomat's function to argue his country's "brief." Despite his role as an intermediary in conflicts between his country and another, the diplomat is not a mediator, except in certain rare cases. He is a bargainer for one side, an entirely committed participant in the negotiations, and he must secure the best possible advantage for his side. To recall once more the counsel of de Callières, the diplomat should "distill drop by drop into the minds of your competitors those causes and arguments which you wish them to adopt. By this means your influence will spread gradually through their minds almost unawares."

NEGOTIATION—THE ART OF DIPLOMACY

The Purposes and Meaning of Negotiation.   The objects of negotiation between states are as variable as the goals they seek in foreign affairs. In general, we can say that the desired end is the procurement of consent. The goal of negotiation may be to obtain certain privileges for the citizens or traders of one country in the territory of the other; it may be the winning over of the other state to participate in some regional or other organization or in a mutual-security arrangement; it may be securing support for some proposal in the United Nations. Whatever the object, negotiation entails the presentation of views and counterviews, the compromising of differences, the search for areas of mutual interest and common agreement, and the conclusion of some form of accord or agreement, oral or written, formal or informal. This may take the form simply of a minute of a conversation, or it may be embodied in an executive agreement or a formal treaty or convention. Again the words of de Callières have a ring of wisdom about them:

> The surest and best way in which the negotiator can establish good relations is to prove to both courts that their union is of great mutual advantage. It is the essential design of diplomacy to confer such a mutual advantage, and to carry policy to success by securing the cooperation in it of those who might otherwise be its opponents.

Diplomatic negotiation is the politician's art at the international level. The diplomat must navigate between and reconcile conflicting interest groups. Now that diplomacy encompasses the world, the diplomat's task is made more difficult by the diversity of cultural backgrounds which his opposite numbers may have. He must understand the different mentality and value systems of those with whom he is dealing—a task that is not always easy.

Negotiations may be friendly and relaxed, or they may entail protracted and strenuous parleys, with various political pressures being mobilized by one side or the other. The diplomat may have to deliver notes or present demands with which he is not personally in sympathy but which his instructions leave no room to alter or soften. He must be able to submerge his own sentiments while drawing upon his knowledge of the two countries, and summon all the acumen he can command, to enable his government to succeed in its policy. Negotiation can be a difficult and unpleasant task between countries engaged in a bitter power struggle. This has been the case on many occasions between the Soviet Union and the Western powers.

The most difficult negotiation is that between parties engaged in hostilities or which have no formal ties. Merely establishing communication as a preliminary to possible negotiation can be a delicate operation fraught with hazards that can be easily set off by premature publicity. Discussions must precede the establishment of diplomatic relations between countries or regimes that do not recognize one another. These can be very difficult and are usually conducted in an atmosphere of suspicion and political sensitivity.

Diplomatic "Victories." Diplomacy rarely "wins" if one party considers its side to be "losing." Extremely skillful diplomacy, and perhaps even deception and misrepresentation, can on occasion gain temporary diplomatic advantages that are not necessarily an accurate reflection of the relative power positions of the parties concerned. But such "victories" are usually hollow ones, and in fact there may be no such thing as a "diplomatic victory." As long as nations have recourse to war or a means beyond diplomacy for settling conflicts, they can repudiate any agreement harmful to their interests, for which they are willing and able to fight. In this case, agreements become mere "scraps of paper," as a German chancellor contemptuously termed his country's pledge to respect Belgian neutrality in World War I.

Thus the diplomat's task is to find some workable nonviolent arrangement acceptable to both sides, rather than to achieve a brilliant—but almost invariably fleeting—success over other participants in negotiations. Compared to the finality of military victory, diplomatic solutions may offer less than complete satisfaction because of their compromise nature. But in fact the vast bulk of relations and working arrangements between countries are diplomatic, because morally and physically nations simply cannot afford to go to war over every difference of opinion, every conflict of interest with their friends or even their enemies in international society.

Persuasion and Compromise. The basic technique of diplomacy is to persuade the representative of another government by inducements and appeals to reason, magnanimity, self-interest, pride, or even fear. "The faculty of influencing others by conversation is the qualification peculiarly necessary to a diplomatist," observed Lord Lyons a century ago. Through manipulation of words, or statements to the press and radio, statesmen and diplomats seek favorable responses to their policies and actions. If another cannot be persuaded to adopt a position or action desired, attempts are made to ascertain what compromise is feasible. The art of compromise thus is a prominent element of diplomacy. Sometimes this can be achieved by reference to traditions, precedents, or treaties. Sometimes it is achieved by innovation or even by a process characterized by the British practice of "muddling through."

Inducements and Pressures. Where the ordinary forms of persuasion are not sufficient to achieve agreement or to attain desired ends, inducements may be brought into play. These may include offering preferential trade arrangements, loans, investment capital for development projects, or military or technical assistance. Suffice it to mention here that the Marshall Plan and subsequent foreign-assistance programs did give

United States diplomats valuable leverage in negotiating with foreign governments. British governments were long able to sway rulers in parts of the Middle East by giving subsidies and lease payments for naval sites or other strategic facilities.

Communist offers of aid to countries such as Afghanistan, Egypt, India, Indonesia, and Cuba have been handled as a combination of economic credits for development and inducements to bind recipients closer to the Soviet Union. Furthermore, Communist aid and diplomacy have been employed, despite claims to respect the independence of others, as a means of acquiring political leverage in the recipient country or of shaping internal situations in the interests of Communism.

When other means of securing diplomatic objectives prove unavailing, pressures may be tried in such forms as protests against the action of a government, hints of economic or other reprisals, cancellation of trade benefits, recall of the ambassador, or sterner measures. Cuban–United States relations went through such a cycle in 1959–1960. After repeated protests had failed to halt insults and restrictions, the United States was driven to canceling its purchases of Cuban sugar, then to embargoing the export of strategic items, and later to severing diplomatic relations. The impact of United States diplomacy was weakened by Soviet and Chinese loans and purchases of sugar and by Cuban seizure of American properties and assets valued in the hundreds of millions of dollars.

Duplicity, Bluff, and Coercion. Deceit and duplicity were traditional characteristics of older Italian diplomacy and have been accepted as techniques by Communists. Marshal Stalin said,

A diplomat's words must have no relation to actions—otherwise what kind of diplomacy is it? Words are one thing, actions another. Good words are a mask for the concealment of bad deeds. Sincere diplomacy is no more possible than dry water or wooden iron.

A reputation for integrity is now a valuable asset in a world of continuing relationships. Agreements are usually subject to rapid check by the extent of their program implementation. Deceit and duplicity are no longer as common as when Henry IV of France instructed his envoys, "If they lie to you, lie more to them." But they are still present. Hence, for example, the United States insists that provision for inspection be made in any arms control arrangements.

One should, however, distinguish between deceit and bluff, which is as much a part of the art of diplomacy as it is of poker. For example, some might consider the "asking position" at the beginning of a negotiation to be bluffing. Bluff may involve coercion. At the time of the Anglo-French attack on Suez, Soviet Premier Khrushchev threatened to send "volunteers" and to rain rockets upon Britain and France unless they desisted. This was a cynical maneuver, for Khrushchev told the United States Ambassador Charles Bohlen that these threats were not to be taken seriously. A comparable technique was employed when the Soviet Premier said that he would attack the United States with rockets if it attacked Castro's regime in Cuba. This was later explained as having been intended to be only "symbolic."

Adolf Hitler developed a cunning diplomacy that won some tangible results for Nazi Germany before World War II. By making skillful use of propaganda to weaken foreign resistance, and of quasimilitary coups, Hitler produced a series of *faits accomplis,* such as the reoccupation of the Rhineland in 1936—a move it was later learned he had been prepared to retract if the Nazi forces had encountered military opposition. Hitler had previously denounced the "injustices" of the Versailles Treaty and appealed to the Wilsonian principle of "self-determination" to moderate opposition. Many of his moves were made on weekends, when Foreign Offices were not fully operative. To convince foreign diplomats of his adamant resolve to take all necessary steps, including use of force, to incorporate parts of Czechoslovakia into Germany, Hitler indulged in temperamental outbursts. Khrushchev displayed some of these same tactics when he was in office.

Some Soviet Diplomatic Styles. The Soviet Union has employed some of the diplomatic practices associated with Renaissance and Byzantine conduct of affairs. A state generates a sense of insecurity in neighboring countries if it pursues an equivocal course of conduct. Since the Bolshevik Revolution, the Soviets have not hesitated to overthrow governments when they have thought this would advance their interests, as in Poland in 1945, Czechoslovakia in 1948, and Hungary in 1956.

A strategy of ambiguity has been characteristically employed against the Western powers to weaken their response to Soviet moves. However, Communist subversion was countered in Greece and, as a further counter to Soviet policies, the United States took the lead in organizing the Marshall Plan and establishing NATO. Soviet diplomacy with respect to Berlin has similarly been ambiguous, harassing and threatening by its "brinksmanship" tactics in the Berlin Blockade and the erection of the Wall. Yet time and again they have postponed or evaded a showdown involving force.

Another characteristic of Soviet diplomacy has been to invert the customary meaning of words in treaties and agreements, thereby precipitating lengthy disputes. Much of the trouble over the Yalta Agreement centered on differences in interpreting the meaning of such designations as "fascist" and "democratic." The Soviets, consistent with their ideology, used the word "fascist" to rationalize removal of non-Communists from governments and substitution of Communists, whom they called "democrats." Because the agreement failed to spell out the precise meaning of these terms, the Soviet arguments were difficult to deal with, although they constituted gross violation of the Western understanding at the time the agreement was made.

A further part of the Soviet style has been to carry arguments to great lengths in an effort to weary their opponents—a tactic aptly dubbed "diplomacy of exhaustion." Soviet negotiators have frequently shown that they have little or no latitude to modify positions without reference to the Politburo for new instructions. Taciturn Foreign Minister Molotov, known among diplomats as "Old Stony Bottom," symbolized the intransigence and inflexibility of Soviet manners at the conference table. In recent years, however, Soviet diplomacy seems to have lost some of this rigidity.

Vilification and false accusation is another technique. This procedure once so angered the mild-mannered Secretary of State George C. Marshall that he walked out of a conference with the Russians and never came back. Soviet diplomats at the United Nations have at times exhibited a unique disregard for traditional diplomatic protocol, as when Khrushchev pounded the table with his shoe.

The impression given by Soviet diplomacy until the mid-1960's was of antagonism toward the interstate system in general and hostility and suspicion toward foreigners. Yet at Tashkent in early 1966, Soviet Premier Kosygin skillfully and patiently exercised good offices to bring India and Pakistan to an agreement. The Soviet Union was acting as a Great Power accepting some responsibility for maintaining peace.

Soviet decision makers were apparently taken aback by Chinese Communist tactics in 1966 when the latter staged organized demonstrations in front of the Soviet Embassy in Peking and unleashed bands of teen-agers to attack "old ideas, culture, customs and habits," including Soviet ways, in what Peking called a "great proletarian cultural revolution." Moscow lodged a stern protest with the Government of China against the "outrages" and "hooliganism" committed before the Soviet Embassy and the detaining of a car flying the Soviet flag carrying the chargé d'affaires on official business. Reverting to the language of classical Western diplomacy, Moscow advised the Chinese that such actions were a "direct violation of generally accepted standards of international rule." States, it complained, are "bound to show due respect for diplomatic embassy officials and to take steps to prevent any encroachment on their persons, freedom or dignity." Thus, Soviet behavior with respect to the Chinese antics bore witness to its increasing acceptance of the amenities of traditional diplomatic styles once termed "bourgeois" and ignored by early Bolsheviks.

Subversion and Assassination as an Aid to Negotiations. One way to insure friendly negotiations or to resolve an impasse in negotiations with an obdurate government is to remove the negotiators, the government itself, or influential elements within it. Assassination and subversion are not orthodox techniques of diplomacy. But they are sometimes used in international relations.

Diplomacy by assassination flourished among the Renaissance Italian princely states. It is not altogether unknown today. Assassination under foreign auspices is rarely clearly proven. Other Arab states have charged that Egypt has supported assassination plots. During the 1950's several Latin American heads of state made similar charges against Trujillo, the dictator of the Dominican Republic, who was subsequently assassinated.

Assassination has been a major instrument of the Vietcong, but striking at the level of village officials rather than at the higher level of government, and associated with other subversive techniques. In Indonesia the Communist coup failure in 1965 stemmed in part from failure to carry out all of the planned assassinations of military leaders.

Subversion has been a routine instrument of Communist policy. Claiming that it is both justifiable and in their interests to undermine and overthrow non-Communist governments, in order to install their own agents and mold societies in their own pattern, Communists have not hesitated to foment internal disturbances, incite civil wars, and instigate *coups d'état*. The Soviet Balkan satellites supported the Communist guerrillas in the Greek civil war from 1947 to 1950. Soviet diplomats simultaneously sought to block U.N. efforts to get the facts about armed intervention across the northern frontiers.

The Threat of Force in the Background of Negotiations. Military power has always been present in the background of diplomacy, available to be called upon if need be to help protect national interests or achieve policy goals. The use of armed force short of war has been invoked on many occasions when other techniques have failed to provide the protection or satisfaction states have desired. Show of force was used in the nineteenth century to compel China and Japan to "open" their lands to trade and foreign relations, after which gunboat diplomacy became a well-known technique in China to gain extraterritorial privileges for foreigners, or special territorial or trading concessions. Marines were landed in various Caribbean countries during the first two decades of the twentieth century to protect American lives or property in the midst of disturbed political conditions. The Red Army was sent into Hungary in 1956 to put down the popular uprising that threatened to sever the ties with the U.S.S.R.

The chief asset of a diplomat is his country's prestige. The military power of his country is often a major element of that prestige and may speak louder than words. In Chapter 19 we shall discuss the role of armed force as an instrument of national policy. One example that might be mentioned here, nevertheless, has been the presence of American armed forces in Europe, coordinated with European forces through NATO. These forces have been an invaluable support to United States diplomacy. The presence of these forces has facilitated the economic reconstruction of Western Europe, freed the European governments to concentrate upon building new relationships and institutions among themselves, and made possible a German contribution to European defense within a framework of friendly relationships.

Use of Good Offices and Mediation. When nations cannot reach agreement through their own resources, a third party may offer its good offices to help the disputants find a basis for an accommodation or amicable settlement. This mediation is one of the most important procedures that can be employed in disputes between states. An example is the successful interposition made by the President of the International Bank in assisting India and Pakistan to settle the Indus River dispute. This settlement provided terms for distributing the waters for irrigation, and also arranged the necessary funds for completion of this undertaking, said to be the largest irrigation project in the world. The United Nations appointed a mediator for Cyprus at the same time it sent the U.N. Force into the island to bring peace between the Greek and Turkish Cypriot communities. Again, Emperor Haile Selassie of Ethiopia successfully mediated a cease-fire arrangement between Algeria and Morocco in their border dispute over the western Sahara in 1963.

Mediation goes beyond good offices in that the third party not only offers to serve as a channel of communication, but makes suggestions on the substance of the issues dividing the parties. Success in mediation depends partly on the astuteness of the mediator in closing the gaps between the parties and in suggesting acceptable grounds of accommodation. There must also be a disposition among the parties to come to a settlement. Without such willingness no amount of ingenuity by a mediator is likely to be successful. Timing is also important. The mediator must estimate whether the time is suitable for making proposals and must retain the confidence of both sides. He must be persistent but not overly pressing and must know when to be discreet and how far to share confidences. He must also be adept at judging when positions are flexible enough to bring the parties closer, and he must be patient and able to restrain those who would plunge ahead without allowing time to heal troubled relations.

THE LEVEL AND SETTING OF NEGOTIATIONS—NEW STYLES IN DIPLOMACY

The Setting for Negotiations. Negotiations may proceed at any one of several levels and sometimes simultaneously at two or three. They may take place directly between heads of government and constitute "summit diplomacy," or between foreign secretaries through correspondence, private talks, or at Foreign Ministers' conferences. They may proceed through ambassadors' meetings with appropriate officials, through delegates with ambassadorial rank and plenipotentiary powers at international meetings, or between specialists in technical subjects, either as a preliminary to discussions among their superiors or as a conclusive negotiation. Measured by the numbers of meetings, people involved, and agreements reached, negotiations by specialists constitute the majority of diplomatic relationships for the United States. The administration of foreign assistance involves continuous negotiation and currently includes, at any one time, approximately two thousand project agreements with recipient countries.

Negotiations may involve only two governments or many states. Alternatively, several states may, after negotiations among themselves, decide to make a collective or parallel approach to another power or group of powers. The Western powers thus approached the Soviet Union on numerous occasions during and after World War II on war issues.

Again, negotiations may proceed routinely between governments through their established missions, or they may proceed in a special international conference or in some organ of a regional or world organization such as the United Nations. Where the interests of many states are involved they often entail utilization of both procedures. There is no set pattern. Each situation is handled as circumstances, interests, and mutual agreement indicate and make feasible. This is where judgment and a "sense of the possible" must guide the statesman as he seeks to advance his nation's cause.

Personal Diplomacy by Foreign Secretaries. Personal diplomacy by Foreign Secretaries has been found useful on many occasions, but it can be overdone. The personal appearance of a Foreign Secretary flying into a foreign capital when a crisis arises can impair the subsequent effectiveness of the ambassador on the spot and expose the Secretary himself to intrigues and pressures. It is valuable for a Secretary to gain first-hand impressions abroad and exert his influence on others, but any protracted absence leaves his own capital without the individual primarily responsible for planning and directing the nation's foreign policy and strategy and it separates the head of the government and his principal advisor. Furthermore, once a Secretary has made his position clear through a personal appearance, there is no easy line of retreat or disengagement. An ambassador's instructions can be changed, ignored, or reversed. He can even be disavowed. A publicized meeting is of questionable value when there is no clear idea of what can reasonably be accomplished.

There are many gatherings today that demand the personal attendance of a Foreign Secretary, such as meetings of the NATO Council or conferences of the OAS or the ANZUS Pact powers. The Foreign Ministers of most of the United Nations find it desirable to attend at least a part of each annual General Assembly session. With most of their colleagues there for the general debate, the Assembly period allows opportunities for quiet informal talks and serious negotiations on matters not on the formal agendas. By advance planning a Foreign Minister can hold numerous private conversations instead of making separate trips to several countries. The growth of international organization has increasingly drawn Foreign Ministers into conference diplomacy.

Summit Diplomacy. "Summit diplomacy" can be useful if there is a genuine desire for mutual agreement, but requires careful preparation. Meetings of Prime Minister Churchill and President Roosevelt were generally fruitful; those with Stalin developed an overall Allied strategy and sought agreement on the political issues of postwar Europe and the United Nations, but they were much less satisfactory. There was no mutual trust and the West was unable to cope with Soviet expansion.

Summit diplomacy involves large risks. A busy chief executive ordinarily can spend only a limited time away from his capital, and conferences must necessarily be of short duration. The world's attention is riveted on such meetings, creating a tremendous public pressure on the participants for positive results and for some kind of diplomatic "victory." The Khrushchev visits to the United States and the abortive Big Four Paris gathering in 1960 assembled an enormous news and propaganda apparatus around the participants, making confidential parleying almost impossible. If there is no agreement, the participants generally try to place the burden of failure on the other side and to arouse world sentiment against the opponent.

Before he became Secretary of State, Dean Rusk wrote,

> Such experience as we have had with summit diplomacy does not encourage the view that it contributes to the advancement of American interests. . . . I conclude that summit diplomacy is to be approached with the wariness with which a prudent physician prescribes a habit-forming drug—a technique to be employed rarely and under the most exceptional circumstances, with rigorous safeguards against its becoming a debilitating or dangerous habit.[6]

Mr. Rusk then felt that summit conferences divert "time and energy from exactly the point at which we can spare it least."

Summit talks may be fruitful in finding solutions to impasses at lower levels, on specific questions. They are often useful in finalizing an agreement whose content has already been negotiated. However, experience has shown that an aggressive power with a closely geared propaganda apparatus can turn the talks into a device for gaining worldwide publicity for its own views and posture while embarrassing others and putting them on the defensive.

Conference Diplomacy. Much of the business of international relations is conducted by international conferences and periodic meetings of international organizations. This technique is termed "conference diplomacy."

Conference diplomacy goes back at least to the Congress of Westphalia (1642–1648), which laid the foundations of the modern state system. Other similar historical landmarks are the Congress of Vienna in 1815, the Congress of Berlin in 1884, the two Hague Peace Conferences in 1899 and 1907, the Versailles Peace Conference in 1919, and the United Nations Conference at San Francisco in 1945.

A regularly convening conference system was introduced by the League of Nations. The United Nations has continued this with its annual meetings of the General Assembly and more frequent meetings of the Security Council and other bodies. The Security Council is organized so it can function continuously, and the General Assembly can convene on one or two days' notice.

[6] Dean Rusk, "The President," *Foreign Affairs*, Vol. 38, No. 3, April 1960, p. 361.

Regional and other groupings, such as NATO, the Organization of American States (OAS), and the European Unity Movement, also utilize conference diplomacy. Negotiations within these limited groupings are sometimes difficult because they are so intimate; dealing with friends can at times be more difficult than dealing with political opponents and rivals.

Public involvement in international politics has stimulated conference diplomacy. The Great Powers now feel constrained to give small states a voice and an equal vote and they require their support for action. One of the problems encountered in such arrangements is that small powers may demand that votes be taken criticizing or condemning other states in circumstances where the larger powers would have to take any enforcement measures. The larger powers can thus be placed in awkward positions by not wishing to offend the smaller states, yet at times questioning the wisdom of such votes.

Conference diplomacy has enhanced collaboration in particular areas by using combined planning and activity. For example, one of the unique achievements of NATO has been the development of peacetime operational military cooperation. Despite the divisive and serious problems that are unresolved, the NATO organization has nonetheless succeeded in developing significant partnerships of effort, joint thinking, and combined activities that are most important to the security of the North Atlantic community.

A second development of conference diplomacy has been the growth of the concept of community. This has been particularly evidenced by the formation of the European Economic Community and its related bodies. With this has also emerged "parliamentary diplomacy," which has become a permanent part of the diplomatic scene.

Conference diplomacy tends to be "open diplomacy," although "open disagreements openly arrived at" can damage the interests of the parties involved and the conference or organization in which they occur. Discussion and disagreement may sometimes be preferable to keeping a question out of the public light, for it may sharpen and clarify issues and the positions of parties, as in the discussions of such controversial problems as the Hungarian uprising, the conquest of Tibet by China, and the Vietnam War.

One hundred years ago there were few international conferences and almost none that met on a continuing basis. Today the United States participates in nearly 400 conferences a year, many involving technical discussions and participation of officials from various departments of government. Such an effort places a heavy strain upon the diplomatic services of nations.

Lack of adequate preparation for conferences can cause a breakdown or failure. There is a dangerous tendency to use conference diplomacy for propaganda purposes and to exploit strengths and weaknesses to the point of exacerbating differences.

Limitations of Conference Diplomacy. Many Americans favor conference diplomacy because of its resemblance to the New England town meeting or a session of Congress. But there is a considerable difference between legislative-type gatherings of this kind and conferences of sovereign states. Aside from the differences in power and significance of various states, their representatives are not free agents but are bound by instructions from their governments, and their function is to protect and advance the interests of their state.

Conference diplomacy beween Communist states and Western powers requires agreement among the allies on when to negotiate, what is negotiable, what concessions and agreements can be made, and when to stand firm. Important agreements must be approved by the governments concerned. In some instances negotiating positions may have to be explained to legislators whose support is vital to the government. And James Reston comments, all this "must be done with one eye on a resourceful and inquisitive democratic press still operating on the assumption that all diplomatic maneuvers are news."

Officials of authoritarian states are not under comparable pressures from a political opposition or the press. It is feasible to reverse previously inflexible demands at any time. Furthermore, the press does not pry behind government positions or investigate private conversations without the consent of the authorities. Nor does it try to reveal disagreements and compromises among decision makers or speculate on the details of carefully planned strategies lest this give intelligence to the other side.

During the 1961 Berlin crisis when the Western Foreign Ministers were meeting prior to their talks with the Soviet Foreign Minister, James Reston commented in *The New York Times* that the Soviet Foreign Minister would come to the talks "with a concealed hand of cards. He will meet with Secretary of State Rusk knowing most of the compromises that have already been discussed in the West and prepared to meet them when and if they come up. It is clearly an unequal system," Mr. Reston added, "most favorable to a closed society, and it will continue this way until the West, in its own interests, devises new procedures for handling diplomacy and information in a state of semi-war." [7]

[7] James Reston, "Problem of Negotiating in the Open," *The New York Times,* September 15, 1961.

Parliamentary Diplomacy. Dean Rusk is credited with coining the phrase "parliamentary diplomacy" to describe U.N. meetings where discussions are governed by rules of procedure resembling those of national parliaments. The debates and actions on draft resolutions, elections of officers, determination of the budget, the Secretary-General's annual Report, similar to a State of the Union Message, and the political maneuvering by organized blocs of states resemble national legislative procedures.

Regional and political blocs try to influence the outcome of deliberations such as political parties, regional blocs, and special interest groups in parliamentary systems. The operations of these groups are not dissimilar to the logrolling that goes on in national legislative bodies. In U.N. corridors delegates exchange opinions, urge their positions, and try to gather votes. Discussions and lobbying also take place in the delegates' lounge, the bar, and the dining room whenever meetings are in progress. During Assembly sessions and in international crises there is more diplomatic activity within New York City than in any capital.

Parliamentary diplomacy has its limitations. It tends to create the illusion that a problem can be solved by exposure of an issue to debate and the mere passage of resolutions, when in practice tensions and national sentiments are increased. A state may vote on a draft resolution without having much understanding of the underlying issues or possible consequences. Abstention from voting may be significant in the total ballot. Bloc politics may become a kind of power politics unrelated to responsibilities involved.

On the other hand, parliamentary diplomacy can be useful in focusing world opinion. It can facilitate multilateral collaboration and lay foundations for collective action. This form of diplomacy is no substitute, however, for other methods.

All forms of diplomacy—whether traditional, personal, summit, conference, or parliamentary—are intertwined. None is a completely sufficient technique for carrying out policies and programs. Traditional diplomatic negotiations may change overnight into "personal diplomacy" by the intervention of a Foreign Minister while bilateral negotiations are proceeding. A party may decide to raise the question in the United Nations or some other organ, thereby changing the scenario and the actors, bringing the matter to the attention of the entire world, and paving the way for other political forces to exert pressures upon it.

SUCCESSFUL DIPLOMACY: SOUND POLICY AND EFFECTIVE PROGRAMS

The task of diplomacy continually becomes more complicated. Virtually every state is now involved in the discussion and settlement of international problems. A diplomatic move often requires simultaneous action in scores of capitals as well as in the U.N. Effective diplomacy requires care in correlating actions to avoid inconsistencies and the possibility that one move may contradict or cancel out another. Careful timing is needed in order to take the right step in the right place. Particular skills are needed to encourage concerted actions and, sometimes, the use of collective armed forces. Modern diplomats must also be able to function effectively under public scrutiny in open assemblies. Cultivation of friendly, mutually beneficial relationships is a function no diplomat can overlook.

Negotiations between states must be supported by concrete actions if they are to be effective. The end products of successful diplomacy are in accords and agreements, which may be in any form ranging from informal understandings to treaties and conventions. Measures to implement agreements include ratification of treaties, approval of agreements, formulation and execution of programs, and appropriation of resources. In addition, required economic and technical assistance must be sent to where they are needed. Propaganda must be directed to places where it will serve a useful purpose, and military power maintained as a background supporting the diplomatic instrument of policy. In all of these respects, programs give weight and meaning to the words of the diplomat. Furthermore, additional actions and more diplomacy flow from almost any successful diplomatic move. In democratic societies public opinion must be generated to support government policies.

Ability to adjust techniques and programs to changing circumstances is important for successful diplomacy. A foreign aid program that is successful in one part of the world will not necessarily accomplish the desired purposes in other regions. The Marshall Plan was well suited to the needs of postwar Europe. Different types of assistance are needed in Asia, Africa, and Latin America. Organized command structures under NATO have been useful in Europe, but such procedures have not been possible in SEATO. Effective statesmanship depends on clever choice of techniques and on ability to sense the crucial stage in negotiations and when new ways should be sought to handle situations.

In the game of power politics the effectiveness of a nation's diplomacy is limited by its willingness to take necessary measures to demonstrate its intent. The United States did not deter Japanese militarism in the Far East in the 1930's by merely announcing a policy of nonrecognition of the fruits of aggression. By contrast, the Berlin airlift gave unmistakable support to American diplomacy striving to maintain a free and open Berlin and was instrumental in deterring reckless action by the Communists.

Aside from the qualities already mentioned, the statesman seeking an effective diplomacy must have certain finely attuned sensibilities in dealing with others. He must be able to pursue his course with calm and steady nerves, determined to succeed. He must know when the bounds of bargaining have been reached as well as how to turn weakness and opportunities to strength. He must be patient in living with uncertainty and conflict, knowing that these have always characterized world affairs. And he must know when and how to bring other states and other assets to the support of his negotiations and policy.

International relations represent a flow of actions and interactions by which problems are tackled, adjusted, compromised, settled, and new ones created. Few are ever completely erased. In thinking about the handling of international affairs, it is necessary to bear in mind that although diplomacy is at the heart of the system of international politics, it is dependent for its success upon the support of other instruments of political, economic, and military strength and the ability of the statesman to meld all of his assets and tools with an informed public opinion. As Lester Pearson has said, "Strength without skilled diplomatic action may lead you straight against a stone wall. But diplomacy, without strength behind it, may be merely an aimless exercise." It is to those instruments of policy that put "muscle" into diplomacy that we turn in the next chapters.

CHAPTER 17

International Communication as an Instrument of Policy

INTRODUCTION

Because the actions of men and of states are shaped by the attitudes and the ideas which people hold, as we pointed out in Chapter 3, it is not surprising that governments should concern themselves with the extension of ideas and the formation of cultural ties abroad. By such means they strive to influence the minds and emotions of foreign peoples, while their diplomacy operates at the more formal level of interstate relations. In order to condition responses or stimulate political pressures abroad, many states use public information, propaganda, and cultural relations programs that are coordinated with their diplomacy. These are psychological instruments of policy.

ATTITUDES AND IDEAS IN WORLD POLITICS

Images are formed from knowledge of another state's or people's deeds and statements. Tourist behavior, news reports, speeches and activities of national leaders, a state's responses to crises, and propaganda are bases for the formation of such images.

340

Pictures in Our Heads. Walter Lippmann has observed, "What each man does is based not on direct and certain knowledge, but on pictures made by himself or given to him. Inevitably our opinions are pieced together out of what others have reported and what we can imagine." [1] The pictures people form about others do not always correspond with reality. Because men act by what they believe or by what their emotions incline them to favor, most states endeavor to create favorable attitudes in the minds of others, rather than let images and attitudes develop randomly.

Objectives in Attitude Formation. The most common objective in molding ideas is the promotion of a reliable and impressive image. States try to assure others that they adhere to principles, act morally and in good faith, and seek friendly relations with others. These values are the basis for cooperation among states.

Respect is another goal, especially of states that wish to be considered as a model to be followed by others. At the other end of the spectrum, states sometimes seek to evoke fear of themselves, or induce feelings of insecurity, hopelessness, or panic in other countries. The psychological instruments are sometimes employed in order to break existing ties between other peoples and their governments or between other states. Efforts are also on occasion made to subject other governments to pressures in order to force their policies to move in certain desired directions.

United States information and cultural relations activities have tried to picture the United States as the leader of the free world, a champion of freedom and liberty, an invincible power, a friend of subject and underprivileged peoples, and a nation standing for justice, fair dealing, equality among states, and orderly processes in international relations. The French have stressed their civilizing mission. British programs have often sought to evoke images of reliability, accuracy, fair play, solid strength, and political stability. Soviet propaganda seeks to present a picture of a powerful nation built upon a planned economic and revolutionary system that is a successful model for developing countries.

A White House Committee on International Information Activities observed some years ago that the psychological aspect of policy is not separable from policy itself and is inherent in every diplomatic, economic, or military action. There may be specific psychological plans and activities directed toward national objectives, but there are no separate national psychological objectives. National objectives are comprehensive and all-embracing.

---

[1] Walter Lippmann, *Public Opinion* (New York: Macmillan, 1922), p. 25.

PROPAGANDA AS AN INSTRUMENT OF POLICY

Two generations ago propaganda was a minor instrument of statecraft, although the techniques were used by the representatives of Corinth and Corcyra in appealing to the people of Athens at the time of the Peloponnesian wars. Thucydides in his *History of the Peloponnesian War* refers to the employment of the arts of political persuasion. The Roman Catholic Church first developed the concept of propaganda in founding the Jesuit order, whose goal is the propagation of the faith. Propaganda is now used extensively by states to influence opinion and decisions in other nations.

Growth of Propaganda.   In the United States the use of propaganda as a coordinated instrument of government policy began during World War I. After that war it was discontinued until World War II. The Soviet Union was the first modern state to develop a massive propaganda system for internal and external use in peacetime. Since then propaganda activity has become an integral part of the Communist system. Propaganda programs were extensively used by Benito Mussolini's regime in Italy and by Nazi Propaganda Minister Joseph Goebbels.

The creation of networks of rapid communication, increasingly urbanized populations, more widespread literacy, and improved techniques of propaganda have facilitated greater use of this instrument and the temptation to exploit it. Propaganda activity has received added stimulus from the political competition to influence the developing countries and the threat of nuclear war. In an era of what former Secretary of State Dean Acheson has called "total diplomacy," propaganda has come to occupy a prominent place among the external programs of states. Moral pressure upon a negotiator, a show of force, and the offering of economic inducements have long been means of influencing the minds and actions of others. Today they are supplemented by the sophisticated and complex operations of the psychological instrument.

The Nature and Psychology of Propaganda.   Propaganda consists, according to Professor Paul M. Linebarger, of the "planned use of any form of public or mass-produced communication" designed "to effect the minds, emotions, and action of a given group for a specific public purpose."

Frederick S. Dunn says in his book *War and the Minds of Men* that, "if only the right things are communicated by some people to some other people, a change can be effected in the attitudes of nations toward each other." This is, as he points out, a "technical proposition which rests upon our knowledge of the processes of using ideas or symbols to modify the behavior of men."

Much has been learned recently about the art and science of communication through improved identification of audience targets and the kinds of messages and symbols that appeal effectively to different audiences and induce various outlooks, dispositions, and motivations. Appeals to loyalties, animosities, emotions, stereotypes, and tradition may prove more successful than logical argument. The sort of communication that appeals to the political elite is ineffective with the general public. Another approach is needed for the illiterate audience in a tropical village. Effective public information programs must identify with the value systems of their audiences.

Barriers to Foreign Audience Appeal. Foreign propaganda almost automatically has to overcome skeptical and disinterested attitudes. Prejudices are easily aroused when the source of slanted messages is recognized. Reception is hindered even more where there are differences between countries.

Language is sometimes a barrier, although this can usually be overcome by using bilingual broadcasters and script writers. Most countries with foreign information and propaganda programs distribute their materials and direct their broadcasts in many different languages and dialects in order to reach the widest audiences.

Censorship and electronic jamming of foreign broadcasts have been widely practiced by Communist countries as weapons against propaganda from abroad. These barriers have forced others to relay broadcasts from mobile transmitters aboard vessels that move about seeking weak spots in the circumference of interference in efforts to have propaganda reach the target audiences. Fewer problems are encountered in sending information to free societies.

Requisites for Effective Propaganda. Among the most fundamental requisites for effective propaganda are simplicity, interest, credibility, and relevance. The propagandist must be able to employ the tools of sociology, psychology, and group analysis in order to select and appeal effectively to his particular target. Effectiveness also depends upon repetition of the theme through various media to impress it on the minds of audiences through seeing, hearing, and reading, creating what Harold Isaacs has called "scratches on the mind."

[1] SIMPLICITY. Simple slogans such as "Ban the Bomb," "General and Complete Disarmament," "Capitalist Imperialists" do more to form subconscious images than reasoned arguments about the comparative

virtues of various political and economic theories. Accusations of "geno-cide" directed at the Chinese Communists in Tibet or praise of the "freedom fighters" in Hungary and the terms *free world* and *cold war* become common usage.

[2] INTEREST. Propaganda is ineffective if it does not interest the recipient. Some United States propaganda has emphasized concern over Communism in countries where the primary concern is with economic development and nation building. Psychology has shown that people are most interested in subjects that touch themselves and that the intensity of their interest diminishes in proportion to their remoteness from the subject.

The United States Information Agency's publication *American Out-look* has stressed African problems in an effort to reach African audiences. Articles have dealt with such subjects as, "Secretary Discusses African Neu-trality," "U.S. African Aid Rises," "Senator Cites Africa's Needs." These stories have generally been reprinted from American newspapers and the African feels a sense of American interest in African affairs.

[3] CREDIBILITY AND VISIBILITY. An appeal is effective only so far as it is credible to the audience to whom it is directed. If propaganda appeals are artificial or of a dubious nature, they are not likely to achieve results. Most propaganda must in the long run be subordinated to policy because the credibility of its proclamations depends upon their being reinforced by actions.

When the Soviet Union put its first Sputniks into orbit, it was able to make effective propaganda both because this was a novel accomplish-ment, and millions in many parts of the world were able to see the satellite with their own eyes. Many people associated the capability to orbit a satellite, and later to orbit a human being, with great scientific and military achievement. The prestige value associated with achieving a "first" in space can be very considerable. The United States gained much prestige when television viewers the world over were able to watch the Gemini VI and VII rendezvous in space and come within a foot of each other. Simi-larly, the pictures transmitted from near the planet Mars were a propaganda feat for American science, as were the pictures sent from the moon.

The presence of American military forces in Western Europe makes real the declarations of United States interest in Europe by evidence that Europeans can see for themselves. The Soviet Union, exploiting the propaganda value of spectacular aid projects, has placed more emphasis than the United States on the visibility and tangibility of its foreign aid projects, although the United States has also sponsored some "impact projects."

[4] IDENTIFICATION WITH LOCAL EXPERIENCES OR OUTLOOKS. Western peoples have thought that Communist propaganda is "beating a dead horse" by continually calling Britain and the United States exemplars of "imperialism" and "monopolistic capitalism." In the underdeveloped countries, where efforts are being made to eliminate Western influences, these descriptions can be persuasive. This is because of their simplicity and the visibility of some of the things described, such as low wages and large foreign landholdings and investments. The test of effective propaganda is not whether everybody believes it, but whether it is sufficiently credible to those to whom it is directed to achieve the desired results.

[5] CONSISTENCY. Propaganda need not always be inherently consistent. Messages directed to a particular audience over a specific issue or type of situation must have some consistency, nevertheless, or there will be repercussions.

Arthur Krock has remarked in *The New York Times* that a democratic government must substantiate its statements by actual deeds if its propaganda is to be effective, and cannot conceal its failures, while an autocratic government can and does conceal both failures and inconsistencies. Furthermore, the policies of the latter can both be inconsistent with its professions and be reversed overnight.

Types of Information and Propaganda Appeals. The purposes or objectives of information programs are numerous and can vary from time to time depending upon the intent of the originator. The following are among the numerous purposes that may be sought:

[1] NEWS AND INFORMATION. Much so-called propaganda does no more than communicate information and invite the listener or reader to reach his own conclusions. This approach is typical of Anglo-American efforts in political communication. United States activities in World War II followed what was called a "strategy of truth." Today the United States Information Agency uses facts and explanations as the major tools in its efforts to portray the United States abroad and to influence other peoples. On becoming Director of USIA, Mr. Carl Rowan was told by President Johnson, "tell the truth." Mr. Rowan replied, "Mr. President, that's all I know how to do." The British Broadcasting Corporation (BBC) maintains the same principle in its overseas newscasts.

Confidence based on accurate reporting can be "banked" as a permanent attribute, as in the case of the BBC, for public confidence is a significant asset. The availability of accurate news and information can be beneficial to the sender through its imposition of limits on possible distortion.

[2] DISTORTION THROUGH SELECTION.   Distortion is prevalent in much official communication designed to manipulate foreign opinion. This communication ranges from stark honesty to sudden shifts to untruths for strategic reasons to the technique of the "Big Lie." A middle-course approach emphasizes the favorable aspects, ignores or attempts to anticipate or distract attention from the unfavorable aspects, and frequently employs emotionally loaded description which cannot be directly proved.

In this type of propaganda each side operates from an implicit assumption of its own innocence and seeks to fashion a presumption of an opponent's guilt. Each stresses its peace-loving posture, leaving it to others to disprove this. Where one fails to conform to the image put out by another, it may be denounced as "aggressive" or "imperialistic." This form of propaganda is frankly designed to condition attitudes abroad, and to generate pressures upon others.

In this middle form of propaganda there is a kernel of fact or near-fact on which interpretation or distortion is based. A sample can be taken from *American Outlook* (USIA), June 1960. This presents a bright picture of the American economy, including the high standard of living attained by American workers. Under the headline "Record Outlay Set by United States Business," the paper wrote as follows,

NEW YORK—U.S. business has been steadily increasing capital outlay plans for this year to a record high, with the emphasis heavily on modernization for greater efficiency rather than on expansion of output. However, manufacturers are planning to expand production capacity by about 5 per cent this year, and contemplate further expansion for the next few years.

This was reported recently by the economic staff of the McGraw-Hill Publishing Co. of this city on the basis of a recent survey. . . .

All U.S. business, the McGraw-Hill report said, plans to spend $37,863 million (about £13,000 million) this year on new plants and equipment. This represents a 16.4 per cent increase over the 1959 actual total of $32,543 million. It is also $852 million higher than was reported in an earlier Government survey made in late January and early February.

The Communist powers were at the same time presenting foreign audiences a different picture of the American economy. According to a statement issued by the Moscow Conference of Communist and Workers Parties in December 1960, broadcast to many parts of the world,

The decay of capitalism manifests itself chiefly in the principal country of contemporary imperialism—the United States. Monopoly capital in the

United States reveals its obvious inability to make full use of the available productive forces: The richest country among the developed capitalist countries, the United States has become the country of particularly large-scale chronic unemployment. Increased unemployment in industry has become a permanent feature in that country. Despite the enormous increase in military appropriations, carried out at the cost of lowering the living standards of the working people, the rate of post-war production growth is slowing and now rarely outstrips the population growth. Over-production crises have become more frequent.

Neither of these attempts to convey impressions contained a fact which could not have been supported by careful selection out of a number of indices. The projection of business investments in the United States, carefully selected to contain favorable data, later proved to have been somewhat optimistic.

[3] COVERT PROPAGANDA. Propaganda is sometimes conducted by covert or undercover means or is deliberately designed to propagate untruths. Foreign governments have purchased newspapers or news agencies in other countries to infiltrate biased news and distorted stories into channels of public communication. Similarly, specially prepared films concealing or obscuring their source of origin are circulated in various parts of the world to manipulate mass concepts and images.

The pure lie is generally an unacceptable propaganda technique on grounds of expediency as well as morality, for when discovered, the lie is likely to redound to the discredit of the user. Some dictators have not hesitated to employ the technique of the Big Lie. Adolf Hitler argued in his book *Mein Kampf* that if a lie were big enough and repeated often enough, at least part of it would be believed because the masses are too unimaginative to think anyone would dare to tell such stories unless true. Hitler maligned the Jews and spread fantastic stories of the discovery of new "super" weapons. For a short time the propaganda was effective, serving as an adjunct to the rapid and violent military technique of the blitzkrieg. But under conditions of more sustained competition, states seeking respect have found that blatantly false propaganda is disadvantageous.

Information may be inserted into communications media to distract or attract attention. Particular troop or ship movements may be reported as a feint when other movements are in fact occurring. Questions at news conferences may be designed to draw attention to particular matters, and stories may be altered before release to emphasize certain points.

Special vehicles of communication are sometimes created for this type of propaganda in order not to impair the reputation of well-known media. If such activities become apparent, governments can maintain silence or deny responsibility when certain concealed propaganda is observed.

[4] APPEALS TO IDEALISM. A favorite Communist method of conducting propaganda is to set up or to infiltrate youth movements or organizations or gain leverage in socialist groups that appeal to idealist causes. The Communists in Japan, for example, have penetrated student and Socialist Party mass demonstrations. International Youth Festivals afford opportunities to entice young people into a web of personal involvement so they can later be used to spread propaganda in their own countries.

[5] "THOUGHT REFORM." In some Communist countries, notably China, propaganda has been widely used to bring about "thought reform" on a nationwide basis. Attempts are made through a general process of guided thinking to engender bitterness toward the West and to reorient popular attachment to the Communist cause, while preaching loyalty to the native society, institutions, and basic values. The Communist Chinese now use this technique against Soviet "revisionism."

PROPAGANDA AND POLICY

The discussion thus far has focused upon the characteristics of the propaganda instrument. The purpose of propaganda, whatever its form and the technique employed to disseminate it, is to further policy and national objectives. Thus the policy maker must look ahead in his utilization of the propaganda instrument, analyzing its immediate usefulness and estimating its longer-run consequences and preparing suitable measures for dealing with future contingencies. This is a difficult task, especially in a democracy where policy makers are continually under pressure and where policy is formulated under the glare of publicity.

Domestic Information Programs and Foreign Policy. One of the uses of domestic information is to strengthen the negotiating position of the statesman by mobilizing public sentiment. Domestic information can be employed to justify radical or hazardous measures, as was Hitler's practice, or to reinforce resistance to foreign demands, as in Iran in 1951 when the Anglo-Iranian Oil Company properties were nationalized. Premier Mossadegh permitted, or perhaps even covertly aided, mob actions to occur in the streets and bazaars of Teheran to convey an impression of Iranian resolution against Britain.

Communist and some non-Communist countries have used "spontaneous demonstrations," usually by students, as a method of showing displeasure and making propaganda against United States policies. In a well-policed state, these demonstrations can occur only with government consent. Use of these procedures makes it difficult for statesmen to withdraw from extreme situations without bringing relations nearly to the breaking point or suffering political reversal in their own countries if concessions are made. Government encouragement of extremist attitudes or actions can embitter relationships with neighboring countries until accommodation or reconciliation is impossible, as in Arab-Israeli relations. Proverbially, if a statesman mounts a tiger, he may find it impossible to dismount. The wise statesman leaves himself some alternative.

John Foster Dulles stated during the 1952 American Presidential campaign that it would be the policy of the Eisenhower Administration to "roll back the Iron Curtain." These remarks were later said to have encouraged Eastern Europeans to believe that American support would be given if the people rose against Moscow. Disillusionment and criticism followed American failure to do more than verbally condemn Soviet actions in the Hungarian revolution. Democratic statesmen must carefully consider interpretations that may be attached to statements meant for domestic consumption.

Content Analysis. Governments must subject propaganda to an exacting content analysis to reveal significant attitudes or responses. A nation's program may unwittingly give away strategic or political information or prematurely expose attitudes or plans that should be withheld or couched in different language. Systematic analysis includes a count of the frequency with which certain symbolic words or subjects appear, and information can be gained about situational factors influencing decision makers, their estimates of situations, and their policy intentions.

Hong Kong houses one of the most intensive propaganda analysis operations in the world. Experts systematically sift through and analyze virtually every printed publication from mainland China for whatever clues they can find to Chinese thought, intentions, and trends within the domestic scene.

Relation of Message to Policy. The content of the message communicated by the propaganda instrument must be consistent with the overall thrust of national policy. It may be useful on occasions to create ambiguity by authoritative expressions of apparently contradictory policy views, although this generally leads to an impression abroad that the government is weak and divided or paralyzed by an absence of strong executive leadership.

Liberal democratic societies have a propensity for the publication of divergent views. Freedom of expression and of the press are core values. The democratic process depends on sufficient public information to enable informed judgments to be made. Attempts to stifle public debate are resisted by the press and those who regard these efforts as trends toward totalitarianism. As a result the governmental decision-making process often takes place in full view of the public, and differences of opinion make news that is quickly sent abroad and may be misinterpreted there. Senator Bourke Hickenlooper reported to the Senate Foreign Relations Committee some years ago,

It should be borne in mind that the opinion of the world regarding the United States and its objectives is being affected continuously by news developments in the United States. In that news, the official efforts [of the United States Information Agency] play but a relatively small role. Infinitely larger is the role played by Congress, by the Executive branch, the Judicial branch, and by the organizations and individuals on the American scene acting on issues which might once have been considered domestic but which are now of deep international significance. A single action by an American organization, a speech by a Member of Congress or by an official of the Executive branch, or an Executive order, administrative regulation or law, can produce—in and of itself—an impact throughout the world of vast and enduring proportion.

The fact is that inconsistent and unfavorable items of information which may be turned against them by opposing propagandists are provided almost indiscriminately to the world's press by the open societies. Thus open decision making in which the public is able to participate may place the liberal societies at a competitive disadvantage with totalitarian regimes which screen out news they do not wish to publicize. As a result of these opposing forces, there is a continual tension between the desires of a democratic government to restrict or guide news and to have a fully informed public.

Measures to increase consistency and strength without greatly infringing freedom of information require that the operators of the propaganda instrument be brought into all levels of national decision making. If their pronouncements are to meet standards of truth and consistency, they must know what is taking place and what is planned. To avoid un-popular consequences they must also be able to contribute their opinions to the making of choices among policy alternatives.

Evaluation of Programs. The potentialities of the information and propaganda instrument are limited. It may not be possible to do more than color the image of reality held by persons abroad. In the long run the basic image must be formed and maintained by actions and behavior, rather than be dependent upon words and the manipulation of symbols. Propaganda programs can play down, distract attention from, or attempt to justify unpopular actions or events. They can call attention to accomplishments and actions that mesh with policy, but they cannot perpetuate misconceptions forever.

We have tried to suggest that propaganda is by nature difficult to operate and is often unpredictable. Its effectiveness is conditioned by many interwoven factors of timing, sequence, content, emphasis, and surrounding conditions. Because the effects of propaganda take place in the minds and conversation of others, assessment of its results in any situation may be difficult or uncertain. The user must base his calculations on the messages sent abroad and their implications, on any distortions that may emerge as the messages are transmitted, and on the probable effects these distortions will have on policies and actions.

Successful propaganda efforts can inform a government about the usefulness of its expenditures of resources and can help provide a reappraisal of governmental policy. Senate and presidential committees and private agencies repeatedly investigate the United States information programs. In general, they have concluded that this sort of activity is useful, although the precise usefulness at a given time is often uncertain.

To counter the effectiveness of the United States efforts, the Soviet Union and its satellites have used hundreds of transmitters to jam American broadcasters and to interfere with their reception behind the Iron Curtain, although such jamming by the Iron Curtain countries was suspended in 1963. The use made of Information Service facilities abroad where they are permitted, the flow of refugees and mail from the target areas, and the views expressed by those who have come from these regions testified that the American message succeeded in penetrating the Communist-controlled areas, despite efforts to exclude it.

On the other hand, James Reston, writing in *The New York Times,* in January 1961, affirmed that "no country ever had a better story to tell or failed so lamentably to tell it well as the United States in the sixteen years since the end of the war."

THE OPERATION OF INFORMATION AND PROPAGANDA SYSTEMS

United States Information Program. The United States program is operated by the United States Information Agency (USIA), which is under the policy supervision of the Secretary of State. Overseas activities are under the supervision of the local ambassador as part of each embassy "country team." There are offices in over 200 foreign cities and more than 10,000 persons are employed in the operation, over two thirds of whom are overseas.

The purpose of the USIA is to promote United States foreign policy objectives by influencing public attitudes in other nations, and by advising the United States foreign policy formulators and executors about the effects on the foreign public of existing and proposed policies and programs. The methods used include personal contacts, radio, television, libraries, book publication and distribution, press releases, including a daily Wireless Bulletin for distribution by every United States embassy, motion pictures, exhibits, English-language instruction, and other means of communication.

The best-known program operated by USIA is the Voice of America, which broadcasts in many languages. The advent of communications satellites further increases the potential for using radio and television for propaganda purposes.

Activities of Other States. By utilizing indigenous Party members, front organizations, and segments of populations dissatisfied with existing conditions in their own societies, Communism is able to enlist a whole range of native supporters sensitive to local issues and people's responses. Through these channels propaganda is directed to undermining the will to resist Communist policies and to encourage movements looking toward the overthrow of existing institutions.

Many other states conduct operations varying from simple information programs, perhaps primarily designed to encourage tourism, to massive propaganda programs such as those of Egypt and Cuba. The British conduct a peacetime overseas publicity program, with some materials emanating directly from government agencies and some from the nominally independent BBC. Propaganda is a relatively cheap instrument of foreign policy.

CULTURAL RELATIONS AS AN INSTRUMENT OF POLICY

In addition to information programs, many states engage in cultural relations activities.

It has been said that the "most effective way to exchange knowledge is to wrap it up in a person." One thinks of the very successful efforts to strengthen bonds among Great Britain, the United States, and the Commonwealth by means of such educational arrangements as the Rhodes, Commonwealth, and Marshall Scholarships. These have made it possible for thousands of talented young men to study in each other's countries.

Cultural relations conducted by the British in the former Empire not only aided the orderly transition of many territories to independence, but also laid the basis for continuing association through the Commonwealth. Similar French efforts in the former French African territories may prove remunerative in the same way. In both instances, the training younger leaders of these territories received in the United Kingdom and France contributed to their sense of appreciation of British and French values and basic political and legal institutions.

France was possibly the first of the Great Powers to develop cultural relations as an official activity. France's example was followed late in the nineteenth century by the initiation of programs by Britain and Germany. Tsarist Russia attempted to use pan-Slavism as a vehicle for the intrusion of Russian imperial influence and politics into Central Europe. British foresight, and the educational activities of American missionaries and later of the United States government, enabled over ten million members of the elites in the underdeveloped countries today to read English as their second language. This is a valuable asset in the competitive efforts of the liberal democracies to communicate with leaders in these pivotal regions.

The United States Cultural Relations Program. A Division of Cultural Relations was set up in the Department of State in 1938 and first devoted attention to Latin America, where Nazi and Fascist influences were then making advances. Through both public and private initiative the Institute of International Education was developed to facilitate student exchanges and foreign study.

United States government-assisted cultural relations programs now extend across a wide front from government-financed student exchanges and similar activities to massive tourism permitted by a liberal passport and visa policy.

Because of the leading role educators and students often play in national politics, especially in the underdeveloped countries, where trained manpower is in high demand, persons receiving some of their education in this country may come to exercise political influence or become national leaders. United States students and professors studying abroad have a similar opportunity to establish contacts with many who will ultimately reach positions of high regard and responsibility in their countries. The Fulbright Act of 1946 providing scholarships to foreign students, and the Smith-Mundt Act of 1948 providing leadership exchange arrangements, brought the federal government into these activities for the first time. The overseas operations programs (economic assistance, military assistance, USIA) include education and orientation trips to the United States. The private foundations have given strong support to international education and exchange. Exchanges of students, teachers, scientists, and leaders in business, the professions, and government, under both public and private aegis, are considered a vital part of the overall United States program.

In 1965 over 80,000 foreign students from 159 different political entities were studying in the United States. About 10,000 of these were receiving U.S. government assistance. Approximately 18,000 American students were studying abroad, and 4,000 American faculty members were teaching abroad while some 9,000 foreign faculty and scholars were working on American campuses. The cost of the student-professor exchange was about $350 million, of which $50 million was contributed by the federal government and the remainder by foundations, foreign governments, universities, and the students themselves. Seventy American universities were conducting technical assistance projects overseas under contracts with the government totaling over $100 million.

There are over a million and a half Americans living abroad, a measure of the extent of American contact with people in other countries. Most of these are in or accompanying the armed forces, but more than half a million are associated with private enterprises. These enterprises range from oil companies and engineering and business firms to mission schools. A million Americans a year have been going to Europe as tourists. These contacts further friendly relations with foreign countries and peoples, but can be a liability if those who go abroad do not endeavor in their personal conduct to represent the better sides of American life and to show appreciation for the local culture.

One of the striking features of the United States cultural relations program has been the sending of books to foreign countries. Each year the USIA arranges for publication and sale abroad of several million low-priced books.

Direct cultural exchanges between the United States and the Soviet Union have been greatly expanded since the death of Stalin. Since 1958, the number of Americans visiting the Soviet Union has more than doubled, with somewhere between 10,000 to 15,000 persons entering the Soviet Union a year. Simultaneously the flow of Soviet visitors to the United States has increased.

One view of the usefulness of cultural interchange has been expressed in the inimitable language of jazz trumpeter Louis "Satchmo" Armstrong. "Yeah," grumbled Satchmo, "I'd like to crawl under that Iron Curtain. Let all them foreign ministers have their summit conferences—Ol' Satch, he might get somewhere with them cats just havin' a basement conference. . . . Well, maybe ol' Uncle Sammy won't let me do like I want to, but man, I'd really like to exchange some two-beat culture with them Russian cats. They ain't so cold but what we could bruise 'em with the happy music." He ultimately got his way with the result that American jazz has since then swept the U.S.S.R. There have also been highly acclaimed tours of such eminent American orchestras as the Boston, Philadelphia, and Cleveland Symphonies to Russia.

The Peace Corps. Early in his administration President John F. Kennedy initiated a Peace Corps for service in developing countries. By congressional enactment the objects of the Corps are "to promote world peace and friendship . . . to help the peoples of such countries and areas in meeting their needs for trained manpower, and to help promote a better understanding of the American people . . . and a better understanding of other people on the part of the American people." The objectives of the program are both development and cultural relations.

Volunteers normally serve for two years, living with the people they are helping. By the mid-1960's there were over ten thousand Peace Corps volunteers overseas in forty-six countries, about half of whom were teaching. Most of the others were engaged in community development, health projects, agriculture, and public works. The long-run contribution of the Peace Corps to development has yet to be determined. But there is no doubt of the success of Peace Corps volunteers in being accepted by countries where they serve and in projecting a favorable image of the United States at the grass-roots level.

The Soviet Cultural Program. It is impossible to state with accuracy what the Soviet government expends for cultural relations. Professor

Frederick Barghoorn in his book *The Soviet Cultural Offensive* points to what he calls the massive "logistical support" behind the Soviet effort. The Soviet Union is said to have been spending about $2 billion as far back as 1953. This has certainly increased and may amount to more than the combined total of all other countries' expenditures for this purpose.

Extensive research, language, and other specialized training, together with the writing, processing, and supplying of materials, go into Soviet endeavors to export culture and to exert influence in the developing countries.

The structure of the Soviet political system enables a singleness of purpose to be given to Soviet activities that few others can duplicate. Soviet academic work, cultural-relations activities, and communications research attempt to create an image of a powerful yet cultured and "peace-loving" state that has produced great achievements as a result of its economic, social, and political system. Exchanges are always intended to constitute what Professor Barghoorn calls "unilateral dissemination," a process in which others are influenced by what the Soviets do, but in which Soviet citizens are largely curtained off against the accomplishments of others. This represents a crude definition of power in terms of the Soviet construct of politics: he who exerts influence has power, and he who permits himself to be influenced does not. Within the Soviet Union the converse of the cultural exchange is the guided tour to which foreign visitors are subjected.

A major component of the Soviet cultural program is the publication of low-cost books in many languages, the provision of Soviet films, records, and exchanges of dancers, pianists, composers, scientists, and other creative or performing artists. Among the most effective devices employed have been mass meetings and other appeals to idealism through such gatherings as the Vienna Youth Festival and the Stockholm Peace Appeal, which sought worldwide signatures in support of the slogan "Ban the Bomb." Among other efforts having a large appeal have been the tours of such companies as the Bolshoi Ballet and the Moscow Philharmonic, and of such eminent artists as Miroslav Restropovitch.

Professor Barghoorn comments on the risks of exchanges with the Soviet Union in these words,

Perhaps the most dangerous of these risks is that of distraction of free world attention from the frightening realities of Soviet policy. The Bolshoi Ballet could not make a Leninist out of a Rotarian, but it might help him to forget that irreconcilable conflict is basic to the Communist creed. Soviet scientific displays could not convert Egyptians to socialism, but they might make it easier for them to forget the price paid by the Soviet people for forced-draft industrialization. . . . Soviet political advertising, in a word, features attractive packaging but offers no price tag.[2]

One of Moscow's ventures has been the establishment of a Friendship of Nations University distinct from the University of Moscow. The youth of Asian, African, and Latin American countries are invited to apply to this university to be trained in the Russian language, science, and the arts, and for political indoctrination. Through such contacts the Soviets hope to fashion activists with whom they can work for Communist interests when they return to their own lands. American educators who have had opportunities for private talks with high-level Soviet academicians and scientists have been left in no doubt that Moscow intends to give the Western powers a "hell of a hard go" in the underdeveloped world. The Friendship University is one facet of a long-range scheme. The liberal democracies are being challenged to expand cultural relations activities and to provide education and better hospitality than they have in the past for those who come from foreign lands.

CONCLUSION

A decision to have public information and cultural relations programs presents policy-making problems and at the same time stimulates decision making. These programs must be geared to an overall policy. Choices must be made among the long- and short-run objectives that policy makers seek to obtain.

The goal of effective manipulation of opinion is to create responses favorable to the general policies and objectives of the state. The appeal to sentiment abroad is not an end in itself but a means by which public pressures may be developed to the advantage of the state employing the psychological instrument. This appeal seeks to get beyond the "we are good" and "they are bad" type of imagery to the eventual stimulation of favorable attitudes and official actions that will bring tangible benefits to the initiating state. A government must have a clear picture of where it wishes to lead others and what it hopes to accomplish.

In addition to the more conventional uses of the psychological

[2] Frederick C. Barghoorn, *The Soviet Cultural Offensive* (Princeton: Princeton University Press, 1960), p. 336.

instrument, it can be applied for other purposes. If, for example, an international arms control arrangement becomes an accomplished fact, involving agreed limitations within categories of weapons, the public information instrument might become an important supplementary tool in the process of inspection and enforcement. An international inspecting organization would have to employ the media of communications to enlist the co-operation of the authorities and populace of states being inspected and to inform the world about evasions.[3]

Taken in sum, the information and cultural relations programs add a "fourth dimension" to foreign relations in providing additional avenues of contact among peoples and states. They are not to be viewed as ends in themselves, but as one among other forms of implementing policy or fostering understanding across international borders.

[3] See Ithiel de Sola Pool, "Public Opinion and the Control of Armaments," *Daedalus*, Vol. 89, No. 4, Fall 1960.

CHAPTER 18

The Economic Instruments of Foreign Policy

INTRODUCTION

In Chapter 8 economic factors that underlie the capabilities and interests of states were discussed. In this chapter we shall examine economics as a "force," an instrument, in international politics. Economic resources are a means of exercising power. As such they are one of the tools of foreign policy. With the increasing interdependence of national economies, the economic instruments have become increasingly significant in the relations among states.

Definition and Scope of the Economic Instrument. An economic instrument may be defined as any economic capacity, institution, or technique explicitly or implicitly applied to foreign policy goals. The goals toward which it is directed may be economic (securing needed raw materials or expanding an export trade), political (support of orderly change or development in a less-developed state), military (securing bases), or psychological (demonstrating sympathy with or support of another nation's policy).

The adjustment of economic ends to means and of means to ends is one of the most complicated aspects of international affairs. The complications arise partly because in free-world countries private initiative is a dynamic element in generating economic activity. Private initiative actuated by prices and profits may, or may not, be consistent with national objectives of security, welfare, and development. The powerful forces of nationalism which have been generating the explosion of states, and producing so many of the conflicts among countries, cut across traditional economic objectives such as security and welfare.

The world of economic relationships is full of paradoxes. Each state seeks an international economic order shaped to its own interests, yet it must cooperate with other states that are often both its best customers and strongest competitors. Again, the economically weaker states have been receiving more international economic attention because of concern for their rate and direction of change. Economic relationships result in a labyrinth of international interchanges and agreements which exceed the total of all other interstate relationships and have a sensitivity surpassing that of other relationships, except perhaps those stemming from nationalism and security—which sometimes materially condition economic affairs.

National Objectives, Economic Resources, and Foreign Policy. Economic power is vital for a sustained influence in world affairs. A weak economy may lead to political instability and perhaps become a target for Communism. Internal economic affairs are therefore often of pressing international concern. The great economic competitors are also economically and politically dependent on the health of each other's economies. Numerous United States corporations, for instance, would like to have Britain's overseas trade, but the United States could not afford to see its British ally founder economically.

The economic strength of the United States has been the predominant factor in world power since World War II. Some argue that nuclear power has been *the* most predominant power element. Nuclear power was made possible by United States economic power, which has also made the United States chief supplier and chief customer of many countries. United States economic power provided the principal leadership in international economic affairs and the capital to rehabilitate Japan and many European countries after World War II. It still provides half the foreign-government capital assisting the developing countries. Its economic strength has been a principal support of the free-world military posture against Communism. The United States economy is a primary support of all United States instruments of foreign policy. It is so important that government officials have argued that inflation and subsequent depression are as dangerous to security as the direct threats of Communism.

The status of particular national economies affects world affairs. Increasing economic strength enables more resources to be used to further foreign policy objectives. Demonstrated success in their development plans may increase the appeal of the methods used. Economic relationships create political influences. If Chinese heavy-industry output in the 1970's should exceed that of Japan and India combined, and Chinese attitudes remain rigid, there would be a serious possibility of resulting economic and political disruptions on the Chinese perimeter. On the other hand, increased economic association with the free world might affect the doctrinaire militancy of Communism.

Economic strength is an essential pillar for building national military power and total national strength. Today manpower is a less critical component of military power than in previous generations. Military power now depends more on technology, industry, and public finance, underlining the fact that domestic economic institutions and resources are important in determining a state's policies and programs in foreign affairs. Many states cannot have significant military instruments without the support of the industry of some other state, nor could they sustain major hostilities without such support. The Pakistan-India clash over Kashmir, for example, would have soon been limited by losses of military equipment and depletion of other supplies if it had not been halted by political action.

POLICIES AND INSTRUMENTS AFFECTING INTERNATIONAL TRADE

Most states make their greatest economic impact on external affairs through their position and power in international trade. A state may use its trading position to enhance its own strength and development, to help develop an international community favorable to its interests, and to weaken and constrict the influence of competitors and potential enemies. During hostilities, states direct these approaches for the purpose of victory. Economic operations connected with an open conflict include a number of positive techniques, known collectively as economic warfare, that are not quite the same as peaceful economic relations. The distinction between economic warfare and peacetime economic technique has blurred, however, as the boundary area of conflict lying between peace and hostilities has widened and become more complex. In this section we deal with orthodox and traditional measures by which a state can strengthen itself and favorably influence the international environment.

Policies Pertaining to International Trade. Most nations follow policies that combine other considerations with that of international trade. These include national defense, the protection of particular industries, and the furtherance of external political objectives. By trade policies states seek to change a world free-market situation toward their particular, and often differing, objectives.

TARIFFS. The tariff or import tax is the most familiar device employed for influencing the flow of international trade. Some states also levy taxes on exports, a practice which the Constitution prohibits in the United States. Tariffs are of four general types, according to their intent: (1) revenue, (2) protection of local industry, (3) changing the terms of trade, and (4) retaliation or negotiation.

The revenue tariff has become less important in more-developed countries but remains an important instrument in many less-developed countries. In an economy which is partially nonmonetized and in which the bureaucratic efficiency and public attitudes necessary for adequate internal taxation are absent, the tariff is a comparatively simple means of raising public revenues and may be one of the few reliable means. It was, in fact, the primary source of revenue in the United States until the passage in 1913 of the Sixteenth Amendment, legalizing the income tax. A revenue tariff needs to be low enough to avoid discouraging imports and must be imposed on items for which there is a strong demand. A revenue tariff is therefore unlikely to be compatible with other tariff objectives mentioned above. As a state improves its ability to raise internal taxes, it adopts other objectives for its tariff program, and makes less use of it for revenue.

One of the more exasperating problems in helping less-developed countries toward modernization has been that of their export and import regulations. Most of these countries are not underdeveloped in bureaucracy, which does, at times, frustrate both exporters and importers.

Protective tariffs have had the biggest impact on international trade. Historically, there have been a number of arguments to justify protection by tariff for a state's producers against foreign competitors. Most of these arguments have been based on economic fallacies; of the arguments, two have some economic validity. One is the argument that a new or "infant" industry deserves protection from foreign competitors until it grows sufficiently to employ efficient, large-scale production techniques and to orient itself to mass markets. The argument is valid if the underlying resource position can support an infant industry that is given this protection, as was the case with many American industries in the nineteenth century and in some less-developed countries today. There is a danger that protection will be lavished on new industries that cannot grow or survive without continued protection or that will insist upon continuing tariff shelter indefinitely.

A second argument for protection is based on national security: a particular industry deserves protection from foreign competitors if its product is essential to the nation's defenses should foreign supplies be curtailed. This is valid for certain key products if the state cannot protect its foreign sources of supply and the transportation lines to them, and if a conflict is likely to continue until existing stocks are exhausted. One difficulty with the argument today is that it depends on debatable assumptions: of protracted, non-nuclear hostilities, of nonavailability of foreign supplies, and, sometimes, of static technology.

The national security argument has been stressed particularly for raw materials. There are interesting points on both sides of the debate. Peacetime production of nonreplaceable raw materials makes smaller deposits of these available for war. On the other hand, it is argued that protection may be necessary to encourage domestic producers to find and develop new domestic deposits or to develop more efficient methods of utilizing existing lower-grade deposits.

In any case, whenever either the infant industry or defense argument for a tariff is valid, a more effective and less costly method of providing protection may be a subsidy to the domestic producer.

The benefits derived from international trade are not equally divided. The ratio of export prices to import prices, known as the terms of trade, largely determines how the benefits from trade are shared. Tariffs can and have been used to improve a country's terms of trade. Success depends on the country's command of the market and on the avoidance of retaliation.

Tariffs have been used as bargaining weapons for retaliation or negotiation. An existing schedule of high rates permits a state to make concessions in those rates in exchange for similar ones by other states or for a political *quid pro quo*. The ultimate goals of the bargaining must be to improve the terms of trade and to increase the quantity of trade. A country does not profit from an improvement in the terms of trade if a decline in trade is not offset by the gains per item traded. Although use in negotiation could be a short-run argument for an existing high-tariff schedule, it is unconvincing in the long run. Such action invites retaliation by other powers. Although a nation will benefit economically by lowering tariffs if other nations follow suit, and may benefit even if they do not, the converse does not hold; no single nation can gain economically by raising tariffs if thereby it generates a cycle of retaliation.

These four types of tariffs not only reduce imports but indirectly reduce exports. If a state does not buy from others, the others cannot earn that state's currency and buy its goods, except through grants and loans from the selling state. For small proportions of trade, however, reserves of gold and foreign exchange can be used to settle accounts. A state with domestic industries dependent upon foreign markets injures those industries if it raises tariffs to protect other industries. In the United States 15 to 25 per cent of the output of the coal, construction equipment, civilian aircraft, and certain light machinery industries is sold in foreign markets. An even higher proportion (25 to 50 per cent) of certain agricultural products such as tobacco, cotton, and wheat is exported. Over 3 million United States workers' jobs depend directly on exports; about 4½ million on both import and export trade.[1]

The United States has relaxed considerably the very high Hawley-Smoot tariff of 1930. The first Trade Agreements Act was passed in 1934, giving the President authority to negotiate tariff reductions with other nations subject to reciprocal concessions. These are embodied in Reciprocal Trade Agreements. Although the Congress has limited Presidential discretion and has from time to time added clauses to protect industries subject to "serious injury" or deemed vital to national security, tariff rates have decreased markedly. The ratio of duties to value of dutiable imports has moved from 50 per cent in 1931–1935 to 14 per cent in the early 1960's. Much of this drop can be attributed to price rises which cut the percentage yield of fixed duties. But the trade agreements have also been a major factor.[2] The Trade Agreements Act was replaced in 1962 by the Trade Expansion Act with provisions, not immediately executed, for a liberal trading policy.

There is a basis for reasoned speculation that the tariff is becoming less important as a technique of economic policy compared to other methods. Regional economic arrangements, like the European Economic Community; wide international arrangements such as the General Agreement on Tariffs and Trade (GATT); various types of state trading; the controlled movement of capital for economic development; and other methods of control support the suggestion that the free-trade–protection controversy is no longer the principal problem in foreign economic affairs that it once was.

[1] *Statistical Abstract of the United States* (1965), p. 889.
[2] *Ibid.*, p. 890.

QUANTITATIVE CONTROLS. Quotas, or physical limits on the amounts of various imports, are the most common alternative to tariffs. Quotas are essentially devices for protecting domestic producers and conserving foreign exchange, although they can also be used as weapons of economic warfare. Because they can end at short notice all imports, or all of a particular import, they are even more restrictive than tariffs. The immediacy of their response and the accuracy with which their direct effects can be calculated make them a favorite technique of states trying to isolate some parts of their economy from the world economy. Thus a state engaging in extensive national planning, in heavily subsidizing particular industries, or in channeling imports into certain sectors of the economy is likely to turn to quotas as the simplest and surest means of controlling imports.

The United States uses mandatory quotas for some agricultural products and mineral raw materials, including oil, excepting imports from Mexico and Canada which are controlled by a voluntary agreement. The United States arguments for quotas are partly based on protection of industry and partly on reasons of national security. However, access to Canadian and Mexican sources can hardly be blockaded and both countries are linked to the United States by formal defense arrangements. The United States has negotiated some voluntary quotas on beef in response to pressure from United States cattlemen and has been a member of a multilateral voluntary quota arrangement of twenty-one countries, arranged by GATT, for cotton textiles.

Exchange control is a common means of both quantitative and qualitative limitation. A nation trying to conserve its supply of foreign currencies or seeking to maintain a particular exchange rate for its own currency may do so by skillful and continued regulation of import quotas. Less-developed countries needing imports but lacking adequate foreign exchange to secure all their wants sometimes adopt import quotas in order to direct whatever purchases they can afford in terms of available foreign currencies toward goods which have highest priority. A state generally uses a more direct method of controlling foreign currencies. This is accomplished by requiring exporters to sell their foreign exchange earnings to the government at an established rate. The currencies obtained are then rationed out to importers in amounts and at rates the government considers sound. These controls can be applied unrestrictedly to imports or to selected kinds of transactions when combined with import licensing. Different exchange rates can be established for different types of exports and imports. Multiple exchange rates have the advantage of providing a means of influencing the direction of trade as well as its volume. They also tend to develop a Pandora's box of increasingly unmanageable complications.

After World War II, when the American dollar was in short supply throughout the world, most nations adopted exchange controls to discriminate against dollar imports. With the reversal of the dollar shortage toward the end of the 1950's, these discriminatory controls were generally dismantled, except in new and developing countries. The declining use of exchange and other controls, which had greatly hampered traditional multilateral trading practices in the 1940's and 1950's, contributed to a big expansion in world trade, which expanded from $101 billion in 1959 to $169 billion in 1964.

The widespread use of quantitative restrictions has at times given them an even more important role in shaping modern international trade than have tariffs. The tariff is probably a preferable measure from the standpoint of free enterprise. Whereas a tariff shifts prices, thereby shifting the pattern of production and consumption, consumers do retain some power of choice and market mechanisms continue to operate. It is collected comparatively easily at the nation's ports and requires a minimum amount of policing and secondary controls. Quantitative controls dispense with the market mechanism altogether, substituting government fiat. These controls also entail considerable administrative effort to decide who gets what, how much of it, and at what rate, and to enforce compliance by both exporters and importers.

Both tariffs and quantitative controls are often employed by a nation in an attempt to strengthen its own economic position, with little regard for their impact on other nations. Despite arguments in favor of trade liberalization, the growing tendency of states, particularly developing states, to plan and manage their internal economies may discourage them from relaxing controls on foreign trade. Yet the increasing interdependence of national economies indicates that the logical trend is toward much greater international economic cooperation—control on a multinational basis.

DIRECTED TRADE. Directed trade and international agreements are measures designed to shape the external environment in a favorable manner. Directing trade, rather than letting patterns develop according to market criteria, has two kinds of advantages. First, trade is a *de facto* instrument of cultural and political penetration; for along with goods move businessmen, traders, technicians, and communications. Second, if one state can achieve a dominant position as a supplier or customer of another, it can hope to exercise some influence on the other's political and economic policies. Even if the state does not intend to use its potential leverage, suspicion by others that it might do so can affect interstate relations. The cry for economic freedom and the anti-Dutch feeling in Indonesia in its early years of independence were due partially to these fears—as have also been some of the expressions of anti-American feeling in Latin America.

Direction of trade can serve several national objectives. It may be employed to strengthen colonial ties, support alliances or other political arrangements, extend influence in certain regions, or develop a self-sufficient economic system. Bilateral trade agreements, preferential tariff and quota treatment, special credits or other financial arrangements, and manipulation of prices are typical means by which states can shape the direction of their trade. The United Kingdom has used "imperial preferences," by which the members of the British Empire and Commonwealth have had a lower tariff rate levied against their imports into the United Kingdom and to each other than have outsiders. Authoritarian states have been the principal users of trade direction. The National Socialist government of pre-World War II Germany used cartel arrangements by which the foreign holdings of German industries were materially managed for political and military purposes, particularly in southeast Europe.

When a strong power has a major part or all of the trade of a lesser state, it can exercise political and other pressures often called "economic imperialism." A large and variegated economy such as that of the Soviet Union provides a versatile instrument to further political objectives. Such a state can purchase the entire production of a given country's key export commodity and can couple the action with a payment arrangement which may contain political as well as economic strings. Whether for security, ideological, or other reasons, Communist trade was for two decades after World War II aimed principally at Soviet bloc self-sufficiency except for the few items it could not produce, such as natural rubber, or the cases where trade outside the bloc might yield political dividends.

About two thirds of the total trade of the Soviet Communist system was still intrabloc in the mid-1960's as compared to three quarters in 1960. But the trend is to increased out-of-bloc trading, particularly by the Central European countries, which used to conduct about two thirds of their trade with Western nations. Purchases of Canadian and Australian wheat by both Russia and China have also indicated some thaw on the economic front of the cold war generated by the shortfalls in Chinese and Soviet agriculture and the desire of some Western countries to market their surpluses.

Communists do consider economic advantage, generally driving fairly hard bargains over trade matters. With alertness to the opportunities presented by temporary export problems such as those involving Burmese rice, Egyptian cotton, Ceylonese rubber, Cuban sugar, and with the flexibility inherent in centralized control over trade, the Soviet leaders have sought to create the image of an economically powerful, helpful neighbor ready to protect its less-developed friends from the instabilities of capitalist markets.

The less-developed countries have not become heavily dependent on Soviet markets or supplies. By 1964 only a half dozen free-world countries—Afghanistan, Guinea, Iraq, Mali, Syria, and the United Arab Republic—traded significantly with the Soviet bloc. Nevertheless, the large Soviet bloc economy, its leaders' complete control over trading activities, and their ability to accept economic losses for political advantage mean that the Soviet economic complex can have considerable influence on the international environment through trade direction.

Communist China is employing the same techniques for comparable objectives in various parts of Asia, Africa, and Latin America. Its moves have not been coordinated with those of the Soviets, lending further credence to the proposition that China is pursuing its own goals. This Chinese "go it alone" policy tends toward increasing rivalry and conflict with the Soviet Union as the industrial and military power of China rises.

States that emphasize private, rather than state, trading practices can direct their foreign trade to some extent by manipulating tariffs, as in the imperial preferences of the United Kingdom, or by selective quotas, as in the sugar imports of the United States. By preferential taxes or other special treatment, they can also direct the efforts of private investors where national as well as private interests will be served. At the turn of the century the French government encouraged its citizens to lend to Russia by buying Russian state bonds, in order to strengthen the Franco-Russian alliance of 1894. As a more recent example, the United States has provided special guarantees and tax concessions for private foreign investment into the less-developed countries.

INTERNATIONAL AGREEMENTS

Two major instruments of post-World War II international economic cooperation were created at the Bretton Woods conference in 1944: the International Bank for Reconstruction and Development (IBRD) often called the World Bank, and the International Monetary Fund (IMF). The latter, with over 100 members including practically all non-Communist countries plus Yugoslavia, is a mechanism for consultation and collaboration in monetary and trade measures and assists its members in meeting short-run foreign exchange difficulties. The International Monetary Fund has become increasingly important as a source of emergency help. Advice on economic and monetary reforms is more easily received from an international agency, and bilateral assistance is more gracefully made contingent on reforms that the IMF recommends. Advice and assistance have been given to a number of less-developed countries with inflationary or other monetary problems, for example, Turkey in 1954 and several Latin American countries in the 1960's. As another example of IMF action, in cooperation with the United States and Western European countries, the IMF loaned one third of the $3 billion provided England in the fall of 1964 to support the pound sterling.

A third major device of international economic cooperation is the General Agreement on Tariffs and Trade, known as GATT. This agreement among most of the major trading nations is designed to provide a forum for the development of mutually beneficial trade principles and practices and for negotiations to reduce trade barriers. By 1965 GATT had increased to sixty-six members, with thirteen additional nations participating partially, and had contributed to the reduction or stabilization of duties on tens of thousands of internationally traded items. Members of GATT agree that, with some exceptions, concessions granted by any of them to a "most-favored" nation will be extended to all of them, thus spreading the benefits of any trade liberalization.

Despite the general compatibility of GATT's objectives and methods with those of the United States, this country has been cautious in the degree of its involvement. Congress has not formally approved United States participation in GATT or endorsed it.

In addition to these arrangements, there are a number of organizations of a partially economic nature under the aegis of the United Nations. These include the United Nations Educational, Scientific, and Cultural Organization (UNESCO), the Food and Agricultural Organization, the International Labor Organization, and others. Although not important in terms of their budgets, these organizations provide a forum for international cooperation and contribute technical assistance to less-developed nations.

A state may prefer to join in smaller groupings based on regional, or special economic interests. The European Economic Community (often called the Common Market) is a prime example. The somewhat looser grouping known as the European Free Trade Association, or "Outer Seven," has eliminated substantially all trade barriers between its members. These groupings gained their impetus from the Organization for European

Economic Cooperation (OEEC), which coordinated the Marshall Plan. The Organization for Economic Cooperation and Development (OECD), consisting of the Western European countries, Canada, Japan, and the United States, is another descendant of the OEEC. The purposes of the OECD include promotion of policies for economic stability and growth, expansion of world trade, and extension of assistance to developing countries. There is a Central American trade organization and a Latin American Free Trade Association (LAFTA).

Such regional arrangements are apparently becoming an increasingly important part of the economic scene. The more limited ones may increase trade within the confines of their restricted membership and so speed economic growth. These gains may occur, however, at the price of wider trade relations and of benefits for the larger international community.

The Communist states' Council for Mutual Economic Assistance represents another form of politico-economic grouping. The Soviet Union has used this mechanism as the Communist answer to the Marshall Plan, to coordinate the trade and economic development policies of the Soviet bloc. The pulls of trade opportunities external to the bloc are, nevertheless, loosening some of the bonds of this arrangement.

International commodity agreements are specialized instruments of economic cooperation. In 1964 there were wheat, tin, and coffee agreements on prices and quotas and another dozen or so agreements to compile statistics, exchange information, and promote cooperation. These commodity arrangements directed to stabilization of price fluctuations apply to only a portion of the materials for which world price stabilization would be helpful. Individual states have found it extremely difficult to establish minimum and maximum prices or buffer stock arrangements acceptable to both producer and consumer interests. Such arrangements on an international basis are even more difficult. International stabilization is made more important when so many small countries (and some large ones, for example, Brazil's dependence on coffee) rely on one or a few commodities for their foreign exchange earnings.

Economic Warfare.   The use of economic means to weaken a potential or actual opponent is often referred to as economic warfare. Traditionally associated with hostilities, its use short of war is not new. Clausewitz observed, "disarm your enemy in peace by diplomacy and trade if you would conquer him more readily on the field of battle."

Each state operates along a front in its international affairs extending from subtle persuasion through a range of pressures to open violence. Economic techniques and resources are widely applicable along that front. As an example, it seems reasonable for the International Monetary Fund to link exchange credits to economic reforms within a country, but the withholding of such credits from a country judged to be an aggressor is a clear economic sanction and might be called economic warfare.

Prior to World War II the world had considerable faith in the efficacy of economic sanctions. The League of Nations voted these against Italy in 1935 for its aggression against Ethiopia but they were ineffective. Similar sanctions were invoked by the United Nations General Assembly in 1951 against Communist China for aggression in Korea. These too were ineffective. Britain imposed economic sanctions on Rhodesia in 1965 and the United States cooperated as did most other countries. A paper blockade is unlikely to be persuasive unless one or more of the states supporting it dominates some critical economic resource involved, such as oil, food, or arms. Even then the flow of international trade is so complex and persistent that in the long run supplies flow increasingly to the country that is the target of economic sanctions. The seemingly obvious action is then to couple a paper blockade with a physical blockade.

A physical blockade is an overtly hostile act against the country blockaded and moves the level of conflict upward to include countries which are the sources of intercepted ships and goods. The international sensitivities involved in such procedures are recorded in the history of the traditional concern of the United States over freedom of the seas, resulting in the strange development of United States operations in Vietnam which employed bombing of North Vietnam without any interception of the steady flow of international shipping to that country. Britain felt it necessary to obtain a United Nations Security Council resolution endorsing its action in intercepting oil tankers bound for Rhodesia.

Most techniques of the paper blockade are directed to controlling exports and imports of the target country. These controls are simple to operate for a state trading country. Where trade and the flow of investment capital proceeds by private means, countries must erect a system of controls to conduct economic warfare. The controls are generally always in existence for trade in arms and there has been no problem over prevention of export of weapons from Western countries to Communist countries. Other types of goods can be considered "strategic," such as scientific instruments that might be useful in making weapons. The United States has had limited success in persuading agreement on control of export of these to Communist countries. The difficulties begin with the definition of "strategic." Food is the most strategic item for a country suffering from a food shortage.

Economic sanctions (economic warfare) short of war can have a severe short-run effect on the target state. But over the longer run many defections are likely among any group of allies. The search for profits, the priority given to balance of trade considerations, and the skepticism concerning the effectiveness of such sanctions tend gradually to erode their effectiveness. Furthermore, there is a persistent line of argument to the effect that trade relations dull the edges of political conflicts and move toward increased understanding among nations—a rationalization neither proven nor certainly refuted. Peacetime economic warfare now needs to be allied in character. It involves much diplomacy and adjustment along with a continual appraisal of whether the gains are worth the increasing strains.

Summary on Policies and Instruments. The preceding discussion has dealt with a considerable number of measures that states employ in the conduct of international trade. These measures are rarely used alone, are complex in their interaction, and are certainly not clearly predictable in their outcome. There is usually reasonable assurance about the general direction of trade resulting from one, or a combination of, these measures. The underlying reasons for the measures are often more pertinent to the study of international affairs than the technical aspects of the measures. For the measures are ways in which a state operates to utilize the economic factor as an instrument of policy. The objectives of that policy may pertain to internal economic or political matters, to security, to building of ties with another state, to strengthening other states, and so on.

FOREIGN ECONOMIC ASSISTANCE

The boundaries between foreign trade, foreign aid (or assistance), and foreign investment are blurred. These foreign activities are intertwined in their operation. For instance, United States economic assistance programs grant or lend dollars, but usually only for purchase of goods in the United States. The grant or loan is often for a specific purpose such as the construction of a power plant which might have used United States private funds. If United States private funds are used, the government may still "assist" by giving some tax advantage to the lender or by providing guarantees against such hazards as expropriation. The citizen willing to make foreign investments who has his profit motive in step with the needs and objectives of his country is often a fortunate man.

Definition, Objectives, and Types of Assistance. Economic assistance is the provision of economic resources by one state to another. This broad definition may be refined to book length by discussing the objectives of this provision, the methods used, and the various forms of economic assistance.

The objective of economic assistance is furtherance of national self-interest. If the profit motive impels private individuals toward desirable foreign lending, as in the case of the large overseas British investments in the nineteenth century, so much the better. The resulting trade and the return flow of interest and capital payments benefited Britain greatly. Since World War II there have been three general types of foreign assistance. Relief and economic rehabilitation were required for the war-torn world. Then the emerging nations needed assistance in their drive for social, political, and economic modernization. Some countries require assistance to help resist Communist pressures, to help deal with internal chaos resulting from an inability to organize their economic affairs, or to overcome poor harvests and other happenings beyond the country's control. The last two objectives have sometimes overlapped, for example, in Korea and Taiwan. Assistance may be given as a *quid pro quo* in international dealings; some such arrangements may be judged by skeptics to be bribery.

It has been argued that assistance does not assuredly gain continuing friendship and support or even insure development. But power relationships are guided by the yardstick of self-interest, not gratitude. Assistance does often buy time, however, for events to develop in a less unsatisfactory way than they otherwise might.

The United States has provided large assistance for all three objectives. During the period from 1945 into the early 1950's over $20 billion went into rebuilding Western Europe, mostly under the Marshall Plan. The success of this program is proven by the strong competition in world trade and the current Western European capability to contribute to development of the emerging states. Most of the Marshall assistance took the form of grants of dollar exchange and capital goods. Only a limited amount of technical assistance was needed, for Western European states already possessed most skills.

Since 1950 most foreign assistance has moved toward (1) increasing contributions from international agencies, particularly the World Bank; (2) a shift toward the developing countries; (3) a shift away from grants toward increasing emphasis on loans; and (4) an expansion of participation in technical assistance by states, foundations, and United Nations agencies. Coordination among different assistance programs within a developing country is a new, and often important, problem of international affairs.

The spectrum of types of assistance is indicated by two examples: the hard loans provided by the United States Export-Import Bank to finance purchases in the United States and the food sold for local currency, or given away, under the Food for Peace Program—Public Law 480. The local currency from food sales is then used to pay local United States expenses and for capital investment in the country. Capital and technical assistance are often mutually supporting and unlikely to be successful separately. On the other hand, capital for such purposes as expanding electrical output or building roads may need little supporting technical advice. Assistance for improved administration, customs reforms, and control of disease often needs little capital.

The methods of providing assistance are very diverse. In some instances a donor may contribute to a multilateral agency such as the Inter-American Development Bank, which then lends to the recipient country. It may grant funds to a United Nations agency, which then supports technical assistance. The provider may operate on a bilateral basis with recipient countries. Or it may join with a consortium of other countries and international agencies to provide a "package" of assistance. This last may be really a coordination of bilateral dealings, as in the Colombo Plan for South Asia. Assisting countries now generally tie the expenditure of both grants and loans to their own production. But funds provided through multilateral agencies are not readily so tied—thereby indicating an argument for bilateral assistance when the providing country has balance of payments problems.

The receiving country can use the funds for purchasing manufactured imports, construction of plants, communications, schools and hospitals, provision of capital for banks to lend to private enterprise and cooperatives, education and development of human skills, and so on. To be successful, the assisted state must usually cooperate by self-help actions which make the assistance effective.

In sum, foreign assistance has become big international business measured in terms of money. It has also triggered a significant proportion of the vast mass of relationships among states and between states and international agencies.

Who Provides the Assistance and How. In 1963 the emerging free world states received economic assistance of $8.1 billion in loans and grants of over five years' maturity. The United States provided 60 per cent of this assistance, $4 billion bilaterally, and a proportion of the $1.4 billion loaned by international agencies. Other developed countries, most of them associated in the Development Advisory Committee (DAC) of the OECD, provided $2.7 billion. Oil-rich Kuwait provides a higher portion of its gross national product for assistance (all to Arab countries) than any other state. The United States also provided approximately $1 billion for military

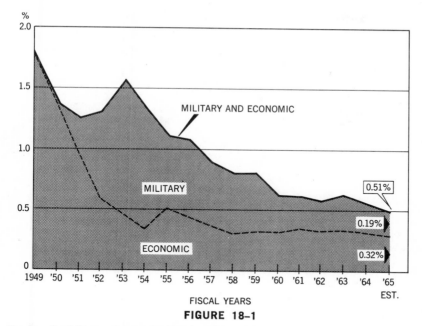

FIGURE 18–1

Foreign Assistance Act Expenditures as Per Cent of U.S. Gross National Product
(*From Agency for International Development, Summary Presentation
to the Congress, March, 1965*)

assistance. Statistics alone can be misleading. There are also short-term loans to assist in exchange stability. Nor is either the flow of private capital or the repayment problem reflected in these statistics. Assistance-receiving countries had a public foreign debt of about $30 billion in 1965. Interest and payments will soon be a significant portion of the foreign exchange earnings, which will also continue to be needed for more development investment. Hence, lending terms at low interest with a long time to pay will be increasingly important and problems of debt renegotiation and threatened default will increase. Meanwhile, the consensus of experts is that net assistance lending will still need to be increased by $3 to $4 billion annually.

In 1964 Communist countries committed about $1.5 billion to assistance—several times the 1963 amount.

The people in the assistance business as administrators, technical advisors, and students being educated to return to their homeland may be as important as the money. About 14,500 Soviet technicians were working abroad in 1964 in some thirty countries. Thousands of foreign students were going to school on scholarships in Communist countries. Communist

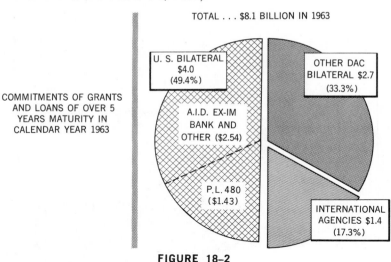

FIGURE 18-2

Assistance Received by the Developing Countries (*From Agency for International Development, Summary Presentation to the Congress, March, 1965*)

China has been expanding its assistance program in Africa and some other parts of the world. The United Nations agencies had thousands of technicians in the less-developed countries. Of 18,000 United Nations personnel, some 16,000 are engaged in social and economic activities. The United States in 1965 had assistance programs for seventy countries, most of the expenditures being concentrated in a dozen countries, and economic missions in forty-eight countries. The number of United States personnel overseas in assistance operations is difficult to estimate because of the use of contracts to universities and other agencies to carry out assistance projects. The number certainly tops the Communist overseas personnel.

Motivations for Providing Assistance. Generosity does exist in international relations, particularly in the American style of conducting them. But not to the worldwide extent of $8 billion a year being provided by industrialized countries to developing countries. Some of that amount is, of course, in the form of bankable loans and some is in agricultural surpluses. But there must be other reasons. The argument that short-term costs for development provide longer-term markets for goods is sound but not a sufficient explanation of the motivation to provide aid. The principal reason is political. The emerging states are determined to modernize quickly. The situations of many of them are revolutionary, disorderly, and could be disastrous. The United States and some other developed countries consider that assistance is a matter of hard-headed self-interest. The conflict in the world between Communism and the West over the emerging countries, and the conflict between the Communist blocs, has made it impractical for the greater powers to ignore the assistance instrument of foreign policy. President John F. Kennedy, in a message to Congress on May 25, 1961, said,

> The great battleground for the defense and expansion of freedom today is the whole southern half of the globe—Asia, Latin America, Africa and the Middle East—the lands of the rising peoples. Their revolution is the greatest in human history.

The President went on to state that the adversaries of freedom did not create the revolution but are striving to capture it. He cited the instruments of concealed aggression—arms, agitators, aid, technicians, propaganda, subversion and support of insurgency—and then said,

> With these formidable weapons, the adversaries of freedom plan to consolidate their territory—to exploit, to control, and finally to destroy the hopes of the world's newest nations; and they have ambitions to do it before the end of this decade. It is a contest of will and purpose as well as force and violence—a battle for minds and souls as well as lives and territory. And in this contest we cannot stand aside.

The Issue of Foreign Assistance.   No other United States foreign program since World War II has been debated either so long or so vigorously. The foreign assistance program is an excellent example of the effect of American public opinion on policy. It is unpopular and therefore limited in size and hampered by criticisms and administrative strictures.

There is little understanding that programs are predominantly loans and less understanding that the many strings on the U.S. bilateral programs include the requirement that any goods be purchased in the United States. The cost is low compared to costs of arms and small wars. Yet the informed people who conduct our foreign affairs, both Democrats and Republicans, have considered it a most useful policy instrument. Secretary of State Rusk is reported to have told the House Foreign Affairs Committee that economic assistance is "essential to United States security and national interest," and that without it, "many countries undoubtedly would have been subverted or overrun in the past two decades. The frontiers of freedom would have shrunk and Americans would be living in a less stable and more threatening world." [3]

There is some question as to what extent assistance has generated

---

[3] *The New York Times*, March 18, 1966.

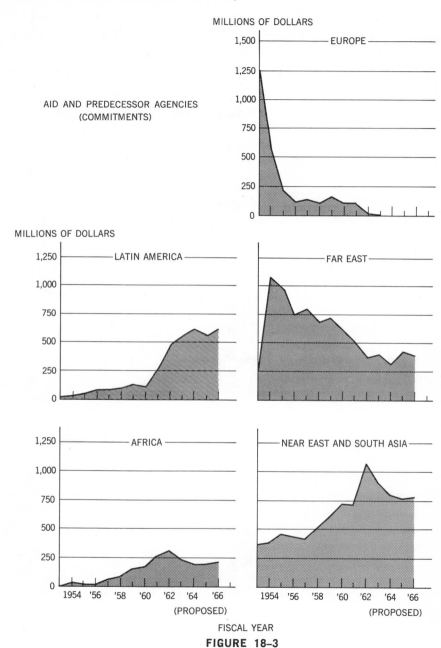

FIGURE 18-3

Trends by Area of U.S. Assistance (*From Agency for International Development, Summary Presentation to the Congress, March, 1965*)

lasting political influence with the recipient countries, a doubt underlining the point that, in international affairs, gratitude is often a pleasurable anticipation of a favor about to be received. In 1965 one Latin American diplomat commented that but for the Alliance for Progress to which the United States had in 1961 committed $20 billion in assistance over a ten-year period the inter-American system would probably not still be in one piece.[4] The Communist countries have had their disappointments, as seen in the suppression of the Indonesian Communist Party in 1965, despite all the Chinese and Soviet assistance. Chinese Communist personnel have also been expelled from several African countries which have received assistance from Communist China.

Designing and operating assistance programs involves many choices for which there are no formulas. To aid or not to aid? Should there be more or fewer strings? Should emphasis be on long-term or on more dramatic short-term projects? Should there be special attempts to promote private investment and private enterprise? Should there be competition with others in assistance programs? Should emphasis be on bilateral or multilateral channels? This question has been debated by using the argument that use of multilateral channels, including the World Bank, enables greater leverage to be brought to bear on countries for needed reforms, avoids the detailed involvement of the United States, and also avoids the controversy over programs in which Congress often becomes involved. But, on the other side of the argument, will Congress be willing to appropriate as much money for multilateral administration as for U.S.-managed assistance when other industrialized countries are not willing to increase their contributions to international assistance agencies? And can U.S. funds provided to international agencies be tied to expenditure in the United States? And some will argue that U.S. assistance is useful as a policy instrument.

How are the effects of an assistance program measured and priorities set among programs? There is grave difficulty in tracing and presenting the economic effect of a program. Certainly, success turns partly on political and psychological factors which cannot be quantified.

Pressures for assistance are strong, and design and operation of programs has created a new function for public servants, something of a new type of foreign service. Some seventy emerging countries are a large and worrisome number. Development takes a long time even when programs are successful, hence judgments are difficult today. History is likely to judge, however, that the assistance programs helped development, helped to buy time, and gave the United States useful associations with others.

[4] *The New York Times,* December 5, 1965, p. 4E.

CASE STUDY—THE UNITED STATES
BALANCE OF PAYMENTS

The balance of payments is the most universally used single reference by each state for gauging the management of the economic instrument in interstate affairs. It is roughly equivalent to the household account of a family or the operating statement of a business. The payments situation of the United States, or any other country, is always in a dynamic state of "balance." Surpluses or deficits in the flow of goods, services, and capital are continually compensated by a flow of gold, foreign exchange, and of debt instruments. When the regular transactions, the goods and services exported, the earnings on foreign investments, and the capital received do not equal the sum of the goods and services imported and the capital exported, then there is a payments deficit. The United States had a payments surplus from World War II until the late 1950's. An annual payments deficit followed and this caused continual pull on United States gold reserves.

If the United States were only concerned with the traditional types of foreign economic activity—export and import of goods and of services such as shipping—the balance of payments would show a large surplus. And if the United States were not the major world economic power, the situation would be less difficult and less delicate. The United States is to a considerable degree the free world's banker and its monetary and economic stability is a major factor in free-world security.

Turning to the nontraditional foreign economic activities of the United States, first, the private citizen has become a tourist, resulting in more than tripling the tourist expenditures abroad between 1950 and 1964 when they were about $2.5 billion. Second, the government supports United States foreign policy by significant military and economic expenditures abroad. This export of dollars has been rigorously curtailed by a "Buy American" policy in these programs, so that net dollar outflow through this avenue had by 1964 been cut to $2.1 billion for the military and in 1965 to $700 million for all economic assistance programs—a total of the same order of magnitude as the cost of tourism.

Much of the outflow due to military expenditures, and some of that due to economic assistance expenditures, was offset by German and other agreements to purchase U.S. manufactured arms and by the return flow of assistance dollars to purchase U.S. goods—the precise situation was difficult to quantify.

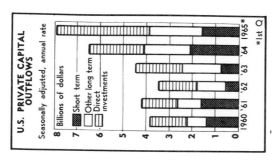

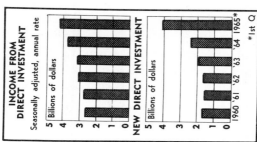

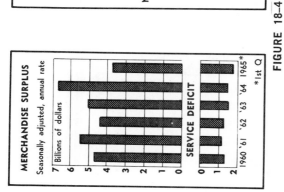

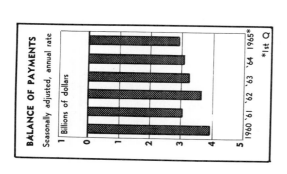

FIGURE 18-4

United States Balance of Payments *(From The New York Times, August 8, 1965. Reprinted by permission)*

The Buy American policy includes stocking Army Post Exchanges in Germany with United States goods, pressure on military personnel overseas to put their pay into savings bonds rather than the local economy, and tying of direct assistance grants and loans to purchases in the United States.

The third large nontraditional (because of its magnitude) area of activity is the export of capital to other countries. The short-term capital goes partly because of higher foreign interest rates, conflicting with the general policy of the United States to keep internal interest rates low. Long-term capital, as well as some short-term, goes to finance increasing exports and because earning prospects overseas are more attractive. About two thirds of the capital outflow has been going to Western Europe. The net outflow in 1963 and 1964 was between $4 and $5 billion a year. These investments will, over the long run, produce earnings which, if repatriated to the United States, will help the balance of payments in future years. In sum, the payments outflow in 1965 included approximately 12 per cent for tourism, 14 per cent for government programs, and 20 per cent for capital export.

The payments deficit is now a pressing problem. The special steps to cut down the dollar outflow due to government programs have been mentioned. Little has been done thus far about tourism. There is a "See America First" program. An effort is being made to increase foreign tourism in the United States, and customs exemptions on imports by tourists have been drastically reduced. The United States wants capital outflow to less-developed countries to continue. To decrease outflow to other countries there have been checks on foreign borrowing in the United States and an appeal, initially effective, by the government to businesses to exercise voluntary restraints on their foreign investment in already industrialized countries. Efforts will continue to check inflation, keeping United States price levels down and thereby helping to make United States goods competitive and attractive abroad. But the United States balance-of-payments problem will almost certainly continue to be a key item of concern to the country's foreign policy makers.

CONCLUSION

Many of the economic policies and actions resorted to by nations in the past reflected the political and economic arrangements of a world now no longer with us. As we pointed out in Chapter 8, the economic world of pre-World War II has been transformed by technology and by political and social factors. We cited three trends evident in this transformation: (1) an increased political fragmentation of the economic world brought about by the emergence of newly independent but underdeveloped nations, which seek rapid economic growth and political status; (2) the increasing commitment of governments to responsibility for both internal and external economic welfare and stability leading to the growth of international arrangements to promote the "common welfare"—thereby reflecting at least a limited community with respect to this value; and (3) the rise of Communist economic power, providing Communist states with increased means to pursue political and economic objectives in the underdeveloped countries as well as in the remainder of the free world.

The flexibility of the economic instrument of policy makes it very powerful. A case can be made that more orderliness has been achieved in international economic affairs than in political and other affairs, even though all types of affairs are closely linked. The future use of the economic instruments of policy must be viewed in the context of a world in which more national affairs are being managed by governments and in which economic instruments will have a larger political content.

CHAPTER 19

The Military Instrument and Its Management in Foreign Affairs

THE MILITARY INSTRUMENT DESCRIBED

Definition. Military force is the final arbiter in conflicts among nations. Military power in the broad sense—i.e., military resources of all types together with their purposes—is an integral part of the backdrop of international affairs and will continue to be so even if some measure of arms control is achieved. Therefore the foreign policy and supporting programs of every state are materially concerned with the military instrument of policy. We define this instrument as the policies and programs, external and internal to a state, concerned with the raising, maintenance, and use of military power.

Purpose. The uses of military power vary from state to state and era to era. Military power is used by some states in lieu of different types of resources, for example, as a police force for the preservation of internal order. Like other power, it has meaning only in the accomplishment of objectives. The following are the objects of military power today.[1]

[1] DETERRENCE. This involves prevention of the use by another state of its military power—and of other instruments of policy as well.

---

[1] Amos A. Jordan, "The Elements of National Power," *Army*, April 1966.

"Deterrent power is the ability to prevent certain threats or actions from being carried out by posing an equivalent or greater threat." [2]

[2] DEFENSE. This involves resisting military attack if deterrence fails. There is some dichotomy between deterrence and defense. For example, deterrence forces, such as offensive nuclear missiles, may be ill-suited to defense and vice versa.

[3] COERCION. This involves the active use of force, ranging from shows of force, blockade, and nonviolent measures to seizure of territory and political control to ultimate destruction.

[4] BACKDROP FOR NEGOTIATIONS. The possession of powerful forces lends weight to diplomatic bargaining. Louis XIV engraved his cannon with the inscription, "The last argument of kings." A modern version is supplied by China's Mao Tse-tung—"political power grows out of the mouth of a gun." If, for instance, the U.S. lacked adequate military power it could have little hope of progress in arms control negotiations with the U.S.S.R.

[5] CONTRIBUTOR TO NATIONAL PRESTIGE. Secretary of the Navy Paul Nitze has observed that prestige is a multiplier of power. "If they [people] believe we will be able to do, and will in fact do, what we indicate our intention of doing, they will accommodate themselves to our intention (even if they disagree with it) without forcing us in most instances to prove our point by doing it." Mr. Nitze also comments that friends are thereby more inclined to add their strength to ours. He might further have added that internal confidence in available military force is essential to gaining public support for some policies and programs. The drive of France, China, and others toward a nuclear capability has been in part a drive for prestige.

[6] SHIELD. Military power can provide a protective structure behind which other instruments can operate and political and economic institutions can grow and new ideas take root. Admiral Mahan wrote that the "purpose of military power is to provide time for moral ideas to take root." This shield purpose is particularly applicable to the military forces of new and developing states in which the social and political fabrics are often still weak and vulnerable to destructive tactics of militant minorities, insurgents, and subversive elements backed by foreign powers. The shield of United States military power after World War II, operated after 1949 through NATO, made possible the growth of the European community. That shield has been extended by arms assistance, alliances, and merely by its existence to many developing states.

[2] Henry A. Kissinger, *Problems of National Strategy* (New York: Praeger, 1965), p. 3.

[7] CONTRIBUTOR TO LEADERSHIP AND DEVELOPMENT. In new and changing societies military power can contribute to leadership and development. Many of the newer states are gravely deficient in administrative skills and in strong institutions. The military instrument often has these skills and an institutional strength which can help to fill critical voids during the modernizing transition.

In summary, states use the military instrument to influence their external environment and to support the stability of their internal programs. The long-run effectiveness of the instrument is not to be read in battle histories but in the position and prestige of the country possessing it.

Changing Nature of War.   Military force is meaningful only as a means to achieve national ends. Military power is not an end in itself. This principle of political primacy has been summarized by von Clausewitz's famous dictum "that war is nothing but a continuation of political intercourse with an admixture of other means." If military means become ends in themselves, dominating political objectives, "we have before us a senseless thing without an object." The United States War Department stated the same view in General Order No. 100 of April 1863: ". . . Modern wars are not internecine wars in which the killing of the enemy is the object. The destruction of the enemy in modern war, and, indeed modern war itself, are means to obtain that object of the belligerent which lies beyond the war."

If military force is to continue as a manageable means to political ends, both the means and the ends must remain limited. The bitter religious wars of the sixteenth and seventeenth centuries reflected the lack of limitation of ends. Even with the relatively low destructive power of military weapons of that day, the totality of the ends pursued resulted in a series of wars so destructive that the original purposes of the conflicts were submerged.

The Napoleonic Wars again demonstrated the consequences of restraining neither the ends nor means of war. The involvement of the entire French nation rather than narrow dynastic interests in the ends of the war and the use of large conscript armies rather than small professional armies combined to produce a "monster" which threatened to alter radically the nature of the European state system.

Perhaps partly because of the lessons learned from the Napoleonic Wars, the European powers succeeded in limiting the nineteenth-century wars which followed the Treaty of Paris in 1815. The ends were limited to settling specific issues. The fate of a nation was not made to hang on the outcome. The powers generally limited the means of war as well, reverting to the use of small (except for the British fleet) professional forces. It is instructive to recall that the greatest single military instrument of the nineteenth century, the British fleet, fought no major battle between Trafalgar (1805) and Jutland (1916). The one inordinately destructive war of the nineteenth century, which in retrospect was the first of the modern wars, involving relatively unlimited means and ends, was the American Civil War.

Initially, many thought that World War I was another in a series of limited wars in Central Europe. But, as Raymond Aron points out in *Century of Total War*, World War I expanded primarily because of "technical excess": the machine gun, the tank, heavy artillery, the airplane, the submarine, and poison gas. The unrestrained use of means resulted in such an increase in violence that, in part, the means shaped the ends. Only *total* victory, it seemed, could justify the slaughter resulting from modern weapons systems and the total mobilization of industry and population.

World War II further illustrated the total nature of modern general war. The almost complete lack of restraint in the use of means (the nonuse of gas warfare was the notable exception), and the unconditional nature of the ends sought, resulted in the most destructive war in history. Yet, at great price, the war generated as many issues as it settled. World War I destroyed the traditional European order; World War II destroyed the existing international order, leading to a new Great Power system and to the rapid disappearance of colonialism on a worldwide basis.

Any lingering beliefs that general war remained a practical means of resolving disputes between major powers have been dispelled by the enormous jump in the destructiveness of war with the development of nuclear weapons. For the first time it has now become clear that the destructiveness of the means has become disproportionate to the attainment of any ends save national survival and any other vital interests of the same order of value. The balance of terror resulting from potential opponents possessing the capability for mutual annihilation has resulted in general war becoming less likely. The clash of two nuclear powers has been likened to a battle between two scorpions (each of whose sting is lethal) in a bottle. But, although nuclear weapons serve as a deterrent to nuclear war, they have not provided a means of settling conflict.

During our era—still marked by unsettled issues of World War II, the ideological confrontation between Western ideas and Communism, and the revolution of the emerging nations—conflicts involving violence have become commonplace.

Violence internal or external to a country is often questionably categorized as "war." There were over twenty identifiable conflicts involving violence under way at the beginning of 1958. Two thirds of these were still in existence at the beginning of 1966 when the total conflicts under way had doubled. During this period (1958–1966) there were altogether some 150 insurgencies (broadly defined as a violent challenge to governmental authority or to the existence of the regime), some 40 per cent involving Communism. During the same period there were only some fifteen conventional military conflicts between two states.

There has been a clear correlation between frequency of occurrence of significant conflicts, particularly insurgency, and low per capita product countries. Thus, in seventy countries which according to the World Bank have less than $250 annual per capita product (thirty-eight of them below $100), over fifty conflicts occurred between 1958 and 1966. For twenty-seven "rich" countries (over $750 annual per capita product) only two experienced internal violence and these twenty-seven were involved in only ten conflicts altogether. One might speculate that internal security problems are correlated with low per capita income and hence such countries have particular need of military or other force for internal security. Or the statistics may argue that economic progress is a pacemaker for peace. The correct generalizations are unclear; perhaps there are none.

Thus, the present era is marked by the threat of a war of annihilation and the actuality of limited, even ambiguous, hostilities. In this environment, the creation and management of military forces to achieve the multiple purposes discussed at the beginning of this chapter pose a multitude of complex problems which are discussed in the following sections.

The Adjustment of Military Means to Purposes and Vice Versa. The relation of power to purpose and of purpose to power in the military area constitutes one of the critical tasks of statecraft. Because each state has only limited resources, it seeks to do the best it can with the military resources it has. Needed change in military resources is usually slow, being checked by traditionalism and by social and economic costs. Yet changes in technology and in national policy goals may occur relatively rapidly. Thus, for example, the United States for a few years after World War II lagged in creating military resources consistent with its purposes and later lagged somewhat again in shifting policies and resources to meet the Communist policy of "wars of liberation." As a second instance, the "national style" of Indian thought, stemming from Gandhi, contained a significant element of pacificism and nonresistance, creating a preference for a policy of nonalignment and an unwillingness to arm the nation. The quarrel with Pakistan and the ominous shadow of an aggressive China looming over the Himalayas are inconsistent with this "style" and at length forced the government to face up to some of the realities of establishing a modernized defense.

No state can now provide alone all of the military resources needed to achieve the security and other purposes listed at the beginning of this chapter. Nor is any one of those purposes likely to be achieved by military resources alone. Hence, each state needs to devise a pattern of policies and programs, which are not necessarily purely military but almost always have major military components, to further these purposes.

The long-term objectives of most states envisage ultimate elimination of war as an instrument of policy and a decrease in emphasis on the use of force in international relations. But national leaderships are generally conscious of the overriding short-term necessity for maintaining military programs designed to support present values. Otherwise the state or its society may not be around to answer "present" at the roll call of that world toward which we aspire.

The Military Instrument and the Emerging Nations. The complexities of managing the military instruments are particularly severe in the emerging nations where national income and skills are low, where change is certain to involve social and political conflicts, and where opportunities are present for militant minorities and insurgent elements to exploit weaknesses. Under such circumstances nation preserving invariably involves nation building. The problem and the direction of United States' policy in these new conditions are described in the statements of three United States leaders. President John F. Kennedy characterized the emerging nations as the "great battleground for the defense and expansion of freedom today, the whole southern half of the globe." A few years ago, Secretary of State Dean Rusk spelled out our national strategy on that battleground with these words,

We must encourage the less developed countries to move forward on their own as smoothly as possible, and we must simultaneously assist them against the threat of subversion. The success of this strategy requires new insights and techniques. We must become guardians of the modernization process rather than custodians of the status quo. We must be pro-modernization as well as anti-communist.

The United States has significant military relationships, including military missions, with many of the emerging nations. Following the thrust of the preceding statements, the Chief of Staff of the U.S. Army, in the official Army magazine, pointed out that activities to promote stability and progress in the modernization process of emerging nations had become a mission of the Army. He went on to point out that success lies beyond the reach of military means alone and requires concerted political, economic, and social action. These in turn require knowledge of public administration and economic development—as well as the military skills to deal with insurgencies.

THE NUCLEAR DILEMMAS

Secretary of State Dean Rusk, in presenting the Nuclear Test Ban Treaty to the Senate Foreign Relations Committee in 1963, commented, "The hard fact is that a full-scale nuclear exchange could erase all that man has built over the centuries. War has devoured itself because it can devour the world." Nuclear military power consists of both nuclear weapons and their delivery systems. Having one without the other is of restricted value, as when France had a nuclear device but lacked the missiles for its delivery. Similarly, Communist China had after 1964 some nuclear power but lacked a delivery system. Defense Secretary McNamara is reported to have told a NATO meeting that Communist China could be expected to have some medium-range missiles by the late 1960's and intercontinental missiles by 1975. Mr. McNamara is said to have estimated that, despite a "near-famine" economy, the Chinese were devoting 10 per cent of their gross national product to military expenditures.[3] Germany and some other United States allies have planes capable of delivering nuclear warheads but control no warheads. From the standpoints of cost and technology, the modern delivery capabilities (missiles, planes, and atomic artillery) are more difficult and time-consuming to provide than a small inventory of nuclear materials. The United States and the U.S.S.R. possess both weapons and delivery capability to achieve a quick and vast destruction. Few other states are likely to acquire large nuclear power soon, but several have a potential nuclear capability.

The progress of technology now gives two of the Great Powers a capability to destroy one another. As long as there is no effective arms control, this mutual power of destruction can, with little or no warning, be triggered by miscalculation or an irrational act. Others can acquire a ready nuclear arsenal. The problem of nuclear weapons will be exacerbated as third, fourth, and nth parties acquire them, together with the ability to deliver them. Britain, France, and China have detonated nuclear weapons. Washington and Moscow have thought the situation sufficiently critical to

[3] *The New York Times*, December 16, 1965.

provide a "hot line," a direct telephone connection, between the White House and the Kremlin, but some time may pass before Peking is included in the network. The bizarre possibility exists that a third party could trigger a nuclear interchange between two other states.

Nuclear proliferation creates a number of dilemmas. Might a lesser nuclear power, by threat or action, trigger a major nuclear exchange? Because its allies (Britain, France) are developing a nuclear capability and others can develop one, should the United States accept the realities and provide them with the means in some form? The NATO Multilateral Force (MLF) in which there would be joint allied control of a nuclear military force has been one proposed expedient. The MLF has proven difficult, both politically and administratively, to arrange. The extent of nuclear sharing with allies is a major U.S. dilemma. In the minds of some statesmen nuclear weapons are undoubtedly a Great Power status symbol, as well as a deterrent. President de Gaulle, for instance, has insisted that France's status as a Great Power requires her to have her own *force de frappe*. Facing an uncertain future, statesmen are reluctant to renounce the acquisition or retention of nuclear weapons. A theoretically desirable arrangement would be a complete banning of further proliferation. But, with Red China and perhaps others near the nuclear power threshold the chances of an effective compact along these lines seem small.

Theoretically, two nuclear powers could engage in limited-objective hostilities without escalating to a massive nuclear exchange. But the advantages of getting the nuclear jump or "first strike" on an opponent may be so great, and the hazards of being hit first so high, that a crisis confrontation of nuclear powers is likely to lead to escalation. This situation emphasizes the delicacy of mutual deterrence. In order for a nation to retain the capacity, and hopefully to forestall a first strike, a sufficient part of its own nuclear force must be invulnerable. This is essential if it is to retain the capacity to retaliate, or to launch a "second strike." Only by maintaining a credible ability, and will, to respond after being hit first can deterrence be reasonably assured to the nuclear power. The developing tendency may be to strive to keep the level of tension well below the threshold which might trigger a nuclear confrontation, regardless of the depth of the controversy.

THE MANAGEMENT OF THE MILITARY INSTRUMENT

Military Management in a Nuclear World. Once nuclear weapons are possessed, how are they best managed for maximum effectiveness?

TABLE 19-1
How Vulnerability Affects Deterrence

State of Retaliatory Force		Outcome of All-Out War		Ability of the U.S. Retaliatory Force to Deter:	
U.S.	U.S.S.R.	U.S.	U.S.S.R.	ALL OUT WAR	LIMITED AGGRESSION
1. Vulnerable	Vulnerable	1st strike wins 2nd strike loses	1st strike wins 2nd strike loses	Highly Unstable	Uncertain—but unstable
2. Vulnerable	Invulnerable	1st strike— stalemate 2nd strike loses	1st strike wins 2nd strike— stalemate	Very low against deliberate surprise attack	Almost useless
3. Invulnerable	Vulnerable	1st strike wins 2nd strike— stalemate	1st strike— stalemate 2nd strike loses	Deterrence against all-out war high	All-out capability can discourage limited aggression
4. Invulnerable	Invulnerable	1st strike— stalemate 2nd strike— stalemate	1st strike— stalemate 2nd strike— stalemate	Mutual deterrence	All-out war threat almost useless

From *The Necessity for Choice* by Henry A. Kissinger (New York: Harper & Brothers, 1961). .

Thus far, nuclear weapons have had only indirect application to conflict, acting as a backdrop to any threatened involvement of nuclear powers in support of local conflicts and internal wars. There are at least two discernible hazards in applying nuclear strength to local conflicts. First, pressures of support from the great nuclear powers may quickly escalate to a massive nuclear exchange. Second, a small number of nuclear weapons in the possession of allies may generate initial actions which would trigger a massive nuclear exchange. A war that is "limited" from the standpoint of a great nuclear power is likely to seem unlimited to the leadership of a small state facing extinction. "There is no human activity that stands in such constant and universal contact with chance as does war," wrote von Clausewitz.

Nuclear military power has made the technological race more critical. There is always a question that stabilized mutual deterrence, if achieved, will continue. A technological breakthrough in missile defense, in megaton-loaded satellites, or in some other bizarre weapon system not necessarily in the nuclear family, could critically upset the military balance.

Nuclear military power poses other grave problems. Is it worth its high costs? Should dependence be placed on it for a wide variety of military purposes? Such power can be provided in other than megaton units, for example, in small tactical weapons, but there is little consensus on the effects, of the use of these smaller weapons. The subsequent program of building multiple-purpose forces for "flexible response" signified a conclusion that nuclear military force is not technically and/or politically suitable for all the military purposes to be served. Yet, all United States military activity is inevitably viewed against the existent backdrop of great nuclear power.

Historically, one of the characteristics of a revolutionary change has been that it took between a generation and a century before men agreed on what had happened and why, if they did then. Obviously we do not now have the perspective needed to assess the full meaning of nuclear weapons. There are, however, at least two definite trends in the use of military force, which are related closely to the nuclear dilemma.

1. There is a turn to military programs which bypass the nuclear dilemma. An illustration is the shift of Communist emphasis to ambiguous conflict situations, such as internally generated "wars of national liberation" ("fraudulent civil wars" as some have called them).

2. There is greater emphasis, discussed in the next chapter, on conflict control and arms control. These approaches ask for initiatives which may be risks in the present to achieve a less bleak future for the world.

What and Who Constitute Military Management?   The purposes of the military instrument overlap. Furthermore, a particular military program is almost certain to further two or more of these purposes; for example, nuclear power deters, provides prestige, and may coerce or defend. The two categories of management problems of the military instrument also overlap: first, creation and maintenance of the instrument in accordance with some strategy; second, methods of employment including the decision-making process. There is not a neat division of management into policy making and execution, with the first handled by politically responsible officials and the second by professional military men. Political theories about management of the military instrument and management itself differ among states. In the United States emphasis is placed on civilian control at the top. This is not the case in many of the developing countries.

Because the implementors of policy are usually also architects of policy, decision makers and operators in each state must work together in the foreign policy field. Each must support the other for success in policy. Thus, if a country's strategy requires bases, diplomacy must help to obtain them.

The head of government generally has the authority to employ the military instrument, although action by the legislative body may be needed to declare a formal state of war and to provide funds and other resources. Planning and employment of forces in support of foreign policy has become an increasingly complicated operation between the military establishment and the political arm of government. Recognition of this point occasioned the creation of the National Security Council in this country. It has also led to joint schooling of United States military and foreign service officers, and to a multitude of policy, organizational, and administrative measures within the United States government.

The Military Instrument and Diplomacy.   As well as being an active instrument of the political arm of the state, armed force is a visible resource standing behind the shoulder of diplomacy. Employment poses delicate problems in decision making. Had the United States not responded with force for the defense of the Republic of Korea in June 1950, its policy in the Far East would have been undercut and the entire political balance in the area affected. Because total United States military power was not committed in Korea, there was a reserve supporting political action in the cold war struggle elsewhere. The management of armed force in conjunction with diplomatic endeavors is among the most difficult activities of statecraft. As another example, President Johnson, in late 1965 and early 1966, was able to vary the level of violence (Christmas and New

Year's truce pause and then resumption of bombing of North Vietnam) as part of his "peace offensive." Such orchestration when hostilities are under way is both difficult and unusual.

With a world always in an endemic crisis situation, at least by definition of Chinese Communist ideology, there is a need for a particular variety of show of force, namely, a continuous effort to impress both friends and others with the magnitude of military power and the firmness of resolution to use that power if pressed. Here enters the problem of distinguishing between resolution and sabre (missile) rattling. A "show of force" in the old sense has been affected by technological advances. The most massive types of military power are no longer always readily visible. The observer must depend either on uncertain intelligence, or on statements by the possessor, to estimate the true significance of what is "shown." Hence it seems that the use of military power through "show of force" is coming increasingly to rely on the onlooker's estimate of the power in being, coupled with statements of resolution, or even of threat, by the possessor.

Overt Force and Its Restraints. Active employment of the military instrument covers a spectrum of possibilities ranging from some varieties of show of force, through guerrilla fighting and limited war, to the grim capability for all-out nuclear exchange. Most states do not need to handle the entire spectrum of actions insofar as their own territory is concerned. But the Great Powers, particularly the United States and the Soviet Union, are concerned with the entire spectrum because of their strategic interests in allies and neutrals.

The inhibitions against open use of armed force are now much stronger than a generation ago. The restraints are (1) institutionalized in the United Nations; (2) implicit in alliance systems, which by being designed to involve associates may cause the associates to place brakes on a militant member; and (3) due particularly to the fear of escalation toward nuclear war. This third concern is compounded out of possible irrationality of leadership, operational mistakes, and miscalculation as to capability and/or intent of another party. An outstanding historical example is the drift of the Great Powers into World War I—the "war nobody wanted." The large number of uses of force in recent years show that these restraints have not deterred recourse to armed conflicts. But there is no doubt that world opinion focused in the United Nations is increasingly opposed to unilateral and unwarranted attack upon others.

Ambiguous military force makes matters more difficult for the country that is the target because the intent of involvement is unclear. It can lead to confusion in world opinion, as is illustrated by the divided views in the United States over Vietnam. Also, if the effort does not prosper it can more easily be recessed or called off without face-losing formal negotiations. Formal declarations of war seem now to have gone the way of the dreadnought and muzzle loader. Not that undeclared wars have been unusual. C. L. Sulzberger, writing in *The New York Times* in March 1966, commented that government researchers had counted 162 cases in United States history in which the President instructed the military forces to act against opponents without Congressional authorization, including a three-year conflict with France starting in 1798.

Ambiguity, Readiness, and Credibility. Communism has developed ambiguity of force to a high point of sophistication. By cloaking actions with obscurity and doubtfulness as to the reasons for the conflict, as well as concealing the sources of the forces used and the political objectives sought, Communist elements have been able to sow much confusion. With carefully prepared and cleverly launched moves, ambiguous situations can be created on short notice, requiring readiness to meet them on the spot and quickly demanding hard political decisions to counter them. This was the case in the Dominican crisis in 1965, when hasty action was required to cope with a situation of civil strife in which arms were being widely distributed to the populace. The movement of U.S. and other OAS forces into the Republic seemed imperative if a revolutionary situation were not to result in another Castro-type take-over.

Credibility in the use of force turns in large measure on the view of other states (friend and opponent) as to (1) whether the military power available is adequate, and (2) whether the states concerned have the political will to use the power in support of their purposes. "If therefore one of two belligerents," wrote von Clausewitz, "is determined to take the way of great decisions by arms, he has a high probability of success as soon as he is certain that the other does not want to take it. . . ."

The Rationale of Military Planning. The simplistic model of rational military planning is that the political leadership states the purposes to be achieved by military forces. The professional military then prepares a plan on which are based estimates of resources required to achieve the purposes. The political leadership then provides the resources and the country's military agencies act as and when directed by political leadership.

The first step in moving from the simplistic model toward reality arises from the fact that for any country armed forces have a traditional component and, under any circumstances, change slowly because of both cost and inertia. Hence such planning as is done has, in the shorter run, a large element of shaping existent means to achieve the ends sought and vice versa. American tradition has been one of small land forces in peacetime, a tradition undoubtedly contributing to the effort in the 1950's to find a viable long-range strategy with emphasis on strategic air, and also naval, power.

Secondly, domestic as well as foreign goals compete for resources. Furthermore, because absolute security cannot be insured by unilateral military strength, security planning must include consideration of political and economic measures contributing to the same purposes as those sought through military forces. These measures are, in varying degrees, components of or related to the military instrument of policy—neutrality, alliances, regional arrangements, support of peacekeeping measures by the UN and other conflict control measures, arms control, military assistance (given and received), and other measures. Conversion of plans or policy into real military power then also requires concrete actions in interstate relations through diplomacy.

Military Assistance. The technique of military assistance is not new. France provided arms to the revolting American colonies during our Revolutionary War with England. The United States provided tens of billions in lend-lease aid to allies during World War II. What is new is the widespread use of this technique in peacetime. On the order of fifty states were receiving military assistance—arms or military training missions or both—from the United States, the Soviet Union, or Communist China in the mid-1960's. The United States provided over $30 billion of arms assistance in the first twenty years after World War II, initially principally to NATO countries but, more recently, primarily to countries on the Asian rimland threatened by Communism. By the mid-1960's the annual grant assistance was on the order of $1 billion a year (see Figure 18–1). But sales of arms, mostly to NATO countries, were approximating another billion. These sales illustrate one of the confusing aspects of military assistance. When is the arrangement an employment of the military instrument; when is it a commercial transaction perhaps pressed to help the balance of payments situation; when is it both?

The reasons for military assistance need to be analyzed from two standpoints, that of the recipient and that of the provider. The recipient may lack the technology, the production capacity, or the financial resources to provide for himself the arms or the skills judged desirable. Because military resources, in the minds of the possessor, tend to be directed to specific purposes, arms and technical advice are wanted for specific purposes, for example, prestige or use in connection with a specific potential opponent. On the side of the provider, the reason for military assistance is the furtherance of national interest, for example, strengthening the recipient country against a third party, support of internal security in the complicated milieu of change in many nations, and even *quid pro quos* for political cooperation. Testifying before Congress in 1966, Secretary Rusk defended the military assistance program, in part, as helping "to build the shield behind which economic growth can take place." Theoretically the recipient and the provider are agreed on purpose; in fact they may be collaborating when their respective purposes overlap only partially. A state receiving arms for the stated purpose of security against external aggression may sometimes also have internal security as an objective in the minds of its leaders, and vice versa.

As another example, a military advisory group may be provided, in part, because of the political and institution-building influences it can have in a country where the military institution is important. Military assistance sometimes includes aspects of a cultural relations program. For example, a large number of foreign officers have attended United States military schools which include some orientation in United States concepts of democracy; military mission personnel work closely with their opposite numbers in the host country.

There are now producers of arms other than nuclear weapons, both outside and inside the Communist countries, who are eager to sell. Hence, if a country perseveres in a will to procure arms, the matter is essentially one of funding. If foreign exchange is not available, then a credit sale may be arranged. Faced with this situation, and the political as well as military undertones of having U.S. military equipment used by another country, the United States can be placed in a dilemma, doubly so since U.S. equipment is high in cost compared to that from other countries—to sell or not to sell; if to sell, under what terms.

MILITARY STRATEGY

Characteristics of Strategy. "Strategy," wrote von Clausewitz, "is simple but not thereby very easy." There are three main characteristics of national military strategy, which is the art of employing armed force to secure policy objectives.

[1] SPECIFIC PURPOSES. A military strategy stems from the twin roots of national objectives and the estimate of the environment. By its

nature, a sensible military strategy and the force to implement it are somewhat geared to specific purposes, that is, to meet specific threats and to deal with specific situations. Hence the military force of a state is often not impersonal vis-à-vis other states or, if charged with an internal security mission, vis-à-vis militant internal groups. It is not likely to be viewed as friendly by the targets toward which it seems to be directed—even though no state ever presents its military power as being other than for the defense of its vital interests.

[2] CAPABILITY SETS LIMITS. In selecting a military strategy, the choices of a state are limited by its capability to raise and support military forces, to obtain allies, and to keep up in the technological race. Many states cannot devise an adequate military strategy independent of an alliance or other political association with states having similar objectives. Furthermore, military strategy is conditioned by the allocation of resources between internal and external requirements.

[3] MILITARY STRATEGY, PART OF A LARGER WHOLE. Military strategy is inseparable from the policies guiding economic, psychological, and diplomatic instruments of policy. Crisis diplomacy, for instance, an aspect of the political instrument of policy, is frequently accompanied by overt, or threatened overt, use of the military instrument.

Historical Discontinuity in Strategy. The traditional pattern of strategy envisaged time for mobilization and for concerting detailed arrangements with allies. The rapidity with which modern military force can be applied and hence the readiness required to be prepared to counter such force effectively make such a pattern no longer appropriate. Arrangements with allies for command, communications, bases, and other operational matters need to be concerted in advance of tension situations. Modern strategic requirements tend to generate systems of relationships among states mutually dependent for security.

A further aspect of change in strategy is its geographical dispersion with increasing emphasis on the southern half of the globe and on ambiguous situations such as "wars of liberation" and other forms of insurgency which avoid nuclear confrontation and combine violence with social, political, and economic measures. Military strategy to be applied in the area needs to be consistent with the anticolonial environment that is more interested in development than in an ideological struggle.

The discontinuity in strategy derives in part from technology. Technology, for instance, has changed the significance of control of the seas. Any area of the globe can now be quickly attacked by missiles launched from other areas and by military force transported by air power. The discontinuity in strategy is underlined by the lack of experience with modern weapons on which to base judgments concerning concepts and military programs. Clausewitz warned that the art of war belongs to the empirical sciences, that we can only learn the nature of war from experience, and that "effects can never be completely discerned from the mere nature of the means."

Each state plans and builds for its use of military power in a conceptual framework of its own selection from among the practical choices. The conceptual framework is shaped in considerable part by the momentum of yesterday's concepts. Britain, for example, clung to a strategy detached from Europe too long prior to 1914; the United States clung to neutrality, isolation, unpreparedness, and faith in other than military measures against Japan too long in the 1930's.

The Choice of a National Strategy.   The range of grand strategies extends from nonresistance, neutralism, nonalignment, and unilateral military programs, through various forms of collective security, to the rarely announced aggressive use of the military instrument to expand state power and prestige. The environmental background against which the choice of strategy is made has undergone the revolutionary change described in the preceding section.

The choice of a strategy is now difficult and the outcome is often unsatisfactory, even for the Great Powers, as shown by the uneasy alliances of the U.S.S.R. and Communist China and of France and the other NATO powers in the mid-1960's. The new realities include a proliferation of national interests and far-reaching changes in the strength of many powers. The equation of world power is now significant for every state; a military crisis anywhere is usually a potential threat to the interests of many states.

A Unilateral Approach Underlying Military Strategy.   Self-sufficiency in military power has generally been associated with a discernible group of attitudes toward conflicts among other states—aloofness, isolation, and variant types of neutrality of which modern day neutralism or "nonalignment" by African and Asian leaders, is the most important. The different policies flowing from these attitudes obviously overlap. Neutrality may be related to isolation. Switzerland, Sweden, and probably Eire exemplify this policy, which has as its core the maintenance of correct formal attitudes and actions toward all the participants in any international conflict. Neutralism does not mean that a state does not prepare to defend itself as best it can. Sweden and Switzerland maintain some of the more efficient armed forces in Europe.

The present-day minimum purposes of any state's military program, whether or not accompanied by some type of neutrality, would appear to be (1) adequacy to prevent a quick *fait accompli* and to assure time for international agencies and tacit allies to act, and (2) assurance of internal security sufficient to preclude ambiguous and confusing situations over such matters as legitimacy of governments and issues of an internal conflict, as occurred both in Laos and in the Congo in 1960. A superficial self-sufficiency derives from being in the shade of nuclear power and of supporting, as a principle, nonintervention by outside powers or agencies. Some states can proceed upon a formally unilateral way, counting on a *de facto* ally waiting in the background if military trouble develops, as India did until attacked by China.

Coalition or Alliance Approaches.   Alliances are one method of balancing the strength of a potential opponent or of attaining a preponderance of military power. The military component of power is, of course, only one element in the balance-of-power equation. But it is usually a quite visible element, and hence important. The search for a military balance may be regional or global. Thus the United States, after World War II, abandoned the outmoded Jeffersonian doctrine of "no entangling alliances" and became a leader in nine alliances (see Chapter 22 and Figure 22–3) directed against threats of aggression.

There is usually some definition, vague or specific, of the respective commitments of the participants and of the machinery for an alliance. Viable alliances are grounded in mutuality of strategic interests. Although each partner's interests overlap, they are rarely completely the same. Thus Norway certainly did not wish to be involved in the United States problems in the Western Pacific through NATO. Nor did the ANZUS partners in the South Pacific want to be obligated to act outside of that area. Regional arrangements, sanctioned in the United Nations Charter, are a species of alliances directed to concerting collective action for security within a region. Both NATO and the Rio Pact are regional arrangements.

A coalition approach to security is a greater political problem for each nation involved than a unilateral approach. Even the most friendly states are bound to differ over the nature and relative importance of specific security objectives and the threats thereto. This is clearly seen in the differing views held by Washington and General de Gaulle on the need for integration in NATO. Differing estimates result in differences over policies and programs. Even in wartime, where there has been agreement on the threat, the building and management of collective military power is difficult indeed—as shown by the many World War II memoirs emphasizing differences over strategy between Britain and the United States and even more so between the Western allies and the Soviet Union. Napoleon once said: "If I must make war, I prefer it to be against a coalition." Churchill's comment has a political nuance: "Only one thing is worse than fighting with allies, and that is fighting without them." [4]

The problems of alliances are even greater in a situation short of war and require the most patient and talented practice of the diplomatic art. When interests other than military are not compatible, and the pressing danger decreases or disappears, the centrifugal forces can disband or weaken an alliance—witness the quick disintegration after World War II of the alliance between Moscow and the West, also the weakening of NATO as the Russian "coexistence" policy took effect and France felt free to pursue policies which, although weakening NATO, gave the French a much more independent position in world affairs.

Global Collective Security.   The concept of a universal collective security—a global alliance of all states for peace—is written into the United Nations Charter and will be discussed in Chapter 23. Here we note only that there are serious problems in concerting large collective forces under the United Nations. Aside from whatever political and psychological measures the U.N. can employ to check a nation's use of military power, the United Nations is dependent on contributions of such forces from member states. In addition to the political and financial difficulties involved in such a process, illustrated by the United Nations operation in the Congo crisis, there are operational difficulties in handling a collective force, usually hastily assembled from different states. The Charter provides that the United Nations use of armed force must be initiated by the Security Council, in which the Great Power veto may block any proposed action. Clearing this hurdle can be not only time-consuming when time is of the essence, it can also be fatal to any action. It is for this reason, as we shall see in Chapter 23, that the member states passed the Uniting for Peace Resolution in 1950 to enable a matter blocked in the Council by the veto to be taken to the General Assembly. But as the world has seen, this has not solved all problems when there is Great Power disagreement.

The approaches to national strategy discussed above are not mutually exclusive. Most states are pragmatic in following the pattern which best fits their interests in particular situations. Thus the United States at the same time it is allied to some forty states supports the universal approach

[4] Quoted by John L. Snell, in *Illusion and Necessity* (Boston: Houghton Mifflin, 1963).

through the United Nations. And it certainly would not hesitate in a grave situation to take unilateral action if it felt this to be necessary (for example, in the Cuban missile crisis). Only Switzerland comes to mind as a truly doctrinaire "unilateral" state, not even choosing to join the United Nations. With very few exceptions, states support, in principle, conflict control and arms control discussed in Chapter 20. Once a state commits itself to one or more of these policy patterns (unilateral, coalition, global), its military strategy and supporting programs are inevitably somewhat captive. Orderly changes are slow and difficult.

United States Security Policy. Prior to World War II, the U.S. defense strategy was characterized by small armed forces, unpreparedness, a dependence on slow mobilization, and an assumption that some other power, essentially Britain, would make any needed quick military response while the United States armed. Strategic interests were not clearly defined but were implicitly accepted as being confined, under usual circumstances, to the Western Hemisphere and the Pacific Ocean area.

Following World War II the initial hopes of a universal security arrangement under the United Nations faded by 1947. The United States faced a world having large areas which had become partial power vacuums as a result of the war. The strength of Britain and France had declined sharply. There was economic prostration. The old colonial empires were falling apart. Power, like nature, abhors a vacuum. The pressing threat was that Communist power would flow in to fill the vacuums, as it tried to do in Iran and Greece, and as it did in China. The United States was accordingly compelled to make a drastic and quick shift from its traditional strategy, using first massive economic resources, then shifting to development of large ready military power, and then entering into unprecedented peacetime commitments such as NATO.

The cost of this shift in strategy could be measured in several ways, one way being in the service of Americans in the armed forces and in the military, foreign assistance, atomic energy, and other security programs totaling over half the federal budget.

U.S. strategy became, and continues to be, a subject of wide public discussion, political controversy, and of study by civilian scholars and research institutes. One of the outcomes of this has been the appearance of terms such as *containment, graduated deterrence, flexible response, escalation*, etc., which capsulize the description of complex strategic concepts and military programs. Many of these terms, which not long ago would have been merely military jargon if existent at all, have found their way into the lexicon of political scientists and other scholars.

The United States' basic political-military strategy in the past twenty years, starting in 1947 with the Truman Doctrine and the Greek-Turkish assistance program, has been containment of Communism. This policy has been supported by alliances, massive assistance programs, and a maintenance of forces overseas, sometimes described as a "forward strategy." The great nuclear capability which the U.S. developed in the 1950's supported a corollary strategic policy: *deterrence*. In 1954, deterrence strategy was given a particular interpretation, namely, *massive retaliation*, when Secretary of State John Foster Dulles announced that the United States would retaliate against any aggression "at times and places of our own choosing." This policy statement implied the possible use of nuclear weapons in response to non-nuclear military action. The statement also implied the reluctance of the United States government to meet the costs and other implications of building a multipurpose family of military instruments.

The rising nuclear power of the Soviet Union brought mutual deterrence progressively into the global strategic picture. Also Soviet strategy shifted to peaceful coexistence coupled with support of "wars of liberation," that is, subversion and insurgency. The credibility of the U.S. nuclear position and resolution was apparently still adequate to prevail in the Cuban missile crisis of 1962. But the changing strategic situation in the early 1960's required a new or, more correctly stated, an expanded strategy and military resource base to support that expansion. The nuclear deterrent, increasingly in the form of an enormous ready missile capability, was maintained. Efforts to develop arms control and conflict control were continued along with the alliances and accompanying assistance programs. A counterinsurgency program was instituted to help new nations strengthen their ability to deal with Communist-supported internal aggression. And U.S. military instruments were made more versatile in order to support the strategy of "flexible response"—in effect a tacit admission that nuclear power has only a limited range of application in the spectrum of conflict situations.

The orchestration of military power with other instruments of foreign policy and with other countries has been the object of scholarly attention and a continual concern of United States leadership. The statements of two Presidents to West Point graduating classes summarize the problem. In 1955, President Eisenhower said, "No mastery of command can substitute for an intelligent comprehension of the economic goals, the political impulses, the spiritual aspirations that move tens of millions of people. But your greatest opportunity for enduring contribution to America may well be the council table, far removed from war." Then, in 1962, President Kennedy said,

> You will need to understand the importance of military power and also the limits of military power—to decide what arms should be used to fight and when they should be used to prevent a fight—to determine what represents our vital interests and what interests are only marginal. . . . Our forces therefore must fulfill a broader role—as a complement to our diplomacy—as an arm of our diplomacy—as a deterrent to our adversaries and as a symbol to our allies of our determination to support them. . . .

Soviet Military Doctrine. Technological change has an important effect on Soviet doctrine, which has traditionally held that war with capitalism is inevitable. That doctrine toward war was publicly revised from both theoretical as well as realistic considerations. In October 1960 a leading Soviet military strategist and theoretician, Major General Nikolai Talensky, wrote that "war as an instrument of policy is becoming outdated" because the "process of development of techniques in the destruction of peoples makes it impossible now to use weapons for the solution of political tasks, as has been the case in the course of thousands of years." [5] The Moscow Conference of representatives of Communist and Workers Parties in December 1960 assessed the "historical" forces now operative in the international arena, and declared that "real forces which can wreck [the] aggressive plans [of 'imperialism'] have taken shape. There is no fatal inevitability of war." However, the conference left no doubt about continuing conflict in the future. Emphasizing their currently chosen version of war, the conference report continued, "The Communists have always recognized the progressive, revolutionary importance of national-liberation wars, and are the most active champions of independence. . . . they consider it their international duty to cooperate with the peoples struggling for liberation and those who have liberated themselves from the imperialist yoke of oppression." Premier Khrushchev underlined this "duty" by pledging Soviet support for "wars of national liberation." [6] It should be noted as Chinese nuclear and missile capability increases, that the Sino-Communists (see Chapter 14) have not renounced war.

The Future of Military Strategy. Clearly, military strategy must now be devised within guidelines which are designed to prevent nuclear war. It has been suggested that military strategy had reached a "dead end"

---

[5] *The New York Times,* October 13, 1960.
[6] *The New York Times,* January 19, 1961.

with the development of nuclear power. Professor Henry A. Kissinger of Harvard University observes that some of the "most vocal and passionate advocates of arms control" would dismiss "strategic considerations impatiently as representing the attitude of short-sighted or power-mad men." He goes on to add, "Thus the absolutism that identifies safety with physical power all too often has been countered by another absolutism which pretends that arms control is an alternative to our security effort rather than a complement to it." [7] It seems, therefore, that military strategy is not obsolete, but has taken on a new direction. The strategy of total war may be at a dead end. The search for arms control is now part of the strategic context in which military power must be viewed. The strategy of using military power to achieve national goals remains a vital part of the art of statecraft and is at the heart of the international political process.

[7] Henry A. Kissinger, *Necessity for Choice* (New York: Harper, 1961), pp. 281–282.

PART V

Organizing the International Community

Preamble

WE COME NOW *to the last part of the text. In Part I of the book we suggested that notwithstanding the powerful forces for change at work within the international environment, it is possible to develop a realistic and useful model of the political relationships of modern states. A theory can be built around the exercise of power, the pursuit of purposes, and the recognition of a community of interests, although it cannot provide a complete description of contemporary world politics.*

In Part II we examined the dynamic factors or "forces" which constitute part of the international environment and are the basis of relationships. In Part III we discussed the processes by which governments make decisions on national policy in order to protect and advance their interests. in Part IV we considered various types of instruments states use to pursue their policies and attain their goals.

We complete the framework of analysis in Part V by turning to the formalized aspects of the world order. They can be classified by purpose, as the search for peace, security, and welfare; and by method, as international law and international organization.

The modern state system has always had some order and accepted methods for conducting international affairs, although these have been marked by disorder, crisis, and conflict. Today there is a tendency to institutionalize international political processes through multinational operating agencies and programs. The increasing complexity of world forces generates added need for orderly, reliable, and routine ways of conducting international relations. Individual states have less ability to manage their external environment, and increasing interdependence leads to a community of shared values and common objectives, in regional and worldwide associations.

We commented in a previous chapter that scientific knowledge has recently been doubling as rapidly as once every ten years. There is some doubt whether man's political competence, particularly in dealings among states, doubles as often as once in a century. Considering the rapidly changing world, it is perhaps remarkable that the state system is progressing as well as it is in evolving systems for furthering peace, security, and welfare. In the remaining chapters we shall turn to the institutional efforts of states to introduce a measure of order and organization into international affairs.

CHAPTER 20

The Search for
International Peace

INTRODUCTION

Peace—the absence of the use of force in conflict over values—is a shared value of almost all people and an announced major purpose of almost all governments. President Johnson stated in his 1965 State of the Union message, "The most urgent business for all of us remains strengthening the foundation of world peace." Yet violence and declared and undeclared wars continue. Not too long after President Johnson made this statement he was committing Americans to battle in Vietnam, while at the same time exploring avenues for an acceptable peaceful solution. As this example illustrates, peace is not necessarily synonymous with security; although nations value peace, security or the achievement of some other objectives are sometimes more valuable to peoples and governments.

The stated objective of peace implicitly raises a question: what kind of a peace? For peace can always be achieved by capitulation to the opponent. Peace can be imposed by coercive power. Peace may be the consequence of a sufficient agreement on values. Or it can be an agreement that the value of the existent order transcends the importance of the points in conflict. International law cannot create peace or order. It can only reflect the order that exists because of a consensus or power balance. Peace is a precondition for an international order upon which law can be based.

The Search for Peace.   The search for peace goes forward through a wide variety of means. Treaties and agreements, such the United Nations Charter, bind states to limit their use of force and to follow certain procedures in disputes. States arm themselves and enter into alliance systems in order to discourage others from attacking them. An explosive situation or the actual outbreak of hostilities usually generates an international effort to control the conflict and reduce it below the level of violence. Peacekeeping techniques have been evolving for maintaining cease-fires, once conflict has been brought under control. There are recognized techniques, principally founded on the practices of diplomacy, for trying to settle disputes peacefully. Since World War II there has been persistent international effort to effect control of the arms which make war a feasible and acceptable policy choice to states, and also to control the use of nuclear weapons which make war an ever more dangerous policy choice.

The search for international peace is partly a search for ways to effect, or to resist, change in interstate affairs without resort to violence. It is also a search which must recognize that shifts in internal affairs affect international affairs. Hence violence in internal affairs, or even a non-violent shift threatening the external power balance, can also become a problem of international peace. This search for peace implicitly recognizes that recourse to violence will not soon be eliminated. The pragmatic approach is to work forward along lines that reduce the number of instances of violence, minimize the destruction, and return conflicts to negotiation at the earliest possible stage.

The preceding approaches to the search for peace do not include the religious and idealistic approach of pacifism, which makes peace the overriding value. Pope Paul VI recognized the difference between a religious or idealistic and a political approach when in appealing for peace in Vietnam, he was careful to note that "judgment of political questions and temporal interests" was outside his competence. He also distinguished his appeal from "pacifism which ignores relative rights and duties in the conflict in question."

The wide variety of activities in the search for peace are illustrated by the interests and activities of the United States Arms Control and Disarmament Agency, established in 1961 to operate under the supervision of the State Department. The Congressional act establishing the Agency stipulates that its policy "must be consistent with national security policy as a whole." In addition to development of policy and the conduct of arms control negotiations, the Agency's report to Congress cites interest in research activities, arms control implications of new weapons technology, means to prohibit the threat or use of force to change boundaries, methods to reduce the danger of war by accident and by surprise attack, methods to check escalation of violence, the peaceful settlement of disputes, and the inhibition of regional arms races.[1]

The Causes of War. Case studies are available to support the proposition that wars are caused by misguided leaders, by aggressive states, by lack of balance of power, by arms races, by accident or miscalculation, by deep-seated differences, and by other causes. Statesmen have long struggled against these alleged causes. Citing an example, Metternich's willingness to restore a defeated France to Great Power status in 1815 was probably a recognition that a balance of power in Europe would in the long run contribute to peace. The League of Nations and the United Nations were launched with peace as a primary purpose.

Wars, it can be argued, are often caused by weakness which tempts pressures and aggression. Hence counters to this cause of war are the arms program and the alliance which provide countervailing power and hence deterrent force—peace maintained by threat of unacceptable counter action. Again, some maintain that war is inescapable in the anarchic international system of sovereign states and that the increase in the numbers of states has thereby enlarged the opportunities for friction, conflict, and war.

Various solutions have been proposed for changing the present system. Using the analogy of internal order in most states, it is argued that war could be reduced or averted if international law were strengthened. Others have proposed world government as a solution. These can only be academic proposals as long as there is neither international consensus on these proposed courses nor any permanent international force to compel "law and order." The attitudes of the Great Powers are the single most important factor in determining whether there will be peace or war.

Even as great an idealist as Woodrow Wilson did not envisage that peace would be achieved in another way than by the deterrence of mobilizing, through the League of Nations, overwhelming power against an aggressor.

---

[1] United States Arms Control and Disarmament Agency, Fourth Annual Report to Congress, January 1, 1964—December 31, 1964 (Excerpts), *Department of State Bulletin*, Vol. LII, No. 1340, March 1, 1965.

It is worth noting that in his analysis of the military requirements for such a league, Wilson was among the first to appreciate that arms control was not synonymous with disarmament. Although the Fourth of his Fourteen Points had called for the reduction of armaments "to the lowest point consistent with domestic safety," Wilson also believed that the stability of the postwar world would depend on the League's ability to coerce its strongest members (and among them the strongest naval power, Great Britain). Accordingly, when he applied his "disarmament point" to the United States, he ended up asking Congress in December, 1918, to triple the size of the battle fleet the Navy had afloat in November when the shooting stopped.[2]

SOME ASPECTS OF CONFLICT CONTROL

The underlying concept of the United Nations Charter, with its primary objective "to save succeeding generations from the scourge of war," was that the Great Powers, acting in unison, would prevent war or stop it quickly if it occurred. This concept has not been proved basically wrong, and strong arguments point to the soundness of the concept for maintaining peace among over 100 states which are not Great Powers. The integration of world affairs today—economic, monetary, military, etc.—and the dominance of these factors by the Great Powers gives them a potential leverage which can under many circumstances bring violence to a halt. This is not to say that the concerted action of the Great Powers could quickly eliminate all conflicts and causes of violence. The Cyprus conflict is a case in point. Nor, in today's world, can we be optimistic about the likelihood of concerted action among the Great Powers. Pacific settlement of disputes is a different and often more difficult matter than preventing, or compelling, a cessation of hostilities.

It is generally accepted, except among doctrinaire Communists, that conflicts should be resolved by other than violent means. Resourceful diplomacy is the first preventative of conflicts. But the use of the negotiating and persuasive powers of diplomacy has limits; to be effective the diplomatic arm must be supported by other means of persuasion and compulsion. Violent conflicts, and the threat thereof, extend from nuclear war through limited war, that is, war with conventional weapons. The spectrum also includes overt and covert military interventions by one state in the affairs of another, together with insurgency and guerrilla activities about which there may be great ambiguity as to the source, the type, and the extent, if

[2] Warner R. Schilling, "Weapons, Doctrine, and Arms Control: A Case from the Good Old Days," *Journal of Conflict Resolution*, Vol. VII, No. 3, September 1963.

any, of external support. Scholarship and techniques of statecraft have traditionally been directed to seeking ways to prevent and control interstate conflicts. As indicated by the brief discussion in the previous chapter of insurgencies and other internal violence, conflict control may now have a new dimension of great importance for which insufficient methods of collective intervention have been devised. Internal violence, particularly if it does not have an element of genocide or of ideological conflict, seems more likely to be exempt from external intervention than formal wars between states. Generally tolerated methods for intervention do exist; for example, the withholding of recognition and of different types of assistance.

Recent history has had examples of attempts at conflict control by third parties. The Great Powers have sometimes acted as third parties, using their own power to intervene in order to stop hostilities. This power has been in various forms: diplomatic and psychological pressures, such as United States action in the British-French attack on Suez in 1956; exertion of economic pressures, as in the cutting off of United States aid in the Indian-Pakistani war in 1965; and rapid military intervention ("peace enforcement" followed by "peacekeeping"), as in the civil war in the Dominican Republic in 1965. On occasions the middle powers, such as Canada and India, have lent their positions and influence to halt conflicts and to provide, under the U.N. flag, an international presence between fighting parties, as at Suez and in Cyprus. One of the sobering aspects of attempts at conflict control is the difficulty of disengagement once an effort has been launched. For example, there is a U.N. Commander and a military headquarters under the U.N. flag in Korea thirteen years after the armistice.

The instances of the use of military force by third parties to effect conflict control by compelling the cessation of hostilities are rare. United States and OAS combined intervention did succeed in the Dominican Republic in stopping violence, enforcing peace, and permitting a peaceful election to be held. In the larger context of the world power struggle, a case can be made that the intervention prevented the establishment of a second Communist government in the Western hemisphere. In general, however, the spread of nationalism, the propaganda effectiveness of charges of imperialism, and sometimes the danger of counter-intervention by a rival power have increased reluctance both to undertake and to accept such interventions. Economic sanctions and adverse world opinion are other available measures for conflict control. Except in specialized situations their effectiveness is doubtful. Italy continued its war against Ethiopia despite the partial economic sanctions applied to it by the League of Nations. One factor prompting an Indian-Pakistani cease-fire in 1965 was the power of the United States to stop its very considerable food assistance program for each country. Diplomacy backed by power is the most effective method of stopping hostilities between states. In some instances time, and the impact of the costs of fighting it out for a while, are needed for contestants to come to a point of willingness to accept third party intervention.

The circumstances might indicate an increasing trend toward the use of international organizations, both regional ones, such as the Organization of American States, and the universal United Nations, as a means of conflict control. But international organizations depend upon their member states for power resources, including finances, and have limited diplomatic and psychological influence as separate entities. The Secretary-General of the United Nations possesses some power and may be useful in certain situations. In the Congo situation the United Nations Force was comprised of troops from neutral and nonaligned states, mostly colored, though these forces were often ferried and supplied by United States airpower. The feasibility of intervention and the use of force turns in part on the flag under which the operation occurs. Experiences such as those in the Congo, the Near East, West New Guinea, Cyprus, and elsewhere, where U.N. forces have helped maintain or restore peace, have caused some to turn toward an international police force, a subject which we shall consider further in connection with arms control.

A conflict, either threatened or reaching violent action, is not necessarily eliminated by being controlled. There are two more steps to achieve a stabilized solution. First, there must be a period of peacekeeping while diplomacy works toward a more permanent settlement of the underlying causes of the conflict. Second, the settlement must assure that the fighting will not be renewed. The advancement of such a settlement may take a long while, as evidenced in the continued Arab-Israeli and Kashmir disputes.

PEACEKEEPING

The *Pax Britannica* of the nineteenth century, implemented in great part by the British fleet, was a peacekeeping contribution to that world order.[3] The remaining presence today of Britain east of Suez continues to contribute to peacekeeping in that area.

The term *peacekeeping* has in recent years referred to the use of

[3] See Ruth B. Russell, *Development of Peacekeeping Rules* (Washington: Brookings Institution, 1965).

military personnel for preventing or controlling violence within or between states. Peacekeeping is essentially a holding operation to try to create a favorable situation and to gain time for a peaceful settlement of the issues involved. The first step, achievement of a cease-fire, generally has to be achieved by diplomacy. Secondly, the consent of the state or states in which it is proposed to station a peacekeeping force must be secured through diplomatic channels. Thirdly, contingents of forces must be sought from states that are acceptable to the country or countries in which they are to be posted. Fourthly, arrangements must be completed for moving the forces from their home bases, and assembling and supplying them. Operations such as these are not easily arranged on the spur of the moment. They require intense diplomatic effort.

Enforcement of a cease-fire, or of peace, against the will of the parties is a difficult business. Of the eleven peacekeeping efforts of the United Nations in the first two decades of its existence,[4] the only case involving enforcement has been Korea.

Peacekeeping efforts can be unilateral, multilateral, regional, or under the control of the United Nations. The attitude of the host country or countries is particularly important. If there is not some sort of invitation to undertake a peacekeeping effort, the intervention is made much more difficult. Once an invitation is received, because practically all states feel they must espouse the cause of peace, the dispatch and use of peacekeeping supervisory forces becomes much more practicable. The functions of such forces are generally observing, policing, patroling, and the installation of a "presence" to deter further violence.

The presence of peacekeeping forces is likely to affect the outcome of a dispute. The forces are generally inclined to favor the status quo unless the leadership of the force is motivated toward a change. Such change can be subtle, as for example, when there is a subversive movement in the country or area concerned. Hence the matter of who commands the peacekeeping forces is of paramount importance.

Peacekeeping since World War II has been a useful but not very decisive instrument in international politics. As many as 200,000 individuals from over fifty nations participated in United Nations peacekeeping activties in the first twenty years of its existence. The political difficulties in getting the operation underway, the problems over personnel involved, the relations of the peacekeepers with the contesting parties, and the financial and other support of the peacekeeping forces are some of the difficulties

[4] Greece, Arab-Israeli 1948, Korea, Indonesia, Kashmir, Lebanon, Egypt and Gaza Strip (Suez), Congo, West New Guinea, Cyprus, Yemen.

that must be overcome. Peacekeeping and the peaceful settlement of disputes will be mentioned again in Chapter 23 because these two functions are primary missions of the United Nations.

PEACEFUL SETTLEMENT OF DISPUTES

Most states prefer bilateral diplomacy to settle their disputes and Article 33 of the United Nations Charter states explicitly that this method should be tried first. But when disputes reach the level of actual or threatened violence, the interposition of third parties or some international instrumentality can be helpful in establishing effective communication between the contending parties, in searching for bases of settlement, and in bringing public opinion to bear in favor of peaceful settlement.

There is a variety of traditional techniques for dealing with disputes peacefully. Under good offices a third party may bring the disputants together but does not attempt to propose a solution. Through mediation a third party may attempt to conciliate a settlement by proposing a solution, which is not, however, binding unless or until the parties accept it. Good offices and mediation are often combined as when U.S. Ambassador Ellsworth Bunker mediated between the Dutch and Indonesians when the latter were struggling for their independence. Conciliation can be described as institutionalized mediation, whereby the disputing parties submit their dispute to a formally constituted commission which attempts to suggest an acceptable solution. Commissions of inquiry can be used to determine the facts of a dispute. Through arbitration the disputing parties agree to use the services of a third party, perhaps an *ad hoc* group of experts or a tribunal such as the Permanent Court of Arbitration to propose a settlement on the basis of respect for principles of law and justice. A dispute which falls within the boundaries of international law can be referred to the International Court of Justice and adjudicated. There is the technique of the plebiscite to establish the opinion of the people concerned in case the dispute is over territory. None of these techniques are self-starting, save in the case of legal disputes that come under the optional clause of the Statute of the International Court of Justice. Otherwise, the techniques must be initiated by diplomatic action. The applicability of the various peaceful settlement procedures is unfortunately lessened in the modern era by the increased ambiguity of disputes, particularly in internal war situations, sometimes supported by external parties. The major instrument for dealing with disputes is therefore still diplomacy. In many cases, time alone can act to solve the basic elements in disputes, witness the lengthy Arab-Israeli and U.S.-Mexican water diversion disputes.

ARMS CONTROL

Definition and Purpose. The term *arms control* encompasses the concepts of disarmament, limitation of armaments, regulation of armament, and both possession and the ways of utilizing arms. For example, arms control could take place without arms reduction, or it could take the form of uncontrolled disarmament. Arms control can be implicit or it can come about through tacit agreement, as in the cessation of nuclear testing by the United States and U.S.S.R. between 1958 and 1961. Or it can result from explicit formal agreement, as in the Nuclear Test Ban Treaty of 1963. The concept of arms control extends beyond the reduction of armaments to include such ideas as nuclear free zones proposed for Africa and Latin America, and the "hot line" between Washington and Moscow to inhibit use of force caused by misunderstanding or miscalculation.

In his book *The Control of the Arms Race*, Hedley Bull, while personally considering that the furthering of security is the chief objective of arms control measures, lists three other purposes: (1) the release of economic resources; (2) the argument that war is morally wrong, although Mr. Bull notes that this argument has to do with the use, not the possession, of weapons; and (3) the argument that "military establishments corrupt liberal and democratic institutions: that the presence in society of military men, of military power and the military ethic, stunts the growth of liberty and stifles the prospects of parliamentary or popular rule." Although these three purposes often have a primary interest for individuals and groups, it does seem that security is the important objective in the realm of international politics today. On this objective Hedley Bull comments, "The extent to which armaments and armaments races provoke international tension and war, and the extent to which arms control can provide guarantees of international security, are often exaggerated. The contribution of arms control to international security may be a modest one, and we must first reflect upon the source of its limitations." [5]

It may be argued that the availability of arms makes the upsetting of constitutional governments more likely. This is controversial, however, since coups and revolutions are often more the product of the discipline

[5] Hedley Bull, *The Control of the Arms Race* (London: Weidenfeld-Nicholson, 1961), pp. 1–2.

and organization of the instigators (whether the military or subversive elements) than of the quantity and modernity of arms available.

Arms-Control Efforts in the Past.   The classical example of successful arms control efforts, employing a sanction that appealed to basic values, is that contained in Aristophanes' play of 411 B.C., *Lysistrata*, in which the ladies banded together and denied the men their favors, thereby stopping hostilities. In the Middle Ages the Church sponsored the "Peace of God," by which adversaries did not fight on Sundays and holy days—an institution reappearing in modern version in the cease-fires in Vietnam for Christmas and the New Year holidays.

Arms control has been imposed by the victorious on the defeated from the time of Rome's wars with Carthage to the post-World War II arrangements. It has been the subject of interstate agreements, freely entered into as in the Naval Limitation agreements of 1922 and 1930. Since the first Hague Conference of 1899, control of armaments has been the subject of frequent, and now continuous, conference diplomacy. The form of the proposals has ranged from control of a specific weapon as in the convention banning use of poison gas, to renunciation of war as an instrument of policy as in the Kellogg-Briand Pact of 1928.

The United States and Canada have been participants in the most successful arms control program. Their border has remained demilitarized since 1817, when the Rush-Bagot Treaty between the United States and Britain limited naval armament on the Great Lakes to three vessels each.

Arms Control Since World War II.   The United Nations Charter makes the Security Council responsible for formulating plans for the "establishment of a system for the regulation of armaments." Discussion of arms control has been almost continuous. Starting in 1962 negotiations went forward in an Eighteen Nation Committee on Disarmament meeting at Geneva.

Contemporary arms control efforts have followed two general lines: "general and complete disarmament," which was the central area of discussion from 1959 until after the Cuban missile crisis in 1962; and control of nuclear armament or, more broadly, stabilizing the nuclear environment. The latter topic has emphasized such aspects as control of technology, warning against surprise attack, insurance against miscalculation, control of the means of delivery of nuclear weapons, and nonproliferation of nuclear weapons as well as nuclear arms limitation. Proposals have included the 1946 Baruch Plan for international control of dangerous fissionable materials, President Eisenhower's Open Sky proposal of 1957, and the limited Nuclear Test Ban Treaty of 1963, which banned all nuclear tests except underground explosions.[6] This treaty was agreed to by over 100 countries including the United States, the U.S.S.R., and Britain—but not the other two members of the nuclear club—France and Communist China. The United Nations has passed a resolution banning the placement in space of weapons of mass destruction.

Formal proposals for comprehensive disarmament have envisaged general disarmament in all categories of weapons but there has been little definition and no agreement on how complete such disarmament can realistically be. Soviet Premier Khrushchev called in 1959 for "complete" disarmament over a period of four years. Other proposals have envisaged a universally accepted treaty with progress by stages, an inspection system, and some sort of peacekeeping arrangement such as an international police force. All of these proposals are complicated in concept and fraught with operational difficulties, even assuming a reasonable modicum of trust among the states concerned. Proposals for general disarmament implicitly premise the creation of a supranational authority having the nature of a world government. These proposals entail negotiated disarmament.

Due in part undoubtedly to the sobering effects of the Cuban missile crisis, and China's achievement of a nuclear explosion in 1963, there has been an increasing tacit acceptance that general and complete disarmament cannot certainly be achieved in time to control the atom. A resulting sense of urgency accordingly has arisen concerning the proliferation of nuclear weapons. In 1965 both the United States and the Soviet Union submitted draft treaties which were referred to the Eighteen Nation Committee for its consideration. Nonproliferation is an area where the interests of the major nuclear powers tend to overlap despite the power struggle in some other areas.

Writing for *Foreign Affairs* in July 1965, William C. Foster, Director of the United States Arms Control and Disarmament Agency, cited three considerations concerning nuclear proliferation from the standpoint of the United States. First, the increased hazard of nuclear involvement might turn the United States back to an isolationist policy at a time when the world is shrinking so as to make such a policy disastrous. Second, nuclear proliferation erodes the margin of power relative to the rest of the world provided by our wealth and industrial base. Third, there is the simple fact that the probability of use of nuclear weapons increases with the number of fingers on nuclear triggers. Mr. Foster concluded that the United States would be justified in accepting rather large costs in an effort to prevent nuclear proliferation. He recognized the possible

[6] For text of treaty see Appendix C.

erosion of alliances resulting from the concern of allies over a nuclear détente between the United States and the U.S.S.R. In addition to nonproliferation the United States has proposed a freeze and reduction of
strategic nuclear delivery vehicles, a cutoff of production of fissionable
materials, a comprehensive test ban treaty, a "bomber bonfire" of obsoles-
cent aircraft, and demonstrated destruction of nuclear weapons to obtain
fissionable materials for transfer to peaceful uses. The last item underlines
the increasing importance of control of the plutonium produced by the
growing number of industrial atomic energy plants. The international
Atomic Energy Agency and Euratom provide a voluntary means for inspection and safeguards

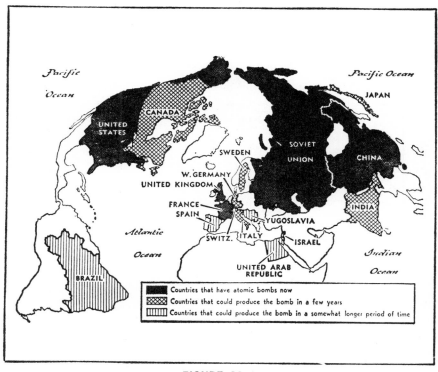

FIGURE 20–1

The Spreading Threat of Nuclear Bombs (*From* The New York Times,
August 1, 1965. Reprinted by permission)

Some Obstacles to an Arms-Control Program.

The statesman
thinks first of his country's security and of objectives which have been
furthered by the military instrument. Only then does he think of men

and weapons systems as contributing items, and for these there are few agreed yardsticks for comparison among countries. No agreed common denominators exist for such elements as men, missiles, alliances, bases, or the very effective secrecy of Communist countries. Besides unpredictable and continuing technological change, there are the hazards of political developments in new countries, changing governments, and new combinations of states.

Inspection for compliance with arms control agreements is a knotty problem. Even with widespread cooperation, a multinational inspection system would be a tremendous and irksome bureaucratic enterprise. Without international inspection the chances that rising distrust might quickly upset an arms control arrangement would be great indeed.

Another difficult area is sanctions in case of noncompliance. There could be at least two forms of noncompliance: refusal to submit to inspection, which might be difficult to establish; and circumvention of the substantive control on arms, resulting in diplomatic controversy. There is a grave question whether states would be willing to use force to coerce a noncomplying state or, having limited their own arms, would be able to use force against a state that violated controls. Moreover, a small time advantage might give one state preponderant military power in its region or even in the world.

The lead time between proof of technical feasibility and provision of operational weapons is generally long. Hence, if a state first learns of a weapon only when another state has acquired it, the resulting time gap in the balance of weaponry may be serious—for example, the secret acquisition of an antiballistic missile system by one, but not the other, of the two nuclear superpowers.

There has been discussion of an international police force to help overcome some of the difficulties just mentioned. Such a force would be truly international and not a force of national units operating under the United Nations flag. In addition to the problems of recruiting, replacement, logistical support, transportation, and financing there is a problem of command. It is problematical how many states would be willing to accept an arms control arrangement that required trusting vital interests to an unprecedented international police force which, like the unicorn, no one has yet seen.

Viewing the history of arms control, some aspects stand out. Imposed arms control, as on Germany after World Wars I and II, has been transitory. Negotiation of detailed agreements has been exceedingly difficult. Technology and other changes have overtaken agreed-upon details.

When mutual trust or a community of interest has been lacking progress has been almost impossible. There have been instances of *de facto* arms control. The United States–Canadian and United States–British situation is a tacit control based on trust. The Western European countries maintained forces below their capability during the 1950's and 1960's, probably because they relied on United States strategic nuclear power. Many lesser states have possessed fewer arms than they aspired to because manufacturing states would not provide them. This has been an embryonic and unstructured system of arms control which has been implicit in restrictions in legislation by the United States Congress on provision of arms to Latin American countries.

Possible Guidelines for Arms-Control Progress. There is wide consensus of purpose on preventing massive nuclear exchange—the possible exception being Communist China. Although there may be no mutual trust between Communist powers and Western powers, there can be mutual assurance of adequate retaliatory power. The first step toward arms control may be a nonproliferation arrangement combined with a stable nuclear situation in which both sides know that no power's nuclear capability is likely to be wiped out in a surprise nuclear "first strike."

Arms control should be as self-regulating as possible. Rather than conceal its inventory of nuclear arms, a state might wish to display that inventory as a part of its deterrent strategy—thereby providing *de facto* inspection.

There is a case for viewing sweeping proposals concerning arms control with caution. "Maximum disarmament, down to the level of a national police force, is not synonymous with maximum stability and may in fact be inconsistent with it. In a totally disarmed world even a small number of secreted or clandestinely manufactured nuclear weapons could disrupt the international order and allow one power to dominate its more trusting adversaries." [7] Each state in discussing arms control tends to look for measures which improve its relative power position or, at the minimum, do not adversely affect that position. For example, in early post-World War II arms control discussions, the U.S.S.R. placed heavy emphasis on United States bases and the United States made proposals which might continue its lead in nuclear weapons. The pragmatic approach to arms

[7] *United States Foreign Policy*, "Developments in Military Technology and Their Impact on United States Strategy and Foreign Policy," Study No. 8, Prepared for the Senate Committee on Foreign Relations by the Washington Center of Foreign Policy Research, The Johns Hopkins University, 86th Congress, 1st Session, (Washington: Government Printing Office, 1959).

control looks for measures which do not change the existing military balance, while reducing arms and the danger of war.

CONCLUSION

Peace with security is the prime objective to which disarmament is secondary. Discussion often focuses on disarmament rather than on control.

There are strong views that the search for peace is in the long run a matter of dampening or eliminating international conflicts while increasing mutual trust among nations. Recognizing that this is a "chicken and egg" situation, Inis L. Claude, Jr., in his *Swords Into Plowshares*, writes, "nevertheless, there are strong indications that the elimination of war is more dependent upon intervention into the vicious circle at the points of political conflict than at the points of military technology." The reasons for conflicts between states threatening or generating violence may be becoming fewer. The dynastic rivals of the past are no longer with us. Trade interests and *Lebensraum* reasons for violent conflict are less significant. Economic and religious excuses for violence are also less important, although they still exist—as in the Arab-Israeli conflict or in the unstable situations of some new states. Although wars are certainly no less dangerous, the causes of war may be lessening.

The "chicken and egg" situation has its brighter side. Certain attitudes are prerequisites for arms control. The gradual achievement of these attitudes results in reduction of tensions and increase in trust, thereby generating tacit disarmament and eliminating the need for formal agreements, inspection, and policing never yet completely successful in the state system.

Arms-control measures need to be teamed with other conflict control means and also with national military strategies. The basic legislation and the interests, cited at the beginning of this chapter, of the United States Arms Control and Disarmament Agency attest to this point. Effective arms control requires managing the military force of the state within certain guidelines. The search for arms control is now part of the strategic context in which military power must be viewed and shaped, and vice versa. Viewing arms control as encompassing control of devastation as well as arms reduction, the United States shift from a strategy of massive retaliation to armed forces permitting a flexible response was a stabilizing measure. The preservation of a nuclear balance may be argued to be an arms control measure. Any arms control proposal unsettling the military balance that is an integral part of the balance-of-power equation is almost certain to be unacceptable to the states concerned.

Any existing military balance is most unlikely to be a negotiated arrangement. Rather it is a tacit arrangement or an unstable equilibrium, likely to be upset by contending states each striving for preponderance rather than equilibrium. Perhaps the best that can be hoped for is a combination of formal actions such as the Nuclear Test Ban and of tacit understandings, while an increased consensus evolves among conflicting states—as in the development of consensus on nonproliferation of nuclear weapons.

Professor Robert Bowie stresses that "no arms control plan will remain effective and dependable unless it continues to serve the national interests of each of its parties, as its leaders conceive those interests. . . ." It is not useful to consider the world community of states as an undifferentiated whole. The problem of peace is inextricably tied to the conflict and power relationships of specific states, and formulas for seeking peace must be shaped to this specific context.

CHAPTER 21

The International Rule
of Law

INTRODUCTION

Two generations ago the study of international relations was principally
concerned with international law. From the middle of the seventeenth
century until World War I, statesmen and scholars regarded the law of
nations and diplomatic history as the most exact and logical approaches
to international affairs.

The outlook has changed since then. Violence and disregard of the
rights of weak and neutral states and of international obligations during
World Wars I and II, the lawless actions of Fascist and Communist
forces, and modern nationalism have fostered widespread skepticism about
international law. Ideological competition and the increasing role of the
many African and Asian states that have neither a tradition of adherence
to international law nor a part in its creation have added to this skepticism.
Politics holds the world spotlight. Policy makers have become preoccupied
with the revolutionary forces operating in the international scene and
these are beyond the scope of generally agreed rules of international law.
World leaders do not often refer to international law, nor do incidents

occur that give rise to public debates about it. Appeals to the International Court of Justice and to arbitration are comparatively few.

However, practically all states in the community of nations have affirmed their recognition of the principles of international law. Treaties, agreements, national pronouncements, court decisions, and provisions incorporated into their own legal systems are explicit acknowledgment of the potential of international law. The fact that a law of nations exists and is accepted by the majority of states must not blind us, however, to the fact that it is still a relatively weak and primitive form of law.

THE NATURE OF CONTEMPORARY INTERNATIONAL LAW

International law may be defined as the sum of the rules, principles, customs, and agreements states accept as having the binding force of law for the regulation of aspects of their international relations.

The Preamble to the United Nations Charter attests to the central place of international law in the scheme of international relations. It declares that one of the four main ends for which the organization exists is "to establish conditions under which respect for the obligations arising from treaties and other sources of international law can be maintained." More than 117 states have acknowledged this objective by adhering to the Charter.

International law is a unique body of jurisprudence. It is based on practice and usage, and is a *corpus juris* that is still in evolution. It did not spring full-blown from any single legislative or diplomatic act but has grown slowly, one precept at a time.

Early Concepts of a Law of Nations.   The idea of a law applicable to relations among states can be traced far back into history. Greek poets and philosophers spoke about principles and customs common to all Greeks whatever their city-state. Thucydides spoke of the "law of the Hellenes" and again of the "laws of all mankind." The Greeks had no concept of international law in the modern sense, however, of a body of principles enforceable in courts of law.

The Romans moved a step further. The *jus gentium,* a body of law and equity applicable to foreigners resident in the Roman Empire, was a system of private international law that came to encroach upon portions of the field of public international law. Livy says this law was applicable to peoples of all nationalities. But it did not include a concept of a body of sovereign states equally subject to law. The Roman *jus civile* was applicable to citizens and drew heavily upon rudimentary concepts of a national law.

During the Middle Ages the canon law of the Roman Catholic Church, together with the existence of the Holy Roman Empire and the perseverance of the *jus civile* and *jus gentium*, implanted in the minds of Europeans the consciousness of a common law independent of local political rule. Some of the mercantile codes that developed in areas around the Mediterranean and in the North and Baltic Seas in the thirteenth century are also part of the foundation of international law. Most famous of these were the *Consolato del Mare* in Barcelona and the Laws of Wisby applied among the towns of the Hanseatic League. Originating in the practices of merchants and seamen and later applied by courts, these rules were widely accepted and became a common law of the sea.

The Founders of International Law. The actual founders of international law were a few jurists, theologians, and scholars in the sixteenth and seventeenth centuries. The most illustrious of these was Hugo Grotius, a Dutch jurist and statesman, to whom international law owes its inception as a systematized body of principles, rules, and usages. His celebrated work, *De Jure Belli ac Pacis,* was published in 1625 and became one of the world's most widely read books. Marshaling impressive evidence from the writings of others on the practice of rulers and states, Grotius declared what was the law. He argued that enlightened interest and right reasoning dictated that rulers and states should submit to principles and rules of law in their international conduct. He fashioned the outlines of a system statesmen were willing to accept and upon which succeeding generations of jurists could build a living law.

Roscoe Pound, former Dean of the Harvard Law School, once epitomized the origin of the law of nations in these words, "International law was born of juristic speculation and became a reality because that speculation gave men something by which to make and shape international legal institutions and a belief that they could make and shape them effectively."

The Nation-State System—Cornerstone of the Law. Grotius' formulation of the law of nations coincided with a fundamental political change in Europe. With the Protestant Reformation, new states arose or broke away from the Catholic Church and refused to acknowledge the authority of the Pope. His allocation of the colonial world to Spain and Portugal was disregarded by England and other powers, and the special rights of Papal envoys at international gatherings were challenged. Europe was politically divided and a system of higher law was unacceptable to all. The Thirty Years' War marked a transition to another stage of political relationship in Europe. This was embodied in the Treaty of Westphalia (1648). By its terms the leading states of Europe acknowledged the equality of sovereign states as the basis of the new political order and the bedrock of international law. Statesmen and writers joined in establishing that states are the subjects of the law and that before the law all states are juridically equal, whatever their size, origin, religion, or form of government. These are the cardinal principles of international law.

Sources of the Law.   Since the seventeenth century, writers on the law have examined the practices and usages of states for evidence of what they regard as law. From these and from natural law and Roman law, concepts of status, persons, title, and jurisdiction have been developed. These are the contractual bases of agreement, rights, and obligations of states. In practice, additional principles evolved relating to the treatment of ambassadors and the sanctity of treaties. To writings and practice were added treaties, state papers, court decisions, and utterances of responsible leaders as further sources of international law. Because most of the countries of Asia and Africa did not until recently qualify as nation-states, very few of the rules had Asian or African participation in their formulation.

The Central Issue of Sovereignty and Consent.   The central issue of the law of nations is the reconciliation of sovereignty and obligation in a system predicated upon common consent.

In the early stages of international law, Grotius and others contended that there was a natural law binding on all men and states, irrespective of their will, divinely implanted in the minds of men or inherent in society and discoverable by right reasoning. This theory was challenged by the positivists, who claimed that because the nation-state possesses the supreme political power above which there is none other, it cannot be obligated under law except by its own consent. This school of thought has insisted that international law consists of only those rules and principles which are formally agreed to by states, through such means as treaties and agreements, and are clearly evidenced by state practice.

Statesmen generally have acted upon the latter view. But an examination of what is widely accepted among states as international law shows that some aspects of it rest upon tacit consent, whereas other parts are incorporated into treaties and agreements. The body of international law that is applicable today to disputes referred to the International Court of Justice is declared by Article 38 of the Court's Statute to include:

a. international conventions, whether general or particular, establishing rules expressly recognized by the contesting states;

b. international custom, as evidence of a general practice accepted as law;

c. the general principles of law recognized by civilized nations. . . .

Sometimes the law is expanded when a state takes a step and others do not object to it. An example is the orbiting of a satellite over the territory of others without protest. In such a manner a principle of "freedom of space" may have been inaugurated. Communications satellites and the formation of the quasipublic Comsat Corporation introduce a new field of legal relationships, as do the arrangements among the cooperating states in the Antarctic.

Another principle may have been evolved out of the formation and stationing of international peacekeeping forces under U.N. auspices. The "thin blue line" has operated in such strife-torn areas as the Gaza Strip, Cyprus, and the Congo, with the consent of the local sovereigns.

Development of supranational institutions holding powers of regulation and enforcement over both individuals and corporations and providing access for individuals to an international Court of Human Rights in the European community has brought new forms of international liability, responsibility, and authority.[1]

The Binding Force of Law. Domestic law is normally considered to be a rule of conduct promulgated by an authority entitled to make it binding upon a subject. This authority may be a sovereign, a legislature, or a court. In international law where sovereign states comprise the subjects, there is no superior authority that legislates for states or possesses the power to bind them without their consent. Because of this situation some think that international law is not "true law." However, statesmen declare it to be law, and governments assert rights and obligations based upon it. National courts and international tribunals give effect to the law of nations when it is invoked before them. Governments use the instruments of policy available to them to maintain their rights under the law. And such widely accepted agreements as the Charter of the United Nations and the Statute of the International Court of Justice specifically provide for actions and decisions predicated upon the binding force of international law.

[1] There are precedents for the right of the individual to seek redress directly through the European Commission of Human Rights to the European Court of Human Rights, as for instance in Lawless v. Ireland (1961) and de Becker v. Belgium (1962). See Wolfgang Friedmann, *The Changing Structure of International Law* (New York: Columbia University Press, 1964).

International law is not always observed or enforceable. States from time to time violate or refuse to uphold it, as do individuals and groups in the case of domestic law. Thus, Germany in World Wars I and II sank unarmed passenger vessels and neutral ships, contrary to generally understood precepts of international law.

Fundamentally, the binding force of international law rests upon a willingness of states to observe it. They will abide by the law if it seems to be in their interest. Where states consider their national survival or independence to be at stake, or where their security and interests demand action in contravention of the law, they may ignore or disregard it. Expediency, mutual convenience, respect for the rights of others, prestige, and the possibility of suffering retaliation or being exposed to forceful actions, all motivate support and observance of the law in relations among sovereign states.

Western political ideas and institutions no longer dominate. The current clash of ideologies and political systems and the many different cultural patterns now represented in the international arena result in less consensus on the basis of law. African and Asian states in particular feel that because they had no part in forming it, the law is not necessarily always their law. Lack of agreement on basic principles of conduct and comity deprives international law of one of the fundamental elements of an effective legal system.

Marxist-Leninist dogma denounces the principles of justice, reason, and obligation generally accepted by Western states as underlying international law.[2] The basic values of independence, integrity, civil stability, and respect for the rights of other nations represented in international law are denied by their dogmatists. Soviet leaders and jurists have alleged that Western interpretations and applications of international law are a "bourgeois product," designed as a tool for the exploitation of oppressed classes and the destruction of socialist states. This interpretation implies that Communist states need observe international law only when they wish to do so, and that they may release themselves from obligations toward others on the grounds of sovereignty, self-interest, and dogma. This deprives the law of the universal binding force it enjoyed during much of the nineteenth and early twentieth centuries, and makes it difficult or impossible for law to function in relationships between Communist and non-Communist states.

The Soviet Union's position is ambivalent, for it has not formally

[2] See Hans Kelsen, *What Is Justice?* (Berkeley: University of California Press, 1960).

denied the existence of international law. The Soviet government has repeatedly taken refuge in the principles of sovereignty, territorial jurisdiction, and diplomatic and consular privileges and immunities to protect and advance its interests and objectives. Only by agreeing to abide by some of the generally accepted rules of international law is it possible for the Soviet Union and its Communist allies to have diplomatic relations with other states. The Soviet Union has adhered to the Charter of the United Nations with its Preamble expressly stating that members will seek to establish conditions under which "respect for the obligations arising from treaties and other sources of international law can be maintained." Yet the Soviet Union, as well as France, has refused to accept the validity of the International Court's finding in its 1962 advisory opinion on certain U.N. expenses that states are obliged to pay peacekeeping assessments voted without their consent by the General Assembly. Until Soviet legal scholars provide a theoretical justification for observance of the law, one can only be certain that the Soviet Union will be guided by what it believes its national interests require under the circumstances.[3]

Institutional Inadequacies of International Law. One of the major differences between international and domestic law is the relative lack of institutional support in the international system.

There is no international government to formulate new law when the situation demands it. There is no world congress with authority to pass laws binding on states as national legislatures enact laws for individuals, corporations, and inferior political and administrative units. The United Nations General Assembly does not have this power.

There is no international police force to administer or enforce the law, and no internationally elected and responsible district attorneys or prosecutors. Each state acts for itself in these capacities. States are both originators and subjects of the law, as well as its enforcers, prosecutors, interpreters, and judges.

The International Court of Justice has been comparatively little used. When its judgments and advisory opinions are handed down, they depend largely upon the good faith and the pledged word (note Article 94 of the Charter) of the parties to uphold them.

Most of the significant decisions relating to international law come

---

[3] See Friedmann, *op. cit.*, pp. 327–340. Soviet views on the law are set forth in A. Vyshinsky, *The Law of the Soviet State* (New York: Macmillan, 1948). See also M. Chakste, "Soviet Concepts of the State, International Law, and Sovereignty," *American Journal of International Law*, January 1949, pp. 21–36; Jan F. Triska and Robert M. Slusser, *Theory, Law and Policies of Soviet Treaties* (Stanford: Stanford University Press, 1962).

from the high courts of national states, such as the Supreme Court of the United States, the Hight Court of Judicature, and the Law Lords of the Privy Council in Britain. Here have been enunciated many of the "landmark" opinions and decisions that have contributed heavily to the development of international law.

The United Nations General Assembly and Security Council may censure or castigate a state that fails to abide by its obligations under international law, or refuses to comply with a decision of the International Court of Justice to which it is a party. Articles 41, 42, and 94 empower the Security Council to recommend or "decide" what "measures" should be taken to maintain or restore international peace if it is determined that a threat to the peace, breach of the peace, or act of aggression exists as a result of the refusal of some state to abide by a decision of the International Court. In the last analysis, however, the United Nations depends upon the member states, individually or in concert with regional organizations, to execute such measures as the Security Council may call upon them to take. (See Article 25 and Chapters VI–VIII of the Charter.)

International law must depend upon the support of powerful nations. In the eighteenth and nineteenth centuries it was often British influence and power which upheld the development and enforcement of international law, often furthering British self-interest. The changes that have occurred in world power since 1939 require American support and the combined support of many nations for enforcement at this time. In this connection it may be observed that the U.N. action in Korea is a first example of a collective use of armed force, following a formal decision by a world body, to uphold the independence of a state against aggression and to enforce respect for international law. And the actions by U.N. forces in the Near East, the Congo, and Cyprus, under the direction of the Secretary-General, to help maintain peace and order may be other historic precedents. It should be mentioned that in each instance the permission of the sovereign on whose territory these forces were employed was obtained in advance.[4]

The fact that the enforcement of the law is, by and large, decentralized and dependent upon the actions of individual states results in uneven application and enforcement. When small and large states are involved in a dispute, the more powerful may be tempted to compel settlement on its terms, unless the larger state has a strong respect for law, for the rights

[4] See Lincoln P. Bloomfield, *International Military Forces* (Boston: Little, Brown, 1964), Chapter 1; Gabriella Rosner, *The United Nations Emergency Force* (New York: Columbia University Press, 1963), pp. 32, 50–59.

of small nations, or for world opinion. Britain and the United States have deep-rooted traditions of respect for legal procedures, and have generally settled disputes involving legal questions by peaceful methods, including the use of arbitration and judicial settlement.

A Law with Diverse Interpretations. Although the law of nations has been widely acclaimed, there are many differences over its precise meaning and its application in particular situations. There is no code embracing all the rules, principles, customs, and usages comprising the law, and there are often differences over the interpretation of treaty clauses.

Diplomacy is normally the first means used to adjust disputes. The American Republics have reached several multilateral agreements on contents of the law which they are willing to accept, as in the Convention on Rights and Duties of States. Another instance of creating law through diplomacy was the conclusion of the Convention of International Civil Aviation at Chicago in 1944. This clarified the right of national jurisdiction in air space and provided for the regulation of international commercial air transport. Many of the principal states engaged in international air traffic, including the United States, adhered to this convention, but the Soviet Union did not do so.

The U.N. International Law Commission has been concentrating on codifying portions of international law. Out of its efforts have come the Geneva Conference on the Law of the Sea and the Vienna Conference on Diplomatic Privileges and Immunities, both of which have led to multilateral treaties now in force. It appears, however, that states are very slow to give formal agreement to codification of custom and practice, lest this impose limitations upon them they may later find unacceptable.

THE OBSERVANCE AND ENFORCEMENT OF INTERNATIONAL LAW

Observance of the Law. Widespread violation of law gives evidence of a weak body of jurisprudence. It does not establish that there is no law. No matter how weak or primitive a legal system may be, it embodies law if there is common consent that it should be so regarded by the community to which it applies. Some municipal law systems are notoriously weak. Crime is rampant in many metropolitan areas. Even national and constitutional laws are not always enforced if there is public apathy. Yet the law still exists.

In reality, the violations are relatively few compared to the magnitude of interstate relations and issues. A government determined to have its way at the expense of another is unlikely to be deterred by international law if its policymakers think they have sufficient power to impose its will. But governments usually attempt to prove that their actions are based upon some tenet of international law, or they seek an interpretation that is favorable to their interests and policies.

Enforcement, Self-Help, and War. Traditional international law has distinguished various means by which international legal rights may be enforced. These include political or economic pressures, the use of embargoes or pacific blockades, reprisals involving the use of force, the severance of diplomatic and consular relations, and declaration of war. These are lawful actions if preceded by a violation of law. There are jurists who maintain that the measure of self-help employed must be proportionate to the gravity of the violation.

Is war legal under international law? Article 2, paragraph 4, of the Charter of the United Nations obligates all members to "refrain in their international relations from the threat or use of force against the territorial integrity or political independence of any state, or in any other manner inconsistent with the purposes of the United Nations." [5] The Charter does not prohibit the use of force; it expressly provides for use of force coordinated by the United Nations organization for the maintenance of international peace and security and the enforcement of international law under Chapters VII–VIII and XVII of the Charter. The use of force to end aggression is authorized by the Charter, and the Korean War was fought for this purpose. Article 51 expressly sanctions the use of national armed force in pursuit of the "inherent right of individual or collective self-defense if an armed attack occurs." And Articles 52 and 53 envisage the use of force by regional arrangements or agencies at the direction of the Security Council. Whether or not Article 53 requires "prior" authorization by the Security Council of such uses of force is a disputed matter.

ROLE OF LAW IN INTERNATIONAL POLITICS

International law has several interacting purposes. We will discuss some of them briefly.

---

[5] The late Judge Lauterpacht believed that the terminology of the Charter makes it possible to distinguish between "just" and "unjust" (or lawful or unlawful) wars— "the latter being those waged in breach of the obligations of the Charter." L. Oppenheim, *International Law*, 7th ed. by H. Lauterpacht (London: Longmans, 1952) vol II, p. 223.

Establishment of Norms of Conduct. Law is generally thought of as existing primarily to establish norms of conduct for the guidance of relationships between or among individuals, groups, or organizations. International law, like municipal or constitutional law, was originally accepted by states as a means to introduce order and regularity into the conduct of relationships. This remains the primary purpose of the law. If there were not an international body of law, one would have to be invented. Without the frame of reference of agreed norms of conduct, there could be no orderly international relationships. International law does not encompass all relationships. It applies primarily to peaceful intercourse.

Facilitation of Peaceful Settlement of Disputes. If differences over conduct or respective rights and commitments are to be adjusted on their merits, there must be another basis than a contest of power. Law provides a consensual framework by which the parties to a dispute may ascertain or test the propriety of their respective positions and actions, their rights and obligations. Law provides a basis on which they can agree to refer their differences to a third party or institution for mediation, conciliation, arbitration, or judicial settlement.

The good offices of another state may be offered to two or more disputing parties in order to bring them into contact or to assist them in finding a peaceful settlement. The actual basis on which agreement may be sought may be political or expedient, or equitable, rather than a strict interpretation of rights and duties under international law. Nevertheless, it is through the system of international law and its procedures of arbitration and judicial settlement that states do seek peaceful settlement.

Law as an Instrument of National Policy. States are willing to agree to a law of nations because it contributes to their means of securing their objectives in international relations. They may be able to advance their interests by appealing to the moral force of the law, by invoking its provisions as a sanction for their own actions and policies, or by challenging on the basis of legal principles the legitimacy of actions taken by others. Law then serves as an instrument of national policy.

Limitation on Power Politics and Aggression. Law also functions as a means of restraining the power struggle among states. In combination with the restraints imposed by world opinion, agreed norms and rules of conduct contained in the law and approved by common consent establish limits upon the exercise of sheer power by the strong against the weak, without which international relations would be anarchic.

The law does not prohibit states from defending their territorial integrity or political independence or from protecting their vital interests by force, if need be. Nearly all states have agreed through adherence to the United Nations Charter that "acts of aggression or other breaches of the peace" are to be "suppressed" and that "effective collective measures" are to be taken by the members of the United Nations "for the prevention and removal of threats to the peace." There is, however, no agreed definition of aggression. Each situation involving a charge of aggression has to be examined on its own merits and only such action can be taken as an appropriate majority of the U.N. members can agree upon, either in the Security Council or in the General Assembly. Eventually a workable definition may evolve from case practice, although Moscow, Peking, and the representatives of Communist Parties in eighty-one countries have agreed that wars of "national liberation" are "just" wars and may be encouraged and supported under their concept of world order. This concept makes it questionable whether international law will significantly limit violence except among non-Communist states.

Law as an Integrating Force in World Community.   The idea of community implies the presence or creation of shared values and purposes and some machinery for resolving differences, facilitating agreement, and promoting mutual interests. The law helps to crystallize and give meaning to whatever internationally shared values of political order exist. It also strengthens the proposition that foreign affairs should be conducted within a framework of legally ordered relationships. And the application of the law through diplomacy, arbitration, judicial proceedings, and self-help is indispensable in resolving international differences and achieving agreement within the community.

SOME CONTEMPORARY PROBLEMS OF INTERNATIONAL LAW

International law is composed of rules, each of which conveys some expectations. Neither the International Court nor states regard themselves as being formally bound by prior decisions in similar cases (the doctrine of *stare decisis*). International law cannot therefore be "fully comprehended." An approximate understanding can be gained from texts, treaties, and cases.

The most difficult problems are due to uncertainties in the law itself or to states choosing not to accept particular rules. In these areas politics and law merge and the security, welfare, or freedom of action of states are most directly concerned.

Recognition under International Law.   Nonrecognition of an emergent state, or of a revolutionary government, produces important political consequences. Isolation of an unrecognized state inhibits its effectiveness by precluding normal diplomatic relations with others. Revolutionary movements or rival governments seek the international approbation which recognition conveys. Nonrecognition of one of two claimant governments, as in the case of the Nationalist and Communist Chinese, constitutes powerful support for its rival. In a civil war situation the recognized government may be aided by other states against the unrecognized faction. If general hostilities develop, other states may have to recognize a condition of belligerency and assist one party or adopt a position of neutrality. Nonrecognition of others enables states to keep their legal relations fluid and to retain a certain freedom of action.

The rules of international law provide crude standards by which to determine whether a new political entity is to be regarded as a state. Usually such an entity must possess a defined territory, have an effective government, and be able and willing to assume the obligations of an independent state under international law. Other states must decide whether the new entity meets these qualifications and whether recognition will serve their interests.

1. DE FACTO AND DE JURE RECOGNITION.   Under the prevailing positivist view, recognition is at the discretion of each state. The United States has been a leading exponent of the doctrine that recognition or its withholding is primarily a political act with *de jure* effect. For these reasons many states, including the United States, withheld recognition of the Soviet Union during the 1920's, when they disapproved of its policy. Similarly, recognition was withheld from the government of Communist China during the 1950's and early 1960's and from the government of East Germany.

The Soviet Union customarily extends early recognition to newly established regimes—as in Iraq, Guinea, and the Congo. This policy provides it with opportunities for establishment of diplomatic missions, and propaganda and intelligence activities, and the chance of gaining a political foothold where governments are not yet firmly rooted.

The United Kingdom takes the position that recognition should be extended "as a matter of legal duty and not of policy," as soon as a new entity or regime has given evidence of being firmly established, regardless of its political coloring. This policy leads to the concept of recognition as being merely declaratory of a fact of existence and involving no moral judgment or political approval of the regime. It is *de facto* recognition.

It is for decision which is the more correct and the more advantageous view of recognition—the *de facto* or the *de jure* approach. Many Latin Americans have objected to the recognition policy of the United States, which was initially employed by President Wilson as a political device for influencing the shape of governments in the countries of Central and South America, feeling that the granting or withholding of recognition on a political basis amounts to interference in their internal affairs. Foreign Minister Estrada of Mexico said in 1930 that,

. . . such a course . . . offends the sovereignty of other nations, implies that judgement of some sort may be passed upon the internal affairs of those nations by other governments, inasmuch as the latter assume, in effect, an attitude of criticism, when they decide, favorably or unfavorably, as to the legal qualifications of foreign régimes.

Nevertheless, with some inconsistency with the preceding, more than half of the Latin American countries have for political and religious reasons never extended *de jure* recognition to the Soviet Union.

2. THE UNITED NATIONS AND RECOGNITION.   Some have suggested that governments are accepted automatically into the world legal community when a state is seated at the United Nations. This is in a sense true. But it is doubtful whether the principal states are ready to amend the Charter to give the U.N. authority to make such action binding on their behalf so far as bilateral relationships are concerned. An attempt to resolve the question of recognition in the General Assembly would probably lead to bitter differences, although many of the newer states have chosen to follow the *de facto* formula.

The seating in the United Nations of a new political entity or the representatives of a regime involved in a domestic contest for power may raise the question of whether such a move becomes a constitutive act of recognition. The Charter gives the world organization no authority to act on behalf of its members to determine whether they should or should not recognize a state or government. That prerogative remains with and is claimed by the individual member states. The United Nations does have to make a judgment for itself when an entity applies for membership, when competing delegations with separate credentials arrive from a member state, or when a group of states presses for the admission or seating of a country.

The difficult problems that can arise in conjunction with admission or seating are illustrated by the protracted issue over Communist China.

Those favoring its seating have stressed the regime's *de facto* control of mainland China since 1949. They also argue the "inevitability" of the move and the desirability of having communication with the Chinese and of bringing them within the obligations of the United Nations Charter. Some think Communist presence would ease international tensions and resolve basic conflicts, despite deep-seated and diametrically opposed fundamental elements. The United States, and others opposed to this view, have pointed to the prestige the Communist Chinese would acquire from a permanent seat on the Security Council; the political defeat this would administer to the Nationalist Chinese on Taiwan and the millions of overseas Chinese; and the effect this action could have upon free world security and the balance of power in Asia.[6]

State Jurisdiction. The national territory of a state is acquired under the rules of international law by (1) discovery and effective occupation; (2) cession or purchase; (3) conquest and annexation; (4) prescriptive usage; or (5) accretion, where boundaries are changed slowly by natural forces, and by meandering rivers or the gradual buildup of deltas by waterborne soil deposits. National jurisdiction extends to the limits of the state's land boundaries and to its possessions abroad: Within these boundaries it exercises freedom of action, except for treaties with foreign powers and protection of the rights of aliens and immunities accorded to foreign diplomats and armed forces. Since the seventeenth century, international law has recognized the right of each state to exercise jurisdiction over a belt of marginal, or territorial, waters surrounding its territories. Within this belt international law recognizes a right of innocent passages for merchant vessels of foreign states. National revenue and customs authorities patrol these waters, and sometimes more extensive contiguous areas, in order to prevent smuggling or other violations of local law and jurisdiction.

The Law of the Sea. The United Nations Conference on the Law of the Sea (1958), attended by eighty-six nations, sought to bring order out of the many concepts and claims that have threatened the freedom of the high seas. Formulas were reached for determining the baselines from which territorial seas and contiguous zones extend. It was agreed that there shall be "no suspension of innocent passage of foreign ships through straits which are used for international navigation between one part of the high seas and another part of the high seas or the territorial sea of a

[6] The hearings conducted by the United States Senate Foreign Relations Committee on the China question, beginning with the testimony of A. Doak Barnett and Professor John Fairbanks of Harvard on March 8, 1966, throw light on the arguments for and against recognition and U.N. seating. See Chapter 23 for distinction between admission to membership and seating.

foreign state." Terms were drawn up on which food and mineral wealth may be gathered from the sea bed and from subsoil areas of the continental shelf without prejudice to the rights of others freely to use the sea and skies above. Comprehensive provisions were also made for international conservation of the animal and plant life of the sea.

The Conference was unable to reach agreement, however, on the width of territorial waters. Changes in the nature of weapons and in man's ability to exploit formerly inaccessible areas brought into play a variety of economic, biological, political, and strategic factors which caused the differences of states to remain unresolved.

Assertions of national rights have included claims to sovereignty over the continental shelf, however far from shore this may extend. Peru, Chile, and Ecuador claim that their territorial seas extend 200 miles out from their shores. Korea claims jurisdiction out to 150 miles. The Communist states have customarily asserted exclusive rights out to at least twelve miles. Some states, such as Iceland and Canada, have claimed a right to regulate fishing in areas on the high seas to which they feel they have special rights by reason of custom, geography, or economic necessity.

American support of the traditional three-mile limit has been based on a desire to protect the rights of American fishermen on the high seas, to facilitate use of narrow passages such as those leading to the Baltic and Mediterranean Seas, and to forestall the creation of rules which would permit enemy submarines to lurk submerged in waters near the coasts of neutral states in time of war. Because agreement could not be reached on the width of the territorial sea, this remains subject to the vagaries of practice, with each state asserting and enforcing what it can.

Jurisdiction in the Air. The episode of the American U-2 reconnaissance aircraft which was shot down, allegedly from approximately 60,000 feet over the Soviet Union in 1960, raises a problem analogous to that of jurisdiction in the territorial seas. The prevailing view is that a state has complete jurisdiction and may exclude or regulate the movement of all aircraft in the air space above its territories, possessions, and marginal waters. For security reasons there is no right of innocent passage in the air. Permission must be obtained from state authorities for foreign aircraft to enter or fly over the area of national jurisdiction. This concept is affirmed in the Chicago Convention on International Civil Aviation.

Outer Space and International Law. Permission has not been sought in advance for transit rights over foreign states by earth satellites utilizing outer space, nor has any state objected to the passage of satellites over its territory. By tacit consent a regime has been established in outer space which is more or less analogous to that on the high seas, that is, outer space is open for exploration and use by all states and subject to the national appropriation of none.

As more sophisticated hybrids between aircraft and orbiting vehicles come into use, the problems of demarking the line between air space and outer space may become increasingly vexing. Satellites that can scan and photograph the earth and possibly eavesdrop on or interrupt communications within or between countries from outer space may cause states to invoke new rules. But until others are able to remove such objects from the sky, protests are unlikely to affect the use of outer space.

The Antarctic Treaty signed at Washington in 1959 may provide a model for the removal of the dangers of an active arms race in outer space. It permits the conduct of scientific research, without prejudicing overlapping national claims to possession of sectors in the Antarctic, and it forbids the importing of military equipment into the area or the conducting of nuclear explosion. It also provides for exchange of information about activities undertaken there. Following this principle, the U.N. General Assembly in 1961 called on states not to place atomic weapons in outer space.

On December 13, 1963, the Eighteenth General Assembly adopted a Declaration of Legal Principles Governing the Activities of States in the Exploration and Use of Outer Space. This declaration set forth the following major principles: (1) the exploration and use of outer space is open to all states on an equal basis and no part is subject to national appropriation; (2) space activities will be conducted in accordance with international law; (3) states and international organizations bear international responsibility for activities in outer space and any effects therefrom on earth.

Law and the Observance of Treaties. The main rule of international law in respect to the binding force of treaties is *pacta sunt servanda*, meaning that treaties are made to be observed. Under this doctrine no state has the right to terminate a treaty unilaterally before its fixed term of expiration or otherwise than as provided in its text. It has been suggested that actions necessary for the preservation of the state are permitted under a principle of "state necessity," although this interpretation has been resisted. Another debatable proposition in the law is whether a state may nullify or demand mitigation of a treaty if circumstances have changed since the treaty was concluded. This is known as the doctrine of *rebus sic stantibus*. Brierly states that "there seems to be no recorded case in which its [the doctrine's] application has been admitted by both parties to a controversy, or in which it has been applied by an international tribunal." [7]

According to international law, treaties prevail in cases of conflict with national law. This principle is controversial, and to avoid both domestic and international problems the United States has tried to construct laws and treaties that are mutually compatible.

Should an international arms-control system be established, the problems of inspection could raise issues of overlapping and conflicting jurisdiction. The doctrine *pacta sunt servanda* would then assume unprecedented importance because the slightest infraction of such a treaty could become a matter of great danger to the adhering states. However, if the infraction is a "substantial breach" of a multilateral treaty, the other parties would probably be justified in terminating the treaty between themselves and the defaulting party.[8]

It is theoretically clear that under international law states are generally deemed free to nationalize foreign property on condition that the act of expropriation (nationalization) is neither retaliatory nor discriminatory. Many states have, however, found the requirement for prompt payment difficult to fulfill, and the meanings of "adequate" and "effective" compensation have been subject to dispute. It has been argued that even outright confiscation represents no real loss to investors who may already have received much more than their original investment. On the other hand, it may be argued that some intrinsic investments cannot be repaid "adequately" except by return of the expropriated property to the investor.

Confiscation of foreign property has not been unusual in the past. Communist states and some underdeveloped countries have seized foreign assets to which they had access. For example, Premier Castro's government seized United States-owned assets estimated at approximately $1.4 billion in Cuba with little promise of repayment.[9]

The means of pressing for redress open to capital-exporting states range from verbal protest to the breaking of diplomatic relations or the imposition of economic sanctions which are difficult to coordinate internationally against offenders. The British and French attempt to recapture

---

[7] J. L. Brierly, *The Law of Nations* (Oxford: Clarendon Press, 1963), p. 335.

[8] See American Law Institute, *Restatement of Foreign Relations Law of the United States* (Tentative Draft, 1959), Section 143.

[9] See *Expropriation of American Owned Property by Foreign Governments*. Report prepared for the Committee on Foreign Affairs, House of Representatives, July 19, 1963. 88th Congress, 1st Session. (Washington: Government Printing Office, 1963).

the Suez Canal after Egyptian nationalization and seizure was contrary to the United Nations prohibitions against the use of force. Present international law does not provide standards for determining the fair value of foreign investments and the means of repayment in case of expropriation. Bilateral negotiations and treaties afford the best reliance there is in most instances. For American investors the program of U.S. government guarantees affords some insurance of a return in the event of expropriation. Finally, the desire for further foreign investment by underdeveloped countries is likely to make their governments pause before carrying out expropriations in the future.

International Law and the Individual. International law has traditionally been a law of states which are its subjects. It deals only indirectly with private individuals. This aspect of the law may be undergoing a modification as a result of the Nuremburg war crimes trials and the U.N.'s Human Rights Declaration and Convention. Following this a European Court of Human Rights has been established. Individuals may take disputes to this court concerning the denial or infringement of their rights under the European Convention of Human Rights. A larger role may ultimately be recognized for the individual under international law, although it will probably always remain essentially a law among states.

The Problem of Change. A serious problem connected with international law, as with any system of law, is to balance the maintenance of existing rules and the progressive development of new principles as society changes.

Legislatures and courts generally correct legal inequities in their domestic societies within a reasonable time. In the international realm these institutions are lacking and there is little provision for peacefully changing legal obligations. The International Court of Justice can proclaim that the terms of treaties and other rules of international law must be observed. A provision in the Statute empowering the Court to decide cases according to justice rather than law, known as rendering judgment *ex aequo et bono*, requires the consent of both parties but has never been used. When the law is so inflexible that it cannot easily admit desirable changes without the consent of all parties to a dispute, there is decreasing respect for law and use of legal processes.

The law is essentially a conservative force for preserving existing rights and obligations, and because international law tends to support the status quo it is sometimes regarded by emerging states as an instrument of repression, a reflection of former relationships of power. Consequently, political and economic challenges to the status quo become combined with legal challenges unless the law provides remedies. Where there is no remedy, states must either acquiesce in what they regard as an injustice or employ methods of self-help, some of which may contravene the law. Analogous examples in domestic society may be seen in the violence which preceded the legal right of labor to organize or in the behavior of civil rights demonstrators against what they believed to be injustices.

It is remarkable how much change does occur under the existing structurally inadequate system. The majority of the new states have emerged peacefully, and through the machinery of international conferences and organizations a large number of multilateral conventions and agreements have been adopted, altered, and replaced.[10]

International law, like United States constitutional law, makes a distinction between legal and political disputes. Both the International Court of Justice and nation-states recognize that the judicial process is not an appropriate means of settling political issues. But the area of international relations touched by the law continues to expand. The rise of international organization has led the law to recognize the judicial personality of the United Nations and its specialized agencies and the role of these organizations in enlarging the sphere of international law and broadening the range of matters in its concern, such as the status of individuals before the law, statelessness, refugees, minority rights, labor, and the treatment of nonself-governing areas.

THE INTERNATIONAL COURT AND INTERNATIONAL LAW

The establishment of the Permanent Court of International Justice in 1920, and its continuance as the International Court of Justice under the Charter and Statute adopted at San Francisco in 1945, gave to international law a permanent international court, competent to decide on a basis of law "any dispute of an international character" which states agree to submit to it and "all matters specially provided for in treaties and conventions in force." Article 36 of the Statute gives the Court competence, where states have deposited declarations accepting its compulsory jurisdiction, to decide any or all classes of legal disputes concerning "any question of international law," or the existence of any fact which, if established,

[10] Professor Manley O. Hudson compiled a list of 670 agreements of this nature signed between 1919 and 1945, terming this process *international legislation*. See M. O. Hudson, *International Legislation*, nine volumes, (Washington and New York: Carnegie Endowment for International Peace, 1931–1950).

would constitute a breach of international obligation, and the nature and extent of reparation to be made therefor.

Many have expressed dissatisfaction with this optional clause arrangement by which states can accept compulsory jurisdiction subject to any reservations or conditions they see fit to attach. Article 36 was a compromise arrangement. Professor Julius Stone in *Legal Controls of International Conflict* argues that this was a "reasonable compromise," and it was, in fact, the only one that could be accepted at San Francisco. States may "avoid an indefinite submission to judicial sanctification of a legal status quo which may become intolerable to them, while allowing the traditions of judicial settlement and judicial expansion of the field of settled law to build up." In Professor Stone's view, "it is more important for the court's turnover of business to grow steadily, than it is to have tidy schemes of broad compulsory settlement." [11]

The existence of the Court has contributed to the peaceful settlement of a substantial number of cases involving legal questions, although in the totality of contemporary world politics it has played a secondary role. The Court has prestige and a reputation for impartiality. The major conflicts of peace and war have not been referred to it, but have been handled instead by political means through direct negotiation or conference-type diplomacy, as in the Palestine situation, the Berlin blockade, the Korean War, and the Congo situation.

The reasoning employed by the Court in its judgments and opinions contributes to the literature and case law of international relations. Jurists refer to the actions of the Court, and its dicta have been cited in litigation before national courts as evidence of what is the law. States cannot be compelled to go to the Court as can individuals within a domestic society. Nor can they, against their will, be made to abide by the decisions of the Court until such time as the international community is prepared to employ collective means for their enforcement. The true significance of the Court lies in the fact of its existence and in the willingness of some states to take certain of their disputes to it.

TOWARD WORLD LAW

In the preceding pages we have examined some of the features of the law of nations. This law among states is still a fragmentary and primitive

---

[11] Julius Stone, *Legal Controls of International Conflict* (New York: Holt, 1954), pp. 151–152.

system of jurisprudence. It has grown haphazardly through the actions of states and organizations and has had no central organ concerned primarily with its orderly development until the last forty years. Such a process has characterized the development of most primitive law, however, as has leaving enforcement to the injured party. Centralized enforcement has traditionally been the culminating stage in legal development. The shortcoming of international law is not that it is not law, but that it is an incomplete system with many of its provisions ill-defined. There remain abundant opportunities for evasions and for miscarriages of justice. In a world divided by a cold war, international law can move only slowly toward world law. One significant step is the recognition given by the International Court of Justice that the United Nations is an "international person" and has a legal personality even as do states.[12]

Students of international law have maintained that before international law can become "true world law," provision must be made for a world constitution and the development of more effective institutions in the international community. These propositions may be useful bases for constructive deliberation on far-distant ways of achieving a more orderly world. However, the creation of any one particular organization is unlikely to provide the complete answer to the problem of a more peaceful and orderly world based upon law and justice.

Realism in world politics requires the clarification of existing differences in interpretation and meaning, the removing of tensions and conflicts that exist between large segments of the community, and the gradual strengthening of the institutions we already have. The words of Professor Brierly of Oxford summarize the problem, "[although] the problem of world community remains eventually a moral problem it is also in part a problem of statesmanship and . . . international society needs institutions through which its members can learn to work together for common social ends." To this phase of international politics we shall now turn.

---

[12] Reparation for Injuries Suffered in the Service of the United Nations. International Court of Justice, Advisory Opinion of April 11, 1949, in connection with the assassination of Count Folke Bernadotte in Palestine. I.C.J. Reports, 1949, p. 174.

CHAPTER 22

Limited-Purpose
International Organizations

COMPLEX PATTERN OF ORGANIZATION

Another dimension is added to international politics by the increasing web of international organization. This web is composed of two different types of associations: the less than universal associations of a regional and limited-purpose nature, and the general world organization polarized around the United Nations. The limited-purpose organizations standing midway between the national state and world community may strengthen the latter as they assist further cooperation between particular groups of states, but this concept is not yet proved. Regional and specialized organizations and the United Nations overlap and even compete.

We shall make no attempt to foretell the future of this web of developing structures and collaboration. It has been generated by the need for groupings limited both in membership and in the portion of the world they serve, and designed to serve less than universal needs and purposes. So long as this need is felt, and so long as states believe they are better served by limited rather than general and universal organs or associations, these are likely to prevail.

Types of Limited-Membership Organizations. There are no clearly defined categories of limited-member organizations. They are generally regional in membership, such as the Organization of American States, or in their purposes and objectives, such as the Southeast Asia Treaty Organization, or both.

They can be described by their functions, which include economic, social, peace and security, and political-consultative, and these functions overlap. The bond may be ideological, religious or racial, rather than primarily functional, as in the Soviet bloc or the Arab League.

Some of these organizations are competent to discuss, and even to act upon, a wide range of problems and functional activities. This is true of the Commonwealth of Nations and also of the North Atlantic Treaty Organization. Others are limited or technical in their cognizance. The Colombo Plan, for example, is restricted to providing development aid to the nations of South Asia.

Recognizing that no method of cataloguing these arrangements is altogether adequate, we can, nevertheless, suggest four broad categories into which they tend to fall. There are orthodox regional organizations such as the European Community and the Organization of African Unity. Then there are the macroregional arrangements such as the North Atlantic Treaty Organization, SEATO, and the ANZUS Pact (Australia, New Zealand, and the U.S.). These tend to have fairly specific geographical objectives, but their membership includes nations in different regions. There are associations with limited or no geographical affinity but membership drawn together by historic, political, cultural, or other ties. These include the Arab League, the Commonwealth, and the French Community. Finally, there are arrangements whose only discernible integrating characteristic is emphasis upon a functional purpose, often economic. The Organization for Economic Cooperation and Development (OECD), consisting of the Western European states, the United States, Canada, and Japan, is in this category. The object of this association is to assemble resources to assist development in less-developed countries.

Table 22–1 lists some of the limited-purpose organizations or arrangements of the preceding types.

A Fluid System. Any organized international arrangement can be defined by its purposes, together with the relationships established to accomplish those purposes. The purposes of the various organizations and arrangements just noted include one or more of the following: (1) establishing machinery for consultation through multilateral diplomacy, (2) encouraging and arranging peaceful settlement of disputes between

TABLE 22–1

Sample Contemporary Regional and Other Limited-Membership Organizations

1. Regional-Type Organizations

Organization of American States *
Organization of Central American States
United States–Canadian Permanent Defense Board *

Latin American Free Trade Association
Central American Common Market

Council of Europe
Western European Union
Community of the Six
   European Economic Community (Common Market)
   European Coal and Steel Community
   Euratom
Benelux Customs Union
Nordic Council
European Free Trade Association
Central Rhine Commission
Danube River Commission

Warsaw Pact (U.S.S.R. and European satellites)
Council for Economic Mutual Assistance (Communist)
Organization of African Unity

South Pacific Commission *

2. Macroregional Arrangements

North Atlantic Treaty Organization *
South East Asia Treaty Organization *

Antarctic Treaty Arrangement *
ANZUS Mutual Defense Treaty *
Central Treaty Organization *

3. Nonlocalized Political Associations

League of Arab States
Commonwealth of Nations

French Community
Association of Socialist States (Communist)

4. Multilateral Functional Arrangements

Colombo Plan *

Organization for Economic Cooperation and Development *

* Signifies United States participation or association.

members without outside intervention, (3) facilitating political and cultural relationships, (4) improving economic cooperation, and (5) promoting mutual security.

The mechanics vary from periodic meetings to having permanent staffs and integrated operational procedures such as the EEC High Authority and the NATO Military Commands.

Many of the less-than-universal organizations are of limited duration; of those in existence before 1940, few remain. Some may be superseded by arrangements more suited to the interests and values of their members.

There is a seemingly random adoption of the approaches to

international collaboration. Professor Inis L. Claude, Jr., in his book *Swords Into Plowshares*, suggests that approaches to international collaboration reflect "distrust of the accuracy of anyone's aim at a solution and preference for releasing a shower of shots in the general direction of the problem." Statesmen try all approaches, being uncertain of what is best. Claude suggests that there is practicality in this "organizational eclecticism, this dedication to randomness."

WELLSPRINGS OF ORGANIZED COOPERATION

Basic Elements.   Cooperation in international organization depends upon an awareness of common interests and agreed purposes. National self-interest is the primary generating force, and particular situations do not have the same concern for all states. It is for this reason that the United Nations is not always the best place in which to seek a solution of a problem.

Geographical propinquity may suggest the utility or desirability of forming an international association. Shared aspirations and difficulties, or the presence of an external threat can stimulate associations. Practical arrangements for international cooperation have become more significant as states have become less self-sufficient and more interdependent.

The strength of international organizations derives in large measure from present-day activities rather than from long-term objectives. In general, the strength of any arrangement bears a direct relationship to the depth and span of the mutuality of interests of the parties. It also depends on the diplomatic competence of statesmen and the efficiency of joint programs or activities.

The relationship of shared objectives to cooperation is seen in the failure of the wartime association of the Western powers and the Soviet Union to survive the war, whereas inter-American arrangements and Nordic cooperation have grown over the years into fuller collaboration. NATO cooperation has remained meaningful for most of its members, notwithstanding the ups and downs of Soviet policy, save for General de Gaulle, whose sense of values and personal ambitions led him to withdraw French forces from the NATO commands and to demand that NATO headquarters be removed from France.

States have different reasons for participating in international arrangements. The United States, for example, has directed its concern in connection with the SEATO countries to the threat of Communist aggression in Southeast Asia. Pakistan, on the other hand, is more concerned with the dispute with India over Kashmir.

Regionalism as a Basis for Organized Cooperation. Regionalism has been advocated as preferable to universal cooperation for problems that are of special concern to a limited group of states in a region. It is argued that within the confines of a region there are likely to be more shared values and common purposes, hence cooperation can be more readily attained than through a broad, universal forum such as the United Nations. With the large increase in the membership of the United Nations, and the accompanying shift of interests, the world organization is unlikely to translate general principles into concrete actions as effectively as a smaller group of states. Distant nations can use the United Nations to interfere in local affairs regardless of the wishes of the states involved.

Organized cooperation does not necessarily thrive simply because geographers have referred to a particular part of the globe as a region. The cultural and political affinities of the states that exist in an area, the measure of trust and communication, the consensus on values and objectives among them are significant along with geographical propinquity. Strong animosities between neighbors, as between Israel and the Arab states, can make collaboration impossible. South and Southeast Asia form a distinct natural region, yet there has thus far been considerable conflict among the emerging states. The shift of Indonesia away from Communism and an aggressive posture may presage an increasing regionalism.

The Pacific Ocean area has been considered as a possible locus for regional collective security. Some states adjoining the area feel there are insufficient common interests on which to found an association. Instead, limited-member mutual-security pacts have been concluded between the United States and Japan, between the United States, Australia, and New Zealand, and between the United States and Korea. But there are indications of an increasing sense of community among the non-Communist states of the Western Pacific as Japan, the one non-Communist Great Power of the area, begins to emerge from the shock of defeat and gives signs of interest in taking a leadership position.

The evolution of international political arrangements would be easier if the basic elements of common purpose and shared values mentioned previously were found more widely. But such is not the situation. Hence the term *regionalism* is limited in meaning and application unless these elements are present in at least a minimal degree. There have been no successful attempts to formulate a precise definition of regionalism and regional arrangements.

Regional arrangements are recognized in the United Nations Charter as appropriate for preserving international peace and security and settling disputes (see Articles 33, 52–54 of the Charter, contained in Appendix E). The right of collective self-defense provided for in Article 51 implicitly recognizes arrangements that are neither universal nor regional. The Charter of the Organization of American States refers to the OAS as a "regional agency within the United Nations." The North Atlantic Treaty refers to the right of collective self-defense under Article 51. There are no fixed lines for determining what is regional and what is not. The term *regional* is usually applied to a cooperative arrangement among a group of states if the parties so designate their arrangement.

Functionalism as a Basis for Organized Cooperation. Some writers have insisted that the gradual evolution of special-purpose organizations is the soundest way of building a more stable world system. David Mitrany of Oxford has commented on this approach.

> Sovereignty cannot in fact be transferred effectively through a formula, only through a function. By entrusting an authority with a certain task, carrying with it command over the requisite powers and means, a slice of sovereignty is transferred from the old authority to the new, and the accumulation of such partial transfers in time brings about a translation of the true seat of authority.[1]

Mitrany stated that "the problem of our time is not how to keep the nations peacefully apart but how to bring them actively together."

Functional activities that take place across national lines according to needs may overstep traditional links between authority and a specific territory. However, states usually form cooperative arrangements for specific objectives, such as promoting welfare and security. Limited transfers of authority do occur in some of the arrangements where multinational agencies have been created, for example, in the European Economic Community.

The functional system is flexible and can be applied where it is most suited to needs and desires, irrespective of geographical lines. It permits gradualism, assisting the growth of consensus and community where parties are ready for it. The activities of the special-purpose organs of the European Economic Community helped increase the consensus among most of the states of Western Europe.

[1] D. Mitrany, *A Working Peace System* (New York: Oxford University Press, 1946), pp. 9, 14.

Regionalism and Functionalism Fuse. There is no distinct division between regional and functional organizations. It might be argued that regional arrangements tend to be military and political, whereas functional organizations operate chiefly in the economic and social fields. In practice, however, these concepts break down. Almost any international arrangement, whether regional or universal, can be described in functional terms also. Most arrangements are based on some political consensus, and most functionally defined arrangements, such as the Inter-American Development Bank, are more than purely functional.

THE MECHANISM OF COOPERATION

Organized international cooperation requires institutional machinery to guide programs of action. Relationships extend from political consultation and accommodation to the establishment of institutions and procedures and to the development of operational activities. If the organization develops effectively, it will acquire a staff of officials and technicians that form a kind of international service.

The process of integration is a two-way street. The mechanism of cooperation is affected by the constituent parties, who in turn are affected by it. If there are differences over basic concepts and values, there is unlikely to be much delegation of power to operating echelons or reciprocal influence of the central institutions on the parties. When there is sufficient trust and consensus among the parties, statesmen are willing to delegate functions to the organizational structure and to give administrators and technical experts freedom to cooperate. Organized cooperation on the management level is almost certain to strengthen the order initiated by political agreement.

NATO has a permanent council with members of ambassadorial rank, a Secretary-General and international secretariat, several Supreme Commands, a Military Committee, a NATO Staff College, and many operational arrangements. (For text of Treaty see Appendix B.) During its first fifteen years, interests and activities were closely interlaced as the membership shared common values and apprehensions. After President de Gaulle came to power in France, French collaboration decreased. French forces were withdrawn from NATO commands. French officers ceased to participate in some of NATO's activities. And President de Gaulle requested that American and Canadian forces and NATO Headquarters leave French soil. His main objection was to the "integration" of forces, which he held to be degrading to French honor and sovereignty. This may represent only a passing phase. Or it may represent the intrusion of a longer-range division among the NATO partners that will in the end result in this alliance becoming but one more in the long succession of passing arrangements between states. Some feel the machinery should be adjusted to accord a greater sense of equality. Others prefer to leave the machinery alone and trust to flexibility of arrangements.

Organized international cooperation requires leadership, and this tends to be provided by the most dynamic power. Egypt has provided the leadership for the Arab League, and the United States for NATO and SEATO. Inis L. Claude, Jr., comments that "regional organizations tend to be built around the local great power, and thus take on the character of a solar system." This tendency can theoretically lead to a "sphere of influence" if carried too far. The character of the relationship is determined in final instance by the disposition of the partners and the environment in which they operate.

In the succeeding sections we shall examine a series of cooperative arrangements of varying types. Space does not allow a full examination of all existent regional and functional organizations. Those discussed here are taken as being illustrative of some of the main types that are found in the contemporary world.[2]

WESTERN EUROPEAN COOPERATION

The cooperative efforts required to fulfill the Marshall Plan of European recovery led to an extensive network of cooperation in Western Europe.

The Community of the Six (EEC).   The most distinctive arrangement is the European Economic Community composed of France, the Federal Republic of Germany, Italy, Belgium, the Netherlands, and Luxembourg, commonly known as the Community of the Six or EEC. The Community has three related components, the Coal and Steel Community (ECSC) formed in 1951, the Common Market or European Economic Community (EEC) established by the Treaty of Rome, 1958, and the European Atomic Energy Community (Euratom), formed in 1958.

There is a European Parliament formed by the amalgamation of the three Assemblies of the Communities. This has supervisory functions

---

[2] The reader is referred to the bibliography at the back of the book for suggested readings on these and other arrangements. Specialized bibliographies are found in such periodicals as *International Organization* and *Foreign Affairs*.

including the right to consult, to hold hearings, and to require reports. The Parliament, by a two-thirds vote, can compel any of the executives to resign. There is a European Court of Justice to interpret the treaties involved. The executives of the three Communities were merged into a single Fourteen-member group by a 1965 treaty. Each Community has a Council of Ministers, similar to a board of directors, which handles major policy decisions and is the link between the governments on policy matters. The European Community is not a federation, but it is a supra-national organization much more integrated than any other yet existent. The most salient supranational aspect is that the executive has the right to act on majority decisions of the members rather than requiring unanimity on major issues, as is traditional in most international organizations.

The individuals appointed to the High Authority by their governments act together and are responsible to the European Parliament. The Council of Ministers coordinates the work of the Authority with governmental economic policies, and a Consultative Committee links it with employer and employee groups in the industries.

The European Economic Community provides for the creation of a common market among the six countries through progressive reduction of tariffs and restrictive quotas over a transitional period extending for twelve to fifteen years, beginning from 1960. It is hoped that it will also be able to harmonize economic policies. The Commission of the EEC constitutionally possesses a smaller range of power than the High Authority of the ECSC, but until the crisis of 1965–1966 raised by General de Gaulle over the right of the Commission to fix agricultural quotas contrary to the views and interests of France, the Commission had been functioning in a manner exceeding the hopes of many integrationists.

The Euratom Community is organized along lines similar to ECSC. Its functions are to develop research, establish nuclear industries, obtain and hold fissionable materials, and concern itself with health and safety from radiation. It maintains close relations with the Atomic Energy Commissions of Canada, the United Kingdom, and the United States. Euratom has provided a means of fostering joint effort on atomic matters among the six countries and of maintaining a measure of control over independent national effort in this field. Euratom seeks to coordinate developments in its field in such a way that activities in one country will not become a nuclear threat to the security of others.

The EEC is something less than a federation but is more integrated than regional associations such as the OAS and the Organization of African Unity. Sovereign states have, by treaty, surrendered carefully restricted increments of sovereignty, the principal element being the right to act by majority vote. The European Economic Community began functioning through mutual self-interest and has been moving toward what may be a new type of political entity. Walter Hallstein, President of the EEC Commission, writes, "Just as language precedes grammar, so politics precedes political theory; and disputes as to the proper terminology for what we are doing in the European Community sometimes seem to me as academic as grammarians' controversies." [3]

President de Gaulle, resisting encroachments on French sovereignty, has questioned the right of the EEC to override the veto of a state where there is an issue of vital concern to that state. It seems likely that the members will in the long run be able to resolve their differences sufficiently to permit the Community to move ahead along the lines already patterned. The inference that can be drawn from the experience of the European Community is that what counts in international organization, as in other facets of international politics, is not so much the legal bases for action, but the underlying desires of the member states to further the idea of community. Collaboration and integration advance when states are disposed to move in these directions. They are slowed down and cooperation becomes disappointing when the spirit of nationalism prompts leaders to stress national rights and glory. Europeans as a group have glimpsed, however, the advantages of the larger community and are likely to return to this again when de Gaulle has had his day.

The European Free Trade Association (The Seven).   The development of the Common Market presented serious economic problems for the Western European states that were not members of the EEC. After consultation it was decided that seven nations—Austria, Denmark, Norway, Portugal, Sweden, Switzerland, and the United Kingdom—should join in forming the European Free Trade Association (EFTA), which was established in 1959. These states, known as the Seven or the Outer Seven, pledged themselves to promote economic expansion, to insure fair competition in trade, to prevent disparity in the supply of raw materials, and to progressively remove tariff barriers. Each retained its own tariffs with respect to other countries. The central institution of EFTA is a ministerial council which meets in Geneva and has a small secretariat. Although this group has considerable economic leverage, it has not become as cohesive as the EEC or moved as far in consolidating its organization. This may have been because some of its members, particularly the United

[3] Walter Hallstein, *Challenge and Opportunity* (Cambridge: Harvard University Press, 1962), p. 28.

Kingdom, felt it to be a temporary instrument to meet the competition of the Six, which would ultimately give way to a merger of the two organizations.

FIGURE 22-1

The Two European Trade Areas (*From* The New York Times, *January 15, 1965. Reprinted by permission*)

The formation of the EEC and EFTA aligned the principal trading states of Western Europe into two camps that were "at sixes and sevens." Although all of these states are joined in the Organization for Economic Cooperation and Development (OECD), along with some others, this has not brought them together into a single economic community. The main obstacles to an expansion of the European Economic Community have been Britain's reluctance to loosen its ties with the Commonwealth and perhaps with the United States, and General de Gaulle's reluctance to have Britain become more of a continental power and thus threaten France's hegemony. Britain's trade has shifted from the 1956 pattern of 40 per cent Commonwealth and 25 per cent Western European to more trade with the EEC and EFTA countries than with the Commonwealth. In 1964 32 per cent of her trade was with Western Europe and only 30 per cent with the Commonwealth. Britain and other members of EFTA applied unsuccessfully for membership in the EEC in 1962. Since then

President de Gaulle has moderated in his views toward British membership, and Prime Minister Wilson of Britain appears to have become
somewhat more interested in accession. If the two associations merge,
Europe will become an economic power center comparable to the United
States.

European Political Cooperation. There are many difficulties on
the pathway to European political integration. There are differences over
the direction in which Europe should move, whether toward the ideas of
the Six or of the Seven or even of some larger circle of states. There are
differences over the desirable degree of federation and the rate of progress
that should be attempted.

President de Gaulle checked the formal progress toward a European
political community by his re-emphasis of French nationalism. Rapid
integration of Western Europe may decrease the chances of weakening
the Soviet domination of Eastern Europe. Notwithstanding the weakening
of the European Community and NATO ties which French policy has
been seeking, something quite unprecedented has been happening in
Europe since 1950 that must be reckoned with on both sides of the Atlantic, and on both sides of the Iron Curtain.

NONLOCALIZED POLITICAL ASSOCIATION

Statesmen are impelled to invent new forms of relationship as the forces
of change alter the structure and management of power. Among the innovations aimed at bringing together policy and political power among
groups of states is the Commonwealth of Nations.

The Commonwealth. The Commonwealth is comprised of states,
once parts of the British Empire, that have chosen to remain in an organized association. In 1966 it had a membership of twenty-two countries,
including nine African states that were simultaneously members of the
Organization of African Unity. In the words of the 1949 London Declaration, the members are "in no way subordinate to one another in any
aspect of their domestic or external affairs," and are "united as free and
equal members of the Commonwealth of Nations, freely cooperating in
the pursuit of peace, liberty and progress." The Commonwealth possesses
no permanent institutions other than a secretariat, and its members are
not bound by formal treaties. There is no central control of foreign or
economic policy. The British sovereign is recognized "as the symbol of
the free association of its independent member nations and as such the

Head of the Commonwealth." Consultation is carried on at many levels. Meetings of the Prime Ministers are held when considered necessary. There are numbers of committees coordinated by a Commonwealth Relations Service. The Commonwealth is a unique political arrangement. It is not a league, like that of the Arab States; neither is it a federation.

Commonwealth members benefit from sterling bloc membership, tariff preferences, some special forms of development aid from Britain and other economically advanced member states, and some insurance on security. The English language provides a considerable bond.

The Commonwealth has survived the withdrawals of Eire in 1939 and South Africa in 1961. It was badly strained by the British-French attack upon Suez in 1956, when there was no prior consultation with members. It is not able to impose a common policy on one or more of its members. In 1965 the India-Pakistan war, and Tanzania's and Ghana's breaking of diplomatic relations with Britain over the refusal of Britain to use armed force in the Rhodesian situation, were policies opposed by Britain. The security position of the Commonwealth has altered as British power has declined and United States power in the Pacific and South Asia has increased. Commonwealth members have joined other security arrangements, sometimes without British participation, as in the case of the ANZUS Pact between Australia, New Zealand, and the United States. Britain's appraisal of her security interests can be different from the appraisal African and Asian Commonwealth members make, particularly in the case of those following a nonalignment policy. The future of the Commonwealth is unclear.

The uniqueness of the Commonwealth is in its adaptability to changing circumstances. For Britain, the Commonwealth is a means of continuing its world influence. It is a moral substitute for Empire. Britain's economic problems may lead to closer ties with Europe and consequent increased strains on the Commonwealth relationship. There are also strains as a result of conflicts between member states, the need to find security through other associations, and development by members of external bonds with other arrangements such as the OAU. Commonwealth members do not form a voting bloc in the United Nations.

Only the future can determine whether the Commonwealth, in being the most worldwide arrangement other than the United Nations, is thereby so disparate that it is not permanently viable.

The French Community. The French Community, founded by General de Gaulle in 1959, consists of twelve states, formerly parts of the French Empire in Africa. These countries are freely associated with the

French Republic. The central organ of consultation is a Council made up of the heads of government, with headquarters in Paris. By 1966 the French Community was no longer an effective formal instrumentality of international politics. For most of the African states pan-Africanism has a more powerful appeal than the formal political ties with France as the strains and divisions of African politics have swayed the governments of these states. The cultural and economic ties remain strong, however, with a continuing significant French presence in these states.

The League of Arab States.　The League of Arab States, formed in 1945, is another example of a nonregional political association. This group of, technically, eleven Arab states extending from Iraq and Saudi Arabia in the Middle East to Algeria and Morocco in North Africa embraces most of the Arab and Islamic states. These countries are preponderantly populated and ruled by Arab peoples and culturally attached to Islam. There are varying degrees of unity, however, in this group. Tunisia has virtually ceased to cooperate with the League because of differences with Egypt. Saudi Arabia and the United Arab Republic (Egypt) have clashed over their rival interests in Yemen, resulting in UAR troops being sent into that country.

Under the leadership of the UAR, the Arab League focuses opposition on the state of Israel, and seeks political influence at the United Nations, as well as economic and technical assistance from abroad. The common racial, religious, and cultural background is a cohesive element, but is not always sufficient to allay national differences. It can be argued that the only strong common interest is opposition to Israel, and that conflicts such as that over Yemen and on the Moroccan-Algerian border undermine the League's usefulness. Even in the case of the Arab-Israeli conflict there are differing degrees of support for active opposition. The League has a fairly extensive institutional machinery on paper, including Council meetings called when situations demand summit-level consultations and a tightly organized caucus with a permanent chairman at the United Nations. Although economically and militarily the League is weak and subject to internal jealousies, it is a considerable political force within the United Nations.

The Organization of African Unity (OAU).　Africa is a vast continent consisting of at least two regions: the Islamic Arab portion north of the Sahara and the varied Negro peoples and states south of the Sahara. Yet in 1963 practically all African countries joined in forming the Organization of African Unity (OAU), patterned in many respects after the Organization of American States. This continental association is designed to consolidate the interests of the African states and to help preserve and express their African-ness in regional and world affairs.

The Charter of the OAU provides for coordination of policies in political, economic and other areas, furthering emancipation of all non-independent African territories, nonalignment, and settlement of disputes by peaceful means. The Charter provides for an Assembly of heads of state, a Council of Ministers meeting at least twice yearly, a permanent secretariat with a Secretary-General, and a permanent Arbitration and Conciliation Commission.

The OAU's first years were somewhat turbulent ones, with the Congo problem dividing the members. The organization considered border disputes between Ethiopia and Somalia, and between Kenya and Somalia, and contributed to ending the hostilities between Morocco and Algeria. There is consensus on anticolonialism, illustrated by concerted action to force the withdrawal of South Africa from most of the United Nations agencies and to exert the maximum possible political and economic pressure upon it because of its racist policies. The OAU has a Liberation Committee and a small Liberation Fund directed to the liberation of the Angolan, Mozambique, and South African black peoples. In the Rhodesian situation the OAU Council demanded that Britain use armed force against the rebellious white government, and when this was not forthcoming put pressure upon members to break diplomatic relations with Britain. This demand by the more radical elements, led by Nkrumah of Ghana and Touré of Guinea, emphasized divisions among the African states, and few complied. Ghana reversed its policy when Nkrumah was overthrown and re-established relations with London. Continued Portuguese rule in Africa is another target of the OAU anticolonialist drive.

The OAU has a membership comprising nearly one third of the voting membership of the United Nations, and overlapping with the Commonwealth, the French Community, and the Arab League.

The OAU has additional concepts to those underlying other international arrangements. It reflects national self-interest and the feeling of the relatively weak nations that by standing together they can exercise more power than separately. But the OAU is also a manifestation of pan-Africanism, of "Africa for the Africans," and has some of the subjective aspects of nationalism and of communal ideology. It has few effective bonds of cohesion and may function principally as no more than an international political association for some time.[4]

[4] See Norman J. Padelford, "The Organization of African Unity," *International Organization*, Vol. XVIII, No. 3, Summer 1964, pp. 521–542.

THE UNITED STATES AS A FOCUS OF
ORGANIZED COOPERATION

The United States is the center of a network of organized cooperation, including OAS, NATO, OECD, and security arrangements of various kinds with more than forty states. It is also a member, or part of the backdrop, of practically every non-Communist international association, such as SEATO. These relationships have tended to increase in depth, both in the security area and also in the fields of economic and political concerns.

The Organization of American States (OAS).   The thesis of a Western Hemisphere community, possessing a wider and deeper consensus than that shared with the remainder of the world, is the basis of the organized cooperation of the Latin American countries and the United States. The formal agreements and institutions stem from the First International Conference of American States held in 1889. The strength of the association developed slowly, marked by periodic conferences, the development of a permanent secretariat in the Pan-American Union, and the formulation of agreed principles such as consultation in case the peace or security of the Western Hemisphere is threatened or disturbed. World War II gave impetus to the association and in 1945 the Act of Chapultepec set the stage for the Inter-American Treaty of Reciprocal Assistance—the so-called Rio Pact of 1947—and the adoption by twenty-one states of the Charter of the OAS at Bogota in 1948.

The Rio Pact was the first regional security arrangement based on Article 51 of the United Nations Charter. (For text of Pact see Appendix D.) It is a broad commitment against armed attack and includes a pledge to consult in cases of aggression by means other than armed attack. As in the NATO treaty, the members assert that an attack on one is an attack on all. Unlike the NATO treaty, no explicit reference is made to a response including the use of force. There has been discussion of an OAS peacekeeping force such as the *de facto* OAS Force sent to the Dominican Republic in 1965, but thus far differences have prevented agreement upon this, the principal one being apprehensions that this would be used to interfere in the internal affairs of member states.

The Charter of the OAS sets forth purposes extending from peace and security to the promotion of economic and cultural development. It affirms the juridical equality of states and accepts the principle of nonintervention in internal affairs—a policy of deep concern to the Latin

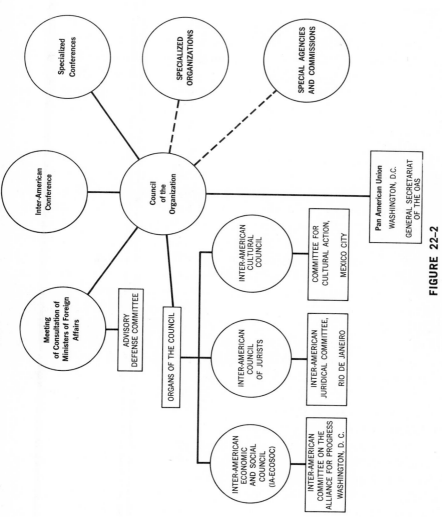

FIGURE 22–2

Organization of American States

American states. The Charter also provides for a continuing organization which in turn generates periodic conferences at the level of heads of government and foreign ministers.

The supreme organ is the Inter-American Conference, which corresponds to the United Nations General Assembly, although it is scheduled to convene only every five years. There is a Council, similar to the Security Council of the U.N., but its powers are more limited.

There is no established practice for determining which matters will be handled in the OAS and which in the United Nations. The Council of the OAS dealt with over twenty disputes in its first twelve years, and there has been a tendency to use the regional organization whenever there are problems relating particularly to the American states.

Prior to the Alliance for Progress program, the United States was primarily interested in security against overt aggression and against internal Communist insurgency. Cooperation in security matters is coordinated through the Inter-American Defense Board, located in Washington. In 1954 the OAS adopted a Declaration of Solidarity for the Preservation of the Political Integrity of the American States against the Intervention of International Communism. However, in 1960, at the Santiago Conference of Ministers, the United States was unable to obtain adoption of an unequivocal resolution against Communist infiltration into Cuba. The OAS supported the United States in the Cuban missile crisis of 1962 and, with dissenting votes, joined the action to stop fighting in the Dominican Republic in 1965. In the latter case, the only significant contributor of troops other than the United States was Brazil, which also provided the force commander. Operationally, the Dominican action was a success with peace being restored and maintained, a democratic election achieved, and withdrawal of the force in the summer of 1966 agreed to by the OAS and the Dominican Republic. The meaning and applicability of this precedent remained to be argued.

Latin American states have placed great emphasis on economic cooperation, pressing for actions in the area of economic development, for which the United States must provide much of the capital. The Inter-American Development Bank, established in 1960, and the Alliance for Progress program proposed by President Kennedy and formalized in the Punta del Este Charter in 1961 were in response to these pressures. The Alliance for Progress also stresses social development. Emphasis is placed on self-help in social, agrarian, and fiscal reforms. The United States made a general pledge to provide $20 billion over ten years and by 1966 was recognizing that the Alliance program would need to continue after 1971 to assure "take-off" in development. The OAS added an Inter-American Committee on the Alliance for Progress (CIAP), composed of economists. This persuaded most Latin American countries to present development plans for review and criticism to enable programming United States assistance in a manner similar to Marshall Plan procedures in Europe. Making criticism and suggestion a multilateral process lifted some onus from the United States and stimulated social and economic thought. The Alliance target is 25 per cent per capita increase in production, which Latin America, as a whole, achieved in 1965, although several countries did not.

Although not components of the OAS, mention should be made of the Latin American Free Trade Association (LAFTA), even though this has as yet accomplished little, and the Organization of Central American States, a regional political organization under which some functional cooperation has been developing. The principal advance in integration is the Central American Common Market, composed of Guatemala, El Salvador, Honduras, Nicaragua, and Costa Rica, with a combined population of 12 million. These countries are making solid progress toward becoming an economic region. Cooperation is already developing in education and other specialized areas.

The OAS represents progress toward hemispheric community but still has major problems in organized cooperation. It has had considerable success as a consultative arrangement and as a forum for regional political activities, and has brought combined action short of force to bear on several hemisphere problems. It has no ready instruments of power except those contributed on the particular occasion by its members. Finally, the OAS is an association in which individual states act in concert for differing, although not necessarily conflicting, objectives. It can be argued that the primary interests of the United States are in the political and security areas, whereas the primary interests of other members are in development and deterrence to outside intervention in case of internal instabilities. The political and social heterogeneity of its members, even among the Latin American members who share a common language (except for Brazil and Haiti), limits the degree of community.

North Atlantic Treaty Organization (NATO). Of all the post-1945 arrangements into which the United States has entered none is more significant than NATO. This first expression of the emerging North Atlantic community is an international association which extends from broad political agreement, through continuous consultation, to combined technical and operational activities of a most advanced nature.

The North Atlantic Treaty, signed in April 1949, was generated by the Soviet threat to Western Europe. The Communist coup in Czecho-slovakia in February 1948 led to the Brussels Pact of Western European Union in which Britain, France, and the three Benelux countries joined in mutual defense. A resolution introduced into the United States Senate by Republican Senator Arthur H. Vandenberg shortly thereafter author-ized the United States to enter mutual defense agreements that would con-tribute to its security. The United States then entered the first peacetime alliance in its history. The twelve original members, comprising Belgium, Canada, Denmark, France, Great Britain, Iceland, Italy, Luxembourg, the Netherlands, Norway, Portugal, and the United States were joined by Greece and Turkey in 1952 and by the Federal Republic of Germany in 1955.

The treaty (see Appendix B) provides for the peaceful settlement of disputes without the use or threat of force, economic collaboration, prepa-ration for resisting aggression by individual effort and mutual assistance, and consultation and mutual assistance in case of armed attack. Invoking the right of collective self-defense, recognized by Article 51 of the United Nations Charter, the signatories agreed that "an attack against one or more of them in Europe or North America shall be considered an attack against them all," and agreed to respond in concert, with force if necessary.

Building armed strength jointly on the basis of "self-help and mutual aid," NATO has approached the problems facing the directorship of a supranational state. Combining United States arms assistance with allied manpower, stationing of troops on allied soil, the creation of integrated allied military command structures and headquarters, and the program-ming of fiscal and production matters in each state to contribute to the common objective, are complicated and unprecedented in peacetime. Even the NATO military strategy is a sophisticated approach to use of military power.

There are difficulties in proceeding from generalities and general pledges to effective operational details of increased international coopera-tion. Success in this collaboration requires considerable mutual trust as each nation learns the secrets and problems of the others. Success also de-pends on the development of some common reference points and proce-dures; otherwise collaboration is slow and difficult. The experience of United States-British combined military planning in World War II, and of the OEEC economic planning, stood NATO in good stead.

The permanent NATO Council and International Staff under the Secretary-General were located in Paris for the first twenty years. Foreign Ministers, Defense Ministers, and others attend key meetings. The Military

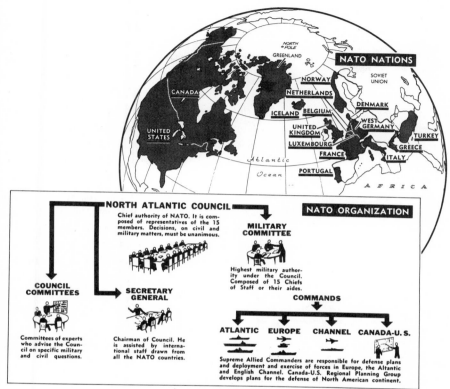

FIGURE 22-3

The North Atlantic Treaty Organization (*Adapted from* The New York Times, *December 13, 1964. Reprinted by permission*)

Committee is composed of the Chiefs of Staff of all member nations and commanders of NATO forces. Most of the tactical planning and policy arrangements have been products of the several Commands [Atlantic, Europe, Channel], which must cope with the problems of cooperation among sovereign governments. The Supreme Headquarters of the Allied Powers in Europe (SHAPE) was located in France until it was moved to Belgium in 1967. NATO has an intricate set of installations embracing communications, supply bases, airfields, and the like.

It might be argued that NATO could, or should, evolve into political and economic areas. Some of the functional economic areas allied to security have been filled by other international arrangements, principally the European Economic Community and the OECD. There are conflicts within NATO that cannot be overlooked, such as the conflict between

Greece and Turkey over Cyprus. Another difficulty, extending beyond NATO, results from the drive of the anticolonialist states for the liberation of Portugal's African territories. Hence NATO has remained essentially a security arrangement.

NATO's security problems are complex. The nuclear environment requires close operational coordination and arrangements for quick flexible response. Sovereign governments, nevertheless, tend to want to reserve freedom to consider and consult. The military pre-eminence of the United States provides an atmosphere of association with a Great Power, unless the lesser powers of Western Europe act as a group. United States pre-eminence provides a nuclear umbrella regardless of individual contributions and degrees of cooperation. The United States strategic hegemony has been a source of dissatisfaction and resentment to France, which has taken a more independent course as the Soviet threat has apparently decreased.[5] The problem of possession and/or control of nuclear weapons within NATO has increased, particularly since France has acquired nuclear power. The United States has attempted to provide for a degree of NATO participation in nuclear policy through a proposed multilateral force. But there have been objections to this from various sides, not the least being fear that this would give Germany a "finger" on the nuclear trigger.

Difficulties arise from the United States being a world power and viewing NATO as only one important part of its security context. For example, the United States became involved in South Vietnam, which is of little concern to most NATO countries. NATO is practically the entire security context for its other members, except for the North American Air Defense Command (NORAD), which controls Canadian and United States air defense; the Central Treaty Organization (CENTO), which the United States supported but did not formally join, linking Britain and Turkey with Iran and Pakistan; and the Southeast Asia Treaty Organization (SEATO), reflecting the security interests of only three NATO members, Britain, France, and the United States.

NATO has been the cornerstone of the United States system of cooperation for security. Yet in 1965 Henry A. Kissinger titled his book on the Atlantic alliance *The Troubled Partnership*. Part of the trouble comes from United States success in promoting a stronger, more integrated Europe, deterring and containing the Soviet threat. The NATO Treaty was made

---

[5] See *The Atlantic Alliance: Basic Issues*, a study submitted by the subcommittee on National Security and International Operations to the Committee on Government Operations, United States Senate. 89th Congress, 2d Session (Washington: Government Printing Office, 1966).

to run for twenty years, but the agreement continues after 1969, although a member may then withdraw after one year's notice. The mechanisms and habits of NATO consultation have been deeply ingrained; the operational arrangements are close and detailed. The changing security situation in Western Europe, and sense of increased freedom of action on the part of the allies, the rising power and nationalist views of France, and the fact that the United States is now the only true global power, continue to press for changes in NATO. Yet the fundamental community of interests in security remains substantially unchanged. NATO is the only clearly discernible operating institution of the Atlantic community. As the security impetus diminishes, some additional political arrangements may become reasonable if this grouping is to become more of a community.

President de Gaulle's decision to withdraw from the military organization of the alliance, and to have SHAPE and all American military installations withdrawn from French soil, placed the alliance in a difficult position. The military installations could be relocated, and American forces could be removed from France. General de Gaulle's power to request these steps was not questioned, but some did question whether France should be held accountable for the cost of relocation of the facilities in Europe. Should the political headquarters, the NATO Council, be left in France, despite the liabilities, or be removed with the military headquarters to another country? What steps should be taken to realign NATO forces, including nuclear arms, to maintain the military effectiveness of the alliance? To what extent was the French President's move a tactical negotiating one designed to obtain a larger voice in NATO affairs or some rearrangement of its structure? Should the other nations urge France to remain, or should they proceed on the basis of leaving a "vacant chair" for France to reoccupy after de Gaulle? To some it appeared that President de Gaulle, through his various maneuvers, was trying to establish France in the preferred position of the "balancer" in the world power equation. To others this seemed out of the question with France's limited power.

These were difficult questions to answer. As an initial move the heads of government of fourteen member states declared that the Atlantic Alliance was "essential and will continue." They emphasized that NATO was effective as an instrument of defense and deterrence "by the maintenance in peacetime of an integrated and interdependent military organization in which, as in no previous alliance in history, the efforts and resources of each are combined for the common security of all." No system of bilateral arrangements, they declared, can be a substitute.[6] On this note the parties

[6] Text in *Department of State Bulletin*, Vol. LIV, No. 1397, April 4, 1966, p. 536.

began searching for an accommodation that would permit the alliance to continue functioning as an effective organization in keeping with its purposes.

Southeast Asia Treaty Organization (SEATO).   The SEATO collective defense arrangement, formed at Manila in 1954, complements NATO on the global scene by joining eight powers (Australia, New Zealand, Britain, France, Pakistan, Thailand, the Philippines, and the United States) for mutual defense of the Southwestern Pacific and Southeast Asia. The Western nations were unable to persuade neutralist India, Indonesia, and Burma to join in the pact. By a special protocol the states of Laos, Cambodia, and South Vietnam, which were precluded from joining such a pact by the terms of the Geneva agreement of 1954, are nonetheless brought within the treaty area of concern.

The SEATO agreement provides that each member, in the event of armed aggression in the treaty area, "will act to meet the common danger" in accordance with its constitutional processes. The United States was explicit that this commitment was meant to apply only to Communist aggression. Otherwise, it would only consult in the event of some other aggression or armed attack. The purposes of the treaty also include countering subversive activities, strengthening free institutions, and furthering economic development.

The United States implemented its SEATO commitment, which was coordinated with support already being given South Vietnam in 1965, with a major military effort against the insurgent Vietcong and North Vietnam. The weak aspects of the disparate SEATO alliance were quickly apparent. Pakistan was immersed in troubles with India and took no action. Britain supported the United States politically, but British ships continued to carry goods to North Vietnam. France declared that the United States' choice of action was unsound, and remained aloof and critical. The ANZUS allies, the Philippines, and Thailand, gave strong support. And Korea, not a member of SEATO but allied bilaterally with the United States, sent a significant force.

Multilateral Coordination Through United States Bilateralism. The United States has bilateral defense treaties and mutual assistance arrangements with many countries in different parts of the world. Yet there are no connecting links between some of these. For instance, the United States has separate defense treaties with the Nationalist Republic of China, Japan, and Korea. Relations among these countries, however, have not reflected the same degree of community of interests that exists between each and the United States. There is an agreement by which the

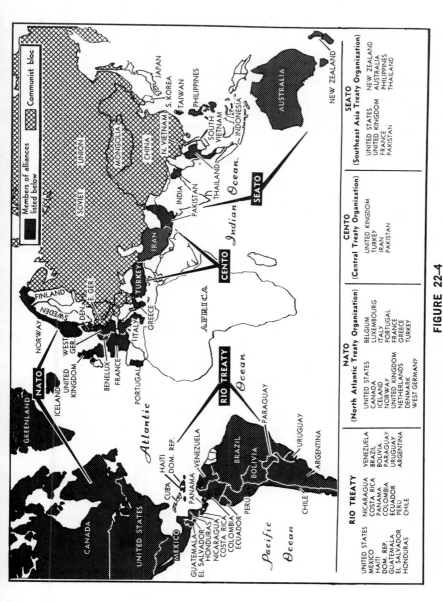

FIGURE 22-4

Western Alliances—The Major Mutual Defense Treaties (*From* The New York Times. *Reprinted by permission*)

United States uses air facilities in Spain, which certainly contribute to NATO support, yet Spain remains outside of NATO and has a difference with Britain over Gibraltar. There are usually serious reasons for these situations that place the United States in the position of the hub of a wheel that has spokes but no continuous rim. Nonetheless, these bilateral associations often provide the United States with opportunities for increased influence in persuading cooperation among its friends and allies who do not enter into institutionalized cooperative arrangements among themselves.

Consensus and Leadership in Organized Associations. The United States has moved a long way since 1945 in public and official attitudes concerning alliances and other organized cooperation. The multilateral association that reflects the strongest sense of community is NATO, the only institutional arrangement other than OECD formalizing the Atlantic community. With a common foundation of culture, history, and social and political concepts which facilitate effective communication, these states have a comparatively wide consensus on values and objectives, and a high order of trust, which is a limited commodity in international affairs generally. Yet there are many inadequacies and problems in NATO. Except for the rather special Canadian-United States relationship, the consensus among the parties to other arrangements is narrower. Differences do exist on the primary objectives of states, which makes consensus difficult to achieve.

Leadership, contributed sometimes by predominant power, is a most important element in organized cooperation. By entry into security arrangements the United States has, *ipso facto*, accepted an enormous and unprecedented leadership role. This is inevitable in any primarily military association because in the final analysis the Great Power (or Powers) holds the responsibility for peace or war, and victory or defeat. It is optimistic to say that the United States "can exploit its central position to convert formal alliances or bilateral relationships into an entente—a common way of looking at problems that are increasingly shared in common—especially among those eight or ten middle powers on four continents on whose support and initiative a polycentric world makes the United States increasingly dependent." [7] But the leadership position is clear and involves enormous difficulties in seeking common denominators of interest and in insuring that both greater and lesser associates have a sense of participation and responsibility and have an effective voice in decision making.

[7] See Alastair Buchan, "The Atlantic Debate," *Foreign Affairs*, Vol. 43, No. 4, July, 1965, pp. 574–586.

INTERNATIONAL COMMUNIST ORGANIZATION

It has been noted in Chapter 14 that policy execution of the great Communist states is supported by an international apparatus of Communist parties and their members. From 1919 to 1943 this apparatus was headed by the Comintern (or Third Communist International) subject to Moscow. Since World War II the leadership in Moscow has used a variety of instruments, in addition to the Red Army and Soviet dictatorship, to link the Communist-ruled countries and Communist parties. From 1947 to 1956 the Cominform, from which Yugoslavia was expelled by Stalin in 1948, was principally a means of controlling the European Communist parties. Recently the methods of transmitting policy are Party conferences attended by representatives of national parties and through clandestine channels. At the Twenty-third Communist Party Congress in the Soviet Union in 1966, representatives of eighty-six national party groups joined in calling for united action.

In Eastern Europe the Soviet Union has tried to parallel regional developments in the West by forming with the satellite states a Council for Mutual Economic Assistance (COMECON or CEMA). COMECON made only limited attempts toward integration until 1962, when the challenge and attraction of the Common Market became apparent. Soviet leadership then turned to molding this agency into a heralded "world socialist market" that would presumably be self-sufficient. But the concept was resisted by the Eastern European states, whose trade with the West was becoming profitable and attractive. Also, the Middle European states resisted the Soviet concept of "socialist international division of labor" by which they might be denied the possibility of diversified industrialization. The future of COMECON depends on the course of East-West trade, which is likely to become more extensive barring a renewed hardening of East-West divisions. The signposts for that course are in the indicated interest of European countries in increasing this trade rather than in moving toward autarchy. Another signpost may also have been put up by President Johnson when he said in his State of the Union Message for 1966 that he favored expansion of U.S. trade with Eastern Europe. This may encourage freer actions by these states.[8]

For security, the U.S.S.R. has a series of bilateral alliances with the Eastern European states and with Communist China. Security is also

---

[8] See statement of Secretary Rusk, *Department of State Bulletin*, Vol. L, No. 1290, March 16, 1965.

furthered by the Warsaw Pact arrangement linking the European satellites with the Soviet Union in a system somewhat like that of NATO, with a leader of the Soviet Army as its commander. The Warsaw Pact was formed in 1955 as a counter to West Germany's rearmament and admission to NATO. It afforded a new basis for keeping Soviet troops in Eastern Europe and for holding the Soviet bloc together in a common security system. Military coordination is advanced through a Joint Armed Forces Command, comprising a Soviet Commander-in-Chief, together with the Ministers of Defense or other military leaders of the satellite countries, and a General Staff headed by a Soviet officer. According to a United States Senate subcommittee study, a Political Consultative Committee, composed of the first Secretaries of the several Communist Parties, in addition to the heads of government and their ministers of defense and of foreign affairs, serves as a forum for articulating common stands on key international issues as proposed by the U.S.S.R. Although some of the Eastern European countries have been able to loosen relationships with the U.S.S.R. in late years, the Warsaw Pact still provides a basic treaty obligation linking these states with the Soviet Union.[9]

International Communism is a pervasive force that has penetrated most areas of the world. It is unclear whether the cooperative arrangements that exist within this system are as strong as those within the free world. The Communist strength has been affected by the competition for leadership between Peking and Moscow, making a "socialist commonwealth" an even more complicated matter, by the decrease in cohesion generated by the Sino-Soviet split and by the polycentric forces operating in Eastern Europe. But quoting Professor Z. K. Brzezinski of Columbia University, "While many obstacles still remain and others may arise [in Communist collaboration], particularly with the further development of China, the West would do well not to underestimate the importance of the organizational development of the Communist camp."[10]

CONCLUSION

International organization below the universal level includes many organizations that have been established and much experimentalism in forms, procedures, and activities.

[9] See *The Warsaw Pact: Its Role in Soviet Bloc Affairs*. A Study submitted by the Subcommittee on National Security and International Operations to the Committee on Government Operations of the United States Senate. 89th Congress, 2d Session (Washington: GPO, 1966).

[10] Zbigniew K. Brzezinski, "The Organization of the Communist Camp," *World Politics*, Vol. XIII, No. 2, 1961, pp. 175–209.

There are many other limited-purpose organizations in addition to those discussed in this chapter. These include the Colombo Plan in South Asia, the South Pacific Commission, the loosely formed grouping of the Afro-Asian states, and the Nordic Council among the Scandinavian states. Limitations of space preclude discussions of these and others. The reader is referred to the specialized literature of international organization.

We have tried to illustrate features of the salient types of international organization that operate at less than the global level. There are complex questions confronting the nations in this whole area. These problems have been tackled in a fairly random manner. There has been, however, a great deal more building upon precedent, with other experiments in mind, than is readily apparent. But it is a fact that in the search for solutions under pressures of time and of a multitude of other concerns, states have tried several approaches simultaneously, not always certain which would serve best in a given situation.

Organized cooperation is a response to a sense of need that is mutually shared in varying ways and with differing outlooks. The present diverse patterns of organization are likely to be perpetuated. States are likely to prefer putting their eggs in several baskets rather than in one, keeping at the same time regional, functional, nonlocalized, and universal organizations in the picture as well as bilateral associations. The relative weights among these different types will shift as states appraise the degree of effectiveness of action through one or another type in the service of their objectives.

CHAPTER 23

Organizing the World Community:
The United Nations

There is a world community of states, sometimes called the society of nations. Relationships within this society have been marked by recurrent conflict, disorder, and crisis, although the mass of relations are routine and orderly. In the community today there is a trend toward increasing use of institutional procedures moving through international organizations, the major one being the United Nations.

THE RATIONALE OF UNIVERSAL
INTERNATIONAL COLLABORATION

During the nineteenth century, states began to feel a common concern about a number of problems which led some of them to coordinate their actions, examples being to suppress piracy and the African slave trade. As other examples there was also common interest in facilitating the flow of mail across national frontiers, regulating telegraphy, and collecting meteorological data to improve weather prediction. As transportation increased

476

disease proved to have no respect for national boundaries. A rudimentary sense of community developed from dealing with these problems.

The resulting limited-purpose organizations, which were formed to facilitate cooperation in these areas, established routine methods of operation and a corps of officials who were the forerunners of an international civil service. By 1911 there were as many as forty-five administrative organizations, such as the European Commission for the Danube, the Universal Postal Union, and the International Red Cross. Successes in limited functional spheres encouraged application of the cooperative approach to wider areas of mutual concern.

Less progress was achieved at the time in political affairs, although the equilibrium erected at the Congress of Vienna in 1815 was maintained for a century by the Concert System among the Great Powers. Notwithstanding occasional large gatherings, such as the Congress of Berlin in 1878 and the two Hague Peace Conferences, there were no permanent organs for continuous diplomacy or collective action. The need for such institutions was not generally accepted until World War I. Then common interests formed the basic rationale for another step in the development of international cooperation.

The League of Nations and Collective Security. The League of Nations was a product of the Paris Peace Conference in 1919 and was conceived of as a general organization to assure international peace and security through institutionalized international cooperation. Its chief architect, President Wilson, thought the League would be a permanent association of powers to maintain peace and enforce peaceful settlement of international disputes. The League was a continuation of the balance-of-power concept, but was to have the preponderance of power and to function on the principle of collective security. The refusal of the United States to join contributed to depriving the League of the required power and prestige to act effectively in situations involving aggression and challenges to the established order.

The objectives and structure of the League were the direct antecedents of the United Nations. Its three principal organs were an Assembly of all member states, a Council of the Great Powers and members elected by the Assembly, and an international Secretariat with headquarters in Geneva. There was also a Permanent Court of International Justice, empowered to "hear and determine any dispute of an international character which the parties submit thereto," but this was not originally connected with the League.

The League dealt with some forty-five cases involving peace and security during its twenty years. In the area of political change and conflict involving the Great Powers, the League did not attain the objectives of its founders.

One of the principal innovations of the League of Nations was the concept of collective security incorporated in the Covenant. By this principle the members agreed that an attack upon any state, or a threat to the peace, would be regarded as a threat to all members, and they agreed that if the Council or the Assembly found that such an attack or threat had occurred, they would join in applying economic, political, or military sanctions against the offending state.

Although they condemned Japanese aggression in Manchuria in 1931, the League members were unwilling to match power with power. The United States for its part played a separate, ineffectual, role in connection with this aggression. The League again failed to act firmly against Italian aggression in Ethiopia in 1935. Although some economic sanctions were applied against Italy, they were not adequate to halt the conquest of Ethiopia. By 1939 Japan, Germany, and Italy had left the League and other members were weak or divided. The organization was ineffectual by the beginning of World War II. The League's success or failure depended on an adequate consensus among the larger members and on the will and competence to support consensus with action. These requisites were not present when the major crises overtook the League in the 1930's. The League was formally terminated in 1946 and its assets transferred to the United Nations.

THE NATURE AND POLITICS OF THE UNITED NATIONS

As had been the case with the League of Nations, United States leadership gave the primary impetus to the formation of the United Nations. Early in World War II President Roosevelt accepted the idea of a collective system of international security for the postwar world. This principle was expressed in the 1941 Atlantic Charter agreement between Roosevelt and Churchill. Here began the definition of differences and development of compromise solutions that paved the way for a widely acceptable agreement on postwar organization. Certain major differences with the Soviet Union were resolved at Dumbarton Oaks in 1944 and at Yalta in 1945. Some Latin American states were initially reluctant to support the plans because they wanted to preserve regional integrity. The differences with these states were resolved at a meeting held in Mexico City after the differences with the U.S.S.R. had been resolved at the Yalta conference. After two months of negotiation at San Francisco in the spring of 1945, representatives of fifty governments reached unanimous agreement on the Charter of the United Nations. The United States Senate, which had rejected the League a generation before, approved United States membership in the new organiation by a vote of 89 to 2. The text of the Charter will be found in Appendix E. It is recommended that the reader familiarize himself with it.

Assumptions and Characteristics. The functions of the new organization and the responsibilities accepted by its members represented the practical limits of formalized collaboration attainable at the time. A basic premise underlying the arrangement was an assumption that the Great Powers would continue to cooperate despite any divergent interests and ideologies.

The Charter specifies that the United Nations is a multipurpose instrument to assist states in solving international disputes, to maintain international peace and security, to promote international cooperation in solving economic, social, and cultural problems, and to function as a center for harmonizing the actions of nations. These are the broadly stated purposes of the organization. But within them virtually every type of question affecting relations among states may be brought before the U.N. As the late Adlai Stevenson said, it is the purpose of the United Nations to be the "forum and safeguard of peace."

Despite the hopes of idealists, the United Nations was not insured a preponderance of power to replace the traditional balance-of-power system. The organization is a limited collective-security system. Chapter VII provides for national armed forces to be put at the disposal of the Security Council under certain circumstances and provides for the use of collective or multinational forces under its authorization or direction. But the special agreements provided for in the Charter to implement these provisions have not been concluded, although states have responded to requests by the Security Council or the General Assembly for forces to be made available on a voluntary basis for specific peacekeeping missions. Some countries —for example, Britain, Canada, and the Scandinavian states—have taken steps to earmark small units of their forces to meet urgent U.N. requests. The United Nations is an improvement on the League of Nations in this respect.

Despite the symbolic implications in its name, the United Nations is an association of sovereign states and restricts the sovereign power of these states only to the extent of the pledges given in the Charter. The organization may take only actions permitted by the Charter or agreed on by the members. The United Nations was not conceived as a world government and specifically safeguards national rights by affirming that, except in peace-enforcement measures, the organization shall not intervene in matters essentially within the domestic jurisdiction of any state. It is not made clear in the Charter, and it remains a controversial question, what is within the "domestic jurisdiction" of states. There has been extended debate on this point. The right to possess armed forces and to use them for individual and collective self-defense is expressly retained. The only decisions that can be made binding upon member states are those of the Security Council on measures to maintain or restore international peace and security, and these decisions can only be made by unanimous vote of the Great Powers. Resolutions of the General Assembly relating to the maintenance of international peace and security, even when taken under the provisions of the Uniting for Peace Resolution (1950), are only recommendations to states and do not have binding force, although they may carry moral weight.

The six principal organs of the United Nations are the General Assembly, in which all members are represented; the Security Council, comprising both permanent and elected members; the Economic and Social Council (ECOSOC), elected by the General Assembly; the Trusteeship Council; the International Court of Justice; and the Secretariat, headed by the Secretary-General.

The United Nations and National Interests.   The United Nations is one means by which states can advance and protect their national interests. It exists for the purpose of facilitating relationships, concerting efforts, reconciling and, where possible, adjusting their differences. United Nations actions depend upon the cooperation of states, and the organization is responsive to the national interests of states. The U.N. is subject to the impact of the competing interests of members, and open disagreement or stalemate may result. There has been a succession of conflicts between East and West in the Security Council, the General Assembly, and ECOSOC, and the U.S.S.R. has vetoed many resolutions. The clash of interests is evident in the negotiations on disarmament and in the confrontations between the new and older states, the have-nots and the haves. It is an indispensable function of the United Nations to find and develop complemetary interests.

The U.N., the Balance of Power, and Collective Security.   Secretary of State Cordell Hull is reported to have said in 1944 that a United Nations organization would eliminate the need for balance-of-power

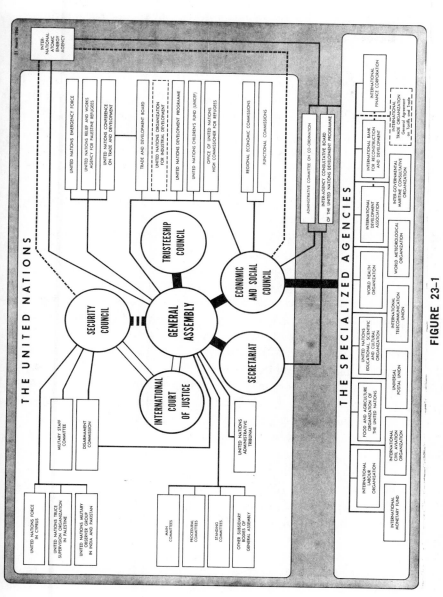

FIGURE 23-1

The United Nations and Related Agencies (*Office of Public Information, The United Nations*)

politics. On the contrary, the United Nations immediately became one of the mechanisms through which balance-of-power politics operates. By giving permanent seats on the Security Council to the five principal wartime allied powers, with the right to veto any action by the Council, the Charter incorporated the postwar balance of power in the heart of its system. By giving the Great Powers a right to veto the admission of new member states, the Charter insured that politics would govern the seating of new members. The U.N. has inevitably become involved in balance-of-power politics because it is an association of states, authorized to hear, discuss, and to take action on any threat to peace, any act of aggression, or any matter of concern to any state. Power politics operate continuously in the forums of the United Nations, in every action of the U.N., and in the voting alignments of states and groups of states.

The organization is built around a concept of collective security, that is, collective interest in, and responsibility for, maintaining international peace and security. The limited provisions for enforcement and use of armed force are the most the powers were able to agree on in 1945. There is no present indication that members are willing to extend the powers of the organization. Differences have increased among states since 1946, and new political elements have been introduced through the admission of many new nonaligned states. These may decrease the prospects of agreement on a formula to increase the powers of the organization.

Membership in the World Organization.   The United Nations looks in the direction of membership by all states willing to accept the obligations of the Charter. By 1956 the original membership had grown to eighty. A dramatic increase took place in 1960, when the independence of many African countries brought the enrollment to ninety-nine. In 1966 there were 119 members. It is possible the U.N. may eventually have as many as 140 members.

A few states have chosen not to apply for membership. For Switzerland, the obligations under the Charter seem incompatible with strict neutrality. Some entities, such as the divided states of Germany, Korea, and Vietnam, as well as Communist China, have had their acceptance delayed as a result of Great Power divisions. Most newly independent states have sought membership in the world organization as a token of political achievement and sovereign equality, particularly with respect to former ruling states.

The political problem of membership involves recommendation by a majority of the Security Council, including all of the permanent members, and then admission by vote of the General Assembly. The desire of the

Great Powers to support the developing countries has accelerated admission of most new entities.

Several significant political changes have occurred with the admission of the many new states. The organization is now nearly universal and voices the closest approximation to "world opinion." Many members are able to make only insignificant contributions to the financial and military resources of the organization, yet its responsibilities and activities are multiplied. The accession of the large number of Asian and African states has changed the balance of the membership. Two thirds of the votes represent only 10 per cent of the world's population and 5 per cent of the financial contributions to the U.N.—a great disproportion between voting strength and real power.

Originally, European and Latin American states predominated in the U.N. There were only four African members. By 1966 there were sixty members from Africa, Asia, and the Near East. This was more than half of the membership, and it was sufficient to prevent General Assembly action when these states were able to concert their votes. The African, Asian, and Latin American states can exercise a considerable influence by caucusing and forming a united front. At one time the Western states, Israel, and Nationalist China made up the majority of the U.N. They now comprise only 40 per cent of the total.

The increase in membership and the development of voting blocs has not tipped the voting and the general climate of view within the organization, for the most part, except in two major areas of interest. These are on matters relating to colonialism and racial discrimination. Otherwise, the blocs tend to split. The voting patterns are complex and tend to reflect views of their individual interests on particular situations. The low-income countries favor measures that promise help for their countries. The African states oppose U.N. intervention in African affairs, except where it is directed against white elements, as in Rhodesia, South Africa, and the Portuguese territories.

The present membership has the effect of requiring a good deal of politics to line up votes before resolutions can be sure of a two-thirds vote. The situation is complicated by the fact that representatives of the new countries are often without instructions on how to vote on specific questions and therefore may be in a dilemma until the final moment on how to cast their votes or whether to abstain.

The Communist take-over of mainland China in 1949, and the withdrawal of the Chiang Kai-Shek government to Formosa, raised the problem of Chinese representation at the U.N. The issue involved the prestige of the Nationalist Chinese, who were allied to the United States, and the representation of Communist powers in the U.N., and particularly the distribution of power in the Security Council, because the Republic of China is declared by the Charter to be one of the five permanent members of that organ. The issue of seating Communist China has been one of the most controversial and sensitive questions before the U.N. The distinction between "seating" a delegation of a country already a member of the U.N. and the admission of a state to "membership" should be kept clear. Seating requires the acceptance of credentials and a favorable report by the Credentials Committee, which can be handled as a procedural matter with a simple majority vote unless the Assembly decides, as it has heretofore in the China case, that the question is an "important one" and should have a two-thirds vote. Formal admission to membership requires a two-thirds vote. Presumably it would take a similar vote to drop any country, including Taiwan, from membership.

The Charter makes no provision for withdrawal from membership. Each state therefore retains this right. Indonesia withdrew in 1965 but, in 1966, resumed its membership. Provision is made for the suspension or expulsion of members that "persistently" violate the Charter, although no member has yet been dealt with in this manner.

Politics in the General Assembly.   As membership has increased, consensus within the General Assembly has become a more serious political problem. The environment created by the differences among the older states has been compounded by rivalries among the newer states. Attempts to bridge differences are made by continuous diplomatic effort within and outside of the U.N. Persuading others of the justice of one's own position and the reasons for supporting it is the essence of the political process in parliamentary diplomacy.

A glance at the distribution of the membership listed in Table 23–1 will show that no single geographic group or bloc has enough members to insure an Assembly majority. The game of politics that is played year after year at the Assembly consists of stating one's position with utmost clarity and precision, trying by every means of persuasion to obtain the support of others, and lining up as many votes as possible for key ballotings. In this process there is bound to be much bargaining for mutual support of the various items that are before the U.N.

Voting patterns are not consistent, for many different points of view are represented in the groupings. Individual states are often persuaded to vote differently than with the majority of their group. Only the Soviet bloc states have shown a disposition to follow the U.S.S.R. regularly, and even here some of the members have at times abstained rather than voting with

TABLE 23-1

United Nations Members by Regional Groupings

African 36	*Asian* 26	*Commonwealth* 8 (+15)
*Algeria	Afghanistan	Australia
Botswana	Burma	Britain (U.K.)
Burundi	Cambodia	Canada
Cameroun	†Ceylon	Jamaica
Cent. Afr. Rep.	†Cyprus	Guyana
Chad	†India	Malta
Congo (Brzvle.)	Indonesia	New Zealand
Congo (Leopdvl.)	Iran	Tobago
Dahomey	*Iraq	Trinidad
Ethiopia	Japan	
Gabon	*Jordan	*Eastern European* 10
†Gambia	*Kuwait	
†Ghana	Laos	‡Albania
Guinea	*Lebanon	Bulgaria
Ivory Coast	†Malaysia	Byelorussian SSR
†Kenya	†Malé	Czechoslovakia
Lesotholand	Mongolia	Hungary
Liberia	Nepal	Poland
*Libya	†Pakistan	Rumania
Malagasy	Philippines	Ukrainian SSR
†Malawi	*Saudi Arabia	Soviet Union
Mali	Singapore	‡Yugoslavia
Mauretania	*Syria	
*Morocco	Thailand	*Western European* 15
Niger	Turkey	
†Nigeria	*Yemen	Austria
Rwanda		Belgium
Senegal		Denmark
†Sierra Leone	*Latin America* 20	‡Finland
Somalia		France
*Sudan	Argentina Peru	Greece
†Tanzania	Bolivia Uruguay	Iceland
Togo	Brazil Venezuela	Italy
*Tunisia	Chile	Luxembourg
†Uganda	Colombia	Ireland
*UAR (Egypt)	Costa Rica	Netherlands
Upper Volta	‡Cuba	Norway
†Zambia	Dominican Rep.	Portugal
	Ecuador	Spain
	El Salvador	Sweden
Others 4	Guatemala	
	Haiti	
China	Honduras	
Israel	Mexico	
South Africa	Nicaragua	
United States	Panama	
	Paraguay	

* Arab League
† Commonwealth
‡ Does not always associate with group

their associates. The Latin American, Afro-Asian, and Scandinavian states frequently divide in their voting, notwithstanding their caucusing. Groupings permit political manipulation in the General Assembly, and in other representative bodies, according to multiple interests.

The Secretary-General and the Secretariat.   The Secretariat, under the Secretary-General, is an international civil service with some of the characteristics of a foreign office. It staffs meetings, arranges translations, processes reports, and performs other administrative tasks. As mentioned previously, of the present 18,000 employees of the U.N., some 16,000 are engaged in the economic and social activities of the organization.

The Secretary-General is an important international statesman in his own right. Conflicts among the members have by default permitted him to exercise considerable initiative on problems involving threats to the peace. The Secretary-General is appointed for a five-year term by the General Assembly on the recommendation of the Security Council, an action requiring a majority of at least nine including all of the permanent members. A Great Power veto can prevent a recommendation, and a group of one third plus one of the members can block approval by the General Assembly. It is clear from the composition of the Assembly that future secretaries are more likely to come from the new states, and from the Afro-Asian area, than from Europe or the Commonwealth.

Neither the Secretary-General nor members of the staff are to seek or receive instructions from any government or external authority. Each member of the U.N. undertakes to respect the international character of the office and its responsibilities. This means that the Secretary-General and his staff are intended to be impartial, neutral officials, and that states are not to try to influence them in the discharge of their duties. The Soviet assertion that blocs should be represented at the Secretary-General's level is contrary to the Charter.

The power and position of the Secretary-General are not defined in the Charter, but have developed by precedents. The first Secretary-General, Trygve Lie of Norway, established such practices as communicating with states and making independent proposals to the principal U.N. organs. The second Secretary-General, Dag Hammarskjöld of Sweden, elaborated these precedents, used his good offices among disputing states, established a "United Nations presence" in disturbed countries by sending high-ranking members of the Secretariat, and exercised vigorous executive leadership in the Suez and Congo situations. The third holder of the office, U Thant of Burma, extended the mediating role of the Secretary-General and sought to make himself available for the promotion of peace and cooperation.

The Secretary-General always faces the possibility of incurring the hostility of a Great Power, as did both Lie and Hammarskjöld with the Soviet Union. Mr. Lie resigned, partly because of Soviet noncooperation, which was seriously diluting the effectiveness of the United Nations, and Mr. Hammarskjöld may have reached the height of his effectiveness at the time of his death in the airplane crash on the borders of the Congo. The Secretary-General holds a very important position, yet is politically vulnerable. His role is important in the U.N.'s attempts to further international peace and promote economic progress of the developing nations. The office is a paradoxical combination of strength and weakness.

United Nations Financing. The expenses of the organization are met by contributions of the member states. These are of two kinds: (1) fixed contributions, assessed against members for support of the regular budget according to a sliding scale based on relative ability to pay, and (2) voluntary contributions to special funds designated by the General Assembly.

The General Assembly has decided that in principle no state should pay more than 30 per cent of the total ordinary expenses of the organization. Actually, the United States has recently been paying about 32 per cent. The smallest assessment has been fixed at 0.04 per cent. These assessments are adjusted as capacity to pay changes. From 1946 to 1958 total outlays amounted to $2.435 billion, of which the United States contributed 47.7 per cent. The regular annual budget now is about $100 million.[1]

The financial demands upon the United Nations are likely to increase. Economic growth in many parts of the world is accompanied by mounting demands upon the resources of many of the newer and underdeveloped countries, so that they are unlikely to increase their contributions for a long time to come. The minimum assessment is heavy for some small countries, for they must also maintain a costly mission in New York.

The United Nations has in recent years faced a grim financial outlook. Its regular budgetary requirements have grown by $40 million since 1959. Technical assistance costs add about $100 million annually which are covered by separate voluntary subscriptions. Major problems have arisen in financing peacekeeping and other emergency measures. Special funds have been set up for these activities, but expenses have not been completely met. The U.N. force in the Congo cost over $400 million for the four-year period

[1] See John G. Stoessinger and Associates, *Financing the United Nations System* (Washington: Brookings Institution, 1964); also Norman J. Padelford, "Financial Crisis and the Future of the United Nations," *World Politics*, Vol. XV, No. 4, July 1963, pp. 531–568.

it was there. The United States, Britain, and others made substantial contributions to these funds, with the United States contribution exceeding 35 per cent of the total. The Soviet Union and its allies have refused to pay any part of the peacekeeping costs, and France refused to contribute to the Congo costs. The funds for the United Nations force in Cyprus were raised by the uncertain method of periodic voluntary subscriptions.

The 1965 financial crisis involved the question of the right of Great Power members to refuse to pay for expenses of which they did not approve, and their retention of the right to vote in the General Assembly when they were more than two years in arrears. The issue also tended to return the responsibility for peacekeeping more toward the Security Council, with its Great Power veto, and away from the Assembly, where a majority of smaller states might press resolutions for actions not desired by one or more Great Powers—and which could only be executed by Great Power support.

A second aspect of the crisis at the Nineteenth Assembly session was the unwillingness of the majority to suspend the voting right of France and the U.S.S.R. under Article 19, though these states were then more than two full years in arrears on their payments of the special peacekeeping assessments. The United States argued that the Assembly should take this action, but it did not press for a vote. One of the first actions of Ambassador Goldberg was to announce a reversal of the United States position. The reluctance of the members to vote on this issue vindicated again the right of dissent, and acknowledged that the application of a denial of the right to vote under Article 19 to Great Powers would split the organization and the consensus on which it is based.

The financial situation conditions the future of the United Nations and the nature and scope of its operations. For mainly political reasons, the Great Powers are reluctant to make higher contributions. This reflects their views of the role and usefulness of the United Nations to their interests. The many small states, which can dominate voting and which value the U.N. highly, are unable to provide the necessary financing.

THE UNITED NATIONS AND THE MAINTENANCE OF INTERNATIONAL PEACE AND SECURITY

The opening clause of the Charter makes it apparent that the overriding purpose of the United Nations is to prevent war. In nearly every chapter there is some provision relating the other objectives of the organization to this prime concern.

The Charter does not precisely define a threat to international peace and security, a breach of the peace, or an act of aggression. It is left for the Security Council or the General Assembly to determine in each situation whether a given action or set of actions involve aggression or threats of aggression, and what measures should be taken to cope with them.

Role of the Security Council. The primary responsibility for dealing with situations involving threats to international peace and security resides in the Security Council. While an alleged threat to peace or act of aggression is under consideration, other organs cannot interfere. The Council may refer some or all aspects of the problem to the Assembly, and it may ask the Assembly and Secretary-General for a recommendation or for assistance. It may refer legal questions to the International Court of Justice. If the Security Council is blocked by a veto, as it has often been, the question may be dropped from its agenda by a procedural vote of any seven members, and, under the terms of the Uniting for Peace Resolution, the Assembly may then be summoned to deal with the situation. This is a second line of action if decision making in the Security Council breaks down.

When the Security Council decides what measures to take to maintain or enforce peace under Chapter VII, including the use of economic, political, or military measures, these are obligatory for member states. They are more than recommendations.

The Council may take a variety of steps to deal with situations threatening peace or security. It must first determine whether there is a threat or breach of the peace, or an act of aggression. This is a substantive matter and subject to the veto, and requires an affirmative vote of seven members of the Council, including the permanent members.

The Council may then decide to take "provisional measures" while it is studying a crisis. It might, for example, call upon the parties to settle their dispute peacefully. If fighting is occurring, the most common action is to call for a ceasefire and withdrawal of forces. This procedure was used for Palestine in 1948 and at the outbreak of the Korean War in 1950. The Council may go further and appoint a United Nations Mediator to try to arrange a truce or settlement. The Council may set up an Investigating Commission, as it did when guerrilla forces crossed the northern borders of Greece in 1947. It may appoint a Good-Offices Committee to negotiate with the disputing parties, as it did for Indonesia in 1948, when the Dutch were using force to prevent Indonesian independence.

The Council may decide to call for an international force to maintain or restore peace and order, as it did for the Congo, and for Cyprus. Or it may request the Secretary-General to place economic or technical services at the disposal of a country or to employ the facilities of his office to seek a peaceful solution.

Chapter VII of the Charter envisages a military fighting force under the aegis of the U.N. This has never been created, however, because of the failure of the members to conclude the necessary special agreements with the Security Council. The forces requested from states for the several peacekeeping operations differed from the contemplated military fighting force in that they were volunteered on an *ad hoc* basis and were authorized to use force only as a last resort in self-defense. Their mission, furthermore, was to police and pacify, rather than to enforce. Because forces of this nature are not strictly provided for in the Charter, states are at liberty not to volunteer contingents. And states, such as France and the Soviet Union, have argued that they are not obligated to pay for the costs of such a force when they are opposed on political grounds to the missions of such forces.

The Council may call upon states to refrain from assisting a party, as it did with respect to the white minority regime of Rhodesia, and at the time of Korea. It may call for an embargo, breaking diplomatic relations, expelling a state from the United Nations, or aiding a state attacked. It may request direct help for a victim of aggression, or it may set up a United Nations Supreme Command, as it did for Korea, and request members to make forces available to the commander. If the necessary majority can be secured, the Council may call for military "enforcement" action, in which the members are obligated by the Charter to cooperate with the U.N.

With this wide range of possibilities, the Security Council must decide in each circumstance what will best serve the needs of the time and the interests of member states. The veto principle and the necessity for obtaining a majority vote operate in all of these steps.

Composition of the Council. Two main questions confront members in any crisis. Will the Great Powers—that is, the United States, Soviet Union, Britain, France, and China—be able to unite or will one or more of them block Council action by a veto? Secondly, in view of the neutralist policies of the Asian and African states, will the Security Council be able to muster a majority for measures that involve a use of force or affect neutralist states? The veto is an integral part of the system, and the elective membership of the Council has become increasingly important. The

Charter provides that, in electing members, "due regard" must be paid to the "contribution" of member states to the maintenance of peace and security and to the other purposes of the organization, and to "equitable geographical distribution."

Many states have been elected to the Security Council that have been unable to make a contribution to maintaining peace and security. There has also been a tendency for the Assembly to elect smaller powers from Asia or Africa for political and prestige reasons, irrespective of their ability to contribute substantively to maintaining or enforcing international peace. This situation seems likely to continue given the politics of the General Assembly. Meanwhile, able middle powers such as Canada, Australia, and India have been elected to the Council less frequently than formerly.

An amendment to the Charter, now approved by the principal powers, increases the size of the Security Council from eleven to fifteen. This should provide a more equitable distribution of elective seats, but it is uncertain whether mature, stable, and resourceful powers will fill them or whether voting blocs will place more of their numbers upon the Council. It is likely that elections to the Security Council will continue to be strongly contested, and that the composition of the organ will significantly affect its ability to maintain and enforce international peace and security.

The Veto Problem. The veto power given to the permanent members of the Security Council by the Charter applies to all substantive decisions, except when one or more of them may be parties to a dispute. In this case they must abstain. The veto provision was written into the Charter in order to protect the rights and interests of the Great Powers from actions by majorities of lesser powers, and it was designed to give the Great Powers a controlling voice in any situation which might ultimately require them to employ their own manpower to enforce international peace. The veto right means that if a Great Power chooses to associate itself with an aggression, the Council will be paralyzed.

The Soviet's use of the veto on more than a hundred occasions has led to repeated protests of its abuse. The Uniting for Peace Resolution (1950) was devised to avoid the paralyzing effect of a veto in times of emergency. There are indications, however, that the larger powers are now less enthusiastic about going to the Assembly than they were in the 1950's under the threat of a veto, so there may be more efforts to resolve differences between the powers within the Security Council.

Since 1947 the practice of not counting an abstention from voting as failure to concur has eased the situation by permitting the Council to adopt a proposal for which one of the Great Powers does not explicitly desire to cast a negative vote. Suggestions have been made that the Charter be amended to eliminate the veto, but there are no indications that any Great Power wants to give up this valuable prerogative. Hence, means must be sought for securing agreement within the Council, or the General Assembly if the problem is transferred there.

The General Assembly and the Maintenance of International Peace and Security. The distinctions between the powers and role of the Assembly and the Security Council are important. The jurisdictional power is not coequal. The Assembly can only make recommendations, although a resolution passed through the Assembly by a large majority carries considerable political and moral weight. But the Assembly has no authority to make its actions binding upon member states except in the case of the annual budgetary assessments and a few minor matters. Even here the U.S.S.R. and others have defied the authority of the Assembly, refusing to pay for items to which they are opposed. The Assembly has no explicit authority under the Charter to call for armed forces and enforcement measures. It is true that under the Uniting for Peace Resolution, the Assembly may invite states to make armed forces available for peacekeeping actions when the Security Council is blocked by the veto. It did this when British and French vetoes prevented the Council from undertaking efforts to stop the hostilities at Suez—thereby authorizing a force which is still in existence (UNEF). The Resolution also was utilized during the Congo crisis. But the Assembly can do no more than *request* states to make forces available, and in the light of the political and financial crisis over financing peacekeeping, it appears doubtful that the Assembly can require states to pay for such forces financed by assessment, when this action is opposed by a Great Power.

The Assembly can call for investigation or for peaceful settlement. It can appoint a conciliation commission to negotiate with parties, or send an observation group to a troubled spot. It can take other "provisional measures," such as calling for a ceasefire. The full scope of the Assembly's powers has yet to be probed. The majority of the Assembly has accepted its expanding role in emergencies, although the United States and some others have been less enthusiastic since it became apparent that Assembly resolutions can be passed by a majority which is primarily unable to execute the actions required. There are two further considerations in relation to the maintenance of peace and security. A two-thirds majority must be obtained for an important action, and Assembly actions are now influenced by nonalignment in the clashes between Communism and strongly anti-Communist states. Compromise is generally necessary, and the presence of many voting groups makes political maneuvering inevitable. Resolutions tend to be diluted unless there is a wide consensus of world opinion, as upon South Africa's apartheid policies and the repressive measures of the Rhodesian white minority.

Provisions for Pacific Settlement of Disputes. Existing or threatened violence indicates a conflict or dispute. The process of pacific settlement includes adjustment of the causes as well as control of the violence.

Chapter VI of the Charter relating to pacific settlement of disputes is a key element of the U.N. system. This obligates all parties to a dispute or situation "the continuance of which is likely to endanger international peace and security," to try to settle the dispute by peaceful means.

Under Chapter VI settlement is to be sought first by the parties themselves, through negotiation, inquiry, mediation, conciliation, arbitration, judicial settlement, resort to regional arrangements, or other means. States may bring a matter to the U.N. at any time for discussion and recommendation. The provisions of the Charter are very general and allow many alternatives. The Security Council or the General Assembly may discuss the situation, hear the parties, and deliberate on what should be done. Airing of disputes is often sufficient to induce parties to try to reach settlement. If this does not succeed, the discussion may open up other avenues of solution. A resolution may be passed recommending measures to ease the situation. Good offices or mediation may be proposed. Or the legal aspect of a dispute may be referred to the International Court of Justice.

The Charter does not make the Security Council as responsible for promoting pacific settlement as it does for the maintenance of international peace and security. The Assembly and the Council complement one another in this area of responsibility, and appeals may be made to either. If a matter goes first to the Security Council and runs into a veto there, it may be taken off the agenda of that organ and brought before the General Assembly. This option permits flexibility in pacific settlement procedures.

The International Court of Justice. The International Court of Justice, also discussed in Chapter 21, is intended to play a major role in the settlement of justiciable disputes. Chapter XIV of the Charter provides that all members of the United Nations are *ipso facto* parties to the Statute of the Court. The Court may hear any legal dispute the parties agree to refer to it. In addition, it may be asked by the General Assembly or the Security Council for an advisory opinion. Its jurisdiction comprises all matters specially provided for in the Charter or in treaties and conventions that are in force.

The most controversial issue relating to the competence of the Court is the extent to which it should have compulsory jurisdiction in legal disputes. The Connally Amendment attached by the United States Senate to American acceptance of the Statute excludes from the Court any question which the United States government declares to be within the "domestic jurisdiction" of the United States. Many lawyers have urged repeal of this amendment, arguing that the United States is protected by Article 2, paragraph 7 of the Charter. But actions of the General Assembly asserting U.N. jurisdiction in matters that some states have felt to be within domestic jurisdiction have left others uncertain that such protection does exist. The Court has taken the position that it will stop proceedings if a party formally objects on grounds of domestic jurisdiction, although it may examine the merits of such a point if one of the parties requests it to do so.

Sufficient cases are referred to the tribunal at The Hague to indicate that the Court is filling a useful place in the settlement of justiciable disputes. On the other hand, the refusal of France, the Soviet Union, and others to accept the Court's advisory opinion on peacekeeping expenditures, which had no obligatory force, and its closely divided bench on the Liberian-Ethiopian case against South Africa over the treatment of Southwest Africa, show that the work of the Court cannot be separated from international politics.

The Balance Sheet on Pacific Settlement. These are some of the ways in which the United Nations attempts to promote pacific settlement of international disputes. The continuing disputes between the Arab states and Israel, between Egypt and Saudi Arabia over Yemen, between India and Pakistan, and between the African states and South Africa, all of which have been before the U.N. repeatedly, illustrate the difficulty of translating general principles into practical settlements. The United Nations has, nevertheless, been instrumental in assisting some states to reach a pacific settlement of disputes. One such instance was the dispute between the Netherlands and Indonesia over West New Guinea. This territory was eventually transferred to the latter under the supervision of a U.N. Temporary Administrator aided by a special U.N. force. The record is one which ranges from failure to success in a long sequence of disputes and situations threatening international peace and security. The vital importance of having an agency available to hear and consider disputes is accepted. This function is one of the reasons why the

U.N. would have to be invented if it did not exist. The responsibility for seeking international peace and security is a many-faceted, and often thankless, task.

PROMOTION OF DEVELOPMENT

Another major concern of the world organization is the promotion of cooperation in the economic, social, cultural, educational, and health fields, and the realization of human rights and fundamental freedoms. This concern is now focused heavily on the problems of development. The U.N. declared the 1960's to be the Decade of Development, in which a concerted effort should be made to help the developing countries to achieve minimum standards of economic growth and social advancement.

ECOSOC and Its Related Commissions. The organ chiefly responsible for the consideration of development problems is the Economic and Social Council (ECOSOC), which operates under the direction of the General Assembly, by which it is elected. The Council is composed of twenty-six states (formerly eighteen) broadly representative of the U.N. membership.

ECOSOC initiates studies and reports and makes recommendations to the General Assembly, to members, and to the Specialized Agencies. It prepares draft conventions, calls conferences, and correlates the programs of many agencies. Its agendas comprise many difficult problems associated with economic growth and collaboration. A series of regional and functional commissions, including the Economic Commissions for Europe (ECE) and Africa (ECA), assist the Council. These commissions overlap the activities of regional organizations such as the European Economic Community and the Alliance for Progress described in the preceding chapter.

Through their studies of economic conditions and long-range planning, these groups deal with fundamental problems, facilitate trade and investment, and help to evolve national plans for economic development and suggest ways to utilize technical assistance. ECOSOC has functional commissions to deal with human rights, population, status of women, transport, and communications. The Human Rights Commission formulated and implemented a Universal Declaration of Human Rights. The Transport and Communications Commission has promoted the adoption of uniform road signs and signals, international driver licensing arrangements, meetings of experts on passport and visa formalities, and the like

—steps not noted on the front pages of the world press, but valuable practical aids to international circulation and communication.

Much constructive work is being done by the so-called Specialized Agencies which have been brought into relation with the United Nations —the International Labor Organization (ILO), the Food and Agriculture Organization (FAO), UNESCO, the World Health Organization (WHO), the World Bank (IBRD), and the International Monetary Fund (IMF).[2]

These organizations vary a good deal in importance, depending upon the criteria of judgment. A few samples may serve to illustrate the range of services being rendered. The International Monetary Fund and World Bank have been mentioned in a previous chapter. The International Labor Organization seeks to improve working conditions through adoption of international agreements. It also tries to facilitate settlement of labor disputes and further the laboring man's rights and interests. The World Health Organization coordinates a worldwide attack on epidemic diseases and malnutrition, and its medical teams are helping the underdeveloped countries to improve their own medical services. The Food and Agriculture Organization assists states to conserve natural resources and improve agricultural production, processing, and marketing. UNESCO's literacy program is aiding local leaders in teaching basic reading and writing skills to uneducated peoples. Each of these agencies is rendering specific services to countries having different levels of economic and technological growth. Their efforts are linked through the Expanded Program of Technical Assistance, and the U.N. Development Program.

Development Assistance.   The United Nations has moved strongly into development assistance through technical assistance and helping countries to find capital to facilitate growth.

Developing countries often prefer to take assistance from an international source, which avoids the political and economic relationships incident to dealing with the United States or other Great Powers.

The principal multilateral assistance comes from the World Bank and through the "soft loan window" of the International Development Association. The World Bank, which has loaned over $5 billion, operates on a strictly businesslike banking basis, including advisory services, economic surveys, and loan supervision.

The Expanded Program of Technical Assistance (EPTA), later

[2] Descriptions of these organizations and their activities will be found in the *United Nations Yearbook,* in current issues of the *U.N. Monthly Chronicle,* and in the factual summaries and articles contained in *International Organization.*

merged with the Special Fund in a U.N. Development Program under the overall direction of Mr. Paul Hoffman, operates a program of the order of $30 million a year pledged outside the regular United Nations budget, and provides technical assistance to underdeveloped countries "to ensure the attainment of higher levels of economic and social welfare for their entire populations." The Special Fund, similarly financed at a level of over $100 million a year, makes loans for development services, and for activities which would not meet the World Bank's strict criteria. The target set by Secretary-General U Thant for the Development Program is $200 million a year, a small proportion of the need of the developing countries. This target has not so far been met, because of the reluctance of the principal donors to channel larger amounts through the less readily controlled hands of the U.N.

The ultimate test of the United Nations was originally conceived as its ability to maintain international peace and security. But its contributions to the advancement of human welfare and to the alleviation of want are significant and can help to lay foundations for peace, friendship, and security.

The U.N. and National Political Development. The United Nations is also concerned with the political advancement of the peoples of non-self-governing territories. It has publicized issues of colonialism, furthered efforts toward self-government and independence, and served as an intermediary at the birth of new states.

Problems of political development can be brought to the U.N. through the right of any member to bring up "any matter" affecting peace or security for debate or recommendation. Policies of ruling states toward dependent territories in which there are nationalist movements can be alleged to be causing threats to peace, justifying United Nations concern. The African nations have repeatedly laid these charges against Portugal for its handling of Angola and Mozambique, and have obtained resolutions condemning that country.

The United Nations is involved through the Declaration Regarding Non-Self-Governing Territories in Chapter XI of the Charter, and through the International Trusteeship System provided for in Chapters XII–XIII. The core of these provisions is the responsibility placed on administering states to lead the peoples in these territories toward "self-government" by means of the "progressive development of free political institutions" and to promote their political advancement.

The trusteeship system has functioned effectively as a means of aiding transition from dependence to statehood. Since 1960 the number of territories remaining under trusteeship has rapidly declined, and today there remain only a few trust areas, including the United States Trust Territory in the Pacific and the Australian-administered territories of New Guinea and Nauru. Given the widely scattered, sparsely populated, and economically dependent nature of most of the islands and atolls encompassed in these territories, it is difficult to foresee their independence. The problem is to find a solution that will meet the pressures and requirements of the interests of the inhabitants, the administering powers, and the anticolonialist forces in these tiny possessions. Progress has been made in improving educational and self-government facilities, but there are still long steps to be taken before most of them can hope to become viable independent states.

One of the most difficult problems associated with political development is the question of Southwest Africa, a territory originally mandated to South Africa after World War I which that country refused to place under U.N. trusteeship. African and Asian states have protested South Africa's application of racial discrimination policies in this territory. In 1963 Ethiopia and Liberia charged South Africa with violation of the Charter and requested of the World Court a judicial interpretation of the rights and duties of all parties, a request which the Court refused to act upon. There are likely to be more problems involving the Portuguese territories of Angola and Mozambique, and possibly other lands before the goals of the 1961 Declaration on Ending Colonialism are attained. Professor Rupert Emerson of Harvard has cautioned, nevertheless,

Abhorrent as the thought may be to the most ardent anti-colonialists, it can also not be left out of account that there are occasional instances in which continued association with the metropolitan power on appropriate terms is more acceptable to the people of a territory than is independence.[3]

The most difficult and frustrating phases of decolonization may lie ahead. The U.N. still has immense tasks before it in the realm of assisting political development.

CHANGE IN THE UNITED NATIONS

Any political organization that is to remain viable in the changing world must be adaptable.

[3] Rupert Emerson, "Colonialism, Political Development, and the U.N.," in Norman J. Padelford and Leland M. Goodrich (eds.), *The United Nations in the Balance* (New York: Praeger, 1965), p. 135.

Formal and Informal Change. The founders of the United Nations made provision for change through amendment and usage. Only two amendments have had sufficient support to become effective thus far. One of these authorized an enlargement of the Security Council and the other increased the size of ECOSOC.

Proposals for other changes, such as abolishing the veto power and introducing weighted voting into the General Assembly, have failed to gain the necessary support. But tinkering with the Charter will not produce order where there is none. The difficulties of the U.N. lie in the cross-purposes and conflicting objectives of the members. Time, goodwill, and enlightenment are needed to resolve these.

The system can be modified in limited ways through practice and usage, as in the practice of not counting a Great Power abstention from voting in the Security Council as preventing the passage of a resolution. The provisions of the Uniting for Peace Resolution are another innovation. Precedents have also been established in the form of U.N. peacekeeping forces assembled in response to requests by the Security Council and the General Assembly. The role of the Secretary-General has been substantially expanded by usage and acceptance. Practice and usage are fashioning what might be called a living Charter, and this process can be extended with the agreement of the members.

A Struggle for Change. The Congo crisis was the setting for a struggle over both the concept of the United Nations role in the preservation of peace and security, and over the position of the Secretary-General. The U.N. role as enunciated by Secretary-General Hammarskjöld was to keep "newly rising conflicts outside the sphere of bloc differences." Assessing the political uncertainties in the newly independent and nonaligned nations, Mr. Hammarskjöld said that,

. . . temporarily, and pending the filling of a [power] vacuum by normal means, the United Nations enters the picture on the basis of its non-commitment to any power bloc, so as to provide to the extent possible a guarantee in relation to all parties against initiatives from others.[4]

Recognizing the voting strength of the nonaligned nations, their interests in the U.N., and that "it is extremely difficult for the United Nations to exercise an influence on problems which are clearly and definitely within the orbit of present day conflicts between power blocs," the Secretary-

[4] From Introduction to the Secretary-General's Fifteenth Annual Report to the General Assembly, September, 1960.

General conceived that the United Nations should seek a principal role in conflicts not already entwined in bloc differences.

The Soviet Union rejected this concept. Khrushchev declared that in the struggle between Communism and capitalism there could be no neutrals, and he applied this view to the United Nations. He called for the replacement of the Secretary-General by a presidium of one representative of the Western bloc, one from the Communist bloc, and one neutral. The Soviet proposal was an effort to establish a Soviet veto over the actions of the Secretary-General similar to the Great Power veto in the Security Council. Thereby the United Nations could be prevented from engaging in future activities to which the Soviets objected, such as those in the Congo.

The death of Secretary-General Hammarskjöld precipitated a debate on the Soviet troika proposal. When the African and Asian states firmly opposed this plan, the Soviet Union withdrew the proposal, permitting the election of neutralist U Thant, on condition that he consult with his senior aides on the Secretariat. The Soviet proposal can, however, be made again.

History seems to support the concept of Mr. Hammarskjöld on the areas where the United Nations may operate effectively. But the difficulties over the Congo make it unlikely that peacekeeping operations dependent on assessments will be launched again if they are opposed by one or more of the Great Powers.

The Future of the United Nations.   The constitutional, operational, and financial difficulties confronting the United Nations are a symptom of more fundamental political situations in interstate affairs. The U.N. exists as an instrument to further, and to help reconcile where possible, the national interests of its member states. It is not a supranational world government.

The founders assumed the United Nations would be a means for furthering peace and security to the extent that substantial agreement could be found among the Great Powers.

In thinking about the future of the U.N. we thus return to a point from which we started in this book. Peaceful relationships depend upon the measure of consensus that exists among states. Where there is a sharing of views on goals and objectives, a sense of community can develop. The absence of this consensus reduces interstate relations to a struggle for power among competing and conflicting parties. Consensus among the powers has been strained and influenced by the dynamics of contemporary world politics, the forces of revolutionary change operating in the international environment, the ending of colonialism, the rise of the new nations with their nationalistic and economic drives, the conflict of ideologies, technology, and the population explosion.

The Idea of World Government. Some think that wider changes are needed in world organization before international peace and security can be assured.

Advocates of world government argue that violence cannot be contained and war prevented until there is a mechanism empowered to make world law, an executive competent to apply the law, a world police force sufficiently powerful to enforce peace upon states, and a system of courts with jurisdiction over both states and individuals. Supporters of these views usually insist that the world institution should have independent means of revenue, with the right to levy taxes directly upon states, private business, and individuals. To promote the success of such a system, advocates hold that national armed forces must be disarmed as a world police force is built up.[5]

The practical difficulties with this model are that states have yet to be persuaded that national interests will be served by superimposing another layer of government on top of the national state. Aside from the considerable costs this would entail, none could be sure that those who might acquire power in the world government would employ it as conscientiously to advance and protect the interests of the individual states as would the duly elected or appointed representatives of their own people. Indeed, it would be enormously difficult for an international authority to function as an agent of the entire world community. Sooner or later those in control would come to have interests at variance with those of some states. An immediate difficulty lies in the conflict in ideologies which divides the nations. In the absence of an agreed consensus on the basic values and goals of world government, differences will prevail on objectives to be pursued, and therefore upon programs to achieve them. It does not appear that the kind of world organization proposed by the world federalists can be achieved in the foreseeable future through amendment of the United Nations Charter.

Possibly one step toward what George Washington saw as the need of this continent nearly 200 years ago, a "government for the whole," may first evolve among the Atlantic nations, whose alliance has been suffering what the first President warned was typical of all alliances, "infractions and interruptions." Leaders like Prime Minister Pearson of Canada, former

[5] See, for example, "Declaration of the Second Dublin Conference on World Peace Through World Law," Dublin, N.H., October 5, 1965, Grenville Clark, Secretary.

Secretary of State Christian Herter, and some Congressmen have seen a need for reconstructing, broadening, and more experimentation within the Atlantic community.

CONCLUSION

The uses and limitations of the United Nations became clear in its first two decades. It functioned successfully at Suez, in the Congo, in West New Guinea, and to an extent in Cyprus. It was a useful instrument at the time of the Korean War in rallying assistance for a victim of aggression. The United Nations provides a focus for world opinion and diplomacy, particularly for small countries that cannot afford a large diplomatic staff.

When one or more Great Powers oppose an effort to maintain peace and security, progress is problematical. Other multilateral methods, such as the use of regional organizations, can sometimes be employed.

The United Nations today presents increasingly perplexing questions for states whose economic and financial strength underwrites the bulk of its costs, including its development programs, and who provide the trained manpower and material to maintain international peace and security. It is becoming more difficult to obtain the necessary majorities for the political actions needed.

The great increase in membership has changed the balance within the United Nations and its overall character. The voting dominance of the Asian, African, and Communist states may make older powers less ready to go to the General Assembly, or possibly other organs, when their vital interests are at stake.

There has been an East-West confrontation since the United Nations was born. There are indications of a growing North-South confrontation, overlapping and ever diffusing some of the cold war conflict, between the industrialized "have" states and the nonaligned, underdeveloped "have-not" states. Their primary interests, as they see them, are not in the problems of the East-West struggle, but on questions of colonialism, disarmament, development, and the opportunities the United Nations gives them to play a role in international politics. These matters, many having to do with the undramatic but useful activities of the specialized agencies, may be increasingly the stock in trade of the United Nations, in a context stated by the late President Kennedy:

I would address a special plea to the smaller nations of the world—to join with us in strengthening this Organization, which is far more essential to their security than it is to ours—the only body in the world where no nation need be powerful to be secure, where every nation has an equal voice, and where any nation can exert influence not according to the strength of its armies but according to the strength of its ideas. It deserves the support of all.[6]

Secretary of State Dulles once remarked, "Nothing that is practical or desirable would be attained by destroying or undermining the United Nations or losing faith or hope in it." He added that the very fact that relations between the opposing blocs are tense, "that there are many points of conflict, and that war is possible, makes it all the more important to have a place where the tensions can be openly discussed, and where the differences may be fought out with words rather than bombs."

The United Nations today is not what some architects thought they were creating in 1945. But it is an active, universal organization of primary importance. In the area of development it has found a field of concern that may occupy its attention long after the Decade of Development has passed into history. This field is currently affording a constructive challenge to its efforts and resources. The leaders of nearly all free countries, including every president of the United States in recent times, have underlined that their countries seek international peace. In these two spheres United States interests overlap with those of the United Nations.

Professor Inis L. Claude, Jr. of the University of Michigan sums up the existing situation in these words, "We cannot be unconditionally certain that the United Nations has a future. We can only assert that there is a clear need for the Organization." [7]

[6] The State of the Union: Message of President John F. Kennedy Delivered to the Congress, January 30, 1961. House Document 73, 87th Congress, 1st Session.
[7] Inis L. Claude, Jr., "Implications and Questions for the Future," in Padelford and Goodrich, *op. cit.*, pp. 471, 482.

CHAPTER 24

Change and Challenge

In this book we have tried to provide both a framework of analysis of international politics and a perspective on the realities of contemporary world affairs. The point has now been reached to take stock of the principal themes which emerge from this analysis.

THE RAPIDITY OF HISTORIC CHANGE

The future flows out of the present and from the past. Interpretation of the past is one of the main problems confronting those examining the present and looking forward to the future. Since 1900 history has moved so quickly that analyses of the present risk being appraisals of the past.

Many people living today have seen no less than five distinguishable eras in world affairs. In the first decade of the twentieth century, international politics was dominated by the European powers. Parts of the Americas and most of Asia and Africa were under European hegemony.

504

World peace rested on the uneasy balance between the Triple Alliance and the Triple Entente. America was a growing power in world affairs, as yet untested in Great Power politics.

The era of World War I saw a vast Armageddon engulfing the massed manpower of Europe, Russia, the British Empire, and America. The empires in Europe disintegrated under the impact of defeat and nationalism, and some of those outside of Europe were gravely shaken. Revolutionary Communism seized power in Russia. This era also saw the rise of America to a decisive world-power position both in war and in a temporary diplomatic leadership which urged the principle of national self-determination and was primarily instrumental in drawing up the Peace of Versailles and the League of Nations.

A third era followed the Versailles settlement. In this period, from 1920 to 1939, America withdrew behind a façade of isolationism, unwilling to assume responsibility for maintaining and shaping the world order it had helped initiate. This was the period of the worldwide economic depression and the rise of the welfare-state concept. No less significant was the consolidation of Communist power in Russia under Stalin, and the growth of Japan as a Great Power bent on establishing its own exclusive sphere in Asia and the Pacific.

Next, overlapping the previous era, came the era of Fascism, from 1933 to 1945, with its drive for the conquest of Europe and Asia, and Hitler's effort to exterminate the Jewish people. Almost the entire world became involved in the World War precipitated by Nazi actions. The curtain was finally brought down on this dark period of human history by the massed might of the United States, Britain, the Free French, the Soviet Union, and other allies. The most striking results of this war were the power vacuums occasioned by the defeat and occupation of Germany and Japan, the disintegration of the European colonial empires, and the agreement to form a new world system, the United Nations, to replace the League of Nations.

Once again a new era crowded rapidly upon mankind before its predecessor had closed. This was ushered in by the explosion of the first atomic device on the sands of Alamagordo, the dropping of the nuclear bombs on Hiroshima and Nagasaki, and the perfection and testing of much larger weapons systems after the war. This was a period marked by great American power, the founding of the United Nations, initiation of tremendous foreign-assistance programs, the appearance of a distinct bipolarity in world affairs, and the incongruity of neither-war-nor-peace in the new struggle between forces of freedom and of Communism. This period also saw the Berlin blockade, the seizure of China by the Communists, and the war in Korea.

The 1960's introduced a fifth era of twentieth-century international affairs. The leaders of World War II were gone and half of those living did not personally remember that war. There were fundamental shifts in the world power situation. The colonial empires had vanished, leaving in their place dozens of new, weak states, economically and politically immature. The Soviet Union had become a superpower possessed of the most powerful missiles and weapons, but involved in deep controversy and conflict with the other great Communist power, China. NATO, once the most dynamic force in postwar world politics, was in disarray. The sharp postwar clash between the U.S.S.R. and the West seemed slightly softened. Western Europe had recovered economically and become once again a great power center.

In this period a new revolutionary force of nationalism appeared in Asia and Africa, giving rise to over fifty new states with a drive for rapid economic and social development. There appeared at the same time signs of a vast population increase. Many of the new states sought a voice in world affairs but were unwilling to become aligned in maintaining and enforcing world peace. The combination of all these circumstances in turn transformed the United Nations from its original concepts.

The world may now be standing on the threshold of another era as man begins to explore outer space. There have not been any claims to extraterrestrial sovereignty, but the symbols of earthly sovereignty have been landed on the moon and carried into the far reaches of space. Meanwhile, the age of nuclear power moves onward, overhanging the civilization of mankind with its destructive power. A new concern has arisen in the proliferation of nuclear weapons among states, threatening to escalate local hostilities to holocausts. The continued recurrence of conflicts and violence indicates that the nuclear presence does not deter resort to violence and that force remains a major element in international affairs.

The reader may pause for reflection on what might have been. After World War II, the transition from colonialism might have occurred without extremes of danger, disorder, and conflict, if the victorious powers had moved with a substantial consensus. The lessons of the period between the two world wars influenced the development of the United Nations. It was hoped that world peace would be organized, but without the cooperative efforts of the large powers, this was illusory. In addition to the Communist conflict with the West, the surge of new states and the struggles for power and position among new and old have contributed to the strains and disorder of world affairs. The rule of law and collective security measures have, however, carried weight in world affairs. International consultation and organized action has increased, but the unilateral use of national power is still the predominant characteristic of international relations.

THE UNITED STATES IN THE CHANGING WORLD

In abandoning its traditional isolation after World War II, the United States accepted the leadership of the Western world, replacing the war-exhausted Western European powers. Through aid to Greece and Turkey, the Marshall Plan, NATO, and active participation in world councils, the United States asserted its intent to use its economic, political, and military power in the interest of world stability and the containment of Communism. That intention was tested in Korea. The firm and rapid United States response made clear to all that military conquest was an unprofitable and perilous adventure. Another test came in the 1960's in Vietnam, and the United States again responded with significant power in order to contain Communism in Southeast Asia. At the same time, the United States was using its political instruments and its economic resources to further political, social, and economic development in the emerging countries.

The influence of the United States is felt in nearly every country. Having become a great global power, the United States has gradually realized that it has acquired "the imprecise responsibility of maintaining a global power balance during an era of revolution in both political and natural science." [1]

This power balance is not a comparatively simple matter of controlling geographical spheres of influence. The geographic arena is global. The fronts of conflicts and cooperation are diplomatic, cultural, psychological, economic, and military, as well as geographic.

In a more demanding and critical world than that of 1945, the United States can no longer expect to have the same appeal to the world's hopes. It no longer has the almost exclusive image as the country to follow and to imitate, and it no longer enjoys military invulnerability or unchallengeable world power. Although continuing to have tremendous power and influence, the United States has to chart its policy in the light of changes that are occurring now and that will extend into the future.

[1] C. L. Sulzberger, *The New York Times*, February 27, 1966.

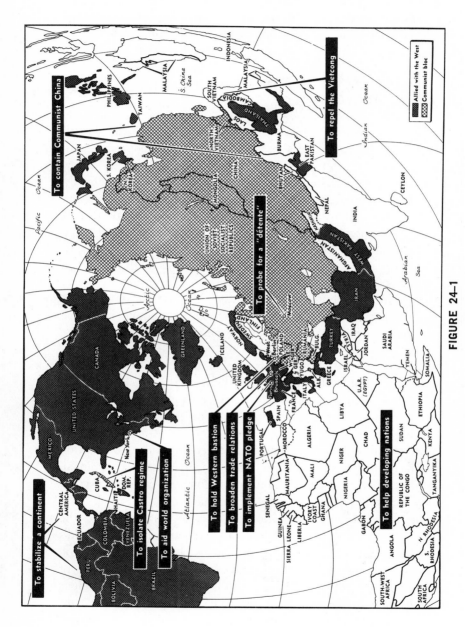

FIGURE 24-1

Ten Major U.S. Foreign Policy Commitments Around the World

(From The New York Times, December 1, 1963. Reprinted by permission)

"These," said President John F. Kennedy, "are extraordinary times. We face an extraordinary challenge. But our strength as well as our convictions have imposed upon this Nation the role of leader in freedom's cause." [2]

The fundamental issues of this challenge extend beyond self-preservation. As Paul Nitze, former Director of the State Department's Policy Planning Council, pointed out, there is a larger issue, which is the "creation of some form of world order compatible with our continued development as the kind of nation we are and believe ourselves capable of becoming." This larger issue makes it necessary for us to focus on what we are trying to construct in the long term as well as what we are defending against immediate encroachments.

Conflict is bound to exist in international affairs because the goals of different states diverge. Any pretense that an order can be created which altogether eliminates conflict is Utopian. Given a reasonable consensus on value systems and interests, conflicts might be managed under an improving system of international order. The conflict with Communism remains critical because of the incompatibility of values and the cross-purposes of states. Pragmatists can compromise and accommodate; dogmatists are unlikely to compromise unless they have no other alternative. In the longer perspective, dealing with the challenges of Communism is only a part of the complex task ahead, but it is a means of buying time to achieve a higher level of sanity and order in world affairs.

Implicit in a policy of buying time is the question of whether America can act with sufficient decision to meet the successive threats and challenges of Communism, and at the same time add new dimensions to its own policy through alleviating the world's other problems and helping to guide on a long-term basis, the events of the future. There is also the question how the United States, and the West, will use that time. It can be frittered away. If this is done, the future will indeed be less secure and more fraught with danger to free institutions and independent choice. There may be "a tide in the affairs of men, which taken at the flood, leads on to fortune." Time may be used to create a world in which even the Soviet, Chinese, and other authoritarian regimes will find that their most attractive alternative is to live on the same principles we do. This situation may be achieved by the combined use of the West's resources, human and material, to frustrate overt military aggressions and covert efforts to undermine the political institutions of others; to strengthen

[2] Special message to Congress, May 25, 1961, on Urgent National Needs, House Document 174, 87th Congress, 1st Session. p. 1.

foreign societies economically and administratively; to shift the competitions of the cold war to the eradication of disease and want; to collaborate in exploring outer space; to strengthen the "preventive diplomacy" and economic- and technical-assistance roles of the United Nations; to build a stronger model in the Atlantic community; to help alleviate tragedy and suffering where these afflict the lives of men and nations.

The last reasonably stable system of international politics was the balance-of-power system of the nineteenth century. That system was underwritten by a group of European powers operating in another environment. The Great Power membership is now global, with more Eastern emphasis, except for the world power position of the United States. The United States is not powerful enough to impose a new system of international order even if it wished to do so. But the creation and shape of any system depends materially on United States power and leadership.

One of the principal problems confronting the United States is the subjective one of how Americans think about foreign affairs. Historical perspective and political understanding are needed in dealing with many problems. The problems of international politics cannot be solved by reference to any abstract moral standard. They must be dealt with by choosing among practical alternatives in the real world. President Eisenhower once commented that policy making generally consists of "choosing the least undesirable alternative." Professor William Lee Miller suggests that in the real world sweeping affirmations of "freedom," "justice," and "peace," and opposing aggression, have limited, and even negative, effects unless they are supported by the intent to act.[3] In the international political world, the ethics that count derive more from the consequences of actions than from the quality of intentions and motives. This is not to suggest that ends justify the means. Rather, the analysis suggests that international politics is an art of the possible. Today there is a high premium on correct judgment as to what is possible, and on the correct appraisal of the means needed to achieve that which is judged possible.

The confusion and frustrations associated with international affairs can lead to disillusionment and contemplation of radical solutions. This is illustrated by some of the proposals put forward in the United States concerning Vietnam (see Figure 11–1). Some proposed escalation of military action to an indefinite end. Others proposed abandoning South Vietnam to Communism. It is hard for people to accept the fact that problems

---

[3] William Lee Miller, "The American Ethos and the Alliance System," in Arnold Wolfers (ed.), *Alliance Policy in the Cold War* (Baltimore: Johns Hopkins University Press, 1959), pp. 31 ff.

in foreign affairs are rarely solved. They are more often worn out or simply replaced by other and more difficult problems.

In a democracy all citizens bear some responsibility for helping their government choose among the practically possible alternatives. Rather than capitulating to disappointments or turning to implausible courses, the task of the responsible individual is to foresee and adjust to changes while striving to influence them.

The price of power may be high and is a difficult one when military force has to be used in defense of freedom. But the test of greatness of past world powers has been their capacity for carrying burdens rather than their wealth or grandeur. When Rome faltered the world was plunged into anarchy for centuries. Britain was in great part responsible for the comparatively stable system of the nineteenth century. Now Britain's power has declined; its withdrawal would have been more disruptive had it not been for the reluctant movement of the United States to take its place as a power for peace.

Some people have looked for gratitude from those assisted. In international affairs gratitude is more often the pleasant anticipation of a favor about to be received. Others have felt America should be loved and trusted for what it has done. We are not loved because we are very rich; we are not completely trusted because we are very powerful. From the standpoint of enlightened national interest the goal is more precisely respect and prestige. Prestige does not always lead to popularity. But it is the responsibility of those with power to preserve the existent order until a better one can be devised irrespective of the popularity of their actions.

For the United States the preservation and strengthening of our freedom and institutions, of our security and welfare, are our primary national purposes. Supporting these purposes are the objectives of attaining a more peaceful and prosperous world in which law and justice may reign in the affairs of nations. Today the Communist threat to the free nations, and the "manifold problems of a changing world which at many points fuse into one," place unprecedented demands upon the United States. The United States must have "the necessary foresight, the ability to organize its policy-making process, and the willingness to commit resources to policies the end results of which are far from clear and [far from] certainly attainable in a short time." [4] Only thereby can purpose be steadily and successfully pursued.

[4] *United States Foreign Policy.* "Basic Aims of United States Foreign Policy," Study No. 7, prepared for the United States Senate Committee on Foreign Relations by the Council on Foreign Relations. 86th Congress, 1st Session (Washington: Government Printing Office, 1959).

The words of two Presidents stress the problems of change and adjustments that face the United States. "I speak today," John F. Kennedy said in his first State of the Union Message, "in an hour of national peril and national opportunity. Before my term has ended, we shall have to test anew whether a nation organized and governed such as ours can endure. The outcome of it is by no means certain. . . ." [5] Abraham Lincoln, in a Message to Congress a century earlier also stressed the necessity for reordering thought to conform to the realities of current times.

The dogmas of the quiet past are inadequate for the stormy present. The occasion is piled high with difficulty and we must rise with the occasion. As our case is new, so we must think anew and act anew. We must disenthrall ourselves and then we shall save our country.[6]

Accepting that the United States' destiny depends on the survival and growth of freedom in the world, the United States has to devise ways of exercising an effective leadership role, for there is no other state which combines the power, purpose, and potential leadership to this end.

In a world containing the divisions and conflict of the present, cooperative relationships offer the best alternative for influencing the external environment. These require time to build and to perfect, for cooperation among sovereign states is always difficult. The differences of culture, tradition, and outlook between France and its NATO partners reveal how true this is in the Atlantic community. It is even more so where national differences are deeper. Although recourse to organizations and institutional forms is often a preferred means of dealing with international problems, it cannot be overlooked that even the most intimate alliances and agencies do have limitations. And these limitations differ from the standpoints of individual states.

It is inescapable that the United Nations, the most cosmopolitan of all cooperative arrangements, should reflect many differences. For it affords many nations a means of advancing divergent and often opposing ideas and interests. At the same time, it provides a channel through which common purposes and joint action can be developed if nations are disposed to use it to this end. As the late Ambassador Adlai Stevenson testified,

---

[5] State of the Union Message, January 30, 1961. House Document 73, 87th Congress, 1st session.

[6] Second Annual Message, December 1, 1862. Text in James D. Richardson, *A Compilation of the Messages and Papers of the Presidents, 1789–1897.* Published by the Authority of Congress (Washington: Government Printing Office, 1897), Vol. VI, pp. 126, 142.

the United Nations does afford "our best hope for fashioning a peace marked with freedom and justice—a peace which accords with the aspirations of free men everywhere." [7] The alternative, as President Kennedy saw it, is "the abandonment of the principle of a world governed by law to a world dominated by force." [8] It is worth remembering that arrangements such as NATO, the U.N., the OAS and other multilateral institutionalized forms are but some among the many instruments of policy that are available to statesmen for dealing with emergent problems. The process of decision making must always encompass the question of which instrument and pattern of policy to employ in a given circumstance for the attainment of national interests and goals. The answers to this question are not always the same, for the inputs of facts and the desiderata of objectives vary between times and situations. Taking these into account, and weighing the advantages and the liabilities of one course against another, the statesman seeks to choose unilateral or cooperative measures that he and his advisers believe are the most likely to insure attainment of the goals desired. The calculus is often far from easy.

CONCLUSION

The preceding chapters have sought to provide a frame of reference for viewing international relations at the present time and for the years ahead of us. Our approach has been essentially pragmatic. It has been dictated in large part by the overriding effects of the rapid change through which the modern world is passing.

As we come to the conclusion of this volume, we are aware that many aspects of international relations have been touched upon only briefly. The whole is too vast and complex to include more than an introduction to selected features in a single volume. Issues and problems that have tried the minds of statesmen and experts for years are not made any easier by glib speculations.

We have not attempted to define what the United States should do in the years ahead. Although we think our country's purpose is clear and lasting, policies are, and will continue to be, the result of many changing forces and factors. They will have to be hammered out in the heat

[7] Testimony of Ambassador Adlai Stevenson at Hearings of Senate Committee on Foreign Relations, January 18, 1961.

[8] State of the Union Message, January 31, 1961; and letter to the American Association for the United Nations, March 12, 1961. *Department of State Bulletin*, March 27, 1961.

of controversy and in the moil of domestic and foreign politics. There are few long-lasting answers, no pat solutions, for the uncertain future in which democratic peoples must exercise responsible judgments as circumstances arise.

Our purpose has been to identify some of the principal forces moving through the scene of world politics at this juncture, to delineate the basic factors that affect the policies and actions of states, and to describe some of the facets of the diplomatic and international process through which states must act to advance their ideas and their interests and to find common purposes with their neighbors in this changeable world.

The United States occupies a central place in the continuum of world politics. It must concern itself deeply with the forces of change at work within the international environment. What the United States does, or fails to do, in the foreign policy field is of vital significance for all nations, large and small. Addressing the American Legion convention in 1966, President Lyndon B. Johnson underscored the old truth that "responsibility is the price of power and influence." Our commitment to stop aggression and to root out the causes of war—"the poverty of man's body, the privation of his spirit, the imprisonment of his liberties"—has grown, he said, "because our responsibilities in the world have grown," because "our understanding has grown," and because "events in the world have compelled it to grow." [9] World politics cannot be studied apart from American policies and actions. Neither can the United States separate itself from international politics, for the two are inexorably linked.

Experience has taught us that no one nation has the power or the wisdom to solve all the problems of the world. Each nation must do what it can to preserve and promote the values it cherishes. No other nation can or will do this for it. But by reasoning and working together, nations can seek practicable solutions to the problems of peace and war and development that outstrip the capabilities of each of them acting separately. For most international problems yield, to the extent that they do, chiefly through prolonged and quiet exploration with others.

Through the World Bank, the Marshall Plan, NATO, the Alliance for Progress, and other programs the United States has shown that it is capable of producing imaginative, long-range programs that are in balance with the challenges of the day and with the resources available to deal with them.

[9] *The New York Times*, August 31, 1966. See also the President's State of the Union Message the same year. *Department of State Bulletin*, vol. LIV, No. 1388, January 31, 1966, p. 153.

In a diverse and torn world, moving with rapid steps toward an end that cannot be seen, fresh thought is needed on how best to deal with the emergent issues of global politics. As the nation faces the differences and conflicts of international politics, it must look to responsible citizens to help find the ways in which to build while at the same time it defends; to seek purposeful uses of power that will help create a workable system of world order that will conserve the values we prize while allowing others to achieve the development they legitimately desire. These are the difficult problems of world order and of progress toward increased world community on which United States policy focuses today.

The Flow of Policymaking
in the Department of State[1]

The Department of State is an organism that is constantly responding to a vast assortment of stimuli. A new Soviet threat to Berlin, a forthcoming conference of Foreign Ministers of the Organization of American States, a request from Poland for credit, a solicitation for support of a candidacy for the Presidency of the United Nations General Assembly, a plea from an ambassador that the head of the government to which he is accredited be invited to visit the United States officially, a refusal by another government to permit the duty-free importation of some official supplies for a U.S. consulate, a request from the White House for comment on the foreign affairs section of a major presidential address, an earthquake in the Aegean creating hardships which it appears the U.S. Navy might be able to alleviate, a request for a speaker from a foreign policy association in California, a transmittal slip from a Member of

[1] By Charlton Ogburn, Jr. (Appendix C) in H. Field Haviland, Jr., and Associates, *The Formulation and Administration of United States Foreign Policy*, A Report for the Committee on Foreign Relations of the United States Senate (The Brookings Institution, 1960). This appeared in Study No. 9, 86th Congress, 2nd Session, January 1960, printed as Senate Document No. 24 of 87th Congress, 1st Session. Revised in 1966 to reflect changes in organization and administrative procedures of Department of State and other agencies concerned.

Congress asking for information with which to reply to a letter from a constituent protesting discriminatory actions against his business by a foreign government, letters from citizens both supporting and deploring the policy of nonrecognition of Communist China, a continuing inquiry by a press correspondent who has got wind of a top secret telegram from Embassy Bonn on the subject of German rearmament and is determined to find out what is in it, a demand by a Protestant church group that the Department take steps to prevent harassment of their coreligionists in a foreign country, a request by a delegation of a federation of women's clubs for a briefing on southeast Asia and suggestions as to how its members might be useful in their planned tour of the area, a request from Consulate General Brazzaville for a revision of cost-of-living allowances, a visit by a commission of inquiry into the operations of U.S. foreign aid programs, a telegram from a U.S. embassy in the Near East declaring that last night's flareups make a visit by the Assistant Secretary for Near Eastern and South Asian Affairs, now in mid-Atlantic, inopportune at the moment, a warning by a European Foreign Minister of the consequences should the United States fail to support his nation's position in the Security Council, and a counterwarning by an African representative at the United Nations of the consequences should the United States do so—this is a sample of the requirements made of the Department of State in a typical day. Of course it does not include the oceans of informational reports that come into the Department by telegram and air pouch or the countless periodicals from all parts of the world that arrive by sea.

What is required to begin with is that the flow be routed into the right channels. This does not apply to press correspondents and foreign embassy officials; they usually know where to go without being directed. For the rest, almost every piece of business—every requirement or opportunity for action—comes within the Department's ken first as a piece of paper. These pieces of paper—telegrams, letters—must be gotten as speedily as possible into the hands of the officers who will have to do something about them or whose jobs require that they know about them.

The telegram and mail branches of the Office of Communications, under the Deputy Under Secretary for Administration, receive the incoming material and, after decoding and reproducing the telegrams, indicate on each communication the distribution it should receive among the bureaus or equivalent components of the Department. With telegrams, the deliveries are simultaneous. Several score copies of a telegram may be run off. A yellow copy, called the action copy, like the original of an airgram or letter, goes to the bureau responsible for taking any necessary action; white copies go to all others interested.

A telegram (No. 1029, let us say) from a major U.S. embassy in Western Europe reports the warning of the Foreign Minister of X country that a grave strain would be imposed on relations between X and the United States should the latter fail to vote with X on a sensitive colonial issue in the United Nations

General Assembly. Such a telegram would have a wide distribution. The action copy would go to the Bureau of European Affairs. The action copy of a telegram to the same purpose from the U.S. delegation to the United Nations in New York, quoting the X delegation, would go to the Bureau of International Organization Affairs. This is a matter of convention.

Information copies of a telegram of such importance would go to all officers in the higher echelons—the Secretary of State (via the executive secretariat), the Under Secretaries, and the Deputy Under Secretaries. They would also go to the Policy Planning Council, to the Bureau of African Affairs because of the involvement of certain territories within its jurisdiction, to the Bureau of Far Eastern Affairs and the Bureau of Near Eastern and South Asian Affairs because the telegram concerns the incendiary question of European peoples' ruling non-European peoples, and of course to the Bureau of Intelligence and Research. Other copies would go to the Department of Defense and the Central Intelligence Agency. The executive secretariat would doubtless make certain that the Secretary would see the telegram. In addition, its staff would include a condensation in the secret daily summary, a slim compendium distributed in the Department on a need-to-know basis. If classified top secret, it would be included in the top secret daily staff summary, or black book, which goes only to Assistant Secretary-level officials and higher.

In the bureaus, incoming material is received by the message centers. There a further and more refined distribution would be made of telegram 1029. Copies would go to the Office of the Assistant Secretary (the so-called front office), to the United Nations adviser, to the public affairs adviser (since the United States is going to be in for trouble with public opinion in either one part of the world or the other), and to whatever geographic office or offices may seem to have the major interest. In the Bureau of International Organization Affairs, this would be the Office of United Nations Political Affairs.

In the Bureau of European Affairs, the yellow action copy of the telegram goes to the Office of Western European Affairs and thence to the X country desk, where it is the first thing to greet the desk officer's eye in the morning. As it happens, the desk officer was out the evening before at an official function where he discussed at length with the first secretary of the X embassy the desirability of avoiding any extremes of action in the United Nations over the territory in question. In the front office of the Bureau, the staff assistant has entered in his records the salient details of the problem the Bureau is charged with and has passed the telegram on to the Assistant Secretary.

The following scenes are now enacted:

The X country desk officer crosses the hall to the office of his superior, the officer-in-charge, and the two together repair to the office of the Director of the Office of Western European Affairs. The three officers put in a call to the Assistant Secretary for European Affairs and tell his secretary that they would like as early an appointment as possible.

The Director of the Office of United Nations Political Affairs (UNP) telephones the Director of the Office of Western European Affairs (WE). He says he assumes WE will be drafting an instruction to the U.S. embassy in X to try to dissuade the Foreign Office from its course, and that UNP would like to be in on it. He adds that they had thought of getting the U.S. delegation to the United Nations (US Del) to present this view to the X mission in New York but that there seemed to be no point in doing so since the latter would already be advising its government to take account of world opinion.

After the Secretary's morning staff conference, where the matter is discussed briefly, a conference is held in the Office of the Assistant Secretary for European Affairs to decide on a line to take with the X government. The X desk officer is designated to prepare the first draft of a telegram embodying it. The draft is reviewed and modified by his officer-in-charge and the Office Director for Western European Affairs.

The telegram instructs the U.S. embassy in X to make clear to the X government our fear that its projected course of action "will only play into hands of the extremists and dishearten and undermine position of elements friendly to West" and suggests that the X government emphasize its policy to take account of the legitimate aspirations of the indigenous population of the territory in order to improve the atmosphere for consideration of the problem by the General Assembly. The Assistant Secretary, after scrutinizing and approving the telegram, finds it necessary only to add the Bureau of Near Eastern and South Asian Affairs to the clearances. Those already listed for clearance are the Deputy Under Secretary for Political Affairs, the Bureau of International Organization Affairs, and the Bureau of African Affairs. He says it can be left to the Deputy Under Secretary for Political Affairs to sign the telegram; he does not see that the telegram need go higher.

It remains for the drafting officer to circulate the telegram for approval by those marked for clearance. In the Bureau of African Affairs the telegram is termed extremely gentle to the X government but is initialed as it stands. The Office of United Nations Political Affairs (UNP) wishes to remind X that the United States, setting an example of its adherence to the principle of affording the widest latitude to the General Assembly, had even accepted on occasion the inscription of an item on the agenda accusing the United States of aggression. The X desk officer states, however, that WE would not favor such an addition, which might only further antagonize the X government. Thereupon, UNP, yielding on this point, requests deletion of a phrase in the telegram seeming to place the United States behind the X contention that the question is not appropriate for discussion in the United Nations. The drafter of the telegram telephones the Director of the Office of Western European Affairs who authorizes the deletion, having decided that he can do so on his own without referring the question to his superior, the Assistant Secretary.

With that, the Director of the Office of United Nations Political Affairs initials the telegram for his Bureau, and the X desk officer "hand carries" the telegram (in the departmental phrase), with telegram 1029 attached, to the Office of the Deputy Under Secretary for Political Affairs and leaves it with his secretary. At 6 o'clock he is informed by telephone that the Deputy Under Secretary has signed the telegram (that is, signed the Secretary's name with his own initials beneath) without comment. The desk officer goes to the seventh floor, retrieves it, and takes it to the correspondence review staff of the executive secretariat, where the telegram is examined for intelligibility, completion of clearances, conformity with departmental practices, etc., before being sped to the Telegram Branch for enciphering and transmission.

The next morning, all offices of the Department participating in the framing of the telegram receive copies of it hectographed on pink outgoing telegram forms. The telegram, bearing the transmission time of 8:16 p.m., has entered history as the Department's No. 736 to the embassy in X. The X desk officer writes "telegram sent," with the date, in the space indicated by a rubber stamp on the yellow copy of the original telegram 1029, and the staff assistant in the front office makes an equivalent notation in his records. The yellow copy is then sent on to the central files, whence in time it will probably be consigned to the National Archives. Only the white copies may be kept in the Bureau's files.

In this case, however, no one is under any illusion that the matter has been disposed of. Scarcely 24 hours later comes a new telegram 1035 from the embassy in X reporting that, while the X government may possibly make some concessions, it will certainly wage an all-out fight against inscription of the item and will expect the United States to exert itself to marshal all the negative votes possible. The question is, what position will the United States in fact take and how much effort will it make to win adherents for its position? No one supposes for a moment that this explosive question can be decided on the bureau level. Only the Secretary can do so—as the Secretary himself unhappily realizes.

At the end of a staff meeting on Berlin, the Secretary turns to the Counselor and Chairman of the Policy Planning Council and asks him to give some thought within the next few days to the alternatives open on the question. The official addressed sets the wheels in motion at once. A meeting is called for the next morning. Attending are: the Counselor and Chairman of the Policy Planning Council himself and several members of his staff (including the European and African specialists), the Director of the Office of United Nations Political Affairs, the Western European officer-in-charge, the X desk officer, a member of the policy guidance and coordination staff of the Bureau of Public Affairs, and three intelligence specialists, namely, the Director of the Office of Research and Analysis for Western Europe, the Director of the Office of Research and Analysis for the Near East and South Asia, and the Director of the Office of Research and Analysis for Africa.

The discussion explores all ramifications of the issues involved and is generally detached and dispassionate. The object of the meeting is to help clarify the issues so that the Policy Planning Council may be sure all relevant considerations are taken into account in the staff paper it will prepare for the Secretary.

The Secretary is in a difficult position. The President's views on what course of action to take are somewhat different from his. The Congress is also of divided view, with some Members impressed by the irresistible force of nationalism among dependent peoples, others by the essential role of X in NATO and European defense. The ambassadors of some countries pull him one way, others another. One of the Nation's leading newspapers editorially counsels "restraint, understanding and vision." At the staff meeting he calls to arrive at a decision, the Secretary perceives that his subordinates are as deeply divided as he feared. He takes counsel with each—the Counselor, the Assistant Secretaries for European Affairs, African Affairs, and Near Eastern and South Asian Affairs. At the end he sums up and announces his decision. Thereupon the following things happen:

The Assistant Secretaries take the news back to their bureaus.

An urgent telegram is sent to the U.S. Embassy in X reporting the decision.

Telegrams are sent to embassies in important capitals around the world instructing the ambassador to go to the Foreign Office and present the U.S. case in persuasive terms.

A similar telegram is sent to the U.S. delegation in New York for its use in talks with the delegations of other United Nations members.

Conferences attended by representatives of the geographic bureaus concerned, of the Bureau of Public Affairs, and of the U.S. Information Agency, are held. Afterward, the representatives of the U.S. Information Agency return to their headquarters to draft guidances to the U.S. Information Service establishments all over the world. Such guidances tell how news of the U.S. decision is to be played when it breaks.

The more important the problem, the more the upper levels of the Department become involved. In a crisis—one brought about, say, by the overthrow of A, a Western-oriented government in the Middle East—the Secretary himself will take over. However, the bulk of the Department's business is carried on, of necessity, by the lower ranking officers. Even when a crisis receives the Secretary's personal, day-to-day direction, the desk officer and the officer-in-charge are always at hand to provide the detailed information only specialists possess, while in the intelligence bureau, country analysts and branch chiefs will be putting in 10-hour days and 6- or 7-day weeks. Generally, moreover, the crisis will have been preceded by a good deal of work on the part of lower-level officials.

In the case suggested, it was apparent for some time that all was not well in A. The U.S. Embassy in A was aware of growing discontent with the regime through its indirect contacts with opposition political elements, from information from Cairo, from evidences of tension, from clandestine publications. Additional straws in the wind were supplied by the public affairs officer in A both to the embassy and to the U.S. Information Agency because of his special contacts among professional groups. On the strength of these reports and of dispatches from American foreign correspondents in the area, and equipped with analyses from the Bureau of Intelligence and Research, all pointing in the same direction, the desk officer at a staff meeting of the Office of Near Eastern Affairs imparts his disquiet. He is directed to prepare a memorandum which, if convincing in its presentation, the Office Director undertakes to put before the Assistant Secretary.

What the desk officer has in mind will require national action, so what he drafts takes the form of a memorandum to the Secretary. It embodies a statement of the problem, the actions recommended, a review of the facts bearing upon the problem, and a conclusion. At the end are listed the symbols of the offices of the Department from which concurrences must be sought. Backing up the memorandum will be supporting documents, especially telegrams from the embassy, each identified by a tab. The mass fills a third of an in-box.

The problem is defined as that of strengthening the present pro-Western regime of A. By way of recommendation, the desk officer is especially sensitive to the problems and needs of the country for which he is responsible. He calls for more detachment of the United States from A's rival, B, expediting U.S. arms deliveries to A and the supply of certain recoilless rifles and jet fighter planes the A government has been requesting, support for A's membership in various United Nations agencies, a Presidential invitation to the Prime Minister of A to visit the United States. Much of what the memorandum recommends has to be fought out in the Bureau and even in the Office since it conflicts with the claims of countries (and the desk officers responsible for them) in the same jurisdiction. While neither the Office Director nor the Assistant Secretary doubts that support of B is a handicap in the region, they consider that a proposal for a radical departure would simply doom the memorandum by preventing anyone from taking it seriously.

As it finally leaves the Bureau with the Assistant Secretary's signature, the memorandum is considerably revised, and further change awaits it. The Department of Defense cannot provide the desired recoilless rifles and jet fighters. The Bureau of International Organization Affairs cannot offer any undertakings at this stage with respect to the question of membership in United Nations agencies. The Deputy Under Secretary for Political Affairs rules out a request of the President to invite the A Prime Minister for an official visit because the number of those invited is already too large.

Among recommendations in memorandums to the Secretary, as among salmon battling their way upstream to the spawning grounds, mortality is heavy.

Almost everywhere in the world, things are far from satisfactory, but the United States cannot be doing everything everywhere at the same time. And A, far from seeming to cry out for attention, looks like the one Middle Eastern country about which it is not necessary to worry.

Then the uprising occurs in A. Early in the morning, the officer-in-charge of A and one other country is awakened by the ringing of the telephone. In a flash, before his feet have touched the floor, he has visualized every conceivable disaster that could have befallen his area and has picked the overthrow of the monarchy in C as the most likely. Or did the security people find a top secret document under his desk?

On the telephone, the watch officer at the Department tells him that a "Flash" (a telegram which means "Get this one read immediately even if you have to rout someone out of bed") is coming off the machine and it looks serious—he had better come down. En route, the officer-in-charge turns on his car radio and picks up a news broadcast, but nothing is said about A. Uncle Sam has beaten the press agencies.

At the Department, he finds the telegram wholly decoded and reads the hectograph master. There is revolution in A. The top leadership has been either murdered or banished. The officer-in-charge could legitimately awaken the Assistant Secretary, but for the moment it seems there is nothing that can be done, so he decides to hold off until 6 a.m. and then call the Office Director and put it up to him. He does, however, call the A desk officer and tell him to get on his way. To share his vigil beside the watch officer's desk there is a representative of the executive secretariat, who will have the telegram ready for the Secretary to read immediately on his arrival. In the Bureau of Intelligence and Research—it being now after 4 o'clock—the morning briefers have arrived to go over the night's take and write up items of importance, with analyses, for the Director's use in briefing the Secretary's morning staff conference. The briefer for the Office of Research and Analysis for the Near East, South Asia and Africa—a GS-11 specialist on India—takes one look at the Flash on A and gets on the telephone to the A analyst.

By the time the Secretary has stepped from his black limousine and headed for the private elevator a good deal has happened. In the Bureau of Near Eastern and South Asian Affairs, everyone concerned with A from the Assistant Secretary down, and including the officer-in-charge of CENTO and Southeast Asia Treaty Organization affairs and the special assistant who serves as a policy and planning adviser, has been in conference for an hour laying out the tasks requiring immediate attention. Two more Flash messages have come in from A, one reporting that so far no Americans are known to have been injured but offering little assurance with respect to the future. The Assistant Secretary has already put in a call to the Director of Intelligence Research to ask that all possible information on the new leader of A and his connections be marshaled and that the Central Intelligence Agency be informed of the need. For the rest, the following represent the Assistant Secretary's conception of what should be done first:

1. The Department of Defense must be apprised of the Department of State's anxiety and be requested to have transport planes in readiness at nearby fields for the evacuation of Americans if necessary in accordance with pre-arranged plans. There must be consultation on what instruments are available if American lives have to be protected by force.

2. The U.S. Embassy in C, a friendly neighbor of A's to which the Flash messages have been repeated, will be heard from at any moment, and the Office of International Security Affairs in the Department of Defense will have to be alerted to the possibility of emergency military assistance for C.

3. Anything in the pipeline for A should be held up.

4. The possibility of a demonstration by the U.S. 6th Fleet in support of C's independence and integrity will have to be discussed with the Department of Defense.

5. A crash national intelligence estimate will be requested of the Central Intelligence Agency, provided the Agency does not consider the situation too fluid for a formal estimate to be useful.

6. The public affairs adviser will get in touch with the Bureau of Public Affairs, the departmental spokesman and the U.S. Information Agency to agree on the kind of face the United States will put on the affair.

7. The B Ambassador will probably have to be called in and apprised of the critical need for his government's acquiescence in overflights of B for the purpose of getting supplies to C. The B and C desk officers had better get busy immediately on a draft telegram to embassy B (repeat to C) setting forth the case the ambassador should make urgently to the B Foreign Office.

At 9:12, anticipating that he will be called to accompany the Secretary to the White House, the Assistant Secretary instructs his secretary to cancel all his appointments for the day, including one with the dentist but excepting his appointment with the C Ambassador. ("Mr. Ambassador, you may assure His Majesty that my Government remains fully determined to support the sovereignty and territorial integrity of his nation.")

At 9:14, 1 minute before the scheduled commencement of the staff meeting, the Assistant Secretary joins his colleagues in the Secretary's anteroom, prepared to hear the estimate of the Director of Intelligence and Research and to give his own appraisal and submit his plan of action.

North Atlantic Treaty, April 4, 1949

PREAMBLE

The Parties to this Treaty reaffirm their faith in the purposes and principles of the Charter of the United Nations and their desire to live in peace with all peoples and all governments.

They are determined to safeguard the freedom, common heritage and civilization of their peoples, founded on the principles of democracy, individual liberty and the rule of law.

They seek to promote stability and well-being in the North Atlantic area.

They are resolved to unite their efforts for collective defense and for the preservation of peace and security.

They therefore agree to this North Atlantic Treaty:

ARTICLE 1

The Parties undertake, as set forth in the Charter of the United Nations, to settle any international disputes in which they may be involved by peaceful means in such a manner that international peace and security, and justice, are not endangered, and to refrain in their international relations from the threat or use of force in any manner inconsistent with the purposes of the United Nations.

ARTICLE 2

The Parties will contribute toward the further development of peaceful and friendly international relations by strengthening their free institutions, by bringing about a better understanding of the principles upon which these institutions are founded, and by promoting conditions of stability and well-being. They will seek to eliminate conflict in their international economic policies and will encourage economic collaboration between any or all of them.

ARTICLE 3

In order more effectively to achieve the objectives of this Treaty, the Parties, separately and jointly, by means of continuous and effective self-help and mutual aid, will maintain and develop their individual and collective capacity to resist armed attack.

ARTICLE 4

The Parties will consult together whenever, in the opinion of any of them, the territorial integrity, political independence or security of any of the Parties is threatened.

ARTICLE 5

The Parties agree that an armed attack against one or more of them in Europe or North America shall be considered an attack against them all; and consequently they agree that, if such an armed attack occurs, each of them, in exercise of the right of individual or collective self-defense recognized by Article 51 of the Charter of the United Nations, will assist the Party or Parties so attacked by taking forthwith, individually and in concert with the other Parties, such action as it deems necessary, including the use of armed force, to restore and maintain the security of the North Atlantic area.

Any such armed attack and all measures taken as a result thereof shall immediately be reported to the Security Council. Such measures shall be terminated when the Security Council has taken the measures necessary to restore and maintain international peace and security.

ARTICLE 6

For the purpose of Article 5 an armed attack on one or more of the Parties is deemed to include an armed attack on the territory of any of the Parties in Europe or North America, on the Algerian departments of France, on the occupation forces of any Party in Europe, on the islands under the jurisdiction of any Party in the North Atlantic area north of the Tropic of Cancer or on the vessels or aircraft in this area of any of the Parties.

ARTICLE 7

This Treaty does not affect, and shall not be interpreted as affecting, in any way the rights and obligations under the Charter of the Parties which are members of the United Nations, or the primary responsibility of the Security Council for the maintenance of international peace and security.

ARTICLE 8

Each Party declares that none of the international engagements now in force between it and any other of the Parties or any third state is in conflict with the provisions of this Treaty, and undertakes not to enter into any international engagement in conflict with this Treaty.

ARTICLE 9

The Parties hereby establish a council, on which each of them shall be represented, to consider matters concerning the implementation of this Treaty. The council shall be so organized as to be able to meet promptly at any time. The council shall set up such subsidiary bodies as may be necessary; in particular it shall establish a defense committee which shall recommend measures for the implementation of Articles 3 and 5.

ARTICLE 10

The Parties may, by unanimous agreement, invite any other European state in a position to further the principles of this Treaty and to contribute to the security of the North Atlantic area to accede to this Treaty. Any state so invited may become a party to the Treaty by depositing its instrument of accession with the Government of the United States of America. The Government of the United States of America will inform each of the Parties of the deposit of each such instrument of accession.

ARTICLE 11

This Treaty shall be ratified and its provisions carried out by Parties in accordance with their respective constitutional processes. The instruments of ratification shall be deposited as soon as possible with the Government of the United States of America, which will notify all the other signatories of each deposit. The Treaty shall enter into force between the states which have ratified it as soon as the ratifications of the majority of the signatories, including the ratifications of Belgium, Canada, France, Luxembourg, the Netherlands, the

United Kingdom and the United States, have been deposited and shall come into effect with respect to other states on the date of the deposit of their ratifications.

ARTICLE 12

After the Treaty has been in force for ten years, or at any time thereafter, the Parties shall, if any of them so requests, consult together for the purpose of reviewing the Treaty, having regard for the factors then affecting peace and security in the North Atlantic area, including the development of universal as well as regional arrangements under the Charter of the United Nations for the maintenance of international peace and security.

ARTICLE 13

After the Treaty has been in force for twenty years, any Party may cease to be a Party one year after its notice of denunciation has been given to the Government of the United States of America, which will inform the Government of other Parties of the deposit of each notice of denunciation.

ARTICLE 14

This Treaty, of which the English and French texts are equally authentic, shall be deposited in the archives of the Government of the United States of America. Duly certified copies thereof will be transmitted by that Government to the Governments of the other signatories.

In witness whereof, the undersigned plenipotentiaries have signed this Treaty.

Done at Washington, the fourth day of April, 1949.

Treaty Banning Nuclear Weapon Tests in the Atmosphere, in Outer Space and Under Water

*Signed at Moscow August 5, 1963;
in force October 10, 1963.*

The Governments of the United States of America, the United Kingdom of Great Britain and Northern Ireland, and the Union of Soviet Socialist Republics, hereinafter referred to as the "Original Parties,"

Proclaiming as their principal aim the speediest possible achievement of an agreement on general and complete disarmament under strict international control in accordance with the objectives of the United Nations which would put an end to the armaments race and eliminate the incentive to the production and testing of all kinds of weapons, including nuclear weapons,

Seeking to achieve the discontinuance of all test explosions of nuclear weapons for all time, determined to continue negotiations to this end, and desiring to put an end to the contamination of man's environment by radioactive substances,

Have agreed as follows:

ARTICLE 1

1. Each of the Parties to this Treaty undertakes to prohibit, to prevent, and not to carry out any nuclear weapon test explosion, or any other nuclear explosion, at any place under its jurisdiction or control:

(a) in the atmosphere; beyond its limits, including outer space; or underwater, including territorial waters or high seas; or

(b) in any other environment if such explosion causes radioactive debris to be present outside the territorial limits of the state under whose jurisdiction or control such an explosion is conducted. It is understood in this connection that the provisions of this subparagraph are without prejudice to the conclusion of a treaty resulting in the permanent banning of all nuclear test explosions, including all such explosions underground, the conclusion of which, as the Parties have stated in the Preamble to this Treaty, they seek to achieve.

2. Each of the Parties to this Treaty undertakes furthermore to refrain from causing, encouraging, or in any way participating in, the carrying out of any nuclear weapon test explosion, or any other nuclear explosion, anywhere which would take place in any of the environments described, or have the effect referred to, in paragraph 1 of this article.

ARTICLE 2

1. Any Party may propose amendments to this Treaty. The text of any proposed amendment shall be submitted to the Depositary Governments which shall circulate it to all Parties to this Treaty. Thereafter, if requested to do so by one-third or more of the Parties, the Depositary Governments shall convene a conference to which they shall invite all the Parties, to consider such amendment.

2. Any amendment to this Treaty must be approved by a majority of the votes of all the Parties to this Treaty, including the votes of all of the Original Parties. The amendment shall enter into force for all Parties upon the deposit of instruments of ratification by a majority of all the Parties, including the instruments of ratification of all of the Original Parties.

ARTICLE 3

1. This Treaty shall be open to all states for signature. Any state which does not sign this Treaty before its entry into force in accordance with paragraph 3 of this article may accede to it at any time.

2. This Treaty shall be subject to ratification by signatory states. Instruments of ratification and instruments of accession shall be deposited with the Governments of the Original Parties—the United States of America, the United Kingdom of Great Britain and Northern Ireland, and the Union of Soviet Socialist Republics—which are hereby designated the Depositary Governments.

3. This Treaty shall enter into force after its ratification by all the Original Parties and the deposit of their instruments of ratification.

4. For states whose instruments of ratification or accession are deposited

subsequent to the entry into force of this Treaty, it shall enter into force on the date of the deposit of their instruments of ratification or accession.

5. The Depositary Governments shall promptly inform all signatory and acceding states of the date of each signature, the date of deposit of each instrument of ratification of and accession to this Treaty, the date of its entry into force, and the date of receipt of any requests for conferences or other notices.

6. This Treaty shall be registered by the Depositary Governments pursuant to Article 102 of the Charter of the United Nations.

ARTICLE 4

This Treaty shall be of unlimited duration.

Each Party shall in exercising its national sovereignty have the right to withdraw from the Treaty if it decides that extraordinary events, related to the subject matter of this Treaty, have jeopardized the supreme interests of its country. It shall give notice of such withdrawal to all other Parties to the Treaty three months in advance.

ARTICLE 5

This Treaty, of which the English and Russian texts are equally authentic, shall be deposited in the archives of the Depositary Governments. Duly certified copies of this Treaty shall be transmitted by the Depositary Governments to the governments of the signatory and acceding states.

In Witness Whereof the undersigned, duly authorized, have signed this Treaty. . . . (Rusk, Home, Gromyko)

Inter-American Treaty of Reciprocal Assistance (Rio Pact)[1]

ARTICLE 1

The High Contracting Parties formally condemn war and undertake in their international relations not to resort to the threat or the use of force in any manner inconsistent with the provisions of the Charter of the United Nations or of this Treaty.

ARTICLE 2

As a consequence of the principle set forth in the preceding Article, the High Contracting Parties undertake to submit every controversy which may arise between them to methods of peaceful settlement and to endeavor to settle any such controversy among themselves by means of the procedures in force in the Inter-American System before referring it to the General Assembly or the Security Council of the United Nations.

ARTICLE 3

1. The High Contracting Parties agree that an armed attack by any State against an American State shall be considered as an attack against all the

[1] Signed at Rio de Janeiro, September 2, 1947, and ratified by the United States on December 19, 1947. Senate document, Executive 11, 80th Congress, 1st Session.

American States and, consequently, each one of the said Contracting Parties undertakes to assist in meeting the attack in the exercise of the inherent right of individual or collective self-defense recognized by Article 51 of the Charter of the United Nations.

2. On the request of the State or States directly attacked and until the decision of the Organ of Consultation of the Inter-American System, each one of the Contracting Parties may determine the immediate measures which it may individually take in fulfillment of the obligation contained in the preceding paragraph and in accordance with the principle of continental solidarity. The Organ of Consultation shall meet without delay for the purpose of examining those measures and agreeing upon the measures of a collective character that should be taken.

3. The provisions of this Article shall be applied in case of any armed attack which takes place within the region described in Article 4 or within the territory of an American State. When the attack takes place outside of the said areas, the provisions of Article 6 shall be applied.

4. Measures of self-defense provided for under this Article may be taken until the Security Council of the United Nations has taken the measures necessary to maintain international peace and security.

ARTICLE 4

The region to which this Treaty refers is bounded as follows: beginning at the North Pole; thence due South to a point 74 degrees north latitude, 10 degrees west longitude; thence by a rhumb line to a point 47 degrees 30 minutes north latitude, 50 degrees west longitude; thence by a rhumb line to a point 35 degrees north latitude, 60 degrees west longitude, thence due south to a point in 20 degrees north latitude; thence by a rhumb line to a point 5 degrees north latitude, 24 degrees west longitude; thence due south to the South Pole; thence due north to a point 30 degrees south latitude, 90 degrees west longitude; thence by a rhumb line to a point on the Equator at 97 degrees west longitude; thence by a rhumb line to a point 15 degrees north latitude, 120 degrees west longitude; thence by a rhumb line to a point 50 degrees north latitude, 170 degrees east longitude; thence due north to a point in 54 degrees north latitude; thence by a rhumb line to a point 65 degrees 30 minutes north latitude, 168 degrees 58 minutes 5 seconds west longitude; thence due north to the North Pole.

ARTICLE 5

The High Contracting Parties shall immediately send to the Security Council of the United Nations, in conformity with Articles 51 and 54 of the Charter of the United Nations, complete information concerning the activities undertaken or in contemplation in the exercise of the right of self-defense or for the purpose of maintaining inter-American peace and security.

ARTICLE 6

If the inviolability or the integrity of the territory or the sovereignty or political independence of any American State should be affected by an aggression which is not an armed attack or by an extra-continental or intra-continental conflict, or by any other fact or situation that might endanger the peace of America, the Organ of Consultation shall meet immediately in order to agree on the measures which must be taken in case of aggression to assist the victim of the aggression or, in any case, the measures which should be taken for the common defense and for the maintenance of the peace and security of the Continent.

ARTICLE 7

In the case of a conflict between two or more American States, without prejudice to the right of self-defense in conformity with Article 51 of the Charter of the United Nations, the High Contracting Parties, meeting in consultation shall call upon the contending States to suspend hostilities and restore matters to the *status quo ante bellum*, and shall take in addition all other necessary measures to reestablish or maintain inter-American peace and security and for the solution of the conflict by peaceful means. The rejection of the pacifying action will be considered in the determination of the aggressor and in the application of the measures which the consultative meeting may agree upon.

ARTICLE 8

For the purposes of this Treaty, the measures on which the Organ of Consultation may agree will comprise one or more of the following: recall of chiefs of diplomatic missions; breaking of diplomatic relations; breaking of consular relations or of rail, sea, air, postal, telegraphic, telephonic, and radio-telephonic or radiotelegraphic communications; and use of armed force.

ARTICLE 9

In addition to other acts which the Organ of Consultation may characterize as aggression, the following shall be considered as such:

a. Unprovoked armed attack by a State against the territory, the people, or the land, sea or air forces of another State;

b. Invasion, by the armed forces of a State, of the territory of an American State, through the trespassing of boundaries demarcated in accordance with a treaty, judicial decision, or arbitral award, or, in the absence of frontiers thus demarcated, invasion affecting a region which is under the effective jurisdiction of another State.

ARTICLE 10

None of the provisions of this Treaty shall be construed as impairing the rights and obligations of the High Contracting Parties under the Charter of the United Nations.

ARTICLE 11

The consultations to which this Treaty refers shall be carried out by means of the Meetings of Ministers of Foreign Affairs of the American Republics which have ratified the Treaty, or in the manner or by the organ which in the future may be agreed upon.

ARTICLE 12

The Governing Board of the Pan American Union may act provisionally as an organ of consultation until the meeting of the Organ of Consultation referred to in the preceding Article takes place.

ARTICLE 13

The consultations shall be initiated at the request addressed to the Governing Board of the Pan American Union by any of the Signatory States which has ratified the Treaty.

ARTICLE 14

In the voting referred to in this Treaty only the representatives of the Signatory States which have ratified the Treaty may take part.

ARTICLE 15

The Governing Board of the Pan American Union shall act in all matters concerning this Treaty as an organ of liaison among the Signatory States which have ratified this Treaty and between these States and the United Nations.

ARTICLE 16

The decisions of the Governing Board of the Pan American Union referred to in Articles 13 and 15 above shall be taken by an absolute majority of the Members entitled to vote.

ARTICLE 17

The Organ of Consultation shall take its decisions by a vote of two-thirds of the Signatory States which have ratified the Treaty.

ARTICLE 18

In the case of a situation or dispute between American States, the parties directly interested shall be excluded from the voting referred to in the two preceding Articles.

ARTICLE 19

To constitute a quorum in all the meetings referred to in the previous Articles, it shall be necessary that the number of States represented shall be at least equal to the number of votes necessary for the taking of the decision.

ARTICLE 20

Decisions which require the application of the measures specified in Article 8 shall be binding upon all the Signatory States which have ratified this Treaty, with the sole exception that no State shall be required to use armed force without its consent. . . .

ARTICLE 25

This Treaty shall remain in force indefinitely, but may be denounced by any High Contracting Party by a notification in writing to the Pan American Union, which shall inform all the other High Contracting Parties of each notification of denunciation received. After the expiration of two years from the date of the receipt by the Pan American Union of a notification of denunciation by any High Contracting Party, the present Treaty shall cease to be in force with respect to such State, but shall remain in full force and effect with respect to all the other High Contracting Parties. . . .

Charter of the United Nations

We the peoples of the United Nations determined

to save succeeding generations from the scourge of war, which twice in our lifetime has brought untold sorrow to mankind, and

to reaffirm faith in fundamental human rights, in the dignity and worth of the human person, in the equal rights of men and women and of nations large and small, and

to establish conditions under which justice and respect for the obligations arising from treaties and other sources of international law can be maintained, and

to promote social progress and better standards of life in larger freedom,

and for these ends

to practice tolerance and live together in peace with one another as good neighbors, and

to unite our strength to maintain international peace and security, and

to ensure, by the acceptance of principles and the institution of methods, that armed force shall not be used, save in the common interest, and

to employ international machinery for the promotion of the economic and social advancement of all peoples,

have resolved to combine our efforts to accomplish these aims.

Accordingly, our respective Governments, through representatives assembled in the city of San Francisco, who have exhibited their full powers found to be in good and due form, have agreed to the present Charter of the United Nations and do hereby establish an international organization to be known as the United Nations.

CHAPTER I   PURPOSES AND PRINCIPLES

ARTICLE 1

The Purposes of the United Nations are:

1. To maintain international peace and security, and to that end: to take effective collective measures for the prevention and removal of threats to the peace, and for the suppression of acts of aggression or other breaches of the peace, and to bring about by peaceful means, and in conformity with the principles of justice and international law, adjustment or settlement of international disputes or situations which might lead to a breach of the peace;

2. To develop friendly relations among nations based on respect for the principle of equal rights and self-determination of peoples, and to take other appropriate measures to strengthen universal peace;

3. To achieve international cooperation in solving international problems of an economic, social, cultural, or humanitarian character, and in promoting and encouraging respect for human rights and for fundamental freedoms for all without distinction as to race, sex, language, or religion; and

4. To be a center for harmonizing the actions of nations in the attainment of these common ends.

ARTICLE 2

The Organization and its Members, in pursuit of the Purposes stated in Article 1, shall act in accordance with the following Principles.

1. The Organization is based on the principle of the sovereign equality of all its Members.

2. All Members, in order to ensure to all of them the rights and benefits resulting from membership, shall fulfil in good faith the obligations assumed by them in accordance with the present Charter.

3. All Members shall settle their international disputes by peaceful means in such a manner that international peace and security, and justice, are not endangered.

4. All Members shall refrain in their international relations from the threat or use of force against the territorial integrity or political independence

of any state, or in any other manner inconsistent with the Purposes of the United Nations.

5. All Members shall give the United Nations every assistance in any action it takes in accordance with the present Charter, and shall refrain from giving assistance to any state against which the United Nations is taking preventive or enforcement action.

6. The Organization shall ensure that states which are not Members of the United Nations act in accordance with these Principles so far as may be necessary for the maintenance of international peace and security.

7. Nothing contained in the present Charter shall authorize the United Nations to intervene in matters which are essentially within the domestic jurisdiction of any state or shall require the Members to submit such matters to settlement under the present Charter; but this principle shall not prejudice the application of enforcement measures under Chapter VII.

CHAPTER II   MEMBERSHIP

ARTICLE 3

The original Members of the United Nations shall be the states which, having participated in the United Nations Conference on International Organization at San Francisco, or having previously signed the Declaration by United Nations of January 1, 1942, sign the present Charter and ratify it in accordance with Article 110.

ARTICLE 4

1. Membership in the United Nations is open to all other peace-loving states which accept the obligations contained in the present Charter and, in the judgment of the Organization, are able and willing to carry out these obligations.

2. The admission of any such state to membership in the United Nations will be effected by a decision of the General Assembly upon the recommendation of the Security Council.

ARTICLE 5

A Member of the United Nations against which preventive or enforcement action has been taken by the Security Council may be suspended from the exercise of the rights and privileges of membership by the General Assembly upon the recommendation of the Security Council. The exercise of these rights and privileges may be restored by the Security Council.

ARTICLE 6

A Member of the United Nations which has persistently violated the Principles contained in the present Charter may be expelled from the Organization by the General Assembly upon the recommendation of the Security Council.

CHAPTER III   ORGANS

ARTICLE 7

1. There are established as the principal organs of the United Nations: a General Assembly, a Security Council, an Economic and Social Council, a Trusteeship Council, an International Court of Justice, and a Secretariat.
2. Such subsidiary organs as may be found necessary may be established in accordance with the present Charter.

ARTICLE 8

The United Nations shall place no restrictions on the eligibility of men and women to participate in any capacity and under conditions of equality in its principal and subsidiary organs.

CHAPTER IV   THE GENERAL ASSEMBLY

Composition

ARTICLE 9

1. The General Assembly shall consist of all the Members of the United Nations.
2. Each Member shall have not more than five representatives in the General Assembly.

Function and Powers

ARTICLE 10

The General Assembly may discuss any questions or any matters within the scope of the present Charter or relating to the powers and functions of any organs provided for in the present Charter, and except as provided in Article 12, may make recommendations to the Members of the United Nations or to the Security Council or to both on any such questions or matters.

ARTICLE 11

1. The General Assembly may consider the general principles of cooperation in the maintenance of international peace and security, including the principles governing disarmament and the regulation of armaments, and may make recommendations with regard to such principles to the Members or to the Security Council or to both.

2. The General Assembly may discuss any questions relating to the maintenance of international peace and security brought before it by any Member of the United Nations, or by the Security Council, or by a state which is not a Member of the United Nations in accordance with Article 35, paragraph 2, and, except as provided in Article 12, may make recommendations with regard to any such questions to the state or states concerned or to the Security Council or to both. Any such questions on which action is necessary shall be referred to the Security Council by the General Assembly either before or after discussion.

3. The General Assembly may call the attention of the Security Council to situations which are likely to endanger international peace and security.

4. The powers of the General Assembly set forth in this Article shall not limit the general scope of Article 10.

ARTICLE 12

1. While the Security Council is exercising in respect of any dispute or situation the functions assigned to it in the present Charter, the General Assembly shall not make any recommendation with regard to that dispute or situation unless the Security Council so requests.

2. The Secretary-General, with the consent of the Security Council, shall notify the General Assembly at each session of any matters relative to the maintenance of international peace and security which are being dealt with by the Security Council and shall similarly notify the General Assembly, or the Members of the United Nations if the General Assembly is not in session, immediately the Security Council ceases to deal with such matters.

ARTICLE 13

1. The General Assembly shall initiate studies and make recommendations for the purpose of:

a. promoting international cooperation in the political field and encouraging the progressive development of international law and its codification;

b. promoting international cooperation in the economic, social, cultural, educational, and health fields, and assisting in the realization of human rights and fundamental freedoms for all without distinction as to race, sex, language, or religion.

2. The further responsibilities, functions, and powers of the General Assembly with respect to matters mentioned in paragraph 1 (b) above are set forth in Chapters IX and X.

ARTICLE 14

Subject to the provisions of Article 12, the General Assembly may recommend measures for the peaceful adjustment of any situation, regardless of origin, which it deems likely to impair the general welfare or friendly relations among nations, including situations resulting from a violation of the provisions of the present Charter setting forth the Purposes and Principles of the United Nations.

ARTICLE 15

1. The General Assembly shall receive and consider annual and special reports from the Security Council; these reports shall include an account of the measures that the Security Council has decided upon or taken to maintain international peace and security.

2. The General Assembly shall receive and consider reports from the other organs of the United Nations.

ARTICLE 16

The General Assembly shall perform such functions with respect to the international trusteeship system as are assigned to it under Chapters XII and XIII, including the approval of the trusteeship agreements for areas not designated as strategic.

ARTICLE 17

1. The General Assembly shall consider and approve the budget of the Organization.

2. The expenses of the Organization shall be borne by the Members as apportioned by the General Assembly.

3. The General Assembly shall consider and approve any financial and budgetary arrangements with specialized agencies referred to in Article 57 and shall examine the administrative budgets of such specialized agencies with a view to making recommendations to the agencies concerned.

Voting

ARTICLE 18

1. Each member of the General Assembly shall have one vote.

2. Decisions of the General Assembly on important questions shall be made by a two-thirds majority of the members present and voting. These questions shall include: recommendations with respect to the maintenance of international peace and security, the election of the non-permament members of the Security Council, the election of the members of the Economic and Social Council, the election of members of the Trusteeship Council in accordance with paragraph 1 (c) of Article 86, the admission of new Members to the United Nations, the suspension of the rights and privileges of membership, the expulsion of Members, questions relating to the operation of the trusteeship system, and budgetary questions.

3. Decisions on other questions, including the determination of additional categories of questions to be decided by a two-thirds majority, shall be made by a majority of the members present and voting.

ARTICLE 19

A Member of the United Nations which is in arrears in the payment of its financial contributions to the Organization shall have no vote in the General Assembly if the amount of its arrears equals or exceeds the amount of the contributions due from it for the preceding two full years. The General Assembly may, nevertheless, permit such a Member to vote if it is satisfied that the failure to pay is due to conditions beyond the control of the Member.

Procedure

ARTICLE 20

The General Assembly shall meet in regular annual sessions and in such special sessions as occasion may require. Special sessions shall be convoked by the Secretary-General at the request of the Security Council or of a majority of the Members of the United Nations.

ARTICLE 21

The General Assembly shall adopt its own rules of procedure. It shall elect its President for each session.

ARTICLE 22

The General Assembly may establish such subsidiary organs as it deems necessary for the performance of its functions.

CHAPTER V   THE SECURITY COUNCIL

Composition

ARTICLE 23

1. The Security Council shall consist of eleven Members of the United Nations. The Republic of China, France, the Union of Soviet Socialist Republics, the United Kingdom of Great Britain and Northern Ireland, and the United States of America shall be permanent members of the Security Council. The General Assembly shall elect six other Members of the United Nations to be non-permanent members of the Security Council, due regard being specially paid, in the first instance to the contribution of Members of the United Nations to the maintenance of international peace and security and to the other purposes of the Organization, and also to equitable geographical distribution.

2. The non-permanent members of the Security Council shall be elected for a term of two years. In the first election of the non-permanent members, however, three shall be chosen for a term of one year. A retiring member shall not be eligible for immediate re-election.

3. Each member of the Security Council shall have one representative.

Functions and Powers

ARTICLE 24

1. In order to ensure prompt and effective action by the United Nations, its Members confer on the Security Council primary responsibility for the maintenance of international peace and security, and agree that in carrying out its duties under this responsibility the Security Council acts on their behalf.

2. In discharging these duties the Security Council shall act in accordance with the Purposes and Principles of the United Nations. The specific powers granted to the Security Council for the discharge of these duties are laid down in Chapters VI, VII, VIII, and XII.

3. The Security Council shall submit annual and, when necessary, special reports to the General Assembly for its consideration.

ARTICLE 25

The Members of the United Nations agree to accept and carry out the decisions of the Security Council in accordance with the present Charter.

ARTICLE 26

In order to promote the establishment and maintenance of international peace and security with the least diversion for armaments of the world's human and economic resources, the Security Council shall be responsible for formulating, with the assistance of the Military Staff Committee referred to in Article 47, plans to be submitted to the Members of the United Nations for the establishment of a system for the regulation of armaments.

Voting

ARTICLE 27

1. Each member of the Security Council shall have one vote.
2. Decisions of the Security Council on procedural matters shall be made by an affirmative vote of seven members.
3. Decisions of the Security Council on all other matters shall be made by an affirmative vote of seven members including the concurring votes of the permanent members; provided that, in decisions under Chapter VI, and under paragraph 3 of Article 52, a party to a dispute shall abstain from voting.

Procedure

ARTICLE 28

1. The Security Council shall be so organized as to be able to function continuously. Each member of the Security Council shall for this purpose be represented at all times at the seat of the Organization.
2. The Security Council shall hold periodic meetings at which each of its members may, if it so desires, be represented by a member of the government or by some other specially designated representative.
3. The Security Council may hold meetings at such places other than the seat of the Organization as in its judgment will best facilitate its work.

ARTICLE 29

The Security Council may establish such subsidiary organs as it deems necessary for the performance of its functions.

ARTICLE 30

The Security Council shall adopt its own rules of procedure, including the method of selecting its President.

ARTICLE 31

Any Member of the United Nations which is not a member of the Security Council may participate, without vote, in the discussion of any question brought before the Security Council whenever the latter considers that the interests of that Member are specially affected.

ARTICLE 32

Any Member of the United Nations which is not a member of the Security Council or any state which is not a Member of the United Nations, if it is a party to a dispute under consideration by the Security Council, shall be invited to participate, without vote, in the discussion relating to the dispute. The Security Council shall lay down such conditions as it deems just for the participation of a state which is not a Member of the United Nations.

CHAPTER VI   PACIFIC SETTLEMENT OF DISPUTES

ARTICLE 33

1. The parties to any dispute, the continuance of which is likely to endanger the maintenance of international peace and security, shall first of all, seek a solution by negotiation, enquiry, mediation, conciliation, arbitration, judicial settlement, resort to regional agencies or arrangements, or other peaceful means of their own choice.

2. The Security Council shall, when it deems necessary, call upon the parties to settle their dispute by such means.

ARTICLE 34

The Security Council may investigate any dispute, or any situation which might lead to international friction or give rise to a dispute, in order to determine whether the continuance of the dispute or situation is likely to endanger the maintenance of international peace and security.

ARTICLE 35

1. Any Member of the United Nations may bring any dispute, or any situation of the nature referred to in Article 34, to the attention of the Security Council or of the General Assembly.

2. A state which is not a Member of the United Nations may bring to the attention of the Security Council or of the General Assembly any dispute to which it is a party if it accepts in advance, for the purposes of the dispute, the obligations of pacific settlement provided in the present Charter.

3. The proceedings of the General Assembly in respect of matters brought to its attention under this Article will be subject to the provisions of Articles 11 and 12.

ARTICLE 36

1. The Security Council may, at any stage of a dispute of the nature referred to in Article 33 or of a situation of like nature, recommend appropriate procedures or methods of adjustment.

2. The Security Council should take into consideration any procedures for the settlement of the dispute which have already been adopted by the parties.

3. In making recommendations under this Article the Security Council should also take into consideration that legal disputes should as a general rule be referred by the parties to the International Court of Justice in accordance with the provisions of the Statute of the Court.

ARTICLE 37

1. Should the parties to a dispute of the nature referred to in Article 33 fail to settle it by the means indicated in that Article, they shall refer it to the Security Council.

2. If the Security Council deems that the continuance of the dispute is in fact likely to endanger the maintenance of international peace and security, it shall decide whether to take action under Article 36 or to recommend such terms of settlement as it may consider appropriate.

ARTICLE 38

Without prejudice to the provisions of Articles 33 to 37, the Security Council may, if all the parties to any dispute so request, make recommendations to the parties with a view to a pacific settlement of the dispute.

CHAPTER VII ACTION WITH RESPECT TO THREATS TO THE PEACE, BREACHES OF THE PEACE, AND ACTS OF AGGRESSION

ARTICLE 39

The Security Council shall determine the existence of any threat to the peace, breach of the peace, or act of aggression and shall make recommenda-.

tions, or decide what measures shall be taken in accordance with Articles 41 and 42, to maintain or restore international peace and security.

ARTICLE 40

In order to prevent an aggravation of the situation, the Security Council may, before making the recommendations or deciding upon the measures provided for in Article 39, call upon the parties concerned to comply with such provisional measures as it deems necessary or desirable. Such provisional measures shall be without prejudice to the rights, claims, or position of the parties concerned. The Security Council shall duly take account of failure to comply with such provisional measures.

ARTICLE 41

The Security Council may decide what measures not involving the use of armed force are to be employed the give effect to its decisions, and it may call upon the Members of the United Nations to apply such measures. These may include complete or partial interruption of economic relations and of rail, sea, air, postal, telegraphic, radio, and other means of communication, and the severance of diplomatic relations.

ARTICLE 42

Should the Security Council consider that measures provided for in Article 41 would be inadequate or have proved to be inadequate, it may take such action by air, sea, or land forces as may be necessary to maintain or restore international peace and security. Such action may include demonstrations, blockade, and other operations by air, sea, or land forces of Members of the United Nations.

ARTICLE 43

1. All Members of the United Nations, in order to contribute to the maintenance of international peace and security, undertake to make available to the Security Council, on its call and in accordance with a special agreement or agreements, armed forces, assistance, and facilities, including rights of passage, necessary for the purpose of maintaining international peace and security.

2. Such agreement or agreements shall govern the numbers and types of forces, their degree of readiness and general location, and the nature of the facilities and assistance to be provided.

3. The agreement or agreements shall be negotiated as soon as possible on the initiative of the Security Council. They shall be concluded between the Security Council and Members or between the Security Council and groups of

Members and shall be subject to ratification by the signatory states in accordance with their respective constitutional processes.

ARTICLE 44

When the Security Council has decided to use force it shall, before calling upon a Member not represented on it to provide armed forces in fulfillment of the obligations assumed under Article 43, invite that Member, if the Member so desires, to participate in the decisions of the Security Council concerning the employment of contingents of that Member's armed forces.

ARTICLE 45

In order to enable the United Nations to take urgent military measures, Members shall hold immediately available national air-force contingents for combined international enforcement action. The strength and degree of readiness of these contingents and plans for their combined action shall be determined, within the limits laid down in the special agreement or agreements referred to in Article 43, by the Security Council with the assistance of the Military Staff Committee.

ARTICLE 46

Plans for the application of armed force shall be made by the Security Council with the assistance of the Military Staff Committee.

ARTICLE 47

1. There shall be established a Military Staff Committee to advise and assist the Security Council on all questions relating to the Security Council's military requirements for the maintenance of international peace and security, the employment and command of forces placed at its disposal, the regulation of armaments, and possible disarmament.

2. The Military Staff Committee shall consist of the Chiefs of Staff of the permanent members of the Security Council or their representatives. Any Member of the United Nations not permanently represented on the Committee shall be invited by the Committee to be associated with it when the efficient discharge of the Committee's responsibilities requires the participation of that Member in its work.

3. The Military Staff Committee shall be responsible under the Security Council for the strategic direction of any armed forces placed at the disposal of the Security Council. Questions relating to the command of such forces shall be worked out subsequently.

4. The Military Staff Committee, with the authorization of the Security

Council and after consultation with appropriate regional agencies, may establish regional subcommittees.

ARTICLE 48

1. The action required to carry out the decisions of the Security Council for the maintenance of international peace and security shall be taken by all the Members of the United Nations or by some of them, as the Security Council may determine.

2. Such decisions shall be carried out by the Members of the United Nations directly and through their action in the appropriate international agencies of which they are members.

ARTICLE 49

The Members of the United Nations shall join in affording mutual assistance in carrying out the measures decided upon by the Security Council.

ARTICLE 50

If preventive or enforcement measures against any state are taken by the Security Council, any other state, whether a Member of the United Nations or not, which finds itself confronted with special economic problems arising from the carrying out of those measures shall have the right to consult the Security Council with regard to a solution of those problems.

ARTICLE 51

Nothing in the present Charter shall impair the inherent right of individual or collective self-defense if an armed attack occurs against a Member of the United Nations, until the Security Council has taken the measures necessary to maintain international peace and security. Measures taken by Members in the exercise of this right of self-defense shall be immediately reported to the Security Council and shall not in any way affect the authority and responsibility of the Security Council under the present Charter to take at any time such action as it deems necessary in order to maintain or restore international peace and security.

CHAPTER VIII   REGIONAL ARRANGEMENTS

ARTICLE 52

1. Nothing in the present Charter precludes the existence of regional arrangements or agencies for dealing with such matters relating to the main-

tenance of international peace and security as are appropriate for regional action, provided that such arrangements or agencies and their activities are consistent with the Purposes and Principles of the United Nations.

2. The Members of the United Nations entering into such arrangements or constituting such agencies shall make every effort to achieve pacific settlement of local disputes through such regional arrangements or by such regional agencies before referring them to the Security Council.

3. The Security Council shall encourage the development of pacific settlement of local disputes through such regional arrangements or by such regional agencies either on the initiative of the states concerned or by reference from the Security Council.

4. This Article in no way impairs the application of Articles 34 and 35.

ARTICLE 53

1. The Security Council shall, where appropriate, utilize such regional arrangements or agencies for enforcement action under its authority. But no enforcement action shall be taken under regional arrangements or by regional agencies without the authorization of the Security Council, with the exception of measures against any enemy state, as defined in paragraph 2 of this Article, provided for pursuant to Article 107 or in regional arrangements directed against renewal of aggressive policy on the part of any such state, until such time as the Organization may, on request of the Governments concerned, be charged with the responsibility for preventing further aggression by such a state.

2. The term enemy state as used in paragraph 1 of this Article applies to any state which during the Second World War has been an enemy of any signatory of the present Charter.

ARTICLE 54

The Security Council shall at all times be kept fully informed of activities undertaken or in contemplation under regional arrangements or by regional agencies for the maintenance of international peace and security.

CHAPTER IX   INTERNATIONAL ECONOMIC AND SOCIAL COOPERATION

ARTICLE 55

With a view to the creation of conditions of stability and well-being which are necessary for peaceful and friendly relations among nations based on respect for the principle of equal rights and self-determination of peoples, the United Nations shall promote:

a. higher standards of living, full employment, and conditions of economic and social progress and development;

b. solutions of international economic, social, health, and related problems; and international cultural and educational cooperation; and

c. universal respect for, and observance of, human rights and fundamental freedoms for all without distinction as to race, sex, language, or religion.

ARTICLE 56

All Members pledge themselves to take joint and separate action in cooperation with the Organization for the achievement of the purposes set forth in Article 55.

ARTICLE 57

1. The various specialized agencies, established by intergovernmental agreement and having wide international responsibilities, as defined in their basic instruments, in economic, social, cultural, educational, health, and related fields, shall be brought into relationship with the United Nations in accordance with the provisions of Article 63.

2. Such agencies thus brought into relationship with the United Nations are hereinafter referred to as specialized agencies.

ARTICLE 58

The Organization shall make recommendations for the coordination of the policies and activities of the specialized agencies.

ARTICLE 59

The Organization shall, where appropriate, initiate negotiations among the states concerned for the creation of any new specialized agencies required for the accomplishment of the purposes set forth in Article 55.

ARTICLE 60

Responsibility for the discharge of the functions of the Organization set forth in this Chapter shall be vested in the General Assembly and, under the authority of the General Assembly, in the Economic and Social Council, which shall have for this purpose the powers set forth in Chapter X.

CHAPTER X   THE ECONOMIC AND SOCIAL COUNCIL

Composition

ARTICLE 61

1. The Economic and Social Council shall consist of eighteen Members of the United Nations elected by the General Assembly.

2. Subject to the provisions of paragraph 3, six members of the Economic and Social Council shall be elected each year for a term of three years. A retiring member shall be eligible for immediate re-election.

3. At the first election, eighteen members of the Economic and Social Council shall be chosen. The term of office of six members so chosen shall expire at the end of one year, and of six other members at the end of two years, in accordance with arrangements made by the General Assembly.

4. Each member of the Economic and Social Council shall have one representative.

Functions and Powers

ARTICLE 62

1. The Economic and Social Council may make or initiate studies and reports with respect to international economic, social, cultural, educational, health, and related matters and may make recommendations with respect to any such matters to the General Assembly, to the Members of the United Nations, and to the specialized agencies concerned.

2. It may make recommendations for the purpose of promoting respect for, and observance of, human rights and fundamental freedoms for all.

3. It may prepare draft conventions for submission to the General Assembly, with respect to matters falling within its competence.

4. It may call, in accordance with the rules prescribed by the United Nations, international conferences on matters falling within its competence.

ARTICLE 63

1. The Economic and Social Council may enter into agreements with any of the agencies referred to in Article 57, defining the terms on which the agency concerned shall be brought into relationship with the United Nations. Such agreements shall be subject to approval by the General Assembly.

2. It may coordinate the activities of the specialized agencies through consultation with and recommendations to such agencies and through recom-

mendations to the General Assembly and to the Members of the United Nations.

ARTICLE 64

1. The Economic and Social Council may take appropriate steps to obtain regular reports from the specialized agencies. It may make arrangements with the Members of the United Nations and with the specialized agencies to obtain reports on the steps taken to give effect to its own recommendations and to recommendations on matters falling within its competence made by the General Assembly.

2. It may communicate its observations on these reports to the General Assembly.

ARTICLE 65

The Economic and Social Council may furnish information to the Security Council and shall assist the Security Council upon its request.

ARTICLE 66

1. The Economic and Social Council shall perform such functions as fall within its competence in connection with the carrying out of the recommendations of the General Assembly.

2. It may, with the approval of the General Assembly, perform services at the request of Members of the United Nations and at the request of specialized agencies.

3. It shall perform such other functions as are specified elsewhere in the present Charter or as may be assigned to it by the General Assembly.

Voting

ARTICLE 67

1. Each member of the Economic and Social Council shall have one vote.

2. Decisions of the Economic and Social Council shall be made by a majority of the members present and voting.

Procedure

ARTICLE 68

The Economic and Social Council shall set up commissions in economic and social fields and for the promotion of human rights, and such other commissions as may be required for the performance of its functions.

ARTICLE 69

The Economic and Social Council shall invite any Member of the United Nations to participate, without vote, in its deliberations on any matter of particular concern to that Member.

ARTICLE 70

The Economic and Social Council may make arrangements for representatives of the specialized agencies to participate, without vote, in its deliberations and in those of the commissions established by it, and for its representatives to participate in the deliberations of the specialized agencies.

ARTICLE 71

The Economic and Social Council may make suitable arrangements for consultation with non-governmental organizations which are concerned with matters within its competence. Such arrangements may be made with international organizations and, where appropriate, with national organizations after consultation with the Member of the United Nations concerned.

ARTICLE 72

1. The Economic and Social Council shall adopt its own rules of procedure, including the method of selecting its President.

2. The Economic and Social Council shall meet as required in accordance with its rules, which shall include provision for the convening of meetings on the request of a majority of its members.

CHAPTER XI   DECLARATION REGARDING NON-SELF-GOVERNING TERRITORIES

ARTICLE 73

Members of the United Nations which have or assume responsibilities for the administration of territories whose peoples have not yet attained a full measure of self-government recognize the principle that the interests of the inhabitants of these territories are paramount, and accept as a sacred trust the obligation to promote to the utmost, within the system of international peace and security established by the present Charter, the well-being of the inhabitants of these territories, and, to this end:

a. to ensure, with due respect for the culture of the peoples concerned, their political, economic, social, and educational advancement, their just treatment, and their protection against abuses;

b. to develop self-government, to take due account of the political aspirations of the peoples, and to assist them in the progressive development of their free political institutions, according to the particular circumstances of each territory and its peoples and their varying stages of advancement;

c. to further international peace and security;

d. to promote constructive measures of development, to encourage research, and to cooperate with one another and, when and where appropriate, with specialized international bodies with a view to the practical achievement of the social, economic, and scientific purposes set forth in this Article; and

e. to transmit regularly to the Secretary-General for information purposes, subject to such limitation as security and constitutional considerations may require, statistical and other information of a technical nature relating to economic, social, and educational conditions in the territories for which they are respectively responsible other than those territories to which Chapters XII and XIII apply.

ARTICLE 74

Members of the United Nations also agree that their policy in respect of the territories to which this Chapter applies, no less than in respect of their metropolitan areas, must be based on the general principle of good-neighborliness, due account being taken of the interests and well-being of the rest of the world, in social, economic, and commercial matters.

CHAPTER XII   INTERNATIONAL TRUSTEESHIP SYSTEM

ARTICLE 75

The United Nations shall establish under its authority an international trusteeship system for the administration and supervision of such territories as may be placed thereunder by subsequent individual agreements. These territories are hereinafter referred to as trust territories.

ARTICLE 76

The basic objectives of the trusteeship system, in accordance with the Purposes of the United Nations laid down in Article 1 of the present Charter, shall be:

a. to further international peace and security;

b. to promote the political, economic, social, and educational advancement of the inhabitants of the trust territories, and their progressive development towards self-government or independence as may be appropriate to the particular circumstances of each territory and its peoples and the freely expressed wishes of the peoples concerned, and as may be provided by the terms of each trusteeship agreement;

c. to encourage respect for human rights and for fundamental freedoms for all without distinction as to race, sex, language, or religion, and to encourage recognition of the interdependence of the peoples of the world; and

d. to ensure equal treatment in social, economic, and commercial matters for all Members of the United Nations and their nationals, and also equal treatment for the latter in the administration of justice, without prejudice to the attainment of the foregoing objectives and subject to the provisions of Article 80.

ARTICLE 77

1. The trusteeship system shall apply to such territories in the following categories as may be placed thereunder by means of trusteeship agreements:

a. territories now held under mandate;

b. territories which may be detached from enemy states as a result of the Second World War; and

c. territories voluntarily placed under the system by states responsible for their administration.

2. It will be a matter for subsequent agreement as to which territories in the foregoing categories will be brought under the trusteeship system and upon what terms.

ARTICLE 78

The trusteeship system shall not apply to territories which have become Members of the United Nations, relationship among which shall be based on respect for the principle of sovereign equality.

ARTICLE 79

The terms of trusteeship for each territory to be placed under the trusteeship system, including any alteration or amendment, shall be agreed upon by the states directly concerned, including the mandatory power in the case of territories held under mandate by a Member of the United Nations, and shall be approved as provided for in Articles 83 and 85.

ARTICLE 80

1. Except as may be agreed upon in individual trusteeship agreements, made under Articles 77, 79, and 81, placing each territory under the trusteeship

system, and until such agreements have been concluded, nothing in this Chapter shall be construed in or of itself to alter in any manner the rights whatsoever of any states or any peoples or the terms of existing international instruments to which Members of the United Nations may respectively be parties.

2. Paragraph 1 of this Article shall not be interpreted as giving grounds for delay or postponement of the negotiation and conclusion of agreements for placing mandated and other territories under the trusteeship system as provided for in Article 77.

ARTICLE 81

The trusteeship agreement shall in each case include the terms under which the trust territory will be administered and designate the authority which will exercise the administration of the trust territory. Such authority, hereinafter called the administering authority, may be one or more states or the Organization itself.

ARTICLE 82

There may be designated, in any trusteeship agreement, a strategic area or areas which may include part or all of the trust territory to which the agreement applies, without prejudice to any special agreement or agreements made under Article 43.

ARTICLE 83

1. All functions of the United Nations relating to strategic areas, including the approval of the terms of the trusteeship agreements and of their alteration or amendment, shall be exercised by the Security Council.

2. The basic objectives set forth in Article 76 shall be applicable to the people of each strategic area.

3. The Security Council shall, subject to the provisions of the trusteeship agreements and without prejudice to security considerations, avail itself of the assistance of the Trusteeship Council to perform those functions of the United Nations under the trusteeship system relating to political, economic, social, and educational matters in the strategic areas.

ARTICLE 84

It shall be the duty of the administering authority to ensure that the trust territory shall play its part in the maintenance of international peace and security. To this end the administering authority may make use of volunteer forces, facilities, and assistance from the trust territory in carrying out the obligations towards the Security Council undertaken in this regard by the administering authority, as well as for local defense and the maintenance of law and order within the trust territory.

ARTICLE 85

1. The functions of the United Nations with regard to trusteeship agreements for all areas not designated as strategic, including the approval of the terms of the trusteeship agreements and of their alteration or amendment, shall be exercised by the General Assembly.

2. The Trusteeship Council, operating under the authority of the General Assembly, shall assist the General Assembly in carrying out these functions.

CHAPTER XIII   THE TRUSTEESHIP COUNCIL

Composition

ARTICLE 86

1. The Trusteeship Council shall consist of the following Members of the United Nations:

a. those Members administering trust territories;

b. such of those Members mentioned by name in Article 23 as are not administering trust territories; and

c. as many other Members elected for three-year terms by the General Assembly as may be necessary to ensure that the total number of members of the Trusteeship Council is equally divided between those Members of the United Nations which administer trust territories and those which do not.

2. Each member of the Trusteeship Council shall designate one specially qualified person to represent it therein.

Functions and Powers

ARTICLE 87

The General Assembly and, under its authority, the Trusteeship Council, in carrying out their functions, may:

a. consider reports submitted by the administering authority;

b. accept petitions and examine them in consultation with the administering authority;

c. provide for periodic visits to the respective trust territories at times agreed upon with the administering authority; and

d. take these and other actions in conformity with the terms of the trusteeship agreements.

ARTICLE 88

The Trusteeship Council shall formulate a questionnaire on the political, economic, social, and educational advancement of the inhabitants of each trust territory, and the administering authority for each trust territory within the competence of the General Assembly shall make an annual report to the General Assembly upon the basis of such questionnaire.

Voting

ARTICLE 89

1. Each member of the Trusteeship Council shall have one vote.
2. Decisions of the Trusteeship Council shall be made by a majority of the members present and voting.

Procedure

ARTICLE 90

1. The Trusteeship Council shall adopt its own rules of procedure, including the method of selecting its President.
2. The Trusteeship Council shall meet as required in accordance with its rules, which shall include provision for the convening of meetings on the request of a majority of its members.

ARTICLE 91

The Trusteeship Council shall, when appropriate, avail itself of the assistance of the Economic and Social Council and of the specialized agencies in regard to matters with which they are respectively concerned.

CHAPTER XIV THE INTERNATIONAL COURT OF JUSTICE

ARTICLE 92

The International Court of Justice shall be the principal judicial organ of the United Nations. It shall function in accordance with the annexed Statute, which is based upon the Statute of the Permanent Court of International Justice and forms an integral part of the present Charter.

ARTICLE 93

1. All Members of the United Nations are *ipso facto* parties to the Statute of the International Court of Justice.

2. A state which is not a Member of the United Nations may become a party to the Statute of the International Court of Justice on conditions to be determined in each case by the General Assembly upon the recommendation of the Security Council.

ARTICLE 94

1. Each Member of the United Nations undertakes to comply with the decision of the International Court of Justice in any case to which it is a party.

2. If any party to a case fails to perform the obligations incumbent upon it under a judgment rendered by the Court, the other party may have recourse to the Security Council, which may, if it deems necessary, make recommendations or decide upon measures to be taken to give effect to the judgment.

ARTICLE 95

Nothing in the present Charter shall prevent Members of the United Nations from entrusting the solution of their differences to other tribunals by virtue of agreements already in existence or which may be concluded in the future.

ARTICLE 96

1. The General Assembly or the Security Council may request the International Court of Justice to give an advisory opinion on any legal question.

2. Other organs of the United Nations and specialized agencies, which may at any time be so authorized by the General Assembly, may also request advisory opinions of the Court on legal questions arising within the scope of their activities.

CHAPTER XV THE SECRETARIAT

ARTICLE 97

The Secretariat shall comprise a Secretary-General and such staff as the Organization may require. The Secretary-General shall be appointed by the General Assembly upon the recommendation of the Security Council. He shall be the chief administrative officer of the Organization.

ARTICLE 98

The Secretary-General shall act in that capacity in all meetings of the General Assembly, of the Security Council, of the Economic and Social Council, and of the Trusteeship Council, and shall perform such other functions as are entrusted to him by these organs. The Secretary-General shall make an annual report to the General Assembly on the work of the Organization.

ARTICLE 99

The Secretary-General may bring to the attention of the Security Council any matter which in his opinion may threaten the maintenance of international peace and security.

ARTICLE 100

1. In the performance of their duties the Secretary-General and the staff shall not seek or receive instructions from any government or from any other authority external to the Organization. They shall refrain from any action which might reflect on their position as international officials responsible only to the Organization.

2. Each Member of the United Nations undertakes to respect the exclusively international character of the responsibilities of the Secretary-General and the staff and not to seek to influence them into the discharge of their responsibilities.

ARTICLE 101

1. The staff shall be appointed by the Secretary-General under regulations established by the General Assembly.

2. Appropriate staffs shall be permanently assigned to the Economic and Social Council, the Trusteeship Council, and, as required, to other organs of the United Nations. These staffs shall form a part of the Secretariat.

3. The paramount consideration in the employment of the staff and in the determination of the conditions of service shall be the necessity of securing the highest standards of efficiency, competence, and integrity. Due regard shall be paid to the importance of recruiting the staff on as wide a geographical basis as possible.

CHAPTER XVI   MISCELLANEOUS PROVISIONS

ARTICLE 102

1. Every treaty and every international agreement entered into by any

Member of the United Nations after the present Charter comes into force shall as soon as possible be registered with the Secretariat and published by it.

2. No party to any such treaty or international agreement which has not been registered in accordance with the provisions of paragraph 1 of this Article may invoke that treaty or agreement before any organ of the United Nations.

ARTICLE 103

In the event of a conflict between the obligations of the Members of the United Nations under the present Charter and their obligations under any other international agreement, their obligations under the present Charter shall prevail.

ARTICLE 104

The Organization shall enjoy in the territory of each of its Members such legal capacity as may be necessary for the exercise of its functions and the fulfillment of its purposes.

ARTICLE 105

1. The Organization shall enjoy in the territory of each of its Members such privileges and immunities as are necessary for the fulfillment of its purposes.

2. Representatives of the Members of the United Nations and officials of the Organization shall similarly enjoy such privileges and immunities as are necessary for the independent exercise of their functions in connection with the Organization.

3. The General Assembly may make recommendations with a view to determining the details of the application of paragraphs 1 and 2 of this Article or may propose conventions to the Members of the United Nations for this purpose.

CHAPTER XVII   TRANSITIONAL SECURITY ARRANGEMENTS

ARTICLE 106

Pending the coming into force of such special agreements referred to in Article 43 as in the opinion of the Security Council enable it to begin the exercise of its responsibilities under Article 42, the parties to the Four-Nation Declaration, signed at Moscow, October 30, 1943, and France, shall, in accordance with the provisions of paragraph 5 of that Declaration, consult with one another and as occasion requires with other Members of the United Nations with a view to such joint action on behalf of the Organization as may be necessary for the purpose of maintaining international peace and security.

ARTICLE 107

Nothing in the present Charter shall invalidate or preclude action, in relation to any state which during the Second World War has been an enemy of any signatory to the present Charter, taken or authorized as a result of that war by the Governments having responsibility for such action.

CHAPTER XVIII   AMENDMENTS

ARTICLE 108

Amendments to the present Charter shall come into force for all Members of the United Nations when they have been adopted by a vote of two-thirds of the members of the General Assembly and ratified in accordance with their respective constitutional processes by two-thirds of the Members of the United Nations, including all the permanent members of the Security Council.

ARTICLE 109

1. A General Conference of the Members of the United Nations for the purpose of reviewing the present Charter may be held at a date and place to be fixed by a two-thirds vote of the members of the General Assembly and by a vote of any seven members of the Security Council. Each Member of the United Nations shall have one vote in the conference.

2. Any alteration of the present Charter recommended by a two-thirds vote of the conference shall take effect when ratified in accordance with their respective constitutional processes by two-thirds of the Members of the United Nations including all the permanent members of the Security Council.

3. If such a conference has not been held before the tenth annual session of the General Assembly following the coming into force of the present Charter, the proposal to call such a conference shall be placed on the agenda of that session of the General Assembly, and the conference shall be held if so decided by a majority vote of the members of the General Assembly and by a vote of any seven members of the Security Council.

CHAPTER XIX   RATIFICATION AND SIGNATURE

ARTICLE 110

1. The present Charter shall be ratified by the signatory states in accordance with their respective constitutional processes.

2. The ratifications shall be deposited with the Government of the United States of America, which shall notify all the signatory states of each deposit as well as the Secretary-General of the Organization when he has been appointed.

3. The present Charter shall come into force upon the deposit of ratifications by the Republic of China, France, the Union of Soviet Socialist Republics, the United Kingdom of Great Britain and Northern Ireland, and the United States of America, and by a majority of the other signatory states. A protocol of the ratifications deposited shall thereupon be drawn up by the Government of the United States of America which shall communicate copies thereof to all the signatory states.

4. The states signatory to the present Charter which ratify it after it has come into force will become original Members of the United Nations on the date of the deposit of their respective ratifications.

ARTICLE 111

The present Charter, of which the Chinese, French, Russian, English, and Spanish texts are equally authentic, shall remain deposited in the archives of the Government of the United States of America. Duly certified copies thereof shall be transmitted by that Government to the Governments of the other signatory states.

IN FAITH WHEREOF the representatives of the Governments of the United Nations have signed the present Charter.

DONE at the city of San Francisco the twenty-sixth day of June, one thousand nine hundred and forty-five.

Protocol of Entry into Force of the Amendments to Articles 23, 27 and 61 of the Charter of the United Nations Adopted by the General Assembly Resolutions 1991 A and B (XVIII) of 17 December 1963

Whereas Article 108 of the Charter of the United Nations provides as follows:

Article 108

Amendments to the present Charter shall come into force for all Members of the United Nations when they have been adopted by a vote of two thirds of the members of the General Assembly and ratified in accordance with their respective constitutional processes by two thirds of the Members of the United Nations, including all the permanent members of the Security Council,

Whereas the General Assembly of the United Nations adopted on 17 December 1963, in accordance with the said Article 108, the amendments to Articles 23, 27 and 61 of the Charter of the United Nations as set forth in resolutions 1991 A and B (XVIII),

Whereas the requirements of the said Article 108 with respect to the ratification of the above-mentioned amendments were fulfilled by 31 August 1965, as shown in the Annex to this Protocol, and the said amendments entered into force on that day for all Members of the United Nations,

And whereas the text of Articles 23, 27 and 61 of the Charter of the United Nations as amended reads as follows:

Article 23

1. The Security Council shall consist of fifteen Members of the United Nations. The Republic of China, France, the Union of Soviet Socialist Republics, the United Kingdom of Great Britain and Northern Ireland, and the United States of America shall be permanent members of the Security Council. The General Assembly shall elect ten other Members of the United Nations to be non-permanent members of the Security Council, due regard being specially paid, in the first instance to the contribution of Members of the United Nations to the maintenance of international peace and security and to the other purposes of the Organization, and also to equitable geographical distribution.

2. The non-permanent members of the Security Council shall be elected for a term of two years. In the first election of the non-permanent members after the increase of the membership of the Security Council from eleven to fifteen, two of the four additional members shall be chosen for a term of one year. A retiring member shall not be eligible for immediate re-election.

3. Each member of the Security Council shall have one representative.

Article 27

1. Each member of the Security Council shall have one vote.

2. Decisions of the Security Council on procedural matters shall be made by an affirmative vote of nine members.

3. Decisions of the Security Council on all other matters shall be made by an affirmative vote of nine members including the concurring votes of the permanent members; provided that, in decisions under Chapter VI, and under paragraph 3 of Article 52, a party to a dispute shall abstain from voting.

Article 61

1. The Economic and Social Council shall consist of twenty-seven Members of the United Nations elected by the General Assembly.

2. Subject to the provisions of paragraph 3, nine members of the Economic and Social Council shall be elected each year for a term of

three years. A retiring member shall be eligible for immediate re-election.

3. At the first election after the increase in the membership of the Economic and Social Council from eighteen to twenty-seven members, in addition to the members elected in place of the six members whose term of office expires at the end of that year, nine additional members shall be elected. Of these nine additional members, the term of office of three members so elected shall expire at the end of one year, and of three other members at the end of two years, in accordance with arrangements made by the General Assembly.

4. Each member of the Economic and Social Council shall have one representative.

Now, therefore, I, U Thant, Secretary-General of the United Nations, sign this Protocol in two original copies in the Chinese, English, French, Russian and Spanish languages, of which one shall be deposited in the archives of the Secretariat of the United Nations and the other transmitted to the Government of the United States of America as the depositary of the Charter of the United Nations. Copies of this Protocol shall be communicated to all Members of the United Nations.

Done at the headquarters of the United Nations, New York, this thirty-first day of August, one thousand nine hundred and sixty-five.

References

CHAPTER 1 THE INTERNATIONAL POLITICAL SYSTEM

Aron, Raymond, *The Century of Total War* (Garden City, N.Y.: Doubleday & Company, 1954).

Boulding, Kenneth E., *The Meaning of the 20th Century* (New York: Harper & Row, 1965).

Carr, Edward H., *The Twenty Years' Crisis, 1919–1939* (New York: The Macmillan Company, 1948).

Dahl, Robert A., *Modern Political Analysis* (Englewood Cliffs, N.J.: Prentice-Hall, 1963).

Duchacek, Ivo D., *Conflict and Cooperation Among Nations* (New York: Holt, Rinehart and Winston, 1960).

Herz, John H., *International Politics in the Atomic Age* (New York: Columbia University Press, 1959).

"The International Political System: Theoretical Essays," *World Politics*, Special Issue, Vol. XIV, No. 1, October 1961.

Lanyi, George A., and Wilson C. McWilliams, *Crisis and Continuity in World Politics: Readings in International Relations* (New York: Random House, 1966).

Niebuhr, Reinhold, *The Structure of Nations and Empires* (New York: Charles Scribner's Sons, 1959).

Wright, Quincy, *The Study of International Relations* (New York: Appleton-Century-Crofts, 1955).

CHAPTER 2 TOWARD A THEORY OF INTERNATIONAL POLITICS

Fox, William T. R. (ed.), *Theoretical Aspects of International Relations* (Notre Dame: University of Notre Dame Press, 1959).

Hoffmann, Stanley (ed.), *Contemporary Theory in International Relations* (Englewood Cliffs, N.J.: Prentice-Hall, 1960).

Kaplan, Morton A., *System and Process in International Politics* (New York: John Wiley & Sons, 1960).

Liska, George, *International Equilibrium* (Cambridge, Mass.: Harvard University Press, 1957).

Machiavelli, Niccolo, *The Prince and the Discourses* (New York: Random House, 1950).

McClelland, Charles A., *Theory and the International System* (New York: The Macmillan Company, 1966).

Morgenthau, Hans J., *Politics Among Nations*, 3rd ed. (New York: Alfred A. Knopf, 1960).

Rosecrance, Richard N., *Action and Reaction in World Politics: International Systems in Perspective* (Boston: Little, Brown and Company, 1963).

Rosenau, James N. (ed.), *International Politics and Foreign Policy: A Reader in Research and Theory* (New York: The Free Press of Glencoe, 1961).

Schelling, Thomas C., *The Strategy of Conflict* (Cambridge, Mass.: Harvard University Press, 1960).

Snyder, Richard C., H. W. Bruck, and Burton Sapin (eds.), *Foreign Policy Decision-Making: An Approach to the Study of International Politics* (New York: The Free Press of Glencoe, 1962).

Thompson, Kenneth W., *Political Realism and the Crisis in World Politics* (Princeton, N.J.: Princeton University Press, 1959).

Waltz, Kenneth N., *Man, the State, and War* (New York: Columbia University Press, 1959).

CHAPTER 3 ATTITUDES, BELIEFS, AND INTERNATIONAL POLITICS

Benedict, Ruth, *Patterns of Culture* (Boston: Houghton Mifflin Company, 1959).

Brzezinski, Zbigniew K., *Ideology and Power in Soviet Politics* (New York: Frederick A. Praeger, 1962).

Cohen, Carl (ed.), *Communism, Fascism, Democracy: The Theoretical Foundations* (New York: Random House, 1962).

Corbett, Percy E., *Morals, Law and Power in International Relations* (Los Angeles: John Randolph Haynes and Dora Haynes Foundation, 1956).

Etzioni, Amitai and Eva (eds.), *Social Change: Sources, Patterns, and Consequences* (New York: Basic Books, 1964).

Kautsky, John H. (ed.), *Political Change in Underdeveloped Countries: Nationalism and Communism* (New York: John Wiley & Sons, 1962).

Klineberg, Otto, *The Human Dimension in International Relations* (New York: Holt, Rinehart and Winston, 1964).

Lasswell, Harold D., *Psychopathology and Politics* (New York: The Viking Press, 1960).

——, and Abraham Kaplan, *Power and Society* (New Haven: Yale University Press, 1950).

——, and Daniel Lerner (eds.), *World Revolutionary Elites: Studies in Coercive Ideological Movements* (Cambridge, Mass.: M.I.T. Press, 1965).

Lippmann, Walter, *Public Opinion* (New York: The Macmillan Company, 1921).

Lerner, Daniel, *The Passing of Traditional Society: Modernizing the Middle East* (New York: The Free Press of Glencoe, 1964).

Niebuhr, Reinhold, *Moral Man and Immoral Society* (New York: Charles Scribner's Sons, 1960).

Pye, Lucian, *Aspects of Political Development* (Boston: Little, Brown and Company, 1966).

——, *Politics, Personality and Nation-Building* (New Haven: Yale University Press, 1962).

United States Senate, Committee on Foreign Relations, *United States Foreign Policy*, Study No. 10, "Ideology and Foreign Affairs," prepared by the Center for International Affairs, Harvard University (86th Congress, 2nd Session, Washington: GPO, 1960).

United States Senate, Committee on Foreign Relations, *United States Foreign Policy*, Study No. 12, "Economic, Social and Political Change in the Underdeveloped Countries and its Implications for United States Policy," prepared by the Center for International Studies, M.I.T. (86th Congress, 2nd Session, Washington: GPO, 1960).

CHAPTER 4 NATIONALISM AS A FORCE IN INTERNATIONAL POLITICS

Barghoorn, Frederick C., *Soviet Russian Nationalism* (New York: Oxford University Press, 1956).

Bossenbrock, William J. (ed.), *Mid-Twentieth Century Nationalism* (Detroit: Wayne University Press, 1965).

Brzezinski, Zbigniew K., *The Soviet Bloc: Unity and Conflict* (Cambridge, Mass.: Harvard University Press, 1960).

Carr, Edward H., *Nationalism and After* (New York: St. Martin's Press, 1945).

Coleman, James S., and Carl G. Rosberg, Jr. (eds.) *Political Parties and National Integration in Tropical Africa* (Berkeley: University of California Press, 1965).

Deutsch, Karl W., *Nationalism and Social Communication* (New York: John Wiley & Sons, 1953).

Eban, Abba, *The Tide of Nationalism* (New York: Horizon, 1959).

Emerson, Rupert, *From Empire to Nation* (Cambridge, Mass.: Harvard University Press, 1960).

Kohn, Hans, *Nationalism: Its Meaning and History* (Princeton, N.J.: Princeton University Press, 1955).

——, and Wallace Sokolsky, *African Nationalism in the Twentieth Century* (Princeton, N.J.: Van Nostrand, 1965).

Laqueur, Walter Z., *Communism and Nationalism in the Middle East* (New York: Frederick A. Praeger, 1956).

Shafer, Boyd C., *Nationalism: Myth and Reality* (New York: Harcourt, Brace & World, 1955).

Shepherd, George W., Jr., *The Politics of African Nationalism: Challenge to American Policy* (New York: Frederick A. Praeger, 1962).

United States Senate, Committee on Foreign Relations, *United States Foreign Policy*, Study No. 10, "Ideology and Foreign Affairs," prepared by the Center for International Affairs, Harvard University (86th Congress, 2nd Session, Washington: GPO, 1960).

Whitaker, Arthur P., *Nationalism in Latin America* (Gainesville: University of Florida Press, 1962).

Ward, Barbara, *Nationalism and Ideology* (New York: W. W. Norton & Company, 1966).

CHAPTER 5   IMPERIALISM, COLONIALISM, AND ANTICOLONIALISM

Barnett, A. Doak, *Communist Strategies in Asia* (New York: Frederick A. Praeger, 1963).

Brzezinski, Zbigniew K., *The Soviet Bloc: Unity and Conflict* (Cambridge, Mass.: Harvard University Press, 1960).

——, (ed.), *Africa and the Communist World* (Stanford: Stanford University Press, 1963).

Cooley, J. K., *East Wind over Africa: Red China's African Offensive* (New York: Walker, 1965).

Easton, Stewart C., *The Twilight of European Colonialism* (New York: Holt, Rinehart and Winston, 1960).

Emerson, Rupert, *From Empire to Nation* (Cambridge, Mass.: Harvard University Press, 1960).

Hobson, J. A., *Imperialism, A Study*, 3rd ed. (London: Allen and Unwin, 1938).

Niebuhr, Reinhold, *The Structure of Nations and Empires* (New York: Charles Scribner's Sons, 1959).

Snyder, Louis L. (ed.), *The Imperialism Reader* (Princeton, N.J.: Van Nostrand, 1962).

United States Senate, Committee on Foreign Relations, *United States Foreign Policy*, Study No. 12, "Economic, Social and Political Change in the Underdeveloped Countries and Its Implications for United States Policy," prepared by the Center for International Studies, M.I.T. (86th Congress, 2nd Session, Washington: GPO, 1960).

Wainhouse, David W., *Remnants of Empire: The United Nations and the End of Colonialism* (New York: Harper & Row, 1964). For the Council on Foreign Relations.

Ward, Barbara, *Five Ideas That Change the World* (New York: W. W. Norton & Company, 1959).

CHAPTER 6   PHYSICAL ENVIRONMENT AND THE STATE

Bidwell, Percy W., *Raw Materials, A Study of American Policy* (New York: Harper & Row, 1958).

Carlson, Lucile, *Geography and World Politics* (Englewood Cliffs, N.J.: Prentice-Hall, 1958).

Earle, Edward M:, *Makers of Modern Strategy* (Princeton, N.J.: Princeton University Press, 1952).

Gyorgy, Andrew, *Geopolitics, The New German Science* (Berkeley: University of California Press, 1944).

Jackson, William A. D., *Politics and Geographic Relationships* (Englewood Cliffs, N.J.: Prentice-Hall, 1964).

James, Preston E., *A Geography of Man*, 2nd ed. (Boston: Ginn and Company, 1959).

Mackinder, Halford J., *Democratic Ideals and Reality* (New York: W. W. Norton & Company, 1962).

Mouzon, Olin T., *International Resources and National Policy* (New York: Harper & Row, 1959).

Sprout, Harold H. and Margaret Sprout, *Foundations of International Politics* (Princeton, N.J.: Van Nostrand, 1962).

——, *The Ecological Perspective on Human Affairs with Special Reference to International Politics* (Princeton, N.J.: Princeton University Press, 1965).

Spykman, Nicholas J., *The Geography of the Peace* (New York: Harcourt, Brace & World, 1944).

Weigert, Hans W., *et al., Principles of Political Geography* (New York: Appleton-Century-Crofts, 1957).

CHAPTER 7   POPULATION AND WORLD POLITICS

Brown, Lester R., *Increasing World Food Output: Problems and Prospects* (Washington: U.S. Department of Agriculture, Economic Research Service, 1965).

Cipolla, Carlo M., *The Economic History of World Population*, rev. ed. (Baltimore: Penguin Books, 1964).

Clarke, John I., *Population Geography* (London: Pergamon Press, 1965).

Freedman, Ronald (ed.), *Population: The Vital Revolution* (Garden City, N.Y.: Doubleday & Company, 1964).

Hauser, Philip M. (ed.), *Population and World Politics* (New York: The Free Press of Glencoe, 1958).

—— (ed.), *The Population Dilemma* (Englewood Cliffs, N.J.: Prentice-Hall, 1963). For the American Assembly.

——, *World Population Problems* (New York: The Foreign Policy Association, "Headline Series, No. 174," December 1965).

Mudd, Stuart (ed.), *The Population Crisis and the Use of World Resources* (Bloomington: Indiana University Press, 1964).

Ng, Larry K. (ed.), *The Population Crisis: Implications and Plans for Action* (Bloomington: Indiana University Press, 1965).

Organski, Katherine, and A. F. K. Organski, *Population and World Power* (New York: Alfred A. Knopf, 1961).

Population Bulletin. Published monthly by the Population Reference Bureau, Inc.

Russell, Sir John E., *World Population and World Food Supplies* (London: Allen and Unwin, 1954).

Sauvey, Alfred, *Fertility and Survival: Population Problems From Malthus to Mao Tse-tung* (New York: Collier Books, 1963).

Thomlinson, Ralph, *Population Dynamics: Causes and Consequences of World Demographic Change* (New York: Random House, 1965).

United Nations, Department of Economic and Social Affairs, *Provisional Report on World Population Prospects, As Assessed in 1963* (New York: United Nations, 1964).

CHAPTER 8 THE ECONOMIC BASE OF POWER AND FOREIGN POLICY

Aubrey, Henry B., *The Dollar in World Affairs* (New York: Frederick A. Praeger, 1964).

Fourastie, Jean, *The Causes of Wealth* (New York: The Free Press of Glencoe, 1960).

Galbraith, John Kenneth, *Economic Development in Perspective* (Cambridge, Mass.: Harvard University Press, 1962).

Kindleberger, Charles P., *International Economics* (Homewood, Ill.: Richard D. Irwin, 1958).

Lary, Hal B., *Problems of the United States as World Trader and Banker* (Washington, D.C.: National Bureau of Economic Research, 1963).

Millikan, Max F., and Donald L. Blackmer (eds.), *The Emerging Nations: Their Growth and United States Policy* (Boston: Little, Brown and Company, 1961).

Myrdal, G., *Beyond the Welfare State* (New Haven: Yale University Press, 1960).

Nurkse, R., *Problems of Capital Formation in Underdeveloped Countries* (New York: Oxford University Press, 1955).

Organski, A. F. K., *The Stages of Political Development* (New York: Alfred A. Knopf, 1965).

Rostow, W. W., *The Stages of Economic Growth* (New York: Cambridge University Press, 1960).

Tinbergen, Jan, *Shaping the World Economy* (New York: The Twentieth Century Fund, 1962).

Triffin, R. F., *Gold and the Dollar Crisis* (New Haven: Yale University Press, 1960).

Williams, John H., *Economic Stability in a Changing World* (New York: Oxford University Press, 1953).

CHAPTER 9 THE TECHNOLOGICAL FACTOR

Bloomfield, Lincoln P. (ed.), *Outer Space: Prospects for Man and Society* (Englewood Cliffs, N.J.: Prentice-Hall, 1962). For the American Assembly.

Brodie, Bernard, *From Crossbow to H-Bomb* (New York: Dell Publishing Co., 1962).

Foster, George M. (ed.), *Traditional Cultures and the Impact of Technological Change* (New York: Harper & Row, 1962).

Gilpin, Robert, *American Scientists and Nuclear Weapons Policy* (Princeton, N.J.: Princeton University Press, 1962).

——, and Christopher Wright (eds.), *Scientists and National Policy-Making* (New York: Columbia University Press, 1964).

Ginzberg, Eli (ed.), *Technology and Social Change* (New York: Columbia University Press, 1964).

Goldsen, Joseph M. (ed.), *Outer Space in World Politics* (New York: Frederick A. Praeger, 1963).

Haskins, Caryl P., *The Scientific Revolution and World Politics* (New York: Harper & Row, 1964). For the Council on Foreign Relations.

Mead, Margaret (ed.), *Cultural Patterns and Technical Change* (New York: The New American Library of World Literature, 1955).

Piel, Gerard, *Science in the Cause of Man* (New York: Alfred A. Knopf, 1961).

Price, Don K., *Government and Science: Their Dynamic Relation in American Democracy* (New York: New York University Press, 1954).

——, *The Scientific Estate* (Cambridge, Mass.: Belknap Press, 1965).

Snow, Charles P., *Science and Government* (Cambridge, Mass.: Harvard University Press, 1960).

United States Senate, Committee on Foreign Relations, *United States Foreign Policy*, Study No. 8, "Developments in Military Technology and Their Impact on U.S. Strategy and Foreign Policy," prepared by the Washington Center of Foreign Policy Research (86th Congress, 2nd Session, Washington: GPO, 1959)

United Nations, *Science and Technology for Development*, Vol. I: *World of Opportunity*. Report on the United Nations Conference on the Application of Science and Technology for the Benefit of the Less Developed Areas (New York: United Nations, 1963), E/Conf. 39/1, Vol. 1.

Wiesner, Jerome B., *Where Science and Politics Meet* (New York: McGraw-Hill Book Company, 1965).

Wohlstetter, Albert, "Scientists, Seers and Strategy," *Foreign Affairs*, April 1963.

CHAPTER 10   THE SEARCH FOR SECURITY

Acheson, Dean, *Power and Diplomacy* (Cambridge, Mass.: Harvard University Press, 1958).

Eccles, Henry E., *Military Concepts and Philosophy* (New Brunswick: Rutgers University Press, 1965).

Herz, John H., *International Politics in the Atomic Age* (New York: Columbia University Press, 1959).

Hoffmann, Stanley, *The State of War* (New York: Frederick A. Praeger, 1965).

Kahn, Herman, *On Thermonuclear War* (Princeton, N.J.: Princeton University Press, 1960).

Kissinger, Henry A., *The Necessity for Choice* (New York: Harper & Row, 1960).

Osgood, Robert E., *Limited War: The Challenge to American Strategy* (Chicago: University of Chicago Press, 1957).

Ropp, Theodore, *War in the Modern World* (Durham, N.C.: Duke University Press, 1960).

Rostow, W. W., *The United States in the World Arena* (New York: Harper & Row, 1960).

Seton-Watson, Hugh, *Neither War Nor Peace: The Struggle for Power in the Post-War World* (New York: Frederick A. Praeger, 1960).

Sokolovsky, V. D. (ed.), *Military Strategy: Soviet Doctrine and Concepts* (New York: Frederick A. Praeger, 1963).

Waltz, Kenneth N., *Man, the State and War* (New York: Columbia University Press, 1959).

Wolfers, Arnold, "National Security as an Ambiguous Symbol," *Political Science Quarterly*, December 1952.

CHAPTER 11 THE NATURE AND ROLE OF FOREIGN POLICY

Cohen, Bernard C., *The Political Process and Foreign Policy* (Princeton, N.J.: Princeton University Press, 1957).

Coombs, Philip H., *The Fourth Dimension of Foreign Policy: Educational and Cultural Affairs* (New York: Harper & Row, 1964). For the Council on Foreign Relations.

Jacobson, Harold K., *America's Foreign Policy*, rev. ed. (New York: Random House, 1965).

Kennan, George F., *American Diplomacy, 1900–1950* (Chicago: University of Chicago Press, 1951).

Lerche, Charles O., Jr., and Abdul Said, *Concepts of International Politics* (Englewood Cliffs, N.J.: Prentice-Hall, 1963).

London, Kurt, *The Making of Foreign Policy East and West* (Philadelphia: J. B. Lippincott Company, 1965).

Marshall, C. B., *The Limits of Foreign Policy* (New York: Holt, Rinehart and Winston, 1954).

Morgenthau, Hans J., *In Defense of the National Interest* (New York: Alfred A. Knopf, 1951).

Osgood, Robert E., *Ideals and Self-Interests in America's Foreign Relations* (Chicago: University of Chicago Press, 1953).

Rostow, W. W., *The United States in the World Arena* (New York: Harper & Row, 1960).

CHAPTER 12   THE UNITED STATES DECISION-MAKING PROCESS

Almond, Gabriel A., *The American People and Foreign Policy* (New York: Harcourt, Brace & World, 1956).

Barnet, Vincent M., Jr. (ed.), *The Representation of the United States Abroad* (New York: Frederick A. Praeger, 1965). For the American Assembly.

Carleton, William G., *The Revolution in American Foreign Policy* (New York: Random House, 1963).

Carroll, Holbert N., *The House of Representatives and Foreign Affairs*, rev. ed. (Boston: Little, Brown and Company, 1966).

Cohen, Bernard C., *The Press and Foreign Policy* (Princeton, N.J.: Princeton University Press, 1963).

——, *Foreign Policy in American Government* (Boston: Little, Brown and Company, 1965).

Crabb, Cecil V., Jr., *American Foreign Policy in the Nuclear Age* (New York: Harper & Row, 1960).

Dahl, Robert A., *Congress and Foreign Policy* (New York: Harcourt, Brace & World, 1950).

Elder, Robert E., *The Policy Machine* (Syracuse, N.Y.: Syracuse University Press, 1960).

Hilsman, Roger, and Robert Good (eds.), *Foreign Policy in the Sixties: The Issues and the Instruments* (Baltimore: Johns Hopkins Press, 1965).

Jackson, Henry M. (ed.), *The Secretary of State and the Ambassador* (New York: Frederick A. Praeger, 1964).

Jones, Joseph M., *The Fifteen Weeks* (New York: Harcourt, Brace & World, 1965).

Lerche, Charles O., Jr., *Foreign Policy of the American People*, 2nd ed. (Englewood Cliffs, N.J.: Prentice-Hall, 1961).

McCamy, James L., *Conduct of the New Diplomacy* (New York: Harper & Row, 1964).

Neustadt, Richard E., *Presidential Power: The Politics of Leadership* (New York: John Wiley & Sons, 1960).

Price, Don K. (ed.), *The Secretary of State* (Englewood Cliffs, N.J.: Prentice-Hall, 1960). For the American Assembly.

Robinson, James A., *Congress and Foreign Policy-Making* (Homewood, Ill.: Dorsey Press, 1962).

United States Senate, Committee on Foreign Relations, *United States Foreign Policy*, Study No. 7, "Basic Aims of United States Foreign Policy," prepared by the Council on Foreign Relations (86th Congress, 1st Session, Washington: GPO, 1959).

United States Senate, Committee on Foreign Relations, *United States Foreign Policy*, Study No. 9, "The Formulation and Administration of United States Foreign Policy," prepared by The Brookings Institution (86th Congress, 2nd Session, Washington: GPO, 1960).

Villard, Henry S., *Affairs of State* (New York: Thomas Y. Crowell Company, 1965).

Westerfield, Bradford, *The Instruments of America's Foreign Policy* (New York: Thomas Y. Crowell Company, 1963).

CHAPTER 13   FORMULATION OF POLICY IN THE PARLIAMENTARY DEMOCRACY

Aron, Raymond, *France: Steadfast and Changing* (Cambridge, Mass.: Harvard University Press, 1960).

Bailey, Sydney D., *British Parliamentary Democracy*, 2nd ed. (Boston: Houghton Mifflin, 1966).

Beer, Samuel H., *British Politics in the Collectivist Age* (New York: Alfred A. Knopf, 1965).

——, and Adam B. Ulam, *Patterns of Government: The Major Political Systems of Europe*, rev. ed. (New York: Random House, 1962).

Dahl, Robert A. (ed.), *Political Opposition in Western Democracies* (New Haven: Yale University Press, 1966).

Dickey, John Sloan (ed.), *The United States and Canada* (Englewood Cliffs, N.J.: Prentice-Hall, 1964). For the American Assembly.

Furniss, Edgar S., Jr., *France, Troubled Ally* (New York: Harper & Row, 1960).

Gelber, Lionel M., *America in Britain's Place; the Leadership of the West and Anglo-American Unity* (New York: Frederick A. Praeger, 1961).

Hoffmann, Stanley H., *et al.*, *In Search of France* (Cambridge, Mass.: Harvard University Press, 1963).

Jennings, Sir Ivor, *Cabinet Government*, 3rd ed. (Cambridge, Engl.: The University Press, 1959).

Pickles, Dorothy, *The Fifth French Republic* (New York: Frederick A. Praeger, 1960).

Rose, Richard, *Politics in England* (Boston: Little, Brown and Company, 1964).

Sampson, Anthony, *Anatomy of Britain Today* (New York: Harper & Row, 1965).

Strang, Lord William, *Britain in World Affairs: The Fluctuation in Power and Influence from Henry VIII to Elizabeth II* (New York: Frederick A. Praeger, 1961).

CHAPTER 14   POLICY MAKING IN THE GREAT COMMUNIST STATES

A. The Soviet Union

Brzezinski, Zbigniew K., *Ideology and Power in Soviet Politics* (New York: Frederick A. Praeger, 1962).

——, and S. P. Huntington, *Political Power: USA/USSR* (New York: Viking Press, 1964).

Dallin, Alexander (ed.), *Soviet Conduct in World Affairs* (New York: Columbia University Press, 1960).

Fainsod, Merle, *How Russia Is Ruled*, rev. ed. (Cambridge, Mass.: Harvard University Press, 1963).

Garthoff, Raymond, *Soviet Strategy in the Nuclear Age*, rev. ed. (New York: Frederick A. Praeger, 1962).

Kennan, George F., *Russia and the West under Lenin and Stalin* (Boston: Little, Brown and Company, 1961).

——, "Polycentrism and Western Policy," *Foreign Affairs*, January 1964.

Laqueur, Walter, and Leopold Labedy (eds.), *Polycentrism: The New Factor in International Communism* (New York: Frederick A. Praeger, 1962).

Rubinstein, Alvin Z. (ed.), *The Foreign Policy of the Soviet Union* (New York: Random House, 1960).

Shapiro, Leonard, *The Government and Politics of the Soviet Union* (New York: Random House, 1965).

Tucker, Robert C., *The Soviet Political Mind: Studies in Stalinism and Post-Stalin Change* (New York: Frederick A. Praeger, 1964).

United States Senate, Committee on Government Operations, Subcommittee on National Policy Machinery, *National Policy Machinery in the Soviet Union* (86th Congress, 2nd Session, Washington: GPO, 1960).

B. China

Barnett, A. Doak, *Communist China and Asia* (New York: Harper & Row, 1960).

Boyd, R. G., *Communist China's Foreign Policy* (New York: Frederick A. Praeger, 1962).

Halpern, A. M., *Policies Toward China* (New York: McGraw-Hill Book Company, 1965). For the Council on Foreign Relations.

Halperin, Morton H., *China and the Bomb* (New York: Frederick A. Praeger, 1965).

Hinton, Harold C., *Communist China in World Politics* (Boston: Houghton Mifflin, 1966).

Hsieh, Alice Langley, *Communist China's Strategy in the Nuclear Era* (Englewood Cliffs, N.J.: Prentice-Hall, 1962).

Rostow, W. W., *The Prospects for Communist China* (New York: John Wiley & Sons, 1954).

Schurmann, Franz, *Ideology and Organization in Communist China* (Berkeley: University of California Press, 1966).

Steele, A. T., *The American People and China* (New York: McGraw-Hill Book Company, 1966). For the Council on Foreign Relations.

Wint, Guy, *Communist China's Crusade* (New York: Frederick A. Praeger, 1965).

Zagoria, Donald S., *The Sino-Soviet Conflict, 1956–1961* (New York: Atheneum Publishers, 1964).

CHAPTER 15 POWER POLITICS AND PATTERNS OF POLICY

Claude, I. L., Jr., *Power and International Relations* (New York: Random House, 1962).

Gulick, Edward V., *Europe's Classical Balance of Power* (Ithaca, N.Y.: Cornell University Press, 1955).

Kissinger, Henry A., *The Necessity for Choice* (Garden City, N.Y.: Doubleday & Company, 1962).

Liska, George, *International Equilibrium* (Cambridge, Mass.: Harvard University Press, 1957).

Merriam, Charles Edward, *Political Power: Its Composition and Incidence* (New York: McGraw-Hill Book Company, 1934).

Morgenthau, Hans J., *Politics Among Nations*, 3rd ed. (New York: Alfred A. Knopf, 1960).

Rosenau, James N. (ed.), *International Politics and Foreign Policy: A Reader in Research and Theory* (New York: The Free Press of Glencoe, 1961).

Schwarzenberger, George, *Power Politics: A Study of International Society*, 3rd ed. (New York: Frederick A. Praeger, 1964).

Seabury, Paul, *Balance of Power* (San Francisco: Chandler Publishing Co., 1965).

Sprout, Harold and Margaret Sprout (eds.), *Foundations of National Power* (Princeton, N.J.: Van Nostrand, 1962).

Thompson, Kenneth W., *Political Realism and the Crisis of World Politics* (Princeton, N.J.: Princeton University Press, 1959).

Wight, Martin, *Power Politics* (London: Royal Institute of International Affairs, 1946).

CHAPTER 16   DIPLOMACY AND THE CONDUCT OF FOREIGN AFFAIRS

Acheson, Dean, *Power and Diplomacy* (Cambridge, Mass.: Harvard University Press, 1958).

——, "The Practice of Partnership," *Foreign Affairs*, January 1963.

Iklé, Fred C., *How Nations Negotiate* (New York: Harper & Row, 1964).

Johnson, E. A. J. (ed.), *The Dimensions of Diplomacy* (Baltimore: Johns Hopkins Press, 1964).

Joy, Admiral C. Turner, *How Communists Negotiate* (New York: The Macmillan Company, 1955).

Kertesz, Stephen D., and M. A. Fitzsimons, *Diplomacy in a Changing World* (South Bend: University of Notre Dame Press, 1959).

Machiavelli, Nicolo, *The Prince* (New York: Oxford University Press, 1906).

Murphy, Robert, *Diplomat Among Warriors* (Garden City, N.Y.: Doubleday & Company, 1964).

Nicolson, Harold, *Diplomacy*, 3rd ed. (London: Oxford University Press, 1963).

——, *The Evolution of Diplomacy* (New York: Collier Books, 1962).

Pearson, Lester B., *Diplomacy in the Nuclear Age* (Cambridge, Mass.: Harvard University Press, 1959).

Plischke, Elmer, *Conduct of American Diplomacy*, 2nd ed. (Princeton, N.J.: Van Nostrand, 1961).

Satow, Sir Ernest M., *A Guide to Diplomatic Practice*, 4th ed. (New York: David McKay Co., 1962).

Thayer, Charles W., *Diplomat* (New York: Harper & Row, 1959).

CHAPTER 17   INTERNATIONAL COMMUNICATIONS AS AN INSTRUMENT

Barghoorn, Frederick C., *The Soviet Cultural Offensive* (Princeton, N.J.: Princeton University Press, 1960).

Blum, Robert, *Cultural Affairs and Foreign Relations* (Englewood Cliffs, N.J.: Prentice-Hall, 1963). For the American Assembly.

Choukas, Michael, *Propaganda Comes of Age* (Washington: Public Affairs Press, 1961).

Daugherty, William E., and Morris Janowitz, *A Psychological Warfare Casebook* (Baltimore: Johns Hopkins Press, 1959).

Dizard, William P., *The Strategy of Truth* (Washington, D.C.: Public Affairs Press, 1961).

Dunn, Frederick S., *War and the Minds of Men* (New York: Harper & Row, 1950).

Dyer, Murray, *The Weapon on the Wall: Rethinking Psychological Warfare* (Baltimore: Johns Hopkins Press, 1959).

Ellul, James, *Propaganda: The Formation of Men's Attitudes*, Konrad Kellen and Jean Lerner, trans. (New York: Alfred A. Knopf, 1965).

George, Alexander A., *Propaganda Analysis* (Evanston, Ill.: Row, Peterson & Co., 1959).

Holt, Robert T., and Robert W. Van de Velde, *Strategic Psychological Operations and American Foreign Policy* (Chicago: University of Chicago Press, 1960).

Kirkpatrick, Evron M., *Target: The World* (New York: The Macmillan Company, 1956).

Lewis, John C., *Communist Propaganda Techniques* (New York: Frederick A. Praeger, 1965).

Linebarger, Paul M. A., *Psychological Warfare* (New York: Duell, Sloan & Pearce, 1954).

Pool, Ithiel de Sola (ed.), *Trends in Content Analysis* (Urbana: University of Illinois Press, 1959).

CHAPTER 18 THE ECONOMIC INSTRUMENTS OF FOREIGN POLICY

Bidwell, Percy W., *Raw Materials: A Study of American Policy* (New York: Harper & Row, 1958). For the Council on Foreign Relations.

Black, Eugene R., *The Diplomacy of Economic Development* (Cambridge, Mass.: Harvard University Press, 1960).

Goldwin, Robert A. (ed.), *Why Foreign Aid?* (Chicago: Rand McNally & Company, 1963).

Hansen, Alvin H., *The Dollar and the International Monetary System* (New York: McGraw-Hill Book Company, 1965).

Hitch, Charles J., and Roland N. McKean, *The Economics of Defense in the Nuclear Age* (Santa Monica: Rand Project R-346, 1960).

Humphrey, Don D., *The United States and the Common Market* (New York: Frederick A. Praeger, 1962).

Kenen, Peter B., *Giant Among Nations* (Chicago: Rand McNally & Company, 1963).

Krause, Lawrence B. (ed.), *The Common Market: Progress and Continuity* (Englewood Cliffs, N.J.: Prentice-Hall, 1964).

Krause, Walter, *International Economics* (Boston: Houghton Mifflin Company, 1965).

Lyons, Gene M., *Military Policy and Economic Aid* (Columbus: Ohio State Press, 1961).

Millikan, Max F., and W. W. Rostow, *A Proposal: Key to an Effective Foreign Policy* (New York: Harper & Row, 1957).

Rowen, Henry, Study Paper No. 18, "National Security and the American Economy in the 1960's." Material prepared in connection with the study of Employment, Growth, and Price Levels for consideration by the Joint Economic Committee, Congress of the United States (86th Congress, 2nd Session, Washington, January 30, 1960).

Schelling, Thomas C., *International Economics* (Boston: Allyn & Bacon, 1958).

Schlesinger, James R., *The Political Economy of National Security* (New York: Frederick A. Praeger, 1960).

Shanks, Michael, and John Lambert, *The Common Market Today and Tomorrow* (New York: Frederick A. Praeger, 1962).

CHAPTER 19 THE MILITARY INSTRUMENT AND ITS MANAGEMENT

Associates in Political Science, U.S. Air Force Academy, *American Defense Policy* (Baltimore: Johns Hopkins Press, 1965).

Bobrow, Davis (ed.), *Components of Defense Policy* (Chicago: Rand McNally & Company, 1965).

Brodie, Bernard, *Strategy in the Missile Age* (Princeton, N.J.: Princeton University Press, 1959).

Challener, Richard D., and Gordon B. Turner (eds.), *National Security in the Nuclear Age* (New York: Frederick A. Praeger, 1960).

Falk, Richard A., and Richard J. Barnet (eds.), *Security in Disarmament* (Princeton, N.J.: Princeton University Press, 1965).

Furniss, Edgar S., Jr., *The Western Alliance: Its Status and Prospects* (Columbus: Ohio State University Press, 1965).

Garthoff, Raymond L., *Soviet Military Policy: A Historical Analysis* (New York: Frederick A. Praeger, 1966).

Ginsburgh, Robert N., *U.S. Military Strategy in the Sixties* (New York: W. W. Norton & Company, 1965).

Goldwin, Robert A. (ed.), *America Armed: Essays on United States Military Policy* (Chicago: Rand McNally & Company, 1963).

Halperin, Michael, *Limited Warfare in the Nuclear Age* (New York: John Wiley & Sons, 1963).

Hammond, Paul Y., *Organizing for Defense: The American Military Establishment in the Twentieth Century* (Princeton, N.J.: Princeton University Press, 1961).

Kaufmann, William W. (ed.), *Military Policy and National Security* (Princeton, N.J.: Princeton University Press, 1956).

Kissinger, Henry A., *Readings in National Security Policy* (New York: Frederick A. Praeger, 1965).

———, *The Troubled Partnership* (New York: McGraw-Hill Book Company, 1965). For the Council on Foreign Relations.

Knorr, Klaus, *The War Potential of Nations* (Princeton, N.J.: Princeton University Press, 1956).

Osgood, Robert E., *Limited War* (Chicago: University of Chicago Press, 1957).

Schelling, Thomas C., *Strategy of Conflict* (Cambridge, Mass.: Harvard University Press, 1960).

Snyder, Glen H., *Deterrence and Defense: Toward a Theory of National Security* (Princeton, N.J.: Princeton University Press, 1961).

Wolfe, Thomas W., *Soviet Strategy at the Cross Roads* (Cambridge, Mass.: Harvard University Press, 1964).

Wolfers, Arnold (ed.), *Alliance Policy and the Cold War* (Baltimore: Johns Hopkins Press, 1959).

CHAPTER 20   THE PROBLEM OF INTERNATIONAL PEACE

American Assembly, *Arms Control* (Englewood Cliffs, N.J.: Prentice-Hall, 1961).

Bechoeffer, Bernard, *History of Arms Control Since 1945* (Washington: The Brookings Institution, 1961).

Bennet, D. W., *United Nations Forces* (New York: Frederick A. Praeger, 1964).

Brennan, Donald G. (ed.), *Arms Control, Disarmament, and National Security* (New York: George Braziller, 1961).

Bull, Hedley, *The Control of the Arms Race* (New York: Frederick A. Praeger, 1961).

Claude, Inis L., Jr., *Swords Into Plowshares*, 3rd ed. (New York: Random House, 1964).

Cleveland, Harlan, *The Obligations of Power: American Diplomacy in the Search for Peace* (New York: Harper & Row, 1966).

Halperin, Morton H., and Dwight H. Perkins, *Communist China and Arms Control* (New York: Frederick A. Praeger, 1965).

Hoffmann, Stanley, *The State of War* (New York: Frederick A. Praeger, 1965).

Jacobson, Harold K., and Eric Stein, *Diplomats, Scientists, and Politicians: The United States and the Nuclear Test Ban Negotiations* (Ann Arbor: University of Michigan Press, 1966).

Lefever, Ernest W. (ed.), *Arms and Arms Control* (New York: Frederick A. Praeger, 1962).

———, *Crisis in the Congo: A U.N. Arms Force in Action* (Washington: The Brookings Institution, 1965).

Millis, Walter, *An End to Arms* (New York: Atheneum Publishers, 1965).

Schelling, Thomas C., and M. H. Halperin, *Strategy and Arms Control* (New York: Twentieth Century Fund, 1961).

———, *Arms and Influence* (New Haven: Yale University Press, 1966).

Shulman, Marshall D., *Beyond the Cold War* (New Haven: Yale University Press, 1966).

Wright, Quincy, *A Study of War* (Chicago: University of Chicago Press, 1942).

Wolfers, Arnold and Others, *The United States in a Disarmed World* (Baltimore: Johns Hopkins Press, 1966).

CHAPTER 21   THE INTERNATIONAL RULE OF LAW

Bishop, William W., Jr., *International Law: Cases and Materials,* 2nd ed. (Boston: Little, Brown and Company, 1962).

Brierly, J. L., *The Law of Nations,* 6th ed. (New York: Oxford University Press, 1963).

Clark, Grenville, and Louis Sohn, *World Peace Through World Law,* 2nd ed. (Cambridge, Mass.: Harvard University Press, 1960).

Friedmann, Wolfgang G., *The Changing Structure of International Law* (New York: Columbia University Press, 1964).

von Glahn, Gerhard, *Law Among Nations* (New York: The Macmillan Company, 1965).

Kaplan, Morton A., and Nicholas DeB. Katzenbach, *The Political Foundations of International Law* (New York: John Wiley & Sons, 1961).

Larson, Arthur, *When Nations Disagree: A Handbook on Peace Through Law* (Baton Rouge: Louisiana State University Press, 1961).

Lauterpacht, Hersch, *Function of Law in the International Community* (New York: Oxford University Press, 1933).

McDougal, Myres S., and Associates, *Studies in World Order* (New Haven: Yale University Press, 1960).

Nussbaum, A., *A Concise History of International Law,* rev. ed. (New York: The Macmillan Company, 1962).

Oppenheim, L., *International Law,* 8th ed. by Hersch Lauterpacht (London: Longmans, Green & Co., 1955).

Ross, Alf, *On Law and Justice* (Berkeley: University of California Press, 1959).

Schwarzenberger, George, *Manual of International Law,* 4th ed. (New York: Frederick A. Praeger, 1960).

Stone, Julius, *Legal Controls of International Conflict* (New York: Holt, Rinehart and Winston, 1954).

de Visscher, Charles, *Theory and Reality in Public International Law* (Princeton, N.J.: Princeton University Press, 1957).

CHAPTER 22 LIMITED-PURPOSE INTERNATIONAL ORGANIZATIONS

Birrenbach, Kurt, *The Future of the Atlantic Community* (New York: Frederick A. Praeger, 1963).

Brzezinski, Zbigniew K., *The Soviet Bloc: Unity and Conflict* (Cambridge, Mass.: Harvard University Press, 1960).

Claude, Inis L., Jr., *Swords Into Plowshares*, 3rd ed. (New York: Random House, 1964).

Deutsch, Karl W., *Political Community and the North Atlantic Area* (Princeton, N.J.: Princeton University Press, 1957).

Dreier, John C., *The Organization of American States and the Hemisphere Crisis* (New York: Harper & Row, 1962).

Haas, Ernst B., *Beyond the Nation-State: Functionalism and International Organization* (Stanford: Stanford University Press, 1964).

Hallstein, Walter, *United Europe: Challenge and Opportunity* (Cambridge, Mass.: Harvard University Press, 1962).

Herter, Christian A., *Toward an Atlantic Community* (New York: Harper & Row, 1963). For the Council on Foreign Relations.

Kissinger, Henry A., *The Troubled Partnership* (New York: McGraw-Hill Book Company, 1965).

Lawson, Ruth C. (ed.), *International Regional Organizations* (New York: Frederick A. Praeger, 1962).

Nye, Joseph S., Jr., *Pan-Africanism and East African Integration* (Cambridge, Mass.: Harvard University Press, 1963).

Plischke, Elmer (ed.), *Systems of Integrating the International Community* (Princeton, N.J.: Van Nostrand, 1964).

Padelford, Norman J., "The Organization of African Unity," *International Organization*, Summer 1964.

Reuter, Paul, *International Institutions* (New York: Frederick A. Praeger, 1961).

Stanley, Timothy W., *NATO in Transition: The Future of the Atlantic Alliance* (New York: Frederick A. Praeger, 1965).

Wilcox, Francis O., and H. Field Haviland (eds.), *The Atlantic Community* (New York: Frederick A. Praeger, 1963).

CHAPTER 23 ORGANIZING THE WORLD COMMUNITY: THE UNITED NATIONS

Bailey, Sydney D., *The General Assembly of the United Nations*, rev. ed. (New York: Frederick A. Praeger, 1964).

——, *The Secretariat of the United Nations*, rev. ed. (New York: Frederick A. Praeger, 1964).

Bloomfield, Lincoln P. (ed.), *International Military Forces* (Boston: Little, Brown & Company, 1964).

——, *The United Nations and U.S. Foreign Policy* (Boston: Little, Brown & Company, 1960).

Burns, Arthur Lee, and Nina Heathcote, *Peace-Keeping by U.N. Forces: From Suez to the Congo* (New York: Frederick A. Praeger, 1963).

Claude, Inis L., Jr., *Swords Into Plowshares*, 3rd ed. (New York: Random House, 1964).

Goodrich, Leland M., *The United Nations* (New York: Thomas Y. Crowell Company, 1959).

Hammarskjöld, Dag, "Two Differing Concepts of the United Nations Assayed," *International Organization*, Autumn 1961.

Hovet, Thomas, Jr., *Bloc Politics in the United Nations* (Cambridge, Mass.: Harvard University Press, 1960).

Kelsen, Hans, *The Law of the United Nations* (New York: Frederick A. Praeger, 1964).

Mangone, Gerard J. (ed.), *U.N. Administration of Economic and Social Programs* (New York: Columbia University Press, 1966).

Nicholas, H. G., *The United Nations as a Political Institution* (New York: Oxford University Press, 1959).

Padelford, Norman J., and Leland M. Goodrich (eds.), *The United Nations in the Balance* (New York: Frederick A. Praeger, 1965).

Rossner, Gabriella, *The United Nations Emergency Force* (New York: Columbia University Press, 1963).

Russell, Ruth B., and J. E. Muther, *A History of the United Nations Charter* (Washington: The Brookings Institution, 1958).

Sewell, James P., *Functionalism and World Politics: A Study Based on United Nations Programs Financing Economic Development* (Princeton, N.J.: Princeton University Press, 1966).

Wainhouse, David W., and Associates, *International Peace Observation: A History and Forecast* (Baltimore: Johns Hopkins Press, 1966).

Sharp, Walter R., *Field Administration in the United Nations System: The Conduct of International Economic and Social Programs* (Princeton, N.J.: Princeton University Press, 1966).

CHAPTER 24   CHANGE AND CHALLENGE

Cleveland, Harlan, *The Obligations of Power: American Diplomacy in the Search for Peace* (New York: Harper & Row, 1966).

Crabb, Cecil V., Jr., *American Foreign Policy in the Nuclear Age* (Evanston, Ill.: Row, Peterson & Company, 1960).

Jackson, Senator Henry M., *The Secretary of State and the Ambassador* (New York: Frederick A. Praeger, 1964).

Jacobson, Harold K., *America's Foreign Policy*, second rev. ed. (New York: Random House, 1965).

Kennan, George F., *American Diplomacy, 1900–1950* (Chicago: The University of Chicago Press, 1951).

Lyons, Gene M. (ed.), *American Purpose and Power* (Chicago: Quadrangle Books, 1965).

Ransom, Harry Howe, *An American Foreign Policy Reader* (New York: Thomas Y. Crowell Company, 1965).

Rostow, Walt W., *The United States in the World Arena* (New York: Harper & Row, 1960).

Thompson, Kenneth W., *American Diplomacy and Emergent Patterns* (New York: New York University Press, 1962).

Westerfield, H. Bradford, *The Instruments of American Foreign Policy* (New York: Thomas Y. Crowell Company, 1963).

Wolfers, Arnold, *Discord and Collaboration: Essays in International Politics* (Baltimore: Johns Hopkins Press, 1962).

INDEX

Acheson, Dean, 192, 230, 245; on policy process, 221–222; on "total diplomacy," 342

Act of Chapultepec (1945), 462

Acton, Lord, 215

Afghanistan, 65; education in, 124; Soviet assistance to, 327; trade with Soviet bloc, 368

Africa, 1, 8, 18; boundary problems, 113, 114; British policy in, 260; and Chinese Communists, 101, 281; and Communism, 26, 98, 102; and international consensus, 14; and International Court, 494; nationalism in, 74–75, 81, 96, 114, 122, 506; neutralism of, 55–56, 192, 490; and new diplomacy, 317; new nations, 23–24, 88; pan-Africanism, 461; party systems, 264; political instability in, 25, 68; population, 125, 127, 128; and Sino-Soviet rift, 64; technical missions, 168; and U.N. membership, 482, 483, 485. See also Organization of African Unity

Afro-Asian states, 475; Bandung Conference (1955), 101; behavior in international affairs, 57; and international law, 425, 428, 430; neutralism, 55–56, 102, 400; nonalignment, 35, 84, 102, 400; and U.N., 483, 486

Aggression, 116; and foreign policy patterns, 310; and law, 435–436; and League of Nations, 477–478; and military assistance, 398; and U.N., 434, 489–491

Agreements, 6; economic, 155, 366, 368–372; executive, 223, 225, 239; and foreign policy, 309; and rules of war, 187; and search for peace, 410. See also Alliances; Treaties

Agriculture, 124–125; detraditionalizing of, 133; and economic base, 136; in less-developed nations, 142; and Soviet Union, 142; surplus programs, 291; and technology, 164, 167; and U.S. foreign assistance program, 131–132

Air power, 109–110, 117, 168; and military strategy, 399; and U.S. capability, 172

Air space, 113; national jurisdiction in, 433, 440

Alamagordo, New Mexico, 505

Alaska, 96

Algeria, 24, 95, 116, 119; and Arab League, 460; and Morocco border dispute, 331, 461

Alliance for Progress, 90, 156, 379, 464, 514; President Kennedy and, 224; Punta del Este Charter (1961), 464

Alliances, 11, 174, 310; and armed force, 395; and balance of power, 301; and collective security, 308–309; and military policy, 397; and military strategy, 399, 401–402; and national security, 177, 179, 189, 192–193, 410; and third party, 188; traditional base of, 204–205. See also United States, treaties and agreements

Almond, Gabriel, 44; on public role in policy making, 242

American Assembly and public opinion, 243

American Samoa, 96

American States: First International Conference (1889), 462. See also Organization of American States

Angola, 96, 497, 498

Antarctic Treaty (1959), 429, 441

Antarctica, 114, 116, 429

Anticolonialism, 14, 36, 51; ambivalence of, 102–103; and colonialism, 88; and military strategy, 399; and nationalism, 81, 84, 144; and Organization of African Unity, 461

ANZUS Pact (1951), 34, 211, 309, 333, 448, 470; and Commonwealth Nations, 459; strategic interests, 401

Apartheid policy; see Racialism

Arab-Israeli dispute, 349, 414, 417, 451; and Arab League, 460; bases for—boundaries, 114, nationalism, 74, population and production, 188; religion, 423; and Nasser's foreign policy, 207; and power politics, 294, 301; and U.N. 494

Arbitration, 416

Arctic, 109, 110, 277

Argentina, 8

Aristophanes, 418

Aristotle, 72, 105; and balance-of-power

ARISTOTLE (cont.)
concept, 296
Armaments, 8, 27, 87, 109, 195; cost of, 173; production, 398; reduction, and Woodrow Wilson, 412; regulation of, 177. *See also* Assistance; Arms control
Armed force, 179, 182, 185, 242; ambiguous use of, 184; capabilities of, 399; and diplomacy, 331; from 1820 to 1929, 183; and internal stability, 180; in Korea, 231; and national security, 191; in World Wars I and II, 185
Arms control, 189, 390, 393, 403, 423–424; definition and purpose, 417–418; guidelines for, 422; international police force, 421; Kissinger on, 406; and military policy, 384, 397; negotiations, 358, 385, 410–411—inspection provisions, 327, 419, 421, 442, and sanctions, 421; obstacles to, 420–422; past efforts, 418; since World War II, 418–420; and technology, 166, 168, 171, 175–176, 237. *See also* Disarmament
Arms race, 22, 191, 411
Armstrong, Louis ("Satchmo"), 355
Aron, Raymond, 387
Asia, 1, 8, 18, 26; boundaries in, 114; and Communism, 98, 102; and diplomacy, 317; and foreign policy, 264; nationalism, 81, 506; neutralism, 55–56, 190; new states of, 81, 88, 122; political conflicts in, 199; population, 124, 125, 130; and Sino-Soviet rift, 64, 281; and Soviets, 276. *See also* Afro-Asian states
Asian Development Bank, 58, 149
Assassination as a political technique, 330
Assistance, 247, 505; agricultural, 131–133; arms, 188; bilateral, 369; and diplomacy, 320, 321, 326–327, 332; and foreign policy formulation, 201, 241, 245; military, 236, 375, 397–398; to new nations, 85, 144–145; and population growth, 130; technical, 84, 104, 133, 166, 237, 374; temporary status of, 240; "tied," 156, 374, 379. *See also* Foreign aid and assistance
Aswan Dam, Egypt, 99, 158
Atlantic Charter (1941), 178, 478
Atlantic Community, 34, 41, 87, 512; and industrialization, 137–139; and NATO, 467–470, 472; and OECD, 472
Atomic energy, 165, 170; peaceful use of, 419–420, 455
Attitudes: effect on behavior of states, 53, 54–59; in emerging nations, 102–103; and foreign relations, 57–58; formation, 341; historical base of, 205; and morality in international affairs, 57; and national

interest, 209–210; and national security, 180–181; and population distribution, 125; and prejudice, 56–57; role of values, 54, 59; stereotyped, 55–56; and war, 185; in world politics, 340–341
Attlee, Clement, 251, 258
Australia, 8, 116, 119; foreign assistance program, 131–132; and Great Britain, 261; population trends, 127, 130; and SEATO, 470; and trust territories, 498. *See also* ANZUS Pact
Austria, 456
Authoritarianism, 60, 67; and national interest, 209; in newly independent countries, 83; population-control policy, 134; and trade direction, 367
Ayub Kahn, 319
Azores, 165

Bacon, Francis, 38
Balance of payments, 138–140, 148, 149; defined, 380; and foreign assistance, 374; and International Monetary Fund, 155; and international trade, 156; in less-developed countries, 156; and military assistance, 397; and national security, 179
Balance of power, 17, 215, 507, 510; approach to international politics, 32–33, 45, 293; and bipolarity, 33; and colonialism, 93; concept of, 296–298; and de Gaulle, 469; as equation of power, 298; evaluation of, 303–306; and foreign policy, 299–302; and Great Britain, 20, 33, 110, 204, 211, 260; historic background of, 20–21, 411; and League of Nations, 477; and military power, 401, 424; and population and production strength, 188; postulates of, 301–302; and Sino-Soviet relations, 290; and Southeast Asia, 199; and Soviet view, 99; Spykman on, 110–111; and U.N., 439, 480–482. *See also* Power politics
Balkans, 308
Ball, George, 230
"Ban the Bomb," 343, 356
Bandung Conference (1955), 101
Barghoorn, Frederick, 356; on U.S.-Soviet cultural relations, 356–357
Barnett, A. Doak, 280n, 439n.
Baruch Plan, for control of nuclear energy, 418
Bases, military, 394; U.S., 117, 165
Bay of Pigs, 207
Bechuanaland: see Botswana
Behaviorism: approach to international politics, 43–45; and national character and

style, 75
Belgium, 73, 117; disintegration of colonial empire, 88, 96; and EEC, 138, 454
Ben Bella, Ahmed, 84, 101
Benelux community, 466
Berlin: airlift (1949), 172, 245, 339; blockade, (1948–1949), 21, 245, 506; crises (1961–1962), 239, 336; and International Court, 445; and Soviet diplomacy, 328; Wall, 113
Bernadotte, Count Folke, 446n.
Bidault, George, 264
Bipartisanship, Congress and, 241–242
Bipolarity, 21, 137, 505; approach to international politics, 33–35, 45; and balance of power, 33; Sino-Soviet, 34; Soviet-U.S., 34
Birth control, 126, 127. See also Population
Bismarck, Otto von, 93, 217
Black, Eugene R.: on population control, 133, 134
Bloomfield, Lincoln P., 432n.
Blum, Léon, 264
Bohlen, Charles E., 328
Botswana (Bechuanaland), 9, 92, 485
Boumadienne, Houari, 84
Boundaries, 411; disputes, 115; ethnic considerations, 115; international, 114; and new states, 112–113; and security, 113–114. See also Jurisdiction
Bowie, Robert R.: on arms control, 424; on policy decision model, 222
Brand, W., 147n.
Brazil, 8, 123, 370; and balance of power, 305; and Dominican Republic, 464; and industrialization, 137, 142–143; and technology, 164
Bretton Woods conference (1944), 368
Brezhnev, Leonid, 271, 272, 273
Brierly, J. L.: on international institutions, 446; on international law, 441–442
Brinksmanship, 328
British Broadcasting Corporation (BBC), 345, 352
British North America Act (1867), 261
Brogan, D. W., 92n.
Brookings Institution, 233; on military impact on foreign affairs, 234–236
Brussels Pact (1948), 466
Brzezinski, Z. K., 60n.; on trends in international Communist organization, 474
Buchan, Alistair, 472n.
Bull, Hedley: on arms control, 417
Bundy, McGeorge, 225, 234
Bunker, Ellsworth, 416
Bureau of the Budget, U.S.: and foreign policy, 227–228

Burma, 101
Byrnes, James F., 230, 319

Callières, François de: on diplomacy, 315–316; on diplomatic negotiations, 324, 325; on professional diplomat, 319
Cambodia, 95, 101; and SEATO, 470
Canada, 8, 16–17; Atomic Energy Commission, 455; discovery of oil in, 116, 119; foreign assistance program, 131–132; foreign policy process, 261–263—consensus in, 262, Secretary for External Affairs, 262, and U.S. Vietnam policy, 262; and Great Britain, 261; and NATO, 108; and peacekeeping, 413; population, 124, 130; relations with U.S., 57, 117, 181, 262, 365, 472; and territorial waters, 440
Capital, 137; controlled movement of, 364; and development, 116, 136; and economic imperialism, 91–92, 149; goods, 140, 147; outflow, 139, 382; scarcity of, 93–94; sources of, 148–150; and technology, 162, 163, 169. See also Balance of payments; Investment
Capitalism, 54, 60; and imperialism, 93–94; and international economic affairs, 136, 141
Caradon, Lord, 96
Carr, Edward H.: on totalitarianism, 185
Castro, Fidel, 66, 180, 207, 328; and Cuban foreign policy, 68, 188; and seizure of U.S.-owned assets, 442. See also Cuba
Catholic Church, 342, 427
Cease-fires, 410, 415; Indian-Pakistani, 413–414; in Palestine, 489; in Vietnam, 418
Censorship, 343, 351
Central American Common Market, 465
Central Intelligence Agency, U.S.: and policy process, 223, 227
Central Treaty Organization (CENTO) (1955), 34, 468; formation of, 108
Chakste, M., 431n.
Chamberlain, Neville, 260, 303
Change, 1ff, 67–69, 171, 504ff; and balance-of-power system, 305–307; economic, 304; and force of nationalism, 70, 78; historic, 504–507; and international law, 443–444; peaceful vs. violent, 18–19; societal, and modern war, 186; and stability of boundaries, 115; technological, 161–164, 217, 304; in transitional societies, 65–66; in U.N., 498–503; U.S. in changing world, 507–515
Chauvinism: Chinese, 80; Great Power,

CHAUVINISM (cont.)
287, 289; Soviet, 79
Ch'en Yun, 283
Chiang Kai-Shek, 483
Chile, 133; and territorial waters, 440
China: U.S. "Open Door" policy toward, 203, 211. See also Chinese Nationalist Republic; Communist China
Chinese Nationalist Republic (Taiwan), 143–144; and foreign policy, 281; Jacoby on, 145; and U.N., recognition problem, 437, 439, 483–484; and U.S.—defense treaty, 470, foreign aid, 373
Chou En-lai, 81, 101, 283
Chu Teh, 283
Churchill, Winston S., viii; 206, 251, 253, 255; and diplomacy, 318, 319; leadership during World War II, 295; meetings with Roosevelt, 333; on national interest, 208–209; on Soviet Russia, 269
Church-state relations: and nationalism, 73
Claude, Inis L., Jr., 298n.; on international collaboration, 450; on need for U.N., 503; on peace with security, 423; on principle of collective action, 309; on regional organization, 454
Clausewitz, Karl von, 40; on credibility of force, 396; on economic warfare, 370; on military strategy, 398; on peacemaker, 181; on war, 386, 393, 400
Cleveland, Harlan: on "era of foreign operations," 238; on long-range foreign policy, 246–247
Climate, 106; and human effectiveness, 116
Coalitions, 177, 263; approach to military strategy, 401–402; French, 264; and national policy and action, 210, 310
Cobden, Richard: on balance of power, 297
Coercion, 14–15, 90; diplomatic, 328; military, 385
Cohen, Benjamin V., 225
Cold War: and bipolarity, 33; and new nations, 85; Shulman on, 64
Collaboration, international, 33; in Antarctic, 114, 429; and nationalism, 70; in outer space, 429
Collective security: concept of, 21–22; League of Nations, 477–478; U.N. and 480, 482
Colombo Plan, 374, 448, 475
Colonialism, 171, 217; defined, 89; and dissolution of empires, 94–97, 506; legacy of, 102; and nationalism, 88; and U.N., 483; and U.S., 90, 92, 104; Western, motives of, 92–93, 130. See also Anti-colonialism
Commissions of inquiry, 416
Committee of One Million on China, 243

Committee on the Alliance for Progress (CIAP), 465
Common Market; see European Economic Community
Commonwealth of Nations, 87, 90, 94, 181, 448, 457; composition of, 458–459; Prime Ministers Conference (1961), 263; security arrangements, 459; South Africa's withdrawal from 94
Communications, 2, 116; and attitude formation, 54, 341; and Communist ideology, 60; cultural relations, 353–357; and diplomacy, 316; and emerging nations, 24–25, 65; international, and foreign policy, 291, 305, 340–341; and international politics, 26, 33, 113; interstate, 6; and nationalism, 70, 75–76, 87; propaganda, 342–353; routes of, 105, 113; studies, 44; and technology, 161, 165, 166, 167–168. See also Mass media
Communism, 1, 16, 161; and bipolarity, 21, 33; conflict with other ideologies, 25–26, 60–61, 210, 278, 301, 387, 509; and economic power, 360; and emerging nations, 24, 96, 144, 189; and geopolitics, 111–112; as ideology, 60, 61–64, 69, 189, 301; and imperialism, 98–101, 310; and insurgencies, 388; international, 80, 474—and Soviet aims, 278–279; national, 79–80; and nationalism, 78–79; and Sino-Soviet rift, 63–64; Soviet, 78; "universal idea," 39, 111; and wars of liberation, 185–186; and world conquest, 18, 26, 117, 210, 258, 405; and world order, 19
Communist bloc (Soviet), 19, 34, 56, 62–63, 98–99, 136, 178, 212, 448; bipolarity, 21, 137; and change, 67; and Communist parties, 473; and diplomacy, 317, 322, 330; and economic policy, 141–142—ties with Soviets, 99; flow of decision making in, 286–287; and force of history, 201; and foreign assistance, 375; and international law, 430; and international trade, 142, 155, 158, 367–368, 473; and military force, 396; and morality in international affairs, 57; and nationalism, 79–80; and new nations, 85–86; and non-Communist states, 108; and polycentrism, 26, 34, 137, 474; propaganda, 352; and rise in economic power, 383; student demonstrations, 349; and territorial waters, 444; theory of international relations, 58; and U.N., 484–486; and U.S. military intervention, 168; and U.S. trade policy, 153; Warsaw Pact, 474
Communist China, 8, 32, 60, 185, 289,

305, 403, 506

ATTITUDES AND IDEOLOGY: attitudes toward West, 58, 179, 281–282; and Communist ideology, 280; and nationalism, 80, 84, 280, 281; and peaceful coexistence, 279; toward Sino-Soviet rift, 289, 301; and wars of "national liberation," 279; world Communist leadership, 102, 279

COMMUNIST PARTY: central role of, 282; institutions and operations of, 282–285; Politburo, 101, 282–285

DOMESTIC AFFAIRS: food supply, 131–132; population, 27, 99, 125, 127, 128, 130, 134, 280, 281, 286, 290; Fed Guards, 329–330; science and technology, 285; as transitional society, 65, 68, 280, 281

ECONOMIC POLICY, 361; consumption, 285; development problems, 145–147; and foreign aid, 376, 379; industrialization, 137, 285; and international trade, 367–368; investment, 285; and the Party, 285; planning, 285

FOREIGN POLICY AND RELATIONS, 268–269; attacks upon—India, 85, 100, 388; Korea, 213; basic factors, 280–281; Constitution and, 282; decision making in, 281–286; and emerging nations, 81, 101–102, 117, 189; National Party Congress, 282; and national defense, 285; nature of, 281–282; and Nuclear Test Ban Treaty, 419; policy flow, 286–287; policy-making machinery, 282–284; propaganda and, 88, 348; and public opinion, 284; and Soviet Union, 282, 329; territorial expansion, 99–101, 111, 269, 290; undeclared wars, 396; and U.N., 438–439, 482, 484; and U.S., 102, 205, 239, 294, 351–352; and Vietnam, 281; and world rule, 18, 26, 117, 122. See also Cuba; India; Indonesia; Korea; Sino-Soviet relations; Vietnam

GOVERNMENT AND INSTITUTIONS, 284–285

MILITARY INSTRUMENTS: armed forces, 281, 285; Kuomintang, 68, 112; military assistance, 397; nuclear power, 99, 102, 164, 281, 285, 390, 405, 419; strategy, 400, 405

Communist organization, international: see International Communist Organization

Community: idea of, 2, 16–17, 512; and consensus in values, 54; and diplomacy, 335; European, 6; international, 35–36, 91, 103, 122, 144; and international law, 436; North Atlantic, 10, 14, 137, 335; organizing international, 407–408; rationale for international collaboration, 476–477; of states (table), 9, 15–16. See also International Rule of Law; Limited Purpose Organizations; Peace; Peacekeeping; United Nations

Community of the Six; see European Economic Community (EEC)

Comsat Corporation, 429

Concert of Europe, 308. See also Triple Alliance; Triple Entente

Conflict, 506; and balance of power, 301; control, 393, 397, 403, 410, 412–414; escalation of, 391–393; and ideology, 198; internal, 198–199; international, British divergence on, 259; on-going, 509; and power, 198; and raw materials, 198; since 1958, 388; Soviet Union and West, 293, 311; territorial objectives, 198; and trade, 198; and unilateral strategy, 400–401

Congo, 8; Communists in, 25, 68; and independence, 96; and International Court, 445; and OAU, 461; political instability, 24, 66, 81, 401; Soviet recognition, 437; U.N. peacekeeping forces in, 91, 402, 414, 432, 487–488; U.S. intervention in, 91

Congress, U.S., 59, 233; advisory functions, 239–240; bipartisanship, 241–242; and foreign policy making, 238–242; leadership in public opinion, 239, 240. See also United States, Congress

Congress of Berlin (1878; 1884), 334, 477

Congress of Vienna (1815), 23, 298, 336, 477

Connally, Tom, 239, 240; amendment to Statue of International Court, 494

Consensus, 14–15, 19, 90; in authoritarian society, 60; and British foreign policy, 260–261; and Canadian foreign policy, degree of, 68; in democratic societies, 67; in developing countries, 144; and exercise of power, 60; in multiparty situations, 263; and national interest, 52, 209; in organized associations, 472; and U.N., 36; and U.S. foreign policy, 196, 221, 224, 239, 247–248; and value clusters, 54, 294; Western, 56

Constitution, U.S., 61, 261; Bill of Rights, 61; executive-legislative functions under, 239; and foreign policy, 223; Preamble, 177; and public expectations, 242; and tariffs, 362

Convention on International Civil Avia-

CONVENTION (cont.)
tion (1944), 440
Convention on Rights and Duties of States (1933), 433
Cook, Robert C., 134n.
Costa Rica, 127
Council for Mutual Economic Assistance (CEMA), 370, 473–474; country team, 237–238
Court of Human Rights, European, 429, 443
Credit, international, 140; and International Monetary Fund, 155
Crimean War, 20, 277
Crowe, Sir Eyre: on balance of power, 299–300
Cuba, 8; agrarian reform, 66; and Canada, 263; and China, 327; missile crisis, 21, 111, 190, 211, 231, 239, 245, 328, 403, 404, 418, 419, 464; propaganda system, 352; relations with U.S., 180, 305, 327; and Soviet Union, 168, 188, 276, 327
Cultural relations, 206; and diplomacy, 320, 340; and foreign policy, 353–357; and military assistance, 398; Soviet program, 355–357; techniques of, 355; U.S. program, 353–355
Cyprus, 74, 175, 412, 413; U.N. peacekeeping forces in, 91, 331, 414, 432
Czechoslovakia, 108, 115, 142, 211, 303, 328

Dahl, Robert, 20n.
Daladier, Édouard, 303
Davis, Forrest: on balance of power, 297–298
de Gaulle, Charles, 21, 87, 253; and Algeria, 95; and American power, 191; and balance of power, 300; and diplomacy, 318; and EEC, 139, 295, 456, 457; and foreign policy, 264–266; and French morale, 295; and French national style, 205; and NATO, 34, 216, 301, 306, 401, 450, 453–454, 469; and nuclear power, 391. See also France
Decision making, 49; and attitude formation, 59; in Communist China, 281–287; historical approach, 30–31; in parliamentary system—Great Britain, 255, Canada, 261–262; and policy planning, 46–47, 195–196, 244–247; social science approach, 45; in Soviet Union, 276, 286–287; and systems approach, 37. See also United States, foreign policy process
Declaration of Independence, U.S., 61, 77
Declaration of Legal Principles Governing the Activities of States in the Explora-

tion and Use of Outer Space (U.N.) (1963), 441
Defense, 116–117; British, 259; and Congress, 241; establishments, 177; Kingston Agreement, 261; and military policy, 385; and NATO, 469; and natural resources, 118; and weapons capabilities, 171. See also Security
Defense, U.S. Department of: decision making in—International Security Affairs, 236, Joint Chiefs of Staff, 224–225, 227, Pentagon, 236, Secretary, 224–225, 236; and foreign policy formulation, 214, 220–222, 231, 234–236
Democracy: asidealogy, 60–61; constitutional, of Great Britain, 253–254; and liberal nationalism, 76–77; political stability of, 67
Demography, 2; U.N. studies on, 125. See also Population
Demosthenes: on morality in conduct of states, 307
Denmark, 117, 456
Desalinization, 120, 133, 167
Deterrence, nuclear, 186, 506; and Great Powers, 391; and military policy, 385; and NATO, 469; and U.S. security policy, 404
Deutsch, Karl W.: on communication and nationalism, 75–76
Developing countries, 23–24, 49–50, 63, 137; and anticolonialism, 88, 96; attitudes of, 60, 102–103; and British foreign policy, 94, 259; and Communists, 58, 60, 81, 84, 99, 101–103, 275; and cultural relations, 357; and economic development, 144–145, 148; effect of foreign propaganda in, 345; and food production, 132–133; and foreign aid, 373, 374, 376–377; and military instrument of policy, 389–390; and new nationalism, 81–86; population in, 24, 65, 125–128; and "revolution of rising expectations," 66, 157; social uncertainties of, 189; and Soviet foreign policy, 275; and trade, 152, 154–155; and violence, 387; and Western technology, 162–163, 166–167, 169. See also Emerging nations
Development, 8, 23–24; capital, 116, 142; economic, 36, 91, 144–147, 168; and economic assistance, 379; and military power, 386; and new nations, 144–145, 203; political, 144; and population, 124–125, 130; and power status, 110, 116; regional problems of, 145–147, 156; social, 144; stages of, 145; technological, 166, 167; and U.N., 495

Development Advisory Committee (DAC), 374

Dictatorship, 68; and foreign policy, 195–196; and totalitarian nationalism, 78

Diefenbaker, John, 263

Diplomacy, 7, 20–21, 22, 206, 338–339
FOREIGN POLICY AND, 291, 309, 313–314, 338, 339; change through peaceful means, 18; conflict control, 412; definition, 314; evolution of, 314–317; negotiation, 324, ff
FUNCTIONS OF, 321–324; observation and reporting, 323–324; protection, 321; representation, 321–323
INSTITUTIONS OF: consulates, 315; legations, 315; permanent missions, 315–316; diplomatic immunity, 315
NEGOTIATIONS, 323–324, 328–329; bluff, 327–328; coercion, 328; diplomatic solutions, 326; duplicity, 327; inducements and pressures, 326–327; good offices and mediation, 331–332; military instrument, 385; new diplomacy, 317; persuasion and compromise, 326; purposes and meaning, 324–325; setting for, 332–333; Soviet style, 328–330; subversion and assassination, 330; threat of force, 330–331
PARTICIPANTS, 20th century: British, 259; Communist, 210; foreign secretaries, 230, 278–279, 319, 328–330, 332–333; heads of state, 318–319; international organizations, 42, 320–321; military and other, 319–320, 332; professional diplomats, 319; special emissaries, 319–320
POLICY INSTRUMENTS, 291ff; balance of power, 21, 22, 33; military instrument, 394–395; national security, 210; recognition policy, 437; technology, 166, 168
TYPES: conference, 334–336, 445; parliamentary, 337; present-day, 317; summit, 318, 333–334

Dirksen, Everett, 241

Disarmament, 42, 85, 212, 259; general and complete, 418–419; post-World War II, 175; U.N. negotiations for, 480; and Woodrow Wilson, 412. *See also* Arms control

Disease: control, 116, 127; and World Health Organization, 496. *See also* Public Health Disputes, international, 310, 410–411; boundary, 112–114; and the law, 435; peaceful settlement of, 416–417; and third party, 416; and U.N., 493–495

Dollar, 138; allocation, 227; drain, 140; and exchange controls, 365–366; export of, 188, 380, 382; in international exchange, 140; stability, 140; and U.S. foreign aid, 372. *See also* Balance of payments

Domestic policy: and foreign policy, 203–204; in parliamentary system, 251

Dominican Republic, 91, 111, 245, 262, 396, 413; assassination plot in, 330; and U.S. Congress, 241

Donham, Wallace B., 160n.

Douglas-Home, Alex, 255

Dulles, John Foster, 85, 229, 230, 256, 319; on executive agreements, 223; on future of U.N., 503; on Iron Curtain, 349; on massive retaliation, 404; on neutrality, 34; and U.S.-Japan peace treaty, 242, 320

Dumbarten Oaks conference (1944), 478

Dunn, Frederick S.: on nature of propaganda, 342–343

East Germany, 142, 294; and U.S. recognition policy, 437

Eastern Europe, 116; Mackinder on, 108; Soviet imperialism in, 98–99. *See also* Communist bloc

Economic Commission for Africa (ECA), 495

Economic Commission for Europe (ECE), 495

Economics, international, 2, 6, 45, 49, 51, 122; and boundaries, 115; change since World War II, 157–159; and foreign policy, 136–159, 291, 310, 359–361; and industrialized states, 137–142; interdependence in, 155–156; investment and, 147–150; and less-developed states, 142–147; and national interest, 198, 209; and national security, 178; and technology, 160, 165, 166; trade patterns, 150–156; trends, 382–383; and Western colonialism, 92, 99

Economy: international, 91, 136–159; Soviet, 140; U.S., 139–140

Ecuador: and territorial waters, 440

Eden, Sir Anthony, 253; and Churchill, 318

Education, 65–66; cultural relations, 353–354; food problem, 133; and literacy, 123–124; and population trends, 125, 127, 128; for potential leadership, 208; for students from underdeveloped nations, 166

Egypt, 65, 116; Arab League, 454; assassination plots, 330; Aswan Dam, 99, 158; and Communists, 84, 204; and

EGYPT (cont.)
control of Suez Canal, 120, 442; propaganda system, 352; Soviet assistence to, 174, 327. *See also* Nasser; United Arab Republic
Eighteen Nation Committee on Disarmament, Geneva, 418; and nonproliferation, 419
Eire, 400, 459
Eisenhower, Dwight D., 178, 190, 214, 223, 253, 256; and Congress, 241, 242; and diplomacy, 318, 320; on national power, 296; Near East policy, 224; 1960 trip to Japan, 216; and NSC, 227, 238; Open Sky proposal, 418; on orchestration of policy, 404–405; on policy making, 510; Presidential advisers, 225–226; and Secretary of State, 229–230
Eisenhower, Milton, 320
El Salvador, 168
Elites, 44, 59, 343: in authoritarian society, 67, 209; Chinese, 282; Communist, 99, 269, 271; in emerging nations, 94, 353; revolutionary, 67–68; in traditional society, 65
Emerging nations, 142–147, 157; and absorption of capital, 166; and balance-of-payments problem, 156, 382; and British foreign policy, 259–260; and control of military power, 394; and industrial technology, 169; and International Monetary Fund, 369; and international trade, 362, 365, 368; middle class in, 83; and military instrument of policy, 389–390; and OECD, 448; and population growth, 135, 142; and public finance, 148–150; and revenue tariff, 362; Sino-Soviet rivalry over, 281; U.S. investment in, 139, 507
Emerson, Rupert: on trusteeship, 498
Energy: U.S. per capita consumption of, 164
England, 77. *See also* Great Britain
Environment, 54, 106; external, 51–52, 177, 182; and foreign policy, 195, 197, 201, 205–206, 218; and military power, 386; and national interest, 211
Escalation, 391, 411, 506; of East-West conflict, 280; of local conflicts, 393; and threat of armed force, 395; and Vietnam, 510
Espionage, 206, 324. *See also* Intelligence
Estrada, Don Genaro: on *de facto* recognition, 438
Ethiopia, 8, 65, 89, 114, 143; case against South Africa, 494; and Italy, 21, 303, 413, 478; -Somalia dispute, 461
Europe, 1; and balance of power, 20–21,

32; decline in international politics, 316; and disintegration of colonial empires, 88, 505; nationalism (19th century), 70, 74; political cooperation, 458; population, 124, 125, 127; and U.S. isolationist policy, 58. *See also* individual countries
European Atomic Energy Community (EURATOM) 41, 87, 420, 454, 455
European Coal and Steel Community (ECSC), 41, 87, 454, 455; and France, 264
European Commission for the Danube, 477
European Common Market. *See* European Economic Community
European Economic Community (EEC), 10, 16, 41, 58, 138, 156, 364, 369, 448, 452, 454–456, 467; and CEMA, 473; and conference diplomacy, 335; and de Gaulle, 139, 265, 266, 295, 456, 457–458; High Authority, 449, 455; organization of—European Court of Justice, 455, members of, 454, Parliament, 455; and shared-value consensus, 90
European Free Trade Association (EFTA), 138–139, 369, 456–458; members of, 457
European Recovery Program, 170. *See also* Marshall Plan
European Unity Movement: and conference displomacy, 335
Exchange, scientific, 165–166
Executive agreements, 225, 239; Dulles on, 223
Expansionism: and patterns of policy, 310–311; and population pressures, 130; territorial, 99, 117
Exports, 92, 121, 137; single-commodity, 154, 188; of surpluses, 148, 154; and terms of trade, 363–364; and underdeveloped countries, 155. *See also* Trade, international
Expropriation, 150, 327; and international law, 442–443
Extremism, political: and change, 67–68

Fainsod, Merle M., 271n.
Fairbanks, John, 439
Federal Bureau of Investigation, 223
Fellows, Lawrence, 85n.
Fénelon, François, 297
Fichte, Johann Gottlieb, 75
Finland, 117, 212; political situation of, 263–264
Finletter, Thomas: on growth of military technology, 173
Food, 124, 125, 128, 167; and population

increase, 131–133
Food and Agriculture Organization (FAO), 132, 369, 496
Food for Peace Program (Public Law 480), 131, 150, 374
Force, 117, 385, 386; ambiguity of, 396; and limited technology, 172; management of, and diplomacy, 394–395; readiness, 396; restraints to, 395–396; threat of, 330–331; and U.N. Charter, 434, 436, 443. *See also* Armed force
Ford Foundation, 243
Foreign aid and assistance, 54, 84, 99, 229, 233, 360; Communist, 375; defined, 372–373; and expansion of Soviet influence, 99; and food for underdeveloped nations, 131–133; growth of, 91; and interdependence, 188; motives, 376–377; objectives, 373; and policy patterns, 310, 338; political influence of, 379; and population control, 130, 134; requirements for receiving, 91–92; sources, 374–376; to transitional societies, 68–69; types, 373; and U.S. public opinion, 224; and World Bank, 373. *See also* United States, economic and assistance policies.
Foreign policy, 6, 106, 197–218
 BASIC ASPECTS OF: decision making, 46–47, 195–196; economic basis, 136–159, 359–360; formulation, 199–201, 214–215, 221; goals and objectives, 197–198, 360–361; idealism and morality, 212–213; limitations, 218; national interest, 197–199, 208–212; national security, 178, 192, 204, 227, 233, 234; policy-planning approach, 47; political realism, 212; uncertainty and risk, 215–217
 INSTRUMENTS OF: diplomacy, 313–339; economic instruments, 359–383; international communications, 340–358 — propaganda, 342–352; military, 384–406; power politics, 293–312
 INTERNAL ELEMENTS: change, 68, 233; elites, 209; geography, 110; private capital, 94; programs and commitments, 202–203; public opinion, 44, 198–199, 207, 219; raw materials, 120; relation to domestic policy, 203–204; science, 236–237; technology, 166–167, 169–170, 236–237
 PATTERNS: content analysis, 349; domestic information, 348–349; evaluation, 351–352; and expansionist objectives, 310–311; and international relations, 310; interrelation, 311, 349–351; and propaganda, 291, 340, 348–352, 357–358; security, 310; and welfare, 310
 SOURCES OF: image of environment, 205–206; intelligence, 206–207; leadership, 207–208; tradition, history, 204–205
Foreign Policy Association, 243
Foreign relations, 2, 3; and attitudes, 57–58; British policy, 255; gauging responses, 58; increase in, 219, 239; in multiparty situations, 263; and the public, 243–244; U.S. approach to, 215
Foreign secretaries: British, 251, 255–256; and diplomacy, 319; and intelligence, 323; personal diplomacy by, 333; U.S., 224, 229–230
Foreign Service, Rogers Act, 316
Formosa, 101, 483. *See also* Chinese Nationalist Republic
Foster, William C.: on nuclear proliferation, 419–420
France, 7, 8, 32, 109, 117, 294; and balance of power, 300; Communist Party of, 63, 264; cultural relations, 261, 353; disintegration of empire, 88, 92, 94–96; and EEC, 138; and emerging nations, 104; foreign investment, 149; foreign policy, 264; Fourth Republic, 205, 210—coalition government, 250, instability, 263, 264; Fifth Republic—policy process in, 265–266; and Germany, 58, 265; and international trade, 368; and League of Nations, 21; military assistance, 397; military power, 400; nationalism, 77; national style, 205; and NATO, 34, 216, 264, 266, 512; nuclear power, 385, 390; Nuclear Test Ban Treaty, 419; power status, 299, 403; religion, 73; Revolution, 77; and SEATO, 470; and Suez, 59, 304, 328; Third Republic, 205, 210, 264; traditional politics of, 264–265; and U.N., 431, 488. *See also* de Gaule, Charles
Franklin, Benjamin, 73
Frederick the Great, 184
French Community, 87, 95–96, 448, 459–460
Friedmann, Wolfgang, 429n.
Friedrich, Carl: on rule, 89–90
Fulbright Act of 1946, 354
Fulbright, J. William, 239; and Johnson's foreign policies, 241
Fulbright Act of 1946, 354
Functionalism: and organized cooperation, 452–453

Gallois, Pierre, 174
Game theory: approach to international politics, 45, 295
Gandhi, Indira, 131
Gandhi, Mohandas K., 94, 264; and national consciousness, 76; and national style, 388–389
Garibaldi, Giuseppe, 75
General Agreement on Tariffs and Trade (GATT) (1948), 155, 364, 365, 369
General Order No. 100, U.S. War Dept., 386
Geneva Conferences: Disarmament, 85, 175, 418; Law of the Sea (1958), 433; Trade and Development (1964), 14, 85, 157
Genocide Convention (1948), 307
Geography, 2, 51, 122; approach to international affairs, 106–112; boundaries, 113–115; elements of—climate, 106, 116, natural resources, 118–122, size and location, 116–117; topography, 106, 112–113; and international associations, 450; and international relations, 105–107; and national security, 190; and power, 295; Spykman on, 110; and technology, 165, 171
Geopolitics, 106; and Communism, 111–112; Haushofer and, 111; Kjellén's definition, 106; Mackinder and, 107–109; Spykman and, 110–111
George, Walter, 240
German Democratic Republic; see East Germany
German Federal Republic; see West Germany
Germany, 5, 8, 21, 73, 117; colonial empire of, 93; division of, 21, 113, 115, 482; and France, 58; and international law, 430; *Lebensraum* thesis, 111, 423; Nazi, 60, 71, 74, 78, 111, 155, 263, 295, 310, 328, 367; nuclear power, 390; post-World War II power, 299; rearmament, 181, 258; reunification, 259; sea power, 109, 110; Weimar Constitution, 263; in World War II, 185, 187. *See also* East Germany; West Germany
Ghana, 83, 101, 459
Gibbon, Edward: on balance of power, 297
Goals, national, 2, 6, 39, 41, 293, 509; Communist Chinese, 282; economic, 359; and foreign policy, 10–11, 197–202; military power and, 388; power politics, 294; and technological advancement, 164
Goebbels, Joseph, 342
Gold, 138; drain, 380; and U.S. balance-of-payments deficit, 380. *See also* Balance of payments
Goldberg, Arthur J., 230, 488
Gomulka, Wladyslaw, 79
Gooch, G. P., 300n.
Good offices and mediation, 331–332
Good Offices Committee, U.N., 489, 493
Goodpaster, Andrew: on relation of policy to program, 202–203
Goodrich, Leland M., 498n.
Government, 65; authoritarian systems, 196; cabinet system, 196, 210; constitutional, 77–78; and foreign policy, 214; presidential system, 196, 209–210. *See also* United States, government
Grants, 372, 373, 397; bilateral, 148–149. *See also* Assistance; Foreign aid and assistance
Great Britain, 7, 8, 116, 294
    FOREIGN POLICY AND RELATIONS: and balance of power, 20, 33, 110, 204, 211, 300; colonialism, 88, 92–94, 211; cultural relations, 353; East-West détente, 259; EFTA, 456–457; emerging nations, 104, 259; foreign aid, 259; foreign exchange, 138; foreign investment, 149, 373; Germany, 181, 300; International Monetary Fund, 369; League of Nations, 21; NATO, 258–259, 300, 466; nature of, 58, 250–261; propaganda, 352; public opinion and, 260–261; recognition policy, 437; Rhodesia, 371; SEATO, 470; Suez, 59, 254, 304, 328; trade, 151, 367; and U.N., 256; and U.S., 258, 260; and Zambia, 91
    GOVERNMENT, AGENCIES AND DEPARTMENTS OF: Atomic Energy commission, 455; Board of Trade, 252, 257; Cabinet committees, 252; Commonwealth Relations Office, 257; Crown, 251, 458; Exchequer, 214, 251–252; Foreign Office, 256–257; Foreign Secretary, 251, 253—aides to, 256, and Prime Minister, 255, and U.S. Secretary of State compared, 255–256; High Court of Judicature, 432; Law Lords of Privy Council, 432; ministers, 256; Minister of Defense, 251, 257
    NATIONAL INTEREST AND POWER: military strategy, 400; nationalism and national interests, 72–73, 211; nuclear power, 390; power decline, 170, 259, 299, 403, 511; sea power, 109, 210–211, 387
    PARLIAMENT AND PARTIES: 251, 253, 257–258; Opposition, 257–258;

parties, 257–260 — Conservative, 258–259, Labour, 251, 253, 258–259
POLICY MAKING: and Cabinet, 251–252; compared to U.S. President, 253–254; coordination and direction of policy, 252–253
Great Powers, 1, 7, 8; and balance-of-power thesis, 303; and colonialism, 92–93; and conference diplomacy, 335; and conflict control, 412; foreign policy programs of, 203; and instruments of policy and power, 117; and interdependence, 174–175; and international law, 432; and international organizations, 42; and lesser powers, 8, 10; military capability, 171–172, 173–174, 391; and military strategy, 400; and new nations, 85, 86; as peacemaker, 181; and population, 123; power struggles, 294; and sea power, 109; and superpowers, 8; and U.N., 402, 482; and war, 186, 306, 390–391; and World War I, 395
Greece, 328, 403; city-states, 29, 317; civil war, 330; and diplomatic immunity, 315; -Turkish dispute, 175, 301; and U.N., 489; U.S. military aid to, 198
Greek-Turkish Aid Program, 21, 224, 245, 404, 507; and balance of power, 299
Grew, Joseph C.: on diplomat's responsibility, 322
Grey, Sir Edward, 255
Griswold, Whitney: on U.S. policy-making process, 220
Gromyko, Andrei, 274
Gross National Product, 8, 10, 151; and insurgency, 388; Japanese economic growth rate, 141; and per capita output, 143–144, 147; and single-commodity export, 154, 188; table of estimates of, 138; as technology indicator, 164, 165; U.S., 138, 139–140, 164, 167
Grotius, Hugo, 41, 187, 427, 428
Growth, economic, 99, 137–142; in developing countries, 144–145; and investment, 147–148; and national security, 188; and new nationalism, 83; requirements for, 145
Guam, 96
Guantanamo Naval Base, 92
Guinea, 83, 84, 168, 368; and Soviet recognition, 437

Haas, Ernst: on conceptions of balance, 298
Hague, The, 187; Peace Conferences (1899, 1907), 334, 418, 477

Haile Selassie, Emperor: and Algerian-Morrocan cease-fire, 331; charisma of, 83
Hallstein, Walter: on EEC, 456
Hamilton, Alexander: on national interest, 208, 211; on power politics, 312; on President's power in foreign affairs, 233
Hammarskjöld, Dag, 486–487; on bloc differences, 499; death of, 500
Hanseatic League, 427
Harding, Warren G., 225–226
Harriman, Averell, 230, 320
Harvard University: Kennedy Institute of Politics, 221; Littauer School of Public Administration, 219, 292
Haushofer, Karl: on geopolitics, 111
Hawaii, 96
Healey, Denis, 259
Health sciences, 167. See also Public health
Hegel, Georg Whilhelm, 39, 75
Herter, Christian, 230, 502; on Soviet foreign policy negotiators, 271
Herz, J. H., 178
Hickenlooper, Bourke: on propaganda, 350
Hilsman, Roger: on men and policy making, 220; on rapidity of technological development, 172
Hiroshima, 505
History: approach to international politics, 30–31; and balance-of-power thesis, 303; in Communist ideology, 60, 69, 111; and foreign policy, 204–205; influence on leadership, 2, 6; rapidity of change, 504–506
Hitler, Adolf, 18, 20, 21, 33, 90, 92, 260, 263, 303, 347, 348; diplomatic cunning of, 328; and Jews, 505. See also Germany
Ho Chih-Minh, 101
Hobson, John A., 93, 93n
Hoffman, Paul, 497
Hoffmann, Stanley: on approaches to international relations theory, 42, 43n, 48; on limitations in power politics, 308
Holmes, Oliver Wendell, 39
Holy Alliance, 189
Honduras, 133
Hopkins, Harry, 225, 319
House, Colonel Edward, 225
Hudson, Manley O., 444n.
Hughes, Charles Evans, 225–226; on foreign policy, 198
Hull, Cordell, 225; on balance of power and U.N., 480–482
Human Rights Commission, U.N., 495
Hume, David, 38; "On the Balance of Power," 297
Humphrey, Hubert H., 209, 225
Hundred Years War, 35
Hungary, 42, 99, 328; national uprisings in,

HUNGARY (cont.)
79–80, 216, 304, 335, 349; U.N. condemnation of Soviet intervention, 42
Huntington, Samuel P., 60*n*.

Iceland, 165; and territorial waters, 440
Idealism, 37; approach to international politics, 39, 49; and foreign policy, 212–213, 215; and propaganda, 348
Ideology, 2, 6, 30, 306; authoritarian, 67; Communist, 60, 61–64, 69, 271, 278; conflict of, 25–26, 60–61, 198, 387; constitutional democracy as, 60, 61, 66–67; deterministic, 39; and foreign affairs, 59–64; and foreign policy, 291; institutionalization of, 70–71; and international relations, 106; and national security, 189; and nationalism, 83–84; power of, 59–64
Immigration, 130–131
Imperial Conference, London (1923), 261
Imperialism, 51, 54, 60; Chinese—and developing countries, 101–102, and territorial expansion, 99–101, and world leadership, 102; cultural, 89; defined, 89–90; economic, 89, 91–92, 367; and nationalism, 88, 94–96; Soviet—Eastern Europe, 79, 98–99, and underdeveloped areas, 99; Western—dissolution of colonial empires, 94–97, and economic theories, 93–94, and motives of, 92–93, 130
Imports, 137; and internal raw materials policy, 120; quotas, 365–366; and terms of trade, 363–364; U.S., 139. *See also* Trade, international
Income, per capita, 130, 145, 151; and investment capital, 147–148. *See also* Gross National Product
Independence, 1, 7, 36, 98; and boundaries, 113; and nation building, 23; and political instability, 96; since 1945 (table), 95
India, 7, 8, 58, 64, 94, 116; and arms, 388–389; and balance of power, 300–301, 305; boundary disputes, 115; and China, 85, 100, 174, 281, 388; Communists, 84, 204; Congress Party, 76, 264; development problems, 145–147; education, 124; industrialization, 137; and Kashmir dispute, 57, 87, 114, 115, 278, 294, 301, 311, 361, 389, 413; language of, 72; military strategy, 401; nationalism in, 74, 76; population, 99, 127, 130, 134; purchase of weapons by, 174; religion of, 73, 123; and Soviet economic aid, 99, 146, 327; and technology, 164; as transitional society, 65, 66; U.S.

food to, 131, 146
Indian-Pakistan dispute, 57, 87, 114, 115, 278, 294, 301, 311, 361, 389, 451, 470, 494; cease-fire, 413–414; and Great Britain, 459. *See also* Tashkent meeting
Indochina, 94; Communist Chinese in, 281
Indonesia, 59, 66, 67, 83, 123, 305; and Chinese foreign policy, 281; and Communism, 68, 101, 330—overthrow of, 379, 451; independence, 96, 367; Soviet foreign assistance, 327; and technology, 164; and U.N., 484, 489. *See also* Sukarno, Achmed
Industrialization, 8; and balance of power, 305; Chinese, 102; and economic base, 136–137, 169; in emerging nations, 23, 65, 152, 157; and international politics, 26–27, 109; Japanese, 141; and national strength, 118; politics, 26–27, 109; and population trends, 124–125, 128; and raw materials, 118, 119; Soviet, 99; and stages of development, 145; and technology, 169
Instability, political, 24, 25; and French political system, 264; and population size and distribution, 128; in traditional societies, 65; in transitional societies, 66. *See also* Stability
Institute of International Education, 353
Intelligence: and diplomacy, 323–324; and foreign policy, 206–207, 214, 274; and military power, 395; and Soviet recognition policy, 437; technological, 166. *See also* Central Intelligence Agency
Interaction: economic, 116; ideological, 116–117, political, 2; social, 116
Inter-American Alliance for Progress: *see* Alliance for Progress
Inter-American Defense Board, 456
Inter-American Development Bank, 374, 453, 464
Inter-American System, 45, 450; and Alliance for Progress, 379; U.S. support for policies of, 241. *See also* Organization of American States
Inter-American Treaty of Reciprocal Assistance (1947), text of, 532–536. *See also* Rio Pact
International Bank for Reconstruction and Development (IBRD); *see* World Bank
International Communist organization, 473–474. *See also* Council for Mutual Economic Assistance; Warsaw Pact
International Community; *see* Community
International Court of Justice; 36, 41, 115, 416, 426, 431, 443–446, 493–494; and international law, 444–445; jurisdiction of, 493–494; and *stare decisis*, 436;

Statute of, 428–429, 443, 444, 493, 494
International Development Association, 42, 150. *See also* World Bank
International Labor Organization, 36, 369, 496
International law, 16, 22, 37–38, 425–446, 507; air, jurisdiction in, 440; arbitration, 416; binding force of, 429–431; and change, 443–444; *consolato del mare* and, 212, 307, 427; diverse interpretations of, 433; early concepts of, 426–427; enforcement of, 434; and expropriation, 442–443; founders of, 427; and individuals, 443; institutional inadequacies of, 431–433; and International Court of Justice, 425–426; in international politics, 434–436; *jus civile*, 427; *jus gentium*, 426–427, 444–445; as normative theory, 41–43; observance of, 433–434, 441–443; and outer space, 440–441; *pacta sunt servanda*, 441, 442; and peace, 409, 411; and policy patterns, 309; and power politics, 307–308, 434–436; *rebus sic stantibus* doctrine, 441; and recognition, 437–439; and rules of war, 187; seas, 439–440; and self-defense, 184; sources of, 428; sovereignty of, 428–429; and space satellites, 166; *stare decisis*, 436; and state jurisdiction, 439–440; and U.N. Charter, 426, 429, 431; Wisby, law of, and, 427; and world law, 445–446
International Law Commission, U.N. 433
International Monetary Fund (IMF), 155, 371, 496; creation of, 368–369
International organization, 10, 21, 87, 161, 198; approach to international politics, 42–43; and balance of power, 301, 308–309; Communist, 473–474; cooperation in—basic elements, 450, functionalism, 452–453; regionalism, 451–452; and diplomacy, 321, 333; experimentalism in, 474–475; limited membership, 448; limited purpose system, 447ff.; as mechanism of cooperation, 453–454; and national security, 193; philosophy of, 35–36, 39; and policy, 217, 309; and political process, 27. *See also* individual organizations
International politics, 2–5; approaches to—author's, 48–50, eclectic, 47–50, historical, 30–31, normative, 37–43, policy science, 43–47, systemic, 31–37, universalism, 35, 36; change in, 504–506; and Communism, 25–26; and community concept, 16–17; diplomacy, 313–317—dynamic elements of, 23–26, functions, 321–324, negotiations, 324–339, partici-

pants, 318–321; economic factors, 136–150, 359–379; environmental factors—ideas and ideology, 59–69, physical, 105–121, values, 54–59; idealism in, 212–213; international communications—cultural relations, 353–357, propaganda, 342–353; and military instrument, 384–406; morality in, 22–23, 37, 212–213; and national security, 177–193; and nationalism, 70–87; nature and composition of, 6–10, 19–23, 69; and order vs. change, 17–19; and outer space; 117–118; and political realism, 212; and population, 123–135, 144; and power politics, 11–15, 294–312; role of law in, 434–436; rules of the game, 22, 23; setting of, 1–4; and technology, 26–27, 159–176; theories of, 29–50; and trade, 150–156
International Red Cross, 477
International relations, 1–2; Communist theory, 58, 278–279; factors affecting, 51–59; post-World War II balance of power, 299; theories of, 29–50
International trade: agreements, 368–370; economic warfare, 370–372; policies pertaining to, 361–368. *See also* Balance of payments; Foreign aid and assistance
Intervention, military, 168, 412–413; by third parties, 413
Investment, 152, 157; capital—and population control, 127, 130; and regional cooperation, 156, and transfer of technology, 169–170, transfer problem, 148–150, U.S., 139–140; governmental, 91, 149; and growth, 147–148; Japanese, 141; in less-developed countries, 139, 148–150, 203; private, 91, 92, 148–150. *See also* Capital
Iran, 66, 69, 117, 348, 403
Iraq, 368; and Arab League, 460; and Soviet recognition policy, 437
Ireland, nationalism in, 72. *See also* Eire
Iron Curtain, 351; Dulles on, 349
Isaacs, Harold, 66n.
Isolationism, 11, 105, 110; U.S. policy, 58, 164, 214, 217, 245, 400, 505
Israel, 74, 114, 120; and Arab League, 460; Gaza Strip, 429; growth rate, 188; multiparty system, 263; nationalism in, 72; U.S. dollar assistance to, 188. *See also* Arab-Israeli dispute
Italy, 8; colonial empire of, 93; Communist Party, 63; and EEC, 138, 454; and Ethiopia, 21, 303, 413, 478; Fascist, 60, 71, 78, 342, 505; Fiat Company, 169; power status, 299; religion, 73; *risorgimento*, 71

Jackson, Andrew, 46
Jackson, Henry M., 240
Jacoby, Neil: on Nationalist China's economic growth, 145
Japan, 8, 21, 32, 112, 116, 217, 451, 505; Communists in, 348; economic growth rate, 141; economic policy, 141, 148; and League of Nations, 478; and Manchuria, 92, 94, 203, 303, 478; and Pacific Trust Territories, 91; population, 125, 127, 130, 133–134; power status, 299, 305; productivity, 137; religion, 73; and technology, 162–163; treaties, 242, 309, 320, 451, 470; in World War II, 110, 185, 186, 305
Jefferson, Thomas, 36, 61, 75, 166; on balance of power, 297; and humanitarian nationalism, 76
Jessup, Philip C., 41
Jews: and Nazi policies, 74, 347; in World War II Germany, 44, 505
Johnson, Lyndon Baines, 19, 111, 214, 230, 247, 318; appointment of Senior Interdepartmental Group, 227, 238; and Congress, 224, 238, 241, 242; and diplomacy, 320; and NSC, 227; Presidential advisers to, 225, 226, 234; on responsibility of power, 514; 227, 238; State of the Union Address (1966), 124, 142; and trade with Eastern Europe, 142, 473; and U.S. food for India, 131; and Vietnam, 209, 224, 225, 238—peace offensive, 394–395; on world peace, 409
Joint Chiefs of Staff, 224–225, 227
Jones, Joseph M., 233n., 245
Jones, Stephen B., 107
Jordan, Amos A., 384n.
Jurisdiction, state, 439; air space, 133, 433, 440; outer space, 440–441; seas, 439–440

Kadar, Janos, 84
Kahn, Herman, 173
Kaiser Wilhelm, 109
Kant, Immanuel, 38–39
Kashmir dispute, 57, 87, 114, 115, 278, 294, 301, 311, 361, 389, 414. *See also* India; Pakistan
Kellogg-Briand Pact (1928), 418
Kelsen, Hans, 41, 430n.
Kennan, George F.: on definition of diplomacy, 314; on diplomatic negotiations, 324; on foreign policy, 205–206, 213, 215; on power politics, 311–312
Kennedy, John F., 35, 46, 214, 253; and Alliance for Progress, 224, 464; on change and adjustment, 512; and Congress, 241, 242; and Cuban missile crisis,

111, 211, 231, 245, 302; and diplomacy, 318, 320; on emerging nations, 389; on foreign aid, 377; and free trade, 151; on limits of military power, 405; and National Security Council, 227; and Peace Corps, 355; and Presidential advisers, 225, 226 on the press, 244; on U.N., 502–503, 513; on U.S. leadership role, 509
Kennedy, Robert F., 225
Kenya, 66, 81, 84, 94, 114; -Somalia dispute, 461
Kenyatta, Jomo, 66, 76, 81, 94; charisma of, 83; on nonalignment, 85; rejection of Communism by, 84
Khruschev, Nikita, 61, 98, 141, 253, 302, 334; and de-Stalinization, 79; disarmament proposal, 419; fall of, 273; and Soviet foreign policy, 271; and Suez, 328; and summit meetings, 318; on trade, 152; Troika proposal, 500; on wars of liberation, 405
Killian, James R.: on science and foreign relations, 236–237
Kindleberger, Charles P., 147n.
King, William Lyon Mackenzie, 261
Kingston Agreement (1942), 261
Kissinger, Henry A., 175n.; on deterrence, 392n.; on military power, 385; on military strategy, 406
Kjellén, Rudolf: on geopolitics, 106, 111
Knox, Frank, 242
Kohn, Hans, 71
Korea, 115, 216, 482; and Soviet Union, 299; and territorial waters, 440; U.N. military headquarters in, 413; U.S. forces, 207, 231, 245, 289, 432; U.S. foreign aid, 373; -U.S. mutual security pact, 451, 470; and Vietnam, 470. *See also* North Korea
Korean War, 21, 34, 184, 434, 506; and Communist China, 281; and International Court, 445; and U.N., 22, 184, 489–490; U.S. forces in, 207, 231, 245, 289, 507
Kosciusko, Thaddeus, 75
Kosygin, Alexei, 98, 271; at Tashkent, 318–319, 329
Krock, Arthur W., 345
Kurile Islands, 111
Kuwait, 10, 374

Language; and nationalism, 72–73
Lansing, Robert, 256
Laos, 95, 101, 401; and SEATO, 470
Lasswell, Harold: on foreign policy action programs, 291

Latin America, 8, 68, 301; agriculture, 142; anti-American feeling, 56, 367; and assassination plots, 330; and Communism, 98, 281; and Cuban experience, 188; and IMF, 369; and League of Nations, 478–479; nationalism in, 77, 81; population, 125, 127, 128; and U.N., 486; and U.S. —arms restrictions, 422, cultural relations, 353, recognition policy, 438

Latin American Development Bank, 150

Latin American Free Trade Association (LAFTA), 370, 465

Lauterpacht, Sir Hersch: on U.N. Charter, 434n.

Law: see International law

Leadership, 44, 293; and attitudes, 59–60; charismatic, 83; Chinese, 102, 282; and decision-making process, 46; and foreign policy, 207–208, 214; and internal security, 179, 181; in international organizations, 454; and international relations, 106; and military power, 187, 386, 389; and morality, 57; and nationalism, 74–75; in organized associations, 472; and power status, 116; and rapid change, 68; Soviet, 44, 99, 111; U.S., and military strategy, 404. See also Elites

League of Arab States, 448, 454, 460

League of Nations, 16, 21, 36, 261, 505; and collective security, 308, 477–478; and conference diplomacy, 334; and economic sanctions, 371; and peace, 411; principal organs, 477; termination, 478. See also Wilson, Woodrow

Leites, Nathan, 44

Lenin, Vladimir Ilyich, 39, 61, 62, 68, 93, 99; and self-determination, 78; and Soviet foreign policy, 271

Lesotho (Basutoland), 9, 485

Less-developed countries; see Emerging nations

Liberia: Ethiopia vs. South Africa; International Court case, 494

Libya, 24, 69, 92, 116, 119

Lie, Trygve, 486–487

Limited purpose organizations, 447–475; basis of, 450–453; table of, 449. See also individual organizations

Lin Piao, 102n.; on Communist Chinese geopolitical strategy, 112; Minister of Defense, 283; on support of revolution, 281–282

Lincoln, Abraham, 61, 75; on reality of the times, 512

Linebarger, Paul M., 342

Lippmann, Walter, 54–55; on attitudes, 341; on national security, 178; on policy formulation, 201; on status quo, 98

Liska, G., 298n.

Literacy, 116; in less-developed countries, 123; and population control policy, 134; and technology, 162; and UNESCO, 496

Literature; and nationalism, 72–73, 75

Liu Shao-chi, 283

Livy, 426–427

Lloyd George, David, 253

Loans, 148–149. See also Assistance

Locke, John, 76

Lodge, Henry Cabot, 324

Lovett, Robert, 236; on foreign policy machinery, 220

Lumumba, Patrice, 84

Luxembourg, 73; and EEC, 138, 454

Lyons, Lord, 326

MacArthur, General Douglas, 258

Machiavelli, Niccolò, 37, 39; and balance of power, 297; and diplomatic technique, 315

Mackinder, Sir Halford, 107–109, 277

Macmillan, Sir Harold, 253, 255

Madison, James, 36; and balance of power, 296

Magna Carta, 61

Mahan, Admiral Alfred Thayer, 109–110; on military power, 385

Makarios, Archbishop, 74

Malaysia, 67

Maldive Islands (Malé), 8, 10

Mali, 368

Malik, Dr. Charles, 52

Manchuria, 21, 281; and Japan, 92, 94, 203, 303, 478

Mausfield, Mike, 239, 240, 318

Mao Tse-tung, 26, 62, 68, 80, 102, 280–281; Chairman of Party, 283; and Chinese revolutionary strategy, 112; on military power, 385; in Moscow, 84

Marshall, C. B., 199

Marshall, General George C., 192, 230, 236; reaction of to Soviet diplomacy, 329

Marshall Plan, 58, 138, 166, 240, 241, 245, 369–370, 373, 507, 514; and balance of power, 299; and diplomatic inducement, 326–327; and France, 265; as a viable foreign policy program, 203, 231, 328, 338

Martin, Paul, 262

Marx, Karl, 39, 44, 61

Marxism-Leninism, 56, 79, 98, 102, 268, 278; and international law, 430; and Sino-Soviet conflict, 287–288; and universal peace, 213

Mass media, 26, 166, 168–169; and diplomacy, 317, 336; and foreign affairs, 243–244, 247
Massachusetts Institute of Technology, 236
Mazzini, Giuseppe, 75
McNamara, Robert, 171, 236; on Chinese nuclear capability, 390
Mediation, 416; good offices and, 331–332; U.N., 493
Mediator: U.N., 489
Mendès France, Pierre, 266
Mesabi: ore supplies, 119–120
Mexico: nationalism in, 74; U.S. trade in, 365; -U.S. water diversion dispute, 417
Mexican War, 74
Middle East, 68; boundaries of states of, 112; economic efforts in, 91; new states of, 81, 88; oil reserves of, 119; religious differences, 123. *See also* Near East
Middle powers, 8
Miller, William Lee: on policy supported by action, 510
Military assistance, 397, 398
Military establishment: and diplomacy, 320; and peacekeeping, 414–415; and policy formulation, 214, 220–222, 231, 234–236
Military instrument: and emerging nations, 389–390; management, 391–398; nature of, 384; nuclear power and, 390–393; purposes of, 384–386. *See also* Strategy
Military power, 30, 361; adjustment of, 388–389; and balance of power, 306–307; conceptual framework, 400; defined, 384; and diplomacy, 330–331, 338, 394–395; and emerging nations, 389–390; and foreign policy, 291, 310; inhibitions to use of, 395–396; and limited-war force, 172; Mahan's seapower thesis, 108–110; management of, 391–394; and modern technology, 170; and national security, 178, 182; nuclear, 390–391, 393; planning, 396–397; projection of, 117; purpose—coercion, 385, defense, 385, deterrence, 384–385, leadership and development, 386, national prestige, 385, and negotiations, 385, protectivity of, 385; and restraints, 395–396; and show of force, 395; Soviet, 275, 276; and third party, 174. *See also* Strategy, military
Mindszenty, Cardinal, 321
Mini-states, 8, 10, 94
Missiles, 109, 117, 173; and defense, 385; and military strategy, 399; Soviet, 278
Mitrany, David: on special-purpose organizations, 452
Molotov, Vyachyslav, 274, 318; and Soviet

"diplomacy of exhaustion," 329
Mongolia, 8, 281
Monroe, James, 36
Monroe Doctrine, 198, 211, 224
Montesquieu, Charles, 76
Morale; as a component of power, 294–295
Morality, 22–23, 37, 57; and foreign policy, 212–213; and power politics, 307
Morgenthau, Hans, 40; on national interest, 208
Morgenthau, Henry, 225
Morocco, 84, 116; and Algeria, cease-fire, 331, 461; and Arab League, 460
Moscow Conference of Communist and Workers Parties, 346–347, 405
Mosley, Philip E., 287n.
Mossedegh, Mohammed, 348–349
Mozambique, 96, 497–498
Muller, Herbert J., 103n.
Multilateral Nuclear Force (NATO), 391
Munich Conference, 212
Murville, Maurice Couve de, 264, 265
Mussolini, Benito, 78, 92, 342
Mutual Security Program, 192
Mutual-security pacts, 451

Nagasaki, 505
Nagy, Imre, 79
Napoleon, 20, 32, 75, 184; on wars, 402
Napoleonic Wars, 33, 386
Nasser, Gamal Abdel, 66, 85, 165, 174, 207; charisma of, 83; and Egyptian diplomacy, 318. *See also* Egypt
Nation building, 23–25; and technology, 166
National defense; *see* Defense
National income; *see* Gross National Product
National interest, 22, 39, 49, 261; articulation of, 209; and bipolarity, 34; changing conception of, 210–211; Chinese, 280; and consensus, 52; and foreign aid, 373; and foreign policy, 197, 198–199, 208–212; gauging of, 210; and geography, 107; governmental deadlocks over, 210; and international cooperation, 450; Lord Palmerston on, 58; Machiavelli's view, 37–38; and military assistance, 398; and power politics, 294, 307; and Sino-Soviet relations, 290; and U.N., 480; and war, 185
National Security. *See* Security; Defense
National Security Act of 1947, 226, 238
National Security Council: 223, 238; and control of military power, 394; and foreign policy, 226–227
National style, 75, 204, 224, 293; French,

205; Indian, 388–389

Nationalism, 1, 11, 18, 33, 51, 67, 122, 293, 506; and anticolonialism, 88, 96; as antifeeling toward West, 24; and balance of power, 305; birth of, 35–36; and boundaries, 114; character and style, 75; communication, 75, 76; and Communist, 78–80, 84, 99, 157, 279; definition of, 71; and economic goals, 360–361; and economic growth, 83, 84; and international law, 425; and international relations, 106; internationalism and supranationalism, 86–87; liberal, and national self-determination, 76–78, 87; and nation building, 23; and national security, 189; nature and composition of, 70–71; new, non-Western—features of, 81, 83, and neutralism, 84, 85; political, 76–86; and popular armies, 184, 185; and population explosion, 128–130; and racialism and xenophobia, 74–75, 86, 87; roots of, 72–76; and Sino-Soviet dispute, 34; symbols of, 75; and technology, 161; totalitarian, 78, 87; and trade, 78; underlying factors of, 72–76

Nationality, 74–76

Nation-state: *see* State system

NATO; *see* North Atlantic Treaty Organization

Natural resources; *see* Raw materials

Naval Limitation Agreements (1922), 418

Nazi-Soviet Non-Aggression Pact (1939), 279

Near East, 91; U.N. peacekeeping forces, 414, 432, 492. *See also* Middle East

Negotiation; *see* Diplomacy

Nehru, Jawaharlal, 24, 94, 264; on population growth, 130

Nelson, Viscount Horatio, 75

Netherlands, 8, 73, 116, 117; and EEC, 138, 454; and Indonesia, 96; multiparty system, 263; relation of trade to GNP, 151

Neumann, Franz, 20n.

Neumann, Sigmund, 44; "crisis strata," 68

Neustadt, Richard: on institutional arrangements for foreign affairs, 221

Neutralism, 1, 11; in Asia and Africa, 55–56, 102; of emerging nations, 24, 105; limitations of policy, 85; and military policy, 397; and military strategy, 400–401; and nationalism, 84–86; and SEATO, 470; and security, 174, 192; and view of world order, 19

New Zealand, 127, 130; and Great Britain, 261; and SEATO, 470

Nicolson, Sir Harold, 314, 315–316

Niebuhr, Reinhold, 39; on ethnic kinship, 74–75; on hierarchy of authority, 103n.; on morality in power politics, 307; on traditional cultures, 65

Nielsen, Waldemar: on Black Africa vs. White rule, 96

Nigeria, 59, 66, 116, 123

Nitze, Paul, 236; on creation of world order, 509; on military power, 385

Nkrumah, Kwame, 83, 101, 461

Nonalignment, 1, 11, 14; and Afro-Asian states, 35, 84, 102; and balance of power, 300, 306; and military strategy, 400; and national security, 189; and patterns of policy, 310; and U.N., 499–500, 506; and view of world order, 19, 21

Nordic Council, 450, 475

North American Air Defense Command (NORAD), 262, 468

North Atlantic Community, 10, 14, 137; and NATO, 335

North Atlantic Treaty Organization (NATO), 10, 14, 17, 34, 45, 87, 309, 338, 448, 453–454, 465–470, 472, 506, 514; and balance of power, 21, 299; and Canada, 262; and coexistence policy, 402; and collective self-defense, 452; and de Gaulle, 34–35, 216, 264, 266, 401, 450, 453–454, 468, 469, 512; and diplomacy, 320, 328—conference, 335, foreign secretaries, 333; and Germany into, 260; and Great Britain, 258, 259, 300; military commands, 449; and military power, 385, 400–401; and military technology, 174, 175; Multilateral Force (MLF), 391; organization of, 453, 466–467; and policy planning, 231; public support for, 224; and security, 467–470; and shared-value consensus, 108; Supreme Allied Commander, political role of, 320; Treaty (1948), text of, 525–528; and U.S., 58, 211, 241, 258, 331, 403, 454, 468, 507; and U.S. military assistance, 397

North Korea, 98, 100, 115, 213. *See also* Korea

North Sea; gas supplies, 170

North Vietnam, 95, 98, 101, 184, 199, 209; and Tonkin Gulf encounter, 239. *See also* Vietnam

Norway, 117, 401; and EFTA, 456

Nuclear Test Ban Treaty (1963), 239, 390, 417, 418–419, 424; text of, 529–531

Nuclear weapons, 8, 54, 58, 109, 110, 117, 183; control of, 410—Baruch Plan, 418, Open Sky proposal, 418, U.S. proposals, 419–420; and geography, 113; and NATO, 468; proliferation, 163, 174,

NUCLEAR WEAPONS (cont.)
259, 391, 418, 419, 422, 506; in space, 118; and war, 178, 212, 289, 302, 342, 387
Nuremburg Trials, 443

Office of Emergency Planning, U.S., 226
Oil, 91, 116, 119, 139; and technological advances, 165, 167. *See also* Raw materials
Oppenheim, L., 434*n*.
Order, international; and collective security, 21–22; concept of, 17–19; and national security, 19, 177; and peaceful vs. violent change, 18, 67–69; and "rule of law," 41
Organization for Economic Cooperation and Development (OECD), 139, 370, 448, 457, 467, 472; and aid to emerging nations, 374; and expenditures in technology, 162
Organization for European Economic Co-operation (OEEC), 265, 369–370, 466
Organization of African Unity (OAU), 41, 87, 448, 458, 460–461; Charter, 461
Organization of American States, 10, 17, 41, 42, 448, 462–465; Charter, 452, 462; and Communism, 464; and conference diplomacy, 335; and conflict control, 414; and Dominican Republic, 91, 245, 413, 462, 464; and foreign secretaries, 333; Inter-American Conference, 464; Pan-American Union, 462; *See also* Rio Pact
Organization of Central American States, 465
Osgood, Robert: on national interest, 208
Outer Mongolia, 98
Outer Seven; *see* European Free Trade Association
Outer space, 117–118, 237, 506; and international law, 166, 429, 440–441; Soviet achievements, 276, 278

Pacific Trust Territories, 91, 96
Padelford, Norman J., 461*n*., 487*n*., 498*n*.
Pakistan, 8, 123, 305; division of, 216; Kashmir dispute, 57, 87, 115, 278, 294, 301, 311, 361, 388, 413; nationalism in, 74; and religion, 73; and SEATO, 470; as transitional society, 64, 66
Palestine, 22; and International Court, 445; partition of, 74; and U.N., 489. *See also* Israel
Palmerston, Lord, 58, 253, 255; on balance-of-power policy, 302

Pan-American Union, 462
Papacy: authority of, 427
Parliamentary system: 249–267; Cabinet, 249, 250–254; Parliament, 250; policy making in, 249–261; Prime Minister, 249, 250–254
Paul VI, Pope, 27; appeal for peace, 410
Pax Britannica, 414
Peace, 19, 54, 409–424; arms control and, 417–424; and boundary disputes, 115; British view, 260; conflict control, 412–414; and international law, 41–42; philosophical view, 38; search for, 410–411; and U.N., 178. *See also* United Nations, peacekeeping
Peace Corps, 323, 355
Peaceful change, 12–19
"Peaceful coexistence," 26, 63, 181, 402, 404; and Communist dogma, 279
Peacekeeping, 410, 414–416; and nuclear power, 186; and temporary intervention, 91, 96; and U.N., 22, 42, 186, 190, 192; and unilateral intervention, 91. *See also* United Nations, peacekeeping
Pearl Harbor, 60, 184, 207, 308
Pearson, Lester, 262, 501–502; on diplomacy and policy, 313, 317; on expert personnel, 320; on relationship of strength and diplomacy, 339
Permanent Court of Arbitration, The Hague, 36, 416
Permanent Court of International Justice, 444, 477. *See also* International Court of Justice
Perry, Commodore Matthew C., 217
Peru, 8; and territorial waters, 440
Philippines, 90; independence, 96, 204; and SEATO, 470
Poland, 8, 98, 115, 212, 303, 328; church-state relations, 73–74; uprisings in, 79–80
Policy, 117; geopolitical approach to, 107–112; instruments of, 291–292; law as instrument of, 435; patterns of, 309–311; planning, new nations, 144; technology as instrument of, 166–167. *See also* Strategy, military
Policy-science: approach to international politics, 43–47
Political Entities with Qualified Status, 9, 10
Polycentrism, 26, 34, 80, 306
Pool, Ithiel de Sola, 358*n*.
Poole, DeWitt C., 298*n*.; on balance of power, 304
Population, 2, 8, 51, 105, 506; and colonialism, 93; control, 124, 127, 130, 133–134, 141, 167; and economic development, 147–148; estimates of, 107, 125–

127, 134–135; "explosion," 24, 27, 65, 119, 127–130, 144, 158; and food production, 124, 125, 128, 131–133; Malthus prophecy, 135; migration, 130–131; military-age, 188; and national security, 188–189; and power status, 10, 110, 116, 123, 295, 304; and technology, 160, 165, 167; and world politics, 123–130

Portugal, 96; and EFTA, 456

Pound, Roscoe; on origins of law, 427

Power, 5–8, 14, 37, 92, 117; and balance, 296, 298–299; and boundaries, 113–115; and communications, 168; concept, 294–296; defined, 11, 293; and development, 110, 116; economic base of, 10, 136–159, 305, 309, 360–361; elements of, 11, 110, 116–118, 168; geopolitical analysis of, 107–112; in international politics, 293, 305; and leadership, 116; nature of, 11–15; negative, 188, 191, 305; nuclear, 360, 506; and population, 10, 110, 116, 123; and prestige, 15–16, 198; projection of, 117, 165; and raw materials, 116 and responsibility, 103–104; and size, 116

Power politics, 2, 20, 37; approach to international politics, 40–41; and diplomacy, 338–339; historical U.S. suspicion of, 204, 215; as instrument of policy, 291, 293–296; limiting forces in—collective measures, 308–309, international law, 307–308, 435, morality and world opinion, 307, tradition and internal opinion, 308; and nationalism of Communist satellites, 80; Soviet pragmatic approach to, 58, 111. *See also* Balance of Power

Powers, categories of, 8–10

Pragmatism, 57; British, 58; Soviet, 58, 111

Prejudices; see Attitudes

President of the United States, 223–226. *See also* United States, President and Executive branch

President's Material Policy Commission (1952), Report of, 122

Prestige, national, 15–16, 198, 293; and diplomacy, 292, 331; and imperialism, 92; and military power, 385, 400; Soviet, 276; and support of peaceful methods, 181; and technology, 162, 164, 166; and U.N., 84

Price, Don K.: on diplomacy, 292; realism in foreign policy, 220

Production, 137; capital goods, 140; consumer goods, 140; costs, 116; and national security, 188–189; per capita, 143–144, 147

Proletariat, 39; in Communist ideology, 62, 98, 111; and internationalism, 80

Propaganda, 26, 60, 63, 122, 206, 352; anti-imperialist, 88, 102; and communications, 166, 168–169; and diplomacy, 317, 334, 338; domestic, relation to, 348–351; evaluation of, 351–352; and foreign policy, 29, 340, 348–352, 357–358; as instrument of policy, 342–348—barriers to, 343, growth of, 342, nature of, 342–343, requisites for, 343–345; Soviet, 79, 99, 437; types of appeals, 345–348; U.S. and other, 352

Protectionism, 38, 78. *See also* Trade, international

Psychology: and national security, 178, 190

Public administration, 237; and diplomatic training, 321

Public health, 127; and international diplomacy, 320; in less-developed countries, 123–124

Public inforamtion programs, 206, 343; and foreign policy, 291, 340; types of, 345–348. *See also* Propaganda

Public opinion, 6, 22–23; and armed force, 395–396; and British foreign policy, 260–261; and Communist China's foreign policy, 284; congressional leadership in, 239; and internal security, 181; and international law, 435; manipulation of, 291; and power politics, 307, 308; Presidential leadership in, 224; and U.S. foreign aid program, 377; and U.S. foreign policy, 44, 207, 224, 338

Puerto Rico, 90; independence, 96; population pressures, 130

Quadruple Alliance, 20

Quebec, 261

Quemoy and Matsu, 100–101

Quotas, 365–366; and EEC, 455; and exchange control, 365

Racialism, 6, 54, 86; Genoside Convention, 307; and nationalism, 74–75; Nazi view of, 111; and South African, 84, 94, 96, 263, 494, 498; and U.N., 483; and U.S. Negro, 86; and world politics, 123

Rakosi, Matyas, 84

Raw materials, 105, 116, 151; and conflict, 198; depletion and expansion of supplies, 119–120, 147; and economic base, 136; and industrialization, 118–119; and interdependence, 176, 188; minerals, 118–120; and national policies, 120–122; and national security, 363; and

RAW MATERIALS (cont.)
policy patterns, 310; and population, 125; and power status, 110, 116, 293; and synthetics, 170
Realism: moral, 213; political, 87, 212, 446
Recognition, 437–438; and U.N., 438–439
Reform: agrarian, 66; economic, 91, 150; educational, 66; social, 91
Regionalism, 447ff; and international cooperation, 451–452; and functionalism, 453
Reischauer, Edwin, 305
Religion, 6, 22; and nationality, 73–74; and world politics, 123
Renan, Joseph Ernest, 75
Reston, James, 98; on conference diplomacy, 336; on long-range Asia policy, 199; on U.S. public information, 351–352
Restropovitch, Miroslav, 356
Revisionism, 18, 63, 287
Revolutions, 18, 268; American, 74, 77, 185, 397; Bolshevik, 57–58, 78, 269, 328; charismatic leadership of, 83; and early nationalism, 77–78; elite of, 68; French, 184–185; Lin Piao on, 112; and patterns of policy, 310–311; "of rising expectations," 66, 157, 163, 164
Rhodesia, 85, 86, 89, 94, 459; British peacekeeping forces, 91; and U.N., 371, 483, 490, 492, 493; and Wilson, 257
Richardson, James D., 512n.
Richelieu, Cardinal, 315
Rio Pact (1947), 34, 211, 309, 401; text of, 532–536
Rogers Act (1924): and U.S. Foreign Service, 316
Roosevelt, Franklin Delano, 46, 61, 208–209, 256, 478; Churchill meetings, 333; and congressional bipartisanship, 242; and diplomacy, 318, 319; and Kingston Agreement, 261; and Presidential advisers, 225, 226
Roosevelt, Theodore, 109, 165; and diplomacy, 318
Root, Elihu, viii, 247
Rosner, Gabriella, 432n.
Rossiter, Clinton, 239
Rostow, W. W., 94; on national interest, 208; on national style, 205; on stages of economic growth, 145
Rousseau, Jean Jacques, 38, 76
Rowan, Carl, 345
Rumania, 80; trade with Britain and France, 158
Rush-Bagot Treaty (1817), 418
Rusk, Dean, 218, 230, 319, 336, 473n.; on foreign aid, 377; on nuclear war, 390; and parliamentary democracy, 337; on summit diplomacy, 334; on U.S. and emerging nations, 389; on U.S. military assistance program, 398
Russell, Richard, 240
Russell, Ruth B., 414n.
Russia; see Soviet Union

Salisbury, Lord, 255
Saltonstall, Levertt, 241
Samoa, 10
Satellites, space, 109, 118, 276; communications, 429; and international law, 166, 429, 440–441; Telstar, 169; weather, 169
Saudi Arabia, 65, 116, 143; and Arab League, 460
Schlesinger, Arthur, N. Jr., 46–47
Schilling, Warner R., 412; on Soviet scientific prestige, 161
Schuman, Robert, 264
Sea, U.N. Conference on Law of, 439–440
Sea power, 117; Mackinder on, 108; Mahan on, 109–110; Spykman on, 110–111; and technology, 399
Security, 10, 19, 43, 51, 106, 177–193; and air space, 440; and arms control, 417–418; collective, 21–22, 117, 174–175, 177, 192, 308, 400, 402–403, 506 —and U.N., 482; and diplomacy, 321; and economic affairs, 136, 144, 360, 363; feelings and attitudes of, 180–181; and foreign policy, 178, 192, 204, 221, 234, 277, 310; fundamental objectives of, 181–182; and geography factors, 113, 116–117; and insecurity, 191–192; internal, 179–180, 388; meaning of, 178, 179; and military assistance, 398; and military power, 182–187, 192, 399; and Mutual Security Program, 192; and national interest, 198, 211; and negative power, 188; and nonaligned nations, 189; nonmilitary aspects of, 187–190; and social uncertainties, 189; state as instrument of, 192–193; and technology, 160, 161, 166, 173; and values, 178–179. See also Strategy, military
Self-determination, 76–78, 87, 505; and Hitler, 328; Lenin's declaration of, 78–79
Sen, B. R., 131n., on food shortages, 132
Seymour, Sir Harold, 322
Shafer, Boyd, 71
Shakespeare, William, 72
Shannon, William V., 47n.
Shaposhnikov, Marshal Boris M., 40
Shastri, Lal Bahadur, 319

Shotwell, James, 171–172
Simulation: approach to international politics, 295
Sinkiang, 281
Sino-Soviet relations, 22, 26, 49, 56, 63–64, 99, 293, 306, 377, 506; and bipolarity, 34–35; and Communist leadership, 80, 102, 278–279, 474; and difference in national interest, 290; future of, 287–290; ideological factor, 80, 279; and international trade, 368; and national Communism, 79–80; underlying factors, 80, 279–280
Sino-Soviet Treaty of Alliance (1950), 280
Slusser, Robert M., 431n.
Small powers, 8, 10
Smith, Adam, 38, 153
Smithies, Arthur: on budget and national policy, 229
Smith-Mundt Act (1948), 354
Snell, John L., 402n.
Social organizations, stages of, 65–67
Social structure, 64–68; and power status, 110
Societies: modern, 66–67; traditional, 65; transitional, 65–66
Somalia, 65; disputes, 461
Somaliland, 92, 114
Sontag, Raymond, 161
Sorensen, Theodore C., on Kennedy's Presidential advisers, 225n.; on Kennedy and the press, 244n.
South Africa, 94, 96; and Commonwealth, 459; and Great Britain, 261; industrialization, 137; and OAU, 461; racialist policies of, 84, 86, 263, 494, 498
South East Asia Treaty Organization (SEATO), 34, 309, 338, 448, 454, 468, 470; formation of, 108; and public support, 224; and U.S. containment policy, 451; U.S. leadership, 454
South Pacific Commission, 475
Southeast Asia, 58, 100; and Vietnam, 199
South Vietnam, 7, 111, 198, 209; and SEATO, 470. *See also* Vietnam
Sovereignty: in air space, 440; extraterrestrial, 506; and international law, 428–429; of nation-states, 6, 20, 431, 708; in outer space, 440–441; overseas, 439–440; and U.N., 479
Soviet bloc; see Communist bloc
Soviet Union, 8, 39, 60, 109, 311
    ALLIANCES, 473; Communist China, 473; economic, 370, 473–474; Warsaw Pact, 79, 473, 474
    ATTITUDES AND IDEOLOGY: after Bolshevik Revolution, 57–58, 78–79; and Communism, 78, 505; and

foreign policy, 277; liberalization, 269; nationalism, 84; toward West, 58, 376–377
    COMMUNIST PARTY (CPSU): All-Union Congress, 272–273; apparatus, 79, 89, 473; Central Committee, 271–273, 288; Cominform, 473; Comintern, 473; and foreign policy, 270–271, 279; and ideology, 271; Politboro, 270, 271–272, 273; Secretariat, 272, 273; Twentieth Party Congress (1956), 79; Twenty-first Party Congress (1959), 141; Twenty-third Party Congress (1966), 271, 289n., 473
    DIPLOMACY, 328–330; with Communist China, 329; at Tashkent, 318–319, 329
    DOMESTIC AFFAIRS: Constitution, 269–270; industrialization, 122, 137, 277; language, 72; population, 99, 125, 127, 128, 130, 134; raw materials, 119
    ECONOMIC AFFAIRS: assistance (CEMA), 370, 473–474; economic growth, 140, 141, 147, 275; foreign investment, 148, 149; foreign trade and assistance, 142, 146, 153, 155, 275–276, 327, 367–368, 370; sales of foreign wheat, 132, 367
    FOREIGN POLICY: basic factors, 276–280; and Communist dogma, 279–280; and expansionism, 269, 277; and government, 273–276; and international Communism, 278; policy flows, 276, 286–287
    INSTITUTIONS FOR POLICY DECISIONS: Ministries—Committee for Foreign Economic Relations, 275–276, Council of Ministers, 271, 273, of Defense, 275, of Foreign Affairs, 272, 273–274, of Foreign Trade, 275–276; Party, 270–273—Politboro, 271, 272, 329, Supreme Soviet, 273
    INTERNATIONAL RELATIONSHIPS: bipolarity, 33–34; cessation of nuclear testing, 417; cultural relations, 355–357; and international law, 430–431; polycentrism, 26, 80; propaganda, 79, 88, 342, 344–345; recognition of new nations, 437; U.N., 329, 431, 480, 488; and underdeveloped nations, 84, 99, 275, 280; and U.S., 35, 49, 325, 506: in World War II, 185, 278, 305
    MILITARY STRATEGY, 405; "peaceful coexistence," 26, 63, 181, 279, 402.

SOVIET UNION (cont.)
404; "wars of liberation," 7, 19, 40, 102, 185, 186, 279, 388, 393, 397, 399, 405
NATIONAL SECURITY, 277, 473–474; nuclear power, 278, 404
POWER STATUS, 8, 57, 110, 111, 117, 165, 189, 277, 299, 305, 506; imperialism in Eastern Europe, 98–99, 277, 328, 458; military power, 275, 390, 400
RED ARMY, 79, 98, 108, 212, 473; in Hungary, 331
SCIENCE AND TECHNOLOGY, 166, 167; Academy of Science, 278; scientific advancement, 276, 277–278, 344; scientific prestige, 161; space technology, 118
Spain, 96, 112; U.S. air facilities in, 472
Spengler, J. J., 134n.; on population explosion, 135
Sprout, Harold and Margaret: on effects of technology, 162
Spykman, Nicholas J.: on geographical determinism, 106–107; on geopolitics, 110–111; on power politics, 40, 117, 302
Stability, political: 54, 66–67; and crisis, 67–69; and internal security, 180; in multiparty system, 250; and power structure, 110; in two-party system, 250. See also Instability
Stalin, Josef, 58, 61, 62, 79, 98, 146, 269, 274, 505; on diplomacy, 327; and Politboro, 272; purges (1937–1938), 275; and Soviet foreign policy, 271; and summit meetings, 318, 319, 333
Standard of living, 23; in developing countries, 144, 157; and economic growth, 147; and natural resources, 118; and population, 124–125, 127, 128
Stassen, Harold, 242
State, U.S. Department of, 219; and Arms Control and Disarmament Agency, 410–411; foreign policy functions of, 230–233; Policy Planning Council, 220, 222, 229, 231, 236; responsibilities of, 221, 229–230; Secretary, 224, 229–230—compared to Britain's Foreign Secretary, 255–256. See also United States, government agencies and departments
State system, 23, 48; and bipolarity, 35; Communist view, 278; and community concept, 15–16; defined, 7–10; and geography, 112–113, 116–117, 193; increase in number of, 87, 95–97, 306, 411; interdependence, 217; and international law, 427–428; and national interest, 10–15; and prestige, 15–16

States: as actors, 7–10; categories of, by power, 8, 10; definition of, 7; list of, 9
Statesmanship, 18; and balance of power, 32, 33, 293
Status quo: Kennedy on, 302; Lippmann on, 98
Stettinius, Edward, 256
Stevenson, Adlai E., 230; on U.N. as hope for peace, 512–513
Stewart, Michael, 259
Stimson, Henry L., 203, 242
Stockpiling, 295; U.S. policy for, 120–121, 153–154
Stoessinger, John G., 487n.
Stone, Julius: on judicial settlement, 445
Strategy, military, 107; characteristics of, 398–399; coalition or alliance approach, 401–402; future, 405–406; global collective security, 402–403; historical discontinuity of, 399–400; national, 400; Soviet doctrine, 405; unilateral approach to, 400–401; and U.S. security policy, 403–405
Subversion, 187; Communist, and diplomacy, 324, 328, 330; Communist, and wars of liberation, 185–186; and internal security, 180, 182, 189
Sudan, 8, 66, 68, 80
Suez, 7, 22, 119, 120, 216, 258, 263; British-French attack on, 59, 253, 304, 328, 442, 459; U.S. action in, 413
Sukarno, Achmed, 66, 68, 215; charisma of, 83. See also Indonesia
Sulzberger, C. L.: on Soviet diplomacy, 274; on undeclared wars, 396; on U.S. world influence, 507
Summit conferences, 253, 255, 260; and diplomacy by heads of states, 318, 333–334
Superpowers, 8, 10
Supreme Headquarters of Allied Powers in Europe (SHAPE), 467, 469
Sweden, 8; and EFTA, 456; neutrality, 321, 400
Switzerland, 72, 116, 193; and EFTA, 456; neutrality, 321, 400; and U.N., 403, 482
Systems: approach to international politics, 31–37
Syria, 368

Taiwan; see Chinese Nationalist Republic
Tannenbaum, Frank: on U.S. attitudes, 181
Tanzania, 459
Tariffs, 204; and EEC, 455; and international trade, 362–364; vs. quotas, 365–366; and world affairs, 233. See also

General Agreement on Tariffs and Trade; General Conferences

Tashkent meeting (India-Pakistan), 278, 318–319, 329

Technology, 2, 24, 26–27, 37, 51, 60, 158; and arms control measures, 175–176; and change, 161–164; communications, 161, 163; control of, 418; development, 167, 176; defined, 160–161; and diplomacy, 316; and export earnings, 166; and foreign policy, 166–167, 236–237; industrial, 116, 162, 163, 167, 169–170; and international affairs, 106, 122, 160–161, 164–169; international flow of, 162–163; military, 34, 162, 163, 167, 170–175, 388, 390; and military strategy, 399; and obsolescence, 173; and privacy of states, 169; sharing, 166–167; Soviet, 276; space, 118, 162; and underdeveloped countries, 163; weapons, 411

Telensky, Major General Nikolai: on war and policy, 405

Temperley, H., 300n.

Teng Hsiao-p'ing, 283

Territorial position, 6; and conflict, 198

Territorial waters, 439–440; U.S. position on, 440

Thailand, 101; and SEATO, 470

Thayer, Charles W., 317

Thirty Years' War, 74, 428

Thompson, Kenneth: on policy planning, 215; on political realism, 212

Thompson, William ("Big Bill"), 103

Tibet, 100; and Communist Chinese, 281, 335

Tito, Marshal (Josip Broz), 79, 84

Tocqueville, Alexis de: on foreign policy process, 246

Togo, 8, 10

Tojo, Hideki, 92

Totalitarianism, 71; and nationalism, 78, 87

Touré, Sékou, 461

Tourism, 114; and U.S. balance-of-payments problem, 380, 382

Trade, international, 137–139, 147; and balance of payments, 156; Communist, 99, 142, 473; and conflict, 198; economic warfare, 361, 370–372; free, 151–153, 209; government controls, 152–154; interdependence in, 155–156, 157; international organizations, 368–372; Japanese, 141; and nationalism, 70, 78; and natural resources, 118–119; and policy patterns, 310, 361–368; and protectionism, 38, 78, 209, 362–363; rationale of, 150–152; trends in, 152–154; of underdeveloped countries, 154–155; and U.S., 139–140. *See also* General Agreement on Tariffs and Trade

Traditions, 53, 54; and diplomacy, 314, 317; and foreign policy, 204–205; and policy patterns, 311; and power politics, 308; and social organization, 65

Transport and Communications Commission, 495

Transportation, 125; air, 168, 211; and technology, 165

Treaties, 6; and foreign policy, 309; and international law, 441–443—*pacta sunt servanda* doctrine, 441, 442, *rebus sic stantibus* doctrine, 441; and limitation on power politics, 308; President's responsibility for, 223; and rules of war, 187; and search for peace, 410; Senate's responsibility for, 223; and State Department, 231

Treaty of Paris (1815), 386

Treaty of Rome (1958), 454

Treaty of Westphalia (1648), 33, 35–36, 41, 428; and balance-of-power concept, 298; Congress, 334

Trinidad and Tobago, 10

Triple Alliance (Germany, Austraia-Hungary, Italy), 20, 505; and balance of power, 298

Triple Entente (Britain, France, Russia), 20, 505; and balance of power, 298

Triska, Jan F., 431n.

Trujillo, Rafael, 330

Truman, Harry S., 230, 247; and Congress, 241, 242; containment policy, 108; and diplomacy, 318, 320; and Greek-Turkish policy, 224; and Korea, 231; on U.S. foreign policy, 213, 238, 245

Truman Doctrine (1947), 108, 198, 245, 404

Tshombe, Moise, 84

Turkey, 32; and Eastern Question, 308; and Greece, dispute over Cyprus, 175; and IMF, 369; and NATO, 57; population, 130; Straits, 113, 117; as transitional society, 65, 66, 69. *See also* Cyprus

Thucydides, 342, 426

Union of the Soviet Socialist Republics (U.S.S.R.); *see* Soviet Union

United Arab Republic, 83, 318, 460; and Israel, 74, 114; and projection of power, 165; trade with Soviet bloc, 368. *See also* Egypt; Nasser

United Kingdom: *see* Great Britain

United Nations
    CHARTER, 28, 103, 115, 401, 479; amendments to, text of, 566–568; diplomacy, 416; and domestic juris-

UNITED NATIONS (cont.)
diction, 480; drafting of, 239; and global security, 402; idealism in, 39, 213; international law, 426, 429, 431; regional arrangements, 452; and restraint of force, 434, 436, 443; San Francisco Conference and, 242, 337, 444, 445, 479, 505; and search for peace, 410, 412, 414; text of, 537–565

DECLARATIONS AND RESOLUTIONS: condemnation of Soviet intervention in Hungary (1956), 42; Declaration of Human Rights (1948), 443, 495; Declaration on Ending Colonialism (1961), 498; Declaration on Exploration and Use of Outer Space (1963), 42, 419, 441; Declaration Regarding Non-Self-Governing Territories (1945), 497; Uniting for Peace Resolution (1950), 402, 489, 491, 492

AND DEVELOPMENT, 495–496; assistance, 496–497; Development Fund, 496; Expanded Program of Technical Assistance, 496–497; political, 497–498

DIPLOMACY: diplomatic missions, 315; foreign secretaries at, 333; as forum, 309; functions, 16, 332; mediation, 331; parliamentary democracy, 337; policy development, 217–218

DISARMAMENT, 42, 85

ECONOMIC AND SOCIAL COUNCIL (ECOSOC), 133, 480; demographic studies, 125; and development problems, 495–497; Economic Commissions, 495; enlargement of, 567–568; Specialized Agencies and, 496

ECONOMIC DEVELOPMENT, 42, 86; GATT, 155, 364, 365, 369; technical advisory programs, 166, 373, 374, 376, 487

FINANCES, 483, 487–488; Britain, 488; crisis at Nineteenth Assembly, 488; fixed contributions, 487; and peacekeeping, 431, 487–488; and Soviet Union, 488; and technical assistance, 487; and U.S., 487, 488; voluntary contributions, 487

FOOD AND AGRICULTURE ORGANIZATION, 493

FORCE: authorizations of, 489–490, 493; in Congo, 487–488, 490; in Cyprus, 490; in Korea, 490; in Near East, 414, 432, 492

FUTURE OF, and changes in, 498–501

GENERAL ASSEMBLY: economic sanctions, 371; foreign ministers, 33; and international law, 431, 436; issue of seating of Communist China, 438–439; Khrushchev at, 318, 333–334; and maintenance of international peace, 492–493; new nations in, 8, 85, 317; and pacific settlement of disputes, 493; politics in, 484–486; Pope Paul at, 27; Uniting for Peace Resolution, 480, 491; U.S. representation, 242; voting in, 484, 486, 492–493

HUMAN RIGHTS COMMISSION, 495

INTERNATIONAL COURT OF JUSTICE, 493–494; advisory opinion on financing peacekeeping, compulsory jurisdiction of, 494; judgment in South-West Africa case, 494

AND INTERNATIONAL LAW, 426, 429, 431; and censure, 432; Conference on Law of the Sea (1958), 439–440; enforcement of, 434; and General Assembly, 431, 436; and International Court of Justice, 446, 480, 489; International Law Commission, 433; legal personality, 444; and peacekeeping, 429; and territorial recognition, 438–439

INTERNATIONAL LAW COMMISSION, 433

INVESTIGATING COMMISSION, 489, 492

MEMBERSHIP, 482–484; list of members, 485

MILITARY ENFORCEMENT, 490

NATURE AND POLITICS OF, 478–480, 482–484; African states, 8, 14, 84, 317; Arab League, 46; Canada, 262; Commonwealth Nations, 459; and Communist China, 438–439, 484; Great Britain, 256; Great Powers, 402; lesser powers, 103–104; new nations, 1, 84–85, 451; Soviet Union, 329, 431, 480, 488; U.S. participation, 58, 230, 241, 402–403

PACIFIC SETTLEMENT OF DISPUTES, 493–495

PEACEKEEPING, 42, 192, 397, 478; assessments, 431, 487–488; and boundary disputes, 115, 493; boycott of Rhodesia, 85; in Congo, 91, 168, 402, 414, 490; and Cyprus, 91, 331, 414, 432, 490; and Hungary, 42; and international law, 429; and intervention, 91, 96; in Korea, 22, 184, 415, 490; and maintenance of peace, 18, 180, 186, 190, 308–309, 330, 395, 411, 488–495; military force, 402; and restraint of armed force, 395, 482; temporary administration in West New Guinea, 96, 414, 494

POWER: and balance of power, 298, 301, 309; struggles, 21, 294

REGIONAL ARRANGEMENTS AND, 401

SECRETARIAT, 480, 486–487

SECRETARY-GENERAL, 480, 486–487, 489; Troika proposal for, 500

SECURITY: collective, 21–22, 308–309, 480, 482; facilitation independence, 96; of nonaligned states, 189–190

SECURITY COUNCIL, 301, 324, 334, 371; composition of, 489–491; East-West conflicts in, 480; enlargement of, 566–567; and international law, 436; and regulation of armaments, 418; role of, 489–490; and use of armed force, 402, 480; veto problem, 482, 491–492; voting—abstention from, 491–492

SPECIALIZED AGENCIES, 133, 496. *See also* names of individual agencies

SUPREME COMMAND: in Korea, 490

TRANSPORT AND COMMUNICATIONS COMMISSION, 495

TRUSTEESHIP COUNCIL, 480, 497–498; trust territories, 90–91, 498; U.S. trust territory, 498

VETO PROBLEM, 491–492

VOTING PATTERNS IN, 484, 486

United Nations Educational, Scientific and Cultural Organization (UNESCO), 369, 496

United States, 1, 5, 8, 16–17, 294, 305, 507–515

CONGRESS: House of Representatives, 238—Armed Services Committee, 171, 240, Foreign Affairs Committee, 230, 240, 377; Senate, 238, 239, 479—advisory functions, 239–240, Appropriations Committee, 240, bipartisanship, 241–242, and foreign policy formulation, 238–242, Foreign Relations Committee, 171, 233, 234, 239, 240, 350, 390, and public opinion, 239, 240

CONSTITUTION, 61, 177, 223, 239, 242

DECLARATION OF INDEPENDENCE, 61, 77

ECONOMIC AND ASSISTANCE POLICIES, 360, 373–376; agricultural surplus, 131, 154; and balance of payments, 138–140, 148, 149, 380–382; "Buy American" policy, 382; controversies over, 377–379; domestic, and cost of war, 179; economic growth, 140, 147, 155; and economic sanctions, 371–372; Export-Import Bank, 373–374; Food for Peace (PL 480), 131, 150, 374, 414; foreign assistance, 91, 156, 372–379; GATT, 369; investment abroad, 139–140, 148–149; Marshall Plan, 58, 138, 373; and military assistance, 374–375, 397; Point Four Program, 169; quotas, 365–366; reciprocal trade agreements, 364; Trade Agreements Act, 364; Trade Expansion Act, 364; trade pattern, 151, 152; tariffs, 360–364; in world economy, 120–122, 139–140, 158–159

FOREIGN AND SECURITY POLICY, 403–405; categories of decisions for, 244, 245; and China, 203, 211, 239, 243; containment, 168, 299, 468, 470, 507; and Cuba, 207, 327; cultural relations, 341, 353–355; deterrence, 404; and economic power, 227, 360–361; and foreign aid, 104, 124, 168, 221, 224, 229, 245; isolation and neutrality, 58, 164, 214, 217, 245, 400, 505; League of Nations, 21, 477; Monroe Doctrine, 108, 198, 211; moral principles in, 213; and NATO, 468–469; Peace Corps and, 355; Presidential, 318–319; propaganda and, 342–352; Truman Doctrine, 108, 198, 245; Vietnam, 199, 203, 204

FOREIGN POLICY PROCESS, 219–248, 516–524; budget and, 227–228; Congress and, 214, 221, 223, 224, 226, 238–242; coordination of, 237–238; Defense Department and, 214, 220–222, 231, 234–236; flow of in State Department, 220, 221, 229–233, 516–524; and Foreign Service, 223, 227, 231, 236, 316; formulation, 221, 223; national security and, 178, 192–193, 221, 234–236; National Security Council and, 226–227; outside agencies, 233–234; Presidential advisers, 224–226; Presidential role, 220, 221, 223–224, 225, 239; and public, 242–244

GREAT SOCIETY PROGRAM, 199

GOVERNMENT AGENCIES AND DEPARTMENTS, 223–242; Armed Services, 223; Arms Control and Disarmament Agency, 410–411, 423; Atomic Energy Commission, 224, 236; Bureau of the Budget, 224,

UNITED STATES (cont.)
227–229, 237; Central Intelligence Agency, 223, 227; Commerce Department, 233; Defense Department, 214, 220, 221, 222, 236—Joint Chiefs of Staff, 224–225, 227, Secretary of, 224–225, 236; Export and Import Bank, 373–374; Federal Bureau of Investigation, 223; Information Agency, 344–346, 350, 352, 355; Military Academy, West Point, 237, 404; National Aeronautics and Space Agency, 224, 233, 236; Senior Interdepartmental Group, 227, 238; State Department, 219, 220, 222, 229–230, 231, 236, 516–524—Foreign Service, 223; Policy Planning Council, 220, 222, 229, 231, 236; Supreme Court, 432; Treasury Department, 233. *See also* Congress, U.S.; President of the United States

INTERNATIONAL RELATIONSHIPS: with Canada, 57, 117, 262, 472; with Communist China, 281; with Congo, 91; in changing world, 168, 507–513; with Dominican Republic, 91; with emerging nations, 25, 104, 124, 389; and limited purpose organizations, 462–472; and Pacific Trust Territories, 91, 498; recognition policy, 437; with Soviets, 35, 49, 299; and U.N., 58, 230, 241, 242, 402–403, 487–488

MILITARY POWER AND POSITION, 385; armed services, 223; and balance of power, 21, 110–111, 189, 297–298, 299; bases, 117, 172; between World Wars, 308; civilian control of, 394; global commitments, 109–119; "hot line" to Moscow, 391; in Korea, 21, 168, 184, 216, 432; and national security, 173, 190–191; nuclear capability and policy, 172, 219, 390–393, 417; Presidential responsibility for, 223–224; prestige and, 15, 190, 204, 213, 344; rearmament (post-World War II), 299; sea power, 109, 371; and space race, 118; stockpiling policy, 121, 153–154; strategic position of, 110–111; and technology, 162, 164, 166, 167; in World War II, 185; in Vietnam, 21, 117, 168, 239, 371, 396

POPULATION, 124, 127; population-control assistance abroad, 134

PRESIDENT AND EXECUTIVE BRANCH, 221–226; Executive branch, 220, 221, 223–224; National Security Council, 223, 226–227, 238, 384; Powers of President and British Prime Minister compared, 253–254; Presidential advisers, 224–226—on Science and Technology, 224; special assistants, 226

RACIAL PROBLEM, 86

TREATIES AND AGREEMENTS, 401, 404; Alliance for Progress, 224, 464–465; ANZUS, 34, 211, 309, 451; CENTO, 108; Inter-American Treaty of Reciprocal Assistance (Rio Pact), 532–536; Kingston Agreement (Canada), 261; mutual security, with—Japan, 242, 309, 320, 451, 470; Korea, 451; North Atlantic Treaty, 465–470, 525–528; Nuclear Test Ban Treaty, 529–531; SEATO, 108, 309, 470; U.N. Charter, 536–568

U Thant, 486, 497, 500; on Communist China, 64

Universal Postal Union, 36, 477

Universalism, 35–36, 45

Uranium, supplies, 120

U–2 incident, 440

Values: and attitudes, 53; and balance of power, 32; and community concept, 16–17; and international political behavior, 54–59; and national interest, 11; and national security, 178–179; shared—and consensus, 14–15, 90, and international community, 40–41, 54, and regional cooperation, 451, and new nationalism, 81

Vandenberg, Arthur H., 239, 240, 242, 466

Vatican State, 10; and diplomacy, 315

Venezuela, 68

Versailles: and Hitler, 328; Peace Conference, 108, 210, 224, 334, 477; Treaty of (1919), 17, 18, 298, 505

Vienna Conference on Diplomatic Privileges and Immunities (1963), 433

Vienna Youth Festival, 356

Vietnam, 21, 64, 101, 245, 259, 262, 335, 468, 510–511; ambiguity of conflict in, 184; and Chinese foreign policy, 281; and Congress, 241; division of, 95, 482; and national interest, 209; Soviet containment, 299; U.S. military buildup in, 117, 168, 203, 409, 507; U.S. policy for, 198–199, 203, 204; Vietcong, 7, 68, 198, 330, 470. *See also* North Vietnam

Violence, 182–184, 506; internal, and in-

ternational peace, 410, 413; and negative power, 188
Virgin Islands, 92, 96
Vishinsky, Andrei, 274, 431n.
Voltaire, 76; on violence, 182
Von Ranke, Leopold, 297

War, 6–7, 54; accidental, 391, 411, 418; and balance of power, 302, 303; causes of, 411–412; changing nature of, 386–388; and Communist dogma, 279; guerrilla, 186, 395, 412; insurgencies, 185–186, 412; and law, 434; "of liberation," 7, 19, 40, 102, 185, 186, 279, 388, 393, 399, 436; limited, 117, 171, 172, 393, 395; and national interest, 211; and national unity, 74–75; and nationalism, 185; numbers of, 183–184; objectives of, 186; philosophical view, 38; and population trends, 128, 135; rules of, 187; since World War II, 183–184; and Sino-Soviet rift, 289, 301; Shotwell on, 171–172; and superpowers, 87, 174; and technological advances, 164; thermonuclear, 178, 212, 289, 302, 342, 390–391, 395, 405–406; twentieth-century, 185–186; U.S. engagement in (since 1775), 183
Ward, Barbara: on economic imperialism, 91
Warsaw Pact (1955), 79, 474
Washington, George, 61, 75, 213, 501; Farewell Address, 224
Weapons, 116, 163; capabilities, 171, 399; and technology, 170–174, 411. *See also* Nuclear weapons
West Germany, 294; and EEC, 138, 454; industrialization, 137
West New Guinea: U.N. temporary administration in, 96, 414, 494
Western Europe, 116, 147; and foreign investment, 148, 149; and foreign trade, 152; productivity, 137–138
White House Committee on International Information Activities, 341
Whitehead, Alfred North, 160n.
Wight, Martin, 20n.

Wilson, Harold, 254, 257; and EEC, 458; and U.S. Vietnam policy, 259
Wilson, J. Tuzo, 285n.
Wilson, Woodrow, 21, 210, 224, 226, 256, 477; on balance of power, 303–304; and Colonel House, 225; Fourteen Points, 412; and "liberal idealism," 39, 212–213, 311; and open diplomacy, 316–317; and U.S. recognition policy, 438. *See also* League of Nations
Wolfers, Arnold, 510n.; on foreign affairs, 213; on national security, 178, 179
Wolsey, Cardinal, 299
World Affairs Councils, 243
World Bank (IBRD), 10, 42, 85, 92, 133, 149–150, 320, 331, 373, 496, 514; on conflicts in low per-capita countries, 388; creation of, 368; and reforms, 379; "soft loan window," 496
World Court; *see* International Court of Justice
World government, 36, 164; idea of, 501–502, U.N. not a, 480
World Health Organization, 42, 320, 496
World War I, 185, 505; Aron on, 387; and balance of power in Europe, 20, 33; Great Powers, 395; objectives of, 186; and sea power, 109
World War II, 18, 20, 79, 128, 168, 185; Allied-Axis bipolarity, 33, 402; Axis, 189, 302; and balance of power, 21, 299, 387; and Great Britain, 295; objectives of, 186; and sea power, 109, 110; U.S. lend lease, 397
Wright, Quincy, 6–7

Xenophobia, 55, 83, 86

Yalta Agreement (1945), 329, 478, 479
Yemen, 65, 460, 494
Yugoslavia, 79; expulsion from Cominform, 473; and International Monetary Fund. 368

Zambia, 9

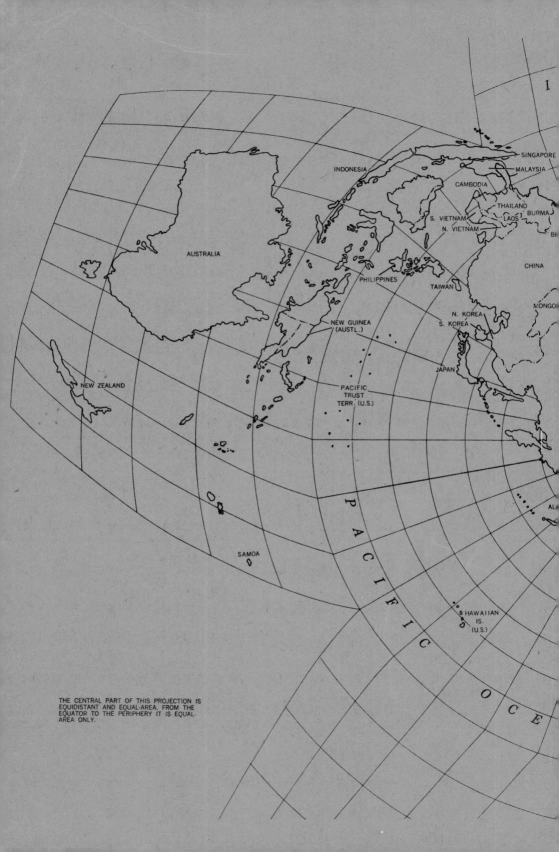

I

SINGAPORE
MALAYSIA
INDONESIA
CAMBODIA
THAILAND
BURMA
S. VIETNAM
LAOS
N. VIETNAM
B
CHINA
AUSTRALIA
MONGO
PHILIPPINES
TAIWAN
NEW GUINEA
(AUSTL.)
N. KOREA
S. KOREA
JAPAN
NEW ZEALAND
PACIFIC
TRUST
TERR. (U.S.)
AL
SAMOA

HAWAIIAN
IS.
(U.S.)

THE CENTRAL PART OF THIS PROJECTION IS
EQUIDISTANT AND EQUAL-AREA, FROM THE
EQUATOR TO THE PERIPHERY IT IS EQUAL-
AREA ONLY.

P
A
C
I
F
I
C

O
C
E